# HOW WE ARE GOVERNED

# HOW WE ARE GOVERNED

## THE BASICS OF CANADIAN POLITICS AND GOVERNMENT

**James John Guy**

University College of Cape Breton

HARCOURT
BRACE
CANADA

**Harcourt Brace & Company, Canada**

Toronto   Montreal   Fort Worth   New York   Orlando
Philadelphia   San Diego   London   Sydney   Tokyo

Requests for permission to make copies of any part of the work should be mailed to: Permissions, College Division, Harcourt Brace & Company, Canada, 55 Horner Avenue, Toronto, Ontario M8Z 4X6.

Every reasonable effort has been made to acquire permission for copyright material used in this text, and to acknowledge all such indebtedness accurately. Any errors and omissions called to the publisher's attention will be corrected in future printings.

**Canadian Cataloguing in Publication Data**

Guy, James John, 1943–
    How we are governed

Includes bibliographical references and index.
ISBN 0-7747-3200-8

1. Canada — Politics and government    I. Title.

JL75.G8 1995      320.971      C94-931436-6

Publisher: Heather McWhinney
Editor and Marketing Manager: Daniel J. Brooks
Projects Co-ordinator: Megan Mueller
Director of Publishing Services: Jean Davies
Editorial Manager: Marcel Chiera
Supervising Editor: Semareh Al-Hillal
Production Manager: Sue-Ann Becker
Production Supervisor: Carol Tong
Copy Editor: Beverley Beetham Endersby
Cover and Interior Design: Steve Eby Production and Design
Typesetting and Assembly: McGraphics Desktop Publishing
Technical Art: New Concept Complete Printing & Publishing Services Ltd.
Printing and Binding: Best Book Manufacturers, Inc.

Cover Art: Charles Pachter, detail of *The Painted Flag* (1981). Acrylic on canvas. Private collection, Toronto. Reproduced with permission of the artist.

♾ This book was printed in Canada on acid-free paper.

1  2  3  4  5    99  98  97  96  95

*For my mother, Patricia, and in memory of my father, Victor*

# PREFACE

In my more than twenty years as a professor who loves to teach introductory political science courses, I have been struck repeatedly by the realization that the only good textbook is one that students can and will read. Political science may seem to come naturally to those of us who profess it, because we relish the world of politics and government. We talk about it every day, write about it from time to time, and sometimes even get involved in it. It is great fun — for *us*. But, when it comes to good teaching, it's really for *them* — the students.

As I wrote this book, I had in mind an image of its readers. This group is diverse, but one characteristic its members have in common is that they are students with many different interests and career goals. They are attending a college or university and are enrolled in an introductory Canadian politics and government course that is either an elective or the beginning of a major or honours degree in political science. Some students take a course at this level because they intend to be political science graduates. Others are already in government service. Still others are simply interested in how government works — something they will want to know if they become accountants, bankers, doctors, social workers, or teachers.

A first course in Canadian politics and government should enlighten these students on the subject of how our governments are structured and behave. All students need to know how they personally relate to the many components of government in Canada, and what political issues will directly affect their lives. That is who this book is for and what it is about.

Experience has taught me that not all who want to learn at the university level regard the study of politics as essential to their lives.

The writer of an introductory textbook on Canadian politics and government cannot assume, therefore, that there is an eager audience out there that can hardly wait to read about the subject. The implications of not making this assumption should be clear: Any good text on Canadian politics and government worthy of the name should combine solid factual content with stimulating presentation.

Because so many students in an introductory course will never take another in the discipline, it is essential that the text they use be especially readable, comprehensive, and instructive. This textbook is written with the assumption that its readers know little about how Canada is governed. It is also written with the belief that, if information is presented in a clear, understandable, and interesting way, students will like what they learn. They may even be enticed to continue their studies in the field of political science.

These are interesting times for students of Canadian politics and government. Against a backdrop of dramatic change throughout the world, Canada is experiencing its own forces of disunity and political disarray. Canada cannot escape the influence of global crisis in the 1990s. It is not surprising that recent international power shifts were bound to rekindle the historic forces that have divided Canada since it was established. As we now must confront the issue of our national survival in this last decade of the twentieth century, the study of Canadian government takes a key place on the podium of academe. Never has the study of Canada's political and governmental systems been as important as at this time. Students should *feel* this urgency, and the excitement of our unique political experience, while attending university or college.

This text is about governing and the ability to do it well — about the institutions, processes, and policies that are involved in Canadian politics and government. *How We Are Governed: The Basics of Canadian Politics and Government* is designed for the uninitiated and undecided student who may be contemplating an important career choice. The book carefully analyzes Canada's political institutions — the electoral system, political parties, Parliament, the bureaucracy, and the courts — because the ability to govern depends on the qualities of the people who make up these institutions. Students must feel that how we govern ourselves matters; how things are done or have been done, and how they are seen to be done, are often as crucial as what is done. One of my goals was to show that the study of Canadian politics is a discipline with both a history and a contemporary vitality. I wanted to provide real-life cases of the governing system at work by making the text rich with historical and current examples of policy-making and politics.

Every student who chooses to study introductory Canadian political science begins a long journey. It takes some time for us to understand Canada's elaborate system of government and politics. We need time to think about the information that comes to us. And we must bring our values to bear on the complex political systems that structure our lives. Accordingly, textbooks have a special obligation to present and teach this wonderful subject well.

In preparing this textbook, I endeavored to cover all of the *traditional* topics common to other Canadian politics texts, but I also *added* many new important topics that rarely, if ever, find their way into such textbooks. I wanted to write a textbook that students not only could read and enjoy but would later credit for shaping their thinking about Canadian politics and government. Thus, included in the following pages is a comprehensive basic core of information about how Canada governs itself. But this text goes beyond others in three additional ways. First, it focusses on the theme of governability at a time when many Canadians are asking themselves whether the present institutions of government will be able to hold the country together. I believe that students will use the framework of governability to analyze their political universe long after they have completed this course. The framework of governability provides a way for professors and students to put information into a broader perspective. Most important, the framework enables students to recognize and think critically about the difficult choices involved in governing a society as large and as complex as Canada. The thematic approach adopted here will teach students how to organize, analyze, and interpret political events, trends, and problems.

Second, the text offers students a broader exposure to the various forces at work in Canadian politics and government: to the various levels of government, to the provinces, to the municipalities, to the role of the media, and to the relationship between economics and politics; to how debts and deficits affect us, and how we manage our fiscal and monetary affairs. A special effort has been made to use many current resources, which will help keep students abreast of recent developments with significance for the future. For example, each chapter opens with a *vignette* that focusses on an actual personality or event that relates to the subject being presented. The scope and variety of political study are also introduced. Basic concepts are presented and highlighted in a *glossary* that defines them for the beginning student. When an important concept is introduced in the book, it is identified and defined. The student can thus review all the major concepts in a chapter by checking the end of that chapter.

Because the study of political science involves both knowledge of concepts and a familiarity with research evidence, it is important for the beginning student to understand statistical data. *Charts, graphs, lists,* and *tables* found throughout the book present statistical information in a clear and attractive way. Where appropriate, *profiles* of people in prominent offices of government have been featured in boxed inserts to draw students into the reality of the information presented. Reading about the daily routines of government officials gives the unitiated reader an excellent in-depth learning experience. *Photographs* and *cartoons* have been carefully selected to highlight each chapter to give students an attractive and exciting portrayal of the information they are reading and discussing in class. Under *Recommended Reading*, the works of the most credible and respected political scientists in the country are cited, with annotations. Most professors assign readings to supplement and illustrate the textbook they have chosen. These suggested readings have been carefully selected for the beginning student. A comprehensive list of *bibliographical references* at the end of the book includes items not only by political scientists but also by writers in related fields, such as economics, psychology, and sociology. No textbook

should be published without an *index*. Students will find the name and subject indices provided in this book very helpful.

Third, the book is designed to meet the needs of both professors and students. Instructors will find this textbook easy to use, and students will find it easy to understand. The most important components of the Canadian political system are organized in a sequence that potential adopters will discover fits readily into their course agendas. Most adopters will not have to restructure their courses in order to use this book. Although there is a logical order in the topics and chapters, I realize that teaching priorities differ among professors who adopt a text. Some may prefer to discuss the constitution at a different point in the course, for instance. They should encounter no major problems in reordering the content of this book to suit their courses.

With all of these pedagogical features just described, this book offers students one reference source that provides a coherent and thorough introduction to the field.

## ACKNOWLEDGEMENTS

Even though there is only one author's name on the cover of this book, it could never have been completed without the assistance of many capable individuals on and off of the campus of the University College of Cape Breton.

A superb team of artistic, editing, and marketing professionals at Harcourt Brace & Company, Canada, made this book a pleasure to write. I especially want to acknowledge the assistance I was given by their competent and creative staff. I am grateful to Dan Brooks, editor and marketing manager, who took command of the development of the proposal and shepherded it through the mass of administrative steps that accompany any project of this scope. And, Megan Mueller, the projects co-ordinator, remained a very close companion throughout the entire period of writing the

book. Her positive counsel and belief in the project provided me much reassurance in my moments of uncertainty. Beverley Beetham Endersby, the copy editor, took another run through my prose to iron out the wrinkles that remained. Her wonderful skills added so much clarity to this new book. Someone at Harcourt Brace did me a big favour when Semareh Al-Hillal was assigned to my book as its supervising editor. She was very helpful because she is so good at what she does.

I greatly value the many positive comments I received throughout the writing of this book from several of my colleagues in universities in Atlantic Canada. Their informed suggestions about what they wanted in a new text made the book more relevant and interesting. Thanks also to those colleagues across the country who offered specific ideas regarding approach and coverage at the outset of this project: Peter Woolstencroft, University of Waterloo; Robert Davidson, Mount Royal College; Richard Baird, University of Alberta; Paul Mier, Capilano College; and Peter Boswell, Memorial University of Newfoundland. A special thanks to my principal reviewer, Dr. Peter (Jay) Smith of Athabasca University, for his careful evaluation of the original draft of the manuscript. Needless to say, the book was immensely improved by his scholarly experience and his critical eye. Retired Nova Scotia Supreme Court Justice Denny Burchell provided thoughtful comments and critical insights on the chapter on law and the judiciary.

A number of my colleagues at UCCB deserve special recognition. I have the good fortune to chair a department of highly competent political scientists who like one another and who want to help one another professionally whenever they can. In this regard, I am grateful to Brian Howe and David Johnson for their encouragement and advice on many chapters. Beryl Davis was very helpful with her advice on municipal government. Mohini Gupta provided, as always, her gentle inspiration.

A general sabbatical provided me with the block of time necessary to concentrate on this project. For that, I am especially indebted to our new president, Jacke Scott, who was so supportive and sympathetic; to our director of research, Robert Morgan, whose backing made it possible for me to complete the book on schedule; and to Dean David White, who helped me acquire the most up-to-date computer to get the job done.

Certain individuals must be singled out for a very special "thanks." Two journalists, justice reporter Steve MacInnis and science reporter Todd Verge, shared their thoughts, facts, and suggestions on all sorts of issues I needed to present in this text. Evo Dipiero researched numerous details, frequently calling Ottawa on my behalf and tracking down government documents. Ainslie White faithfully did many of the computer graphics for the original manuscript. Margaret MacLeod patiently answered constant questions about computer glitches and graciously helped with so much of the detail in preparing the original manuscript for the publisher. Penny Marshall, our head librarian, secured many of the books and documents I needed when I thought I would never get them. Marie Antle, at Statistics Canada, always answered my picky questions about numbers and methods of getting them. Brian Doue handled all of my correspondence eagerly and with much dedication. Thank you so much.

A special note of gratitude to Federal Court Chief Justice Julius Isaac and his staff for permitting me to prepare a profile of him. Ruth Hubbard, president of the Royal Canadian Mint, and her staff enabled me to include her profile. The Honourable Joan Sawicki, Speaker of the Legislative Assembly of British Columbia, gave me much insight into her job, which I was able to pass on to our readers.

Last, but not least, thanks to my wife, Patti; my daughter, Katha; my son, Trevor; and Arielle, my faithful Airedale. You know I love you all.

Readers wishing further information on data provided by Statistics Canada may obtain copies of related publications by mail from Publications Sales, Statistics Canada, Ottawa, Ontario, K1A 0T6, by phone at 1-613-951-7277 or toll-free 1-800-267-6677, or by fax at 1-613-951-1584.

## *A Note from the Publisher*

Thank you for selecting *How We Are Governed: The Basics of Canadian Politics and Government*, by James John Guy. The author and publisher have devoted considerable time to the careful development of this book. We appreciate your recognition of this effort and accomplishment.

We want to hear what you think about *How We Are Governed: The Basics of Canadian Politics and Government*. Please take a few minutes to fill in the stamped reader reply card at the back of the book. Your comments and suggestions will be valuable to us as we prepare new editions and other books.

# BRIEF CONTENTS

# CONTENTS

# THE BASICS OF CANADIAN POLITICS AND GOVERNMENT

**W**ilfrid Laurier once remarked: "This is a difficult country to govern" — an understatement, in hindsight. In our basic attempts to come to terms with that reality, Canadians have produced a country of many governments and of relatively different political systems. Today, so numerous are our governmental units that Statistics Canada counts them from time to time. The latest count indicates that this country has more than 6000 units of government. There is, of course, only one national government, and there are ten provincial and two territorial governments. But, in addition, there are 697 town governments and 134 city governments across Canada. And, among the many other governing bodies counted by Statistics Canada are such units as regional governments, counties, townships, villages, *villes*, and municipal districts.

Because so many governments affect the lives of Canadians, the governing system is complicated. Even government officials find the numerous categories and organizations difficult to comprehend. Moreover, the fragmentation of powers, functions, and responsibilities among the federal, provincial, and municipal governments makes governing very complex and expensive for Canadian taxpayers. The question of how much diversity our political system can tolerate to stay united and function effectively is an important one.

The difficulties of governing Canada have followed a roller-coaster course since the country was federated in 1867, but especially since the 1960s. In Canada's centennial anniversary year, 1967, there was unbridled confidence, but that was soon to be checked, by the 1970 October Crisis; again, in 1980, with the Quebec referendum; and, in the 1990s, with the failure of the Meech Lake and Charlottetown accords, and the spectre of a separatist government in Quebec. Taken together, these are some of the events that have laid the foundations for the emergence of an independent Quebec, to be included in the international community as **sovereign** and distinct from Canada.

By the 1990s, Canada could no longer improvise in the ways that had allowed it to survive so many crises in the past. Canadians faced an uncertain future in an unpredictable world, with no guarantees of how long the country could remain a federated **nation-state**, stretching without disruption between shores washed by three oceans.

The very fabric of Canadian society appeared to unravel as the same dynamics that marked the world's power struggles began to unfold nationally, bringing with them a renewed prospect of Canada's dissolution into semi-independent and independent states.

New visions of the country called for aboriginal "self-government," a sovereign Quebec, gender equality, an internationally competitive economy, downsized governments, a new constitution, a reformed federal system, and a more efficient and effective Parliament. Is the governing system failing, hurtling Canadians toward a constitutional precipice that could send Canada into the next century in fragments? Must we reinvent how we are governed if Canada is to remain a united country?

## *INTRODUCTION*

The political universe in which all Canadian governments must perform is changing dramatically from day to day and from minute to minute. In the last decade of this century, we see every one of our governmental systems wavering under the increasing pressure of the fiscal forces of federalism. Canadian governments are withdrawing from their traditional involvement in society and in the process are transforming the dimensions of Canada's social safety net.

The architecture of our governments is changing as well, now that Canada exists in a global political village that none of its governments can ignore. The world itself has become one large **political system** to and with which all our governments must adapt and interact. But many Canadians detect the seeds of political disorder within Canada, germinated by the gap between the things Canadians expect and the ability of our governments to deliver them.

Since Confederation, government has grown to become a powerful and pervasive force throughout Canada. But that growth has been accompanied by a change in the way Canadians look at government. In the 1960s and 1970s, a broad-based consensus favoured a large and active set of Canadian governments, at the federal, provincial, and municipal levels. Today, Canadians want to keep the political and economic benefits they believe they derive from all their governments, but are also aware that government must be paid for by everyone and that current economic circumstances may mean that the numbers, size, and services of governments are no longer affordable.

Where once there was optimism that our governments could competently manage, direct, and steer society along its desired paths, today pessimism is increasing as the public's faith and trust in government decline to very low levels.

To provide a framework for understanding Canada's challenging problems in a fast-changing world, this book develops the theme of governability in each chapter. The hypothesis that we may or may not be governable, given our unique set of circumstances, is one means of explaining the various institutions, processes, and policies that affect our lives. It makes us think about the performance of governments and the power of the political system to help us survive as a modern nation-state in a competitive international community.

For more than a century, questions have recurred about our ability to govern this complex society of ours. Can our governing systems produce responsive, timely policies that address public issues while holding the country together in light of Quebec's special demands to be regarded as a distinct society? Frustra-

tions expressed today about the inability of the federal government to deal with budget deficits and mounting debt echo concerns over the potential dangers to the country's ability to remain sovereign and united.

In this Introduction, we present the framework of the book, outlining how Canada's governability is reflected in how our governments perform, the various political elements that contribute to our ability to govern ourselves, and the debates over what the proper roles of our governments are.

Chapter 1 tells us about the environment of Canadian government, the nature of our federal system, and how geography affects the way we govern ourselves, and focusses on the distinctive features of Canadian democracy. Chapter 2 informs us that the ways we think about politics and government always affect how governments are structured and how they perform. In the realm of government and public policy, ideas and ideologies are powerful forces that cannot be ignored and must be understood. Chapter 3 tells us about the evolution of our constitution: Canadian politics has been shaped significantly by the constitution and the institutions it has summoned into being.

Chapter 4 presents Parliament as a fused executive and legislative institution of government in Canada. The power of bureaucrats and how we administer the policies of government are the focus of Chapter 5. The nature of our court system and how judicial decisions affect government are the subjects of Chapter 6.

Chapter 7 examines the electoral process in Canada from the perspectives of the voters and the candidates, and how the rules determine the results. Chapter 8 focusses on why people get involved in politics not just as individuals, but also as groups; it examines the uniquely important role that political parties play in the Canadian political system and shows how they train our leaders, identify issues, and set the governing agenda of the country. Most chapters of this book focus on political institutions, leaders, and the things they do: Chapter 9 examines the "mass media," particularly journalists — the people who write, gather, edit, and report the news that people absorb.

Chapter 10 tells us about how we are governed at the provincial level, the role the provinces play in Canadian politics, and the nature of Canadian federalism. The most overlooked, yet perhaps the most influential, level of government in our lives is the municipality, which is the subject of Chapter 11. Finally, in the Conclusion, we look at how we govern ourselves by means of fiscal and monetary policy, why our governments are in so much debt, and what they must do about it.

## GOVERNABILITY: WHAT CAN GOVERNMENTS DO?

Canadians know that the ability to govern a country as vast as ours is crucial, because our national survival in a competitive international system depends on competent and efficient government. In this book, *governability* is the ability of a political system to make authoritative decisions in the public interest, to transform these decisions into effective and efficient public policies, and then to maintain the public's confidence that the governing system is doing the right things.

Richard Simeon (1976, 543) defines "governability" as "the ability of governments to respond to citizens' needs, to formulate policies which are more or less responsive to existing problems, and to be able to secure support and compliance in the implementation of these policies."

The idea that national survival is a product of our ability to govern ourselves has become particularly relevant for Canadians in the latter part of the twentieth century. Most Canadians believe that Quebec is an essential part of Canada, but many are concerned that

it may not remain a province within Canada's original governing system. Many are also concerned about the level of national debt, which has risen over the years as a result of the increasing costs of operating Canada's various governing units. Such concerns force us to look critically at the elements that constitute our governing system, and how it works in relation to the overall political system.

To understand governability we should bear in mind that governments are both "human" and "institutional." A *government* is an organized group of people who — for a time — control the executive, legislative, and administrative institutions of the **state**, who make authoritative decisions and steer the political system in the direction of specific policy or social goals.

Governments are also institutional. They always have an "executive component" that takes a decisive, leading, and responsive governing role in a complex world, and they usually have a "legislative branch" that deliberates and votes on questions of social importance and urgency; a "judicial branch" that settles social disputes and interprets constitutions; and an "administrative branch" that carries out the instructions and expectations of the other branches. (Under the terms of our constitution, Canada's administrative branch of government is subordinate to the executive and is not a distinctively separate branch of government.)

Given that human beings make up governmental institutions, governments can be very successful and advance the societies they lead; however, equally, governments can be toppled by human disruption and violence; they can be defeated in elections; and they can fail as a result of human incompetence, incapacity, and inertia.

### Performance

How well does Canada's political system work? Do our institutions of government perform adequately? How responsive are governmental institutions to the changes taking place within Canada and in the rest of the world? Do we have too many governing institutions? too few? Can Canadians afford their system of government as it now functions? Are Canada's representatives competent? And are they really representative, according to gender, race, ethnic background, education, occupation, and income?

Do Canadians feel that they are involved in their political institutions at all levels of government? Are our political parties competitive, and do they deal with the issues of Canadian society well? Are the rules of the electoral system fair, and do they permit the participation of minorities as well as the majority?

How and why do interest groups function? Are they more effective than political parties in getting things done? Do Canadians understand their constitution and respect both the letter and the spirit of its contents? These questions must lead us to evaluate the capacity of the political system to work proficiently, and ultimately to judge how well we are governed, given the institutions and the capabilities of the officials who run them.

For students of political science, evaluating and judging the ability of a political system to govern is an essential task. The performance of our governing system is a product of the type and organization of the system itself (e.g., parliamentary government combined with a federal system), the skills and competence of the people who comprise the government as well as the electorate, and the political environment in which they must function.

Performance has two dimensions: effectiveness — the extent to which the government can achieve its objectives — and efficiency — the efforts expended and costs incurred in reaching goals. We must ask not only if our government or our political system is likely to be capable of performing, but also what economic and social costs accrue to the public.

## Evaluating Our Governments

Political scientists as well as the general public usually make two types of observations about governments: **empirical** and **normative**. Empirical questions are objective and are based on statements of fact about the reality of a situation rather than the theory behind it. Accordingly, empirical observations about government focus on how *the* government really works. Normative questions are subjective and are based on value judgements about the theory behind a situation. Thus, normative observations about government focus on how *a* government should work, according to some moral or philosophical standard.

Judging the performance of any political system and its ability to work involves both empirical knowledge and normative values. Empirical statements about a particular government describe and explain its nature, components, and performance. We can learn about government by simply describing what we see. Then, we can use that empirical knowledge of how we are governed, proceeding logically from simply describing "what" we see to explaining "why" what we see is happening. For example, we have empirical evidence that, in the short term, policies that address debt and deficit normally create unemployment. In order to evaluate the government's performance in setting these policies, we can then apply normative values that prescribe the ways in which the governing system "should" perform; in terms of the example above, some might say that Canadian governments should pay less attention to the debt and deficit so that the economy will permit a level of employment to stimulate spending and growth.

The concept of governability encourages us to describe and explain the problems of governing our cities, provinces, and the nation. In doing this, we can more satisfactorily locate the strengths and weaknesses in our system of government. Governability gives us a starting point for analyzing and evaluating the nature and performance of governments at all levels — municipal, provincial, and federal. It also enables us to compare how our political system works relative to those of other democracies that have undergone unique institutional and national changes and have either survived or failed.

## THE ELEMENTS OF GOVERNABILITY

Governability involves much more than just institutions of government and how they perform. Other factors work in tandem with those institutions to govern a community of people or peoples. In Canada, geography, the environment, aboriginal rights, the emergent nationalism of Quebec, the advocacies of women's groups in a multicultural nation-state — all condition our ability to govern ourselves and to survive in a competitive international system.

Consequently, Canadian governments do not operate in isolation, unaffected by the society from which they emerge. In fact, the governability of Canada has often reflected the tensions and turmoil of a diverse society in search of political integration. How positively or negatively Canadians feel about their governments is vital to how well we are governed. And, while governmental institutions might appear to be prominent in the political system, they are only a part of it. Politics — the powerful interplay of all interests, values, and goals in our society — constitutes the rest.

### Politics

How does politics affect how we are governed? Politics seems to permeate everything we do in Canada. Every day, our lives are invaded by political forces operating at home, at work, in a university or college, and in our provinces and municipalities. If Canadian governments are to function and survive, they must be attentive not only to the politics within them but also to the political forces around them.

*Politics* is a human behavioural phenomenon that involves the use of social skills, such as bargaining, competition, compromise, negotiation, and sometimes even violence, by which people try to influence others in order to achieve certain desirable social goals. Politics as a social force can help us attain goals that individuals or private groups find it difficult to reach by themselves.

The power of politics is that it communicates our needs to a wider audience. It is fundamentally a persuasive activity: People convince themselves to mobilize and attempt to persuade governments to build universities and colleges; to support the publishing industry, and farmers or fishers; to protect wildlife; to build parks; to support the arts; and so on.

As such, politics involves far more than government and the selection of people to govern our society. It exists because people live together and seek to act collectively. When they act collectively, their individual actions must be co-ordinated in order to get things done. Accordingly, politics is a way to organize numbers of persons to do things together that they could not have done separately.

Most people associate politics with the formal institutions and processes of government, including the ways in which governing elites are selected, how laws are made and enforced, and how the relations between and among governments are conducted. Although much of what we think of as politics has to do with the activities of governments, the realm of politics actually involves a great deal more.

Aristotle observed that human beings are by "nature" political animals. By this, he meant that politics and political behaviour come from inside us and do not just happen outside of, or to, us. In today's world, the practice of politics is not limited to international, federal, provincial, or local governments. We speak of office politics, campus politics, and church politics. Even within the structure and inter-relations of a family, political behaviour is observable. Accordingly, between or among individuals, politics is a detectable phenomenon. In the 1990s, power is a factor in the workplace and at home; as a result, men and women often engage in a political relationship, one that is conditioned by the politics of gender, equality, and affirmative action.

Harold Lasswell (1936) defined politics as "who gets what, when, and how." Canadian professors R. Jackson, D. Jackson, and N. Baxter-Moore (1986, 8) concurred with Lasswell's definition when they stated that "politics embraces all activity which impinges upon the making of binding decisions about who gets what — when and how."

Sometimes, we focus mainly on the "who" of politics — the premiers, the voters, the pressure groups, and the political parties. But "how" Canadians "do" politics — the bargaining, compromising, **lobbying**, and competing — is important too. The "what" of politics refers to policy, the stuff of political conflict, and the **political patronage** in the system — the jobs, the opportunities, the contracts, and so on, that are awarded to people who have political "connections."

Governments are prominent in the politics of our communities. They are the institutions that possess the authority and bureaucratic capacity to convert politics into policy for society, and thus to determine who gets what, when and how. They are concerned primarily with what political scientist David Easton (1965, 50) calls "the authoritative allocation of values for a society," including the distribution of wealth, the exercise of power, and the various rights and freedoms people expect to enjoy. By "values," Easton means anything that is considered important to a society, such as protecting people from criminal behaviour, and providing comprehensive medical care. What makes the allocation of values different is that it is "authoritative"; that is, it converts values into laws or regulations at the command of democratically elected governments.

But politics is the way people with different **political values** bargain, co-operate, and compete to influence government with respect to what it should and should not do. The ability to govern our society would be a very simple matter if it involved using the authority of the state only to obtain goals that people favour and that benefit all equally. In fact, making government decisions is nearly always competitive, and usually conflictive. On any given day, thousands of diverse **political interest groups** are pulling and tugging to get the favourable attentions of the governing system.

Not all groups benefit equally from what governments choose to do, or even pay equally in proportion to their use of the collective good. Politics in large measure involves an attempt to reduce conflicts about who gets how much of something when there is not enough of it for everyone.

### Political Culture

How we govern ourselves is a product of what political scientists call **political culture**. It is the way we orient ourselves to politics and government; however, fundamentally, it is the way or ways a society "does" politics and government. Knowing what comprises our political culture enables us to look behind the formal institutions of our governments to the patterns of political beliefs and behaviours people display. The concept enables us to understand why people living in Cape Breton tend to vote differently from those living on the Nova Scotia mainland. It also helps us to see what makes many people in Quebec embrace a nationalism with sovereignist goals and how that can threaten the viability of Canada's national political culture.

The broader "social" culture includes everything people think and do in their society: its art, literature, human relationships, agriculture, horticulture, and music, for example. However, "political" culture has a narrower focus: a society's governmental and political systems, what they do, and how.

As Figure i.1 shows, we can think of a political culture as the totality of a society's political experiences from its remote to its recent past — its symbols, values, beliefs, skills, customs, traditions, expectations, and attitudes. For example, the "customs" we develop that are not necessarily written anywhere, such as when and how a prime minister should consult with the governor general are a unique aspect of Canada's political culture. The "beliefs" we hold, such as whether governments should be more or less regulative, are part of that culture as well. The "skills" we value, such as those of our governments to negotiate with one another, or with foreign governments, are vital to the survival of our political system. How we learn about these components of political culture can have a determining impact on the governability of our society. For example, the failure to negotiate in the best interests of Canada in a treaty such as the North American Free Trade Agreement (NAFTA), or to legislate too many regulations on businesses could seriously weaken the Canadian economy and render it uncompetitive in the global economy.

All aspects of our political culture are preserved and transmitted to new generations by means of what political scientists refer to as **political socialization**, a concept we analyze in Chapter 2. Political socialization is the process through which an individual learns about politics and government, and develops an understanding of and feelings about, and evaluates, the political world.

A political culture includes people's expectations about the proper role of government in their lives. The culture we develop to do politics transmits our hopes and fears about how we are governed. What do we care about? What do we want from our governmental system? What political values do we want our governments to represent and implement? These political values tell us what is good, or right, or wise, or beneficial. They generate the attitudes and standards of judgement about what we consider to be important, desirable, and proper in governing our society.

The components of political culture are found in varying strengths in different segments of the population, or in different regions, where people may hold values quite different from those of the dominant political culture. In such instances, a region is said to have its own distinctive **political subculture**.

In Canada, doing politics and government in Newfoundland is different from doing them in Saskatchewan because Canadians comprise a multitude of aboriginal, ethnic, linguistic, regional, and political subgroups. In most of these subgroups, people hold a particular set of opinions about government, politics, and the goals of Canadian society, and about their political and legal rights. Given the diversity of Canadian society and the wide range of different subcultures within it, how it is that the governing process continues to function is an important question.

**Figure i.1 Elements of Political Culture**

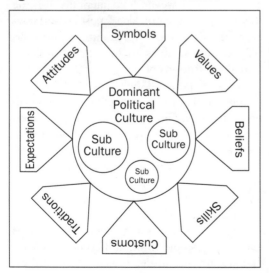

## Political Subcultures

Canada may appear to be a uniform political entity to people and other nation-states outside the country, but students of Canadian politics know that there is little uniformity within the political framework of the Canadian nation-state (see Wilson and Hoffman 1974; Simeon and Elkins 1974; Bell and Tepperman 1979). People in each part of Canada perceive the totality of the political culture differently. While Canada appears to be one national political culture, it is also a union of different political subcultures.

Each province and territory has developed its own political character, traditions, and style of leadership and participation. Public attitudes, the issues, and the political style differ from one part of the country to the next, as do even the procedures used in the legislatures.

The victories of the Parti Québécois in a number of Quebec provincial elections reflect a widespread desire among the people in that province to maintain and extend the uniqueness of Quebec's political culture among all others on the North American continent. Control by the Québécois over the province's territory and its major educational, religious, administrative, judicial, and other governmental institutions has entrenched Quebec as a political subculture that, if it achieves independence, could lead to the unravelling of the governing system in the rest of the country.

The balance of political cultures, and the degree to which they co-exist, constitute some of the most powerful influences shaping our society's political system and the governability of that system. A political system is likely to be more governable, stable, and durable to the extent that its political subcultures can work together, that fundamental political values are acceptable to all of them, and that the public will see the importance of preserving the distinctions without destroying the national political culture.

Conversely, however, instability, disunity, and the possible unravelling of the entire political system will occur when political subcultures are incompatible and/or seek to achieve sovereign independence.

## Political Participation

Governability is related to the degree the governed feel they can participate in the decisions that affect their lives. Individuals and groups attempt to influence the policy process through various forms of political participation. The ability to govern in a society is enhanced when people think they can influence the affairs of government by their actions. This is what some scholars refer to as a person's sense of "political efficacy," by which they mean a person's belief that he or she understands the political system and can influence government decision making. People who feel efficacious are more likely to communicate directly with politicians and government administrators, join political parties, campaign for candidates, and generally seek to steer the political system in their favour. They have a sense of themselves as politically anchored in the system that governs them.

Many Canadians simply view politics and government as an entertaining spectator sport. Most profess to hold a moderate degree of interest in observing political affairs: They frequently discuss politics with family and friends, and may even try to influence the way someone else votes.

But, for Canadians, the most common act of political participation is voting, even though, for many people, it amounts to only a few seconds of actual political involvement. The political system works better when people believe that the vote is an effective instrument for controlling government officials, especially when they feel that those officials are basically accountable to them.

Voting is not the only way people participate in the political system. They also contribute money to political campaigns, go to party conventions, write speeches, give their personal time, stuff envelopes with campaign literature, phone potential voters, put up political support signs, and work at the polls on election day.

People often participate in their political system by contacting government officials — meeting with them, calling them, or writing to them about their concerns. They may send telegrams to a provincial minister of education, asking for more funding for public education. They may telephone their city councillor about fixing a pothole on the street where they live.

Some Canadians participate through less-conventional political acts, such as protesting, demonstrating, or even civil disobedience. Some may deliberately participate in the local underground economy, or deliberately shop across the border as a protest against high taxes and higher consumer prices.

It is often assumed that a large majority of citizens will take part in political life. But, in practice, many Canadians are "apolitical," that is, devoid of political interest and unwilling to participate in politics. Most Canadians do not get involved in campaigns except in a low-key and superficial way. They barely help their political parties between elections, and withdraw their political activism until the next electoral contest. In general, Canadians are more likely to sign petitions, or to write to or call their representatives; only a minority, fewer than a quarter of the electorate, are willing to protest actively, loudly, and visibly within their communities.

How Canada's political system works and whether it survives depends in large part on who participates and how. Political participation is crucial because it enables citizens to communicate their wishes in relation to the conduct of government.

## Political Power

The phenomenon of power is one of the most complex in our lives. Power finds its way into all levels of human interaction — at home, at work, and on the street, and almost everywhere that the public has a voice. But power is especially prominent as the currency of politics and government. Governments are the primary institutions through which political power is exercised, but power is also found extensively and potentially in all social organizations — for example, political parties, pressure groups, interest groups, religious organizations, and corporations — and among individuals.

The search for power is a strong motivation in the world of politics. Those who hold power have the instruments at their disposal to make decisions affecting many human lives. Some analysts see political power as the ability to influence, cause, and control the behaviour of others (Dahl 1957; Deutsch 1967; Holsti 1988). For them, power enables those who exercise it to modify the behaviour of others in certain desirable ways, even in the absence of their consent. Political power may be exercised in many ways — overtly or subtly, legally or illegally, justly or unjustly. In the realm of governability, political power ultimately can compel compliance — if necessary, by the threat or use of force.

However, this perception of power is sometimes identified as "male," in that it posits the doing of something to other people. A feminist view sees power "as the building of capabilities among people to work together to accomplish their goals" (Burt 1990, 214). The former male view is "hierarchical," a top-down approach to decision making in which power is exercised over others; the latter, feminist, view is "circular" in that it seeks a consensus among participants who feel they have been treated as equals in the decision-making process.

Frequently, power, ability, and consent are closely interlocking factors in governability. Power may be exercised by persuasion, command or physical force. As a characteristic of governance, power is the capacity to make decisions that have collective consequences, for example, making a national or provincial budget, setting the bank rate, establishing a university or college, or building a regional hospital.

Political power is exercised by those who participate effectively in the decision-making institutions of society, who feel they have political anchorage in the system, and who can make the political system work for them. The exercise of voting rights, membership in political parties, and, of course, running for government or political office are some of the ways that people realize political power.

In terms of governability, the question to consider is what groups are most likely to use these means of political expression. In Canada, political power is associated with other sources of power that determine the distribution of wealth, prestige, and other resources in the country (Grabb 1988).

Those who, for one reason or another, cannot affect the political and governing process are deemed to be, and usually feel they are, powerless. The powerless feel they have no capacity to be influential in or exert control over government decision making, and those elected to government do not represent them or care about them. They feel, and usually are, excluded from the benefits of the political system. People who regard themselves as powerless are often those on welfare, the unemployed, and those who feel politically alienated from the system that governs them. But, other groups as well, such as business and labour, may feel powerless at times.

In many ways, the governing structure serves to bind together the other bases of power in society. In Canada, there is a sense that the powers of governments are the highest expression and manifestation of political power. Government is the ultimate source of power because, in theory at least, the empowered in all other spheres are answerable to those holding political power. In this view, the government and its administrative apparatus become the repository of the power and will of the people.

Canada's federal government serves to establish and maintain the balance of political power, as between and among provinces, by redistributing the national wealth in the form of transfer payments. Or it can reduce or remove power differences among groups and individuals by passing laws that prohibit race or gender discrimination in hiring practices. In these and other examples, we can see how Canada's governments are a source of power in themselves, and a potential means for establishing, enforcing, or altering power relations in other spheres.

## Political Legitimacy

Democratic governments need legitimacy, the popular acceptance of a government and its officials as rightful authorities in the exercise of power. To survive and operate effectively, a government must enjoy the widely held belief of its citizens that its structures are effective and justified, and that those who exercise governance have the right to do so. The status of rightful power and authority is conferred by the people on a government's officials, actions, and institutions.

On the one hand, if citizens believe that their government is legitimate, they will be inclined to obey its laws and regulations, pay taxes, participate in the electoral processes, and serve willingly in the armed forces. On the other hand, if people think that a government is illegitimate, they will want to change it, break its laws, evade its taxes, ignore its elections, and avoid its calls to military service.

"Legitimacy" is the collective belief that the actions and institutions of government are compatible with public expectations. People must believe that a government's decisions are binding on them because governments have earned the right to make rules and regulations properly.

People will accept the policies and laws of a government as legitimate if it generally meets three criteria: (1) it operates according to certain fundamental legal political procedures and constitutional provisions; (2) it adequately represents the electorate; and (3) its performance is widely viewed as satisfactory.

But government maintains a legal monopoly on armed force, in almost all political systems, and in the end that legal violence can be used to secure compliance. Indeed, at the point where voluntary compliance has to be replaced with systematic governmental force, the legitimacy of the governmental system may soon be eroded. For example, the coercive function of the state can be directed against less-privileged groups and their political allies (e.g., police action against strikers on picket lines or in a specific instance, the use of the Canadian armed forces against the Mohawks).

Governability comes down to the question of whether the government enjoys the support of the people. A government that enjoys legitimacy has little need to use coercion; people will comply without violent confrontations. Only when its legitimacy is in question will a government usually resort to armed force.

## Political Authority

Another important element of governability is political authority, which should be thought of as power plus legitimacy. The concept of authority prevails in both politics and government. Governability depends upon the authority people ascribe to a government because it adheres faithfully to a constitution, and because it performs well. Authority is explicitly conveyed to governments as a legitimate power by those over whom the power is exercised, and who regard it as socially and politically right, proper, and necessary. But when the authority of a government is challenged by its citizens, both the power and the legitimacy of government institutions and personnel are diminished, which can contribute to its failure.

Authority may rest on rational law, tradition, or charisma. For example, a judge's authority rests on rational law, that is, when an individual is granted the right to make decisions for others by means of previously established rules. In contrast, a queen's or a governor general's authority rests on tradition, that is, when an individual is given the right to make decisions for others because of time-honoured customs. Some of a prime minister's or a premier's authority is also based on custom and tradition, such as the power to appoint and remove members of the Cabinet. Finally, people who are perceived to possess extraordinarily compelling personal characteristics enjoy authority based on charisma.

Those given the right to use legitimate power are said to occupy positions of authority. Their authority is strictly limited according to the constitutional or legal definitions of the positions. The police have the authority to write a traffic ticket or to arrest a speeder but cannot convict a criminal. A judge, who cannot issue a traffic ticket or make an arrest, has the authority to try, and sentence, a criminal.

People will accept, usually without question, decisions made by those whom they believe have the right to make them; most people may succumb to raw power because they cannot resist it, but those who do resist and refuse to acquiesce cause the users of raw power greater difficulties than they do the wielders of authority.

In Canada, the right to exercise power normally is vested in a governmental office or flows from the perceived legitimacy of a government function. A prime minister, a member of Parliament, and a federal judge may exercise power and authority because of the legitimacy vested in his or her roles.

One concept closely associated with authority is influence. People who exercise political influence have no automatic right to make decisions. Rather, influence occurs in a political system when someone in a position of power is persuaded to change his or her opinions or to adopt the opinion of someone else.

Influence is not always institutionalized; it rests on individual appeals, based on personal contact. Even people who exercise a great deal of political power must often use influence if they want to affect actions outside the scope of their authority.

All politicians try to exercise influence, by using personal appeals and persuasive arguments to move others to adopt their political positions. Political parties, pressure groups, and interest groups are institutions designed to influence by persuading others of their preferred social goals.

Money can be an important influence in politics and government. At the least, it can buy access to those making decisions. At the worst, it can buy the decisions. Money allows some points of view to be trumpeted while others are forced to whisper. Some candidates or groups can afford to spend a great deal of money for media advertising or to arrange for prestigious people to lobby on their behalf; others can afford only mimeographs or letters.

### Political Leadership

Another essential element of governability is political leadership, a form of public leadership whereby power and influence over, or in co-operation with, other people are exercised, sometimes to mobilize mass support, to achieve sociopolitical goals, and to accomplish ends that are unattainable without public support.

In Canada, where the parliamentary system of government operates extensively, leadership requires putting together the necessary party and governmental support to pass the legislation and to raise the money required to carry it out. Canada's political leaders usually operate in an institutional setting, where they are publicly observed, and where complex rules and constitutional divisions of formal authority limit their individual freedom to lead. The prime minister and the premiers can form and lead a government, determine the size and

composition of the Cabinet, and formulate laws and public policy, but must do so according to the rules, procedures, and traditions of parliamentary democracy.

From the perspective of governability, when leadership is perceived to be in a state of crisis, the political system is vulnerable and will have difficulty governing itself. Indeed, a political system is undoubtedly less effective without acceptable and competent leaders, and in some cases can fail to function as a result of these circumstances.

Responsibility for governing Canadian society is, of course, not evenly distributed, nor is it accessible to all citizens. A particular group of citizens, which may be called the political leadership or the **political elite**, has the task of managing the government, administering the bureaucracy, passing legislation, leading political parties, adjudicating, and mobilizing public action. The identification and presence of a governing elite in Canada has been a focus of social science research for some time.

John Porter, in *The Vertical Mosaic* (1965), found a great deal of evidence to support the view that a highly diverse group of wealthy people controls the dominant institutions in Canadian society. Porter also found that no one single elite exists in Canada. Instead, he found that Canada's political culture is **pluralist**, consisting of competing elites, groups of powerful people found in the economy, the political system, the media, and the military. Others (Olsen 1980; Panitch 1990) have argued that small, powerful social groups have come to dominate the important decision-making institutions in Canadian society.

The most striking fact about political leadership in Canada is how few people are directly involved in it. Within Canada's adult population (18 years of age and older) of about 21 million people, there are somewhere between 700 and 1000 persons directly involved with leadership, including parliamentarians, members of the federal Cabinet, the premiers and their cabinets, deputy ministers, federal and provincial judges, and political party leaders. From the 21 million potential candidates, a very tiny group of political leaders emerges.

The fact that few govern many is a starting point for understanding the nature of *political recruitment*, how people move in and out of government office and positions of political power in Canada. Recruitment is a gradual and continuous process of selection and elimination that narrows the general population to only the few who hold the highest political positions (see Figures i.2 and i.3).

In Canada, some legal qualifications affect the recruitment process. In most cases, any adult citizen is legally qualified to hold public or political office. Other legal qualifications might include residency for MPs, MLAs, MNAs, and senators, and, for certain positions, especially that of judge, professional credentials. Another recruitment criterion

refers to those who are "socially" eligible. No written rules exist concerning this criterion, but there is evidence, as noted by Porter (1965) and others, that a large percentage of our political leaders comes from particular groups in the population.

An examination of the social background of political leaders in Canada reveals that most come from comparatively well-off, middle-class backgrounds. Only a sprinkling of political leaders is drawn from the wage-earning working class. Top government positions are held, for the most part, by English-speaking Caucasian men from successful professional and business families, or by men who themselves have become leading professionals or successes in commerce.

Another group, whom we might call "political activists," are usually middle- and upper-middle-class people who pay close attention to political matters, who serve on committees

**Figure i.2  Which Few Citizens Will Achieve Leadership Roles?**

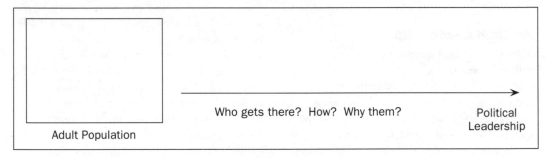

**Figure i.3  Recruitment Criteria for Political Leadership**

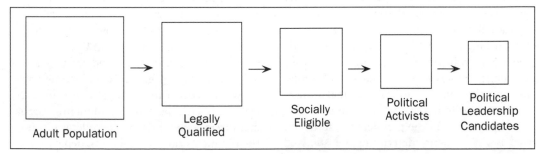

and work in campaigns, who know and are known by people actually holding office, and who are in positions that can supply recruits for public office. And, finally, within the politically active stratum is an even smaller number of people who become the serious candidates for top leadership positions. These include those actually nominated for elected positions, those appointed to cabinets, government executive advisory bodies, the powerful committees of Parliament, the Supreme Court, and so on.

The Canadian agenda is crowded with many unsolved problems of governability: the place of Quebec in a Canadian federation, the relevance and efficiency of our governing institutions, social and economic crises, and the environment. Whom we choose to lead us, and how we choose them are central issues of governability. There can be little question that Canada's success or failure — indeed, its very survival — depends in large part on the quality of the leadership its political system is able to attract.

## Political Trust

The degree to which individuals express trust in government and other political institutions determines the viability of a political system. Democratic governments like Canada's rely upon public support based on trust. *Political trust* is the confidence that people have in the workings of their political institutions, in the way the governments are organized, and in the integrity of the people who work in the political system (see Table i.1). As Michael Ornstein notes, political trust constitutes a citizen's fundamental "relationship" with his or her state (cited in Brym 1986, 54).

People who reveal attitudes of trust display a strong sense of national or provincial identification, even a sense of patriotism toward the geopolitical unit that governs them (see Table i.2).

Those who distrust their governmental system tend to regard leaders as dishonest and

incompetent, and view the political system as wasteful and unrepresentative. Such negative attitudes and ambivalence about the political system is called "political cynicism," and, when widely felt, it can affect the public sense of civic participation. If a significant proportion of a population ceases to trust the political system, the ability of the system to govern is severely threatened.

Mistrust is frequently directed at leaders and policies, but may be targeted at the system of government as well (see Table i.1). In Canada, the highest levels of distrust toward the federal government and the Canadian political system are found in Quebec. *Political distrust* shows itself as a lack of faith in the inte-

### Table i.1 Do You Trust Your Government?

1. How much of the time do you think you can trust the government in your capital city to do what is right?
   a) just about always
   b) most of the time
   c) some of the time
2. Do you think the people in government waste a lot of money we pay in taxes?
   a) waste some of it
   b) don't waste very much of it
3. Most of those running government are smart people who usually
   a) know what they are doing
   b) don't know what they are doing
4. Of the people running government,
   a) quite a few are crooked
   b) not very many of them are crooked
   c) hardly any of them are crooked
5. Government is pretty much run
   a) by a few big interests acting on their own behalf
   b) for the benefit of all people

*Source:* These questions were drawn from Warren Miller and Edward Schneider, *American National Election Studies Data Sourcebook* (Cambridge, Mass.: Harvard University Press, 1980). Reprinted with permission of Harvard University Press.

**Table I.2 "Do You Think of Yourself as a Canadian First or as a Citizen of Your Province?"**

| | Canadian | Provincial |
| --- | --- | --- |
| | (percent) | |
| Quebec | 44 | 55 |
| Newfoundland | 47 | 53 |
| P.E.I. | 57 | 43 |
| Nova Scotia | 63 | 37 |
| Alberta | 74 | 24 |
| New Brunswick | 75 | 25 |
| British Columbia | 83 | 17 |
| Saskatchewan | 83 | 16 |
| Manitoba | 84 | 15 |
| Ontario | 90 | 9 |
| All Canada | 73 | 26 |

*Source: Maclean's,* January 1, 1990. Reproduced with permission.

grity, the representativeness, and the competence of the political elites in the federal system, as well as those in other provinces. People might not want to pay taxes to a governmental system they do not trust. They might refuse to co-operate with the government in supplying census information or accepting jury duty. Or they might refuse to vote.

People with extremely low trust in the political system are said to be "politically alienated." These people feel dissociated from the political system and express attitudes of powerlessness, exclusion, lack of control, and frustration. Alienated citizens do not trust those in power; they may be disenchanted with all politicians; and they may very well be searching for substantial changes in the structures of the governmental system that will make it work better. People who feel alienated do not participate much in the political system, and usually have little of the time, money, and resources to get involved.

In Canada, political alienation depends a great deal on the economic outlook; people seem to trust government more when it pro-

duces economic conditions favourable to their lives. In the province of Quebec, political alienation created by economic forces is compounded by the issue of nationalism. Many Quebeckers feel that their economic hardship is directly related to the extent of governmental control they have over the protection of language and culture.

In the 1990s, political cynicism among Canadians runs much deeper than it has previously. The loss of public confidence in the efficacy of business, labour, education, religion, and the press contributes to more widespread feelings of political alienation among Canadians. And, while the tumbling of political trust has focussed on politicians and government officials, it has generated calls for changes in the system itself. Such calls demand us to reform or abolish the Senate, to adopt a system of proportional representation, to amend the constitution and grant special status to certain groups and Quebec, to alter the rules and procedures of parliamentary government, and to re-examine the fundamental political philosophy behind our system of government.

## GOVERNABILITY: THE UNENDING SEARCH FOR GOVERNMENT'S PROPER ROLE

What is the proper role for government? This question has puzzled the world's political thinkers for several thousand years, and Canadians for well over a hundred years. Why do people put up with government when some of its activities are coercive, regulatory, restrictive, apparently destructive to the national interest, and so on? Governments sometimes make us do things that remove some of our choices and freedoms. Not only can governments restrict you and punish you, they can also tax you, take away your property or freedom if you refuse to pay your taxes, and make the kinds of policy choices that impose great pain in your life.

The contemporary role of Canadian government has radically changed from the days when our grandparents and great-grandparents lived. Evolving from a small farming country of four provinces on the eastern edge of North America to a highly developed economy spanning the continent and exerting its influence in world affairs, Canada has endured massive changes in the role and functions of its governments.

From 1867 to just before the First World War, Canada was transformed from an agricultural society to an industrial and technological society. Originally, our government was small and rudimentary. There were no personal or corporate income taxes, no family allowance cheques, no Canada/Quebec Pension Plan, and no medicare. The Canadian Broadcasting Corporation (CBC) did not exist, nor did the Canada Council, or Atomic Energy of Canada Ltd. The national government consisted of Parliament, a postal service, customs and immigration, a system of courts, and public works.

Today, Canadians are offered radio and television programs whose content is regulated by their federal government. A government marketing board sets the farm gate price of the eggs we crack for breakfast. The car or truck we drive has to meet federal and provincial safety and repair standards. City by-laws ban smoking in municipal government and non-government workplaces. In most parts of Canada, restaurants must supply their customers with "no-smoking" sections in which to sit. Public health officials inspect the foods we eat. Consumer and corporate affairs inspectors check to see if the scales that weigh our food are honest. Customs officials check through our luggage for illegal goods and for illegal quantities of alchohol and cigarettes and undeclared purchases made in foreign countries.

It is hard to imagine today how feeble and uncertain Canada's governments were more than a century ago. The governing institutions that evolved after Confederation have changed in many ways, becoming larger in scale and performing many more complex functions. Considering the enormity of change in modern Canadian society, it is still remarkable that our governing institutions have retained so much of their original form, organization, and procedures.

## Maintaining Law and Social Order

Maintaining order is the oldest purpose of government and was very much a reason for Canadians first to come together in a federal system. Order is part of the purpose of government. The North-West Mounted Police (later the RCMP) was the first symbol of that order in Canada. Most people can identify with the phrase "law and order." Maintaining order in this sense usually means instituting the rule of law to protect the lives and property of people.

The English philosopher Thomas Hobbes (1588–1679) said that sovereign power is essential to protect people from one another, and government must intervene, by force if necessary, if peace and order are to be possible. People could not enjoy the fundamental pleasures of life — a walk in the park, a hockey game, a concert — if, in doing these things, their physical well-being is constantly threatened by others whose violence goes unhindered and unpunished.

Another type of order — social order — is associated with the purposes of government. "Social order" refers to the established patterns of authority in society and to the traditional modes of behaviour that are widely seen as important. It is the accepted way of doing things. The prevailing social order prescribes proper behaviour in many different areas: how politicians should conduct themselves (in both their private and their public lives); under what conditions and at what age people should have sexual relations; what the press should not publish (i.e., pornography). Governments usually act to protect the established social

The frontispiece for Thomas Hobbes's *Leviathan*, published in 1651, illustrates this philosopher's belief that the sovereign is essential to protect society and maintain order. *Source:* The frontispiece for Thomas Hobbes's *Leviathan*, 1651 edition (Oxford: Clarendon Press, 1929).

order, resisting attempts to change social patterns, unless encouraged to do so by means of political pressure.

While anarchists might disagree, most people say that, without some form of government, there would be no "civilized" life. People support the widespread presence of government because it, in turn, gives us law, order, and predictability in our lives. It provides the social context within which our families can be adequately raised; jobs can be safely performed, or even held; education can be equitably acquired; leisure can be securely enjoyed; and our futures can be planned.

We depend on government to supply security and safety, to protect our personal lives, our possessions, our freedoms and privileges. People would be reluctant to be consumers if they thought that the goods they bought would be stolen; a parent would not send a child to school if there were no traffic and criminal laws to make the journey safe; people would not keep their money in banks if their savings deposits were likely to disappear.

More than this, we expect government to protect national borders from foreign invasions and international outlaws, and to manage our natural resources such as the fisheries and the forests. In the absence of these fundamental protections, there would be little reason to make sacrifices, in time, effort, and money, to build our homes, schools, industries, and parks.

But what is the connection between providing basic law and order and other activities of government, such as repaving Highway 401 from Cornwall to Toronto; supporting a Canadian graduate student writing a dissertation on Quebec politics; giving money to Saskatchewan farmers to stave off bankruptcy; publishing brochures naming endangered trees and plants in our provinces; running advertisements for fitness; and sending a monthly cheque to a blind pensioner in Winnipeg?

Obviously, we must look beyond the maintenance of social order to answer such questions about the unending search for government roles. In the modern world of politics, governments are expected to do many other things for the welfare of their people.

### The Public Good

Using their extensive powers to raise money, governments can tax people for money to spend on the public good. Many of the needs and goals of individuals and groups cannot be met without the assistance of the collective power and resources that governments can provide.

What constitutes the public good at any particular time and place depends upon the fundamental habits and values of Canadians and, to a very important extent, upon their scale of priorities — their beliefs about what should come first.

"Public goods" such as the protection of the environment are funded through the general tax system rather than on the "user-pay" principle that is characteristic of "private goods," such as buying a car or going to a play. Governments that represent many interests must often produce or ensure the implementation of collective goods — benefits that are available to all individuals whether any particular individual or group worked to achieve that benefit, or even wants the benefit. Public goods benefit all citizens but are not likely to be produced by the voluntary acts of individuals.

Consider this example: Air pollution caused by automobiles and trucks is, as we all know, a serious problem facing many Canadian communities. Reduction of air pollution would be a collective good in that all would benefit, whether or not they did anything to help reduce it. Suppose a highly efficient pollution-control device is invented that would cost the individual consumer $1000. All Canadians would benefit from the elimination of pollution that resulted from their voluntarily installing such a device on all their vehicles. But it is unlikely that most individuals will install such a device unless forced to by government. Many people would not voluntarily buy such a device because they might conclude that not much difference would be made in the overall pollution rate of the community if they, as individuals, failed to install one. Furthermore, they could use the $1000 for other private purposes. Every citizen would benefit from the installation of those devices purchased voluntarily by some because they would breathe cleaner air, and those who did not purchase the device would enjoy the added benefit of $1000 extra dollars to spend on more personally satisfying goods and services.

If most individuals take this rational approach, a social situation results in which everybody loses. But, if government makes the purchasing and installation of such a device a legal requirement, all citizens gain. In this kind of situation, only when individual choice is eliminated can the overall social good of clean air be achieved.

### The Making of Public Policy

A government's activities range from simply outlining the rules that regulate individual behaviour to the implementation of **public policies** that are intended to fulfil specific social goals. There are many types of public policies. Every law that government passes, every budget it drafts, and every other decision it makes is public policy. Public policy can be defined in many ways, but one of the most useful definitions holds that public policy is the impact government has by either acting or not acting. By acting, for example, a government can pass a law requiring bilingual or unilingual signage, finance AIDS research, send pension cheques to millions of Canadians, raise or cut taxes, send peacekeeping troops to Bosnia, and attempt to clean up toxic waste in our harbours and lakes.

Government also establishes policy by not acting. According to Thomas Dye (1984, 1–3), a decision by a government to ignore the need to address a problem is itself a policy decision. The concept of setting policy through inaction may seem difficult to understand, but it is crucial for discerning the strategies of those who wish to protect a status quo that benefits them. Because the potential power of government is so great, inactivity has the practical effect of being a form of support for things as they are.

Public policy is always a product of governability. Involved in the process are legislators and their lawmaking institutions, the political executive, public administrators, the courts, and parallel institutions such as interest groups and political parties. The policy process in Canada involves many steps and many political actors (e.g., political parties and pressure groups), governmental as well as non-governmental. Every policy carries with it some form of control, like the carrot or the stick, to induce acceptance and compliance (see Figure i.4).

Nowhere is this principle of public policy made clearer than in the area of economic decisions. Budgeting is at the heart of public economic policies. It sets priorities and provides limits for government action. It is also a tangible expression of where government hopes to have an impact on our lives and the decisions we make in the economy.

**Figure i.4  Making Public Policy in Canada**

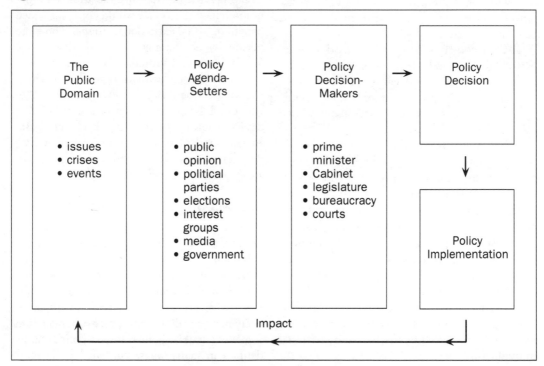

But many policies that people demand are often non-economic and non-material. Some of the bitterest fights in Canada's political history have been over the ways governments impose a set of moral values held by one segment of society upon the whole society, for example, the issues of abortion, the right to choose when we die, liquor laws, Sunday shopping, drugs, and sexual orientation. Choices have to be made among alternative material and non-material goals because no society can do everything, or even all the most worthwhile things, at once. The more painful the choices, the more likely it is that the process of deciding at the government level will generate political conflict.

Governability is enhanced by the three types of public policies governments can use to serve Canadians: (1) "distributive"; (2) "regulatory"; and (3) "redistributive."

*Distributive policies* enable a government to dispense to particular groups something it possesses, for example, land, money, control over aspects of external relations, subsidies to certain industries and corporations, and protective tariffs for manufacturers. Distributive policies usually have low public visibility and produce minimal conflict. *Regulatory policies* apply general rules to whole categories of people, corporate and private. Regulation as a form of policy does, however, establish the political right of government to intervene in the behaviour of corporations or economic sectors (agriculture, aviation, language, communications) that previously could operate subject only to the restraints of a free-market economy. Regulatory policies can protect the public by establishing standards for various private and corporate activities, for example, licensing pilots, placing bans on certain food additives, and setting minimum-wage rates. *Redistributive policies* may stimulate fundamental realignments of social and economic power and benefits in a political system. Policies of redistribution touch upon the most sought-after values in life — money, power, security,

and status — that are shifted from one segment of society and passed on to another.

What the government does or does not do makes the lives of Canadians better or worse. When public policies are in dispute, people disagree over one or more of the following elements: the goals that governments should have, the means they should use to meet them, and governments' perception of the situation.

## *The Promotion of Equality*

The twentieth century has witnessed the emergence of another purpose of government, that is, the promotion and protection of social and political equality. In Canada, where the contrast of poverty amid plenty has moved political leaders to attempt to enhance the quality of life, all governments are expected to level the political and economic playing fields so as to provide equal opportunity for the disadvantaged.

Under the philosophy of the **welfare state**, the role of government has been expanded to provide for the individual's welfare, especially in the areas of education, medical care, and equal employment opportunities for men and women. This contemporary objective of government — to promote equality — has been by far the most controversial. Today, the debt burden for sustaining the kinds of public goods that benefit the welfare of the individual is often the grounds on which they are opposed.

The key issue is government's redistributive role — taking from the rich to give to the poor, from the powerful to give to the less powerful and the powerless. Giving voluntarily to those who do not benefit from the economic and political rewards of the social and economic system, as in charitable donations, has a strong basis in Canada's political history.

Governments make distinctions about the scope of equality. With respect to voting, "political equality" usually means that each voter has one, and only one, ballot. But, when people demand political equality, they usually

Some analysts would argue that genuine equality of opportunity is a precondition for political equality. This young female hockey player might not have been able to participate in the sport ten years ago. What does this suggest about equality of opportunity then and now? *Source:* Cover of *Canada 125: A Special Issue of Destinations and the Magazine Division of The Globe and Mail*, April 1992. Photographer: Gerry Kopelow. Reproduced with permission of the photographer.

want more than equality in casting votes. A Native person and a university president are politically equal simply because each has one vote. But, because of race, occupation, or wealth, some people are more able than others to influence political decisions. Thus, some analysts would argue that equality in wealth, education, security, and social status — that is, social equality — is a precondition for political equality to exist.

Many groups call for the federal and provincial governments to generate "equality of outcome," whereby each person has the same chance to succeed in life. This idea is now deeply ingrained in Canada's political culture. Legislation to remove discrimination and impediments to a fair chance to get a job, to participate in sports, to receive equal pay for equal work, to be eligible for medical care, to have free access to public libraries, and many other features of our society are designed to advance equality of opportunity.

To many people, the conditions for social equality to exist are satisfied by simply offering opportunities for people to advance themselves. According to this conception of social equality, having opportunities is enough; it is not essential for people to end up being equal after using them. For others, however, true social equality means nothing less than equality of outcome. According to this conception, governments are required to implement policies of equality that ensure that people *are* equal.

It is not enough for a government to provide people with equal opportunity for social advancement. Governments are expected to design policies to redistribute national and provincial resources so that economic and social equality are actually achieved. Many Canadians now link the concept of equality of outcome with rights — the idea that everyone is entitled to certain benefits guaranteed by the government or entrenched in the constitution.

Under this conception, the political system guarantees people adequate housing, employment, medical care, and income as a matter of right. Quite clearly, the notion of equality of outcome is fundamentally different from the other two dimensions of equality (political equality and equality of opportunity), and it calls for a much greater degree of governing activity in the social system.

## CONCLUSION

As Canada approaches the next century, the attention of political experts increasingly focusses on the governability of the Canadian political system. Can it hold together, keeping the independence of Quebec within the structure of Canada's federal system? Will our governments be able to reduce their deficits and debts and steer our economies into competitive positions with the rest of the world?

The ways we organize our governments, the competence of our representatives, their lawmaking skills and judgements, the efficiency of our public administrators, the cost-effectiveness of our public services, the co-operation and co-ordination of subnational governments, the activities and creativity of political parties and pressure groups, the political behaviour of individuals — all contribute to the governability of Canadian society.

We should ask how well our system of government works. If it promises to protect the quality of lives of its people, what does it deliver in terms of national unity, employment opportunities, crime prevention, the enhancement of distinctive cultures, and so on? We know that much of what happens in politics and government is the result of the workings of the political system. We can gauge the effectiveness of such a system by the extent to which it is likely to meet social expectations, and we estimate its efficiency by the ratio of its successes to their costs.

The theme of governability is as contemporary as deficit-reduction battles, problems of political-party discipline, and concerns over whether the provinces can continue to deliver their constitutional responsibilities under enormous fiscal restraint. This theme is also as traditional as the so-called Fathers of Con-

federation, who struggled to draft the constitution and establish the balance of powers between the provinces and the federal government. Lastly, the theme of governability is valuable to both instructors and students because it gives us a consistent framework for analyzing and evaluating Canadian politics. In the final analysis, a governing system is the people themselves. We are one another's political fate.

## GLOSSARY

**empirical**  A type of practical activity in which the facts are gathered and their validity is tested against actual experience.

**lobbying**  The various efforts by individuals or groups to contact or communicate with a government in order to influence the decisions it makes.

**nation-state**  A governmental system that weaves together nationalities according to a deliberate political design, determining official languages, creating a uniform system of law, controlling the education system, and creating a bureaucracy in order to foster loyalty to an abstract entity, such as "Canada," the "United States," or "Bolivia."

**normative**  A type of perception based on what should or should not be, referring especially to goodness, justice, virtuous political conduct, and general social propriety.

**pluralist**  The view of political culture that sees it mainly as a competition among groups, each pressing for its own preferred interests.

**political culture**  The patterns of beliefs, symbols, and conduct associated with a political community, its constitutional system, and the government of the day.

**political elite**  A small group of individuals who actually make, or are part of the pro-

cess of making, important government decisions.

**political interest group**  A group formed to address a common political concern or interest that seeks to influence government departments, agencies, policies, or politicians. *See also* **political subculture**.

**political patronage**  A privilege or reward that is usually granted by governments for political reasons, rather than on the basis of merit or competence.

**political socialization**  The complex process by which we learn our political values and ideologies.

**political subculture**  A group that operates within a dominant political culture but differs from it in terms of values, ideology, norms, goals, and strategy.

**political system**  A network of institutions, organizations, activities, and traditions that link people with government.

**political values**  Conceptions that are strongly held about what goals are desirable and what standards for judging actions are appropriate.

**public policies**  Choices that a government makes in response to a social issue, usually experienced as an action or inaction.

**sovereign**  The status of the state whereby its authority and power to make decisions cannot be overturned or reversed by any other agency, body, or person in society.

**state** A set of bureaucratic structures that successfully claim a monopoly on the legitimate use of coercion and physical force within a territory.

**welfare state** A governing system that assumes responsibility for the welfare of its citizens, redistributing income to reduce social inequality, and establishing policies that favour the disadvantaged in society.

## RECOMMENDED READING

Chodos, Robert, Rae Murphy, and Eric Hamovitch. 1991. *The Unmaking of Canada*. Toronto: James Lorimer. This book offers an overview of Canada's political history since 1945, focussing on Quebec and the rest of Canada, regional tensions, and relations between Native peoples and the Canadian state.

Crick, Bernard. 1992. *In Defence of Politics*, 3d ed. London: Weidenfeld & Nicolson. This updated version of a political science classic considers the crisis of governability in Eastern Europe and its impact on the global political climate.

Danziger, James. 1991. *Understanding the Political World*. New York: Longman Publishing Group. This very readable and well-organized work introduces the uninitiated student to the complexities of world affairs.

Gagnon, Alain. 1993. *Quebec: State and Society*. Scarborough, Ont.: Nelson Canada. This collection of original articles serves as an introduction to Quebec politics and Quebec's relationship with the rest of Canada.

Mancuso, Maureen, Richard Price, and Ronald Wagenberg. 1994. *Leaders and Leadership in Canada*. Don Mills, Ont.: Oxford University Press. This book examines the question of leadership in Parliament and in politics. It analyzes the responsibilities and pathways of leadership at all levels of government, in the public service, the provinces, and the municipalities.

Peterson, Steven. 1990. *Political Behavior: Patterns in Everyday Life*. New York: Sage Publications. A good, readable introduction to the dynamics of political behaviour as a sociological phenomenon, considering how social change affects the ways we think about politics.

Pryke, Kenneth, and Walter Soderlund. 1991. *Profiles of Canada*. Mississauga, Ont.: Copp Clark Pitman. The contributors provide a multidisciplinary approach to Canadian studies, examining geography, Native peoples' cultures, Canadian governmental institutions, and Canadian history.

Taras, David, Beverly Rasporich, and Eli Mandel. 1993. *Passion for Identity*. Scarborough, Ont.: Nelson Canada. This collection of interesting articles focusses on the Canadian identity, providing some historical perspectives, examining Quebec and aboriginal issues, and touching on the political sociology of Canada's social diversity.

Watts, Ronald, and Douglas Brown, eds. 1991. *Options for a New Canada*. Toronto: University of Toronto Press. This book offers the reader an independent and illuminating analysis of the values, assumptions, and forces — social, economic, and political — that divide Canadians.

Young, Robert, ed. 1992. *Confederation in Crisis*. Toronto: James Lorimer. Six contributors discuss the post–Meech Lake era, highlighting constitutional politics in a state of crisis throughout Canada.

# 1

# THE NATURE AND ENDS OF CANADIAN GOVERNMENT

CHAPTER

# CANADA: THE STRUGGLE TO GOVERN

### INTRODUCTION

A GOVERNING SYSTEM OF COMPROMISE
A STATE OF MANY REGIONS
SEPARATISM AND REGIONALISM
QUEBEC'S DISTINCTIVENESS
OLD STRUCTURES FACE NEW PROBLEMS

### CANADIAN DEMOCRACY AND GOVERNABILITY

HOW IT ORIGINATED
HOW CANADIANS SEE DEMOCRACY

### THE FEATURES OF CANADIAN DEMOCRACY

CONSTITUTIONALISM AND THE SUPREMACY OF LAW
REPRESENTATIVE DEMOCRACY
RESPONSIBLE GOVERNMENT
THE PARLIAMENTARY SYSTEM OF GOVERNMENT
FEDERALISM AND GOVERNABILITY

### GOVERNING OUR RESOURCES

GEOGRAPHY AND GOVERNABILITY
RESOURCES AND GOVERNABILITY
THE ENVIRONMENT AND GOVERNABILITY

### GOVERNING A PLURALISTIC SOCIETY

WOMEN AND GOVERNABILITY
THE FIRST NATIONS AND GOVERNABILITY

### CONCLUSION

### GLOSSARY

### RECOMMENDED READING

Perhaps the greatest threat to how we are governed is the separation of Quebec from Canada. Some fear that Canada could go the way of the Soviet Union and Yugoslavia and fracture along regional, ethnic, and linguistic lines. The issue of Quebec separation represents the malaise of Canada's governing system. And, by the early 1990s, the battle lines had been clearly drawn. The powerful presence of the Parti Québécois pressing the separatist option within Quebec, and the Bloc Québécois articulating the sovereigntist and separatist ideology in Canada's federal Parliament, is a force that challenges the legitimacy of Canada's governing system.

For Canadians, the issues are no longer just those of giving Quebec what it wants so that it will remain within the federal system. Ensuring that Quebec stays is not just a matter of tinkering with the powers of government to appease people living in Quebec. Nor is it just about the role of government: how much power it should have over the individual, over the various groups to which individuals belong, and over the economy. No one doubts that the question of government is important, but it is central to Quebec's identity as an independent nation-state.

Sovereignty is not a political act of God. The real issue is whether Quebeckers have the political will to go it alone out of a sense of cultural security and economic self-assurance. That is a collective decision that only Quebeckers can make. Any further efforts by the federal government to accommodate Quebec's ambitions will be seen as an act of desperation by all Canadians and will, at one and the same time, fail to satisfy Quebec and infuriate much of the rest of Canada. Ultimately, it is Quebec's decision and there is not very much that the rest of Canada can do to influence it.

And so we face many questions. We know that Quebec's separating would have profound effects on the rest of the country. But few people really understand the conflicts that will arise over questions about assets and liabilities, geographical and political boundaries, and matters of economics and trade. The rest of Canada might still hold together as a country, though this is by no means certain, but a painful period of transition in Quebec and Canada would last through much of the 1990s and well into the next century.

What would the uncertainties bring? Would there be a crisis over the Canadian dollar, an increase in interest rates to keep financing our large foreign debt and stem the outflow of capital or stem the dumping of Canadian and provincial bonds? What would separating do to the employment picture in Quebec and in Canada? Would we fall back into recession? Would there be massive emigration? How would international investors behave?

Would Quebec emerge as a much more stable political economy than the rest of Canada? Would a sovereign Quebec become the modern, moderate, well-run democratic state sovereigntists are forecasting? Would the remaining provinces want to stay in Canada? Or would some, perhaps British Columbia and Alberta, see a better future as a new nation-state in the Pacific northwest? What would happen to equalization payments, regional development strategies, pensions, and unemployment insurance?

Would Quebec lose large hunks of the territory it now holds? Would Quebec lose the northern sections of the province that were transferred from the federal government in 1898 and 1912? What about aboriginal land claims? What if aboriginals living in Quebec decide to remain in Canada? Will the land they regard as theirs from time immemorial still be part of Canada?

And what about international agreements? Will Quebec have to renegotiate NAFTA? Will it sit on the Organization of American States and other international organizations to which Canada belongs, such as the GATT, the World Bank, the IMF, and the OECD? There are questions, lots of questions.

## INTRODUCTION

There has never been a serene period in the governmental history of Canada. In the more than 100 years that have passed since Confederation in 1867, Canadians have struggled to keep their governing system together despite many divisive forces. Confederation itself was not a very popular union and created problems of governability not anticipated by those who designed it.

The British North America Act (now the Constitution Act, 1867) joined the British colonies of Ontario, Quebec, New Brunswick, and Nova Scotia only after bitter debate in each legislature. Ontario was the most in favour of union from sea to sea because Ontarians saw great opportunities in a growing continental economy. Quebec opinion was divided: In Montreal, the business community fantasized about the great prosperity to come, but many French Canadians felt apprehension, fearing that their unique culture would be absorbed in the wider milieu of English and American influences.

The Atlantic colonies were strongly opposed to the creation of a larger Canada. Many people in Nova Scotia and New Brunswick rejected the idea of uniting Canada from coast to coast because they feared higher taxes and anticipated losing their wealth and influence in an expanded Canada. Newfoundland and Prince Edward Island decided not to join the union at that time. In the Atlantic region, some even thought that they would do better to cultivate their ties with the United States, based on the argument that the U.S. markets were much easier to access.

## A Governing System of Compromise

Federalism was the compromise, and Canada became the third state in the world to adopt a

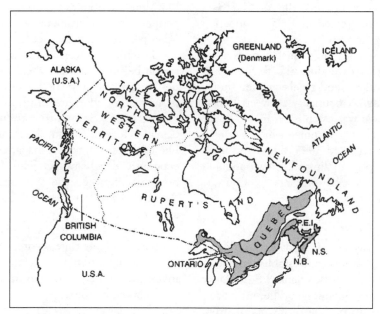

The Dominion of Canada in 1867. *Source:* This map is based on information taken from map sheet number MCR 2036 Index no. 2 edition 6, copyright 1991. Her Majesty the Queen in Right of Canada with permission of Energy, Mines and Resources Canada.

federal system of government, after Switzerland and the United States. Canada began as a federation of provinces with a strong central government; the provincial and federal governments each had certain powers of jurisdiction and all competed with one another for political advantage and economic opportunity.

It was made clear in the British North America Act that other British colonies could, if they wanted to, join Canada in time. In 1870, Canada purchased Rupert's Land from the Hudson's Bay Company and ceded the remaining North-western Territory from Great Britain. The Yukon and North-West Territories were granted only a limited amount of self-government. They still are primarily governed federally. And the division of the territories to provide existing provinces with more land or to create new ones was always a possibility. In fact, some of the North-western Territory became the province of Manitoba in 1870. British Columbia joined Canada in 1871, followed by Prince Edward Island in 1873. The provinces of Alberta and Saskatchewan were created in 1905, connecting a vast country "from sea to sea."

Major boundary adjustments were conducted in 1912, extending the territories of Manitoba, Ontario, and Quebec to the shores of Hudson Bay. A boundary between Labrador and Quebec was established in 1927, but successive Quebec governments have not officially recognized it. In 1949, under the leadership of Joseph Smallwood, Newfoundland became Canada's tenth province by a narrow margin of voter support.

## A State of Many Regions

Because of its vast size, Canada was settled in clusters of population that established themselves in "regions" of the country. Settlement occurred at different times, in different places, by people who, at the time, came mainly from Europe and the United States. Wherever they settled in Canada, people developed a different kind of economy, usually based on access to the resources available and to the technologies of economic productivity prevalent at the time.

The people in these regions often had more social, cultural, and trade connections with neighbouring areas in the United States than with the other regions of Canada. All of the many regional economies were separated by long distances, and usually by natural barriers such as mountains, lakes, and rivers. From Canada's beginnings, governability became identified with the capacity of the federal government to create a national economy out of many regional economies, and to forge a national identity out of social diversity.

Many thought that the Intercolonial Railway (completed in 1876) and John A. Macdonald's **National Policy** would open the markets of Ontario and Quebec to their products (Morton 1983). They were wrong. Industrialists, manufacturers, and shipbuilders in the Maritimes lost out to larger and more efficient competitors in Ontario and Quebec. Maritime economies became vulnerable and peripheral in government decision making in other parts of Canada, especially Ottawa.

Provincial governments in the Atlantic region began to protect their struggling businesses against the strong forces of the centralist national economy and interprovincial competition. Soon after their entry into Canada's federal system, the Prairie provinces, like those of Atlantic Canada, began to show economic disadvantage. The differences in prosperity between the Western regions, the Atlantic region, and central Canada became an important cause of political and economic divisions. These forces became virtually uncontrollable as time went on, creating further regional differences — in family income, investment and job opportunities, inflation, and economic growth.

Canada's patterns of population settlement and provincial resource development, as well as its political and governmental structures, began to reinforce a sense of separateness that Canadians originally felt when the country was first united in 1867. These factors strengthened the belief among various groups that they possessed an identity and a set of social concerns different from those of Canadians in other regions.

Canada's provincial governmental system was, and still is, organized around the notion of a distinctive identity in a region, based on shared territory, economy, and political culture, which is called "regionalism." But, if regionalism becomes strong enough, as it tends to under Canada's federal system, it is sometimes expressed in a movement that favours independence from a larger governing unit. Within Canada's federal framework, a region's (sometimes a particular province's or a group of provinces') desire for political and governmental independence has been reflected in the emergence of **separatism**.

## Separatism and Regionalism

The first separatist movement in Canada occurred in Nova Scotia, just after Confederation, when the anti-Confederates won 36 out of 38 seats. But the British government did not permit the province to separate from Canada, and it took nearly a century before other separatist tendencies surfaced among Canada's provinces. A separatist movement appeared in western Canada in the form of the Western Canada Concept Party in the early 1980s because of dissatisfaction over the federal government's regulation of the petroleum industry.

However, the strongest and most constant separatist movement in Canada occurred in Quebec, where, from the eighteenth century, the "French fact" was legally acknowledged to be a special status of the French within the British Empire, as recognized and embodied in the Quebec Act, 1774. For nearly all of the century that followed, Quebec was able to maintain a unique political and governmental culture, distinguishable from all the other political cultures comprising Canada. With

Confederation in 1867, the constitutional foundation of French language rights was laid under Section 133 of the British North America Act, which recognized the equal status of French with English in the federal parliamentary system and under Quebec provincial law.

By the 1960s, many other developments were perceived to threaten Quebec's unique culture. Quebec remained a traditional society, dominated by the Roman Catholic Church, which controlled the education of French-speaking people, most of the welfare and charity organizations, and almost the entire hospital sector. French-Canadian families were having fewer children; Quebec's immigrants were choosing English over French; and Quebec's business, economic, and cultural development was dominated by anglophones.

The Quiet Revolution of the 1960s was nurtured by the Liberal government of Jean Lesage, whose political style transformed the province of Quebec, bringing it into the same league of public administration already present in most other provinces. Quebec's government modernized and grew quickly to displace the authority of the church in education, health, and welfare. The government placed itself in the centre of the province's cultural activities, business communities, the arts, and the mass media.

A number of political groups that shared these concerns formed a political party called the Parti Québécois. The main agenda of this party was to establish Quebec as a sovereign, independent nation-state, capable of self-determination under international law and almost entirely separate from Canada. The possibility of a separate Quebec became closer to being a reality when the Parti Québécois won provincial elections in 1976 and 1994. The ability to govern Canada was seriously challenged by the presence of a provincial government wanting to break out of Confederation. The Parti Québécois wanted to retain an economic association with the rest of

Canada by means of a common currency, and a free-trade relationship, that came to be known as **sovereignty association**. This proposal was defeated in a referendum conducted in 1980, but the issue did not disappear.

## Quebec's Distinctiveness

When Canada drafted a new constitution in 1982, Quebec refused to sign it because it did not explicitly recognize the province's distinctiveness. The Quebec government passed a law (Bill 101) that forbade the use of English on street signs and storefronts in a legal effort to protect the French language and culture. The new law was divisive everywhere in the country, but particularly for groups such as anglophones living in Quebec.

Many Quebeckers made union with the other provinces conditional upon the passage of a constitutional amendment that would recognize Quebec as a "distinct society" within Canada's federal system. The amendment, the Meech Lake Accord, had to be approved by all ten provinces. The accord was defeated when two provinces — Newfoundland and Manitoba — refused to ratify it because Quebec was seen as "more equal" than other provinces, and because acknowledgement of the distinctiveness of Native peoples and other groups was not included in the final document.

The failure of the Meech Lake Accord reflected on a number of levels a crisis of how we are governed. First, it exhibited the inability of governing institutions and their leaders to alter the framework of Canadian federalism, even after widespread consensus had apparently been achieved: All ten provincial governments and most opposition parties within the provinces supported the accord, as did the federal government and federal opposition parties. But the ratification process collapsed because unanimity was required. Second, Canada's governments could not reach agreement on an acceptable amendment formula for the Canadian constitution, which

weakened the adaptive capacity of the constitution as the first universal law of the land. Third, the Meech Lake experience revealed the profound tensions existing in a governing system that requires federal compromise by means of parliamentary decision making, wherein cabinets regard themselves as the final arbiters of governance. Fourth, Meech Lake challenged the fundamental values of Canada's governability, that is, provincial equality, public participation, and the rights of minorities. The failing of the Meech Lake Accord isolated Quebec and its political system, and severed the linkage of its government to the process of federal compromise.

Canadians distanced themselves from the disappointments of Meech Lake by carefully reviewing the values and structures of their governing system. The fierce challenges that were envisioned, or even dimly perceived, by the architects of the country's governmental framework became the threatening realities of the 1990s. The features of Canada's governing system evolved over a long period of time; some were taken from other political systems, and others grew naturally out of Canada's political experience.

## Old Structures Face New Problems

The founders of Canada's present governmental system thought it was democratic, constitutional, representative, responsible, parliamentary, and federal. These traditional characteristics of governability focussed on Canada's linguistic composition, its regionalism, the division of powers between the federal and provincial governments, and the dynamics of intergovernmental relations. But they have attempted to do so within the context of an aging and cumbersome system of federal–provincial relations, hit hard by duplication, inefficiency, and debt.

The Charter of Rights and Freedoms, 1982, added another dimension to Canadian federalism and parliamentary government — namely, the inclusion of individual, community, and linguistic rights. These rights have altered our governability by placing greater constitutional weight on gender, aboriginal character and identities, **ethnicity**, language, and region. For example, the women's movement, which advocates rights based on individual and collective gender-identity, has politicized a powerful elite who want to represent more than half of the population of Canada; aboriginal claims politicize the identities of Native peoples; and the changing ethnic composition of the country has redefined the traditional assumptions of what Canadian governments should do, and how. By the 1990s, it had become very difficult for the operating structures of Canadian government, carrying such enormous debt and deficits, to withstand the problems barraging them.

## CANADIAN DEMOCRACY AND GOVERNABILITY

### How It Originated

Many of the principles of Canada's democracy did not originate with the so-called Fathers of Confederation. The idea that government is responsible to its citizens, for example, is as old as the Greeks; one can trace the history of human equality before the law to the ancient Hebrews; the guarantee of equal rights and freedoms to both men and women to the tribal democracy of the Iroquois; the right of public access to government-held information and the protection of citizens from bureaucratic abuse to Sweden; and the first written democratic constitution to the United States.

Sometimes, we think of Canada's political experience as starting with the British North America Act. Not so: The circumstances of Canadian life before and during the colonial period shaped and reshaped the political experience of Canada and the democracy that has evolved. But it is important to note that some of the principles shaping our

democracy are rooted in the Judaeo-Christian tradition, and in British and French history.

Democracy as we now understand it was not always so popular among Canadians. In fact, many of those who framed Canada's political system were opposed to it. For decades preceding the country's establishment as a federal state, some even held that any form of democracy would be dangerous, and could lead to instability (Hodgins 1955, 436). Generally, the "masses" were considered not well-enough educated to govern themselves, too prone to the influence of demagogues, and too likely to neglect the rights of those not part of the majority.

### How Canadians See Democracy

Today, Canadians regard democracy not only as a way of thinking about politics but as a form of governance. They emphasize "procedures" for enabling the people to govern themselves at all levels, such as meeting to discuss national issues, voting in provincial elections, and running for municipal office. Canadians also see democracy in the "substance" of government policies and constitutional guarantees, such as medicare and freedom of speech. The *procedural* expectations focus on how decisions are made, for example, in a provincial legislature, municipal council, or the House of Commons; and the *substantive* expectations are concerned with what a government does, for example, the democratic character of laws it passes and the behaviour of officials who are regarded as accountable to citizens.

In Canada, democracy has come to mean a form of government organized according to certain principles that are entrenched in the Canadian political system. The powers of Canadian governments are checked because citizens who know their rights can participate in governing themselves. Thus, Canadians believe that no government is legitimate that does not enjoy the consent and participation of the governed. Some of the most dramatic difficulties Canadian governments have faced have been associated with a public perception that democracy has been ignored by those who govern us.

What people want is linked to what government does. When the air is foul, we expect our governments to clean it up. When we lose our jobs, we want our governments to direct the economy to create more employment. And if the country appears threatened by disunity, we want our governments to keep it together.

Strong democratic values held by a majority of Canadians can sometimes lead to contradictory political results. The victory of the Parti Québécois in a number of provincial elections is Canadian democracy at work. But the twist is that these democratic victories call for the separation of Quebec from Canada, leading possibly to the disintegration of the national governing system that protects our democratic values.

Inconsistencies dominate Canadian democracy. Canadians take pride in their parliamentary form of government but frequently look down on their politicians. We show our children the symbols of our democracy, expecting that they will revere them; at the same time, we do not trust our government officials and tend to describe politics and government as "dirty." Most Canadians agree that their system of government is the best in the world, but few Canadians want their children to participate actively in that system as politicians. Canadians love democracy, yet they often dislike its consequences. We criticize big government, complaining that it overregulates and cannot really solve our problems.

Canada is a diverse nation-state, populated by individuals from all over the world. The Canadian democracy is a conglomeration of different religions, ethnicities, cultural traditions, socio-economic strata, and races. Such diversity exists because most Canadians are immigrants, or descendants of immigrants. Even those we call aboriginal Canadians crossed a land bridge from Asia thousands of years ago.

Diversity produces different perceptions of Canada. As a result, people tend to define society's problems differently and hold conflicting views about what governments should do about them. People also disagree about whether or not government is responsive. Most conflicts in Canadian society must somehow be channelled through government.

## THE FEATURES OF CANADIAN DEMOCRACY

### Constitutionalism and the Supremacy of Law

It is a basic axiom of democracy that a government cannot be accountable to itself. We believe that the role of government is properly constrained by a constitution. According to this principle, which we call "constitutionalism," the organization, conduct, and powers of governments are limited as stipulated in a written charter as well as by unwritten customs and traditions that have earned constitutional status. The principle is extremely important because it makes the constitution supreme, above all government institutions, public policies, and politics itself.

Over the years, in Canada, the constitution has been given supremacy in three areas: over the federal government and the provinces; over whatever laws the federal government might pass; and over the laws of the provinces.

Canadians frequently debate policy questions in terms not only of whether something is good or bad, wise or foolish, but of whether it is "unconstitutional," sometimes referred to as "*ultra vires* [beyond the powers of] the constitution." These kinds of questions are normally decided by the courts. For example, the Supreme Court of Canada has the power of "judicial review," the right to decide what the constitution means; to rule on questions of allocation of powers between the federal government and the provinces; and to decide whether acts of Parliament and those of the provinces are in accord with the spirit and letter of the constitution (Smith 1983).

Although the final document ratified in 1867 is somewhat confusing and sketchy in places, the constitution outlines the organization of government and a great deal about what the governments of Canada can and cannot do (Cairns 1970). Most of the powers, responsibilities, and jurisdictions of Canadian governments are delineated in the original British North America Act, 1867.

This act outlines the powers of the federal and provincial governments and provides a framework within which their jurisdictions may be determined. But many questions about the role and scope of government are unanswered, or are not clearly stated in that document: for instance, it does not mention the role of the prime minister, the Supreme Court, or political parties in Canada's political system. And, while it stipulates that the federal government is authorized to regulate the economy, it also notes that all provincial governments are constitutionally empowered to do the same.

The principle of constitutionalism also sets limits on what governments *can* do, and *how* they can do things. Such limits exist to prevent governments making rash decisions that might further the ambitions of individuals in violation of our basic beliefs about government. Canada's constitution is the mainstay of individual rights: It contains a Charter of Rights and Freedoms that lists things governments may or may not do and proclaims the primacy of certain freedoms that Canadian society enshrines as fundamental law.

Constitutionalism is also symbolic in the eyes of the public in that the constitution is perceived to be greater than the sum of its parts: More than a document that organizes, authorizes, and limits, the constitution is an object of respect. The constitution is both the first and the last resort of democracy; it is where people turn for meaning and relevance

in matters of governance. The political debates that surrounded the Meech Lake Accord before and after its failure, and the extensive cross-country conferencing that exhibited the competing constitutional visions of Canada in the Charlottetown Accord, had an impact on our political system that cannot be exaggerated.

The principle of constitutionalism is still evolving in Canada. It challenges our assumptions about what the divisions of powers are as originally conceived by those who instituted Canada's federal state. The reform of our governing institutions such as the Senate, what constitutes citizenship, how the economy of Canada will be governed — all are evolving components of Canada's constitutionalism.

## Representative Democracy

As distrustful as many nineteenth-century Canadians were about the possible excesses of democracy, they were strongly opposed to arbitrary government. No representative institutions existed when the early Canadian colonies were settled. They were governed by appointed councils directed by a governor who was answerable to France or England.

A number of English political idealists had advanced the philosophy of political representation and popular rule in the seventeenth and eighteenth centuries. These ideas captured the imagination of colonists in North America: Canada's first legislative assembly was elected in Nova Scotia in 1758; Prince Edward Island's was next, in 1773; New Brunswick's, in 1784; and those of Upper and Lower Canada (later Ontario and Quebec), in 1791.

The nineteenth-century English philosopher John Stuart Mill (1806–1873) accepted the necessity of "indirect democracy," wherein citizens participate in government by electing public officials to make government decisions for them. Mill proclaimed such representative government as the best possible form of government (Mill 1958). Today, we think of representative government as a compromise between the principle of "perfect," or direct, democracy (i.e., direct popular participation in making the laws that govern us) and the realities of a complex and huge country such as Canada. From the very beginning, there was no way for all Canadians to assemble, debate, and decide national and provincial problems. The desire to establish government accountability led Canadians to institute representative government, in which a select group of people meet and decide on the issues of the day and remain ever conscious of the wishes and preferences of those who sent them.

In some respects, representative government has taken many turns not conceived of more than 100 years ago, all of which affect governability. Voting for political representatives follows the principles of universal suffrage, universal participation, political equality, and frequent and periodic elections. After the election, however, our elected representatives may not make the same decisions the people would have made if they had gathered for the same purpose. For example, most Canadians favour the use of capital punishment, but since the 1960s parliamentarians have consistently rejected its reinstitution. Thus, in Canada, the principle of *responsiveness*, that is, that those elected should respond to public opinion and do what the people want, is not absolute.

Anyone who has visited Ottawa or a provincial capital to meet with parliamentarians knows the interest taken by them in their constituents. However, in a parliamentary system, "party discipline" affects the representative loyalty of legislators. Political parties demand that their elected representatives vote along party lines, which sometimes run contrary to the interests of constituents. The precise kind of relationship that should exist between Canadian representatives and those who select them is still a matter of debate.

Canada's parliamentary system strikes a balance between the extremes of democratic representation by elites and by direct public participation. Elected representatives act like elites, trying to decide what constitutes the best interests of Canadians. But, in many instances, people want to keep their representatives on a short leash, particularly where highly emotional issues such as capital punishment and abortion are concerned. Legislators must maintain enough discretionary judgement to enable them to act responsibly not only in terms of what their parties want but also in accordance with the wishes of their constituents.

## Responsible Government

Another original feature of Canadian democracy is *responsible government*, whereby Cabinet members must retain the support and confidence of the legislature or resign and stand for election. By the 1830s, most of the British North American colonies had instituted representative government: Nearly 100 years earlier, they had legislative assemblies elected by the colonists that could make laws, raise taxes, and support the governor (Hogg 1985, 189–213).

But the powers of executive government were vested in a governor, appointed by the British Colonial Office, whose members took their instructions from and whose conduct was guided and supervised by the government of the United Kingdom. Colonial reformers wanted the legislative assemblies to enjoy the same powers exercised by the House of Commons in Britain. The rebellions of 1837 forced the British government to consider seriously the demands of the colonists.

Responsible government in which the appointed executive — namely, the governor — would be accountable to the elected assembly was not initiated until the British governor, John George Lambton, Lord Durham, recommended it to his government in 1839, and eventually implemented it — in Nova Scotia, New Brunswick, and Upper and Lower Canada in 1848; in Prince Edward Island and Newfoundland in 1851; in British

Columbia and Manitoba in 1871; and in the North-West Territories, Alberta, and Saskatchewan in 1897.

On the recommendation of Lord Durham, the British model of parliamentary government would be applied in Canada: The governor would be the counterpart of the monarch, the Legislative Council was to be the equivalent of the House of Lords, the Executive Council was to become the Cabinet, and the Legislative Assembly was to be the House of Commons. As D. Milne (1990, 315) summarizes: "Responsible government meant that the governor general ought to appoint and take advice from the executive members who sat in the elected assembly and held the confidence of the members of the assembly."

In effect, the executive branch of government was melded with the legislative branch in an accountable relationship referred to as a **fusion of powers**: Members of the Cabinet must hold seats in Parliament and are "responsible" to it in that the bills they present, the policies they generate, and the actions they take must retain the support and confidence of a majority of members (see Figure 1.1). If not, the Cabinet must either resign or ask the governor general to dissolve Parliament in preparation for an election.

Today, the principle of responsible government is one of the most important components of how we are governed in Canada. It determines the relationship of the governor general to the prime minister and the Cabi-

**Figure 1.1 Fusion of Powers**

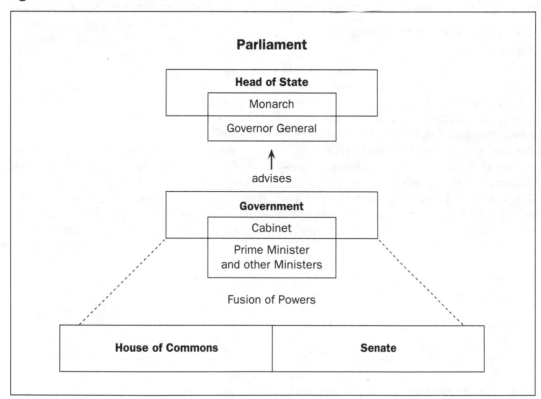

net. It also governs the relationship of the prime minister to the Cabinet, and of the Cabinet to Parliament. It is the principle that underlies the level of confidence in the legislature, the resignation or dismissal of politicians and administrators, the dissolution of Parliament, and the accountability of our leaders to the electorate.

A vital part of our concept of governing is that people who are chosen in free elections are accountable not only to the institutions in which they work but also to the voters. In the contemporary sense, responsible government has everything to do with the decisions governments make or fail to make. If government decisions fail to respond to public opinion, or if they disregard it, and if the government performs poorly by public standards, we can expect support for the government to decline. Should support fall too low, we can expect the public to begin agitating for political, economic, and social change.

## The Parliamentary System of Government

Many of the basic features of British constitutional and institutional practice were adopted by Canadians as instruments for governing a large, complex society. The British North America Act, an act of the British Parliament, not only made Confederation a reality but established British parliamentary procedures, customs, and institutions in Canada. The act created a governing system in which British parliamentary institutions would function in both the national and the provincial governments. This "Westminster model" became a prototype of Canada's political system, modified to suit the political and governmental conditions created by Canada's vast size.

The ability to govern Canada is based on the assumptions that Parliament is legally supreme in the lawmaking process, that it possesses the sovereign right to govern, and that only its members are constitutionally empowered to represent the interests and viewpoints of the people of Canada. In the words of John H. Redekop (1983, 147), "no statutes can be enacted or amended, no taxes legally imposed and no funds legally appropriated unless formally approved by Parliament." Structured and legitimized by a constitution, Parliament is a governing body that consists of the Queen and her Canadian representative, the governor general, an elected House of Commons, and an appointed Senate.

In order to elect members of the House of Commons, Canada is divided into geo-political areas called "constituencies" or "ridings" (at present, there are 295 constituencies nation-wide). In each constituency, political parties choose a person to run in the election, or an individual may decide to run without party affiliation as an independent. On election day, the candidate who receives the largest number of votes is declared elected and is entitled to a seat in the House of Commons; he or she usually represents the platform of a political party as well as the many interests of constitutents. The political party whose members win the most seats will, under normal circumstances, form the government. The leader of that party will be the prime minister.

While the Queen and her representative constitute the **head of state**, the prime minister is the **head of government** (see Figure 1.1). The prime minister and the Cabinet, whose members he or she chooses, are known collectively as "the government." The Cabinet has differentiated itself from Parliament, placing itself in the dominant position to control the lawmaking process, to oversee legislative proceedings, and to plan the general order of business and political agenda the country will consider. Government bills are rarely defeated in Parliament because the governing party almost always musters a majority of its legislative supporters in favour of its legislation.

Parliament itself is not the lawmaking body that many have come to believe; rather, it approves, amends, and rejects government proposals for laws. But Parliament mostly ratifies decisions made by the government, as they are presented by the appropriate minister and supported by a majority of members.

Although its involvement in the preparation of legislation is minimal, Parliament attempts to perform two important functions. The first function is to legitimize the actions of government, but only after rigorous deliberation. Parliament meets to scrutinize, debate, and compromise so as to make laws for all — laws that ideally are in the public interest. Most Canadians accept and obey government decisions because they think laws are made properly and rightfully in the parliamentary forum. Parliament remains the official meeting place in which the government of the day must explain, defend, and justify its policies.

The second function of Parliament is to act as a forum of representation for ordinary citizens. Here the institution may not meet the governing expectations of the public because, like the Cabinet, which is dominated by white Anglo-Saxon males, usually with business and professional connections, Parliament is a model of elite rule and is vastly unrepresentative of the people for whom it is supposed to speak. Usually about 90 percent of MPs are drawn from high-status occupations, compared with only 20 percent of all Canadians (Guppy, Freeman, and Buchan 1987).

Very few women are elected to the House of Commons, and these few are almost all from highly educated and upper-income groups (see Figure 1.2). The character of Parliament as an exclusive club of upper-class white professionals and business persons affects the governability of Canada. Fundamental to the ability to govern is the ideal that Parliament will reflect the sociological composition of the people.

But can aboriginals and people of other ethnic and racial origins be properly represented by white, middle-aged males? Imagine what a more perfectly representative Parliament would look like: It would be 52 percent female, and would include more members of different ethnic and racial backgrounds; the average age would be 38 instead of 50; only about 1 percent, rather than nearly half, would be lawyers and the other 99 percent would be such people as plumbers, steelworkers, schoolteachers, professors, single mothers, and people who qualify for welfare. The representatives, the debates, and the rules processed through Parliament would have a very different character, being far more reflective of the needs of the general population.

The degree to which the membership of Parliament reflects the general population is called "descriptive representation." Taken to the extreme, descriptive representation is unlikely to occur in Canadian society. But it is certainly important for women, in particular, and people from various ethnic and racial backgrounds to feel they have authentic representation in the federal Parliament, in their provincial legislative assemblies, and on municipal councils. For many Canadians, legislatures are microcosms of society and provide visible evidence of whether governments are accessible to all citizens, regardless of gender, race, or national origin.

## Federalism and Governability

One of the most contentious aspects of how we are governed in Canada is the federal–provincial relationship and how it steers the governing system in one direction or another. Canada's federalism has evolved as a system of government in which two levels, national and provincial, have governing authority over the same territory and the people who live and work there.

Frank R. Scott (1977, 35) noted that Canada's was the first governing system to combine parliamentary institutions with a federal structure of government. In this combination, governing institutions may not necessarily be

**Figure 1.2  Distribution of Members of Parliament by Gender, 1980–1993**

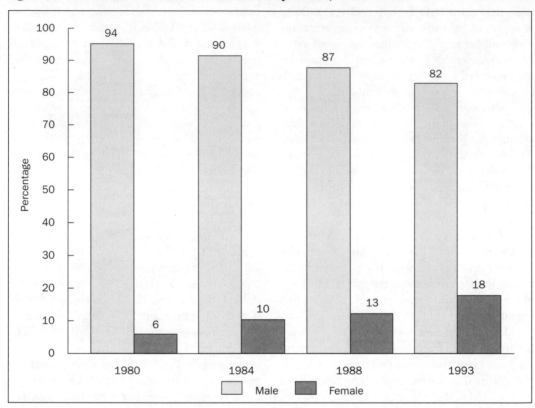

Source: William Mishler and Harold Clarke, "Participation in Canada," in *Canadian Politics in the 1990's,* edited by Michael Whittington and Glen Williams (Toronto: Nelson Canada, 1990), 174. Reproduced with permission of Nelson Publishers.

complementary or may simply compound the difficulties we face in governing ourselves. A parliamentary system in combination with a federal system of government is adversarial; it can place political opponents in a combative and conflictive legislative relationship and make co-operation between levels of government difficult.

Canadians chose federalism because it permits a diversity of governmental organizations, political cultures, and public policies within a single nation-state. The practical problem for the framers of Canada's federal system was to balance the need for a strong central government with the desire of the four

original provinces to retain their decision-making autonomy in regional and local matters. Actually, the constitution makers of the 1860s foresaw a federation in which the central government could eventually exercise control over everything the provinces did. Strong centralizing powers were delegated specifically to, or reserved for, the federal government; other powers and jurisdictions were assigned to the provinces; and some were left for both levels to share.

The character of Canadian federalism has changed a great deal since 1867. Over the years, the provisions of federalism as outlined in the British North America Act, designating which aspects of governability were the jurisdiction of the provinces and which were that of the national government, have remained essentially the same, but the content of Canadian federalism has changed significantly.

Today, Canadian provinces retain remarkable governing vitality. In the course of Canada's federal history, they have become more powerful as subnational units, capable of successfully challenging federal jurisdiction in the courts, and skilful at organizing among themselves to strengthen provincial bargaining powers against Ottawa. Most of the provinces believe that, in many areas, they can govern more effectively and efficiently than can the federal government, especially in protecting and nurturing the health, safety, welfare, and morals of their people.

The constitutional division of powers between the federal government and the provinces has had an impact on the ability to govern. On the whole, federalism has constrained the federal government and continues to limit Canada's governability. Even in the 1990s, the debate continues over which level of government is best able to govern. Although Canada's federal system appears to be highly centralized, the federal government cannot govern Canada alone. It needs the co-operation of the provinces and their municipal governments.

The term "intergovernmental relations" is often used in Canada to refer to the complex web of interrelationships among governments — the federal government, the ten provincial governments, the two territorial gov-ernments, and the thousands of local governments — as they interact far more frequently than ever before.

Since the mid-1980s, one priority of the federal government has been to shift political power and economic responsibility to the provinces. As part of Ottawa's plan to reduce government spending, federal transfer payments and cost-sharing programs have been cut. Provincial and municipal officials have been compelled to look more to their own resources or to find new ones within their jurisdictions.

## GOVERNING OUR RESOURCES

### Geography and Governability

Everywhere one looks in Canada, politics has affected the air, the land, the waters, and the people. One Canadian professor of geography (Hare 1968, 3) noted that "Confederation was, in a very special sense, an act of political geography." Political geography might be thought of as the spatial consequence of politics and government.

In Canada, nation-building has always had something to do with overcoming the enormous challenges of geography. All Canadian governments have played a major role in the building of this large independent northern nation-state from sea to sea. One example of the ability to govern Canada has meant the creation of a national physical **infrastructure**, for example, the Trans-Canada Highway, stretching 7700 km between St. John's, Nfld., and Victoria, B.C., the longest paved national highway in the world. Other geographically challenging facilities of great national significance include the St. Lawrence Seaway, two trans-Canada airlines, and oil and gas pipelines from the West to the East. Governability is also enhanced by major communications systems: Spanning Canada are the Canadian Broadcasting Corporation and telephone, telegraph, and computer-superhighway systems. All these transportation and communications networks unify the country and enhance the effectiveness of how it is governed.

### Size

When Canada was first unified into a single political form, it was immense by European standards: It was larger than France, Germany, and Italy, and many times the size of Great Britain. Although the Atlantic Ocean permitted direct contact with Europe in the early days of Canada's current political system, it was a formidable-enough barrier to restrict contact as well. Thus, the early colonists had access to European goods and ideas but also were protected from being overwhelmed by Europe's strong historical traditions.

Canada's physical size has both advantages and disadvantages in terms of its governability. Size offered Canadians an abundance of natural resources, which are prime requisites for creating national wealth and for achieving international status as a powerful state. However, with vastness in size come problems affecting social cohesion, economic parity, governmental efficiency, and national integration.

Canada spans seven time zones and possesses formidable natural barriers, such as the Appalachians, the Canadian Shield, the Rocky Mountains, the Great Lakes, and the Arctic desert. These natural features can be politically divisive, and present overwhelming problems for governability. Think of the complexities involved in staging a federal election so that everyone can vote and keep or change a government on the same day.

Canadians are committed to maintaining a governing system that covers an area greater than the North Atlantic and Europe combined. Canada stretches nearly 10 million km², from the Atlantic to the Pacific and from the U.S. border to the North Pole. The country occupies this whole area, except Alaska on the Pacific Coast and the small islands of St. Pierre and Miquelon off the shores of Newfoundland.

### Location

Location determines our neighbours, our access to the oceans, our trading partners, and our strategic position in world affairs. Canada is located in a massive, resource-rich land bounded on the east, west, and north by three commercial and strategic oceans. In fact, Canada has the longest coastlines in the world (100 000 km, more than twice the circumference of the earth). These features fostered the development of an independent nation-state comprising many political cultures that were not mere reproductions of parent cultures in Europe. Canada's political cultures are significant components of its political geography as well as major challenges to how it can be governed.

It is an exceptional circumstance that Canada shares a vast border with only one other land neighbour, the United States — a country that happens to be a superpower and the world's largest economy. The proximity of a much larger society that originally wished to annex Canada has been an enduring challenge to our identity and sovereignty. Throughout Canada's history, its geographical position in relation to the United States has had a constant effect on its foreign policy and world view.

Canada employs a large amount of its government resources interacting politically, culturally, and economically with its only neighbour. Those interactions with the United States are the most intense for Canada, which has signed more bilateral treaties with the United States than with any other state in the international system. Its largest embassy is in Washington, D.C., and the United States hosts more Canadian consulates than does any other country. Canada's Department of Foreign Affairs and International Trade funds university research and programs that focus primarily on the United States. Over 75 percent of Canada's two-way trade is with the United States, and Americans are the largest foreign investors in the Canadian economy. Each year, millions of Americans and Canadians cross the border to do business or tour each other's country. No other government in the world communicates more with Canada routinely on a daily basis than does the United States. Citizenship and Immigration Canada, Revenue Canada, and other federal departments that represent Canadian industry, trade, small business, and numerous police departments are in regular communication with their counterparts in the United States.

For these reasons, Canada has used its easy access to the North Atlantic and Pacific oceans to extend its interests globally in an effort to counterbalance the vulnerability of dealing with only one country that has prominence in Canadian affairs. Canada built a strong system of alliances with Europe, the Commonwealth, South America, Central America, and the Caribbean. Canada's geographical location has provided a means for evolving an independent foreign policy and to ward off some of the strong cultural and economic influences of the United States.

### Distance

Closely related to the immense size of Canada are the problems that distance presents to the country's many governments. Notwithstanding the great technological achievements in modern communications, distance is still an important factor in how Canadians govern themselves because it affects the ability of the political system to work effectively and efficiently.

In Canada, most politicians must travel great distances between their constituencies and the capital cities where they do much of their work as the people's representatives. Within most provinces, distance alone can create enormous difficulties for members of legislative and national assemblies (MLAs and MNAs). Even within constituencies, distance is a factor that affects time, cost, convenience, accessibility, and the ability to govern effectively.

Campaigning for election and re-election is a political activity that inevitably comes up against the problems that distance generates. The ability to meet and talk with constituents, and to see where and how they live, is affected by distance in Canada. As well, dis-

tance creates enormous problems for actually staging an election: Redrawing electoral boundaries, placing polling stations conveniently for people at election time, making sure that the electorate is enumerated, and providing access to polls for people with disabilities are just some of the obstacles that distance presents to the political system.

Distance is also a factor in the delivery of government services by the police, courts, and judges; the ability of the government to respond to emergencies; and the presence of government as a symbol of sovereignty. But it is especially a factor in matters of public policy. Where should governments locate their departments and agencies? Should governments subsidize the cost of transporting resources, agricultural products, and other commodities to facilitate economic competition domestically or in the international economy?

### Resources and Governability

Canada has always been blessed with many natural endowments. *Natural resources* comprise all aspects of the physical environment that people find useful: climate, soil, plants, wildlife, minerals and energy resources, such as water, the wind, and the sun. Canadians have always exported their resources — vast amounts of fish, furs, timber, minerals, and farm products, at first primarily to Europe, the Caribbean, and the United States, but now to a wider range of economies in the global community.

The politics of Canada's geography touches these immense resources in particular. Under the constitution, jurisdiction over and responsibilities for natural-resource development in Canada are shared by federal and provincial governments. Actually, the provinces exercise greater control over resource development because they own most of the resources and hold statutory authority to develop them. Many of the responsibilities for environmental management by means of pollution control, environmental-protection legislation, and environmental assessments fall to the provinces.

The federal government has some jurisdiction in the environmental field, and over resources such as the fisheries. The federal government's involvement is limited generally to the management of environments under federal jurisdiction, for example, crown federal lands, Native peoples' reserve lands, the Yukon and Northwest territories, national parks, ports, and airports. By agreement, certain responsibilities for the inland fisheries have been delegated to the provinces, but the federal government retains an overall constitutional mandate to protect and preserve all fish.

Despite the specific delegations of government jurisdictions, Canada's constitution left many questions open, and its language subject to interpretation. Legal battles have occurred among Ottawa, the provinces, and environmental groups over which governments should monitor projects such as Alberta's Oldman River dam, Saskatchewan's Rafferty-Alameda project, and Quebec's Great Whale project. The Supreme Court affirmed Ottawa's power to review the environmental impacts of projects carried out by provincial governments.

The presence of resources as plentiful and complex as those spread across Canada requires a co-operative governing system in order to manage and preserve them properly. But governments, in competition for jurisdiction and power, will inevitably conflict with each other, especially over resources such as oil, gas, the fisheries, Native land claims, and cost-sharing.

## The Environment and Governability

But, just as it is important to consider political geography as a spatial and territorial product of human politics and government, we must also know that our social and economic behaviour has environmental consequences (Bowden 1983). It is governments that make the decisions, formulate the policies, and regulate the economic activities that impact upon the environment and on the quality of life we have within that environment.

Vast quantities of air, water, the earth itself, the fisheries, wildlife, and the forests are vulnerable to what our governments decide to do or not to do. Over the years, the environment has endured the abuses of industrialization and consumption.

The earliest warnings about the destructive environmental consequences of our ways came from Canada's aboriginal peoples, who saw what Euro-Canadians were doing to the places where they settled. In the 1860s, one Micmac chief complained to Queen Victoria about the ways her Canadian subjects dirtied the waters, generated bad air in their cities, and treated wildlife as items of commerce.

The first European settlers in Canada found plenty of pure water, drinkable without treatment; land that was not polluted by toxic chemicals, landfills, and sewage; and fresh air, free from the discharges of automobiles, trucks, and heavy industries. Nineteenth-century Canadians did not worry about harming the environment. The country they came to was largely unsettled, unspoiled, and filled with resources that seemed almost infinite in supply.

The Constitution Act, 1867, contains no hint of concern about protecting and preserving the environment. Indeed, our orientation to the environment, from Confederation to the present, is rooted in the Western, Judaeo-Christian tradition that the physical, plant, and animal world exists to "serve" human needs. In the early twentieth century, concern grew about the affect that the Industrial Revolution, coupled with rapid population growth, might have on Canada's environment. But it took until the 1970s before Canada's governments began to act (Boardman 1992). The Environmental Protection Act was passed in 1970, and the federal Department of the Environment (now called Environment Canada) was established in 1971. Environmental legislation spread throughout the provinces during the 1970s: Ontario's Environmental Assessment Act, 1975, and similar acts were passed, in Quebec in 1977, Newfoundland in 1980, and Saskatchewan in 1980.

By the mid-1980s, governments began to respond to greater public awareness and calls for greater government regulation of polluters (Decima Research 1986). The Canadian Council of Ministers of the Environment (CCME), representing the federal and ten provincial environment ministries, was formed in 1986. Departments and ministries of environment were organized in all provinces by 1990, giving environmental matters a much higher political profile across the country.

Canadian governments have lawmaking jurisdiction over three of the most life-sustaining elements in our environment — air, land, and water. Governments have also taken action to deal with the prevalence of acid rain in Canada. Many provincial governments are passing laws to control acid rain-causing emissions that damage the air, land, the forests, crops, lakes, rivers, animal life, and coastal environments. For example, the government of Ontario legislated against acid rain in 1985, requiring that all major industries in that province reduce their emissions of sulphur dioxide by 60 percent by 1994. The Quebec government enacted regulations to produce a 50 percent reduction in such emissions by the early 1990s. The Atlantic provinces and the New England states agreed to reduce their emissions by 32 percent by 1994. And the federal governments of Canada and the United States have agreed to monitor the levels of acid rain as a continental hazard requiring international governing solutions on both sides of the border.

### The Air

Polluted air also carries damaging chemical agents into the atmosphere, producing two undesirable consequences: the destruction of the ozone layer, and global warming. Serious ozone depletion has occurred over Canadian territory, producing higher risk of ultraviolet radiation directly affecting Canadians, their crops, and animal populations. Environment Canada began to issue weekly ozone reports in 1992, advising Canadians whether to take precautions, such as wearing hats, applying sunscreen, and using sunglasses, to protect themselves from the dangers of ultraviolet radiation. Gases such as carbon dioxide and methane collect in the atmosphere, producing the so-called greenhouse effect and trapping the world's heat and raising temperatures globally. Global warming can result in the kind of climate change that causes flooding around the polar icecap and can alter the water levels in Canada's lake and river systems, threatening coastal communities and their environments.

Canada signed a multilateral treaty to limit emissions of gases causing global warming at the Earth Summit in Rio de Janeiro in 1992. The governments of Ontario, Quebec, and Newfoundland prohibit tampering with emission controls. And, in 1992, British Columbia launched Canada's first motor vehicle emissions-testing program, known as Aircare.

### The Land

The ways Canadians use land has significant environmental consequences as well. The effects of our houses on it, and the agricultural, commercial, governmental, and industrial uses of it are determined by public policy. Land conversions to uses other than those determined by nature can be ecologically damaging. The growth of our cities and the building of highway systems, airports, and communication grids displace agricultural land and affect land generally in more than one way. Industrial and consumer wastes, sewage, garbage — all invade the delicate composition of our lands.

In Canada, land for agricultural purposes is in short supply. Notwithstanding the enormous size of the country, only 13 percent of Canada's land area is suitable for any kind of agricultural production. While terrain and climate limit the amount of Canada's productive land, so do the encroachment on the best farmland by growing cities, expanding highway systems, commercial forestry, and spreading industry. Many of the chemicals used by farmers to control insects and crop quality are eventually harmful to the soil, and some even threaten the ground-water systems deep within the land.

Toxic chemicals absorbed by the soil render it fallow or transmit dangerous chemical discharges into the food chain. Some industries dump their toxic wastes in landfill sites or bury them in the earth. These, and chemicals used to control crop diseases and insects, ultimately are absorbed by the soil and tranferred to people, food, plants, and animals. Soil quality is also conditioned by air pollution, particularly acid rain, which alters the acidity of the soil, affecting the life it sustains.

Soil erosion contributes to what some call "terricide," the killing of the earth as a human habitat. As it occurs in Canada, deforestation disturbs the natural ecosystem, causing soil erosion, preventing the regeneration of the forest, and removing the species of animals that are vital to the life cycle.

Awareness of the effects of unregulated clearcutting and other logging practices has prompted governments to produce public policy directed at protecting the lands and forests of Canada. Provincial governments are expanding provincial parks to preserve forests and are setting limits on the volume of timber that may be harvested on an annual basis. With respect to the challenge of managing the lands and forests of Canada, Canada's governments have a poor record. Most of Canada's timber is located on crown lands owned by the federal and provincial governments. Their ability to govern these resources have long-term consequences for the quality of life not only for Canadians but for populations in the rest of the world as well.

### The Water

Before the first European immigrants came and settled in Canada, pure water that was drinkable without treatment was in plentiful supply. Canada's water supply is still about the same, but much of the water is not clean enough for human consumption and needs to be treated. The ways Canadians have used and treated their water resources have made water a precious natural endowment, testing the capacity of Canada's vast governing system to manage and protect it. Our urban and industrial culture has polluted thousands of Canadian lakes, rivers, and ocean harbours.

Many Canadian communities regularly dump their untreated sewage into rivers and lakes. The food, textile, paper, chemical, metal, and other industries discharge millions of litres of waste water each year. Ground water, which reaches the water table, carries acidity and other pollutants into the underground water system and alters the quality of water supplies in all Canadian communities.

The provincial and federal governments have no comprehensive laws to protect ground water. Ground water, literally the life-blood of our communities, is by and large a sinkhole for much of our pollution. There are no national standards for drinking water either: Most provinces have established guidelines, but only Quebec has laws governing water standards. Because of the convergent growth of cities and industries, the supply of usable water has decreased. The water table is diminishing, and surface waters are being polluted to such an extent that municipal governments are frequently required to restrict water use.

## GOVERNING A PLURALISTIC SOCIETY

Since Confederation, Canadian society has become an ethnic mosaic — a varied composition of many peoples whose distinctive traditions and identities have contributed to the unique blend of political cultures comprising our governing system. About one-half of Canadians descend from one of the two first immigrant groups to establish themselves in Canada — the French and the British.

When Canada took its first census in 1871, about 50 percent of the population was British and 31 percent was French. But, by the 1990s, British and French Canadians comprised only about 25 percent each of Canada's population; immigration had gradually decreased from Britain and France, and that from other parts of the world, especially from Asia, Africa, and the Caribbean, had steadily increased. In 1991, the rank order of these ethnic groups had become: British, French, German, Italian, Ukrainian, Native people and Inuit, Dutch, Chinese, Scandinavian, Polish, Portuguese, Hungarian, Czech, Slovak, Austrian, Belgian, Japanese, and Russian.

The "multicultural" character of Canada's population, the growing numerical strength and voting power of ethnic groups, and the rise of aboriginal nationalism have required governments in Canada to abandon the bicultural bias in their legislation and public policies. The political and governing institutions of Canadian society have begun to grapple with the fact that ethnicity is not just a characteristic of individuals, but is a fundamental characteristic of our entire social system, and a challenge to our governability.

Each group has tended to settle in certain regions of Canada, maintaining their own distinctive culture, social relationships, political attitudes and beliefs, and religion. Most ethnic communities develop institutions — organized, patterned ways of making decisions, behaving, and carrying out social and political interaction — in order to achieve certain goals. Some ethnic groups seek to achieve these goals through religious institutions, separate schools, professional services, social agencies, and cultural organizations.

However, because Canada is a pluralistic society, each ethnic population may hold different political values, generating tensions within the governmental and political systems. Some ethnic groups, such as the descendants of the British in Canada, still dominate positions of social, economic, and governmental power, while others, such as Native peoples, are relatively powerless.

Dominant groups tend to control and restrict the economic, social and political participation by means of "discrimination," the practice of denying opportunity and privilege to members of other groups in society. Discrimination can be protected by law, as in the case of the Indian Act, 1951, or informally by means of attitudes, customs, and traditions that might be applied to gender and other ethnic groups. "Systemic discrimination" can occur when political and social institutions raise barriers that can disqualify equal access to all groups, such as rules about gender participation and promotion in the armed forces, or height qualifications for recruitment into police forces, or language requirements for employment in the government sector.

Once we understand the political ramifications of ethnicity and gender, questions of public policies regarding these groups and their complex implications for Canada's governing system become more apparent. When members of these special groups participate in the political system as a bloc, they force the governing system to accord them recognition and concessions. It appears that demands for autonomy, rather than integration and assimilation, are the modern conditions of Canadian society. Both the need for political self-determination and the need to belong will continue to affect the governability of Canada. The choice between these needs will shape Canada's political destiny well into the next millennium.

### Women and Governability

The capacity of a political system to represent the interests of its citizens and to use their skills in participation is a function of governability. Political systems that fail to represent their members eventually will become ungovernable. To what extent does this statement apply to Canadian women? How are women included or excluded in our political system? Does our political system function less efficiently without their participation? Are we less governable because women are not equally represented in the present system? Can every person be treated equally in a political system controlled primarily by men?

Women have always been involved in politics, but their participation has traditionally been behind the scenes: organizing meetings, raising money, administering election campaigns, and canvassing voters. During the past century, women have become extraordinarily effective at lobbying governments and, by taking independent action, moving the governmental system in a more responsible direction. Suffragists, prison reformers, day-care workers, social workers, nurses, unionists, and managers of women's centres have all been successful in lobbying and effecting changes in government policy.

The first municipal franchise was granted to "widows" and "spinsters" in Nova Scotia in 1893. But a number of federal bills for partial and equal franchise were defeated in the last decade of the nineteenth century. In 1929, Canadian women were declared "persons" under the British North America Act after five Alberta women took their case to the British Privy Council in London, England, which at that time was the final court of appeal after the Supreme Court of Canada. No longer would Canadian women be classed with lunatics and children as people who could not be viewed as responsible for their actions (Anderson 1991, 201). After the famous Persons Case was decided, Canadian women were granted full political freedom. In 1931, Cairine Wilson, from Ontario, became the first woman appointed to the Senate.

Throughout Canadian history, women have constituted slightly more than half of the adult population, but far fewer women than men have run for public office and been elected. Running for political office is still viewed as a traditionally male activity. There is a notion in Canadian society that family life and public life are incompatible. Women, who continue to bear the major responsibility for raising children and managing Canadian households, still face a great deal of societal pressure to keep this their first priority.

As a result, in Canada, women are significantly underrepresented in the federal Parliament and, to a lesser extent, in the provincial legislatures. Women are not equal players in the governing arena, not only because women still face resistance among voters to their having a role in public affairs, but also because they comprise only a small minority among politicians.

For women, the first steps toward political equality led through the ballot box. But once the franchise had been won, it was an upward battle for women in Canada to acquire political power, or even to use their votes to improve their overall social position. However, winning the right to vote and hold public office did not bring women equal status. By the 1990s, even though the opportunities for women to gain access to the political system have never been better, few women seek positions of political and governmental power, and fewer are successful at it.

Though some women hold high political office, they are much more likely to hold honorific posts, such as that of governor general or lieutenant-governor, than to stand a chance of being elected prime minister or provincial premier. Women are most likely to run as candidates and be elected at the municipal level, and least likely to run and be elected at the provincial and federal levels. Yet, the turnout of women voters nationally is higher than that of male voters.

Analyzing the participation of women in government and politics as something that has to do with getting elected may be problematical. Among observers of public affairs, there is a tendency to contrast the political role of women and men within the existing patterns of political behaviour, patterns that historically have been generated, defined, and analyzed by men according to male expectations (Burt 1990, 208). If we compare male and female political participation, we can conclude that women participate "less" than men.

But women have achieved greater influence in Canadian politics in a number of ways, including voting, running for office, and lobbying to have their interests represented. Especially through interest groups and pressure groups advocating their rights, women have altered the fixed attitudes of governments and, to some extent, of society in general. Their aim has been to dismantle gender stereotypes while fashioning public policies that acknowledge relevant differences between men and women. While the National Action Committee on the Status of Women (NAC) fights primarily for women's political and economic rights, other organizations fight more broadly for equality for women in all spheres of life. Together, these organizations keep the issues of inequality and discrimination high on the public agenda.

Until the 1970s, protectionism — the idea that the role of government is to shelter women from life's difficulties — affected the character of Canadian gender law. And protected they were, through laws that discriminated against them in employment and other areas. Women were even "protected" from voting until the first decades of the twentieth century. After nearly a century of broad deference to protectionism, successive Canadian governments began to take a closer look at gender-based distinctions.

By the 1990s, however, legal discrimination had been successfully challenged in some important areas as a result of the advocacy of women's groups. In this regard, the Charter of Rights and Freedoms became the basis for legal challenges to inequality, among other things in Canada's gender relationships.

## The First Nations and Governability

Before the Europeans "discovered" and settled in Canada, 58 aboriginal governments presided over the territory that stretches from the Yukon to the Avalon Peninsula, even including much of what is now the United States. These aboriginal governing institutions long predate the arrival of Europeans on the shores of North America. Each had its own territory and laws, and had developed its own pattern and style of governance. Nonetheless, Native peoples have had to advance and defend their rights to "self-government" since their first contacts with the European colonists (Tennant 1984).

In fact, from the perspective of aboriginal peoples across Canada, their governments have exercised original sovereignty and legitimacy since time immemorial. As the original Canadians, most of the First Nations denied and resisted attempts by Euro-Canadians to assimilate them into Canadian society. The Native peoples did not have to be concerned with becoming Canadians, as they already were. However, Canadian governments promoted and engaged a policy of **assimilation** instead of self-government and separation.

Under the federal and provincial governments, Native language use was often restricted, and religious rituals were curtailed. Native children were sent to residential schools, where they were not permitted to speak their ancestral languages, and many were given non-Native names. Harold Cardinal (1969, 74) noted an official hypocrisy in that Canadians do not ask whooping cranes to become Canada geese, but they want "Indians to become brown white men."

From the perspective of immigrant Europeans, aboriginal political institutions were rudimentary and inferior. As a rule, political leadership was exercised by individuals whose opinions were valued, and whose recommendations had usually worked well in the past. The leadership was subject to a consensus among all of the adult members of a band. The absence of consensus would threaten the survival of the band because, on a day-to-day basis, Native people co-operated with one another to satisfy matters involving basic subsistence. Culture contact with the Euro-Canadians resulted in the erosion of indigenous aboriginal cultures, their political organizations, and their social values, producing a culture of poverty characterized by dependency and despair.

Beginning in the 1830s, aboriginal settlement on reserves separated the two spheres of governability. Many aboriginals saw reserve lands as a place to nurture and protect their threatened cultures from the domination of Euro-Canadians, while many Canadians saw the reserve as the launching pad for the complete assimilation of aboriginal cultures into the national federal political culture.

The politics of aboriginal–Euro-Canadian relations has revolved around two fundamental issues: (1) assimilation into modern Canadian society so that Native claims will disappear, and (2) recognition of the aboriginal as sovereign and self-governing so that land claims will be honoured. Aboriginals view the right to govern themselves as spiritual and **inalienable**, not one that can be assigned to them by Canadian governments. The First Nations have always challenged the widely held assumption that the "two founding peoples" of Canada were the French and the English colonists, and have upheld the primacy of aboriginal claims to territorial sovereignty.

In recent years, the constitutional entitlements of the First Nations and their desire for self-government have moved to the centre of the constitutional stage in Canada. Section 91 (24) of the British North America Act gave jurisdiction over Native peoples and their reserves to Parliament. Not long after, Parliament passed the first Indian Act, giving Canada the power to "manage" the affairs of Native peoples. A few years later, the Indian Advancement Act, 1884, gave limited powers of government at the municipal level to certain Native bands across the country. An amended Indian Act became law in 1951 in an unsuccessful attempt to pacify Native attempts to seek sovereign recognition and greater autonomy in the governance of their affairs.

In the meantime, successive Canadian governments moved to facilitate greater assimilation and gave registered, or "status," aboriginals the right to vote in federal elections. Until that time, they were considered members of tribal nations, whose relations with government were subject to more than 500 treaties of friendship, and hunting and fishing rights with Great Britain, France, and Canada, signed since 1700.

In reaction to the deplorable social conditions of Native life and to the vision of cultural integration shared by successive federal governments, the drive for Native self-government took the form of a **social movement**. Communities of aboriginal peoples began to organize *en masse*, united in their opposition to the proposed termination of their special status.

Most of Canada's land mass below 60 degrees latitude came under treaties signed after 1871 (the last original treaty was signed in 1923) that are still being interpreted and applied today. In these treaties, Ottawa negotiated title to vast swaths of the West in exchange for reserves, gifts such as medicine chests, and annual payments to the Natives.

The Indian Act generated classifications of "Indians" to determine their relationship with the federal and provincial governments. A "status Indian" was registered or entitled to be registered as an Indian under the act. Canada's "status Indians" are "treaty Indians," registered aboriginals who are members of a band whose ancestors signed a treaty with the federal government. A "non-status" Indian is someone who is of Native ancestry, but who is not an "Indian" as defined by the act. His or her name cannot appear on the Indian Register of the federal government.

Treaties have been viewed differently by aboriginals. Some see them as contracts that were forced upon them by a dominant and a more powerful political culture. Others view them as a kind of **social contract** that validates the basis for present and future negotiations between and among sovereign governments. The extensive claims filed with the federal government made the status of Canada's aboriginal peoples a major issue in the constitutional process that unfolded in the late 1970s.

Three sections of the Constitution Act, 1982, related directly to aboriginal peoples. Section 25 promised that the Charter of Rights and Freedoms would not abrogate or derogate from "any aboriginal, treaty or other rights or freedoms that pertain to the aboriginal peoples of Canada"; Section 35 recognized and affirmed "the existing aboriginal and treaty rights of the aboriginal peoples of Canada"; and Section 37 provided for the convening of a First Ministers' Conference on Aboriginal Constitutional Matters, which was held in April 1983. Other First Ministers' conferences were called that focussed on the right of aboriginal self-government.

The struggle to find the solution that will enable the First Nations to govern themselves will undoubtedly continue to challenge the governability of Canada until Canadians are prepared to recognize that right. In 1990, in the so-called Sparrow Case, the Supreme Court of Canada ruled that aboriginal rights include those that protect activity that is essential to the aboriginal community's self-definition. The Court did not draw the conclusion that "self-definition" and "self-government" are the same.

It is almost impossible for Canada's Native peoples to put forward a unified and detailed proposal to which the governments of Canada can relate. The 512 000 status aboriginals and the 32 000 Inuit across Canada have very different demands and expectations from those of Canada's 500 000 Métis and non-status aboriginals, who have no land base and who live scattered across urban Canada. But the natural right to government unites many First Nations. The Assembly of First Nations (AFN), which represents 633 widely diverse status aboriginals, wants the right to choose their laws and to replace specific Criminal Code provisions with their own decrees. This means that the codes of First Nations could overrule the Charter of Rights and Freedoms and provincial codes that govern worker safety, regulation of the environment, and labour relations.

The Canadian government and most of the provinces have moved very slowly on recognizing an already-existing right for aboriginals to govern themselves, a right that precedes them and cannot be conferred by them.

## CONCLUSION

As we have seen, the struggle to govern Canada has many dimensions. To a great extent, the difficulties of governing Canada have been connected with the institutions of government we have developed and the framework within which our governments must operate. Canada borrowed heavily from the British system of parliamentary and cabinet government and created a multiplicity of other governments at the provincial, territorial, and municipal levels to unify the country and manage the affairs of Canadian society.

A federal system can be conflictive but requires the governing units to co-operate if unity is to be achieved out of diversity, and if all levels of government are to exercise authority over the same people and territory. Many Canadians believe the federal system that has evolved is well suited to this large country; in their perception, it has helped to co-ordinate government services, contributing to Canada's political integration. Some hold that the federal system needs to be fundamentally restructured so that it can include more of what is Canada, while others advocate its dismantling so as to create regions of independent states.

But was the adoption of a parliamentary system of government married to federalism genius or folly? The effect of federalism in Canada has been to fragment power and, by so doing, over the years to reduce the ability of the federal government to govern and unite the country.

The territorial concentration of four-fifths of Canada's French-speaking people in the province of Quebec, with its own distinctive political culture, was bound to challenge the ability of the federal government to keep the country unified. Throughout the years since Confederation, Québécois control over the province's territory and its major educational, religious, juridical, and governmental institutions has laid the foundations for the existence of an independent nation-state to emerge from Canadian federalism.

Our ability to govern has also been conditioned by the democratic values underlying the institutions of government we have created. The democratic values Canadians have adopted demand an equalitarian system of government that permits the competition of all governments in Canada and the rivalry of political parties and interest groups, all having the prerogative to block those proposed policies they consider harmful to their interests.

Canadians also believe in the equalitarian political recruitment of people responsive to the demands of society to positions of power and influence. As a result of this dispersion of power in Canadian society, no single leadership group or elite can dominate or control Canadian governments, or Canada's economies. All provincial governments are said to be equal, and should be treated equally. The consequences of holding these democratic values have been an emphasis on urbanization, industrialization, cosmopolitanism, labour productivity, secular education, technological progress, and profit.

However, traditional institutions and values in Quebec have been peripheral to the central thrust of political values in the rest of the country. In order to preserve the distinctive language and culture in that province, Quebeckers have developed a complex system of parallel governmental institutions and informal social networks within which a distinctive national political subculture has emerged. Quebec schools, parishes, credit unions (*caisses populaires*), labour organizations, communications media, voluntary organizations, political parties, and a wide range of other institutions have laid the collective foundations for a very different society within Canada's federal system.

Accordingly, the very same democratic values we hold with such reverence at the national level have also nurtured powerful subcultures within all provinces in different parts of the country. Such forces acting together can pull and tug at the very heart of national unity in the whole country, thus threatening its governability.

The presence of so many divergent interest groups also makes it more difficult to govern Canada's complex political system. There is a powerful influence of certain special interests who compete with political parties and other representative institutions for the attentions of all levels of government. Special-interest groups have developed and grown in power across the country, free to pursue their goals by lobbying the various institutions of government. Some question whether a system of government can work effectively by making special arrangements with the farmers, businesses, labour, and provincial interests is able to make "national" policy. When each group cuts its own deal with a government, will the rules that are made apply equally to everyone? The greater the power of interest groups in a governing system, the more difficult it is for a majority rule to be achieved with any regularity. When interest groups dominate the processes of government and politics, does the ability to govern consequently suffer?

Of course, how we govern ourselves is not just an extension of political and social differences. Geographical factors — such as size, location, and resources — have an important influence on the effectiveness of our government institutions and on the cost of delivering government services and regulation.

Finally, it is important for us to examine how we govern ourselves from the perspective of women and aboriginal peoples. The tendency to separate women as citizens from participating and influencing the structures and policies of Canadian governments is still very pronounced in our political system. It illustrates a critical need for collective action on the part of women to bring about change and access to Canada's system of government. Another great political cleavage that separates from one another is that which isolates aboriginals from the rest of society. Almost whatever variable is being considered — cultural values, gender, income, occupation, or geographical isolation — differences between aboriginals and other Canadians are no less than, and often greater than, those separating other groups. The history of collective action by indigenous peoples exposes much about how we govern ourselves. It is important for students of government and politics in Canada to try to understand the sophistication of aboriginal political leadership and the nature of their government institutions.

## GLOSSARY

**assimilation**  A blending of one group into another by which the minority group is completely absorbed by the majority.

**ethnicity**  The characteristics of a collectivity of people who share an ascribed status based on culture, religion, national origin, or race.

**fusion of powers**  The capacity of the political executive to introduce and to vote for its bills and programs in the legislative branch of government.

**head of government**  In the parliamentary system, the leader of the majority party in the legislature or a person able to form a coalition that will sustain the confidence of the legislature.

**head of state**  The ceremonial executive who formally represents a nation-state, for example, a governor general, a monarch, or a president.

**inalienable**  A type of human rights that cannot be transferred or otherwise removed from an individual or group.

**infrastructure**  Systems of transportation, communication, education, power grids, the industrial and technological base, and the political system.

**National Policy**  The policy advanced by John A. Macdonald in 1870 that led to the economic integration of Canada by building a comprehensive railway system, encouraging immigration, and protecting nascent Canadian industries by means of an external tariff.

**separatism**  In Canada, a political movement that can be traced to the government of Maurice Duplessis in Quebec whose supporters demanded a Quebec, separate and independent from Canada.

**social contract**  A term first used by Plato to posit that social and political obligations are contractual so as to preserve certain inalienable rights to individuals and to ensure the survivability of the society.

**social movement**   A collectivity of people trying to bring about or resist social and political change.

**sovereignty association**   A concept advanced by the Parti Québécois after winning the Quebec provincial election of 1976, calling for a form of semi-independence by retaining economic association with Canada that would include free trade and a common currency system.

## RECOMMENDED READING

Jackson, Robert, and Doreen Jackson. *Contemporary Government and Politics: Democracy and Authoritarianism*. 1993. Scarborough, Ont.: Prentice-Hall Canada. This book examines the fundamental components of comparative government and analyzes the difficulties of governing in a world of constant change.

Beaujot, Roderic. 1991. *Population Change in Canada: The Challenges of Policy Adaptation*. Toronto: McClelland & Stewart. An excellent resource for understanding how the dynamics of Canada's population can affect government policy-making and how Canadian governments are addressing immigration, gender, ethnic composition, urbanization, and health care.

Bell, David. 1992. *The Roots of Disunity*. Toronto: Oxford University Press. This revised edition of a book originally published in 1979 asks whether Canada can hold together in light of the swelling militancy in Quebec, the growing sense of independence among the Western provinces, and the invasion of American industries and culture into Canada.

Canada. Statistics Canada. 1991. *Women in Canada: A Statistical Report*. Ottawa: Statistics Canada. This report on Canadian women compiles about twenty years' worth of economic, social, and cultural data in tables, charts, and graphs.

Coleman, William, and Grace Skogstad. 1990. *Policy Communities and Public Policy in Canada*. Toronto: Copp Clark Pitman. This book examines the development of public policy and how groups in Canadian society influence policy formation.

Dickason, Olive Patricia. 1992. *Canada's First Nations*. Toronto: McClelland & Stewart. This book provides a comprehensive history of the 57 founding peoples of Canada.

Krause, Robert, and R.H. Wagenberg. 1991. *Introductory Readings in Canadian Government and Politics*. Toronto: Copp Clark Pitman. This excellent collection of readings introduces the student to the dynamics of Canada's political culture — its ideologies, federalism, public policy, and Quebec.

Howlett, Michael, and M. Ramesh. 1992. *Political Economy of Canada*. Toronto: McClelland & Stewart. This book offers a survey of how Canada's political and economic system works, the structure and organization of labour, and the nature of Canada's fiscal and monetary policies.

MacDonald, Douglas. 1991. *The Politics of Pollution*. Toronto: McClelland & Stewart. This book examines the worsening environmental consequences of acid rain, radioactive contamination, and toxic chemicals in Canada. It describes the inability of Canadian governments to address environmental problems because of jurisdictional disputes and cost factors.

Nash, Knowlton. 1991. *Visions of Canada*. Toronto: McClelland & Stewart. This book provides a collection of interviews with dozens of Canadians from different walks of life on the subjects of Quebec, the constitution, Native issues, and the future of Canada.

Wine, Jeri, and Janice Ristcock. 1991. *Women and Social Change*. Toronto: James Lorimer. This collection of articles written by leading feminists focusses on the organization of women's groups in Canada and their role in the political process.

CHAPTER

# THE IDEOLOGICAL CONTEXT OF CANADIAN POLITICS

*INTRODUCTION*

*WHAT ARE IDEOLOGIES?*

*OUR POLITICAL SELF: HOW CANADIANS LEARN ABOUT POLITICS AND GOVERNMENT*

*HOW CANADIANS LEARN IDEOLOGIES*

AGENTS OF LEARNING FOR POLITICAL IDEAS

*THE COMPONENTS OF IDEOLOGIES*

RHETORIC
VALUES
BELIEFS AND ATTITUDES
SYMBOLS
PRAXIS

*UNDERSTANDING THE DIMENSIONS OF IDEOLOGICAL THINKING*

RADICAL THINKING
LIBERAL THINKING
MODERATE THINKING
CONSERVATIVE THINKING
REACTIONARY THINKING

*POLITICAL IDEOLOGIES IN CANADA*

DEMOCRACY
LIBERALISM
CONSERVATISM
POPULISM
SOCIALISM
NATIONALISM
QUEBEC NATIONALISM
FEMINISM

*CONCLUSION*

*GLOSSARY*

*RECOMMENDED READING*

**A**ll ideologies make assumptions about the real world. Many contain false premises from which those who hold them reach false conclusions about the real world. But the people who advance them believe the premises and conclusions of their ideology to be "truthful," no matter how others might react. Ideologies become so much a part of us that eventually how we think and how we behave are one and the same. Such is no better illustrated than in the case of Alberta high school teacher James Keegstra, whose ideas, writings, and teachings reveal a pure bigotry and hatred toward Jews and Judaism.

In the early 1980s, James Keegstra was teaching and promoting an anti-Semitic ideology in Alberta. In 1984, he was the first Canadian to be charged, tried, and convicted with willfully promoting hatred. The Alberta Court of Appeal set the conviction aside, reasoning that the anti-hate legislation was unconstitutional. In 1990, the Supreme Court of Canada overturned this ruling. The case was sent back to the Alberta Court of Appeal, which in 1991 quashed the conviction and ordered a new trial, holding that Keegstra should have been allowed to challenge the jurors. At a new trial in 1992, Keegstra was convicted under Canada's hate laws and fined $3000. But, in 1994, the Alberta Court of Appeal struck down his 1992 conviction and ruled that Keegstra was not given a fair trial. The court's decision drew much criticism and was widely viewed as particularly insensitive because the decision was released on the Jewish holiday Rosh Hashanah. Later that same year, Alberta's attorney general sent the Keegstra case back to the Supreme Court for a second time to decide whether the Alberta Court of Appeal erred on a point of procedure when it overturned Keegstra's second conviction for violating Canada's hate law.

Keegstra holds to an elaborate and intense ideology that he believes can explain *everything* about modern world history — once the basic premises are accepted. He posits that past and present history reveal a powerful Jewish-led conspiracy that aims to promote sexual perversion, to destroy Christianity, and to dominate the world. According to Keegstra's ideological premises, the Jews are not only different but have historically been the enemies of Christianity. He assigned his writings to students to "prove" that his assertions about Jews were true. He preached that Jesus was not a Jew because Jews were descendants of some Mongolian tribe, and thus themselves not really "Jewish."

According to the logic of Keegstra's ideology, the Jews caused the French Revolution and were responsible for the American Civil War. He believes and teaches that Jews precipitated the Bolshevik Revolution and conspired to cause the First World War. He teaches that the Nazi Holocaust was a hoax contrived to gain world-wide sympathy for the creation of the State of Israel, while the Jews secretly co-operated with Hitler. Two other Canadians, Malcolm Ross and Ernst Zundel, proclaim similar ideological viewpoints.

Keegstra's ideological premises lead him to believe and teach that this widespread Jewish conspiracy controls universities, publishing houses, the media, and public libraries. He believes that only anti-Semitic literature such as his has escaped the conspiracy of censorship.

The case of James Keegstra is more than just an illustration of prejudice, bigotry, discrimination, and hatred of Jews or other peoples. It represents what his ideology is and how it motivates his behaviour and that of others. Not all ideologies lead their proponents to such insidious conclusions and actions, but, as systems of thought, they have the power to inspire people to do momentous things.

Keegstra's anti-Semitic ideology has deep roots in rural Alberta and can be traced to the Social Credit movement that surfaced there in the 1930s. His ideological premises are based on information that is either illogical or unrelated to reality. It flows from a distortion of current and historical fact and generalizes its conclusions to apply to all members of a particular group — Jews. While all ideologies possess positive and negative attitudes toward certain groups, the information on which prejudice is based initiates behaviour and actions in people that have clear and serious political implications.

## INTRODUCTION

It is sometimes said that Canadians are not very ideological; what that means is that we may not always be aware of the extent to which political ideologies play a role in our lives. Most Canadians do not know precisely where their underlying political values come from, so pervasive is the process by which they are introduced to their beliefs (Lambert et al. 1986). Often people respond to questions in ways that are ideological, even though they may not understand the central political principles of the ideas they use.

Canadians may speak of liberalism, communism, fascism, nationalism, or anarchism, but very few are aware of the full and consistent range of attitudes that comprise these political ideologies. Those who say they are "liberal," "conservative," or "nationalist" often cannot explain what this means in terms of public policy or articulate their views coherently as political thought. In fact, few Canadians order their views on politics and government in inflexible and unchangeable ways.

But we must especially avoid the assumption that Canadian politics is non-ideological. Canadian politics and its governing institutions are ideological in the sense that our political behaviour is shaped, informed, and even dominated by distinctive sets of political beliefs. People's political thoughts are guided and oriented by the ideologies they have absorbed. Ideologies, such as conservatism, feminism, environmentalism, nationalism, or socialism, seep in through all sorts of openings in our minds, conditioning, enriching, and informing us about the ways we see the world.

Most of us are not usually conscious of the fact that ideologies affect the content of our private and social thoughts (Converse 1964, 206). They underlie what we think as well as what we think about. In fact, ideologies are not only outside of us but inside us. They are not things in the objective sense, but are the subjective products of any and all relationships among people in society.

For these reasons, ideologies affect everyone — no one is free from their influences. Ideologies affect how people perceive the world and what they say and do, yet, for the most part, people are not always informed of them and usually, when under their influence, are disinclined to consider them at all critically. Nonetheless, Canadians are predisposed to see the world in certain ways that guide their thinking and their behaviour.

Most Canadians usually do not question the fundamental and pragmatic principles of Canada's political system. They differ on matters only in terms of emphasis and degree. Only a small minority of Canadians are what some would call "hard-core ideologues" — that is, people who have a clear idea what the labels attached to ideologies mean and directly connect their beliefs with their **partisan** choices in elections.

## WHAT ARE IDEOLOGIES?

Conceptualizing about our society can be ideological in that people hold a set of beliefs that are organized and logical, and offer a consistent plan of action and view of the world. *Political ideology*, as it is used interchangeably with the term "political ideas," refers to an acquired set of views about what constitutes the best form of government and the most equitable and just political order. Political ideologies are concerned with the proper functions of government, the kinds of political institutions we have to achieve our social goals, and how we distribute economic, social, and political benefits. All of this has to do with how comfortable we feel about the scope of government activities in our lives (see Figure 2.1).

Like a quilt, an ideology is more than the sum of its parts; it is the joining of those parts in a specified arrangement that provides us

**Figure 2.1 Ideology and the Scope of Government**

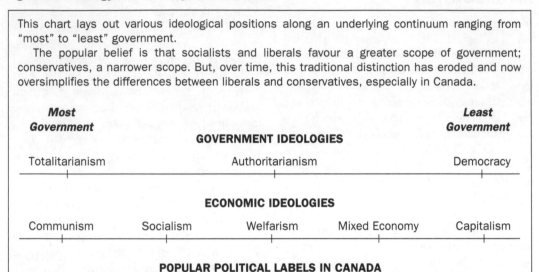

This chart lays out various ideological positions along an underlying continuum ranging from "most" to "least" government.

The popular belief is that socialists and liberals favour a greater scope of government; conservatives, a narrower scope. But, over time, this traditional distinction has eroded and now oversimplifies the differences between liberals and conservatives, especially in Canada.

*Most*
*Government*                                                                  *Least*
                                                                              *Government*

**GOVERNMENT IDEOLOGIES**

Totalitarianism                    Authoritarianism                          Democracy

**ECONOMIC IDEOLOGIES**

Communism          Socialism          Welfarism          Mixed Economy          Capitalism

**POPULAR POLITICAL LABELS IN CANADA**

Socialist          Indépendantiste          Liberal          Conservative          Populist

with a coherent view of the world. For one political scientist, political ideology "spells out what is valued and what is not, what must be maintained and what must be changed" (Macridis 1983, 9). Another group of political scientists (Christenson et al. 1971, 5) defined political ideology as a "belief system that explains and justifies a preferred political order for society either existing or proposed, and offers a strategy (processes, institutional arrangements, programs) for its attainment."

This latter definition suggests that political ideologies are fundamentally "persuasive" political ideas that are goal-oriented and provide our governments with a range of activities in which to engage to create public policies that are acceptable to the governed.

Where there are ideologies, there is "persuasion"; where there is persuasion, there often is the "conversion" of ideological thinking.

Some ideologies cause us to re-examine the very nature of human beings, as do communism, environmentalism, and feminism. For example, many feminists say that a

woman's nature is usually described in male terms, or from a male point of view, or with male interests in mind (Bradshaw 1991). In a world of **patriarchal ideologies**, femininity is portrayed as a lesser masculinity, as is implicit in the often-heard expressions "the weaker sex" and "girl talk." To counter these kinds of assumptions, some feminists assert that femininity should be seen as a distinctive characteristic of female nature, not simply as a weaker version of a characteristic of male nature.

The political power of patriarchal thinking can be seen from another ideological perspective: The emergence of an ideology of environmentalism shows us the relationship between the way people see themselves and the value they place on other natural beings in the hierarchy of existence. Feminists point out that, whenever men are culturally positioned as "masters of the universe" and "masters of nature," they and the systems of government they generate inherit an old and primal permission to be dominant, arrogant, persistent, and even violent in pursuit and exercise of their view of power. In the political context of this human self-perception individual and group life become a competition for power, mostly among men, with daily winners and losers. Victims of this world view are generally women, children, gentle men, and all people culturally different from the power elite.

From another viewpoint, most aboriginals in Canada see "environmentalism" through their own ideological perspective — as a spiritual relationship an individual has with the natural world, which is not distinguishable as a special way of thinking about life. For them, humans are deemed to be part of nature and are not set apart from it or placed above it. Many aboriginals believe in animism, the notion that natural objects — plants, animals, even lakes, rivers, and oceans — contain vital forces that are as real as the human spirit itself. Some aboriginal ideologies see animals as "people" who deserve the same respect as their human neighbours.

Ideologies will portray the way the world is, the way people are or should be, what is and what can be known as a body of knowledge, what has happened and what might happen, what is right and wrong, what is just and unjust, who should lead us, and what is true or false. Answers to these questions have been, and will continue to be, endlessly advanced by *ideologues* — that is, those who faithfully adhere consistently to the tenets of a particular system of beliefs, have a clear idea what labels such as "liberal" and "conservative" mean, and directly connect their beliefs to the party choices they make at election time.

## OUR POLITICAL SELF: HOW CANADIANS LEARN ABOUT POLITICS AND GOVERNMENT

We know that people are not born with a developed set of political beliefs. Men, women, and children acquire their political beliefs and their ideologies after developing a "political self" as they mature.

The concept of political self is a rather vague one as a tool of analysis. But we certainly experience it as real: All of us have some fairly definite notions of how we *feel* about politics. Probably the first political thought to blossom in the mind of a Canadian child is a psychological attachment or identification with a province or region, or with Canada itself. This is by no means a sense of what Quebec or the Prairies, or Canada, is, just a feeling of belonging to it.

But whatever our political self consists of, it is a social product, created and modified throughout life by interaction with other people. The political self in all of us is moulded and shaped by the attitudes, values, and experiences in our families and with our friends, workmates, and schoolmates; and by the media, our communities, our education, and the major political events that affect our lives. At the core of this political self are strong feelings toward the nation-state, its governmental institutions, and certain learned and deeply rooted conceptions about freedom, equality, and rights. Over time, the political self senses how government works, develops impressions and knowledge of politics, and cultivates preferences regarding public policies, political parties, and leaders.

## HOW CANADIANS LEARN IDEOLOGIES

The process of developing the political self by which political beliefs, values, and ideologies are transmitted to individuals, and sometimes carried from one generation to the next, is known as "political socialization." Through political socialization, Canadians internalize, or incorporate into their own thinking, beliefs, feelings, and judgements about whether something is good or bad and about the political world in which they live (Pammett and Pépin 1988). This is the kind of process wherein a political culture is absorbed by people.

Think of the tremendous range of feelings, knowledge, and opinions Canadians have about politics: feelings about Quebec and the fate of Canada, knowledge about federal and provincial political parties, opinions about political leaders and about how or whether to participate in politics. And from where do they all come? The parade and fireworks display on Canada Day? The television debate on Canadian unity? Heated arguments around the dinner table about who is responsible for unemployment? A course in political science? These events and thousands more culminate to produce the political orientations within us.

Just as Canada is not a uniform society, socialization is similar but not an identical process within each province and across the country. Canadian society hosts many political subcultures, and a cross-section of the world's political ideologies are represented almost everywhere in the country. Political socialization differs across regions, between genders, and within provinces and nations of aboriginal peoples. In a multicultural society, political learning takes place differentially, across a wide range of cultural experiences that cherish unique political values, symbols, and skills.

Many factors contribute to the different experiences Canadians have in learning their political ideologies. Canada is a big country with many ethnic and aboriginal groups. In addition to French and English, many other languages are spoken here. And because we live so close to the United States, American political and governmental values cross the border.

Yet, a national political culture does exist, based on the widespread recognition of Canadian symbols, an electoral system that recruits leaders and representatives, a competitive political party system, and institutions of parliamentary government and politics.

## Agents of Learning for Political Ideas

A person growing up in Canada has many teachers from whom to learn about government and political ideologies. Some of this learning is formal: We take courses in Canadian history and government in high school or political science classes at university or college. In such formal settings, we learn generally about the "nuts and bolts" of government, how many MPs each province has, what the governor general does, and so on. Such formal learning can be a limited source of political knowledge. In the sphere of government and politics, formal socialization is to informal socialization as a puddle is to an ocean.

Most of what we learn about our world of politics comes to us without anyone intending to teach it. In fact, there is little evidence that structured learning about politics and government is very long-lasting or that it makes much difference in the attitudes and beliefs of those who are exposed to it. Informal learning seems to be much more effective in transmitting acceptable political ideas throughout our society. It is likely to occur at the dinner table and in front of the TV more than in a school or at political rallies.

Obviously, the paths to political awareness, knowledge, and the development of our political selves will differ among individuals, but most Canadians are exposed to the same influences, or agents of socialization.

### Family

Scholars of political socialization have noted the crucial role of the family in early learning. They inform us that what is learned first is learned best, and what is learned first structures later learning (Beck 1977, 117–18). The family is uniquely situated to be a potent agent of political information, and in Canada the family is far and away the most influential agent of learning.

Not only do the political attitudes and actions of our parents influence our own, but the family also links us to other forces of socialization. We receive from our families our gender, ethnic, and racial identity; our views about social class; our educational opportunities; and our basic beliefs and experiences about life. In the family, we gain positive and negative rudimentary experiences in matters of equality, justice, and personal security. We learn how to negotiate, co-operate, and compete with other members in the family, and carry these lessons with us into the wider social and political arena.

Much political socialization in the family occurs indirectly, however. In fact, Canadian parents are inclined to worry a lot more about the moral, religious, and sexual values of their offspring than they do about a child's political values. The family is not instituted, nor is it usually intended, to be a training ground for politics and government (Kornberg, Smith, and Clarke 1979, 228). The political lessons that take place within the structure of the family are usually given by example, just as family members pass along their dialects, religious beliefs, and attitudes about social class. Party and ideological identification is sometimes adopted by children imitating their parents, such as working for a political party or participating in a demonstration over the issue of a harbour clean-up. This process is more pronounced if the parents are themselves in political agreement and if they participate in the organization of a political party. It is less pronounced when parents are in disagreement.

Politics is, from one generation to another, reasonably, though not always, predictable. Generations do change, but each new generation will, in many ways, reflect the old. However, children are not political clones of their parents. While children do tend to mimic parental reactions to certain highly charged national issues, they usually go their own way on matters affecting them personally, prima-

rily because children are open to counter-influences of political socialization in the school and in the community.

### Schools

Schools can have an influence on political learning that, from an ideological perspective, is equal to or greater than that of parents. The primary and secondary education system is an explicit agent of learning for information and knowledge about politics. Primary schools introduce children to authority figures outside the family, such as their teachers, the principal, school administrators, and police officers. In emphasizing the role of authority and discipline in the education system, schools prepare children to accept and respect the social and political order. Teachers act as authority figures and help their students to become aware of various democratic procedures.

Children learn about the obligations of good citizenship to the extent that the school, the classroom environment, and the teachers stress compliance with rules and regulations. Generally, schools also stress the norms of democratic ideology: to respect the opinions of others, to vote for class priorities, to accept the will of the majority. As well, much of the factual base of Canadian government is learned in the classroom: how the governor general is appointed; the priorities and powers of a prime minister; how many MPs there are in the House of Commons, and senators in the Senate.

Plenty of this early learning is designed to give students positive images about the political system and about the ideas that support the governing system. Schools promote some patriotic rituals, such as singing the national anthem at special events or celebrating national and provincial holidays. Such rituals ensure that youths grow up to be supportive of the basic institutions of government and the accepted ideologies in Canadian society. D. Easton and J. Dennis (1969,

106–107) found that, when young people are exposed to positive messages and images about government and leaders, they are less easily disenchanted with the system when they grow up.

In Canada, schools are the most subtle intrusion of government into our political socialization. Schools are tax-supported public institutions that control teaching standards and curriculum content, and transmit socially and politically approved values. The teachers that are hired, the textbooks that are selected, the facilities that are provided and funded — all are influenced directly or indirectly by government policy. Understandably, governments want schools to promote positive orientations toward the political and economic system they represent.

Mock conventions, model parliaments, elections, and involvement in student government and school newspapers introduce students to the operation of governance in their society. School clubs often operate by democratic procedures and reinforce concepts such as using elections, voting to reach social decisions, and accepting the political will of the majority.

Accordingly, students enlarge their understanding of the political world during these years. They come to understand the differences among federal, provincial, and local governments. For those with a strong interest in political affairs, the high school years are a time for deepening awareness of the larger political system. In effect, students acquire not just facts, but subtle ideological impressions of the way things are and the way things ought to be.

The effect of college and university on political behaviour is more difficult to assess. At this level of education, the effect of the institution — of its rules and authority structure, its curriculum, and its professors — is so intertwined with the influences of the network of peers, and of the family, that the specific effect of the institution is nearly impos-

sible to measure. What is known is that those who complete a university or college education show higher levels of political involvement and political efficacy. In the final analysis, formal education is a powerful influence on an individual's political ideology and on the political behaviour it fosters.

### Peer Groups

Our peers (literally, "equals") are important to our ideological socialization as well. *Peer groups* are groups of people, roughly equal in social position, who regularly interact with one another. Even as children, we tend to associate with people of similar ages and interests.

Students who go to school together and people who work together, play together, and/or live in the same community together — all are peer groups. As parental and school influences decrease, peer groups assume a greater importance in promoting political and ideological awareness. Social pressures on individuals to conform can be quite powerful. People's political opinions are both shaped and strengthened by the groups with which they associate.

Associations among peers are usually nonpolitical. But we know that, in peer groups where people meet face to face, political socialization can result. For example, neighbours can talk up the candidates of one political party and criticize the candidates of another, making it unpopular to voice a dissenting opinion because non-conformity can lead to ostracism. Peer groups of people with similar ethnicity, race, occupational status, or political loyalties can exert strong pressures on members to conform to the dominant characteristics of the group.

Peers are a source of political information. People as peers interpret the world from one another (Bibby and Posterski 1985, 112). Feelings of political cynicism, political trust, and political efficacy flow from our associations with peers. Ethical abstractions such as proper political conduct, fair play, and honesty become meaningful in the give-and-take of peer interaction.

When a person moves up the social ladder, there is a tendency to adopt the ideologies of the new peers; those who move downward on the social ladder tend to continue to hold their former views. Similarly, a change in where we live can also affect our political outlook and orientations because our peer groups often change as well. And entering a new profession or changing occupations provides a new set of peers who can alter our ideological perspectives.

### The Media

Because public knowledge of, commentaries on, and images of political affairs usually come to us from the **mass media**, the media themselves must be considered to be significant agents of socialization. The primary affect of the media is to increase the level of information about politics and government among the general public. Mass communications in Canada are ever-present transmitters of ideological perspectives. The media are not only persuasive but widely educative in our political culture.

In many schools, the mass media, especially TV, are used as classroom tools to educate children. Through the media, they learn about historical figures, ideas, and events. The use of the media as a source of political information is prevalent among high school students in Canada, although less so than among their parents. Parents frequently select political TV programming (and also newspapers, magazines, and radio broadcasts) that their children consume. The media have an effect on what adults think about — that is, the issues, events, and personalities they pay attention to — but also influence ideologies through their coverage of issues and individuals.

The impact of the media on ideological socialization is increasing as communications technologies become accessible to more and more people. Not only do the media provide the information, but they interpret it as well. Research informs us that changes in political opinions tend to follow sentiments expressed by television news commentators (Page, Shapiro, and Dempsey 1987). The mass media in Canada influence the development of political opinions, political activities, and thus the transmission of political ideologies. The interpretive framework that the media may choose to portray can be quickly and subtly absorbed into our existing world of political attitudes and values.

This is not to say that we watch TV and listen to the radio with minds entirely empty of opinions and bias. People will often sort out and reinterpret messages from the media so as to reinforce their opinions, rather than to change them. Moreover, we watch, listen, and read in the midst of family and peers who provide interpretations that can affect the direction and intensity of our opinions. But we perceive the content of the mass-media message selectively, screening out much of the material that conflicts with our values.

Pay particular attention as you watch a budget speech or a prime minister being interviewed. The interpretative frameworks are already in place, and, for most of us, the message is quickly absorbed into our existing ideological views of the world.

We should not conclude that our ideologies and values are utterly impervious to information, or that the media play only a minor role in the formation of our political inclinations. New information, especially if repeated many times, may eventually get through to rearrange the total array of our political judgements and personal beliefs.

### Interest Groups, Parties, and Government

Learning ideologies after adolescence is largely experienced through the media, but other agents exist to facilitate public political education. Interest groups, political parties, and governments themselves are seen to be vital agents of political learning.

These political agents usually have national reach and are able to produce quickly political orientations that are shared widely. Interest groups use public education and information campaigns to gain backing by bringing their ideological perspective to the public's attention. Through their testimony, policy statements, advertisements, fact sheets, and the media coverage of their activities, interest groups are potent teachers of political values.

Political parties play a role as well in educating the public about issues and policies, and in transmitting their ideological positions. By putting candidates up for election to Parliament, successful parties are in a position to shape the policy agenda. The parties operate — at least, hypothetically — as in a marketplace of ideas. They have something to sell (their candidates and their policies), and the voters can, and do, shop around. The way parties think about politics and government can either enhance the legitimacy of the political system or challenge its supportive ideologies.

Governments can produce the same effect by means of their public policies, laws, regulations, and the collection and interpretation of their statistics. Conservative economic policies, the implementation of welfare policies, and the content of policies on external affairs are revealing indicators of the ideologies they represent and teach their citizens. Canadian governments at the federal and provincial levels care very much about the ideologies they represent — they cannot afford not to.

## THE COMPONENTS OF IDEOLOGIES

Ideologies can be disassembled in order to understand what they are and what they do. When one takes an ideology apart piece by piece, one will discover the components that make up a symbolic process of thought and action. We live in a time when the very structures of the political beliefs that have held our society together are crumbling, and the great influence of ideologies throughout this century has brought us to where we are. Ideologies are thus seen to encompass the following dynamic elements: rhetoric, values, beliefs and attitudes, symbols, and praxis (a plan of action).

### Rhetoric

All ideologies abound with rhetorical activity. **Rhetoric** enables people, governments, political parties, and interest groups to transmit messages persuasively, allowing them to establish or restore certain kinds of knowledge about the world around them. It includes spoken and written discourse, as well as nonverbal elements and symbols that have meaning for people, personally and publicly, socially, and politically.

In the third century B.C., Aristotle, in his *Rhetorica*, saw rhetoric as a way of emphasizing social and political reality with a view to acting upon it (Ross 1924, 1354–57). For Aristotle, rhetoric was more than the clever mastery of eloquent persuasion. He saw it as the use of social knowledge to urge and bring about the well-being of a community.

History holds many examples of the power and mastery of rhetoric in the world of politics and government. Through the words of such people as Martin Luther, Martin Luther King Jr., Hitler, Stalin, Gandhi, and Fidel Castro, rhetoric became a mode of altering social reality and of realigning power relationships during times of political upheaval.

The rhetorical dimensions of political and governing power are present in all ideologies, from anarchism to **Zionism**. The command of rhetoric as it is expressed almost universally within ideologies can usually incite powerless individuals to initiate significant political change, even when their efforts to spur reform are resisted by a formidable **establishment**.

Persuasive messages — such as "personal freedom" as part of the democratic creed, "Je me souviens" and *la survivance* in the nationalist rhetoric of Quebec, and "Women are one man away from poverty" and the "Personal is political" in the feminist economic perspective — are designed to attract people to the cause and goals of a patterned way of thinking.

In the end, the purpose of rhetorical persuasion is action: Rhetoric gives voice to those who have power or can empower those who do not; it is a means of sometimes defining, changing, and shifting the nature of power relations in a political culture — "Workers of the world unite!"

Rhetoric is used to signify what the regime of "truth" is in our society (Foucault 1980). What is true becomes both a tool and a product of our way of thinking and our ways of persuading. In Canada, many historians write of "two founding nations," identifying the emergence of the present Canadian governmental system as a product of only the English- and the French-speaking people. All "others" must therefore qualify as "Canadians" by birth, naturalization, or assimilation, according to this way of thinking. The peoples of the First Nations, however, believe that they were the original "Canadians," and therefore should not have to be concerned with *becoming* Canadian or even with being *accepted* as such.

As a technique of modern political expression, rhetoric is used, not only to persuade, but also to control the listener; not only to stimulate thought and action, but also to prevent it; not only to convey information, but also to conceal or distort it; not only to draw public attention, but to divert, or even at times to suppress it.

## Values

As we continue disassembling our ideologies, we discover values. From the individual perspective, values tend to be so general that they are often difficult to identify consciously.

*Values* are socially shared ideas about what is "good," "right," and "desirable." Politics and government are where we find values that are prescribed by people who hold them with great conviction and work toward achieving them with great energy. While political facts and statistics may inform us of what is so, our values inform us what ought to be so. And, thus, we decide what ought to be done on the basis of a cluster of values within us. For example, no political scientist can prove that Quebec should or should not separate from the rest of Canada. But many political scientists have collected facts about the probable consequences of separation and independence, such as the expected economic outcomes, the migrations of people from province to province, and the probable reactions of other nation-states. These predictions of costs and benefits can be used to support one option or another, but the actual goals have to be established on grounds that rise above the facts. A Quebec nationalist might be willing to absorb heavy economic losses to achieve the more important value of independence and self-determination for the Québécois culture in North America.

Many of the prominent political values in society can be deduced from the "dominant ideology," the conventional political wisdom and the political rules-of-thumb present in that society (Abercrombie 1980). The dominant ideology seems to set the value orientations Canadians and their governments adopt as worthy of pursuing for an extended period of time.

Two highly significant value indicators in a dominant ideology are the importance of "freedom" and "equality" as fundamental forces in a political and governing system. Compared with citizens in other countries, Canadians appear to place more value on freedom (see Figure 2.2). In a World Values Survey conducted in the 1980s, respondents in a number of nation-states were asked to rank by preference and importance the values of free-

**Figure 2.2 World Values Survey Ranking of Freedom and Equality, in Percentages**

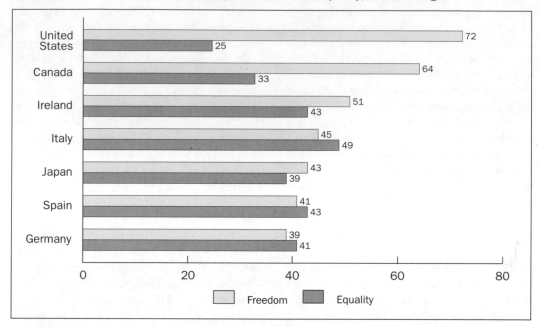

*Source:* World Values Survey, 1981–1982, as reported in R. Inglehart and Scott Flanagan, "Value Change in Industrial Societies," *American Political Science Review* 81 (December 1987): 1289–1319. Reproduced with permission of the American Political Science Association.

dom and equality. Canadians choose freedom by a ratio of nearly 2 to 1; Americans showed an even stronger preference for freedom by a ratio of 3 to 1. But, in most other states studied, respondents ranked freedom and equality much closer together as features of their dominant ideology. The importance of freedom in both Canada and the United States is very clear.

In Canada, the values of freedom, equality, fair play, and the promotion and protection of "Canadian culture" have produced concrete governmental action in these areas. It was a government that created the Combines Investigation Act so as to institute legally equality and fair play in the business and consumer world; it was a government that gave life to the Canadian Broadcasting Corporation, the National Film Board, and many

regulatory and cultural bodies to encourage distinctively Canadian creative pursuits.

Canadians generally cling to the value system that stresses democracy, equality, freedom, humanitarianism, and justice, as entrenched and legitimized in the Canadian constitution and its Charter of Rights and Freedoms. These values have outlined how Canadians should or should not act in certain, if not all, social, political, and international situations. Values inevitably become the yardsticks against which we measure our actions; but they enable us to compare and evaluate our economic and political preferences, sometimes to the extent that they can challenge our governability.

We should also be aware that **counter-ideologies** grow out of the same political and social systems. They germinate out of a critical perspective that recognizes inconsistencies in the dominant ideology. They begin as agents of reform but usually become deviations of the original ideologies, gaining independence in terms of thought and goals. Ultimately, they develop into a self-conscious system of beliefs with an entirely different way of viewing society (Marchak 1988, 5).

Seymour Martin Lipset (1964 and 1986) identified a number of values that, in his view, differentiate Canadians from Americans at the political and governmental levels. He concluded that Canadians are more "collectively oriented" than Americans in that Canadians place a higher value on the groups to which they belong, and on orderly group life in general. In contrast, he found Americans more personalized and "self-oriented," and likely to place greater emphasis on "rugged individualism," competition, and personal achievement. According to Lipset, these values have an impact on our ability to govern ourselves, to reform and build our political institutions, and ultimately to make legitimate decisions in the public interest.

Canadians are more willing to accept government involvement in the economy and to accept government regulation in their lives. Americans living in Canada have noted the number of issues resolved, not by democratic process, but by the decisiveness of executive orders-in-council, for example, the treatment of Japanese Canadians during the Second World War, and gun control, as well as by the great secrecy in which Canadian governments and their civil services often carry out their business (Shackleton 1977).

Lipset concedes that, while some value differences between Canadians and Americans may be on the decline, others are still as prominent as ever. Canadians are still much less wary of big government or of the role of governments in the economic plans of their communities than are Americans.

Lipset also found that, on most attitudinal measures, francophone Canadians are different from both Americans *and* anglophone Canadians. In fact, the attitudinal and value differences Lipset found between francophone and anglophone Canadians are greater in many instances than those between anglophone Canadians and Americans.

### Beliefs and Attitudes

The ideological context of Canadian politics can be further broken down into beliefs and attitudes that are widely held and expressed in our communities. *Beliefs* are one of the cognitive components that help maintain social and political consistency and predictability in the ways we think. For example, many Canadian men and women believe that, on the whole, men have more political power and more social prestige than do women. These beliefs are reflected in our governmental institutions, where men continue to dominate; in our electoral system, where mostly men run for public office; and in our laws, which tend to protect men's interests and assets more than women's.

As functional parts in the anatomy of a political ideology, beliefs are integrated convictions, often "unprovable," based on one or more fundamental assumptions about political behaviour. At the centre of a political ideology is a cluster of well-entrenched, relatively unchangeable beliefs, which literally form the credible core of our political self and how this self comes to see the world.

The character of our belief systems will vary from culture to culture. In the wider Canadian political culture most people believe that "seeing is believing," as manifested by the requirements of evidence in our legal and governmental judicial system, which rely upon witnessing documents and events, and that "getting it in writing" adds to the credibility of an arrangement or promise.

However, in more traditional political cultures, such as those of the peoples of the First Nations, "hearing is believing," and credibility is based on spoken and often nonverbal language, but especially upon the reputation of the speaker. The cultural clash of beliefs is often manifested in the interpretation of treaties transacted "verbally" or in "transcript" many years ago.

If there are hundreds of beliefs that come together to construct our political ideologies, these beliefs are reflected in thousands of attitudes expressed by those in our culture who adopt a certain pattern of thinking consciously or unconsciously. *Attitudes* are the vehicles we use to express what is desirable and undesirable, what is good or bad, what is acceptable or objectionable about the political and social world around us. Many ideologies hold beliefs that women are weaker than men, that women cannot succeed, or even survive, without the aid and protection of men through their patriarchal and political system. Widely expressed attitudes about women as the "weaker sex" are detectable in socially and politically approved gender roles, sport, the family, the workplace, and the "representative" institutions of Canadian government.

The subtle power of these attitudes to spread and sustain unprovable assertions about the status of human beings in Canadian society ultimately affects our abilities to govern ourselves according to the values of freedom and equality that we claim to hold in our national political ideologies.

## Symbols

As the fundamental currencies of political communication, ideologies are often expressed in terms of symbols. A *symbol* is a thing that stands for or suggests something else by way of association. Symbols are the instruments we use to share and transmit certain important ideas in our culture. In the world of politics and government, symbols are anything to which people attach some special value and meaning.

The Canadian flag, the fleur-de-lis, the national anthem, Parliament, the constitution, the courts — all have significant political meanings in our society. It is interesting that Canada is the only country in the world that has a member of a police force — that is, a Mountie — as a national symbol.

Yet, for many years since Canada gained independence from Great Britain, there was a general lack of distinctively Canadian symbols because of our collective desire to maintain ties to Great Britain and France. The Queen's picture appeared on all Canadian money; "God Save the Queen" was sung at important Canadian events; the Union Jack was flown in all regions of the country; and the Queen installed her lieutenant-governors as her representatives at the executive head of both provincial and federal governments.

Retaining close symbolic ties with Great Britain may have been beneficial for many reasons, but it created a necessity for Canadians to develop their own symbols. Canada's dependence on foreign symbols made it difficult for Canadians to perceive what made Canada's political cultures distinct from others. A uniquely Canadian flag with a maple leaf at its centre was adopted on February 15, 1965, after a storm of controversy. The popular acceptance of "O Canada" (written in 1880) as a general expression of national identity by both English and French Canadians led to its adoption as the national anthem.

Other national symbols for Canada are those important documents that guarantee the rights of Canadian citizens. On April 17, 1982, by an act of the British Parliament, Canada got a repatriated constitution, which included a Charter of Rights and Freedoms, as an adjunct to the British North America Act, which was signed into effect on July 1, 1867, creating the "Dominion of Canada."

Gradually our collective identity has been represented in other symbolic expressions. Language (which substitutes words for gestures, things, and events) has had particular ideological and political significance for governing the country. For francophones,

The Canadian flag, as other national emblems, is a patriotic symbol for the country. *Source:* Canada Wide.

language is an integrating and binding force that has provided the French-speaking people of Quebec and other provinces with a strong national identification. Language has given French-speaking Quebeckers a distinctive place in the flow of Canadian history. More important, the French language is especially symbolic for the Québécois who judge their political reality by the meanings they assign to words. For most Québécois, *Assemblée nationale* does not mean the provincial assembly of Quebec; rather, it means the *national* assembly of Quebeckers as a Francophone people. The defence of the French language in terms of legislation is seen as a first-column strategy for the survival of Quebec's unique political and governing culture.

## *Praxis*

Another salient component of ideologies is praxis. **Praxis** may be thought of as acting out the fantasies of an ideology: Doing is believing. The Greeks believed that "praxis" meant "to promote action motivated and stimulated by thought." Aristotle used "praxis" to refer to

practical, as distinct from theoretical, reasoning — to differentiate what humans do from what they think. An "idea whose time has come" is an idea in action, represented by the courage to act upon the conviction.

In the contemporary world of ideologies, praxis is the interrelationship between thought and action — each facilitating the other. Praxis can be seen as purposeful, often voluntary, and goal-oriented behaviour that leads to the fulfilment of a way of life. In this regard, ideologies have consequences in the actions they inspire. They persuade people that they can, and should, do something to achieve the goals of the ideology. A so-called terrorist will plant a bomb in a public place, anticipating the bloody consequences; a feminist might support a magazine or newspaper that publishes only women's views; and environmentalists will lobby the private sector of the economy to change its hazardous packaging of goods in the delivery of its services.

One pronounced manifestation of praxis is **collective action**. In Canada as well as other countries, ideologies provide justification and direction for collective action in social movements. A movement gains success when its interests are fully politicized and institutionalized. The Parti Québécois (PQ) provides an interesting example. During the 1960s, political independence for Quebec was the goal of what was clearly a social movement in that province. From the movement sprang the PQ. The party's twin goals of getting elected and gaining Quebec's independence were both certainly non-institutionalized when it was created in 1968. However, it attained political representation in the provincial elections of 1970 and 1973. By separating its stance on sovereignty association and independence, the PQ earned electoral success in 1976, and again in 1981 and 1994.

In Canada, the feminist movement was the coming of age of a new generation of political thinking about gender relationships in the context of economic, moral, and social reality. Feminism qualifies as a *social movement* — that is, a collective action that is usually politically inspired, involving a large group of people who intend to bring about widespread social change, by promoting it, maintaining it, or resisting it. These organized displays of political concern can come from a variety of issues, such as promoting peace, protecting the environment, women's rights, minority rights, gay and lesbian rights, animal rights, as well as those protesting pornography, cutbacks in social services, and abortion.

The most spectacular form of praxis is *political revolution*. This kind of collective action aims to fundamentally change government, its ideology and institutions, to destroy the power and influence of those groups that support government, and to initiate changes that alter the basic economic, political, and social values in society.

## UNDERSTANDING THE DIMENSIONS OF IDEOLOGICAL THINKING

Despite their frequent use by political analysts, the labels "radical," "liberal," "moderate," "conservative," and "reactionary," do not have strong meaning for many Canadians. But these words are used as if everyone agrees on what they mean and as if they accurately describe the intensity of the ideological commitment held by individuals or by large segments of the Canadian population. That is why it is important for us as students of political ideologies to give these terms special consideration.

Political scientists sometimes place ideas on a continuum so as to better understand the logic of ideological thought (see Figure 2.3).

### Radical Thinking

The radical dimension of an ideology can be defined only in the specific context in which it is used; its meaning varies from time to time and from place to place. "Radicalism" means to get down to the root of the matter, coming from the Latin word *radix*, or "root." The term is most frequently used to refer to an extreme difference from the point of view of those who express the central versions of an ideology. "Radicalism" also refers to a counter-ideology that emerges from a dominant ideology. The radical perspective tends to press its views toward the extreme, and to challenge established ways of thinking about social and political matters. Radicals live for the future; they work to do good as they see it, and to change the world in a fundamental way.

On the whole, it seems fair to say that there are very few independent radical ideologies attracting significant numbers of adherents in Canada today. There are anarchism, fascism, Nazism, and other radical ideologies, but they appeal only to small groups of Canadians. The trials of Ernst Zundel, a Toronto publisher who churned out material which extolled Nazi ideology, attracted support from Nazis across Canada. However, only about half of Canadians even knew why Zundel had been convicted. Moreover, those who were most sympathetic to his positions were least aware of his trials.

People who hold radical views are often associated with the **Left** and the **Right** because

**Figure 2.3  Continuum of Political Thinking**

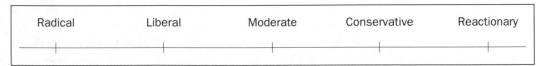

| Radical | Liberal | Moderate | Conservative | Reactionary |

they reject the status quo and want to bring about fundamental changes to the existing governmental, political, and social order. The radical perspective takes notice of the conflicting interests in society and examines the need to maintain social order. It focusses on the injustices of inequality and what must be done to reduce it.

Traditionally, Canadian society has been unreceptive to radical politics. Canada's political and governmental system tends to neutralize the radical dimension of an ideology by stealing its thunder when the public is attracted to its assertions. Elements of radical thought are often absorbed by competing political parties that offer them to the public as policy preferences, such as the "greening" of the Liberal, Progressive Conservative, and New Democratic parties on environmental issues.

## Liberal Thinking

Liberal thinking is reflected in many of the ideologies operating in Canada. Liberal ideas pervade economic, social, and political thought. They call upon us to modify our fundamental beliefs from time to time in all of our ways of thinking. For this reason, liberal thought is always open to change and to the critical review of accepted ideas and practice, and adheres to the dictum that society is evolutionary. It is aimed at social reform that is designed to increase equality and democratic participation in all mechanisms of social decision making, especially government.

The liberal view urges governments to aid the needy, control the powerful, and leave free criticism and non-conformism. It asserts that strong government institutions are necessary to protect individuals from the potential tyrannies of a modern industrial and technological society, such as Canada. The liberal idea holds that the growth of government has enhanced, not diminished, individual freedom. Although the positive state is central in the contemporary liberal creed, lib-

erals do not believe that government should displace the private sector in the economy.

Liberal thinking begins with the assumption that individuals are, in the main, rational beings, capable of overcoming obstacles to progress by peaceful change without resort to violence. The liberal strain of thought advances human dignity in addition to mobility, initiative, and self-control as the desirable means to affect one's own fate. Liberal thought places human rights above property rights, yet regards the two as normally compatible. The liberal dimension trusts human nature as good and has faith in our ability to build a better future, but in all cases sees the meaning of life in doing the best one can do, here and now.

## Moderate Thinking

The moderate dimension in political thinking is reflected by a desire for gradual change and a preference for reform rather than revolution. It is supported by the belief that political transformation should be gradual and involve no violence to governing institutions.

Moderate ideological positions are based on the belief that there exists a consensus — a widely shared agreement — among right-minded people and that the process of politics consists in part in the discovery of this consensus and transforming it into law. The moderate consensus is thought to include a commitment to peaceful resolution of ideological disputes and to reaching compromise when positions appear intractable. Moderate thinking recognizes that a consensus on values may shift with changing circumstances, which is why the process of politics is necessary. The moderate approach wants to give each ideological extreme something of what it wants, so that no ideological group feels totally neglected.

Underlying this way of thinking is a tolerance toward views that may not match the consensus. Ideological thinking is moderate, not necessarily on account of the opinions that motivate it, but because it attempts to balance and conciliate, rather than confront and eliminate, rival systems of thought. A characteristic of moderate thought is that it permits the existence of opposing views, even the radical and reactionary, the liberal and the conservative. The moderate holds that the principal test of an ideology is whether its ideas are credible and workable, even though its belief system seems to be built on many contradictions and complexities. The moderate position emphasizes results, and accepts a realistic view of what can be expected in a complicated world.

## Conservative Thinking

The conservative state of mind relies upon common sense, tradition, and social convention when it considers political and social change. The conservative thinker wants to resist change and maintain the established social and political order because it has proved its survivability. In this regard, conservative thinking emphasizes the value of convention and established practices as guides to the future.

The conservative mind believes that the experience of past generations is a more reliable guide to successful governance than liberal designs to remake society (Oakeshott 1962). The conservative thinker is reluctant to institute changes in the basic fabric of society in order to solve social and political problems. To the conservative mind, society is *homeostatic* — that is, self-changing, self-adjusting, and self-fulfilling. The customs, traditions, and laws embodied in the wisdom of the past should not be carelessly discarded when social change is contemplated. The conservative mindset wants to think carefully before change is unleashed as a desirable technique for human problem-solving.

Property institutions and social arrangements are the essence of society and should not be tampered with whimsically. To the conservative thinker, social and political change is a process similar to the task of rebuilding one's house while continuing to live in it and depending on its uninterrupted protection. The conservative thinker wants to conserve the essence of things, even while certain changes may be installed in them.

The conservative mind is pessimistic about human nature, and has doubts about whether governments can solve social problems (Kirk 1960 and 1982). It believes that people are better off left alone and that most governments will only restrict the resources that exist within the privacy of each person and the resources of the community necessary to solve social problems.

## Reactionary Thinking

The concepts of "reaction" and "reactionary" connote a contrariness to "progress" and "progressive." Frequently, ideologies on the political Right are referred to as "reactionary" and those on the Left as "progressive." Few Canadians would describe themselves as reactionary today because the term's modern connotation is not very positive. It has been employed mainly by the Left to discredit the Right in the realm of political ideologies, especially used against the fascists and Nazis. The goal of reactionary thought is to change what *is*, so as to turn back to what *was* during some real or imagined past.

The reactionary thinker is not merely resistant to change but wants to put the clock back and return to some earlier order of society that is seen as having possessed characteristics (such as honesty, discipline, industrious character, respect for authority and privilege, and an honourable political structure) that the present is felt to lack. The reactionary mind wants to restore cultural traits and political arrangements that are believed to have existed in the past. As a benign sentiment, the reactionary view aligns with the conservative one because it opposes in the extreme any progressive social or political change. All ideologies contain both reactionary and progressive characteristics and want to combine the best of what was with the aspirations to achieve what can be.

## POLITICAL IDEOLOGIES IN CANADA

Most Canadians and their political leaders — whether they know it or not — share elements of, or identify with, mainstream ideologies. These ideological positions do not challenge the existing political and governmental order. For example, most of Canadian liberals, conservatives, and socialists do want to make major changes to Canada's parliamentary system. They accept capitalism Canadian-style as a desirable economic system, and view the economic marketplace as the chief instrument for the distribution of goods and services. Not that everyone in Canada agrees on fundamental issues, but there is a consensus among a substantial proportion of the population.

Canadian ideas about politics and government tend to be loosely interconnected by the fundamental principles of democracy, liberalism, conservatism, nationalism, and socialism. Most people do not neatly separate their ideological positions under general headings simply because this is not the way we think.

### Democracy

Since the earliest days of governing in Canada, the idea of democracy has undergone some transformation and evolution (Watson and Barber 1988). At first, Canadians distrusted democracy itself, especially in view of the American experience, which encouraged the use of violence to achieve democratic ideals. In Canada, the emphasis was on the "peace, order, and good government," based on a legal order designed to encourage the peaceful attainment of government goals. John A.

Macdonald told the first meeting of the Quebec Conference that "we shall have a strong and lasting government under which we work out constitutional liberty as opposed to democracy" (Pope 1895, 55).

Over the years, Canadian politics has moved toward increasing participatory democracy (Hodgins 1955, 17). The Canadian electorate has expanded beyond anything imagined by those who participated in the Confederation Debates. The designers of Canada's parliamentary system of government were suspicious of too much democracy, but they created a framework capable of adaptation to the inevitable demands of popular participation.

Today, Canadians believe that no government is legitimate that does not enjoy the consent of a massive electorate. They also believe that, in some vague way, the ultimate source of political and governing power in Canada is the people themselves. They expect to participate in government, both directly and through their elected representatives. Finally, Canadians think that a political system of stable democratic parliamentary governments must meet not just a few tests, but many, not the least of which is the performance of the governments themselves.

Democracy in Canada is thought to be an idea of means, not just ends — an ideology of "process" (how things should be done) as well as one of "results" (what should be done). Thus, there are two major streams of thought about what constitutes democracy. The first believes democracy is a form of government and emphasizes the procedures that enable people to govern, such as meeting to discuss issues, voting in elections, running for public office. The second portrays democracy in the substance of government policies, in freedom of assembly and speech and protecting people from the abuses of power. The procedural approach focusses on how decisions are made; the substantive approach is concerned with what governments do.

How democratic is Canada? That depends on how you define democracy. If you define it as "rule by the people," Canada is not very democratic, because people do not directly govern here. We have a responsible and representative parliamentary democracy by which we select some of the officials who govern on our behalf. Democratic ideology prescribes certain principles according to which our governments should make their decisions.

### Characteristics of Democratic Ideology

**Importance of the Individual** Influenced by traditional democratic ideas, Canadians have acknowledged the importance of the individual, expanded the rights enjoyed by individuals, and built a vast governing system to serve the needs of individuals, while at the same time protecting collective rights. The Charter of Rights and Freedoms reflects the long tradition of rights enjoyed by Canadians, derived from Great Britain's. Usually, these rights have protected individuals against the governments, such as the freedoms of speech, of assembly, of the press, and of religion. Living in a society with an explicit commitment to individual freedom is a basic tenet of Canadian democratic thought.

**Political Equality** Canadians have always believed that one important role of government is to protect individuals from the excesses of other individuals. From this belief is derived the idea that Canadians have always considered themselves relatively equal politically and socially, if not economically. But there is also a tradition in Canada of looking to kings and queens as people who should be granted special privilege under the parliamentary form of government.

The belief in political equality has led to **popular sovereignty**, or rule by the people. If individuals are equal, no one person or group has the automatic right to rule others; the consent of the ruled must be sought. Of course, not all the people can be prime minister, members of Parliament, or judges. But these officials are not the rulers; they are the representatives of the people, with whom authority to rule is held jointly.

**The Rule of the Majority** Commitments to the principles of individual worth and political equality lead to the ideal democratic notion that the rule of the majority is legitimate; that is, when there are disagreements over policies, majorities rather than minorities carry the decision. If individuals are equal, then policies should be determined according to the will of the greater number.

Those who comprise the minority respect the legitimacy of government decisions but expect to be allowed to convert their positions to the status of majority support. At the minimum, the minority expects the majority to respect their basic rights to become the majority. If these mutual expectations are not fulfilled, minorities are less likely to accept majority rule and tolerate majority decisions. Accordingly, the principle of majority rule necessarily entails minority rights.

**Minority Rights** While the democratic principle of majority rule is important, it can conflict with minority rights, and those who advance it are sometimes threatened by the mere presence of minorities in their communities. In 1989, a button was placed on sale in Calgary that portrayed the stereotyped images of three minority groups — Chinese, Sikhs, and Afro-Canadians — surrounding a beleaguered white person (the personification of a "Canadian"). The insinuation was that the presence of the majority in Canada was threatened by these minorities. In fact, Chinese, South Asians, and Afro-Canadians make up very small proportions of the total Canadian population: 1.5 percent, 1.1 percent, and 0.9 percent, respectively. The Canadian "people" includes members of a majority group and many minority groups.

One hard lesson of Canadian history demonstrated that the majority can harm minority rights, and thus diminish everybody's rights. The expulsion of Japanese Canadians from the West Coast during the Second World War is a case in point. Because they were considered a "security risk," these citizens were rounded up on short notice; their homes and goods, including their fishing boats, were seized; and they were relocated, usually in the secluded areas of British Columbia, Alberta, and Ontario. Not a single breach of security had in fact occurred on which to base such an action. It took until 1988 before the federal government finally apologized to its Japanese citizens and agreed to form a redress, the terms of which included payment of $21 000 to those still living who were affected; the granting of citizenship to persons of Japanese ancestry who were expelled from Canada or had their citizenship revoked; and clearing the names of persons of Japanese ancestry who were wrongfully convicted under the former War Measures Act and the National Emergency Powers Act, or related legislation.

**Pluralism** Pluralism is a fundamental component of democracy in Canada. The very nature of our country nurtures many interests that are theoretically reconcilable within the boundaries of a parliamentary system of government. The pluralist view maintains that, because so many group interests exist, no group or small number of groups can dominate government. This produces, according to the pluralist view, a kind of balance in which no group loses so often that it gives up competing for access to government and political power. Pluralism encourages people to find ways of compromising with each other.

The ideals of pluralist thought have favoured the persistence and diversity of ethnic groups in Canada. In an ideal **pluralist society**, multicultural and ethnic groups may share some aspects of a common culture and participate collectively in economic and political life, while retaining unique cultural aspects in their social networks, residential communities, churches, and languages. Pluralists downplay the problem of ethnic and racial inequality, and advocate the democratic ideal that assumes a basic equality for all groups (Steinberg 1981). But in a society that permits systematic inequalities, pluralism can only be an ideal, as there is no tenable basis for permanent ethnic preservation. Race and ethnicity are important features of this society because most Canadians came from different origins.

### Liberalism

One of the most influential ideologies in Canada is liberalism. Liberalism was not made in Canada; it developed in Europe and was brought to North America by the colonists. What made Canada profoundly different from Europe in regard to this ideology was the speed with which liberal ideas established themselves here, and the extent to which they were modified by Canadian conditions.

There are few words common to our political life that, in the world of ideologies, rival that of "liberal" in their diversity of meaning. Contemporary Canadian liberalism is vastly different from what was known as "classical liberalism," an ideology that migrated from Europe to North America in the late eighteenth century. But Canadian political ideas were shaped in the ferment of political philosophizing that went on during the eighteenth and nineteenth centuries. The ideas of classical liberalism — with their emphasis on the rights of the individual to political freedom, private property, and social and economic opportunity — were particularly adaptive for those settling in Canada.

The liberal ideological tradition seemed relevant, especially to people faced with the necessity of establishing a system of government in the wilderness. For many Canadians, liberalism became an attractive myth to guide individual entrepreneurs in a frontier economy, who, with a good idea and a good deal of effort, could succeed in the marketplace.

When Canada was young, in the nineteenth century, the marketplace was fundamentally unregulated by governments. But, from almost the beginning, the Canadian government had an important role in the marketplace. Indeed, the origins of Canada's federal system lie in active government interventions to create markets favourable to its entrepreneurial class.

Under George Brown's leadership, the Liberal party emerged as a centrist, nationalist, and middle-of-the-road party that has retained many of these characteristics to the present day. In the election of 1874, most of the support came from the countryside, where rural and small-town Canadians gave a decisive electoral victory to Alexander Mackenzie. In leading the party, Mackenzie and his successor, Edward Blake, opposed any restriction on individual liberty, and designed policies against the imposition of protective tariffs and the growth of a shielded factory system that fostered collective and "communistic" production.

The "Canada First" movement in the 1870s added a radical dimension to Canadian liberalism by advancing Canada's total "independence" from Great Britain and its **Tory** imperialism. Canada was viewed as a part of the wider North American economy, where free trade should prevail, and protectionism was unnatural. Some felt that the continental forces of geography, commerce, and language would neutralize, if not undo, the "conservative" character of Quebec society and foster a Canadian nationalism dominated entirely by English Canadians (Smith 1891, 45).

By the end of the nineteenth and the beginning of the twentieth century, liberal attitudes toward government began to change. Wilfrid Laurier succeeded Blake in 1887 and, by bringing support for the party from Quebec, gave liberalism a truly national constituency. Because liberal political ideas were recast by Laurier as a national ideology, they were necessarily subject to a whole host of additional changes. Laurier's embrace of provincial rights and autonomy accommodated Quebec but failed to muster the national will for free trade with the United States. The issue of conscription festered, generating deep divisions within the Liberal party and ultimately leading to Laurier's defeat and resignation.

The divided party was inherited by Mackenzie King in 1919, and he prepared to face the electorate in 1921. The split within the party encouraged liberal radicalism in the form of "progressivism," whose supporters elected 64 members to Parliament from all provinces except Quebec. Progressivism rapidly gained strength in many parts of Canada and advanced an ambitious program of political change. The Progressives included in their ranks men and women from all classes, but they were especially strong in Western rural areas among people who adhered devotedly to democratic principles, wanted governments to limit the power and wealth of private corporations and banks, and generally distrusted the parliamentary system because of its inclinations toward party patronage (Morton 1950, 15). King tried to lure the Progressives back into the Liberal party and was somewhat successful, absorbing them as Liberal-Progressives, but many others eventually took comfort in the Canadian Commonwealth Federation, founded in 1932.

In his ambitions to reunite the Liberal party after the fractious leadership of Laurier, King recast a number of liberal ideas to accommodate a political conciliation of the party's ideology (Christian and Campbell 1990, 59–60). In referring to his liberalism as "positive," King asked Liberals to be concerned about the farmers, the unemployed, and the labour union movement. Liberals no longer saw government as a threat to liberty, or as the inevitable partners of the rich and powerful.

In this "positive" liberalism, which some have called "welfare liberalism," supporters believed that government action should ensure the economic well-being of the country and should provide basic material guarantees (food, shelter, health care, and education) for every individual, and thereby set the agenda for national unity. This would mean ensured protection for the unemployed, pensions for the elderly, and guaranteed prices for the farmers.

By shifting the focus of thought from the virtues of limited government to a belief in the positive state — government activity on behalf of individuals — King's liberalism still saw society as the preserve of individuals who would use collective action to guarantee it. King blamed the presence of inequalities on selfish individuals who ruthlessly protected their own interests at the expense of the public good. Governments, therefore, should act as referees, as mediators and conciliators of social conflict. While serving as prime minister for more than 21 years, King placed the Liberal party on the path of reform that came to symbolize the idea of the positive and interventionist state, and ultimately became the hallmark of contemporary Canadian liberalism.

These factors compelled Liberals to adopt the position that a strong central government was required to hold the country together and to act as a countervailing force to other institutions in the private sector.

Under King's successor, Louis St. Laurent, Liberals developed a boundless faith in strong activist and centralist governments, and propelled the view that the Liberal party was Canada's governing party. The federal government increased shared-cost programs with the provinces and maintained its wartime dominance of the Canadian economy. St. Laurent expanded the support of the party in Quebec, and Ontario, although his continued support of centralist policies created difficulties for the party in Quebec, and the party suffered humiliating defeat in the 1957 and 1958 general elections.

St. Laurent was succeeded by Lester B. Pearson, who upheld the primacy of the individual as a fundamental principle of liberalism. Pearson was never able to command a majority government and, as a result, may not have been in a strong position to assert a particular ideological thrust within the traditions of liberal thought. In hindsight, for this reason, his positions on liberalism appear moderate. But, within the spectrum of welfare liberalism, it was Pearson's government that brought in the Canada Pension Plan and promoted medicare, two of the most fundamental components of reformed liberalism.

His government initiated the Royal Commission on Bilingualism and Biculturalism in response to Quebec's Quiet Revolution, which transformed that province's social structure, stirred nationalistic and separatist currents within French Canada, and stimulated general debate on provincial autonomy and rights across the country.

Pearson's successor, Pierre Elliott Trudeau, while bringing a new charismatic governing style and flamboyant political character to Liberal leadership, was surprisingly faithful to the liberal creed. Trudeau described himself as a "rational" liberal (Trudeau 1968, 48–50) who preserved the traditional tenets of Canadian liberalism, especially in the area of protecting individual rights. As a consequence of the Royal Commission on Bilingualism and Biculturalism, the Trudeau government enacted the Official Languages Act (1969), which sought to extend the use of French within the federal civil service and to make public services available in French wherever concentrations of French Canadians reside.

Individual language rights were also entrenched in the Charter of Rights and Freedoms (Mandel 1989, 1–34). These policy products were logical derivatives of classical liberalism, which preached that the purpose of the state is to serve the individual.

Trudeau defended the universality of social programs already in place and called for new ones to be designed. He advanced economic and cultural nationalism and held that Canadian constitutionalism was incomplete without a patriated constitution. The Trudeau governments' initiatives in the 1970s and early 1980s were focussed on the "Canadianization" of industry, the media, the arts, and education. Under successive Trudeau governments, there was general support for political and social reform; a willingness to engage in extensive government intervention in the economy; the expansion of federal social services; more rigorous efforts on behalf of the poor, minorities, and women; and a greater concern for consumers and the environment.

John Turner tended to swing ideological directions from the right to the centre, to the left side of liberalism. Turner adopted what he called "business liberalism" to harness support within the party, but at the same time he clung to canons of welfare liberalism to keep grass-roots support for the party in the country. Turner launched what he viewed as an extensive re-examination of Liberal thinking in order to discover a successful ideological path for the party in the face of the centralist positions adopted concurrently by the Progressive Conservatives and the New Democratic Party to help them succeed at the polls.

Under Jean Chrétien, Canadian liberalism took on a populist caste that had once been the enduring strength of the Liberals as the "governing party." Chrétien adopted an ideologically centrist position but shifted to the right on reducing the deficit and national debt. His government became committed to reducing the size of the federal government and to withdrawing its presence in the Canadian economy. Unlike previous Liberal governments, Chrétien's reluctantly compressed the welfare state and initiated the most detailed review of the social safety net. In international affairs, his positions are generally seen as opposition to the spread of nuclear weapons, continuing support for development assistance for developing states, and support for international organizations such as the United Nations and the Organization of American States.

### Libertarianism: The Return to Classical Liberalism

The reaction to the reforms of contemporary welfare liberalism is represented in the ideas of libertarians. Although the Libertarian Party remains on the fringe of Canadian politics, its ideas have stimulated considerable ideological interest. The intellectual roots of libertarianism can be traced to the classical liberal movement of the eighteenth and nineteenth centuries in Europe and the United States. Libertarian belief is highly individualistic and favours the expansion of individual freedoms.

Like classical liberalism, libertarianism holds that the state should be kept small, and governments should be limited in power. Libertarians recognize that society needs laws and that legislation and enforcement of the laws are the proper roles for government in a free society. The essential role of government is to enforce private contracts and adjudicate disputes. The government should protect human rights: Libertarians advocate the right to life and abhor the use of violence in society. As well, the right to liberty is advanced on all the traditional freedoms, such as speech, religion, and assembly, and attached especially to ideas, books, films, and any other means of communication. Libertarians also support the property rights of Canadians against confiscation, robbery, trespass, libel, fraud, and copyright violations.

Libertarians oppose the interference of governments in the private lives of citizens, especially of government regulation of the economy. The hallmark of libertarian economics is a belief in the capacity of free markets, not only to perform such tasks as efficient production and utilization of scarce resources, but to do almost everything. Libertarians seek the repeal of laws that they say involve "victimless" crimes, such as prostitution and gambling. They want an unfettered free-market economy and oppose laws that regulate the use of "soft drugs" such as marijuana. Libertarians oppose any laws that regulate the moral or the economic life of Canadians.

Libertarians favour non-intervention in the affairs of other nation-states. They believe that military alliances lead only to war and that the preparation for war leads to a vast increase in the power of government. Libertarians call for cuts in the defence budget, supported by a policy designed solely to defend Canada.

Because the libertarian movement and the party have no immediate prospect of forming a government in Canada, their positions remain ideologically quite pure, without the effect of compromise.

## Conservatism

Canadian society is often described as conservative because of its reluctance to change, its public caution on embarking upon new directions and in taking new symbols (Hogan, 1963). Many point to the slow and uneasy acceptance of a new flag for Canada in the 1960s, of accepting the national anthem, of patriating the constitution, and of developing an acceptable formula for changing it.

Conservatives believe that societies grow slowly and with purpose, so that there is a continuity between the past and the future. Conservatism is naturally suspicious of the public will and its capacity to appreciate the wisdom in tradition and custom. The basic appeal of conservativism in Canada, as elsewhere, is an attachment to habits, language, family, social position, and possessions. Canadian conservatism has been described as an amalgam of business liberalism and democratic Toryism (Christian and Campbell 1990, 103).

George Grant (1965) thought he identified the presence of conservatism among

Canadians who are committed to maintaining an identity distinct from Americans through what he called "conservative nationalism." S.D. Clark (1968, 236) held that Canadians clung to their traditions of language and culture because they made us notably different from the more "open" and "liberal" Americans.

Many of the characteristics of Canadian conservatives are also found in abstract principles. One principle deals with the relationship of politics to economics. Governments should not interfere with the activities of individuals and the rights of property, particularly the latter. When there are conflicts between the role of government and some existing business interest, Canadian conservatives tend to oppose the government — tax officials, government regulations, and the like — and to side with the individual or the corporation, if these represent interests of substance.

For conservatives, formulating new welfare policies, expanding social reforms, and improving the lot of ethnic and racial minorities by initiating public policy do not have a high priority as ends in themselves. But they should be advanced mainly as governing instruments because they increase political and social stability and support the legitimacy of the government.

Generally, conservatives believe that, in economic and social matters, the traditions, liberties, and property rights of individuals and corporations should be strengthened against the state, but in matters regarding crime, subversion, and foreign aggression, the power of the state as well as its liberty of action should be increased against individuals. Courts and police forces should be given more power and discretion to supervise, search, and arrest potential suspects, and more discretion to sentence them to varying lengths of imprisonment.

Canada's first prominent conservative, John A. Macdonald, gave Canadian conservatism a pragmatic character — roughly the notion that true effort is what works — and a readiness to accept whatever seems to be the reality of the Canadian environment (Preece 1984). One fact conducive to the presence of political pragmatism in Macdonald's conservatism was the sheer physical and economic challenge of governing Canada.

This pragmatic orientation would enable Macdonald to incorporate liberal ideas, such as liberty and individualism, tempered somewhat by a Tory reluctance to push them to the extreme. This powerful pragmatism in the early Canadian conservative mind constructed the National Policy, which called for the construction of a transcontinental railway, initiated a strategy of industrialization protected by tariffs, encouraged resource development in the Maritimes and the West, and facilitated business and commercial trade among the existing provinces of the day.

Macdonald gave Canadian conservatism its initial character of loyalty to the Crown and acceptance of privilege in Canada's social and governing system. The choice of a bicameral legislature — one house democratic, the other non-democratic — reflected Macdonald's acceptance of a stratified governing system and the tolerance of conservatives of a propertied elite who may become socially entrenched as the establishment in Canada (Creighton 1966).

Sir Robert Borden was the next Conservative party leader to defeat the Liberals at the polls, in 1911. Borden tried to move the party away from the Tory element of privilege and advanced the idea of equality of opportunity as a way of levelling the most serious displays of social and economic inequality. Borden believed that community interests were more important than the individual interests.

At the same time, the ideas of welfare liberalism were gathering support for the Liberal party and competing with the conservative belief in the fundamental social inequality. Borden still believed that people are naturally endowed with different attributes and are born into different social positions, and that some always acquire more than the rest. It is society's responsibility, based on the principles of compassion and *noblesse oblige*, not the government's role, based on equalitarianism, to extend more opportunities to as many people as possible.

Arthur Meighen, Borden's successor as prime minister, returned the Conservative party to traditional Canadian conservativism. His fidelity to the Crown seemed to insulate him from the liberal influences penetrating his own party as well as those occurring in the general political culture of Canada. His positions were fundamentally conservative, devoted to heritage, defensively proud of Canada's imperial ties, and attached to the British ideals of freedom and justice. He favoured a return to the forces of *laissez faire* and its accompanying myth that older solutions are the best current solutions.

All ideologies were challenged by the Great Depression, but especially Canadian conservatism under the party leadership of R.B. Bennett. In a complex industrial age, the financial traumas of the 1930s inspired a popular belief that only government action could reverse the widespread economic consequences.

Bennett knew that traditional conservative solutions would not be adequate to reverse successfully the economic malaise pervading Canadian communities (Wilbur 1968). He rejected *laissez faire* in favour of "corporatism," a doctrine that favours government action to involve workers, business, and other groups in the planning and implementation of public policy as a collective effort to deal with social and economic problems. Bennett's relatively limited attempts to deal with the momentous catastrophe of the Great Depression earned him severe criticism. The Conservative party was blamed for the disaster that overtook the country during its time in power. Bennett was decisively defeated by Mackenzie King in 1935, and unable fully to implement his vision.

The Conservative party experienced a succession of leaders, R.J. Manion, Arthur Meighen (again), John Bracken, and George Drew, whose common challenge was the ascendancy of Canadian socialism as a credible ideological alternative to the traditional political philosophies unpinning the governability of Canada. Conservatives responded by embracing the idea of progress and attaching it to nation-building. The name of the party was augmented to include the word "progressive" so that the idea of a national party in forward motion would attract people who felt that a dynamic and reformative orientation would make conservative ideology more relevant, and thus more appealing. Conservatives took the name from the dying embers of the Progressive Party in order to attract that party's followers.

After a seventeen-year period of dormancy in opposition, Conservatives won the greatest federal electoral victory in Canadian history, led by John Diefenbaker, whose charismatic political style brought a new dimension to conservative ideology.

Diefenbaker resuscitated conservatism, melding it with some traits of Toryism (loyalty to the British monarchy and Commonwealth) and a strong sense of nationalism and individualism. He articulated his "vision" of Canada, which encompassed a determination to maintain a strong national government, a five-year plan in which to implement the National Development Policy, the Bill of Rights, and his pro-Canadianism (Newman 1963, xii–xiv).

Diefenbaker gave Canadian conservatism a sense of history: Canada had a great destiny that could be achieved with a common political will, guided by proper and dedicated leadership. His government's success in passing a Bill of Rights was driven by his determination to protect the rights of individuals as a matter of social justice and as a component of national and political development.

Diefenbaker supported in principle as well as in practice a modest welfare state because, in his view, a properly constructed and managed social network strengthens the loyalty of people to the country. He thought such a network would have a collective as well as an individual value in that it is an instrument of national unity.

Although Diefenbaker was discredited by his own party, he was largely responsible for developing a broader-based conservative movement in Canada, and for reversing much of its former elitist reputation. Under Diefenbaker, Canadian conservatism was transformed from an elitist philosophy to a more populist cause of the working and middle classes. He gave the party a more positive caste, with a national agenda of its own. In many ways, Diefenbaker strengthened the power of conservatives in the Progressive Conservative party and set the stage for future victories in the 1980s.

Robert Stanfield replaced Diefenbaker as leader of the Progressive Conservatives in 1967. Stanfield's pensive and hesitant political style reflected his devotion to traditional conservative ideals. He presided over a divided party, which made him sensitive to the competing values at the right and left of conservative thought. Stanfield believed that Canada was a uniting of groups that collectively could achieve social justice under one political and governing system. In line with the collective orientation of Canadian conservativism, Stanfield prescribed a national-development strategy involving the participation of many social groups as a solution to unemployment and inflation. As a recommended assault on inflation, he favoured wage and price controls to restore order and confidence in the economy.

His successor, Joe Clark, was much less committed to the traditional conservative ideology. He might be thought of as a **neoconservative**, embracing less rigid ideas than those of such traditional conservatives as Diefenbaker and Stanfield. To describe the ideological stream of conservatism that has so deeply affect Canada as "neoconservative" risks oversimplification. While neoconservatism was an important intellectual force in Great Britain and in the United States, in Canada it was a hand-me-down, a set of broad concepts, slogans, and generalizations that added up to an attack on the role of big government in Canadian life. According to the doctrine, the state must be gradually rolled back, must become more passive. Initiative in society should come, even more than in the past, from the private sector. Canada's governing ideology has generated too much equality and too few risk takers. Neoconservatism calls for a redefinition of priorities regarding the economic and political development of Canada. Indeed, the Free Trade Agreement (FTA) and the possibility of a North American Free Trade Association (NAFTA) became the keystone in the archway of Canadian neoconservatism, because they enshrined Canada's commitment to non-interventionist government.

Clark's new pragmatic vision appealed to both liberals and conservatives in and outside of the party. He believed that liberalism had made government too big and held that liberals had gone beyond the idea that government should provide a "safety net" for the substance needs of Canada's social victims — the unemployed, the disabled, and the elderly. Contemporary liberalism had transformed the modest welfare state into a more intrusive, paternalistic one.

For Clark, modern liberalism had promised too much to too many groups, and a governing system that makes such promises becomes overloaded. Inefficient bureaucracy causes government to lose its authority and to fail to govern effectively. Clark was confident that the private sector would drive the economy into recovery. Incorporating some of the core ideas of business liberalism, he emphasized the **free-market economy** and competition and exalted the option of "privatization" to sell Petro-Canada and other crown corporations to the private sector. This withdrawal of government from the economy would allow the market to pursue its own fiscal and monetary efficiency, and thus produce social progress.

Clark tried to temper the ideological divisions in his party by pursuing a centrist position that employed common sense, pragmatism, and realism. Clark also acknowledged the appropriate role of government in preserving and protecting the rights of individual Canadians in terms of the absence of restraints on individual activity, but not necessarily in expanding their freedoms.

As a candidate for the leadership of the party, and then as a prime minister, Brian Mulroney endorsed most of the conservative propositions that had evolved up to that time. Mulroney emerged as the champion of business liberalism, one who favoured deregulation of business activities, the reduction of the national deficit and the debt, and a return — as much as possible within the confines of Canada's welfare state — to the market and free-enterprise economy. It is difficult to imagine a prime minister who could be closer to the conservatism sweeping North America in the early 1980s while appealing to the centre of Canada's political spectrum.

Ideologically, Mulroney, a pragmatic conservative practitioner who avoided the constraints of doctrine and philosophy, tried to keep a centrist course, both in the party and in the country. As prime minister, he was generally supportive of the status quo and was suspicious of efforts to introduce new governmental formulas and economic arrangements. His obsession with the deficit and national debt confirmed his strong belief that a large and powerful government poses a threat to economic prosperity. He opposed the expansion of governmental activities and asserted that solutions to social and economic problems should be developed primarily in the private sector.

His successor, Kim Campbell, followed closely in the neoconservative tradition launched by Clark. In her short tenure as prime minister, she adopted a smaller cabinet, initiated an extensive government downsizing and reorganization, and promised to engage a new politics in the governing of Canada.

Campbell's goals were to downsize, globalize, and tackle the national debt, promising to eliminate the deficit by 1998. Her policy package included a multibillion-dollar program for job training and adjustment, but regarded the reduction of the federal deficit as the only sure method of creating long-term, economically "meaningful" jobs. For her, the iron rules of market economics would come through for the Canadian economy. She remained committed to the large transfer payments to the provinces but promised to seek cost-cutting efficiencies for all social safety net programs. In Campbell's view, the Canada–U.S. Free Trade Agreement, NAFTA, and the General Agreement on Tariffs and Trade (GATT) were cornerstones of economic growth. She promised to create advisory panels to develop trade strategies for both Latin America and the economies of the Pacific Rim.

In the 1993 federal election, Kim Campbell led the Progressive Conservative party to its most devastating defeat in Canadian history. The old coalitions in Quebec and the Western provinces that had so successfully elected Progressive Conservative governments in the past could not hold together in the face of the Reform Party and the Bloc Québécois.

Never in Canada's electoral history has a governing party been as completely humiliated and overwhelmed in a federal election campaign as were the Progressive Conservatives. The election was billed as "the Conservative collapse" because the party that had reached such heights in the 1984 and 1988 elections was reduced to a rump of merely two members of Parliament. Her successor, Jean Charest, was left to rebuild the Progressive Conservative party from the ground up.

## Populism

The view that the will and abilities of a popular majority should prevail in all matters, including politics, government, science, art, and morals, and that neither experts nor minorities ought to have any valid claims against it can be found in Canadian ideological traditions; it is referred to as "populism." Populism is an ideology based on faith in the ability of ordinary people to overcome political and social difficulties by acting together in a democratic way, and from the cohesion of human interaction gaining an empowerment.

This ideological perspective can produce a consistent political will for limited populations, regions, periods of time, and certain sets of issues. Here the popular **initiative** to move matters toward legislation; the **referendum** to decide on a new law or direction by popular vote; and the **recall**, a device that allows citizens to vote officeholders out of office between elections are regarded by populists as highly effective democratic instruments (Thorburn 1991, 350).

Populism is embraced by those who aim to preserve individual freedom of the small farmer, business people, and labourers. Populists favour using governmental power to enforce their own beliefs on a whole range of issues, even personal moral behaviour. They tend to be small "l" liberal on economic matters but small "c" conservative on social ones.

In Canada, populism grew out of the hard times experienced in the 1920s and 1930s, when people were left to find solutions to complex social and economic problems for themselves. Left-wing populists built a farm–labour alliance and were critical of corporate capitalism and big business. Right-wing populists attacked the power of the banks and big government: The United Farmers of Alberta (UFA) and the United Farmers of Manitoba (UFM) produced governments in their respective provinces. From the Left, the Co-operative Commonwealth Federation (CCF) was created at this time, later to become the New Democratic Party (NDP), as was the right-wing Social Credit Party, founded by William Aberhart, who wanted to pull out of the Depression by giving people purchasing power in the form of social credit. The Progressive Party, led by T.A. Crerar, became the second-largest party in the House of Commons after the election of 1921, and defiantly refused to form the opposition.

The Reform Party has its origins in ideological affinities with the emergence of populism in North America. Initially fuelled by the homespun populism and sense of alienation so predominant in the West, the Reform Party has come to be seen by its members as an anti-establishment voice for all Canadians outside of Quebec.

In Canada, it is a genuine social movement with deep popular roots that calls for adherence to the political values of patience, forward planning, and, above all, good timing. It has served to crystallize dissent against the prevailing orthodoxy across a broad policy front. The policy spectrum of the party touches constitutional reform, representation and electoral reform, economic and fiscal tax reform, environmental reform, and social reforms.

Part of the appeal of the Reform Party is its pressure to make Parliament more responsive to the people, and its stringently folkish platform. It calls for dramatic reform of Canada's democratic institutions, as well as curtailing such previously sacrosanct policies as official bilingualism, publicly sponsored multiculturalism, and liberal immigration policies.

Another populist party is the Confederation of Regions party (CoR) which sees bilingualism as a symbol of what is wrong with Canadian government and politics. CoR supporters believe that bilingualism drains scarce government resources away from public services, that it is responsible for high taxes, and that it is divisive between Canada's two largest linguist groups. CoR has many anti-francophone activists, but it also has attracted many right-wing conservatives who are disappointed with the ideological direction taken by that party. CoR has attracted the support of English-speaking people in the working and lower-middle classes, who resent high taxes and cuts in government services, and who single out those in other linguistic groups who get the jobs.

## Socialism

As it first appeared in Canada, socialism was equated with the values of equality, justice, the end of exploitation of the poor by the rich, and other traits of the high moral ground. Gradually, to many Canadians, the term also came to mean government confiscation of private and corporate property, red tape, government inefficiency, social dependency, and high taxes. Even though there are many varieties of socialist doctrine, they share a sufficient number of common beliefs that we may speak of socialism as a general ideology in Canada.

Canadian socialism has a moral and religious basis. A number of democratic socialist leaders in Canada have been ordained priests and ministers. For them, the "brotherhood" and "sisterhood" of human beings deplores the inequalities of income and prestige, and the insecurity of modern capitalism. The "social gospel" calls for a society to love one's neighbour as oneself, and thus advocate socialism as a means of ensuring the dignity and equality of all people. Socialists reject the ethic of competitive materialism as embraced by capitalism. For them, humans are co-operative before they are consumers and producers.

On the economic side, socialism chooses "economic planning" over the less-constrained dynamics of free markets. Under a central plan, the bill of goods that society will produce is not necessarily determined by consumers. Instead, planners decide and, depending on their beliefs, their decisions may or may not be strongly influenced by what consumers want. Socialist economies allow planners to choose production techniques as well as to determine what to produce and how much. The **planned economy** has more direct control over the rates of economic growth than does the unplanned one because the state determines the volume of investment.

Lacking a private profit motive, socialists must provide incentives, either material or otherwise, for plant managers and workers to perform well. Thus, a socialist economy may produce as much inequality in the distribution of labour income as a capitalist economy does — and for the same reasons: to attract workers to do undesirable or risky jobs, to attract highly skilled people, or to attract people to enter into difficult occupations.

In Canada, the crown corporation is seen as an instrument to address social need by means of public rather than private ownership. As a product of socialist theory, the publicly owned corporation can meet the economic plans of Canadian society and still operate in a market economy.

Canada's New Democratic Party (NDP), with its origins in the 1930s, exhibits several traditional socialist values, although on the whole it works within the existing liberal-democratic and capitalist system. Ideologically, the NDP believes that government is the appropriate instrument for achieving greater equality and security for the average person. In the trade-off between inflation and unemployment, the NDP favours deficit spending to create jobs, with somewhat less concern for any resultant increase in inflation and debt.

With some reservations, public ownership of industrial enterprises is still among the party's policies at the federal and provincial levels. Although the party presents itself as the champion of the worker, it has earned a constituency among professionals, small business, and managers, but attracts only about 20 percent of the popular vote in federal elections.

Nationalism is also espoused by the NDP. It calls for public ownership of Canada's resources, which are dominated by foreign ownership. Nationalism may also have been useful in cementing the NDP's alliance with Canadian labour unions, many of which have been ambivalent about their position as subsidiaries of U.S. unions.

Ideologically, the NDP has never fully adopted the tenets of socialist thought so widely present in the socialist parties of Europe and Latin America. The socialism of the NDP has been very much a liberal socialism. Ironically, the socialism of the NDP has done much to influence the policies and practices of Canadian liberals and conservatives, many ideas and policies being absorbed into the political platforms of other political parties, especially the Liberal and Progressive Conservative parties.

### The Welfare State

The term "welfare state" emerged in Canada during the early 1930s, and therefore is much newer than socialism. As it has evolved in Canada, the welfare state means that governments at the federal, provincial, and municipal levels play a significant role in providing people with security and social well-being through economic and social programs.

A fundamental part of the ideology of welfarism in Canada has been the belief that the state should fight poverty by a variety of redistributive programs collectively known as "social assistance." As well, redistributive taxation and educational opportunity would lessen the inequality of advantage and move the social system toward greater equality.

The development of the Canadian union movement and its political expressions, the CCF and the NDP, have influenced government programs such as unemployment insurance, medicare, and the Canada/Quebec Pension Plan, which have traditionally reflected concerns for the working people and the poor.

Canada's two major political parties, the Liberals and the Progressive Conservatives, successfully initiated and implemented the welfare state in Canada. But much of the social safety net was spawned by the NDP and its predecessor, the CCF. Gradually, one public policy at a time, the social network came to include Old Age Security (OAS), the Guaranteed Income Supplement (GIS), family allowance (now called the Child Tax Benefit), unemployment insurance, health insurance, municipal welfare payments, and provincial Worker's Compensation. In Canada, the social network denotes a government guarantee that certain minimum conditions of human decency and dignity will be made available to all citizens: medical care, education, economic security in old age, public housing, and social-insurance protection against job loss.

Canadians have learned that the welfare state is not identical with socialism. Canadian welfarism has come to mean that every citizen is entitled to at least a minimum of the conditions that characterize the good life, as a matter of right and justice, and that no citizen should be denied those conditions because he or she cannot finance them out of personal resources. There is room for debate among welfarists on the exact type and level of benefits that ought to be guaranteed by the government.

The recessions of the early and late 1980s focussed public attention on the long-standing hardships of social-assistance recipients, especially the growing numbers of unemployed in all provinces, and the proliferation of food banks and soup kitchens across the country (Banting 1987, 316). Hard times widened not only the gap between the rich and poor but also that between government revenues and spending.

As a result, governments were forced to consider reforming Canada's hitherto sacred social safety net. Policy debates began to centre on which existing programs should survive

the deep cuts in government spending, which groups will be hurt or spared, and which groups will shoulder the costs of downsizing government.

## Nationalism

Most Canadians believe they live in a national society, but many also believe they live in more than one society simultaneously. For many people, nationalism is a political doctrine that expects the highest allegiance, more compelling than loyalty to church, social class, race, even family. The psychological attachment of individuals and groups to the nation, with all of its inclusive attributes, can be both destructive and positive (Smith 1979). Nationalism has been the single greatest cause of war this century but has also been the glue of nation-building — what encourages people to travel within the boundaries of their country and what compels them to buy "Canadian," to patronize Canadian companies, and to participate in national ceremonies.

Most agree that nationalism is the ideology people have adopted when they display certain traits. The first is a strong identification with the land, the territory, the boundaries of the country. People manifest an intense psychological identity with and affection toward these physical attributes. Rivers, lakes, mountains, plains, prairies, and coasts evoke powerful feelings. Thus, nationalism might seek recognition as geopolitical entity, defined by boundaries and natural frontiers or by some historical territorial identity.

The second consists of being conscious, to some degree, of being part of a continuous historical entity. This historical consciousness furnishes people with a strong sense of their common roots and a powerful source of resolve to carry on in such a way as not to lose what their ancestors have achieved.

A third trait comprises common language and literature. Most people feel a kinship with those who speak the same language as they do, with a similar accent and in familiar idioms. Often people will judge as "foreign" people who speak a different language or with a different national accent.

A fourth trait is a common culture. Nationalism grows more consistently when people share a particular way of life. Most people conduct their lives — courtship, marriage, child rearing, business, and recreation — in ways generally accepted and approved by all others who share a nationhood. Common culture is a protective and distinguishing characteristic that people know separates them from others who live differently.

Finally, a desire for political and governmental independence generates a full-fledged nationalism. This level of nationalism demands recognition of its status as a sovereign and legal entity in the international community of independent nation-states. It brings with it the consequential right to make all governing decisions without interference or intervention from any other nation-state.

Canada's first political party dedicated to the tenets of nationalism — the National Party — was launched in late 1992 as the institutional projection of a nationalistic movement expressed among Canadians. During the 1960s, the movement had called for greater Canadian protectionism, decreased foreign control of Canadian business; and the assertion of Canadian sovereignty, particularly in relations with the United States. By the 1990s, those dedicated to the preservation of Canadian sovereignty were calling for the repeal of the Canada–U.S. Free Trade Agreement (FTA).

## Quebec Nationalism

Unless one adopts a very narrow perspective, Québécois nationalism can be traced deep into the colonial history of the New World. The movement for responsible government that emerged in Upper and Lower Canada in the 1830s and 1840s was, for the French-speaking people, both a campaign to create a provincial government and a struggle against British colonial domination. Many of those who were active in the movement later supported Confederation, but this did not mean that they had resigned themselves to assimilation with English Canada.

Although Confederation tied the French in Canada to the rest of British North America, it also gave them a separate province in which they were the majority and in which they could protect a common culture, common language, and common history. Indeed, the participation of francophones in Confederation was an expression of nationalism, albeit a nationalism based on quite different premises from those on which the nationalism found in Quebec today rests.

Until the 1950s, Quebec nationalism tended to be conservative, and at times oriented toward conserving the past. These dedicated nationalists felt that the survival of Quebec as a distinctly French culture (*la survivance*) could be achieved by keeping francophones loyal to traditional values. For them, the national survival of Quebec could best be achieved within the terms of Confederation by being vigilant about provincial rights and determined to create a Canada independent from Great Britain.

The most representative of this kind of nationalism was Henri Bourassa (Levitt 1969). Bourassa's politics of nationalism wanted to conserve French culture, especially its Catholicism and, at the same time, to defend a sovereign Canada. His followers organized the Ligue nationaliste with the dual objective of promoting an independent Canada and safeguarding the rights of francophones.

French-Canadian writers such as Jules-Paul Tardivel and Lionel-Adolphe Groulx posited a more separatist brand of nationalism. Groulx was one of the most influential nationalist historians at the Université de Montréal in the first half of the twentieth century. He wrote of the French-Canadian "race," advising them to adhere closely to traditional values and to resist the dynamics of urbanization and industrialization that were affecting Quebec.

Already by 1931, only 42 percent of French Quebec was classified as rural. By 1951, that percentage was reduced to 37, and an even smaller percentage (21) were still living on farms (Posgate and McRoberts 1976, 48).

The lure of material benefits in an increasingly modernized Quebec, coming into greater contact with the English-speaking world, were accelerating the assimilation of the French culture. The old-fashioned approaches to *la survivance* had to be altered in some ways to face the challenges sweeping French-Canadian culture. But the inherent conservatism among French-Canadian elites kept them looking to the past for a model of an ideal nationalistic society. They found political leadership in the Union Nationale government of Maurice Duplessis, who was premier of Quebec from 1936 to 1939, and again from 1944 to 1959. More than any other premier, Duplessis came to symbolize the era of conservative nationalism in Quebec, based on the prominence of the church and family.

But, all through his tenure as premier of the province, fundamental political and social changes continued to erode the traditional culture of Quebec. By 1961, the number of francophones who were classified as rural had fallen to 29 percent, and only 13 percent were still living on farms (Posgate and McRoberts 1976, 48). At the same time, the processes of urbanization and industrialization were generating a new set of elites in the provinces, whose members would reject the basic premises of conservative nationalism.

The new emergent elite did not idealize the past, and wanted to expand the public sector so that the state, not just the church and other institutions, would come to represent the political aspirations of French-speaking Quebeckers. These elites came to be called the "bureaucratic middle class" (Guindon 1964). These elites comprised the educated employees of both private and public bureaucracies, most notably in welfare organizations and educational institutions. These bureaucracies had grown in number and size after the Second World War to meet the needs of urban Quebec, but they were being threatened by the old power groups who clung to the dictates of conservative nationalism.

Paul Sauvé who succeeded Duplessis as leader of the Union Nationale, and then Jean Lesage, the Liberal premier from 1960 to 1966, presided over a dramatic shift in the orientation of politics in Quebec. These political and government leaders were prepared to expand the role of the state in the affairs of Quebeckers to empower them against the powerful presence of federal government dominated by English-speaking Canadians.

The "Quiet Revolution," as this style of provincial governance came to be called in Quebec, had profound implications for the character of Quebec nationalism. The basic principles of *la survivance* had to undergo changes. Supporters of the Quiet Revolution wanted to extend the powers of the provincial government, even at the expense of other institutions, most notably the church. Unavoidably, the new nationalists would generate conflict between Ottawa and Quebec City. Under Quebec premiers Lesage, Johnson, Bertrand, and Bourassa, an intense struggle developed between both levels of government over the powers of the province of Quebec within Canada's federal system.

Their nationalist orientation provided the basis for the rise of the widespread separatist movement in Quebec. The idea of separatism flourished under the ideology of nationalism, but since the 1960s, its popularity expanded. Contemporary separatism grew out of the Quiet Revolution, even carrying its premise a step farther, to the conclusion that the powers necessary to protect French culture in Quebec cannot be achieved within Canada's Confederation. Nationalism was institutionalized in the Parti Québécois and the Bloc Québécois. The Parti Québécois became both a political and a governmental expression of Quebec nationhood. It argues that Quebec possesses all of the necessary social and political ingredients to qualify as an independent nation-state in the Western hemisphere and to function as one in the world community of states. The Bloc Québécois, which is committed to fighting for Quebec's independence in the federal House of Commons, successfully offered sovereignty to Quebec voters as an option in the 1993 federal election, becoming Her Majesty's official opposition. The victory heralded a pivotal confrontation between separatists and federalists, giving Quebec nationalism formal parliamentary representation.

## *Feminism*

Women are not a Canadian minority group. The majority of our population are women. Yet, women share with many minorities in Canada a history of subjugation and abuse. From the emergence of the country until well into the twentieth century, women were not allowed to vote, negotiate contracts, borrow money, serve on juries, freely use all public accommodations, or hold or manage property on the same terms as men. Today, they are still subject to discrimination, stereotyping, and harassment of all kinds in our society. Their earning power is much less than that of men, and most still remain in jobs traditionally considered "women's work."

The first phase of Canadian feminism began in the nineteenth century. At that time, women were excluded from a university education across the country. It was widely held, at that time, that higher education would make women reluctant to accept a socially prescribed domestic role. The first Canadian woman was enrolled in a college in New Brunswick in 1849. Mount Allison University admitted women in 1858, and the University of Toronto kept women out until 1884, for fear of "lowering their standards" (MacLellan 1971).

As Canada was transformed in the twentieth century from a predominantly agricultural to a largely industrial and technological society, the work that men did moved out of the family homestead, from the farms and workshops in or around the home, into factories and other commercial enterprises, leaving women isolated from the economic mainstream, and mostly dependent on men for their financial survival. Women were left to do the housework and to prepare the meals for and raise the children. This environment created an inferior economic and political status for women.

As a result, women were locked out of the decision-making processes of Canadian society. They were assigned a largely powerless role in their communities. Feminine roles and cultural expectations were fixed by patriarchal ideologies, such as capitalism, liberalism, conservatism, and socialism. These systems of thought share the patriarchal bias of power in all social relations in which women's interests are subordinated to the interests of men. One patriarchal component common to all of these ideologies is protectionism — the idea that women must be sheltered from life's hardships as defined by men. This idea grew out of the fundamental belief that women were the property of men, and should be protected and defended by them and the political systems they created.

The women's movement has never been a unified social movement in Canada. Instead, many groups with similar goals have emerged, sometimes working together and other times vigorously competing. The disunited character of the women's movement in Canada is also reflected in diversified ideological perspectives embraced by different groups on the politics of gender relations.

Feminism, in its various manifestations, identifies with some ideological elements in liberalism and Marxism. Liberal feminists focus on the reform of the existing social and political system so as to achieve gender equality. They accept the structures and ideology of the present system but call for political, legal, and economic change to achieve a greater degree of equality. Feminists share with liberalism an awareness of the prominence of the individual in society and a sensitivity toward the ways in which personal relations based on gender create the social world, tending to reproduce male dominance in the workplace, the family, the marketplace, and the bedroom.

In Marxism, feminists share a concern with the structures of power and inequality, and the dynamics of capitalism and production as they relate to women in history. Socialist feminists want to abolish inequalities based on gender. Unlike Marxists, socialist feminists see the fundamental inequities in society as a product of patriarchy, the dominance of men over women. The socialist feminists identify gender differences as a product of the organization of our society around profit, where women are most likely to be exploited. They point out that women and their dependent children are the single largest group of poor people in Canada. Half of all poor people in Canada live in female-headed families, this phenomenon is sometimes referred to as "the feminization of poverty."

Some feminists see the need for a cultural and separate existence for men and women in many areas of life. This ideology, sometimes referred to as "radical," although the term tends not to be used much anymore, is based on biological and psychosocial differences between men and women. It advances the idea that women-centred cultures are necessary to enhance the rightful value of how women think and what they do in society. There are clear lines to be drawn around the social and biological distinctions between men and women. This genre of feminism seeks to redefine the traditional relationship between men and women in virtually every sphere of life, from the workplace to marriage and the family.

One important tenet of feminism is that the personal is political. In other ideologies, "politics" is seen to transpire only within governments and the formal structures of a public political system. Some feminists see this perspective as too restrictive (Smith 1975). They have discovered political elements at every level of human personal interaction. What is "political" is learned and expressed by each and everyone of us in our private lives. It is not just what occurs in the public domain; rather, it is found at the very heart of private interaction, within families and peer groups, at schools, at work, and in our leisure activities. The lines of authority and power in society are drawn and revealed at the personal level. The respect society assigns to women's private space at work and at home; the role of women in social, political, and business decisions; the mindset people retain about gender roles — all dramatize the private as political. Thus, the political is a recognizable characteristic of people relating to each other in both private and public matters. According to this feminist axiom, the most intimate experiences of men and women in their private lives cannot be separated from the wider public context.

Feminists constantly tell us that, in the great fields of human knowledge, women tend to be invisible or are noticed only for the extent to which they deviate from male expectations and male measures of excellence (Frank 1987). The patriarchal world view is reproduced in what is written about and read about, and thus becomes the important substance in the formal structures of academic disciplines. History reports the great achievements and failures of men, and political science and sociology tend to examine only the institutional character of patriarchal societies.

Even within the institution of the family, where women do most of the parenting and rearing, their contribution has been downplayed and trivialized because it takes place in the "private realm" of a patriarchal society.

The work done by women in the home is not publicly and politically recognized as economically productive, whereas men are seen to be active in the public realm, where important things happen economically and politically. Patriarchal ideologies portray men as the breadwinners, rather than as co-parents who share equally in the caring for and nurturing of their children.

Feminism is an ideology that asserts the equality of women with men, the historical contributions of women to public and private life, and a recognized political status of women in society. It asserts the value of both women and humanity. Feminism posits that women should enter into the public world, not to be like men, but to be powerful agents of political change. Feminism stands for women building the power to bring their human concerns to the centre of the political stage with a powerful affirmation of women and women's power, and it has done this since its inception. The marginalization of human concerns in our society has also been the marginalization, trivializing, and devaluation of women. To build a polity where these concerns are central is to build a society in which women are central and powerful.

Feminism is not an organization you can join or a set of rigid principles. It is not a thing, but rather the idea of women coming together, supporting each other and gaining strength to change the political and social world. Feminism is women's way of making and participating in history.

## CONCLUSION

Where do we get our ideas about politics and government? What is the process by which people acquire their political orientations, their political knowledge, their feelings about politicians, and their judgements about the world of politics, economics, and government? All of these questions relate to how we are governed in Canada by its institutions of state (the Crown). How Canadians think about their political system affects how it performs and whether it can adapt and survive.

How we think about politics and government comes to us from many difference sources — our families, schoolmates, friends, colleagues, the media, interest groups, political parties, and the government itself. Think about the tremendous range of knowledge, feelings, and opinions we have about the world of politics. Learning about our political ideologies and what we can do with them is a long and continuing process in our lives.

Ideologies instill beliefs, incite action, and cannot be separated from our concern with fundamental social and political values. Political ideologies give Canadians an underlying imaginative picture of the world and function as a bond to those who embrace them. Ideologies are "suprapersonal" in that they aim to operate beyond the thinking of a single individual, ultimately to unite all like minds within a political culture in its quest for the attainment of a preferred way of life.

Each new generation of Canadians is socialized to a large extent by preceding generations about what political ideologies are tolerable. In many ways, each new generation will look and act like the one before it. In many respects, solidarity and continuity of values are considerable among all age groups in Canada.

While differences in political values are found between generations, they do not necessarily occur on all issues. In this sense, political socialization seems to be biased against radical change. Almost inevitably, this leads to support for and compliance with government and social order. Although many disagree with particular government policies, few will reject the fundamental philosophical justifications for the kind of political system in operation in Canada.

We know that all social movements in Canada have an ideology, a set of beliefs that explains and justifies some actual or potential political arrangement. The ideology provides a diagnosis of the political and social problem the movement wishes to rectify, an explana- tion of how the problem came about and why it persists, a prescription of how to correct the situation, and a scenario on how matters would get worse if the movement failed and its ide- ology were to fail.

## GLOSSARY

**collective action**   Behaviours covering a wide range of group phenomena that are collec- tive responses to, as well as causes of, social and political change, usually occur- ring when ideologies are in a state of flux.

**counter-ideologies**   Countervailing belief systems that challenge the legitimacy of dominant ideologies and often offer alter- native ways of thinking about society, economy, and government.

**establishment**   The group of individuals within a social or political system who clearly possess the major portion of power and are the most influential in directing public policy.

**free-market economy**   An economy that functions on the relatively unhindered interaction of buyers and sellers, whose ex- change of goods and services establish prices, demands, and supplies.

**initiative**   An electoral procedure through which citizens may propose legislation, and even amendments to a constitution, by peti- tions signed by a required number of voters.

**la survivance**   Survival of French Canada as an independent entity.

**Left**   The political designation of persons or groups supporting extremely *liberal* or *radi- cal* economic and political programs with in a political system.

**mass media**   The instruments of public com- munication that transmit political and so- cial knowledge to all members of society.

**neoconservatism**   A mutation of conserva- tism that advocates the belief that liberal- ism transforms the welfare state into an intrusive paternalistic governing system and calls for a re-evaluation of the role of government in the economy and the rest of society.

**partisan**   A strong bias of support for a poli- tical idea, government, political party, cause, or issue.

**patriarchal ideologies**   Social and political arrangements in which only males hold legitimate power or authority vested in their positions.

**planned economy**   Government control and guidance of economic productivity and consumption.

**pluralist society**   A society in which many competing and conflicting groups and ideas have access to government and the politi- cal system.

**popular sovereignty**   The right to govern based on the will of the people.

**praxis**   All actions and behaviours associated with, and carried out from, an ideological commitment.

**recall**   An electoral procedure that enables constituents to remove an elected official from office before his or her term has expired.

**referendum**   An electoral instrument by which the public can directly approve or reject a course of action by society and government.

**rhetoric**   The persuasive ways humans use to communicate with each other.

**Right**   The political term used to indicate persons or groups supporting extremely conservative or reactionary economic and political programs within the governing system.

**Tory** A frequently used nickname for members of the Progressive Conservative party, but also a term referring to the traditional adherences of political conservatism that became the hallmark of the ideology in the nineteenth century.

**Zionism** A movement founded in 1897 by Theodore Hertzl, and later led by Chaim Weizmann, to establish a national home for the Jewish people in Palestine.

## RECOMMENDED READING

Arthur, John, and William Shaw. 1992. *Social and Political Philosophy*. Englewood Cliffs, N.J.: Prentice-Hall. This book gives the student a comprehensive exposure to the gamut of political and social ideas, such as democracy, freedom, justice, and equality.

Bashevkin, Sylvia. 1991. *True Patriot Love: The Politics of Canadian Nationalism*. Toronto: Oxford University Press. The book is organized around the concept of pan-Canadian nationalism. It examines the complex relations between political ideas and public policy in Canada and investigates the limits of Canadian nationalism.

Ebenstein, William, and Alan Ebenstein. 1992. *Introduction to Political Thinkers*. Fort Worth, Tex.: Holt, Rinehart and Winston. The latest edition of this popular, readable classic of political thought from Plato to Rawls is an important tool to initiate students in the ideological dimensions of political theory.

Funderburk, Charles, and Robert Thobaben. 1994. *Political Ideologies*. New York: HarperCollins. This book provides a short but comprehensive introduction for undergraduate students to the world's major political ideologies.

Gruen, Lori, and Dale Jamieson. 1994. *Reflecting on Nature*. New York: Oxford University Press. This anthology presents insightful essays on environmental justice from feminist and naturalist perspectives, focussing on how our ideological views determine the ways we treat nature.

Kroker, Arthur, and Marilouise Kroker, eds. 1991. *Ideology and Power in the Age of Lenin in Ruins*. Toronto: McClelland & Stewart. This important book was written in the shadow of the collapse of communism and the international challenges to capitalism. The contributors present a kaleidoscopic view of ideology at the end of a millennium.

Reinhartz, Jehuda, and George Mosse. 1992. *The Impact of Western Nationalisms*. NewBury Park, Calif.: Sage Publications. This book looks at nationalism historically and applies that perspective to nationalism as a twentieth-century global phenomenon.

Richards, John, R. Cairns, and L. Pratt. 1991. *Social Democracy Without Illusions*. Toronto: McClelland & Stewart. This book traces the renewal of the Canadian Left from the perspective of political culture, nationalism, and economics.

Robin, Martin. *Shades of Right*. 1992. Toronto: University of Toronto Press, This book looks at the extreme Right of the ideological spectrum in Canada, by examining the operations and ideology of Canadian fascists, the Ku Klux Klan, and other right-wing extremist groups.

Whitehorn, Allan. *Canadian Socialism*. 1992. Toronto: Oxford University Press. This collection of nine essays focusses on Canadian socialism, with special analysis of the Co-operative Commonwealth Federation and the New Democratic Party.

CHAPTER

# UNDERSTANDING CANADA'S CONSTITUTION

The great constitutional debates of the 1980s and early 1990s left many people thinking that Canada's constitution must be changed before the country can move forward. The Meech Lake and the Charlottetown accords left the impression that failing to act immediately will leave us frozen in stalemate. Some even argued that, without some quick constitutional accommodation, Canadians will be unable to develop as a people and we will lose Quebec.

However, experience gave us a very different perspective. We learned that altering our constitution is dangerous business. We saw how tinkering and tampering with the first law of the land gave licence to ideologues, racists, and bigots. It risked creating even deeper divisions among linguistic or ethnic groups. Ultimately, it risks the break-up of the country, leaving us with the possibility of civil war.

Not all Canadians feel that we should meddle with the constitution. Many believe that the constitution, left as it is for the time being, still gives us the best option. They feel we should use our collective energies to try to make it work.

One prominent Canadian academic who thinks this way is Michael Bliss, a professor of history at the University of Toronto. He is the author of many books and has recently completed one of particular relevance to the Canadian constitution: *Right Honourable Men: The Descent of Canadian Politics from Macdonald to Mulroney* (Toronto: HarperCollins, 1994). According to him, Canadians should not have opened up their country's constitution so easily and so often. He feels that we have lived well for more than a hundred years with the British North America Act, changing it very few times before presenting it for patriation and adding a Charter of Rights and Freedoms in 1982. It took more than 50 years to implement changes that had been debated periodically since the 1920s. The achievements of 1981–82 made by Prime Minister Trudeau were won only after painful social and political debate. In the wake of Trudeau's constitutional undertaking, a trail of national wounds was evident, notably among the separatists in Quebec and among those who felt disenchanted with the constitutional process.

According to Professor Bliss (interviewed by the author), "The constitution has to be rewritten because we are told it simply isn't working. The one unacceptable option is the status quo. Not so! Our experience since the collapse has shown us what was obvious from 1987, what in fact was obvious in 1982: There is no agreement in Canada to support a better constitution than the one we hammered out thirteen years ago.

"The status quo is the best option we have. We should stop knocking it, start defending it, and get on with making it work. Ottawa should back away and announce a moratorium on schemes for general constitutional reform. It should appoint a royal commission on the constitution, with a requirement not to report before the year 2000. It should continue to work with Native leaders on practical proposals for self-government and real social improvement. While preparing a long-term approach to Senate reform, it should encourage elections to vacant Senate seats. When Quebec holds a referendum on sovereignty, we should try to remind Quebeckers of the benefits of being part of Canada while also telling them the truth about the hard consequences of separation."

## INTRODUCTION

We tend to dismiss those Victorian politicians known as the "Fathers of Confederation" as irrelevant figures from the dim and distant past. But, in 1865, the debates they had over the kind of **constitution** Canada should have were remarkably similar to the those that transpired during the contentious Meech Lake and Charlottetown accords. Newspapers nationwide complained of the monumental dullness of debates in which nearly all the arguments were the same (Waite 1963, Preface).

Then, as now, politicians fought over how best to preserve the French language and culture in Quebec and other provinces. Opinion among French-speaking Quebeckers was split on whether federalism or sovereignty was the answer. They even debated, sometimes emotionally, how to protect official minorities — the English inside Quebec and the French Catholics outside. They worried about whether a fractured Canada would be absorbed by the United States.

Those who framed the original constitution even fought over whether the process of framing it should be conducted privately, behind closed doors, or in an open forum with participation from the public. George-Étienne Cartier, the leading French-speaking proponent of Confederation, remarked that the U.S. Congress on the Constitution sat behind closed doors to prevent public misrepresentations. So, on that principle, the conference at Quebec City sat, very properly, behind closed doors. They even argued over whether to hold a national referendum.

Then, as in the late 1980s and early 1990s, the debate was held in an atmosphere of political and government crisis. The economy was in a slump and all the participating government's were broke. As would be the case in the 1980s, the economy had plunged into recession in the 1860s, after a boom had spurred overspending. The debates even came to blows. Alexander Dufresne of Iberville, Quebec, an opponent of Confederation, was struck in the face behind the Speaker's chair by Joseph Cauchon of Montmorency, who supported Confederation. Confederation opponent Antoine Dorion from Hochelaga, Quebec, complained sarcastically that he would like to be speaking French but most Ontario MPs would not be able to understand what he was saying.

The crucial moment in the process of writing the British North America (BNA) Act came in October 1864, in Quebec City. The delegates met in a nondescript brick building, out of the public eye, approximately where the Château Frontenac now stands. They represented five of Britain's North American colonies: the United Colony of Canada East and West, roughly what we call Quebec and Ontario; New Brunswick; Nova Scotia; Prince Edward Island; and Newfoundland.

The delegates had met six weeks earlier in Charlottetown and had laid out some general principles for Confederation. Later, there would be another conference in London, Ontario. But Quebec is where the deal was done. The 72 resolutions that came out of the Quebec Conference were the draft of the BNA Act — the bones of the constitution that still shapes our destiny today.

Had the BNA Act been subjected to the same degree of public scrutiny as were the Meech Lake and Charlottetown accords, it probably would never have become the primary part of our constitution. The constitution has survived, but is survival enough? After 130 years, is its plan of government outmoded, out of pace with the needs of Canadians? Will it ever accommodate the demands of Quebec? Does it provide our leaders with the means to govern in a world of complex problems that the Fathers of Confederation could not have foreseen?

## THE CONTEXT OF CANADA'S CONSTITUTION

### What Is Our Constitution?

The documents that comprise the Canadian constitution ought to be easy to describe. They are relatively short and written formally but clearly. We know who wrote the constitution and why, and a good deal about what went on during the constitutional debates in the mid-1860s (Bliss 1966, Chap. 1). Yet, when we try to relate what the constitution actually is, the task is not so simple.

No constitution or constitutional tradition can provide for every specific situation that emerges in a society. Our original constitution is not a detailed and complete blueprint for government. Even if it were far more detailed than it is, countless government activities would not be dealt within it, simply because government has grown far more complex in the century since the constitution was written. Discrepancies between what is contained in the constitution and how Canadian governments actually work — for example, parliamentary procedures — are inevitable (Cheffins and Johnson 1986, 118–29).

Such discrepancies can be further explained by the fact that Canada has both a written and an unwritten constitution. The **written constitution** is more than one document, and comprises many legal instruments that qualify as constitutional in their character and effect in Canada. These instruments include British **Imperial** statutes, Canadian statutes, executive proclamations, judicial decisions, and conventions (Maitland 1908). In all, Canada's written constitution includes 14 acts of the Parliament of the United Kingdom, 7 acts of the Parliament of Canada, and 4 **orders-in-council** of the United Kingdom. However, unlike the U.S. constitution, which is a single comprehensive document setting out the fundamental relationships for the functioning of the government, Canada's written constitution is quite incomplete.

Canada's **unwritten constitution** is responsible for a large part of the way our government operates today and for the very existence of democratic practices in our parliamentary system. Like Great Britain, Canada has a constitutional practice that is flexible, relying on unwritten procedures that have come to be accepted as conventions and traditions. For example, there is no mention of the existence of the Cabinet in the written constitution; no mention that the prime minister and the Cabinet must always have the support of the House of Commons; no mention that all members of the Cabinet and the prime minister must have seats in the House of Commons; no mention that the operation of the executive branch of the federal government is duplicated in each of the ten provinces; and no mention that the dispersion of federal and provincial powers can be, as has occurred, changed considerably.

R.M. Dawson (1947) points out that our constitution mainly reflects powerful executive government practices before 1848, not since 1867. A literal reading of the constitution would show Canada to operate as a kind of dictatorial government of one person, the governor, who acts with little control by the people. The governor is the commander-in-chief of the military and makes a vast array of appointments, including all the members of one House of the legislature. The governor can call together and dissolve the other legislative body, the House of Commons, at any time. And the governor has the power to give assent to or refuse legislation.

The great difference between what is written in our constitution and the way Canada is actually governed demonstrates how the English system of law works: It continually evolves. Changes result from common-law development in the courts, acts of Parliament, and the development of the rules and privileges of Parliament.

## Fundamental Constitutional Principles

### Monarchy

Canada is a constitutional monarchy. Some of the features of British royal absolutism have been retained in the constitutional arrangements of Canada's government (Forsey 1985). How we appoint and dismiss our prime minister, how we summon and dissolve Parliament, and how we appoint senators, judges, and the governor general are some of the royal powers that have been constitutionally guaranteed in Canada's system of government. This means that the acts of government and the legislative and political executive must be legitimized by the Crown, that is, the governor general, or on special occasions, and when invited, by the Queen, our formal executive.

By "political executive" in Canada, we generally mean the Cabinet — the senior ministries usually headed by members from the majority party in the House of Commons. The Cabinet has evolved from that group of the monarch's intimate advisers who came to constitute the Privy Council. Canada's Privy Council has survived as the formal machinery through which the monarch exercises royal prerogative powers when necessary, or when invited to do so.

Other inherited monarchical powers are prescribed by our constitution and involve external affairs. The fact that the making of treaties was originally the personal preserve of the British monarch has meant that a Canadian government, although it might feel pressure to offer opportunities to Parliament to discuss an international development, has considerable freedom of action in this field, based on the original practices of monarchs. Today, the negotiation, signing, and ratification of treaties are still executive acts in Canada, and the Cabinet has the authority to bind Canada toward other states by virtue of the royal prerogative.

So powerful was monarchist sentiment among the framers of the BNA Act that they wanted to call the country "the Kingdom of Canada." The British government was reluctant to use this name because it feared offending the Americans, who had repelled monarchy in favour of republicanism, and it insisted that the Canadians find another title. Samuel Tilley, who was a lay preacher as well as a pharmacist, fished the line out of the Bible that contained the phrase "dominion from sea to sea," and the country became the "Dominion of Canada." When the Canadian constitution was patriated in 1982, the entire BNA Act was incorporated into it as the Constitution Act, 1867. So the word *Dominion* continues to be part of the official title of this country — it has only been suppressed, with *federal*, *national*, and *central* substituted as adjectives, and *Canada*, *nation*, and *country* used to replace the noun.

## Responsible Government and the Constitution

The Canadian constitution is inherently democratic, despite the fact that many of the Fathers of Confederation who participated in the writing of the BNA Act were quite reserved about their visions of democracy. As C.B. Macpherson (1965) points out, until about a century ago, Canadians, especially those in public life, regarded democracy with some suspicion because rule by the people was widely viewed as potentially chaotic.

To those who debated the benefits and pitfalls of the BNA Act, democracy had something to do with "responsible government." The formal institutions of government, that is, the monarchy, its representatives, and the executive branch of government, were responsible to elected officials chosen by and representative of the people. This meant that government by the executive was answerable to, and removable by, a parliamentary majority.

As it had evolved in the colonies, responsible government was first put to the test in Nova Scotia, where, after an election, if the House of Assembly could exercise no confidence in the Executive Council, it would resign and the governor would ask the leader of the majority party in the Assembly to form a government (Reesor 1992, 60–90). Under the conventions of responsible government, **political succession** took place, first, in Nova Scotia in 1848, then in New Brunswick in 1848, in Prince Edward Island in 1851, and in Newfoundland in 1855.

These conventions of responsible government were **entrenched** in the BNA Act, in many provisions such as the one that requires the governor general or the lieutenant-governor to act under the "advice" of the ministers who are members of the parliamentary legislatures and hold the confidence of the majority in the elected House. Responsible government has been regarded by many scholars (Dawson 1947; Hogg 1992) as the "most significant" non-federal characteristic of the Constitution Act, 1867.

### Constitutionalism

Canada's constitutional heritage also includes the concept of *constitutionalism*. This concept asserts that government is always limited by constitutional rules, that is, what the law is, and procedures for administering the laws of the state. This limitation does not prevent government from using certain acts of violence that are permitted by the state and its administrators.

Constitutionalism prescribes the way in which such powers can be exercised. The Canadian state, that is, its police, customs, and military forces, can kill someone who, in its view, is an immediate threat to the lives of others.

The concept of constitutionalism establishes the supremacy of the constitution as the first law from which all other laws are made legitimate (Hogg 1992, 115). The BNA Act was not a perfect instrument for establishing its own supremacy because, in effect, it merely outlined the framework of government and the distribution of powers between the federal and provincial governments and left to the discretion of the executive many of the explicit provisions that came to be entrenched much later in the Charter of Rights and Freedoms.

The constitution has continued to evolve and change in two basic ways. First, it has been formally amended, especially by the inclusion of a charter, and will likely be amended again to, among other things, bring Quebec into the constitutional family. Second, court interpretations have imposed important changes on the constitution. The Supreme Court of Canada is the final arbiter of the constitution's meaning or requirements in specific cases. Through the Court's interpretations, the constitution's meaning is changed, enlarged, and updated to meet new conditions in Canadian society.

That the 1867 constitution would remain the vital foundation of Canadian government for more than a century is still an extraordinary achievement. The framers made that possible by confining the provisions of the 1867 document to "government structure" and "division of powers," rather than including an elaboration of rights and policies. But the constitution says nothing about what specific policies the governmental structure and different jurisdictions of government should achieve. These design features are critical factors in the longevity of Canada's constitution; a constitution filled with policy provisions would probably never have survived.

### Egalitarianism and the Charter

Most contemporary observers agree that the Charter of Rights and Freedoms entrenched the concept of egalitarianism into Canadian **constitutional law**. *Egalitarianism* means that there are no relevant differences whereby one person can be supposed to have a greater inherent right to some benefit than another. The charter extends the benefits of the rights that it guarantees to "everyone," "anyone," and "any person" (Hogg 1992, 829–32). The charter's ideal of equality asserts that everyone should have the opportunity to try and to achieve according to his or her efforts and ability, regardless of social background.

As outlined in the charter, these equality rights can be political, legal, and economic. Democratic rights, for example, give the right to every citizen to vote and to freely express his or her political views. These rights reflect the contemporary Canadian belief that all citizens should have an equal chance to influence government policy. The charter affirms that there should be no discrimination on grounds of race; national or ethnic origin; religion; sex; age; or mental or physical disability. A long list of legal rights includes such things as the right to a fair, and reasonably prompt, public trial.

Once the constitution has made a commitment to giving the same political and legal rights to all, is it enough to provide equal opportunity, or is it necessary to assert equality of results in order to overcome disadvantages created by past social discriminations? In this regard, the charter does call for "affirmative action" programs for the socially or economically disadvantaged. The underlying belief behind the inclusion of this consideration is that it is not enough to give rights to people; they must be given benefits as well. Equality of opportunity and results for everyone is, even if entrenched in the constitution, impossible to achieve fully. But the goal of equal opportunity is now a powerful force in our constitutional heritage.

## SOURCES OF CONSTITUTIONAL LAW

### What Is Constitutional Law?

As the most fundamental genre of law in Canada, constitutional law involves the interpretation and application of the constitution (Morton 1984). It is concerned largely with defining the extent and limits of governmental power, and the rights of certain groups and individuals. Final decisions about the meaning of the constitution are in the hands of Canadian courts, especially the Supreme Court of Canada. Constitutional law can be generated only under special circumstances, following complex procedures and involving certain governmental institutions at the federal and provincial levels. Because Canada's constitution comprises many different documents and conventional practices, tracing the sources of constitutional law is important.

### Imperial and Canadian Statutes

One fundamental source of Canadian constitutional law is legislation passed by the British and Canadian parliaments. The expression "Imperial statutes" is used to describe legisla-

tion enacted for Canada by the United Kingdom. Canada followed the British example and recognized the supremacy of Parliament as the ultimate source and maker of law and as having constitutional jurisdiction.

Canada's constitution contains many British statutes. The two most prominent are the British North America Act, 1867, and the Canada Act, 1982. But twelve other British statutes have constitutional status, such as the British North America Act, 1871 (which gave Canada authority to produce new provinces and territories), and the British North America Act, 1886 (which dealt with representation in Parliament of Canadian territories). The Statute of Westminster (1931) is an Imperial statute ensuring the Dominions that no future enactments of the British Parliament would apply to them other than those they requested.

Certain Canadian statutes have constitutional significance. These include the Canadian Bill of Rights (reprinted at the back of this book as Appendix D), the Official Secrets Act, and the Canada Elections Act, all of which have significance in relation to the constitution. All of these statutes are federal, but certain provincial statutes also affect the Canadian constitution. All provinces have passed legislation that addresses the role and function of their formal executives, as well as certain procedures of the legislature and the provincial electoral system. A province's Elections Act, for example, affects the constitutional rights of citizens to register and exercise their vote. And every province has passed human-rights legislation that addresses and replicates most, if not all, of the rights and freedoms outlined in the charter. These statutes may differ somewhat in content, depending on which province has passed them, but they are constitutional.

### Royal Orders and Prerogatives

Another source of Canadian constitutional law is the Imperial royal prerogative and Imperial orders that affect the operation of government in Canada. *Prerogatives* are exclusive privileges, and sometimes peculiar powers and immunities, that are vested in the Crown. Throughout British history, certain prerogatives were accorded to the Crown and adopted in many of the colonies as part of the constitutional framework of colonial governments. In Canada, the Letters Patent of 1947, which creates the office of governor general, outline most of the royal prerogatives as they apply to Canada.

*Imperial orders* are royal prerogatives exercised by the monarch that are constitutional in Canada. They form part of Canada's constitution, but they are instruments of the United Kingdom and will remain so because they are the events of history. Since 1982, Canada has been enabled to repeal all Imperial instrumentation and to re-enact its constitution federally.

## Court Decisions and Judicial Review

If there is disagreement about what the constitution means, who is to interpret it to settle the dispute? Although the constitution does not say so, the judiciary has taken on this role. The Constitution Act, 1867, speaks only briefly about the judiciary, and does not provide much guidance about what it is supposed to do, or how (Hogg 1992, 113–24).

By convention and tradition, courts in Canada have evolved a dual function in government. The most obvious judicial function is to provide an official, impartial forum for the resolution of social disputes. The second function relates to the constitution: **Judicial review** allows courts to review, and sometimes reverse, the decisions of other governmental actors and to declare acts of Parliament *ultra vires* the constitution. To resolve constitutional disputes brought before them, the courts must determine what the relevant provisions of the constitution mean. By deciding that the provisions mean one thing or another, the courts can, in effect, change the constitution.

Especially since the enactment of the Charter of Rights and Freedoms, the court system in Canada has provided a vital forum for testing, and thereby maintaining, the constitutional character of the government. A citizen harmed by an act of government can challenge that action in the courts. The government must show that its action was based on an authorizing law. The police cannot simply arrest people they dislike; they must first charge the person with violating a specified statute, and they must be prepared to specify the legal basis for the arrest. In principle, the courts offer the citizen the means for checking arbitrary power when it violates their constitutional rights.

But the courts play an even more distinctive role in the Canadian system of government. Even if an official can show that a specific act was in conformity with municipal, provincial, or federal law, the act can be reversed if it can be shown in court that the law itself was contrary to the constitution.

## Constitutional Conventions

Another source of constitutional law is *conventions* — widely accepted practices or traditions of parliamentary conduct that stipulate what may or may not be done and that bind certain offices and the institutions of government with the force of constitutional law (Heard 1991). Conventions are distinguishable from constitutional rules in that the latter derive from statutes or from judicial pronouncements.

Constitutional conventions are usually not written anywhere. In Canada, conventions and the practices of formal government adapt themselves to the requirements of contemporary governance, and often do so because the constitution has nothing to say on the matter. Conventions have the character of customs of government but, like law, contain an obligation that is independent of mere habitual implementation.

The political party system is entirely extraconstitutional in Canada, yet who could imagine Canadian politics and government without political parties engaging in competition and forming governments. Most elected politicians represent Canadians under the banner of a political party. Political parties organize and manage elections under the Canada Elections Act, which has constitutional status. However, interest groups also play a major political role in our society because they represent the demands of individuals and groups, and because they influence the decisions governments make or do not make.

Because Canada adopted a form of parliamentary government based on the model of the British constitutional monarchy, most Canadian constitutional conventions reflect powers and prerogatives of the formal executive, that is, the monarch and her or his Canadian representative. For example, it is a convention that the governor general appoints the prime minister and members of Cabinet, members of the Senate, certain members of the judiciary, and members of the Privy Council (Hogg 1992, 17–26).

### Constitutional Change

In order for any constitution to endure, it must be flexible enough to meet the changing needs of a constantly changing society. Canada is a society in rapid transformation, and the ways we have developed of changing the constitution are vital to how we are governed.

Formal amendment procedures are one way of ensuring adaptability, but they are not the only way, or perhaps even the best way, of doing so. Judicial interpretation is sometimes more expeditious and practicable for giving new meaning to old words. The agility of the Supreme Court of Canada in finding ever-fresh significance in the phrases in the Charter of Rights and Freedoms should be proof enough of that. Having the very same words take on new meaning is often quicker than adding an amendment to do the same thing.

But aside from formal amendment and judicial interpretation, the governing system changes by custom and usage. Even the constancy of constitutional wording does not preempt the evolution of the public's expectations of governmental institutions. Socioeconomic conditions, industrialization, urbanization, and communications and technological development have influenced our attitudes and practices. Custom and usage are difficult to interpret as an expression of constitutional will and their bearing is often uncertain: The people speak in mumbles, as it were.

Generally, constitutional changes are made either by formal amendments or by informal processes. Formal amendments change the letter of the constitution, or expand it in some way. Informal processes, including constitutional interpretation and political practice, will also alter the ways government is practised, and ultimately will change the spirit of the constitution.

Accordingly, we must know that the original principles and character of the constitution are not absolute. They have had to be, and will continue to be, shaped and interpreted as the country undergoes the rapid transformations of the twentieth century. It is inevitable that a document which gave powers to different levels of government will sooner or later be caught in a squeeze when the interests of those governments are in sharp conflict, ultimately requiring constitutional change.

Over the years, amendments have been made to the original constitution (Gérin-Lajoie 1950). Each amendment — minor though it may have been — in its own way alters the fabric of the original document and modifies the intentions of those who first framed the constitution. A constitutional amendment in 1992 entrenched the equality of English and French communities in New Brunswick. The Constitution Act, 1982, is, to date, the most influential amendment to Canadian constitutional law, giving Canada independence from Britain in amending the constitution, adopting an independent domestic amendment formula, and including a Charter of Rights and Freedoms. The charter itself has been the most significant instrument of change to Canadian constitutional law.

Both the Meech Lake Accord and the Charlottetown Accord would also have transformed the original constitution and dramatically altered the structures, functions, and interactions of governments in Canada.

These changes would have fundamentally modified the Constitution Act, 1867, by including Quebec and aboriginal peoples in the constitutional framework, and generating a number of amendment formulas to further change the constitution and thus put in place a totally independent and self-generating system of constitutional law.

Today, the continuing debate about the character and meaning of the constitution and the ongoing discussions of constitutional change are part of the evolution of constitutional law in Canada. Since the referendum on the Charlottetown Accord, the issues that gave rise to this amendment, and to the Meech Lake Accord before it, remain with all Canadians, and will persist until they are resolved, one way or another. It must be remembered that the government of Quebec has not yet signed the Constitution Act, 1982, and that Quebec's interests, as expressed in the Meech Lake and Charlottetown accords, have yet to be addressed to the satisfaction of that government.

## THE BASIC DOCUMENTS

### The Constitution Act, 1867

The Constitution Act, 1867, was enacted by Great Britain as the British North America Act, 1867, and was renamed the Constitution Act, 1982. These two enactments, 1867 and 1982, are the two central pieces of the constitution of contemporary Canada.

The 1867 act enshrines the federation of the original provinces of Canada (i.e., Upper Canada [Ontario] and Lower Canada [Quebec]), and Nova Scotia and New Brunswick in a political union. An initial glance will reveal that the 1867 act provided for the direct dominance or supervision of the provinces by the central or federal government (see Figure 3.1). Furthermore, the overall **residual powers** (legislative powers) and other governing powers are given to the federal government, an allocation in sharp contrast to that of the United States, where residual power is vested in the states. The 1867 act also accords several other important powers, including the power to establish the criminal law, to the federal government.

However, in practice, the process of government in Canada proceeds on an "equal and co-ordinate" basis whereby both the federal and the provincial governments share authority.

At the very heart of the 1867 act is the division or allocation of legislative powers between the two levels of government. The key provisions are sections 91 and 92, the former enumerating the powers of Parliament (federal) and the latter the powers of the provincial legislatures. As a consequence, most of the major constitutional cases prior to the 1982 charter concerned the division of legislative powers (Cheffins and Johnson 1986, 118–29).

### Features

Before we deal with the important constitutional and governmental changes since 1982, it is useful to examine several features of Canadian constitutional law that remained after 1867, flowing from linkages and influences between Canada and Great Britain.

**Nature of Government** The preamble to the Constitution Act, 1867, speaks of Canada as having "a Constitution similar in Principle to that of the United Kingdom" within the

**Figure 3.1  The Constitution Act, 1867: What It Does**

1. Establishes a federal system of government and creates a union of Quebec, Ontario, Nova Scotia, and New Brunswick (Parts I and II).

2. Describes and outlines the structure of the federal government (Parts III and IV).

3. Entrenches the office of lieutenant-governor and legitimizes provincial governments (Part V).

4. Divides government jurisdictions between the federal and provincial governments (Part VI).

5. Provides for a judiciary (Part VII).

6. Determines the financial relationships between the federal and provincial governments.

7. Provides for the admission of other provinces.

8. Provides for certain language rights and the construction of the Intercontinental Railway.

structure of a federal system. Basically, this means a monarchy and the British parliamentary system. It reflects the strong **Loyalist** legacy from the earlier generation, rejecting American republicanism, the strict separation of powers in the United States, and entrenched declarations of individual liberties in a **bill of rights**. This fundamental resistance to American values of government was embedded in Canada's constitution with its strong loyalties to the monarchy and British parliamentary practices (Lower 1977, 124).

**The Executive** The executive is perhaps the most confusing branch of Canadian government. Constitutionally, the monarch is the focus of executive power. Queen Elizabeth II is the head of state. Her position is described as "Office of the Queen," and, in addition to being monarch in other realms in the **Commonwealth,** she is "Queen of Canada." The Crown occupies a central place in the Canadian constitution: Legislative power is vested jointly in the Queen and the two Houses of Parliament. The Queen is the head of the executive government, law courts are admin-

istered in her name, and a large number of specific constitutional powers are granted to the governor general as her representative. There has been debate as to whether Canada should continue to be a monarchy, but any change would require unanimity of the federal government and all the provinces under the provisions of the 1867 act.

The Queen is represented in Canada by the governor general federally and by the lieutenant-governors provincially. Today, the governor general is appointed by the Queen under her prerogative power upon the advice of the Canadian prime minister for an official term of six years, but customarily for five years (Ward 1987, 179–80). Lieutenant-governors are appointed by the governor general–in–council — essentially, the federal government, which in practice consults with the government of the province concerned. Today, it is established that the governor general performs the full role of the monarch at the federal level, and the lieutenant-governors do likewise at the provincial level.

Constitutionally, executive power is exercised by the governor general or lieutenant-governors. "The Crown," or "the Crown in the Right of Canada" (federal Crown) or "the Crown in the Right of the Province" (provincial Crown), is the formal expression used to denote the executive bureaucracy of the Canadian state.

**Executive Powers** Executive, or prerogative, powers are privileges and immunities that can be exercised by the Crown. They exist only to the extent permitted under the traditions of **common law**, and may be abolished or modified by Parliament or by the judicial interpretation of the Charter of Rights and Freedoms. They originate from the autocratic power exercised by the monarch before the advent of democracy and responsible government. Since the monarchy is contained within the framework of a constitutional democracy, these prerogatives cannot be broadened. Indeed, in Canada, they are very narrowly confined and apply specifically to the offices of the monarch and the governor general or lieutenant-governors.

Examples of important executive powers included in the constitution are: choosing and appointing the prime minister (or premiers in the provinces) and other ministers; conducting foreign affairs; making treaties; and declaring war and conferring honours. Indeed, much of Canada's constitution was established by the United Kingdom's executive government, or the Crown, through its prerogatives in "colonial affairs." Those prerogatives included the appointment of governors, as today the appointment of governors general is an exercise by the Queen of her prerogative.

Prior to October 1, 1947, certain prerogative powers (e.g., awarding honours or certain aspects of foreign affairs such as declaring war or ratifying treaties) were reserved to the monarch personally, so that there were two divisions — the Crown in Canada (the governor general) and the Crown in the United Kingdom (the monarch) — acting for Canada on the advice of the Canadian Cabinet.

But, by **Letters Patent** effective October 1, 1947, all of the monarch's prerogative powers were delegated to the governor general.

Similarly, lieutenant-governors formerly had federal responsibilities, such as declining **royal assent** to provincial bills and "reserving" them for the governor general's pleasure where the federal government may "disallow" them. Today these powers — although in force in strict constitutional interpretation — are obsolete in practice, and lieutenant-governors are regarded as exclusively the direct representatives of the monarch in the province (Cheffins and Johnson 1986, 84–85).

**Executive Conventions** Executive, or constitutional, conventions allow the continued existence of the monarch in Canada. In essence, the enormous powers conferred on the monarch by legislation, and those available through prerogative, may be exercised only according to rules or traditions called "conventions." The most important convention is that, ordinarily, a governor general or lieutenant-governor will perform his or her functions only upon the advice and with the consent of the prime minister (or premier) and that he or she is bound to take that advice.

Under certain conditions, a governor general or lieutenant-governor can act on his or her own initiative. These are sometimes called "personal prerogatives" or "reserve powers." They concern the selection, appointment, and possible dismissal of a prime minister or premier. Personal discretion can also be used in a decision to dissolve Parliament, that is, to end a parliamentary term and call an election. These kinds of decisions are made in abnormal times, such as when a First Minister loses his or her majority in the legislature or when there is an institutional breakdown.

**The Judiciary** Further to the executive in Canada, the Constitution Act, 1867, makes reference to "the Judicial Committee of the Privy Council," which is a committee of the executive branch of government of the United Kingdom. This committee, through the exercise of the monarch's prerogative in colonial affairs, came to exercise a judicial role for Canadians as a final court of appeal for court decisions in the British Empire. It heard judicial appeals from Canada until 1949, and up to that time was part of Canada's judicial system.

**Privy Council** Another executive body mentioned in our constitution is the "Queen's Privy Council for Canada," which, under the Constitution Act, 1867, is established to advise the government of Canada. The provincial equivalent is the Executive Council. The expression "governor general–in–council" means the governor general "acting by and with the Advice of the Queen's Privy Council for Canada." The provincial equivalent is the lieutenant-governor acting on the advice of the Executive Council.

Today, these institutions have only a ceremonial usage. Real governing power rests with the prime minister or premiers of the provinces and their cabinets. Members of the Cabinet — the ministers of the government in power — are appointed formally to the Privy Council (federal) or Executive Council (provincial) but operate as a cabinet presided over by the prime minister (or premier), not the governor general (or lieutenant-governor).

### The Constitution and Making Laws

**Legislatures** All of Canada's provinces have unicameral (single-chamber) legislatures. Most provinces call their legislatures "legislative assemblies". Quebec has its Assemblée nationale (National Assembly), and Nova Scotia and Newfoundland use the term "House of Assembly." The constitution requires that, before becoming a law, a provincial bill must pass three readings in the Assembly and receive royal assent from the lieutenant-governor.

The federal legislature, known as Parliament, is bicameral (two chambers). Members of the Lower House, the "House of Commons," are elected. Members of the Upper House, the Senate, are appointed by the governor general on the advice of the prime minister. The constitution authorizes Parliament to make laws concerning matters of general public interest, taxation, and federal services. Most legislation is introduced in the House of Commons. The Senate can also initiate legislation, but the constitution states that any bills concerning taxation or the expenditure of public funds are to originate in the Commons.

The parallels between Canada's Parliament and Great Britain's are readily apparent. The appointed Upper House (Senate), with membership for life, was modelled on the British House of Lords, where members of the peerage can sit for life. Senators appointed up to 1965 hold their positions for life. Those appointed after 1965 must retire at age 75.

Similarly, "House of Commons" is also the British Lower House, even though, in Canada, there is no history of formal class divisions in the population. There is no doubt that, when the 1867 act was written, Loyalist emotions and aspirations solidified the strong affinity between Canada and the United Kingdom.

Under the constitution, Senate seats were allocated according to a broad geographic formula with the goal of protecting regional interests. Four regions (Ontario, Quebec, the three Maritime provinces, and the four Western provinces) each have 24 seats. Of the remainder, 6 seats are allocated to Newfoundland, and 2 seats to the territories, for a total of 104 seats.

Overall, the Senate, while performing some useful functions under its original constitutional mandate, has not achieved its goals, and over the years, there have been increasingly frequent calls to reform the institution. As a parliamentary institution, the Senate, not being directly responsible to the electorate, has accepted by convention a role subordinate to

Overall, the Senate has not achieved its goals, and over the years there
have been increasingly frequent calls to reform or abolish the institution.
*Source:* Andy Donato, *The Toronto Sun*, June 25, 1993. Reproduced with
permission of Andy Donato.

the elected House of Commons, even though
it has largely the same authority under constitutional law. However, on occasion, the Senate will review legislation and thereby delay
for months the passage of government bills
already passed by the House.

### The Constitution and Federalism

At the time of Confederation, it was the
intention of the framers of the constitution to
create a powerful central, or federal, government (Cheffins and Johnson 1986).
This level of government was awarded the
strongest governing powers of the time, as
well as authority over the major revenues
sources in the public sector (see Figure 3.2).
Matters of war, external relations, international trade, customs duties, and the postal
service became the jurisdiction of the federal
government.

A strong central government was seen as one that could regulate trade and commerce, navigation and shipping, penitentiaries, weights and measures, currency and coinage, and banking. The residual powers that were not specifically assigned to the provinces were also given to the federal government. Thus Section 91 of the act allows the federal government "to make Laws for the Peace, Order, and good Government of Canada, in relation to all Matters not coming within the Classes of Subjects by this Act assigned exclusively to the Legislatures of the Provinces." In order to match these responsibilities with an ability to pay for them, unlimited taxation power was given to the federal government.

The provincial governments were allocated powers over matters of more direct

**Figure 3.2 Examples of Federal and Provincial Constitutional Responsibilities**

---

**Federal Government**

The legislative authority of Parliament includes:

- the amendment of the constitution
- the public debt and property
- the regulation of trade and commerce
- unemployment insurance
- the raising of money by any mode or system of taxation
- the borrowing of money on the public credit
- the postal service
- the census and statistics
- militia, military, and naval services, and defence
- the fixing of and providing for the salaries and allowances of civil servants and other officers of the government of Canada
- beacons, buoys, lighthouses, and Sable Island
- navigation and shipping
- quarantine and the establishment and maintenance of marine hospitals
- seacoast and inland fisheries
- ferries between a province and any British or foreign country, or between two provinces
- currency and coinage, banking, incorporation of banks, and the issue of paper money
- savings banks
- weights and measures
- bills of exchange and promissory notes — interest
- legal tender
- bankruptcy and insolvency
- patents of invention and discovery
- copyrights
- Native peoples and lands reserved for them
- naturalization and aliens
- marriage and divorce
- the criminal law except the constitution of courts of criminal jurisdiction but including the procedures in criminal matters
- the establishment, maintenance, and management of penitentiaries
- agriculture and immigration
- old-age pensions

*(continued)*

**Figure 3.2** *(continued)*

---

**Provincial Governments**

The legislature of each province may make laws in relation to the following:

- amendment of the constitution of the province, except as regards the lieutenant-governor
- direct taxation within the province
- borrowing of money on the credit of the province
- establishment and tenure of provincial offices and appointment and payment of provincial officers
- the management and sale of public lands belonging to the province and of the timber and wood thereon
- the establishment, maintenance, and management of hospitals, asylums, charities, and **eleemosynary institutions** in and for the province, other than marine hospitals
- municipal institutions in the province
- shop, saloon, tavern, auctioneer, and other licences issued for the raising of provincial or municipal revenue
- local works and undertakings other than interprovincial or international lines of ships, railways, canals, telegraphs, and so on, or works which, although wholly situated within one province, are declared by the federal Parliament to be for the general advantage either of Canada or of two or more provinces
- the incorporation of companies with provincial goals or objectives
- the solemnization of marriage in the province
- property and civil rights in the province
- the administration of justice in the province, including the constitution, maintenance, and organization of provincial courts, both of civil and of criminal jurisdiction, including procedure in civil matters in these courts
- the imposition of punishment of fine, penalty, or imprisonment in enforcing any law of the province relating to any of the aforesaid subjects
- generally all matters of a merely local or private nature in the province
- education
- agriculture and immigration

---

local importance. Provincial jurisdictions are outlined in sections 92 and 93 of the act. Provinces are responsible for hospitals, universities, licensing for business, the management and sale of public lands, and local works (see Figure 3.2).

As these matters were seen to have less importance at the time of Confederation, the provinces were given less command over sources of revenue than was the federal government. Provincial governments were restricted to the collection of direct taxes, that is, any tax paid directly to the government by the taxpayer. In the 1860s, many of the provincial responsibilities were relatively unimportant, but by the 1990s they are of major importance to all concerned. Health and education now comprise the largest portions of total provincial government spending.

### Dual Citizenship

Canadians hold a dual citizenship of a kind: citizenship in Canada, and citizenship in a particular province. This duality stems from our federal system, in which power is shared by the federal government and the ten provincial governments. Under our constitution, the federal government and the provincial governments can claim sovereignty; each of these governments has authority over the persons and resources within its jurisdiction and that authority cannot be taken away by any other government.

Because two governments have jurisdiction over the same space at the same time, authority is divided between the two along constitutional lines. The provincial governments have authority in matters of education. The federal government has authority to coin money. One's driver's licence comes from the province, and one's social insurance number is provided by the federal government. And, if one lives within a county or parish or a city as well, not to mention school and other special districts, those governing bodies are the creatures of the province and cannot claim autonomy on their own. Their power derives from the province and can be taken away at the will of the province. The constitution creates this conceptual division of authority.

Accordingly, dual citizenship has many important consequences, many of which we take entirely for granted. In most provinces, people must pay provincial sales tax as well as federal income tax and the Goods and Services Tax (GST). And because there are ten separate provincial jurisdictions, whenever citizens move from one province to another, they must get a new driver's licence, learn different traffic regulations, and so on. As well, some provinces have more stringent requirements than others for becoming teachers, doctors, and lawyers.

### Shared Responsibilities

There are areas of responsibility in which the federal and provincial governments have shared authority. Under Section 95 of the Constitution Act, 1867, the provinces are awarded responsibility for agriculture and for immigration. The same section of the act gives the federal government the power to legislate in these areas, and asserts that provincial legislation cannot conflict with that of the federal government concerning these matters. In giving the federal government the wide sweep of authority to make laws for the "peace, order, and good government of Canada," Section 91 of the act made it possible for the federal government to intervene in provincial matters, such as natural resources.

Conflicts arise because areas of jurisdiction awarded to the provinces in 1867 have increased in importance, and some matters awarded to the federal government have decreased in importance.

**The Environment** One controversial area of shared constitutional responsibility is the environment. Constitutional jurisdiction over environmental matters is neither federal nor provincial. Rather, it is both. In recent years, this sharing of responsibility has led to a running legal battle among Ottawa, the provinces, and environmental groups over which government should review projects such as Alberta's Oldman River Dam, Saskatchewan's Rafferty-Alameda project, and Quebec's Great Whale project.

The provinces have argued in the courts that the projects under review are largely and exclusively within their territory. But some environmentalists have argued that Ottawa has authority under the Environment Act over these projects because they involve matters for which the federal government has constitutional responsibility and because the projects have environmental effects beyond provincial borders.

Environmental groups have won a number of Federal Court rulings that the regulations require Ottawa to assess projects affecting the environment that involve areas of federal jurisdiction. In a ruling on the Oldman River Dam, the Supreme Court affirmed federal jurisdiction, especially where a project impinges on matters under federal authority.

### Controversial Divisions of Power

From the beginning of our governing history, the federal system has generated tensions between the provinces and the federal government. The constitutional division of powers between the federal and provincial governments has had an important impact on the ability of Canadians to govern themselves. Almost always, the sharing of responsibilities between federal and provincial governments has been controversial. The provinces believe that, in many areas, they can govern more effectively and efficiently than can the federal government.

The responsibilities outlined in Figure 3.2 sometimes overlap, as in the cases of agriculture, immigration, and old age pensions. Social, technological, economic, and political developments create new problems to be dealt with, including aviation, payment for costly innovative medical services, telecommunications, and energy shortages. Problems have had to be resolved over provincial control of natural resources. Disputes have arisen about how mining tax revenues are to be collected and allocated between the federal and provincial governments.

Broadcasting is another area of concern. The Quebec government, in particular, wants provincial control over broadcasting to ensure consistency between programming and the cultural aspirations of Quebec citizens. The government of Canada refuses to give up control of broadcasting in that province.

The federal government enjoys the most extensive taxing powers. Because the costs of some provincial responsibilities, such as education and health care, exceed their revenue-raising capabilities, the federal government has instituted revenue sharing. Thus, the federal, provincial, and municipal governments share expenses in order to deliver many services in the fields of agriculture, education, health care, and telecommunications. But the priority of fiscal restraint by successive Progressive Conservative governments in the 1980s and early 1990s caused political power and economic responsibility to swing back to the provinces.

The return of the federal Liberals to power in 1993 changed very little in the shifting of many financial responsibilities to the provinces. In fact, the concept of federal–provincial cost sharing has been altered in the 1990s: As the federal government has planned to reduce its spending at all levels, the provinces and the many municipal governments have sustained major cuts. The clear signal from Ottawa is that provincial and municipal governments will have to fend for themselves.

The Fathers of Confederation did not foresee that the federalism they instituted in the constitution would fragment power and, by so doing, generally reduce the ability of the federal government to govern. Despite the specific designations of powers and jurisdictions, the constitution left many questions open, and its language subject to interpretation. Over the years, the politics and structure of the Canadian federal system have changed significantly. Populations have shifted, economic and technological advances have been made, investment patterns have favoured different areas of the country at different times. All of these factors have shaped the current federal system.

## The Constitution Act, 1982

The year 1982 gave rise to the three most significant constitutional events in Canada since Confederation in 1867. First, the residual powers of the British Parliament over the constitutional affairs of Canada were terminated. Second, the entrenchment of a Charter of Rights and Freedoms brought to Canada direct judicial review of both federal and provincial legislation as measured against the charter. Third, Quebec refused to sign the charter and isolated itself legally from the constitutional changes.

### Constitutional Patriation

The British government tried to give up its constitutional responsibilities for Canada and its other "dominions" with the Statute of Westminster in 1931. However, it would take another 51 years for Canada to **patriate** an amendment formula. All federal–provincial conferences during that period ended in failed attempts to agree on a common amending formula or on acceptable redivisions of power between federal and provincial jurisdictions.

The efforts intensified after the 1967 Centennial year during a decade of profound political change in Quebec and other parts of Canada. Major federal–provincial constitutional conferences were organized from 1968 to 1971 (known as the Victoria Round); from 1977 to 1979, following the election of the Parti Québécois government in Quebec; and from 1980 to 1982, following the Quebec referendum on sovereignty association. The result — with Quebec's abstention — was the Constitution Act, 1982, with an amending formula and an appended Charter of Rights and Freedoms.

The events of 1982 brought Canadian constitutional affairs completely and exclusively within the control of Canadian institutions. All remnants of the Imperial legislative capacity in the United Kingdom were formally and finally terminated. Thus, Canada became the sole architect of its constitution.

The impasse over settling on an **amending formula** that had so long prevented patriation was overcome by the determination of the federal government and a key decision of the Supreme Court of Canada. The Supreme Court ruled that provincial consent was not legally required for legislation requesting patriation from the United Kingdom to pass. The decision encouraged the dissenting premiers, except Quebec premier René Lévesque, to reach an accord.

The response from the United Kingdom was the Canada Act, 1982 (U.K.), which set out the Constitution Act, 1982, and renamed all British North America Acts from 1867 on as "Constitution Acts." The Constitution Act, 1982, was proclaimed on April 17, 1982, by the Queen at a public ceremony in Ottawa.

### The Amendment Formulas

One of the most unusual characteristics of Canada's Confederation agreement in 1867 was that it did not include a way to change the constitution. It was as if the original framers thought that the governing system they had created was self-adjusting. And so, for more than 100 years, the issue of amending the constitution was both difficult and restricted for the federal and provincial governments.

From 1867 until 1982, when Pierre Trudeau and nine of ten provincial premiers agreed to patriate it, the Canadian constitution remained an act of the British Parliament called the "British North America Act." This act was amended from time to time at Westminster, as ordinary legislation is, sometimes as a result of federal–provincial agreement, sometimes not. Both levels of government really only had the power to change constitutional strictures regarding electoral boundaries. But the 1867 act did not have an amending formula that would enable the government to settle clashes over the constitutional scope of federal and provincial powers or over the more general demands of Quebec.

Constitutional meetings to address Canada's ability to amend its own constitution began in earnest in the early part of the twentieth century, and continued to the 1990s (see Figure 3.3).

Section 52 of the Constitution Act, 1982, declares the Constitution of Canada to be "the supreme law of Canada," capable of amendment only by the amending formula described in the act. Sections 38–45 establish a formula for amending the constitution. Certain sections of the act can be amended only by the federal Parliament; some can be amended by provincial legislatures through a simple legis-

**Figure 3.3  Constitutional Landmarks**

| | |
|---|---|
| 1867 | • Canada (Quebec, Ontario, Nova Scotia, and New Brunswick) achieves dominion status, but cannot make constitutional amendments. |
| 1927 | • A Dominion–Provincial Conference fails to reach consensus on a proposal vesting Parliament with power to amend its own constitution with majority agreement from the provinces. |
| 1935/36 | • In 1935, delegates at the Dominion–Provincial Conference decide Canada should have amending power, provided federal and provincial governments can agree on an amending formula. In 1936, the Continuing Committee on Constitutional Questions fails to reach agreement on formula proposals, but provides the basis for future debates. |
| 1949 | • At Canada's request, Great Britain grants the Parliament of Canada the authority to amend its own constitution, with certain exceptions. |
| 1950 | • A constitutional conference is suspended after a year of discussion of six amending formulas. The provinces object most to giving Parliament unilateral power to amend federal matters. |
| 1960/61 | • Provincial attorneys general come up with an amending formula. Differences prevail, despite majority acceptance of a formula that stipulates unanimity on entrenched issues (minority rights and language) and agreement by two-thirds of provinces with 50 percent of the country's population. |
| 1971 | • At the Victoria Conference, Quebec rejects the amending formula because it does not give the province veto power. Saskatchewan also rejects the formula. |
| 1981 | • Quebec rejects an amending formula that gives no single province a veto, but allows a veto for Quebec and Ontario together. All provincial premiers except Quebec accept an alternative formula: seven provinces with 50 percent of the population. The constitution is ratified without Quebec's endorsement and repatriated with a Charter of Rights and Freedoms. |
| 1990 | • The Meech Lake Accord stipulates unanimity for all major constitutional changes, a veto for every province, and a distinct Quebec clause. It is scuttled by the Newfoundland and Manitoba legislatures. |
| 1992 | • The Charlottetown Accord offers a Canada Clause, recognition of Quebec's distinct society, aboriginal self-government, an elected Senate and other provisions. It is defeated in a national referendum in 1992. |

lative enactment. But the federal government can do the same regarding matters that concern executive government, the Senate, or the House of Commons.

The stipulated general amending procedure requires a resolution of both the Senate and the House of Commons, together with the concurrence of seven provinces having, in the aggregate, 50 percent of the population. Some matters require unanimity, and others can proceed with the concurrence of fewer provinces or are exclusively within federal or individual provincial jurisdiction. In all, there are six mechanisms through which the constitution can be changed (see Figure 3.4).

Quebec's rejection of the constitutional amendment formulas weakened Canada's constitutional framework. However, Quebec's refusal to sign does not prevent the application of constitutional law in that province. In 1982, the Supreme Court of Canada confirmed in *Re Attorney General of Quebec and Attorney General of Canada* (the Quebec Veto Case) that Quebec's consent was not required to fulfil the substantial degree of provincial consent that is necessary to entrench the Constitution Act, 1982.

## The Charter of Rights and Freedoms

Part I (sections 1–34, inclusive) of the Constitution Act, 1982, comprises the Canadian Charter of Rights and Freedoms. With the inclusion of the charter, the Canadian constitution became more than just a historic document, an antique curiosity. The charter has taken on the status of a political symbol — one that adds greater legitimacy to our system of government. Deep respect for the charter has motived many politicians to abandon party loyalty for principles in the charter when constitutional issues are raised (Bryden, Davis, and Russell 1993).

The inclusion of a charter in the patriation package was initially opposed by most provincial premiers. They saw the charter as a constitutional instrument that had the potential

**Figure 3.4  The Six Amending Mechanisms**

1. Only Parliament's approval is required to change the structure of Parliament.

2. Only a provincial legislature's approval is required for changes to its own structure, such as whether to establish a provincial Upper House.

3. Changes that apply to some but not all provinces can be made by passing resolutions in just those legislatures and the federal Parliament (such as resolutions that affect immigration and culture).

4. Changes to the monarchy, the amending formula itself, the composition of the Supreme Court of Canada, or the status of official languages require the *unanimous* consent of all eleven governments, through resolutions of their respective legislatures.

5. The majority of changes apply the 7/50 rule, which requires resolutions for a change from Parliament and the legislatures of seven provinces representing 50 percent of the national population. Resolutions require three years to pass the required number of legislatures. This section provides that as many as three provinces can *opt out* of the amendments, and that the federal government will provide reasonable compensation to them.

6. Changes that apply the 7/50 rule with *no opting out* by provinces involve resolutions for altering the way provinces are represented in the House of Commons; the selection, powers, and representation of senators; the Supreme Court of Canada (other than its composition); the extension of provincial boundaries into northern territories; and the establishment of new provinces.

to erode provincial rights in that the judicial review of provincial legislation would curtail provincial jurisdictions and sovereignty, especially if the Supreme Court of Canada interpreted the Constitution Act, 1867, according to the ideology of the Fathers of Confederation. Some of them expected the provinces eventually to disappear under the awesome powers and jurisdiction of a strong central government.

The compromise that followed was the inclusion of an "override" legislative power (Section 33) with respect to certain provisions of the charter. Thus, Parliament or any provincial legislature has the ability to negate the charter, and thereby regain its legislative supremacy. Quebec used the power to override to protect its Bill C-178, passed by the Parti Québécois government in 1988 to prohibit the use of English on outdoor commercial signs, and Saskatchewan used it in 1987 to protect a back-to-work law. Many believe that the power to override deprives the citizen of constitutional recourse against encroachment on a right that the constitution guarantees, leaving only a legal recourse. A sunset provision in the override assists in this respect by requiring a renewal of the override after five years.

The Canadian Charter of Rights and Freedoms must not be confused with the Canadian Bill of Rights, although they both exist and overlap in content (Tarnopolsky 1975). Distinguishing between these instruments is essential. The Bill of Rights was enacted in 1960, and is merely a federal statute. It is subject to repeal at any time by ordinary federal legislation. To bind the provinces, enactment as a constitutional amendment would have been required. The federal government, therefore, chose to proceed solely within its own jurisdiction to enact the charter.

With the charter now in place, the Bill of Rights is still sometimes used in courts to argue for broader protections for individuals than those found in the charter. One important example is the "due process" protections for those facing criminal charges.

### Rights and Freedoms

The charter entrenches in the constitution human rights that cover a wide spectrum but are by no means all-inclusive. *Fundamental freedoms* include conscience, religion, thought, belief, opinion, and expression; the press and other media of communication; and peaceful assembly and association. *Democratic rights* relate to elections, electoral laws, the vote, and holding membership in elected institutions of state. *Mobility rights* include rights of citizens to enter, remain in, and leave Canada, and to reside and pursue a livelihood in any province. *Legal rights* include numerous and detailed protections in the context of arrest, search, seizure, and other matters of criminal and penal procedures; Section 7 gives everyone the right to life, liberty, and the security of the person, and the right not to be deprived of these rights according to the principles of justice. *Equality rights*, as outlined in Section 15, proclaim the equal status of individuals under the law without discrimination on the basis of race, national or ethnic origin, colour, religion, sex, age, or mental or physical disability.

Section 1 of the charter holds that rights are not absolute and must be balanced against the rights and freedoms of other people. Section 24 authorizes the courts to act as the agents that remedy violations. The success or failure of the charter rests with the judiciary, particularly with the judges of the Supreme Court of Canada. And Section 32 stipulates that the charter applies to Parliament and the government of Canada, and likewise to provincial legislatures.

The power of *judicial review* has been substantially enhanced under the charter, and can involve comprehensive interpretation of the charter itself. The constitutional status of the charter has enabled the courts to review the decisions of the federal Cabinet and provincial cabinets. The scope of such review is not limited merely to matters deriving directly from statutes, but also includes matters dealt with by the executive under the royal prerogative powers. Even charter questions flowing from general public policies, including foreign policy, may be reviewed by the courts.

The charter has two especially significant effects on public policy: It makes some kinds of policy more likely than others, and it creates politics. The charter makes some kinds of public policy more popular and, therefore, more likely to occur than other kinds. Because of its emphasis on the rights of individuals, the charter encourages the adoption of public policies that protect individual rights and freedoms.

### The Meech Lake Accord, 1987

The unanimous accord reached at Meech Lake, Quebec, by all First Ministers (the prime minister and all provincial premiers) was concluded after only one day of negotiations. It was the culmination of an attempt on the part of most governments in Canada since 1982 to include Quebec as a full participant in Canada's constitution. The mission of the Meech Lake Accord was to make such accommodations, including constitutional amendments, that would allow Quebec to give its positive and unreserved political commitment to the Constitution of Canada.

The accord was ratified in Ottawa by all First Ministers on June 3, 1987. Its terms are contained in a bill that would have been enacted as the Constitution Act, 1987. It failed to be ratified by resolutions of the legislatures of all provinces. The important provisions of the accord were:

1. *The Distinctiveness of Quebec*: The Constitution of Canada would recognize that, within Canada, Quebec is a distinct society and that, demographically, French-speaking Canadians are present through-

out Canada but are centred in Quebec, and that English-speaking Canadians are present in Quebec but are concentrated outside that province. The federal Parliament and the provincial legislatures are declared to have a role in preserving these characteristics. The interpretation of the declaration of the "distinctiveness" of Quebec is entirely open and would not be apparent until interpreted by the courts.

2. *The Amendment Formula*: Agreement to meet Quebec's demand for a direct veto power in the constitutional amending formula is achieved by accepting unanimity as the criterion for amendment. Certain amendments require the 7/50 formula — a resolution of Parliament with the support of seven provinces that have 50 percent of the population of all provinces. The formulas for amendments concerning fewer, or particular, provinces, or exclusively federal matters, remain. This change was of particular concern to the Yukon and the Northwest territories, which are evolving toward provincial status. The unanimity requirement in the Meech Lake Accord would have made agreement on such status much more difficult.

3. *The Entrenchment of the Supreme Court of Canada and the Procedures for Appointment of Judges to the Court*: When it was first instituted in 1875, the Supreme Court of Canada was the product of ordinary federal legislation. The Meech Lake Accord entrenched the Court and the appointment procedures for its judges within the constitution, thus protecting this government institution from legislative abolition.

4. *Senate Reform*: The First Ministers responded to demands from the Western provinces that the role and functions of the Senate be modernized, and the method of selecting senators and deter-

mining their representation in the Senate be reformed. Ottawa agreed to select senators from lists of nominees prepared by the provinces. All provinces had a veto on any future changes to the Senate. These contentious reforms required unanimity. Commitment was made to a constitutional conference on Senate reform within one year of the ratification of the accord.

Beyond these specific legal issues, the proposed amendment would have significantly altered the economic relationship between the federal and provincial governments. It would have required the federal government to provide "reasonable compensation" to a province that decides to establish a provincial social program in an area of exclusive provincial jurisdiction rather than to participate in national "shared cost" programs so long as the provincial program is compatible with the federal objectives. This provision had the potential of further decentralizing Canadian federalism by enhancing the capacity of the provinces to establish their own standards as a balance to the development of "national standards."

The Meech Lake Accord required ratification by provincial legislatures by June 1990. The province of Newfoundland initially approved, but then rejected the accord by a narrow margin. In Manitoba, the image of MLA Elijah Harper — former chief of the Cree Red Sucker Lake Band — holding his ceremonial eagle feather stonewalled the vote and prevented the legislature from ratifying the accord before the June 23 deadline. By so doing, he brought aboriginal issues and rights back to the top of any future constitutional agenda.

When the Meech Lake Accord failed to be ratified, a number of nationalist forces in Quebec developed much more radical proposals for constitutional change. The Quebec Liberal party's *Allaire Report* sought massive decentralization of powers to Quebec, demanding exclusive control over 22 jurisdictions and recommending that the federal

government act as a kind of clearing house for the provinces. The Bélanger–Campeau Commission made demands for major transfers of federal powers to Quebec and recommended a referendum to decide between outright sovereignty and a renewed federalism that would respect Quebec's rights to substantial new powers.

Ottawa countered with the Citizens' Forum on Canada's Future (the Spicer Commission), which reported to Parliament and led to federal proposals for constitutional change. The so-called Canada Round of proposals greatly broadened the agenda again, adding the Senate, economic union, and aboriginal rights to Quebec's preoccupation with the division of powers and provincial autonomy. Subsequently, in the course of the public debate, a "social charter" would be added to the list of concerns for the next constitutional agenda. Parliament struck a Special Joint Committee on a Renewed Canada (the Beaudoin–Dobbie Committee) which moved the debate along with its reaction to the federal package. The report kept most of the broader federal agenda alive, including Senate reform, economic union, aboriginal rights, Quebec's distinctiveness, the division of powers, and a social charter.

## The Charlottetown Accord

By 1992, another accord was reached at the Charlottetown Constitutional Conference. In this constitutional agreement, the prime minister, ten provincial premiers, leaders of the territories, and the Chief of the Assembly of First Nations developed a consensus report on the constitution.

This report was the culmination of a long process of constitutional negotiations, which included political representatives from the federal, provincial, and territorial governments, as well as numerous royal commissions, and public meetings held over a two-year period (Monahan and McRoberts 1993). The document produced an agreement to bring

Quebec into the constitutional family, to include a Canada Clause in the constitution, to amend Canada's constitution, to reform the Senate and modify the House of Commons, to entrench the Supreme Court, and to open the way for aboriginal peoples to exercise self-government.

The most important provisions of the consensus report were:

1. *Canada Clause*: The accord would have added a new clause to Section 2 of the Constitution Act, 1867, that would express fundamental Canadian values. The clause would guide the course in the future interpretations of the constitution. Specific references in the clause would identify Canada's parliamentary democracy and federalism. Special mention would be given to aboriginal peoples and related rights and responsibilities. The clause would recognize Quebec's distinctiveness, and describe the linguistic duality of the province and the country. The Canada Clause would also focus on equality of race, ethnicity, and gender. The clause also acknowledges the equality of provinces, while recognizing their diverse characteristics.

2. *Recognition of Quebec's Distinctiveness*: The accord recognized the assertion that the distinctive character of Quebec's society has existed for more than 200 years — since 1774 when the Quebec Act renamed the colony "Quebec" and preserved its religion, language, seigneurial system, and the civil legal code. Under the accord reached at Charlottetown, Quebec's distinctive character was recognized, including the French-speaking majority in the province, the unique culture within Quebec's society, and the civil-law tradition affecting its legal and judicial system.

3. *The Charter of Rights and Freedoms*: The accord would have strengthened some sections of the charter to ensure aboriginal rights and protect the languages, cultures, traditions, and treaties of aboriginal peoples. The constitution would be amended to recognize aboriginal peoples' inherent right to self-government.

4. *Social and Economic Union*: A new provision would have been added to the constitution describing the commitment of governments and legislatures within Canada's federal system to the principle of preserving and developing Canada's social and economic union. Such policies as universal health care, the network of social services and benefits, education, collective bargaining, and environmental integrity would have been entrenched in the constitution.

5. *An Elected Senate*: The constitution would be amended to directly elect senators for five-year terms by means of proportional representation instead of the plurality system used in the House of Commons.

6. *House of Commons Reform*: Reforms would encourage aboriginal representation and facilitate the interaction of the Senate with the House of Commons.

7. *Other Provisions*: Exclusive provincial jurisdiction would be ensured and clarified in the areas of culture, forestry, and mining, but the federal government, through intergovernmental agreements, would be permitted to participate in the operation of these jurisdictions.

In order to build a national consensus for the consensus report, the federal government decided to hold a referendum. For the first time in their history, Canadians were asked to give their approval to a sweeping set of constitutional proposals in a national referendum. The referendum was held in October 1992 and attracted a large voter turnout. The result was that 54 percent of Canada's voters rejected the accord. Only Newfoundland, Prince Edward Island, New Brunswick, and the Northwest Territories chose the "Yes" side of the referendum question by significant margins.

## CONCLUSION

Some of the factors most relevant to how Canadians govern themselves today were determined more than 100 years ago. Canada's governability is given a special caste by the kind of constitution we have, as well as by the social values proclaimed by Canadians.

In reality, the constitution is the primary source of our governability because it determines the government's right to use its authority over us. It enables us to legislate our own laws, to make binding judicial decisions on the ways we behave, and ultimately to carry out all that is necessary for us to survive as a people.

As it has evolved in Canada, the constitution is not a neutral document: It is biased as to where governing powers are lodged, which levels of government can exercise those powers, and ultimately how extensive those powers are. This means that the constitution has a number of significant effects on how we govern such a large country, government institutions, and their public policies and the ways they are made.

Canadian politics and government have been shaped indelibly by the development of the Canadian constitution, however incomplete or imperfect it may be. How do the documents written in the last century fit Canada's needs on the eve of the twenty-first century? Can a set of constitutional documents and conventions conceived by a small circle of men whose fastest mode of travel was horseback or bicycle continue to serve masses of diverse people, some of whom have travelled by spaceship? This is worth pondering in view of the fact that most constitutions do well to survive several decades, much less more than a century. Though by no means the first constitution of a modern independent nation-state, Canada's is one of the oldest original charters in the international community. But, although our constitution has

been responsive enough to have survived, is it responsive enough to allow Canadians to maintain the second-largest governing system in the world?

Intended to construct a government that was representative of the masses of people to a limited extent, the constitution established a constitutional monarchy, which allowed people to elect some representatives who would make their laws. This gave the people more to say in government than those in many other states enjoyed at the time.

But, in reality, the Canadian constitution was originally intended to construct a government that was unresponsive to the masses of the people to a large extent. According to nineteenth-century thinking, government was expected to filter public passions and control our selfish needs. Consequently, the Fathers of Confederation tried to limit public participation in government, allowing people to vote only for members of the House of Commons, not for members of the Senate, or for the governor general and lieutenant-governors.

Since Confederation, changes in the constitution, whether by amendment, as with the inclusion of the charter, or by judicial interpretation, have expanded opportunities for the participation of Canadians in their government. But the changes have done little to modify the original structure of the federal system, which still remains the primary legacy of the Fathers of Confederation. The federal structure has never been deemed satisfactory by Quebec or by many of the provinces in Western and Atlantic Canada.

The Fathers of Confederation were unsure of how to appease Quebec's and other provinces' demands. They thought federalism would eventually resolve these kinds of problems. Accordingly, they left the exact details of the federal–provincial relationship vague, because they could not agree on specifics or foresee the gradual decentralization of Canadian government in the later part of the twentieth century.

The basic thrust of the constitution was to give the federal government as much power as necessary to build and unite a country whose government would one day extend from sea to sea. The Fathers of Confederation believed that the central government of the United States was too weak, and that this weakness had led to a civil war in which millions were killed and the new American state was almost destroyed.

To the makers of Canada's constitution in the 1860s, the "peace, order and good government of Canada" meant the preservation of public order, which was considered one of the most important functions of government. The constitution made it possible, in cases of national emergencies, for the federal government to take on whatever powers were necessary to reach a solution.

Today, with a population approaching 30 million, the demands on all Canadian governments are much more complex than just the preservation of Canadian society. Throughout the twentieth century, the Canadian public has supported the expansion of government beyond merely protecting us to regulating and taking care of us in such areas as business conduct, health care, education, social services, income maintenance, energy, and the environment.

One reality affecting Canada's governability is that the constitution is extremely difficult to change. Short of a dramatic crisis, it is unlikely that any new framework of government could be agreed to in today's fragmented political world, although many attempts have been made. The pioneering 1867 document vested the British Parliament with the power to amend the constitution. And, until 1982, Britain's Parliament held the exclusive power to amend the constitu-

tion. This became a source of embarrassment as Canada earned its independent status in the international community.

The economic and political crises of the twentieth century greatly strained Canada's constitutional structure. By the 1970s, the constitution was respected for its endurance, but also perceived as deeply flawed. It marked a giant step forward for the creation of a massive country in its own time, but it also left many basic questions of government unanswered, and had incorporated some blatantly undemocratic features.

The realities of twentieth-century life had enlarged Canadian conceptions of rights and freedoms. Recognizing that government inevitably plays an active part in modern life, Canadians became concerned about the proper limits of government control, especially with respect to their rights and freedoms.

At best Canada's constitution moves inefficiently, incrementally, and, in the case of Quebec, hesitantly. At worst, it moves barely at all, having legitimized a system of government that is slow to respond to change.

For those whose hope for change centres on the constitution, it must be emphasized that the constitutional-amendment route in Canada is sluggish and painful. For all of its shortcomings, our constitution has established a working system of parliamentary government with the provision of basic rights to citizens and others that places limitations and obligations on the powers of our many governments. To ensure that government is truly constitutional, a constitution must offer some kind of framework that consists of a few principles that cannot be manipulated easily by people in power merely for their convenience. This is the essence of our constitutionalism — principles that are above the reach of everyday legislators, political and ceremonial executives, and politicians, but are not beyond the reach of ordinary people who need their governments to survive.

## GLOSSARY

**amending formula**  The means by which formal changes are made in the language and substance of a constitution.

**bill of rights**  A legislated or constitutional document or set of documents that guarantee fundamental human freedoms, such as the freedoms of assembly, religion, and speech, and specifies basic human rights, such as those of persons accused of crimes.

**common law**  Those unique legal practices that are traced back to King Henry II (1154–1189), who trained representatives called *justices* to administer law, supervise local officials, and gather and administer a body of precedent so as to standardize the administration of justice in all parts of the country and make it "common" to the whole kingdom.

**Commonwealth**  A voluntary association of independent states in Europe, Africa, Asia, the Western hemisphere, and Oceania that were once parts of the British Empire.

**constitution**  A fundamental body of law that prescribes the framework of government and the nature and extent of government authority.

**constitutional law**  Fundamental law that, by convention, tradition, or written documentation, prescribes the framework of government and the nature and extent of governmental authority, and cannot be changed except by formal procedures.

**eleemosynary institution**  An organization created for charitable and benevolent purposes.

**entrenched**  Of a convention or law formally within the protection of the constitution and accordingly subject to change only by formal constitutional amendment and not by ordinary legislation.

**Imperial**  Having to do with the monarch, his or her representatives and administra-tors, and all of the prerogatives of power that are respected and applied in the colonies and independent governments associated formally with the Crown.

**judicial review**  The power of a court, in the course of litigation, to declare the actions of government and the conduct of public officials unconstitutional.

**Letters Patent**  Any official document that is sealed with the Great Seal, by which a person or company enjoys certain privileges. The Letters Patent of 1947 outline the office of the governor general.

**Loyalists**  American colonists of varied ethnic backgrounds who supported the British cause during the American Revolution, many of whom emigrated to Canada in the late eighteenth century.

**order-in-council**  A law issued through the governor general or a lieutenant-governor on the advice of the Cabinet.

**patriate**  To bring home the constitution so that full governing responsibility would be Canada's and no longer that of the British government.

**political succession**  All the ways used by a society to change its political and governmental leaders.

**residual powers**  With respect to the federal Parliament, the powers conferred by Section 91 of the Constitution Act, 1867, to make laws for the "peace, order and good government of Canada," embracing all residuary powers and jurisdictions not specifically assigned to the provincial legislatures.

**royal assent**  The monarchical approval of a bill, public or private, that has passed the readings and committees of both the Senate and the House of Commons.

***ultra vires***  Literally "beyond the powers," describing a statute that is juridically outside of the powers conferred by the constitution.

**unwritten constitution** A constitution that consists primarily of custom, convention, or statute but is not written down as a comprehensive document or set of documents.

**written constitution** The fundamental law as it appears in one or more written documents.

## RECOMMENDED READING

Cairns, Alan. 1992. *Charter versus Federalism: The Dilemmas of Constitutional Reform*. Montreal and Kingston: McGill-Queen's University Press. This book discusses the controversial debates stemming from the effect of the charter on a federal governing system.

Conklin, William. 1993. *Images of a Constitution*. Toronto: University of Toronto Press. This book takes a look at the constitution, using a wide range of judicial decisions as examples. Conklin analyzes Canada's constitutional documents from the perspective of political theory.

Conway, John. 1992. *Debts to Pay*. Toronto: James Lorimer. This book analyzes the power relations, past and present, between English Canada and Quebec. It also explores the traditional divisions of power in order to understand Quebec's grievances.

Foley, Michael. 1990. *The Silence of Constitutions: An Essay in Constitutional Interpretation*. New York: Routledge. This book examines the different ways constitutions develop conventions and unwritten characteristics that are binding under constitutional law.

Gagnon, Alain. 1993. *Quebec: State and Society*, 2d ed. Scarborough, Ont.: Nelson Canada. This collection of original articles serves as an introduction to Quebec politics and history, with a special focus on the Canadian constitution and Quebec's demands within the Canadian federation.

Heard, Andrew. 1991. *Canadian Constitutional Conventions*. Don Mills, Ont.: Oxford University Press. This book is a detailed study of Canada's constitutional conventions in all their complexity and how they affect the governability of the political system under constitutional law.

Knopff, Rainer, and F.L. Morton. 1992. *Charter Politics*. Scarborough, Ont.: Nelson Canada. This book provides a comprehensive examination of the Charter of Rights and Freedoms for beginning students, and features case studies of charter challenges, covering a wide spectrum of legal and philosophical issues.

Milne, David. 1991. *The Canadian Constitution*. Toronto: James Lorimer. This book is an excellent primer on the Canadian constitution, revised over the years to present a readable account of the development of Canadian constitutional law.

Russell, Peter. 1993. *Constitutional Odyssey*. Toronto: University of Toronto Press. This new edition covers the whole story of Canada's constitutional history, from Confederation to the present, and argues that the time has come for Canadians to act as a single sovereign people.

Yates, Richard, and Ruth Yates. 1993. *Canada's Legal Environment*. (Don Mills, Ont.: Prentice-Hall. This book focusses on Canada's constitution and government, the history and sources of Canadian law, and the role of the courts. Sufficient information is provided about the major aspects of constitutional law so that students can appreciate the impact that it has on all aspects of social life.

P A R T

# 2

# THE
# POLITICAL
# STRUCTURE
# OF CANADA

CHAPTER

# CANADIAN PARLIAMENT

Camera one focusses in on the prime minister; camera two is readied on the Speaker. In all, seven remote-controlled cameras prepare to zoom in and focus on the action in the House of Commons. It is 2:00 P.M., and about fifteen minutes before airtime. The TV control room hums with activity. A technician prepares to flash the names of MPs, their ridings, and parties, in both official languages, across the bottom of the screen when members rise to address the Speaker. From the microphone console, perched high in the galleries across from the Speaker, a technician must quickly identify the MP who is recognized by the Speaker and activate the correct microphone. Yet another technician makes sure that all seven cameras are in sync. The crew uses joysticks to pan, zoom, and prepare to focus on the action. Then, as 2:15 P.M. approaches, the TV signal is enhanced at the centre of the House of Commons to stand-by for air. The Hansard tapes are ready to roll. Five, four, three, two, one . . . ON THE AIR!

Daily Question Period has begun. The leader of the opposition rises and demands to know what the prime minister intends to do about unemployment. The prime minister delivers a lengthy defence of the government's policy on the question. Supplementary questions from opposition members come fast and furious on the issues before the House.

Question Period is when heated debate among elected members is likely to take place in Parliament. Opposition members relentlessly confront the government on the issues before the country. And, as the cameras zoom in on democracy, Canadians can judge the performance of their representatives.

The House of Commons Broadcasting Service addresses two audiences in the country. First, all Canadians can, if they choose, watch daily House proceedings and select committee meetings through the distribution network. But the people who work in the House of Commons — members, their staff, and House officials — make up another important audience. The proceedings can be studied, and speeches can be analyzed and used to criticize government and statements made by opposition members.

When television was introduced in the House of Commons in 1977, some people feared that it would disrupt debate and lead to political theatrics just for the cameras. There were dire predictions that publicity-seeking members would engage in ham-acting and long-winded oratory. Some of that has occurred, but not as much as predicted. Nevertheless, the opportunity to posture for political audiences at home has affected the attendance of members and the various ways they deliver their speeches in the House. Even their choice of clothing has been influenced by the critical eye of the camera. Not every member of the public has been impressed by the House in action on TV. For some viewers, the spectacle of debate speaks volumes about the strengths and weaknesses of members of Parliament and about how we make laws in Canada. For others, televised broadcasts are a source of information about how our laws are devised, debated, and passed.

Parliament is a difficult institution for the electronic media to cover. A great deal of parliamentary work takes place over long periods of time in meetings of committees and subcommittees. Such slow, undramatic meetings do not always meet the media's criteria for what is newsworthy. National news reporters tend to focus their attention on the most notorious leaders. Accordingly, when it comes to policy development, television often overlooks some of the most significant aspects of lawmaking.

It is not always easy for Parliament to have its work reported through the televised media. But the instantaneous access television gives the public to parliamentary affairs through the House of Commons Broadcasting Service is essential to keep Canadians informed about their system of government. Zooming in on democracy via television cameras permits Canadians to scrutinize government on a regular basis.

## INTRODUCTION

By the 1860s, the Canadian colonies had gained extensive parliamentary experience with their own legislative assemblies. And they liked what they had. At the time of Confederation, the parliamentary system of government had been operating in eastern and central Canada since the 1840s. Each province in Canada had a legislature, with a lieutenant-governor representing the Queen, and every province except Ontario had an appointed Upper House, called a legislative council or Senate, and an elected Lower House, called a legislative assembly (Assemblée nationale in Quebec).

By creating a federal Parliament, the Fathers of Confederation continued a system of government with which they were familiar, a system that had worked well in England for more than 700 years and in the years immediately preceding the federation of Canada.

Parliament essentially plays two different roles. One is to make laws — the general rules that govern Canadian society — to deal with all the major issues confronting Canada — the economy, the budget deficit and national debt, the tax structure, protection of the environment, and any other problem that has national importance. The other role is to act as a local representative, articulating the viewpoints of various interests in Canadian society and securing tangible benefits for each riding. These two roles often clash and, when they do, the latter seems to suffer the most consequences. Strong party discipline some-

The Parliament Buildings, Ottawa, Ontario, Canada. *Source:* Hans Blohm/Masterfile.

times keeps each elected member of Parliament at odds with local interests. The powerful position of the Cabinet often discounts the ability of MPs to represent their constituents in Parliament.

Canadians, including those who are elected and appointed to serve as parliamentarians, expect Parliament not only to discuss openly the problems of the country but also to advance solutions. Most of the controversy over how well or how badly Parliament performs focusses on its lawmaking function. Members of Parliament, like citizens on the outside, are worried about the ability of Parliament to govern. Many of them are frustrated about the growing difficulty Parliament has in dealing with tough national issues, particularly economic issues, such as controlling the deficit and national debt, and moral issues, such as abortion. Just how does party discipline affect the ability of Parliament to govern?

Parliament is an institution that has called forth extreme assessments. Some heap it with criticism; others regard its performance in making public policy quite remarkable.

Some careful observers are dismayed that Parliament cannot govern effectively. Other equally thoughtful observers believe the critics exaggerate the weaknesses of Parliament and overlook its strengths.

## THE BASICS OF CANADA'S PARLIAMENT

The Parliament of Canada has three components: the Queen, who is the head of state (represented by the governor general when she is not in Canada), the House of Commons, and the Senate. Ultimately, Parliament matters in Canadian government because it is the national lawmaking body. Political parties, individual MPs, and interest groups can all try to influence Parliament, but unless Parliament supports a **bill**, it will remain an idea and does not become law. The legislative process in Parliament is an obstacle course for any government or private member who wants a particular bill to become law.

Parliamentary–Cabinet government is based on the fusion of powers of the executive and legislative branches of government (Atkinson 1990, 336–58). According to this fundamental parliamentary principle, the prime minister and every other minister must, by custom and convention, be a member of one House or the other, or get a seat in one House or the other within a short time of appointment. All government bills must be introduced by a minister or someone speaking on his or her behalf, and ministers must appear in Parliament to defend government bills and answer daily questions on government actions and policies.

The governor general and each provincial lieutenant-governor govern through a **Cabinet**, headed by a prime minister or premier. If a federal or provincial election gives a party opposed to the Cabinet in office a clear majority (more than half the seats) in the House of Commons or the provincial assembly, the Cabinet resigns and the governor general or lieutenant-governor calls on the leader of the victorious party to become prime minister and form a Cabinet. The prime minister chooses the other ministers, who are then formally appointed by the governor general or, in the provinces, by the lieutenant-governor.

If no party gets a clear majority, the Cabinet that was in office before and during the election has two options: It can resign, in which case the governor general or lieutenant-governor will call on the leader of the largest opposition party to form a Cabinet, or it can choose to stay in office and meet the newly elected House, which, however, it must do promptly. In either case, the MPs in the newly elected House will decide whether the newly elected minority government shall stay in office or be defeated in short order.

If a Cabinet is defeated in the House of Commons on a motion of censure, or **want of confidence**, the Cabinet must either resign, whereupon the governor general will then ask the **leader of the opposition** to form a new Cabinet, or ask for a **dissolution of Parliament** and a new election.

In very exceptional circumstances, the governor general can refuse a request for a new election. For example, if an election gives no party a clear majority, and the prime minister asks for a new election without even allowing the new Parliament to meet, the governor general would have to say no. However, the Parliament must meet to see if it can transact public business. If a minority Cabinet is defeated on a motion of want of confidence very early in the first session of a new Parliament, and there is a reasonable possibility that another party can form a government and get the support of the House of Commons, then the governor general can refuse a request for a new election. The same principle applies to provincial legislatures.

No elected person in Canada above the rank of mayor has a term in government office; all such offices are subject only to the limits of parliamentary tenure, which is five years. Thus, MPs and MLAs (MNAs in Quebec) are elected for not more than five years. But the prime minister or premier can usually call an election at any reasonable time within five years. Thus, in effect, the Cabinet has no term.

## CANADA'S EXECUTIVE INSTITUTIONS

### The Sovereign

A very long tradition of sovereign reign over aboriginal and Canadian territory exists in the history of North America. Since the fifteenth century, 32 British and French kings and queens have reigned over Canada (see

**Table 4.1 Sovereigns Reigning Over Canadian Territory, 1485–1993**

| Great Britain | |
| --- | --- |
| 1485–1509 | Henry VII |
| 1509–1547 | Henry VIII |
| 1547–1553 | Edward VI |
| 1553–1558 | Mary I |
| 1558–1603 | Elizabeth I |
| 1603–1625 | James I |
| 1625–1649 | Charles I |
| 1649–1660 | (Republic) |
| 1660–1685 | Charles II |
| 1685–1688 | James II |
| 1689–1702 | William III |
| 1689–1694 | and Mary II |
| 1702–1714 | Anne |
| 1714–1727 | George I |
| 1727–1760 | George II |
| 1760–1820 | George III |
| 1820–1830 | George IV |
| 1830–1837 | William IV |
| 1837–1901 | Victoria |
| 1901–1910 | Edward VII |
| 1910–1936 | George V |
| 1936 | Edward VIII |
| 1936–1952 | George VI |
| 1952– | Elizabeth II |

| France | |
| --- | --- |
| (1515)–1547 | François I |
| 1547–1559 | Henri II |
| 1559–1560 | François II |
| 1560–1574 | Charles IX |
| 1574–1589 | Henri III |
| 1589–1610 | Henri IV |
| 1610–1643 | Louis XIII |
| 1643–1715 | Louis XIV |
| 1715–1775 | Louis XV |

Table 4.1.) Over the centuries, monarchical institutions became permanently associated with Parliament. In the course of these times and events, monarchs gradually lost power to the **Crown** (the organization, machinery, and

public administration of the state), and eventually the Crown lost most of its powers to Parliament. By the time of Confederation in the 1860s, the Fathers of Confederation vested these monarchical traditions and sovereign responsibilities in Canada's parliamentary system of government.

Notwithstanding this powerful historical legacy, most Canadians do not think of the British monarch and her representative — the governor general — as components of Parliament. However, in constitutional law, the sovereign is as much a constituent of Parliament as are the House of Commons and the Senate.

Canada's formal **head of state** is the British monarch or the sovereign who reigns by hereditary right. This person serves as a symbol of national sovereignty for Canadians. The executive authority vested in the sovereign flows not only from the constitution, but also within many statutes passed from the time of Queen Victoria that outline the responsibilities of the sovereign and his or her heirs and successors. Because the sovereign symbolizes the majesty of the Canadian nation-state, all judicial functions are exercised in the name of the monarch.

In effect, the role of the monarch in Canada is to reign but not to govern. The political functions of government are now exercised by political ministers, who are collectively and individually responsible to Parliament, but the monarch still participates in a formal way in some executive and legislative acts. Every royal act having legal governmental effect must be performed on the advice of ministers. The ministers are responsible to the House of Commons, whose members are in turn responsible to the voters. Thus, the monarch has no political powers that she or he can exercise alone.

Because Canada is a constitutional monarchy, the sovereign is in the position of holding extensive formal powers but rarely having to use them. For example, under the constitution, the sovereign chooses the advisers to the Crown, that is, the prime minister and the Cabinet. In fact, in Canada, the legal right of politicians to govern on behalf of the state is delegated to them by the sovereign.

In part because of the desire to remain distinct from the powerful republic to the south, Canadians have little enthusiasm for the idea of an elected president as head of state. Experience has taught the value of a non-partisan head of state, a dignified individual who symbolizes the rule of law, the unity of the nation-state, and the supremacy of the state over the government of the day.

Canada's sovereign is also the head of the Commonwealth of Nations, an international association of 60 member-states from every part of the world community. The Canadian sovereign is a member of a multilingual international partnership of states that share their relationship in the former British Empire. In this regard, the monarch is a symbol of both national and Imperial unity.

## The Governor General

The office of governor general is the oldest continuous institution in Canada, representing Canada's evolution from colony to an independent state within the Commonwealth. The office can be traced to 1627, when the French explorer Samuel de Champlain was appointed the first Governor of New France — that part of North America then ruled by France.

On July 1, 1867, Viscount Monck, who had been governor general of British North America since 1861, became the first governor general of the newly created Dominion of Canada. He was followed by sixteen British governors general — a tradition that was maintained until 1952. In that year, a new tradition was born, that of appointing Canadian governors general, and Vincent Massey was the first to be appointed to that office. In 1959, Georges Vanier was named governor general, beginning the custom of alternating

English-speaking and French-speaking Canadians in the office.

The governor general has two official residences, Rideau Hall in Ottawa, and La Citadelle in Quebec City. When members of the Royal Family visit Canada, they stay at these residences. It is also possible for the governor general to host international conferences, such as the so-called Quebec Conferences of 1943 and 1944, where strategies for ending the Second World War were worked out.

### Roles of the Governor General

Canada is a constitutional monarchy; under the terms of the constitution, Her Majesty Queen Elizabeth II is the head of state (McWhinney 1957). In 1947, under the Letters Patent issued by George VI, all of the sovereign powers and authorities in Canada were delegated to the governor general, the monarch's representative in Canada. Thus, he or she is appointed by the monarch on the advice of the prime minister and, on taking office, is accorded the title "Right Honourable" for life. Both the governor general and his or her spouse are accorded the titles "His Excellency" and "Her Excellency" for the period during which the governor general is in office.

The office of governor general encompasses a number of government responsibilities, both constitutional and ceremonial in nature (Mallory 1984, 40–45). They are functions that flow from the governor general's role in representing the Crown, symbolizing Canadian sovereignty, and officiating on behalf of all Canadians at special ceremonies.

**Representing the Crown** As representative of the Crown, the governor general ensures that Canada always has a prime minister. Making sure that a political executive is in place means that there is always a government in Canada. As a result, the Crown has the right to be consulted and informed by the prime minister, as well as the rights to advise, to encourage, and to warn.

The governor general gives **royal assent** to bills passed by the House of Commons and the Senate, which establishes them as law. He or she can summon Parliament, end its sessions, and dissolve it before an election. The governor general also delivers the **Speech from the Throne** at the opening of a session, outlining the government's legislative plans. He or she signs state documents, such as orders-in-council, commissions, pardons, and diplomatic letters of credence.

The governor general presides over the swearing-in of the prime minister, the Chief Justice of the Supreme Court, Cabinet ministers, and other members of the Privy Council. He or she also receives the monarch and other members of the Royal Family.

**Representing Canadian Sovereignty** In parliamentary democracies like Canada, the jobs of head of state and head of government are done by different people. The governor general represents the monarch as head of state of Canada on visits abroad. Accordingly, as head of state, the governor general is the ceremonial leader and the symbol of the majesty and legitimacy of the Canadian state, leaving political leadership to the prime minister. In this capacity, the governor general receives visiting heads of state and foreign dignitaries, and receives accreditation papers from diplomatic representatives of other governments. These ceremonial activities give the governor general an aura of importance in the Canadian political system and abroad.

Because the ceremonial executive of Canada's government evolved from powerful militaristic English monarchies in previous centuries, the constitution made the governor general commander-in-chief of the Canadian Armed Forces. When the British North America Act was written, Canada did not have — nor did anyone expect it to have — a large standing, or permanent, army. Today, the

Canadian Armed Forces is the responsibility of a minister of defence who, with Cabinet approval, directs the military in matters of external security and peacekeeping.

The governor general issues Letters of Credence to Canadian ambassadors (and Letters of Commission to Commonwealth high commissioners) and receives diplomatic credentials from representatives of other governments. These important diplomatic documents are signed by the governor general in the name of the monarch.

**Officiating** Canada's governor general actively participates in .events across the country, ranging from international conferences to civic receptions, where he or she gives speeches and interviews and discusses those issues that concern Canadians of all persuasions. During such officiating, the governor general may dedicate a public building or attend events held by the organizations to which he or she is formally attached, such as the Boy Scouts of Canada.

Another ceremonial role of the governor general is to present Canadian honours, such as appointments, orders, decorations, medals, and armorial bearings, which are bestowed to Canadians of merit. Approximately 6000 appointments and awards are made annually. Some of the better-known awards are the Order of Canada, the Order of Military Merit, and the Cross of Valour. They recognize achievement, bravery, and exemplary service over a broad range of activities.

### The Privy Council

The Canadian government is a committee of the Queen's Privy Council, once the body that advised the British monarch and was "privy to" secrets of the Crown. It acted as the principal council to the sovereign, comprising trusted friends of the monarch, ministers of the Crown, and other parliamentary officials knowledgeable about the affairs of state.

The Cabinet has developed from that group of the monarch's intimate advisers who came to constitute the Privy Council. As a formal component of executive government in most parliamentary systems, it has survived as the formal machinery through which the monarch exercises his or her prerogative powers when necessary.

In Canada, people who are appointed to the Queen's Privy Council serve for life. Members include people of distinction, such as the Duke of Edinburgh, the Prince of Wales, and the British prime minister (Hogg 1992, 234). Although membership in the Privy Council is extensive, comprising all past and present Cabinet ministers and a number of other public figures — a total of more than 100 — its working character is that of a small number of ministers who are called together to witness the monarch's signing of some formal document, such as the Charter of Rights and Freedoms in 1982. When it meets for more routine matters, the Privy Council conducts its business in the Privy Council chamber in the East Block of the Parliament Buildings.

## THE POLITICAL EXECUTIVE

### The Prime Minister

The prime minister is both an institution and a person. Although the position is not mentioned in our constitution, the office of prime minister has developed institutional character by parliamentary custom and convention, and public expectation. It has become an office of government in its own right, with its own bureaucracy, and roles and functions that have both domestic and international significance. A party leader who wins an election with a majority enters into an institutional relationship with fellow parliamentarians, and with the people of Canada. In the mind of the public, that relationship is stable and permanent.

The prime minister is also a human being who brings a particular personality, political moxy, and style to the position. The decisions and choices made by the person who is called prime minister, and his or her skills and character, profoundly affect the nature of our political life. Of course, prime ministers are captives of the times in which they lead their parties in power — subject to the domestic and international pressures of the moment.

Canada's constitutional and parliamentary conventions do not provide formal written qualifications for either the position of or the person appointed prime minister. All prime ministers confront problems and events they cannot change or wish away. Yet, it is clear that who they are can make a difference. But the prime minister's job is strongly shaped by individuals and groups from the governmental and political spheres, by parliamentary rules and traditions, and by the structural sphere (the economy, the various political cultures across the country, and the internatonal system).

Tradition and practice have established that the prime minister must be a Canadian citizen who is eligible to vote under Canada's electoral laws. The prime minister is one who has been elected to the House of Commons from a federal riding, who is the leader of the major political party that has won a majority of seats in the House of Commons or that can form a government with other parties, and who has been appointed prime minister by the governor general.

Many factors combine to contribute to the powers of a Canadian prime minister and his or her ability to govern, including strength of personality, public popularity, and support from the Cabinet and the political party. The prime minister is carefully watched by everyone — by Cabinet colleagues, the bureaucracy, other members of Parliament, other party leaders, the premiers, and the mass media. Even the most casual of decisions the prime minister makes will affect his or her professional reputation among these groups. In turn, the effectiveness of the prime minister as leader of the country depends on this professional reputation.

In the exercise of parliamentary procedure, the prime minister has available, not only the formal tools accorded the position of "First Minister," but also a broad range of informal tools, of which television has become a powerful example. Modern prime ministers enhance their power to shape public opinion, and their public image, by using television and other news media. With the development of the electronic mass media, prime ministers have learned to make direct appeals to the people, beyond the confines of party and government leadership.

The prime minister can set the **agenda** of government business by determining the procedures by which the Cabinet works and the items to be discussed. The PM advises the governor general and the Crown. By convention, the governor general accepts the PM's advice. By virtue of the right to advise the governor general, the PM may choose the date of the next general election. This power is important for maintaining control in the PM's party, and for taking advantage for any weakness in the opposition.

Although the apparent power of the prime minister tends to overshadow the limitations of the position, we should know that the parliamentary system of government circumscribes that power. As the political executive, the prime minister faces a professional and highly procedural federal bureaucracy as well as a fickle general public. As the head of government, the prime minister usually faces a powerful Cabinet, with many disparate interests and representations. As the country's most prominent diplomat, the prime minister must often negotiate highly complex bilateral and multilateral treaties with very skilled foreign political leaders. The prime minister must also take the heat for everything Canada officially does abroad in military matters, and the peacekeeping operations of the United Nations. Finally, the media may expose corrupt or incompetent government conduct and turn public opinion against the prime minister and the government he or she represents.

### The Symbolic Role of the Prime Minister

No person in Canada — and no public official — is able to command as much public attention as the prime minister. He or she monopolizes the media. This extremely high level of visibility reflects the fact that two roles are combined in the prime minister: He or she is both the head of government and the symbolic political leader of the country.

The Canadian prime minister plays the symbolic role of goal-getter and communicator of national priorities and values. With the growing influence of the mass media on the political executive in Canada, the PM's rhetorical and public relations skills have become essential to this role. Prime ministers strive to set broad priorities for the country, above and beyond the specific policy proposals of their ministers. Tough talk about the deficit and debt or emphasizing a new approach to the conduct of politicians and public officials is quite common from prime ministers in their function as symbolic leaders.

The symbolic nature of the office can cause the Canadian public to turn rapidly on the prime minister when events do not turn out the way they think they should. Most prime ministers fail to live up to the expectations elections produce in the minds of the electorate. The making of decisions — almost any decisions — invariably alienates support, somewhere, among certain groups.

The prime minister so dominates public perceptions of the political world at the federal level that he or she can do little to avoid the critical scrutiny of the informed public. If there is trouble, the prime minister is blamed, no matter how much of the responsibility is under the control of that office.

Because of the symbolic nature of the role of the prime minister, Canadians have come to expect much from this person. Higher public expectations induce prime ministers to make more promises than they can keep, and to assume more power than is intended by the parliamentary system in which they must perform. What Canadians expect from their prime minister is often paradoxical: They apparently want a prime minister to be both tough and gentle. For example, the prime minister is expected to be tough enough to stand up to foreign negotiators but gentle enough to be concerned about the less-fortunate people in Canada and around the world. They want a prime minister to have strong convictions on issues but to be flexible enough to make compromises when necessary. They expect the prime minister to both lead and listen — to initiate new ideas and new ways of doing politics but not get too far ahead of the Canadian people.

Canadians also seem to want a prime minister to be able to inspire the country with high ideals and personal energy. But, at the same time, they believe that prime ministers should not promise more then they can deliver. Although Canadians expect their prime ministers to work well with their Cabinets, they also expect them to have the courage to stand up for deeply held person principles. They want prime ministers to be above politics but to be political enough to put together a Cabinet that can govern effectively. They like a prime minister who is ordinary enough to be "one of us" but extraordinary enough to be distinctive among world leaders. They want a prime minister who can feel confident in the presence of other prime ministers and presidents of the most powerful states in the international system.

Gradually, since Confederation, the office of Canadian prime minister has gained central importance in our system of government (Weller 1985). Neither Parliament nor the courts can command as much public scrutiny. Prior to the Second World War, the prime minister was primarily an elite leader, relatively distant from the people, interacting with parliamentarians often, but with the people only rarely.

After the war, the office of prime minister began to evolve into a more democratic one, primarily because the media, especially TV, focussed more on the personality and powers of the PM. More and more frequently, prime ministers learned to use the media to speak to the public directly about policy. More and more often, prime ministers began to travel outside Ottawa, making public appearances, creating the public perception that the prime minister is a symbol, not only of the government in power, but of the people across the country.

### The Role as Public Policy Spokesperson

The prime minister is the authoritative spokesperson on what is or is not the policy of the government (*The Privy Council Office* 1991). He or she leads the process of setting the general directions of government policy and is responsible for the overall spending program of the government.

The elaboration of government policy is a complex and continuing process, and so a prime minister is always having to explain what the government does or does not do. The complicated relationships that have evolved among the prime minister, the Cabinet, and Parliament have a great deal to do with the different political forces that act on a government at different times — with the ways in which public opinion, the political parties, and organized interests affect what the government does or does not do.

Particularly important is the special relationship that exists between the prime minister and the general public, which has evolved over many years. Through the media, prime ministers have enhanced their power to shape public opinion. A determined prime minister, delivering speeches over a period of weeks and months, can expect to influence the public's support of the policy agenda. However, the relationship between the prime minister and the public is very much a two-way street. Besides leading and directing public opinion, most prime ministers tend to respond to public opinion. Prime ministers want their party to remain in power and to win a favourable place in Canadian history, and they know that neither is likely to be accomplished if they defy public opinion on major issues. Prime ministers are aware, at least in general terms, of what helps or hurts them with the public; they know that they can win public support for their party if things go well, but will face electoral punishment if things go badly. They have strong incentives, therefore, to anticipate public reactions and to do things that will eventually keep the public's support.

The prime minister's Cabinet colleagues identify and propose priorities and initiatives on the basis of their portfolio and other responsibilities. Each minister engages in policy making on behalf of the ministry as a whole. For example, the minister of finance designs economic policy that binds the government to a particular set of fiscal and monetary actions in the economy. But it is the prime minister who has already set the overall agenda and must represent and account for the performance and conduct of each department so that the government appears unified in its goals.

The prime minister also has a particular role in areas of fundamental importance to Canada's national interest (Gwyn 1980). The secretary of state for external affairs is responsible for foreign policy and the activities of the Department of External Affairs. Nevertheless, as head of government, the prime minister maintains a particular interest in external affairs and foreign policy. In that regard, he or she must, from time to time, speak for Canada at the United Nations, the

Commonwealth, the Organization of American States, and the councils many of other international organizations.

In foreign policy, the active roles of both the prime minister and the secretary of state for external affairs require co-ordination of and close interaction with other government departments, such as those involved in trade, tourism, tax policy, and justice. National defence and the solicitor general provide advice to the prime minister on matters of national security and foreign intelligence.

The prime minister's responsibility as public policy spokesperson also extends to intergovernmental relations within Canada. Ministers are involved in federal–provincial relations in their capacities as representatives of the regions of the country. The prime minister, usually with the support of a minister appointed to oversee federal–provincial relations, speaks for Canada and determines the overall management and coherence of relations with provincial and territorial governments.

### The Role as Political Leader

The leadership the prime minister exercises within the Cabinet is of great significance because it drives the system of collective Cabinet decision making (Pal and Taras 1988). An important aspect of political leadership is witnessed when the prime minister selects a Cabinet.

The prime minister is free to appoint to Cabinet whomever he or she pleases. But the prime minister must, in fact, include powerful personalities in his or her party, some of whom may have competed with him or her for party leadership; show appropriate regard for its economic, linguistic, and ideological factions; select men and women who are competent administrators and not just good politicians; and, for the inner Cabinet circle, surround himself or herself with able parliamentary strategists and speakers who can share the burdens of leadership.

The interests of the prime minister and Cabinet are usually the same, but it is a vital for the prime minister to keep his or her colleagues on track at all times. And this sometimes involves forceful persuasion. The prime minister has the power to set the agenda of Cabinet, and certainly has superior opportunities to control the debate within Cabinet once the agenda is established.

The prime minister also influences what Cabinet committees are created, and who shall serve on them, including who shall chair each committee. The ability to control the structure of the Cabinet can be significant if a prime minister expects policy differences to erupt among colleagues on specific issues, or even if he or she wishes to minimize the general role played by an individual or group within the government.

Apart from prestige and powers of persuasion, the prime minister has a vast amount of patronage at his or her disposal. Patronage is a tool of management available to prime ministers in choosing the highest governmental appointees. The PM can fill the top-management positions of government with people who carry out his or her agenda. A high proportion of MPs of a governing party will be able to look for advancement.

Each prime minister is faced with the challenge of creating a Cabinet of manageable size. Candidates for Cabinet minister have their own constituencies not only in the electorate but also in the party and they are often selected by a prime minister because of the party support they can bring. Most prime ministers have found it easier to increase than to diminish the size of the Cabinet, although, in the 1990s, the trend is toward much smaller cabinets, such as those Kim Campbell and Jean Chrétien created in 1993.

The power of a prime minister will normally stem from his or her leadership of the political party that has won a majority of seats in a general election. The potent fact that the PM is the leader of the largest party in the

House of Commons thus confers governing authority in Parliament — although the amount of time that modern prime ministers can devote to the House of Commons has declined since the Second World War, despite the prominence of the prime minister during question period and the occasional set speech on the floor of the House.

The prime minister's responsibility as political leader and head of government also extends to the provinces. Ministers are directly involved with the provinces because their portfolios almost always affect provincial governments. So the prime minister needs to lure the provinces into the national strategy of the federal government because the tendency for provincial government leaders is to focus on issues and policy solutions that benefit only their particular region of Canada. In this regard, the prime minister's principal duty is to create and sustain unity within the country by working with the premiers and their ministers to achieve national goals.

### The Prime Minister's Office (PMO)

Prime ministers do not face their burdens alone; they have many advisers and helpers in a special body called the Prime Minister's Office (PMO). Located in the Langevin Block, near the Parliament Buildings, the PMO is sometimes spoken of as all-powerful. As it is presently organized, the PMO has between 65 and 70 employees, all under the direction of a chief of staff.

The PMO consists of the key executive assistants and personal advisers to the prime minister, who counsel and recommend on matters having to do with general public relations, the media, and relations with Parliament and with party organizations in the provinces (Lalonde 1971).

The PMO is another reflection of how the position of the prime minister has become institutionalized. The PMO provides the prime minister with the staff support he or she needs to do what the public expects.

People in the PMO perform a variety of functions that are essential to the prime minister's political success. It is not easy to generalize about the duties of these people, as they tend to reflect the personal style and political priorities of the prime minister.

Some act as gatekeepers and guardians of the prime minister's time. Others deal exclusively with backbenchers and other MPs. Still others serve as links with the federal bureaucracy and executive agencies of government. Some advise the prime minister on political matters, patronage, and appointments. Others may write speeches, organize the prime minister's schedule, and boost the PM's ego. The PMO also includes a translator, a correspondence unit, and a special projects unit.

A legislative adviser prepares the briefing book — the document the prime minister has on his or her desk when rising in the House of Commons to respond to the opposition. The legislative adviser keeps the prime minister informed about the parliamentary calendar and the flow of legislation through the House of Commons and the Senate.

Staff members review every speech the prime minister delivers, every official announcement, and everything that might have legal bearing on what the prime minister does outside of Parliament. The communications staff manages the prime minister's relations with the Ottawa press gallery and media establishment. It organizes press conferences, supervises media arrangements during prime-ministerial trips, and generally keeps in touch with the media. Some prime ministers find it expedient to designate staff people to link the PMO to certain groups — premiers, mayors, women, and aboriginal leaders.

The PMO comprises the people who owe almost total loyalty to the prime minister, and to whom he or she turns for advice on the mundane and the most serious matters of governance. Good staff people in the PMO are self-effacing, working only for their boss and hiding from the limelight. The people in the

PMO have become increasingly important as the prime minister's connections with the public have grown closer and as the office of prime minister has taken on an institutional life of its own.

## The Cabinet

The most significant members of the government constitute the Cabinet, those who are chosen by the prime minister to attend Cabinet meetings and are made **privy councillors**. In their constitutional capacity as advisers to the Crown, Cabinet ministers are sworn as members of the Queen's Privy Council and hold office at the pleasure of the sovereign, as represented by the governor general. In history, the Cabinet originates from the inner core of privy councillors who gave advice to the English monarchs.

According to Westminster theory, a Cabinet is the highest political decision-making body in the parliamentary system of government. Only members of Parliament may be appointed ministers of the federal Cabinet by the prime minister. The parliamentary system vests legislative initiative and responsibility in the Cabinet — not in individual members of Parliament. In fact, the Cabinet is the government.

When they are chosen, Cabinet ministers are given a portfolio — that is, they are made solicitor general or minister of defence, for example, and placed in charge of one or more public service departments.

In Canada, the Cabinet exists by constitutional convention, as does the position of prime minister (Heard 1991, Chap. 3). It has no written constitutional status. The Cabinet has replaced the Privy Council as the chief source of executive power since the eighteenth century, but the latter still exists as an executive organ, largely giving formal effect to policy decisions made by the Cabinet and making orders-in-council.

One important Cabinet convention is Cabinet responsibility, which requires that

ministers be accountable to Parliament. The direct expression of Cabinet responsibility is found in **question period**. However, by convention, a Cabinet should resign if it loses its majority on the floor of the House of Commons. The opposition will not infrequently table a **motion of non-confidence** in governments, but usually without much hope that the motion will carry. If such a motion is carried, the government should resign and call for an election.

Related to the notion of ministerial responsibility is that of collective responsibility: Ministers can fulfil their personal duties and functions and their obligations as members of the ministry only by acting in concert. The principle of collective responsibility means that all ministers must support and defend government policy and not speak or act against it. If the public perception is that the Cabinet is divided, the government's authority, and ultimately its legitimacy, will be weakened.

Sometimes Cabinet ministers face challenges to their loyalty to the prime minister and other Cabinet colleagues, and to maintaining the loyalty of their department. Understandably, ministers tend to fight in Cabinet for their departmental policies and budgets. Different ideological perspectives within a political party are represented in a Cabinet, and can grate on members who are trying to manufacture consensus. As well, the Cabinet contains the political rivals and possible successors of the prime minister — a situation that alters the interrelationships among ministers, especially with the prime minister.

Canada's legislative processes primarily involve strong Cabinet leadership. The Cabinet exercises a great deal of control over how Parliament spends its time, plans the order in which the government's business is taken up, and can decide when debate will end and when "divisions" (votes) will be taken. As might be expected, the government is sometimes criticized for allegedly high-handed manoeuvres in restricting opposition speeches and for enforced — and nearly complete — silencing of the **backbenchers**.

### Cabinet Size and Composition

Many factors affect the size and composition of the Cabinet. One is the mood of the country about whether the government, as presently constituted, is too big or too small. There is no set limit on the size of the Cabinet; rather, it is up to each prime minister to decide how big it will be. In 1867, John A. Macdonald's Cabinet had thirteen members; however, by the 1990s, Canada had evolved the largest cabinet among the democratic states of the world. Since the 1970s, the wholesale growth of governmental responsibilities prompted the enlargement of Cabinet. Trudeau's largest Cabinet had 37 ministers, 9 more than the largest convened under Pearson. Under John Turner, the size of the Cabinet was reduced to 29, the same number of ministers as in the short-lived Clark government. But the largest Cabinet in Canadian history was assembled by Brian Mulroney in 1984: It totalled 40 ministers, including the prime minister, selected from among 210 Tory MPs. After the 1988 federal election, Mulroney's Cabinet consisted of 39 ministers, including the prime minister, drawn from 169 Progressive Conservative MPs. Kim Campbell, who pledged to tame the size and temper of government, reduced the size of her Cabinet to 24 ministers, and the number of departments from 32 to 23. Jean Chrétien appointed 22 ministers from his caucus of 177 members in 1993.

### Cabinet Representativeness

Another factor of major importance when forming the Cabinet is the principle of representation (Aucoin 1991). Today, the general political criteria a prime minister must follow in striking a Cabinet roster include economic, geographic, gender, linguistic, political, and social factors. In some cases, the choices for representation with major portfolios are well signalled. There is always the difficulty of forming a truly "national" government — one in which, to the extent it is possible, every province or region is allocated at least one Cabinet minister. When this is not possible because representatives have not been elected to the governing party's caucus from every province, the prime minister sometimes appoints senators to the Cabinet to represent these provinces, or gives a minister from a neighbouring province special ministerial assignments in a province with no government representation (Bakvis 1991).

To complicate the job of making a representative government along provincial and regional lines, the prime minister must also try to balance the composition of the Cabinet according to economic, gender, linguistic, and social variables (Bakvis 1991). Every effort must be made to include people to represent the business community, aboriginal people, women, Catholics, Protestants, Jews, and those of French and other non-English origins. John A. Macdonald once said: "Like any cabinet maker, I do the best I can with the lumber you furnish me."

The Cabinet must be representative of women, who make up over 50 percent of Canada's population. In 1984, Mulroney named a record 6 women to his first Cabinet from the 28 elected nation-wide, doubling the previous record of 3. However, these six women comprised only 15 percent of the Cabinet. Prior to the appointment of the six women ministers by Mulroney, only eight women had ever sat around a Canadian Cabinet table. Women were given some tough portfolios — Foreign Affairs and International Trade, Natural Resources Canada, and Environment Canada — a signal that when women with the right credentials are elected, they do not have to sit as backbenchers. In 1989, Mulroney's first Cabinet shuffle again included only 6 women, selected from 39 elected to a larger House of Commons. His successor, Kim Campbell, appointed four women, for a total, including the prime minister, of 25 percent of Cabinet. Jean Chrétien appointed four women, who comprised about 17 percent of his Cabinet.

For backbenchers, the Cabinet is the top of the political ladder, except for the position of prime minister. It constitutes the core of the Canadian political elite — where most MPs want to be — and thus gives Cabinet a very partisan dimension and enhances the loyalty of Cabinet ministers to the prime minister who selected them. After all, careers benefit enormously from an appointment to the Cabinet, and most Cabinet ministers are assured of continued success in either the public or the private sector once they leave the government.

## Ministers and Deputy Ministers

Although Cabinet ministers are appointed by the prime minister and owe their primary allegiance to him or her, they must develop good relations with the departments they run.

Each minister usually heads a government department that is composed of a large bureaucracy with a momentum of its own. These career administrators consider political bosses as birds of passage. From time to time, an order from a minister is seen to be in conflict with the judgement and expectations of their profession. Career administrators do not easily fall in line with each new Cabinet.

Government departments are headed by career civil servants called "deputy ministers," who usually remain at their posts regardless of which political party gains control of the government (Campbell and Szablowski 1979). Deputy ministers advise their political bosses on policy matters, plan and control expenditures in the department, scrutinize the organization and structure of the department, and assume the wider responsibilities of co-ordinating departmental activities with those of other government departments.

### The Interests of the Bureaucracy

Quite understandably, deputy ministers who are the permanent heads of departments will have administrative interests that may differ from those of the minister and the prime minister they serve. Usually, deputy ministers are fiercely dedicated to the programs they administer. They expect that the minister who heads their department will take their advice and avoid the many transient political pressures that cause Cabinet ministers to alter the administration of government and its programs.

Deputy ministers want the minister to represent the interests of the department to the prime minister. As a result, the minister's allegiance to the bureaucratic and the political forces of government is often at cross purposes. Further complication arises from the fact that ministers are responsible only for their part of government, and thus the prime minister has to balance a wider range of interests.

### The Interests of the Government

However, ministers are not totally without ways of dealing with administrative interests of the bureaucracy. For example, Cabinet ministers are accompanied by an entourage of aides, executive assistants, and parliamentary secretaries, who are directly responsible to them. Parliamentary secretaries are members of Parliament who are designated by the minister to assist in the political operation of the department.

In more recent years, ministerial aides, executive assistants, and parliamentary secretaries have played an increasingly important part in the workings of Cabinet. As the complexity and size of the bureaucracy challenge a minister's ability to stay in control, his or her political staff acts as a buffer to the growing influence and potential colonization of politicians by the public service.

One major function of the minister's staff is to protect and advance the political interests of the department and the Cabinet. Performance of this function includes liaison with Parliament, press relations, control of the minister's schedule, travel, and relations with major interest groups and party figures. Ministers also have assistants to perform such inevitable but disagreeable tasks as refusing access, discharging employees and officials, and denying requests for special consideration. The parliamentary secretaries have some input into the development of new programs and legislation. They also serve to take the heat off the minister from time to time in the House of Commons by standing in to answer sensitive questions directed at a department from members of the opposition. Sometimes, as well, when the minister has accepted an engagement to speak in a politically hostile area of the country, the parliamentary secretary is sent instead to deflect political flak away from the minister. Despite such stratagems, all Cabinet ministers are aware of the many difficulties involved in gaining control of the very bureaucracy that is one of the bases of their power.

## The Privy Council Office (PCO)

The Privy Council Office (PCO) is a small executive body called a "central agency" that advises the Cabinet and its committees. Under the Constitution Act, 1867, the PCO was assigned the limited task of preparing and registering orders-in-council. By convention, the PCO greatly expanded its functions, to serve the government in power as a nonpartisan advisory and administrative agency (Robertson 1971).

Since 1940, when it was formally established as a secretariat to the Cabinet, the PCO has been headed by a senior public servant, called the "Clerk of the Privy Council and the Secretary to the Cabinet." This person provides direct support to the Cabinet from the perspective of the values, traditions, and expertise of the public service. As the head of the public service department of the Cabinet, the Clerk of the Privy Council serves as the principal link between the prime minister and the public service.

The Privy Council Office is staffed by career public servants, constituting an executive secretariat. It co-ordinates the activities of the Cabinet with its committees. It also acts as a liaison between the departments of government and the Cabinet as a collective body. As a secretariat to the Cabinet, the professional civil servants in the PCO assist ministers when they must deal formally with their Cabinet colleagues. The content of a minister's proposal is normally not a concern of the secretariat. However, the proper administrative process for presenting a minister's proposal needs the co-ordination of the PCO.

Thus, the PCO provides the Cabinet and its committees with the support required to prepare and conduct meetings. It arranges the meetings, circulates the agendas, distributes documents, provides advice to the chairperson of each Cabinet committee on agenda items, and records Cabinet minutes and decisions. It works with the public servants in other government departments and transmits Cabinet decisions throughout the government ministry.

The PCO also ensures that orders-in-council and other Cabinet instruments are announced officially in order to keep the government informed about its own laws and regulations. In effect, the PCO ensures the efficient organization and flow of information in a complex governmental system.

A key role of the PCO is to support the prime minister in leading and directing the government. The PCO gives advice to the PM on the overall conduct of government business, including how to handle major issues and subjects that are important to the prime minister. The PCO tries to cover all ground so that every important group is consulted and so that a full range of alternatives is known prior to making decisions — that the prime minister and the Cabinet have all the information they need to make decisions. In this context, the PCO works closely with the Prime Minister's Office, the Department of Finance, the Treasury Board, and other agencies of government to give ministers comprehensive briefings on the most central issues before the Cabinet.

## CANADA'S LEGISLATIVE INSTITUTIONS

### The House of Commons

The popularly elected House of Commons is the centrepiece of Canada's parliamentary system of government. It plays three vital roles in the governing of Canadians: First, it is federal lawmaker, making public policies that govern the country; second, it represents local interests, articulating their viewpoints and securing tangible benefits for individual ridings; and, third, it is a forum for the major political and governmental concerns of Canadians.

According Canadian constitutional law, the House of Commons exercises a few fundamental powers that have profound democratic importance. One is majority approval of a proposed bill, making it the law of the land. A second power is that of examining carefully and approving all expenditures of the money that the government collects from taxation and other ways of raising revenues.

Each member of Parliament represents the people of a specific constituency or riding. Collectively, the House of Commons consists of 295 elected members and is responsible for most of the legislation introduced in Parliament. Both members of the House of Commons and senators are members of Parliament. But the term "MP" is usually used to refer to the elected members of the House of Commons. The House of Commons is politically important because its party composition is the basis for the formation of governments. It enables the leaders of one political party to rule and those of the opposition parties to be considered as a possible alternative government.

The pomp and ceremony of parliamentary government (see Figure 4.1) is central to the House of Commons proceedings and its legislative heritage (Franks 1991). Each sitting day begin's with the Speaker's Parade, a ceremonial procession that highlights the Speaker, who wears black robes and a tricornered hat and is escorted to the Chamber by the Sergeant-at-Arms, who carries the symbolic mace (ornamental club).

The Speaker is accompanied by a page (who delivers messages and reading material for members) and followed by the **Clerk of the House** and the **Table Officers**. This British parliamentary tradition was adopted by Canada in establishing its system of government in the nineteenth century. Parliamentary history asserts that the parade was a means of protecting the Speaker from harm during the stormier periods of parliamentary debate.

In order to accommodate all these issues and ensure all opinions are expressed, the House of Commons follows a daily agenda that may vary on certain days but usually follows a predictable order of business.

Monday mornings are usually devoted to private members' business. During this segment, members who are not Cabinet ministers can present bills and make motions for debate. Following the business of private members are Government Orders, which allow the Cabinet to initiate whatever items of business it wants to place on the national agenda. On Mondays, Government Orders take up about two hours of time, from noon until 2:00 P.M. For about fifteen minutes, member's statements consume the daily order of business. During this time, members can speak for up to one minute on matters of importance to them. From 2:15 to 3:00 P.M. is question period, during which time opposition members, and sometimes members of the governing party, ask questions of the government. It is during question period that members can call the prime minister and other Cabinet ministers to account for their actions.

**Figure 4.1  The House of Commons/La Chambre des communes**

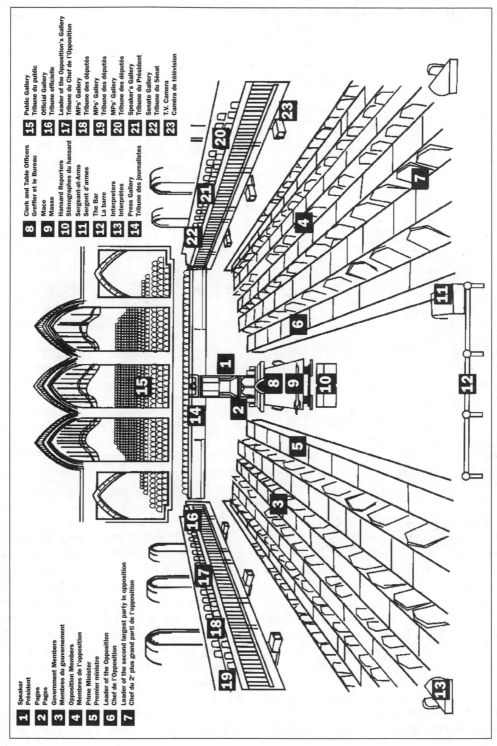

| 1 | Speaker | | 8 | Clerk and Table Officers | | 15 | Public Gallery |
|---|---------|---|---|--------------------------|---|----|----------------|
| | Président | | | Greffier et le Bureau | | | Tribune du public |
| 2 | Pages | | 9 | Mace | | 16 | Official Gallery |
| | Pages | | | Masse | | | Tribune officielle |
| 3 | Government Members | | 10 | Hansard Reporters | | 17 | Leader of the Opposition's Gallery |
| | Membres du gouvernement | | | Sténographes du hansard | | | Tribune du Chef de l'Opposition |
| 4 | Opposition Members | | 11 | Sergeant-at-Arms | | 18 | MPs' Gallery |
| | Membres de l'opposition | | | Sergent d'armes | | | Tribune des députés |
| 5 | Prime Minister | | 12 | The Bar | | 19 | MPs' Gallery |
| | Premier ministre | | | La barre | | | Tribune des députés |
| 6 | Leader of the Opposition | | 13 | Interpreters | | 20 | MPs' Gallery |
| | Chef de l'Opposition | | | Interprètes | | | Tribune des députés |
| 7 | Leader of the second largest party in opposition | | 14 | Press Gallery | | 21 | Speaker's Gallery |
| | Chef du 2ᵉ plus grand parti de l'opposition | | | Tribune des journalistes | | | Tribune du Président |
| | | | | | | 22 | Senate Gallery |
| | | | | | | | Tribune du Sénat |
| | | | | | | 23 | T.V. Camera |
| | | | | | | | Caméra de télévision |

*Source:* Reproduced with permission of the Public Information Office of the House of Commons.

**Figure 4.2 House of Commons: Daily Order of Business**

| DAILY ORDER OF BUSINESS | | | | | | |
|---|---|---|---|---|---|---|
| | Monday | Tuesday | Wednesday | Thursday | Friday | |
| 10:00–11:00 | Private Members' Business | Routine Proceed. Govern. Orders | Caucus | Routine Proceed. Govern. Orders | Govern. Orders | 10:00–11:00 |
| 11:00–11:15 | | | Caucus | | Members' State. | 11:00–11:15 |
| 11:15–12:00 | | | Caucus | | Question Period | 11:15–12:00 |
| 12:00–1:00 | Govern. Orders | | Caucus | | Routine Proceed. Govern. Orders | 12:00–1:00 |
| 1:00–2:00 | | | Caucus | | | 1:00–2:00 |
| 2:00–2:15 | Members' State. | | | | | 2:00–2:15 |
| 2:15–3:00 | Question Period | | | | | 2:15–3:00 |
| 3:00–4:00 | Routine Proceed. Govern. Orders | | | | | 3:00–4:00 |
| 4:00–5:00 | | | | | | 4:00–5:00 |
| 5:00–6:00 | | | | | | 5:00–6:00 |
| 6:00–6:30 | Adjourn. Proceed. | | | | | 6:00–6:30 |
| 6:30–7:00 | | | | | | 6:30–7:00 |
| 7:00–8:00 | | | | | | 7:00–8:00 |

*Source:* Reproduced with permission of the House of Commons.

Following question period are routine proceedings, which comprise many different items, including the tabling of documents, statements by ministers, the presentations of **petitions** and committee reports, as well as the introduction and first readings of bills and the debating of motions. Every day of the week has a place for routine proceedings in the Daily Order of Business. Another hour or so is devoted to Government Orders.

Finally, Monday's session ends with adjournment proceedings. A member who is not satisfied with a reply received during question period can ask, in writing as advance notice, for the matter to be raised again during the adjournment proceedings. A minister or parliamentary secretary attends to respond to the questions.

On Wednesdays, the daily business does not begin until 2:00 P.M., so that each party can hold its caucus. In these meetings, members of the Commons and senators who belong to the same political party meet behind closed doors to discuss policy and the parliamentary agenda.

Decisions are made in the House of Commons in response to a *motion*, a proposal put forward by a member and debated by the

House. After the debate ends, the Speaker asks if the House wants to adopt the motion. If nobody disagrees, the motion carries. If there is disagreement, the Speaker takes a voice vote by asking for those supporting the motion to say "yea" and those opposed to say "nay." Then the Speaker judges whether the yeas or nays have a majority. Any five members who dispute the Speaker's decision or who want to have their names entered on the record can, by rising, call for a recorded "division," or vote. When the division is to be recorded, the division bells are rung to summon members to the House of Commons. Once they return, members rise one after another and bow to the Speaker, with the "yeas" rising first, followed by the "nays." The results are tallied and announced by the Clerk of the House.

The daily record of the debates in the House of Commons is generally referred to as **Hansard**. The official title is "House of Commons Debates." The name comes from T.C. Hansard, who printed the British debates (1812–92). It provides a statement in both official languages in both Houses of Parliament, in part for the immediate convenience of the MPs and in part as a historical record of the proceedings. Hansard is edited, translated, and printed in English and French, and published by the Queen's Printer. The printed copies come from shorthand reports taken on the floor of the House by reporters working in shifts. The House of Commons Broadcast Branch keeps a complete audio and video record of the proceedings.

The Sergeant-at-Arms sits at the end of the Chamber opposite the Speaker. He carries the mace and assists the Speaker when he or she enters and leaves the Chamber. The Sergeant-at-Arms keeps order in the Chamber as directed by the Speaker, and is responsible for the security of the House of Commons. A member who refuses to follow the Speaker's instructions may be "named" (called by his or her last name) and removed from the Chamber by the Sergeant-at-Arms.

## The Opposition

"Her Majesty's Loyal Opposition" exists in many Commonwealth states, such as Great Britain and Canada, in which governments are dependent on parliamentary support to survive. The fact that Canada's government must maintain a majority's support in the House of Commons implies the presence of an opposition waiting to step into the government's shoes either by the unusual occurrence of defection from government ranks or by the more common method of achieving that majority by electoral success. In any event, those who are in power face political rivals who are anxious to replace them, either to change policy or to gain power.

The high profile given by the media to both the prime minister and the leader of the opposition tends to polarize Canadian politics into a struggle between the government and the opposition. The opposition is a key characteristic of the Westminster system of parliamentary government (Ionescu and de Madariaga 1972), since an organized opposition keeps a government on its toes and can provide an alternative government.

In addition to question period, the opposition can use a number of techniques to keep the government accountable. One is to use the mass media to project and propel their objections to government policies and conduct. Raising questions in the House of Commons about the conduct of government MPs attracts the scrutiny of the media. By probing the government in Parliament, the opposition can ensure that issues quickly attract publicity nation-wide.

The opposition's responsibilities include the formation of a "shadow cabinet," which is composed of ministerial counterparts to every major Cabinet post in the existing government. The shadow cabinet provides the leaders of the opposition parties with the opportunity to demonstrate their skills in selecting appropriate alternatives to the government.

In Canada, the more frontal type of attack upon a government will take the form of a vote of non-confidence. A motion of non-confidence is aimed at the government's whole policy and program rather than at any specific item. If such a motion is carried, a government either resigns or calls an election.

The power of party discipline makes votes of non-confidence unlikely to succeed unless the government rests upon some kind of multiparty coalition. Even where a government holds a perilously slim majority, it is difficult for the opposition to win a vote of non-confidence. Nevertheless, a government's advantage of fewer than ten or fifteen seats is considered unsafe because some majority members are almost certainly to be absent occasionally owing to illness or for other reasons.

The death or resignation of an MP means a by-election to fill the vacated seat, and the election can go against the majority to favour the opposition. However, a majority advantage of more than 30 seats heightens the chances of one or more members' defecting from the party's positions during parliamentary divisions.

But it is still a rare event when the cohesion of the parliamentary party does not approximate 99 percent. Voting cohesion declines as the party's **whips** are withdrawn, usually on those issues regarded as raising basic moral questions, such as abortion or capital punishment.

There is a vast amount of compromise, of give-and-take, in the working relationship of oppositions and governments. No Cabinet can realistically draft — let alone introduce — its bills until it has carefully ascertained and weighed the opinions of its opponents in Parliament, of important interest groups (business, labour, agriculture, and the like), and of the general public.

## The Senate

At the time of Confederation, the Senate was created to be a "power of resistance to oppose the democratic element." It has evolved into an institution, unique among states with two levels of government, of "sober second thought." Thus, the Senate is Canada's unelected Upper House of Parliament through which all legislation must pass before it becomes law. Its members, chosen in all ten provinces and two territories, are appointed by the governor general on the recommendation of the prime minister.

The establishment of a Senate gave assurances to Quebec and the Maritime provinces that Ontario, which was growing so rapidly, would not dominate the federal government. Because the seats in the Senate would be distributed by region, it would serve as a permanent check on the elected House of Commons, regardless of how many seats might be allocated to Ontario or any other province on the basis of population size.

The framers of Canada's constitution established specific qualifications for senators. They were to be over 30 years of age, British subjects, and owners of property valued over $4000 in the province they represented. Until the famous Persons Case in 1929, it was assumed that only men would be appointed to the Senate. In 1930, Canada's first female senator, Cairine Wilson, was appointed by Prime Minister William Lyon Mackenzie. Between 1930 and 1993, 35 women had been appointed to the Senate.

There are 104 senators under the following provincial and regional representation: Ontario, 24; Quebec 24; 10 each for Nova Scotia and New Brunswick; 6 each for British Columbia, Alberta, Saskatchewan, Manitoba, and Newfoundland; Prince Edward Island, 4; and 1 each for the Yukon and Northwest Territories.

Unlike the composition of the House of Commons, which is based on representation by population, that of the Senate is based on the principle of regional representation. This regional representation is central to the role of the Senate in Canada's system of government, as the Chamber serves as a forum for the expression of regional concerns.

Senators cannot introduce tax bills or bills to spend money, although they can block their passage once they have come out of the House of Commons. Beyond its traditional responsibilities for reconsidering legislation previously passed by the Commons, the Senate is also involved in other, earlier stages of the parliamentary process. Bills can be introduced in the Senate and are exposed to close scrutiny in Senate committees, which can sometimes result in important improvements and amendments acceptable to both Chambers.

In effect, the Senate's powers are almost identical to those of the House of Commons. No federal bill can become law without the Senate's assent. And the Senate can veto any legislation from the Commons as often as it wants, including budget bills. It has not exercised its veto power very often; however, it has delayed passage of numerous bills and effectively killed bills, as it did when voting a tie on the government's abortion bill in 1991.

The only thing the Senate cannot do is raise taxes or expenditures on its own. It must live with the amounts in the money bills that the House of Commons puts forward. In addition, the Senate cannot prevent its own abolition. The constitution provides that the Senate can be abolished or changed by the House of Commons and seven provinces representing 50 percent of the national population. And the Senate can delay constitutional amendments only for up to 180 days.

In addition to their duties in the Chamber itself, and intensive committee work, senators are also engaged in governmental, parliamentary, and diplomatic activities. The government leader in the Senate is normally a member of Cabinet, and other senators can serve as ministers.

The Senate plays an active research role through special committees, and the results of that work have a major impact on government programs and legislation. The Senate committees develop considerable expertise in improving the legal and technical wording of complicated bills. The Senate is able to conduct special public inquiries into pressing political issues, such as its studies on poverty, mandatory retirement, and the mass media.

The opening of Parliament, the royal assent to bills, and the prorogation (ending of a session) of Parliament take place in the Senate Chamber. On these occasions, the Speaker and members of the House of Commons attend at the Bar of the Senate Chamber after being duly summoned to do so.

The Speaker of the Senate presides at sittings of the Senate, occupying the Speaker's Chair in front of the Throne. The Throne in the centre of the dais (a platform) is used by the Queen or the governor general on ceremonial occasions, such as the opening of Parliament. The leader of the government sits on the side of the Chamber to the right of the Speaker, and the leader of the opposition sits on the left of the Speaker.

Because it is an unelected body, the Senate has never been accorded the degree of respect given to the House of Commons by the Canadian electorate and the media. The Senate has long been treated as a place to put political workhorses out to pasture. The great majority of Canada's senators have their posts because — and only because — of prior service rendered to a dominant political party. When the media are not criticizing its role and functions, they tend to ignore what it does as a legislative body.

### Senate Reform

Interest in changing the Senate has been demonstrated in a wide range of publications and proposals (White 1990). Senate reform was an important provision in the constitutional proposals made by Quebec in its submission to the Constitutional Conference of 1968. The government of Canada drafted white papers on Senate reform in 1969 and 1978. A special joint committee of the

Senate and the House of Commons on the constitution published its report in 1972. But, in 1978, the Supreme Court of Canada struck down an attempt by the Trudeau government to replace the Senate with a House of the Federation because the provinces had not given their consent. And, in 1985, the Mulroney government failed to provide a constitutional amendment that would prevent the Senate as presently constituted from ever repeating its stalling action on important government business.

Over the years, numerous reports have been prepared on reforming the Senate by the governments of British Columbia (1978) and Alberta (1982 and 1985); the Ontario Advisory Committee on Confederation (1978); the Progressive Conservative Party of Canada (1978); the Canada West Foundation (1978, 1981); the Canadian Bar Association (1978); the Pépin–Robarts Task Force on Canadian Unity (1979); La Fédération des francophones hors Québec (1979); the Goldenberg–Lamontagne report of 1980; and the Royal Commission on the Economic Union and Development Prospects for Canada (the Macdonald Commission; 1985).

The future role of the Senate was also a major part of the deliberations of the Federal–Provincial Continuing Committee of Ministers on the Constitution from 1978 through summer 1980. In its "beige paper," entitled "A New Canadian Federation," the Quebec Liberal party recommended an intergovernmental council that would operate independently of Parliament but would perform some of the functions proposed for a reformed Senate.

In 1985, the government of Alberta recommended a "Triple E" Senate: a Senate whose members are directly "elected," based on "equal" representation from each province, and which has "effective" powers (McCormick 1991). Since 1985, important progress has been made toward Senate reform. In 1986, all premiers agreed at the Annual Premiers' Conference in Edmonton that Senate reform is a

priority for constitutional change. In the same year, the federal government pledged to address Senate reform in a new constitutional amendment.

The 1987 Constitutional Accord contained a provision for the Annual Conference of First Ministers to address Senate reform. This was the first time that both the federal and the provincial governments had agreed to concrete measures to reform the Senate. The accord promised that Senate reform would be the next priority in building national reconciliation. The 1992 Charlottetown Accord would have changed the Senate by instituting equal representation from the provinces, with six elected senators each, regardless of population, and the Territories, with one elected senator each. The powers of the Senate would have been expanded to include approval or rejection of government nominations for the governor of the Bank of Canada and the heads of institutions such as the CBC and federal boards and agencies. But the Senate's powers to defeat a government bill would have been reduced and refined.

The architects of a new Canadian Senate have many options from which to choose. To give senators more representative legitimacy in the eyes of Canadians, the federal and provincial governments could share a method of appointment. Another recommended method of appointment would remove the federal government entirely from the process, leaving the power of appointment exclusively with the provinces. Provincial delegates appointed to a reformed Senate could also have review and veto powers over the federal lawmaking process.

Another possible way of choosing senators is by indirect election — that is, by election in the provincial legislatures. In 1978, the federal government proposed a Senate formed on the basis of proportional indirect election. Under the terms of the proposal, the Senate would reflect the proportional popular performance of political parties in the most recent federal election.

In the reports by La Fédération des francophones hors Québec (1979), the Canada West Foundation (1981), and the Macdonald Commission (1985), direct election of the Senate was proposed. The Macdonald Commission advocated an elected Senate, based on proportional representation, with the power to hold up legislation for six months. An elected Senate would be a direct voice of the people from various regions, rather than of political parties or governments. In this regard, the Senate might also be designated to reflect the existence of certain minorities, especially Canada's aboriginal peoples.

There is no doubt that there are many ways to reform the Canadian Senate. What is also certain is that the present means of legislative review and regional representation are inadequate, and widely perceived as such. As a result, many Canadians continue to ask whether they should follow the example of other federations that assign a more functional use to the second Chamber.

## HOW PARLIAMENT MAKES LAWS

### The Legislative Process

The process of making law is basic to our parliamentary system of government, yet it is confusing and poorly understood by most Canadians. No institution receives more attention than Parliament; it conducts its business in full view of the public, especially since 1977, when the daily proceedings of the House of Commons began to be televised.

There are two types of bills: public and private. A bill is a piece of legislation in draft form submitted to Parliament for its consideration. A *public bill* is concerned with matters of public policy and applies to whole classes of persons. A *private bill* relates to matters of a particular interest or benefit to a person or persons, including corporations. Because the legislative process of a private bill is

somewhat different, we will discuss them separately (Jackson and Atkinson 1980, 89–92).

### Public Bills

Public, or government, bills are introduced and sponsored by a minister, and concern policy matters, such as health, the environment, or human rights. Only a minister may introduce a bill for the appropriation of any part of the public revenue or for taxation. Government bills originating in the House of Commons are numbered from C–1 to C–200 in the order in which they are introduced. A government bill is introduced, explained, and defended by the appropriate minister, with the assistance of his or her colleagues.

Sometimes a prime minister will launch a bill that is at the heart of the government program. They may be introduced each day during Government Orders in any sequence the government determines. *Government Orders* consist of any business introduced by the government and considered during the time reserved for the government in a sitting day. Most Government Orders are public bills, and debate on these takes most of the day.

There are three other types of Government Orders: supply proceedings, which are bills concerning the government's annual spending estimates or opposition motions criticizing government policy; ways and means proceedings, which are concerned with taxation and debate on the federal budget; and government business, which are motions on anything the government wants to sponsor.

### Private Members' Bills

In the early days of Confederation, private members' bills took up most of the business of Parliament. But, with the development of a cohesive party structure and a greater burden of government work, private members' time was gradually reduced to about five hours per week. Today private members' bills are unusual because they are not pieces of legislation put forward by the government, through its ministers, but rather through the initiative of an individual MP.

Private members' bills are often associated with the opposition, but, in fact, members of all represented political parties make use of this option in roughly equal measure. Another distinctive feature of these bills is that free voting, without pressure from the party whips to take a stand, is practised to a large extent, and MPs of very different political stripes may even be found on the same side of an issue.

Private members' bills tend to suffer high mortality rates because the government has its own legislative agenda and will pressure its members to give their energies to government bills. For example, of the hundreds submitted for first reading between 1944 and 1984, only fourteen were enacted. But, in 1986, new procedural rules made it easier for this type of legislation to become law. And, in that year, royal assent was given for Bill C–255, the Public Pensions Reporting Act. A number of other bills have become law this way.

Private members' bills may be considered only during Private Members' Hour, a period limited to one hour per day, Mondays to Fridays. During this period, no member may speak for more than ten minutes, unless making a motion, in which case he or she may speak for twenty minutes. At least two weeks must elapse between first and second reading. Such bills operating in the House are numbered from C–201 to C–1000, in the order in which they are introduced, and are considered in the order established by a draw and as set forth in the **Standing Orders**, although this order may be altered by unanimous consent.

Many private members' bills deal with moral and contentious issues, which governments usually want to avoid. Capital punishment, the rights of the unborn, making Canada a nuclear-free zone, and the legalization of marijuana are some of the issue areas that attract private members' legislative initiatives.

Human rights, as in Pat Carney's 1980 Act to Prohibit Discrimination on the Grounds of Sexual Orientation, and freedom of information, as in Bill C–254, which sought access to certain records concerning defence, are other frequent concerns.

In 1993, New Democrat Jim Fulton introduced a bill in the House of Commons to legalize the smoking and growing of marijuana at home, but not for commercial sale, export, or import. The bill would have made marijuana as easy to grow as a lawn and would have erased the criminal records of more than 500 000 Canadians who were convicted of possessing marijuana.

In a parliamentary system filled with restrictions, members of the opposition and backbenchers of the majority party have found in these bills one of the few available means of self-expression. A case in point is that of Jean Chrétien, who drew attention to himself with a bill changing the name of Trans-Canada Airlines to Air Canada in the 1960s. A number of such bills focus on matters of symbolic importance: holiday observances, like the one for John A. Macdonald Day, the flag, or proposals for a new national anthem. The Beaver Bill, introduced in 1974 by the late Sean O'Sullivan, designated the beaver as Canada's sovereign symbol.

### How a Bill Becomes Law

The three stages a bill must go through before becoming law are called "readings" because centuries ago, in Britain, many people, including the members of Parliament, could not read, and the bills were read to the members by the Speaker of the House. Today, the Speaker reads only the title of the bill.

Before a bill becomes law, it goes through the following stages: (1) a member is given leave of the House to introduce the bill; (2) the bill is read for the first time and printed; (3) the bill is read a second time and referred to a committee; (4) the bill is considered in the committee and reported back to the House; (5) the House concurs in the bill at report stage; (6) the bill is read a third time and passed by the House; (7) the bill goes through the same stages in the Senate; (8) finally, the bill receives royal assent (see Figure 4.3).

**Introduce a Bill** To introduce a public bill, a member must give 48 hours' written notice and then, by motion, obtain leave to intro-duce the bill. The motion to obtain leave is automatically adopted without debate, amendment, or question. Normally, ministers introduce bills and do not speak at the intro-duction stage. However, a private member in-troducing a bill will normally make a short speech explaining the purpose of the bill.

**First Reading** First reading follows immedi-ately and is automatically adopted with-

**Figure 4.3 Step-by-Step Stages of a Bill to a Law**

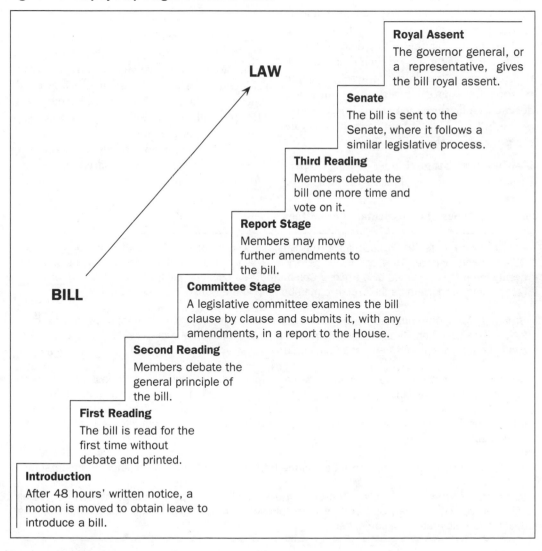

LAW

**Royal Assent**
The governor general, or a representative, gives the bill royal assent.

**Senate**
The bill is sent to the Senate, where it follows a similar legislative process.

**Third Reading**
Members debate the bill one more time and vote on it.

**Report Stage**
Members may move further amendments to the bill.

**Committee Stage**
A legislative committee examines the bill clause by clause and submits it, with any amendments, in a report to the House.

**Second Reading**
Members debate the general principle of the bill.

BILL

**First Reading**
The bill is read for the first time without debate and printed.

**Introduction**
After 48 hours' written notice, a motion is moved to obtain leave to introduce a bill.

out debate, amendment, or question. At this time, the Speaker asks when the bill will be read for the second time, and the response is usually that it will be read at the next sitting of the House. This formality allows the bill to be placed on the **Order Paper** for the second reading.

**Second Reading** Second reading is the most important stage in the passage of the bill. It is then that the principle and object of the bill are debated and either accepted or rejected. The clauses of the bill are not discussed in detail at this stage. Three types of amendments to the motion may be proposed for second reading: First, that the bill be delayed for six months and read a second time then; second, the reasoned amendment, whereby specific reasons for opposing second reading are declared; and, third, that the subject matter of the bill be referred to a committee before the principle of the bill is approved.

**Committee Stage** Under Canada's parliamentary traditions, bills are not at once referred to standing committees. According to the Standing Orders, a bill must be read twice and then referred to a committee (see Figure 4.4). Committees undertake detailed study and possible amendment. Bills based on "supply motions" (money bills) are referred to a Committee of the Whole (all members), which studies in detail all bills dealing with raising and spending money. Other types of bills are referred to a legislative committee, which considers the bill clause by clause. Amendments to the content of the bill are also considered at this stage.

Before beginning a clause-by-clause study of a bill, the legislative committee usually hears the member or the minister sponsoring the bill, and may also receive testimony from outside witnesses on technical matters. Amendments in committee must be in keeping with the principle of the bill, as agreed to at second reading in the House.

The distribution of decision-making power in the Canadian legislative process is a function of political party distribution in the

**Figure 4.4  Types of Parliamentary Committees**

*Standing Committees:* Provided for in the Standing Orders of the House of Commons and the Rules of the Senate. They are investigatory and legislative in nature. Most consist of about twenty members, selected by a Striking Committee, representing political parties in approximately the same proportion as their relative membership in the House.

*Standing Joint Committees:* These are legislative and investigatory committees having both Senate and Commons membership. Committee names reflect the subject under investigation, for example, Agriculture and Trade and Commerce.

*Special Committees:* These function in the same manner as standing committees, but are created in response to specific circumstances and needs. The field of inquiry of special committees is generally narrower in scope than that of standing committees because they are usually appointed to consider a particular topic, petition, or bill. They function as committees until they have presented their final report.

*Special Joint Committee:* A Special Committee having both Senate and Commons membership.

*Committee of the Whole House:* The entire House acting as a committee to study in detail all bills dealing with money, and certain other public interest bills that the House of Commons decides to deliberate as a committee.

House of Commons. Committee assignments are party-based and reflect the percentage of seats a political party commands in the House of Commons. Thus, if the government party wins 70 percent of the seats in the House of Commons, it will occupy approximately 70 percent of the positions on each committee, and opposition parties will also have representation on committees, based on the percentage of seats they won in the last election. Because of the continuing dominant position of the government in the committees, bills are not defeated or killed.

The basic challenge to the House of Commons is how to organize its 295 diverse members in order to get its legislative work done. One major response to the challenge since the mid-1960s has been to establish legislative committees to specialize in parliamentary business. Currently, there are twenty standing committees of the House of Commons and fourteen of the Senate, and three standing joint committees made up from members of the House and the Senate (see Table 4.2). A striking, or selection, committee decides on the membership of the standing and joint committees. Each party caucus provides the striking committee with the names of qualified committee candidates. This practice prevents the government from assigning the least-experienced and least-able opposition members to important standing committees.

Under the Standing Orders of the House of Commons, adopted in June 1978, these committees are permanent and are struck at the commencement of each session of Parliament to consider all subjects arising from the process of lawmaking in Canada. Committee assignments are party-based and reflect the percentage of seats a party commands in the Commons. Committee power is more closely concentrated in the House when there is strong majority government. But opposition parties can be more

## Table 4.2 Standing Committees of Parliament

### House of Commons

Agriculture and Agri-food
Canadian Heritage
Citizenship and Immigration
Environment and Sustainable Development
Finance
Fisheries and Oceans
Foreign Affairs and International Trade
Government Operations
Health
Human Resources Development
Human Rights and the Status of Disabled Persons
Indian Affairs and Northern Development
Industry
Justice and Legal Affairs
National Defence and Veterans' Affairs
Natural Resources
Procedure and House Affairs
Sub-Committee on Private Members' Business
Public Accounts
Transport

### Senate

Aboriginal Peoples
Agriculture and Forestry
Banking, Trade and Commerce
Internal Economy, Budgets and Administration
Legal and Constitutional Affairs
National Finance
Energy, the Environment and Natural Resources
Fisheries
Foreign Affairs
Privileges, Standing Rules and Orders
Scrutiny of Regulations
Selection
Social Affairs, Science and Technology
Transport and Communications

### Standing Joint Committees

Library of Parliament
Official Languages
Scrutiny of Regulations

influential in committees in a minority-government situation.

A number of factors influence MPs' requests for committee assignments. One of these is the desire to be where the action is. They also want to serve on committees that handle the broadest central concerns of government, such as the Public Accounts Committee. Another major motive of House members in requesting committee assignments is to be in a position to influence public policy. Some committees are attractive to members because they play important roles in the key areas of government decision making, like taxing and spending, the economy, and social welfare policy.

The role of committees is essentially to refine and improve measures that the House of Commons has already approved. Nevertheless, committee refinements and amendments frequently necessitate compromises between the committee and the government, which is the author of most bills. These amendments can affect the title, clauses, or schedules in the original bill. Clauses and schedules may be omitted, and new ones added. After a committee has completed its consideration of a bill, it orders the bill to be reported to the House of Commons. When a bill is reported back to the House, it usually passes with little, if any, delay or change, but the bill must still be reported.

**Report Stage** At the report stage, the House receives bills that have been studied, and possibly amended, in committee by considering motions in amendment, of which notice in writing is given. The Speaker is in the Chair, and the general rules of debate apply, with the added restriction that no member may speak for longer than ten minutes on any amendment.

According to the Standing Orders, every bill examined and reported by a committee must be considered by the House at the report stage. Except for those bills considered in Committee of the Whole, the report stage cannot begin sooner than the second sitting day after the bill has been reported, unless the House orders otherwise. Motions in amendment at this stage must be filed no later than the sitting day prior to the beginning of consideration, and placed on the Notice Paper. Ministers of the Crown may, without notice, propose amendments regarding the form of government bills. Once the report stage has begun, no further motions in amendment may be introduced.

Amendments already discussed in committee may be proposed at this stage; the Speaker may select any group of proposed amendments for debate, and may also rule on whether each motion should be voted on separately or as part of a group. This decision is made at the beginning of the report stage. At this time, the Speaker rules on what amendments can be considered. Members who did not sit on the committee that studied the bill can have their amendments considered by the House.

When deliberations at the report stage are concluded, a motion is moved that the bill, with any amendments, be concurred in. The question is put immediately, without amendment or debate. If no amendments are put down for consideration at the report stage, this stage becomes more of a formality, and the report and third reading stages may then occur on the same day.

**Third Reading** The bill is read for the third time, and a motion to pass the bill is made. Amendments considered at this stage cannot contradict the principle of the bill as passed in the second reading. An amendment can be proposed to refer the bill back to committee to be further amended in a specific area, or to reconsider a certain clause or group of clauses.

**Passage by the Senate** After a bill has been passed by the House of Commons, a message is sent to the Senate, requesting that the bill be passed by the Upper Chamber, where procedures for passage of a bill are similar to those of the House. If the Senate passes the bill without any amendment, a message to that effect is sent to inform the House of Commons, and, unless it contains financial provisions, the bill is not returned to the House. If there are amendments, the Senate informs the House by message. In the House, consideration of Senate amendments will appear on the Orders of the Day. If the House agrees to the Senate amendments, a message so indicating is sent to the Senate, and the bill is returned to the Senate for royal assent.

If the House does not agree to the Senate amendments, it adopts a motion stating the reasons for its disagreement, which it communicates to the Senate. If the Senate wishes the amendments to stand nonetheless, it sends a message to this effect to the House, which then accepts or rejects them. If it decides to reject them, the House may adopt a motion requesting a conference between the two Houses, where their respective representatives attempt to resolve the impasse. Twenty-four hours' written notice is required for any motion respecting Senate amendments to a bill.

**Royal Assent and Proclamation** The Constitution Act, 1867, states that the approval of the Crown, signified by royal assent, is required for any bill to become law after passage by both Houses. The ceremony of royal assent is one of the oldest of all parliamentary proceedings and brings together the three constituent parts of Parliament: the Crown (represented by the governor general), the Senate, and the House of Commons. Although the governor general in person may give royal assent to major pieces of legislation and at prorogation, a deputy in the person of the Chief Justice of Canada or a puisne judge of the Supreme Court normally represents the governor general at other times. On all occasions, the Speaker or the Deputy Speaker is present at the Bar of the Senate Chamber, where the ceremony takes place.

The office of the governor general, acting at the request of the government, notifies the House by letter, usually on the day of the event or one or two days before royal assent is to be given. The message is read by the Speaker of the House. It is a notice only and does not constitute a summons, which comes when the **Gentleman Usher of the Black Rod** appears in the Chamber to request the attendance of members in the Senate.

A quorum is not necessary for the Speaker to take the Chair when the Black Rod is at the door; if the House is sitting in Committee of the Whole, the Speaker immediately takes the Chair. After knocking, entering, and delivering the summons, the Black Rod returns to the Senate, followed by the Sergeant-at-Arms with the mace, the Speaker, the Table Officers, and the members, all of whom assemble at the Bar of the Senate.

The ceremony for royal assent consists of the reading by the Senate Clerk, officially styled the "Clerk of the Parliaments," of the short title of the bill or bills to be approved. The formula of assent is then pronounced by the Senate Clerk on behalf of the Crown's representative. If supply bills are to receive assent, the Commons Speaker addresses the Crown's representative, according to an established formula, and presents a copy of each bill to the Senate Clerk Assistant. The Clerk of the Parliaments, in the name of the Sovereign, then thanks the House for its loyalty and benevolence and announces royal assent. At the conclusion of the ceremony, the Speaker returns to the House and reports what has just occurred. The proceeding usually takes fifteen to twenty minutes, after which the House resumes the business interrupted by the arrival of the Black Rod, or adjourns the sitting.

Royal assent is given to a bill when it has passed in exactly the same form by both Houses; it is at this stage that a bill becomes a law. The bill comes into force on the day of assent, unless otherwise stipulated in the bill itself.

## WHO ARE MEMBERS OF PARLIAMENT?

Ours is a representative democracy in which the elected members of the House of Commons and those who are appointed to the Senate serve as our legislative representatives in Ottawa. One way to represent is to be similar to that which is being represented. If it is expected in our political system that women's issues are to be represented, then are there a significant number of women in Parliament? From this perspective, a perfectly representative Parliament would have characteristics similar to those of the general Canadian population in terms of race, gender, ethnicity, occupation, religion, age, and other variables. From this perspective, Parliament is and has been highly unrepresentative.

Women and racial minorities are significantly underrepresented. The first woman to sit in the House of Commons was Agnes Campbell Macphail, who was elected in 1921. The number of women has slowly increased over the years, to about 18 percent of the members of the House of Commons after the 1993 federal election. Between 1930 and 1993, a total of 36 women were appointed to the Senate.

Members of Parliament have historically been far better educated than the remainder of the population. The members of the different parliamentary parties have become similar from the standpoint of social background and career. MPs are increasingly professional in their background and lifestyle, and therefore less representative of their constituents. There has also been a trend for MPs to remain longer in Parliament, and thus to be regarded as "professional politicians." They tend to come from higher-income families and enjoy incomes that are substantially above the national average. Since Confederation, more than half of all parliamentarians have been lawyers. Most of the rest have backgrounds in business, including farming or the professions. Notable for their lack of representation are blue-collar workers, whether skilled, semiskilled, or unskilled. Parliament is thus a more middle-class, better-educated group of people than the citizenry at large, and it contains a disproportionately greater ratio of males to females than is the case among the general population.

Many Canadians feel underrepresented or unrepresented in the most prominent govern-

Although our government is made up of highly educated, middle-class people, it contains a disproportionately high ratio of males to females. However, this ratio is changing. For example, here is Joan Sawicki as Speaker of the British Columbia Legislative Assembly. *Source:* Photograph courtesy of Joan Sawicki.

ing institutions that affect their daily lives. Women, racial minorities, and the poor believe that their interests are not properly articulated in Parliament. The disparities between the Canadian population and the make-up of Parliament reflect a major weakness in terms of one of the tenets of representative democracy, that is, the norm of political equality.

## The Constituents

Ultimately, Parliament is there for constituents. A member of Parliament is a representative of his or her constituents — the people who live and vote in an MP's or senator's riding. Their opinions on issues and the performance of the MP who represents them are crucial in the parliamentary decision-making process. As much as members of Parliament want to please their party leaders by going along with their preferences, legislators have to think about what the voters back home want. If they displease enough people by the way they vote, they might lose their seats in the next election.

The term "constituency" is not as simple as it sounds. Members have several constituencies, including not only their entire riding but also subconstituencies within their ridings, such as those who traditionally vote for their party, special socio-economic groups, and their personal supporters. Sometimes, these constituencies may be in conflict. A pro-choice women's group can be in conflict with the traditional party supporters, both groups expecting their MP to represent their position on the issue of abortion.

In considering the influence of all these factors in a member's environment, it is important to keep in mind that MPs and senators also have strong views of their own. They come to Parliament deeply committed to working on some key issues and do not need to be pressured into acting on them or into voting a certain way when these issues are considered in the government's legislative agenda or are adopted as the party's position. In fact, their strong views on some policy questions can conflict not only with what their party wants but also with what their constituents want. Many constituents vote only for their member of Parliament, notwithstanding who might become prime minister or what party wins the most seats.

All members of Parliament must take positions on matters of public policy when they vote on issues and when they respond to constituents' questions about where they and the party stand on issues. Constituents want them to be experienced, hardworking, and trustworthy — true servants of their constituencies. Party loyalty is, of course, important but what an MP can do for the constituents in the riding determines his or her chances of re-election.

Members of Parliament have worked hard to get themselves known in their constituencies. In the final analysis, constituents want a representative who works hard and gets things done. In the 1990s, the most desirable means of serving constituents is to bring federal dollars and jobs to the constituency. But the job of an MP also entails a great amount of routine work at the riding office. He or she must serve constituents by answering mail and telephone requests. These functions are crucial for members and their staffs, who act as red tape–cutters for everyone from elderly citizens trying to get government pensions to provincial MLAs and MNAs trying to get federal grants for municipal incinerator or water-purification systems.

People turn to their MPs because they see them as allies in their struggles with bureaucrats. Individual members may have limited power in trying to get important legislation passed, but, in dealing with a constituent's problems, their power is much greater because of their ability to deal with bureaucrats. A phone call or a letter to a federal government department can bring attention to a constituent's problem. MPs also provide information to people looking for jobs, as well as to students working on term papers. They help constituents puzzled about which federal government department should be approached or where information can be researched.

Some members say they enjoy their constituency work more than their legislative roles because the results of casework are often more immediate and tangible. Most members are re-elected even if they cannot solve many of the problems their constituents bring to them or cannot obtain federal money for their riding. But members believe that the best way to ensure re-election is to be so good at constituency work, so successful in bringing benefits to their ridings, and so well known to the voters that no serious rival will want to run. Constituency work includes answering mail, solving constituents' problems, making speeches, putting out newsletters and press releases, and meeting with voters as often as possible.

MPs differ widely in how they represent their constituents. Some spend much of their time keeping contacts in their riding. Others channel their energies into legislative tasks and committee work. They let their staffs and assistants handle riding problems. Skilful MPs learn to anticipate voter reactions and to spot the issues of highest concern in their ridings.

## Backbenchers

In the British parliamentary tradition, a backbencher is not a frontbencher. A *frontbencher* is a member of Parliament who holds a ministerial post or an opposition shadow minister. Backbenchers do not hold such posts, and their parliamentary role is largely confined to supporting the leadership of their party as the party whip directs. In Parliament, backbenchers are not expected to have independent minds. Parliamentary activity is largely a contest between the leaders of

the government party and the leaders of the opposition parties (MacGuigan 1978). As a consequence, backbenchers get few opportunities to express themselves independently. However, they may have a chance to ask a question during question period, to contribute to the tail end of a debate, or to take part in a parliamentary committee.

However, if an individual backbencher has the courage to vote against the party direction, he or she may be blackballed by party colleagues. Even more consequential, to cross a parliamentary floor is to terminate one's association with the political party that supported one during the previous election.

In Canada, *government backbenchers* are members of Parliament who belong to the government party but do not perform any special role for the government. They are expected to support their party and its leader in the House of Commons. In meetings of the party caucus, they may question the prime minister and ministers, and take part in the general discussions. In Parliament, they are expected to support the decisions of the Cabinet by both voting and making speeches. They are united by a shared political ideology and the desire for their party to remain in power. Many of them aspire to be Cabinet ministers at some future time. They are also concerned with satisfying the voters who elected them to the House of Commons.

*Opposition backbenchers* share the desires of their leaders to defeat the government party in a general election and thereby have their party form the government. They are expected to make speeches, ask questions, and to cast their votes in accordance with their party's decisions. They also want some day to be in the "front" benches, as members of a Cabinet. Opposition backbenchers will try to gain their party leader's approval in the same way that government backbenchers do. But they want to keep their voters happy with the job they are doing.

## PARLIAMENTARY PRIVILEGE

The growth of parliamentary privilege is linked to the disputes between the Stuart kings and the English Parliament in the seventeenth century. Parliamentary privileges were claimed to protect the House of Commons and its members from the power and influence of the king or queen and the House of Lords. Following the expulsion of James II, the Bill of Rights of 1689 was passed. Among other things, the bill guaranteed that members of Parliament could speak freely and could not be arrested in Parliament. Over time, the House of Commons earned its powers as a deliberative body with special immunities from executive interference.

Parliamentary privileges were formally assigned to Canada's Parliament through the Constitution Act, 1867, and were enacted in a statute now known as the Parliament of Canada Act (Maingot 1982). The most important privilege is that of freedom of speech. MPs may say anything they like about anyone without fear of being sued for libel or slander, provided they say it during the proceedings of Parliament. There are some restrictions about what they can say about each other, however. For instance, to call another MP a "liar" is "unparliamentary language" and may result in the name-caller being suspended from the House or Senate for a period of time. Members who engage in disgraceful conduct, such as hitting another member or making offensive non-verbal signals across the floor, may also be expelled from the legislature.

Provincial parliamentarians also enjoy privilege and may even make disparaging remarks about members of the federal Parliament without penalty. Private citizens outside Parliament may well be called a liar, or worse, by a member without being able to take action about it. However, members are expected to show restraint and good political judgement when speaking about non-members.

It can be argued that, without privilege, members of Parliament could not perform their public duties. It is arguable that the benefit of open and critical examination of any aspect of Canadian life would be impossible to achieve without privilege. However, such benefits must be balanced against what might be seen as the abuse of privilege. In 1992, a Quebec Superior Court judge held that MPs are not above the law, even though they enjoy special privileges in performing their democratic duties. The judge, who deliberated in the case of an MP charged with fraud, breach of trust, and misuse of public money of more than $100 000, held that the Criminal Code must be continued to be enforced, regardless of an MP's parliamentary privileges.

## THE SPEAKER

In Westminster parliamentary history, the role of Speaker was quite dangerous; the Speaker was in the front lines in the battle for supremacy between the monarch and Parliament (Sneddon 1979). There were times when the monarch's displeasure with a Speaker was so great that the latter literally lost his head. Several Speakers were killed or imprisoned. It was in that era that the tradition originated of "dragging in" the reluctant Speaker upon election to the Chair. This custom has been replaced by that of escorting the Speaker to the Chair — a tradition that has continued in Canada with the Sergeant-at-Arms attending the Speaker on entering and leaving the Commons Chamber.

In Canada, the Speaker is the chairperson of the House of Commons or the Senate and has the primary role of conducting meetings and maintaining order. The Speaker holds the position of highest authority in the House of Commons, and usually exercises it from a raised Speaker's Chair at the north end of the Chamber. It is the role of the Speaker to keep meetings orderly and to enforce the rules and procedure of Parliament impartially (Laundy 1984). In so doing, the Speaker protects the rights and privileges of members. Rulings are based on the procedures and interests of Parliament, usually in accordance with the Standing Orders and past precedents of the federal legislatures. The Speaker is not to police but to judge and to intervene to ensure order and fair play.

The Speaker's duties are divided into three categories — ceremonial, quasi-judicial, and administrative. In the ceremonial role, the Speaker is the spokesperson for the House of Commons and the Senate. The Speaker represents Parliament in its relations with the Crown and the Crown's representative, the governor general, and with other authorities and persons outside Parliament. The Speaker reads messages from the governor general and presents bills for royal assent. Next to the governor general, the Speaker hosts and entertains more visiting dignitaries and delegations than any one else in Canada, meeting ambassadors to Canada and attending functions on behalf of the House of Commons. The Speaker is ranked fifth in Canada's order of ceremonial precedence, behind the governor general, the prime minister, the Chief Justice of the Supreme Court, and the Speaker of the Senate.

Perhaps the most prominent role of the Speaker is the quasi-judicial function of presiding over proceedings in the House of Commons. The Speaker acts like a judge in Canada, rather than taking a partisan role in the legislative process as does the Speaker in the United States. Although a member of a party when elected, he or she assumes a neutral posture, and never ostensibly uses the authority of the office to favour his or her own party or any other. The Speaker announces the result of any vote in the House and brings to the attention of the House all matters affecting the rights and privileges of members.

Although the Speaker is the servant of the House, he or she has absolute control over debate during question period. The Speaker calls on members to speak, rules on points of order, decides whether a matter of privilege should take precedence over other business, deals judiciously with a member who is "out of order," and decides whether an emergency debate should be granted. In short, the Speaker interprets the Standing Orders in accordance with precedent, practice, and tradition.

While a legal background is a definite asset in sorting out the intricacies of **parliamentary procedure**, the rendering of a technically correct decision is not the most difficult challenge for the Speaker. The greatest challenge is knowing the mood of the House. Speakers need to be authoritative without being overbearing; dignified, but also humorous and witty; and capable of being neutral without appearing aloof.

Above all, the Speaker must be impartial, showing no alliance with members or a political party. It is true that some Speaker's decisions will be controversial, but it is essential that they not be seen as partisan. The rules of procedure give the Speaker disciplinary powers. Should a member disregard the Speaker's authority — for example, by refusing to withdraw unparliamentary language or causing disorder — the Speaker can "name" the member and expel him or her from the Chamber for the remainder of the day's sitting. The tradition of impartiality is somewhat different for the Speaker of the Senate. Unlike the House of Commons Speaker, he or she may participate in the debates.

The Speaker is also the administrative head of the House of Commons. The Speaker chairs the Board of Internal Economy, which prepares the budget for the House of Commons. The Speaker administers an annual budget and is responsible for about 2000 employees who staff the House. The Speaker of the Senate also carries out many ceremonial and diplomatic functions.

Finally, the Speaker is the member of Parliament for a federal riding. Because the Speaker of the House is not able to debate, question ministers, or vote in the House (unless there is a tie), other parliamentarians know the dilemma a Speaker faces when representing a riding. The Speaker must ask another member of the House of Commons to present petitions to the House on behalf of the Speaker's constituents. The Speaker has the constant support and advice of the principal permanent officers of the House, especially the Clerk of the House and the Sergeant-at-Arms.

Before the parliamentary rules were changed in 1985, the Speaker was nominated by the prime minister and was usually elected without opposition. By custom, the Speaker was chosen from among members of the party in power. Today, the Speaker is elected by secret ballot, and any member, except a minister or a political party leader, may stand for election. It is the only time that a secret ballot is used in Parliament (all other voting by members is done publicly). The Speaker may drop his or her membership in a party and run in the next general election as an independent. In 1985, the Commons adopted a new system whereby any member except ministers of the Crown, party leaders, and anyone holding an office within the House may stand for election as Speaker. The Speaker of the Senate is appointed by the governor general on the advice of the prime minister.

## QUESTION PERIOD

The powers of the Cabinet over the legislative process are significant, but they are tempered by the power of the House of Commons to reject all or part of the Cabinet's legislative program. One device of parliamentary control over the dominance of Cabinet decision making is question period. The daily question period provides Parliament and the public with the principal means for calling the government to account for its actions. It is inconvenient for ministers, wherein lies perhaps its greatest value.

Since Parliament was first instituted in Canada, face-to-face confrontations between political opponents have held a special place in the lore of Canadian legislative politics. But not until the era of television could an entire electorate witness MPs squaring off against each other in the House of Commons. Much of the debate in Parliament is quite predictable. Often the debates are not a series of fiery speeches of point and counterpoint, but, instead, are boring and delivered to sparse audiences, some of whom are reading, conversing, or just walking around. A government with a large majority is not likely to have any of its measures defeated. Opposition parties can delay legislation, but in most cases the will of the government will prevail. Debate is, of course, part of the legislative process, but it is also an effective instrument of control when it is properly focussed on important issues. It is important in parliamentary matters because it produces a record of legislative intent that can have great influence on government conduct as well as on how the public evaluates government performance.

It is not surprising, therefore, that although it lasts for only 45 minutes, question period is undoubtedly the highlight of the parliamentary day, attracting more ministers, private members, journalists, and spectators than most other proceedings of Parliament. By tradition, the first question is asked by the leader of the opposition or a representative acting on his or her behalf. Leaders of other parties are then recognized, followed by other opposition members and, from time to time, an independent or a private member on the government side. At times, it resembles a contest between an irresistible force (a questioner) and an immovable object (the Cabinet). But no matter how large the majority, the government can still be held accountable by a small group of determined opposition members. In the full glare of publicity during question period, ministers and opposition members are eager to score points. Most questions are addressed to the ministers of the Crown, although the Standing Orders permit members to request information from the chairs of committees.

The Standing Orders of the House of Commons provide, among other things, that questions may be put to a minister regarding those areas of public affairs with which he or she is officially connected. The rules of the House seek to ensure that questions will not be improper (e.g., personally insulting attacks). Questions should not be debated, and should not contain arguments, inferences, imputations, epithets, ironical expressions, or hypothetical matter. Supplementary questions should be brief and related to the original question. The answer should be relevant to the question. Although a minister's answers to questions seldom lead to further debate, and almost never to the government's downfall, the knowledge that every phase of their work may be subject to parliamentary questioning keeps ministers constantly on their toes.

Question period is one of the most important aspects of parliamentary procedure because it places the government on the line, or at least that is its purpose. Question period is an opportunity for the opposition parties and independent members to cross-examine the government on its behaviour, its actions, and its decisions. It is supposed to represent the principle of responsible government — government being answerable to the people's representatives in Parliament. However, Parliament is subject to the dominance of the executive and the political party in power.

Nonetheless, question period has been criticized for its tone and style, and there has been much commentary on the nature and length of questions and answers. An immediate step toward improving question period would be the imposition of strict time limits on both questions and answers. The spotlight of publicity is thrown upon the government almost every day that Parliament is in session, leaving no dark corners unexposed where laziness, incompetence, or dishonesty may lurk. As a check on the policies and actions of the executives, question period is a much more reliable form of accountability than the occasional press conference in the United States, convened at the whim of the president and often with reluctance.

## CONCLUSION

Canadians are of two minds about Parliament. As an institution, it is an enigma to most people. Its large size, puzzling procedures, and measured pace, all blur its image. In contrast, individual MPs are better understood and receive higher public approval. Most people think of Parliament in public-policy terms. They expect Parliament, like the government it houses, to solve problems and keep the ship of state on an even keel.

Public approval of Parliament rises and falls with economic conditions in the country — inflation, unemployment, recession, depression, and feelings of optimism or cynicism. If people are unhappy, fearful, or cynical, they blame the government and hold Parliament in low esteem. But people have more detailed expectations for individual MPs than for Parliament as a whole. If Parliament is mysterious and distant, MPs and senators are fairly well known in their provinces and ridings and tend to be judged less on policy contributions than on service to their constituents.

The public's final verdict is, of course, delivered at the polls. Our era is hard on legislatures and legislators. Parliament is subject to severe pressures, some coming externally, that is, in the form of public expectations and fast-moving events. Such pressures challenge Parliament to adapt by altering its practices and work habits. Other pressures come internally — partisan political party wrangling, the power of the government, and a sense of paralysis on the part of the opposition that the legislative process is virtually complete even before a bill is given first reading in the House of Commons. For Parliament to survive, it must relieve these pressures by adjusting its procedures.

Parliament will always be controversial. Unlike the political executive, it conducts its business largely in public. Its faults are out in the open for all to see. No body of politicians can satisfy the demands of all major groups and interests, especially in an age of government cutbacks and scarce resources. And no such body can represent those demands without making tough decisions that are perceived to be incoherent and contradictory. This is the dilemma Parliament faces as a representative institution.

## GLOSSARY

**agenda**  A list of specific items of business to be considered at a legislative or parliamentary session, conference, meeting, or caucus.

**backbenchers**  Elected members of a legislature who do not hold office under the Crown.

**bill**  A proposal for a law that is considered by Parliament in three readings and studied in both the House of Commons and the Senate. After approval by both Houses, it receives royal assent and becomes law.

**Cabinet**  An executive government body composed of the prime minister and the ministers of the Crown or a premier and a provincial executive council that determines the direction of public policy for the government.

**Clerk of the House**  Advises the Speaker and members on parliamentary procedure and practice and sits at the table in front of the Speaker in the Chamber. The Clerk is the most senior executive officer of the Commons and is responsible for keeping the official record of proceedings, preparing Commons documents, and supervising the procedural officers and clerks.

**Crown**  A synonym for the monarch, the governor general, or the government as a whole.

**dissolution of Parliament**  Parliament ceases to exist until a general election is held and a new Parliament is convened.

**Gentleman Usher of the Black Rod**  The personal attendant and messenger of the Queen or her representative when either person is in Parliament. This person summons members of the House of Commons to the Senate at the opening of Parliament and when bills receive royal assent. The "Black Rod" is also responsible for Senate security services.

**Hansard**  The name of the printer in England who began to prepare the reports of Parliament in the eighteenth century. Today, it is the name for the daily official record of debates in the House of Commons, which is edited, translated, and printed in English and French.

**head of state**  Usually a monarch, a representative of the monarch, or a president who symbolizes the majesty of the entire nation-state, and plays a symbolic role in the process of lawmaking and officiates at state events.

**leader of the opposition**  Usually the leader of the party that holds the second-largest number of seats in the House of Commons. This person provides criticism of the government, leads opposition debates in the House of Commons, and suggests amendments to government legislation or alternative proposals.

**motion of non-confidence** One of the motions used in Parliament to decide whether the government or executive should continue in office.

**Order Paper** Is the popular name given to Order of Business and Notices (the daily agenda of the House of Commons).

**parliamentary procedure** The rules and traditions that determine how the House of Commons and Senate carry out their business.

**petitions** Pleas from private citizens or organizations to an official, an agency of government, or a Parliament, requesting that something be done, that some wrong be righted, or that some general grievance be remedied.

**privy councillors** Members of the Queen's Privy Council for Canada, an advisory body to the Crown. The membership is determined by the governor general on the advice of the prime minister, and no minister may hold office without first being sworn to the Privy Council. Privy councillors hold their membership for life, and may use the initials "P.C." after their name.

**question period** The one-hour period during most days when Parliament is in session when ministers have to answer questions raised by the opposition as well as members of the government party.

**royal assent** The approval by the monarch or the representative of the monarch, the governor general or the lieutenant-governor, that makes a bill passed by the legislature a law.

**Speech from the Throne** A speech by the prime minister and the Cabinet that is delivered by the monarch or the governor general at the start of a session of Parliament. The speech is delivered in the Senate Chamber and outlines the government's policies and programs and the legislation it plans to introduce during the parliamentary session.

**Standing Orders** The rules and procedures that regulate the conduct of business in Parliament.

**Table Officers** Parliamentary employees who assist the Speaker to administer the operation of the legislature, facilitate debates, and communicate with members of Parliament.

**want of confidence** One of the notions used in a legislature or other formally organized body to decide whether the government or executive should continue to hold office.

**whips** Named after the "whippers" in the organization of the traditional English fox hunt who kept the hounds from straying, they are chosen in party caucus as special officers of their political parties to ensure that all party members keep the party line and are present for important votes.

## RECOMMENDED READING

Brooks, Stephen. 1992. *Canadian Democracy*. Toronto: McClelland & Stewart. This book covers all of the basic elements of Canadian government but examines in particular the legislative structures of governance.

Clarkson, Stephen, and Christina McCall. 1992. *Trudeau and Our Times*. Toronto:

McClelland & Stewart. The authors provide an excellent treatment of how a prime minister relates to parliamentary colleagues in the House of Commons and the Senate.

Doern, Bruce, and Richard Phidd. 1992. *Canadian Public Policy*. Scarborough, Ont.: Nelson Canada. This book focusses on the making of public policy and analyzes the legislative interactions among the prime minister and the Cabinet, the general policy process, and the role of Parliament in the Canadian policy system.

Dyck, Rand. 1993. *Canadian Politics: Critical Approaches*. Scarborough, Ont.: Nelson Canada. Chapters 15–22 of this book provide an excellent representation and analysis of parliamentary government and politics.

Fleming, Robert. 1992. *Canadian Legislatures 1992*. Agincourt, Ont.: Global Press. This book contains a wide range of articles and presentations on Canada's legislatures, as well as comparisons with the legislative branch of government in the United States.

Gunther, Magnus, and Conrad Winn, eds. 1991. *House of Commons Reform*. Ottawa: Parliamentary Internship Program. This book examines what the House of Commons must do in order to engage in the legislation and debate of the country.

Heard, Andrew. 1991. *Canadian Constitutional Conventions*. Don Mills, Ont.: Oxford University Press. This book focusses on the nature of constitutional conventions and how they affect the powers of the governor general, Cabinet ministers, legislatures, federalism, and the judiciary.

Lijphart, Arend. 1992. *Parliamentary versus Presidential Government*. London: Oxford University Press. This book provides an excellent comparative analysis of the parliamentary and presidential forms of government.

Sproule-Jones, Mark. 1993. *Governments at Work*. Toronto: University of Toronto Press. This book takes a hard look at parliamentary federalism, the underlying arrangements, or "rules," that operate between the levels of government, and the execution of public policy.

White, Randall. 1990. *Voice of Region: The Long Journey to Senate Reform in Canada*. Toronto: Dundurn Press. The author provides a history of Senate reform in Canada, with a thorough analysis of what the reforms can mean.

CHAPTER

# PUBLIC ADMINISTRATION AND CANADA'S BUREAUCRACY

lice, Wina, Aeilidh, Smeorach, Brchaill, and Neoinean were six pregnant purebred Black Highland Scottish cows, imported from the Isle of Mull by Father Bernie MacDonald, who runs a special working farm, called Talbot House, in Frenchvale, Cape Breton. Talbot House is a non-profit rehabilitation farm, geared toward taking recovering alcoholics out of their environment and putting them into a serene setting in which they themselves can develop an alternative lifestyle. Residents at the farm grow their own food, raise animals like these, and participate in self-help programs to improve their chances of overcoming their addictions.

In December 1993, officials of Agriculture Canada ordered the six Black Highlanders killed because they believed that these cows were contaminated with bovine spongiform encephalopathy (BSE), called "mad cow disease" — a non-contagious nervous disorder that eats holes in the cow's brain.

When the first Canadian case was reported in Alberta, Agriculture Canada ordered about 300 cattle destroyed across Canada. Father MacDonald's cows were only suspected of having the disease, and the move to dispose of them by the federal government was a federal strategy for maintaining the integrity of Canada's multimillion-dollar beef industry. The only way for Agriculture Canada to know if a cow has the disease would be to kill it, then analyze the brain of the slain animal to see if the disease was present. In effect, the kill order was given to alleviate concerns among certain of Canada's trading partners (the United States, Mexico, and Japan), who feared infected beef might enter their food supply.

Mad cow disease is believed to be caused when cows are fed meal made from sheep body parts (offal) that is not cooked at temperatures high enough to kill contaminants. Father MacDonald and residents at Talbot House resisted the kill order, arguing that the cows were imported from a farm in Scotland that fed the animals nothing but grass and straw during their quarantine period. They were never fed the contaminated feed believed to cause mad cow disease. Father MacDonald's cows were the only ones of their kind in Canada, and their calves had already been successfully exported to Europe and the United States. None of them developed the disease. Father MacDonald claimed that his cows never showed any of the symptoms associated with the disease — weight loss, unsteadiness, excessive salivation, and moaning. He even demonstrated to officials of Agriculture Canada that all of his pregnant Black Scottish Highland cows were past the age at which the disease was said to manifest itself.

At first, Father MacDonald declined Agriculture Canada's offer to send his cows back to the United Kingdom and to pay all associated costs of the export, up to a maximum of $2000 — the amount designated as compensation for destroying the cows. He and the residents of Talbot House wanted to stand and fight, putting their faith in a Federal Court judge to order Agriculture Canada to cancel the scheduled slaughter of his six Black Highland cows. But, after reviewing the decisions of the Federal Court in two other similar cases, in Ontario and Alberta, they decided to abandon their legal defence and move the cows back to Europe rather than permit the kill order against the cows to take place in Canada. In both the Ontario and Alberta cases, the Federal Court ruled that Agriculture Canada has the right to administer kill orders to protect international trade and to ensure domestic consumer confidence.

Father MacDonald wanted to save the lives of his six beautiful cows. But he knew that the federal bureaucracy was not going to change the kill order, even though it was very unlikely that the Cape Breton cows were diseased. In Canada, bureaucrats are enormously powerful as unelected officials who make decisions that affect the quality of our lives. Sometimes rules and regulations can overshadow common sense. If blindly applied, they will not always function as a means of achieving the best interests of Canadians, but will instead become arbitrary, and perhaps *too* important in their own right.

## INTRODUCTION

Canada's laws and policies are administered, or put into effect, by a variety of departments, agencies, offices, and other government units that together make up its "bureaucracy." For most Canadians, "bureaucracy" means any large, complex organization in which employees have very specific responsibilities and work within a **hierarchy** of authority. The organization of our governments is so complex that most Canadians do not even try to comprehend it, even within their own local communities.

Every day in Canada, government bureaucracies collect, store, and retrieve information about all aspects of our lives. As students of politics and government, we examine government bureaucracies because they play a central role in the governability of the country. The ways our government bureaucracies conduct themselves tell us a lot about how well we govern ourselves, how well we treat our citizens, how we make and implement our decisions, and — when all is said and done — how civilized we are.

How we govern ourselves in Canada owes much to the example of parliamentary government in Great Britain (Hodgetts 1955). Alongside the development of democracy, governing institutions in our culture of public administration came from the British, who struggled to control the bureaucracies of the monarchs themselves. Monarchs could rule over the administrative structure only through their **civil service**: Control of the one could not be asserted without control of the other. For this reason, in Canada, government bureaucracies remain subordinate to the political and ceremonial executive and do not constitute an independent fourth branch of government established under our constitution.

Civil servants were supposed to be loyal to the monarch and not to any policy, party, or special-interest group. They were also expected to be loyal and competent in serving any minister or policy that the monarch commanded. Later, this loyalty became oriented not only to the monarch but to the Crown — that is, to the state — because monarchs come and go, and make mistakes. In effect, the devotion of the civil servant was to the interests of the state and the constitution — if need be, against the errors of monarchs and their cabinets. Under this tradition, any government would expect to be equally well served by a core of professionals in the civil service that have **political neutrality** (D'Aquino 1984).

### How Our Bureaucracy Evolved

As a new country, with simple governing structures, a very sparse population of just over 3 million, a wealth of resources, and remoteness from the political machinations of the old world, Canada in fact needed only a minimal bureaucracy of any kind. In fact, the Fathers of Confederation did not discuss the federal bureaucracy very much, but they did recognize the need for a parliamentary bureaucracy to administer legislative law and to develop expertise in creating and implementing **administrative law**.

Most Canadians adhered to the traditional conception of the governing process as consisting basically of making laws, enforcing them, and going to court to adjudicate them. The idea of a highly trained, highly competent entourage of government employees to keep governability on course was not seen as a priority in the late nineteenth century.

Thus, in 1867, when the new Canadian government began its labours, the bureaucratic establishment comprised only a few hundred people who were hired in the 1860s to serve the fourteen ministries of John A. Macdonald's government. The government had no "career" public servants in today's sense; rather, its bureaucracy consisted mostly of amateurs who were supporters of the party in power. These people were not highly educated experts in the art of governing, and were not even expected to maintain neutrality in relation to the contending political parties.

Today, in Canada, government bureaucracy has become, in every sense, a powerful constituency of government, parallelling Parliament, the Cabinet, and the courts. "Government," as we most often think about it, is the political executive, the legislative, and the judicial organs. In fact, when Canadians talk about government, they tend to overrate the power of the Cabinet as often as they underrate the professional bureaucracy as a forceful element in Canada's parliamentary system of government.

Taken together, these branches do govern, but even given the prominence of their roles, they cannot compare with the constant presence, to say nothing of the sheer numbers, of the public service (Dwivedi 1982, 10). The bureaucracy is, in essence, removed from direct public control, and is often overlooked because of the nature of the decision-making process, which places it behind the scenes in our parliamentary system.

The bureaucracy seldom makes the headlines, and encourages this inattention by the media in order to stay in the background and thus increase its control over the areas of government expertise it manages. Yet, the permanent officials of government — the non-elected clerks and **functionaries** — are encountered by citizens at every turn. In contrast, people generally have no, or very little, contact with the representatives they choose at the ballot box.

The federal government takes a great deal of our national income in taxes and spends the money on a staggering variety of goods and services provided by public servants. Canada's federal government is the country's biggest buyer of almost everything and, likewise, the biggest source of innumerable

services that people consume every day. It patrols Canada's three ocean coasts, and their subterranean depths, and even sends some of its employees into outer space. It operates ferries, some of our institutions of higher learning, museums, and parks. It helps farmers grow better crops, pays for highways, builds airports, and studies weather patterns. It pays people when they are out of work and when they retire. It finances research into the causes of war and peace and AIDS, the consequences of smoking and lovesickness, the mating calls of fruitflies, and the habits of undergraduates. It stockpiles food and maintains an arsenal of weapons.

The people who do these things are called "public servants," "civil servants," or "government employees," if one feels neutral or sympathetic toward them, or "bureaucrats," if one is in a jaundiced mood. The bureaucracy is an easy target for satire and critical rhetoric because it clearly represents both the positive and the negative aspects of Canadian government in action.

All of these employees are individuals who make their careers in governmental organizations that have a variety of political and social purposes. Although the bureaucrats and their organizations are not elected, they can have an enormous impact on the everyday lives of people. To the average citizen, the federal government may seem like an octopus — its tentacles reach just about everywhere.

## THE DYNAMICS OF BUREAUCRACY

Around the turn of the century, a German sociologist, Max Weber; forecasted that bureaucracy might one day dominate societies, permeating to an enormous degree governments and private organizations alike (Harmon and Mayer 1986, 71–74). He called bureaucracy the "iron cage of the future." At the end of the twentieth century, Weber's predictions hold some water, now that bureaucracy affects almost everything we do.

Weber found that government bureaucracies can take on a life of their own and can be powerful quite independent of the governing system within which they are expected to serve. In his description of the ideal type of bureaucracy, Weber identified six principal characteristics:

1. The functions and jurisdictions of the organization are deemed to be "official" and are in compliance with rules, regulations, laws, and directives.

2. Authority is graded and graduated from the top to the bottom in an ordered organization that facilitates the supervision of lower offices by higher ones.

3. The management of the organization is conducted on written documents to ensure uniformity, legitimacy, and efficiency of operations. "Get it in writing" is the key to successful bureaucratic management. Files are an integral part of bu-

reaucratic organization because they are its memory system and can be consulted for guidance on precedence.

4. Bureaucrats are technically trained to perform their jobs, or are experts within fields relevant to the organization.

5. Officials are expected to take an impersonal approach to their "clients" and to treat everyone the same. The impersonality of relationships also applies to other members of the bureaucracy. Decisions are made on the basis of objective criteria rather than personal criteria in what might be called "a zone of indifference" (see Figure 5.1).

6. Officials regard their conditions of employment, their education and training, and their tenure within the organization as components of a career in the civil service.

All of Canada's governmental organizations share certain bureaucratic characteristics: First, *specialization*, or "division of labour," whereby individual jobs or functions have

**Figure 5.1  Zone of Bureaucratic Indifference**

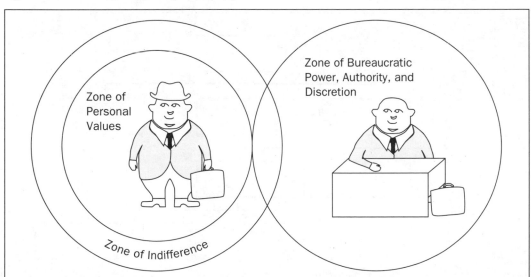

specific tasks assigned to them that can be carried out irrespective of the person who does the job; second, *hierarchy*, or "fixed lines of command" (see Figure 5.2). According to Weber, each government employee knows who the boss is, and whom, if anyone, he or she will supervise. Decisions from the top of the government organization are transmitted to the people who carry them out, and responsibility for carrying out the decisions is fixed and identifiable. This, he believed, adds the dimension of predictability to a government, where each individual is constrained by the mandate of the office and is bound by precedent. Third, incentives exist to attract people to work for the government and to be loyal to its goals. One of the most important incentives is the assurance that job security is absolute, unless a gross transgression is committed.

Weber found that government organizations possess other bureaucratic characteristics as well, including impartiality, that is, devotion to rules instead of individual values; rigidity of attitudes in job performance; extensive paperwork involving the prepara-

tion of files; and, inevitably, red tape. Red tape has continued to be associated with the work of government employees and has come to symbolize the rigid application of regulations that results in delays and frustration for members of the public who are trying to get things done. He noted that bureaucracies work more efficiently when they employ people based on the *merit principle*, according to which demonstrated abilities and credentials, rather than political or administrative patronage, are the criteria for hiring and promotion. Theoretically, advancement occurs without discrimination, based on what, not whom, you know. The organization is staffed mostly by permanent employees whose jobs do not depend on the comings and goings of people at the top.

These features have become the starting point for almost every political analysis of bureaucracy since Weber's. But governments have come a long way since Weber's ideal of a politically neutral and passive bureaucracy that carries out the directives of a democratically elected political executive. Today, in Canada,

**Figure 5.2  A Hierarchy**

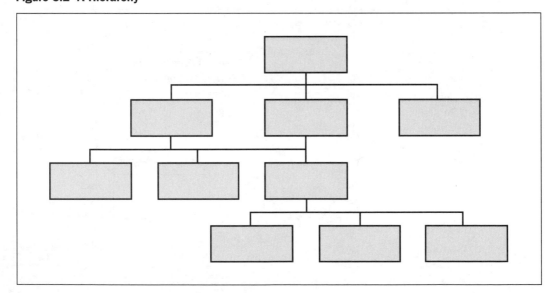

governmental organizations are much more complex, dynamic, and proactive bodies that, many argue, play a major role in making as well as implementing public policy.

The growth of the welfare state has changed most of the functions of government bureaucracy since the turn of the century, functions once performed by religious groups and private organizations. Now government bureaucracies are massive, requiring very extensive organizational and communications systems. The Canadian federal government alone employs more than half a million people, from all walks of life.

## The Growth of Public Administration in Canada

### Times Have Changed

Throughout Canada's history, the agenda of government has changed and grown. In 1867, Canada's annual federal budget was only about $8 million. It has grown steadily since then, and, by the early 1990s, was about $160 billion.

One reason government has grown so much since 1867 is the increasing complexity of modern Canadian society. Almost everything that Canadians do has an immediate economic and political impact in the collective operation of their society. As a general rule today, for every social action there is a governmental reaction. John A. Macdonald did not have a minister concerned about the ozone layer and hazardous materials because these matters were unknown in the 1860s. Early government was much smaller and much less reactive to social need.

### Canadians Think Differently

Another reason governments in Canada have grown so much is that the public's attitude toward the economy has changed since the latter part of the nineteenth century. At that time, there was little or no regulation of the economy or of business behaviour in the marketplace. Entrepreneurs and large industrial and commercial enterprises were generally autonomous, and any government intervention in the economy that might limit the freedom of business was considered inappropriate.

In the twentieth century, many Canadians became aware that the end product of the *laissez faire* approach was not always highly competitive markets that benefited them as consumers. Instead, businesses sometimes formed *oligopolies*, small groups of companies that try to control the entire market. Gradually, government intervention came to be acceptable as necessary to protect the integrity of markets in agriculture, business, finance, manufacturing, and services. And if governments were to patrol effectively for unfair practices in these markets, they needed to expand the role of their administrative bodies.

Over the course of the twentieth century, numerous federal and provincial governmental departments and agencies were organized to regulate the activities of business and specific industries. Examples are the Canadian Wheat Board, the Canadian Radio-television and Telecommunications Commission, Consumer and Corporate Affairs Canada, and the Minister of State for Small Business and for Tourism.

Through bureaucracies such as these, government has become a referee in the marketplace, developing standards of fair business practices and licensing certain businesses for operation. As new social and commercial problem areas have arisen, governments have created new bureaucracies, further expanding the scope of the activities of the public service.

General attitudes about government's responsibilities in the areas of social welfare have changed dramatically since the turn of the century. Running through the fabric of Canada's national political culture is a faith in the ability of government to provide policy solutions to complex social and economic problems. But, at the same time that we criticize the growth of the federal government, we demand its services, highways, airports, job training, consumer protection, and many other benefits. Each of us might be willing to cut benefits for someone else, but most of us want government benefits for ourselves. Canadians have built an elaborate social welfare network chiefly supported by the federal government.

### The Federal Factor

The character of Canada's federal system has had an especially accelerating effect on the growth of government. Two levels of government have a multiplier effect on the size and spending of the federal system. Under Canada's constitution, those powers and jurisdictions not explicitly allocated to the provinces were granted to the federal government. Under this arrangement the federal level of government — unless legally challenged — has grown incrementally as the complex questions of governability tend to fall within Ottawa's jurisdiction (see Table 5.1).

### Table 5.1 The Size of Canada's Federal Government, 1992

|  | Number of Employees |
| --- | --- |
| Departments (Treasury Board employees) | 217 818 |
| Crown corporations | 155 828 |
| Military personnel | 76 319 |
| Canada Post | 73 309 |
| RCMP | 19 521 |
| Total | 542 795 |

*Source*: Adapted from Statistics Canada, *Public Sector Employment and Remuneration*, Cat. No. 72-209; Public Service Commission of Canada, *Annual Report Statistics, 1992*. Reproduced by authority of the Minister of Industry, 1994.

Under the cocoon of federalism, all governments in Canada have experienced growth as a natural bureaucratic phenomenon when organizations and staff take on added responsibilities. Government programs require imaginative ways of implementation, ultimately demanding larger budgets and staffs. Canada's public bureaucracies have grown because they provide important services to many groups of people, and those people — no matter how strongly they are committed to less government — are not willing to sacrifice their own needs to the commitment.

## THE COMPONENTS OF THE FEDERAL BUREAUCRACY

Canada's federal bureaucracy is made up of an extensive array of personnel in federal government departments (e.g., Department of Justice), federal government agencies (e.g., Canadian Aviation Safety Board), central control agencies (e.g., Treasury Board), and **crown corporations** (e.g., St. Lawrence Seaway Authority). Much of the legislation that controls the operation of the federal bureaucracy can be found in the Financial Administration Act and the Public Service Employment Act. These acts and the statutes that create departments provide the legal framework within which the federal government can administer policy and hire those with the necessary expertise to implement it.

Most of the employees of the federal government are recruited by the **Public Service Commission** (PSC), itself an independent central control agency, accountable to Parliament, that is charged with overseeing, examining, hiring, discharging, promoting, and monitoring the working conditions of employees and other agencies operating on the merit system.

The PSC, as it is known today, evolved gradually from the Civil Service Commission (CSC), which was established in 1908 and introduced the merit principle, based on competition. The Public Service Employment Act of 1967 changed the name of the Civil Service Commission to the Public Service Commission. The PSC ensures that government hiring practices do not discriminate against individuals because of their sex, race, national origin, religion, colour, marital status, or age.

The commission plays a very important role in maintaining the professional standards of Canada's civil service and in enforcing the political neutrality of public servants. It provides language training, and staff development in the methodologies of public administration, and administers Canadian regulations on the political activities of public servants.

In 1991, Canada's public servants won the right to engage in politics after the Supreme Court ruled that the Charter of Rights and Freedoms gave most civil servants the right to support political parties and to publicly support candidates during an election. The decision struck down as unconstitutional a section of the Public Service Employment Act that forbade any employee to work for or against a candidate or a party. However, it upheld the section of the act that requires top bureaucrats — those regularly involved in mapping government policy — to remain politically neutral.

## Departments

The oldest, most conventional government organizations are the Cabinet level departments, or ministries, headed by Cabinet ministers. They are the workhorses of the federal government, and of the executive branch of that government. Departments are the largest units of Canada's political executive, each covering substantial areas of government responsibility and hiring thousands of people to implement government decisions.

Departments can be described in management terms as **line organizations**. In contrast to crown corporations and other regulatory bodies, they are directly accountable to a minister of the Crown who can alter the scope, function, and organization of the department. The minister, parliamentary secretaries, and the deputy minister are responsible for the operation and behaviour of the department. The prime minister theoretically has considerable control over the Cabinet departments because they are able to appoint or demote the top officials.

Each of the 25 federal departments has a different mission and is organized differently in terms of its size and administrative structure. They are established to help formulate and administer federal policies in such areas as agriculture, the environment, external affairs, fiscal and monetary policy, justice, labour, and veterans' affairs (see Table 5.2).

Departments are classified as "line departments" when their services and regulations are delivered directly to the public. For example, the Solicitor General and the Transport Canada are two of fifteen such departments. Another group of federal departments are classed as "administrative co-ordinative departments" because they provide their services throughout the government. For example, Revenue Canada raises money to finance government activities, and Public Works manages government property and real estate. A third type, referred to as "policy co-ordinative departments," formulates and implements broad areas of government policy, such as Foreign Affairs and Justice. The last type of department, called "central agencies," assists the Cabinet in its capacity to govern. The Canadian governing system has generated six central agencies — the Prime Minister's Office (PMO), the Privy Council Office (PCO), the Treasury Board Secretariat, the Office of Comptroller General, and the Department of Finance.

The Department of Finance is a good example of one of these powerful bureaucra-

**Table 5.2 Kinds of Federal Departments, Selected Examples, 1994**

| Vertical Co-ordinative Line Departments | Horizontal Administrative Agencies and Departments | Central Departments | Horizontal Policy Co-ordinative Departments |
|---|---|---|---|
| Agriculture and Agri-Food | National Revenue | Finance Canada | Foreign Affairs and International Trade |
| Human Resources Development Canada | Public Works and Government Services Canada | Privy Council Office (PCO) | Industry Canada |
| Citizenship and Immigration | Department of Intergovernmental Affairs | Treasury Board | |
| Natural Resources | | Prime Minister's Office (PMO) | |
| Environment Canada | | | |
| Fisheries and Oceans Canada | | | |
| Indian Affairs and Northern Development Canada | | | |
| National Defence | | | |
| Health Canada | | | |
| Canadian Heritage | | | |
| Solicitor General | | | |
| Transport Canada | | | |
| Veterans Affairs | | | |

cies of government. It acts as a clearing house for the economic activities of all other government departments. Whether it's the Goods and Services Tax (GST), free trade, the new child benefit package, or a crisis at a major Canadian corporation such as Olympia & York, Finance is at the centre of decisions affecting the federal government. It drafts the budget that sets the annual course of government spending, taxation, and economic policies, and has its word to say on everything from child care to the pull-out of peacekeepers from Europe. It is inevitable that the Department of Finance will remain at the centre of the Canadian federal system of government.

## Crown Corporations

Crown corporations make up another major component in the network of Canada's bureaucracy. In the past, these unique public enterprises were created when governments decided that a service was important to the public interest but no private company was willing to provide it or could profit by providing it. While private-sector enterprises are motivated solely by profit, government-owned corporations are organized and financed to withstand economic downturns and to serve the communities for whom they are established.

Crown corporations retain certain common characteristics, whether they are created by the federal government or the provinces, or are jointly owned by private-sector companies: (1) Governments are the major shareholder; (2) The corporation has an independent management structure, outside of direct government control; (3) The goods and services produced enter the private sector; and (4) Prices are set according to natural economic forces.

As agents of public policy, crown corporations are unique forms of enterprise in the Canadian economy (Laux and Malot 1988). Not only are they separate from the central forces of political control, they are also immune from direct government controls in their day-to-day operations. The boards of directors of crown corporations achieve wide public representation by seeking to draw people of diverse economic experience and sociological backgrounds, such as language, ethnicity, religion, and gender. Both the directors and the general personnel are usually drawn from the private corporate and business sector, and bring a business culture into the management and production areas of decision making.

Crown corporations also give governments pathways into the private sector, enabling them to view the sector, with all of its competitive dynamics, and to learn about the market forces that drive successes and failures in the economy. And, finally, when crown corporations make money, they generate revenues for the government in the same way that taxes do. In this regard, they can,

and sometimes do, contribute to the tax base of the country and to the general wealth of the economy.

Prior to Confederation, in 1867, crown corporations were created primarily to manage harbours and meet the demands of nation-building. In 1919, the federal government created the Canadian National Railways in its first major venture in public ownership. Gradually, crown corporations became efficient public management and policy instruments that were seen to function best when they are independent of the governing process. By the 1950s, there were just over 30 federal crown corporations. Over the next 40 years, the federal government gained interest in more than 400 corporations. By the 1990s, approximately one-fourth of Canada's net fixed assets were managed by provincial and federal crown corporations (Gracey 1985, 122). Today, even though some crown corporations have been privatized, their major activities are in areas of finance, insurance, economic planning, resource development, and real estate.

Not all crown corporations are organized in the same way, nor does the government retain the same degree of ownership in all of them. *Mixed enterprises* are public companies that share their ownership with companies in the private sector, or with other governments, provincial or foreign, such as Telesat Canada, and Newfoundland and Labrador Development Corporation is a public enterprise in which ownership is shared by the federal government and the government of Newfoundland and Labrador.

The primary activities for which crown corporations are created have changed throughout the years. But they are fundamentally employed by governments as nation-building instruments in a country of enormous size and complexity. Sometimes they are successful in achieving the goals of their mandates, and sometimes they are not.

## THE PEOPLE IN THE PUBLIC SERVICE

Before discussing in detail the personnel in the public administration, it is necessary to know whom we are talking about. Behind the caricatures of Canada's bureaucrats are men and women. Except for members of the Armed Forces, government employees are known by their positions, for example, assistant deputy minister or information officer. Given the great size and diversity of the Canadian government, public servants vary widely in terms of occupation, place of work, and functional purpose. Among these individuals are computer programmers, biotechnicians, chemists, mathematicians, political scientists, word-processing operators, and receptionists.

Many government employees fit into the stereotypical view of bureaucrats as clerks and office workers. However, practically every occupation represented in Canadian society is performed by someone in the federal government. So, one will find government employees who are accountants, engineers, librarians, and veterinarians.

In order to classify such divergent occupations, the Canadian government groups its employees into human resource categories (see Table 5.3). The administrative support staff of federal departments employ the most people, followed by Canada's foreign and diplomatic service.

Most public servants acquire their positions by meeting the selection requirements for staffing, taking tests to meet administrative and language requirements, and holding the professional qualifications and credentials offered at universities and other special institutions of career training, including the Training Programs Branch of the Public Service Commission itself. As a result of a variety of public and government actions over the past century, the vast majority of government jobs are now filled on the basis of merit.

### Table 5.3 Categories of Federal Public Servants, 1992

| Category | Number |
| --- | --- |
| Management | 4 632 |
| Scientific and Professional | 23 080 |
| Administrative and Foreign Service | 58 812 |
| Technical | 26 058 |
| Administrative Support | 65 112 |
| Operational | 36 402 |
| | 214 096 |

*Source:* Adapted from Public Service Commission of Canada, *Annual Report Statistics, 1992.* Reproduced by authority of the Minister of Industry, 1994.

People enter the public service through a variety of avenues. The Armed Forces has its own system of recruitment. Similarly, other government bodies, such as the RCMP and the Department of External Affairs, have their own separate requirements for hiring and merit.

Most public-service jobs are governed by the determinations of the Public Service Commission. For most positions, competitive examinations are required. But, for some others, individuals are rated on the basis of experience and qualifications. In recent years, federal governments and other agencies have adopted affirmative action hiring practices so as to increase the employment representation of women and visible minorities.

Once hired, most public servants tend to be secure in their jobs, even in the face of government cutbacks and downsizing. Procedures established by the Public Service Staff Relations Board, the Canada Labour Code, and the Public Service Alliance of Canada protect most government workers from arbitrary dismissal. The federal government finds it difficult to fire someone for incompetence, and it can take years to exhaust all avenues of review and appeal.

In terms of the demographics of the general population, high-level administrators in the federal public service represent white anglophone males from the middle and upper classes. White anglophone males have always dominated the federal service and are the majority of government employees in Canada.

Although progress has been made, the federal bureaucracy does not yet fully reflect the social diversity of the Canadian people. In terms of linguistic representation in the public service, the proportion of francophones in the federal government is reflective of that in the total population — that is, about 30 percent — but, in the "Management" category, francophones comprise only about 23 percent. The total federal public service is made up of about 6 percent visible minorities and about 44 percent women: Women fill 12 percent of management positions, and 83 percent of the "Administrative Support" and "Operational" categories of the public service, sometimes referred to as the "pink ghetto" and as employing "pink-collar" workers. Most women work at the bottom of the federal bureaucracy and do predominantly clerical and service tasks (Winn 1985).

Those who start their careers as "professionals" are most likely to reach the highest positions in the public service. These top-level decision-makers have certain traits and attitudes in common. They tend to work well in groups, and not as individual achievers. They accept the restrictions of working in large complex government organizations, and generally understand and willingly accept the need for co-ordination and co-operation. They usually hold high ideals and believe that they are responsible for programs that reflect high social values (Kernaghan and Langford 1990). In doing their jobs, Canadian public servants believe they are working on your behalf.

These attitudes are not at all surprising. The public service wants to attract people who believe in the parliamentary institutions of government and who think that the rules of the game of governability should be played

fairly. However, professional decision making is essentially bureaucratic, not highly visible to the public, and is once removed from Canada's democratic political process. Most public servants carry out their work with little sustained direct public accountability and, as a result, can perform in their jobs without the immediate consequence of public backlash (Laframboise 1983).

Within the structure of Canadian politics and government, bureaucrats are themselves a constituency of power. They support what they do, and do not want to have their jurisdictions arbitrarily changed or, worse still, eliminated. The principal supporters of diplomacy are the diplomats themselves. And the RCMP are the prominent spokespersons for the cause of law and order. Like most public servants, they are interested in their positions, their salaries, their chances for promotion, and their professional working conditions.

Generally speaking, those who dispense Canada's federal government services are committed to the value of those services. They believe that they know how to provide their services better than do laypersons, legislatures, and business professionals. They consider themselves valuable experts. For these reasons, they tend to resist efforts to subordinate their programs to government controls and to rigorous public scrutiny.

## What Deputy Ministers Do

The administrative head of a federal government department is the deputy minister (DM), whose position is the Canadian version of the British "permanent head." Sometimes in Canada, a deputy minister may be called an "undersecretary," as in the Department of External Affairs, a "president," as in the Treasury Board; or a "master," as in the Canadian Mint (see Box 5.1).

Unfortunately, when used in Canada, the term "deputy minister" can be confusing because it suggests that the political minister has a deputized minister to act in his or her

# Profile: Master of the Mint

**M**ost of what government does is seen as enterprise that loses money. But one government body actually makes a lot of money — the Royal Canadian Mint (RCM). The Royal Canadian Mint Act requires that this government corporation operate profitably. The Royal Canadian Mint is the crown corporation responsible for minting coins for Canada and for about 30 other countries. In 1992, for example, the Mint produced more than a billion circulation coins for Canada and nearly 800 million pieces for foreign governments.

First established in 1908 as a branch of the British Royal Mint, it became a Canadian government agency in 1931, and a crown corporation in 1969. Since it began, the RCM has earned an excellent international reputation by successfully diversifying its operations and marketing its coins, tokens, medals, and trade dollars around the world.

The Royal Canadian Mint is managed by a public administrator, who is appointed the Master of the Mint. This person is like a CEO of a major corporation who manages and directs the affairs of a public-owned business and reports to the government of Canada. The position of Master of the Mint is analogous to that of a deputy minister who manages the operation of a government department.

Ruth Hubbard was appointed Master of the Mint in 1993. After graduating with a Bachelor of Arts degree in mathematics and Spanish from Queen's University, Ms. Hubbard completed a Master of Science degree in mathematical analysis at Ohio State University. Her strong background in mathematics and statistics would open doors for her in the public service. She began her career in Canada's public service in 1963 as a senior systems analyst with Statistics Canada. She served as Assistant Director, Methodology Group, Business Survey Methods Division, in this special government agency. She also served for two years as Assistant Secretary in the Treasury Board. In 1984, she accepted a position at the Foreign Investment Review Agency, becoming Executive Vice-President of its successor agency, Investment Canada. In 1988, Ms. Hubbard was appointed Deputy Minister of Customs and Excise for Revenue Canada, and, in 1992, Deputy Minister of Employment and Immigration Canada. Prior to her accepting the position of Master of the Mint, she served briefly as Deputy Minister of Supply and Services and Deputy Receiver General of Canada.

The following is one day's work for the Master of the Mint:

8:45 A.M.  Various phone calls

9:00 A.M.  Meeting with other executive and production officers for a briefing to implement the corporate plan for the Mint

10:00 A.M.  Meeting with company officials in respect of an up-coming Interna-

Ruth Hubbard was appointed Master of the Mint in 1993. Her strong background in mathematics and statistics opened doors for her in the public service. *Source:* Photograph courtesy of Ruth Hubbard.

tional Monetary Fund Conference of governors of central banks and ministers of finance

10:30 A.M.  Meeting with the four vice-presidents of the Mint; VP of Marketing, Finance, Human Resources, and Legal Council

11:00 A.M.  Meeting with official visitors from other states who might be customers of the Mint

12:00 P.M.  Lunch with members of the Conference Board of Canada

1:00 P.M.  Meeting with the auditor general whose accountants are conducting a special examination of the books

2:00 P.M.  Meeting with union representatives to discuss new technologies and how they will affect jobs at the Mint

3:00 P.M.  Marketing meeting on the Special Coin Program for the 1996 Olympics in Atlanta

4:00 P.M.  Approval of certain coin designs to commemorate special Canadians and events.

Unlike other civil servants, the Master of the Mint retains an administrative position "at the pleasure" of the government. She does not enjoy permanent tenure and may be shuffled, demoted, or fired at the will of the prime minister. The two most important skills of Master of the Mint — that of advising and departmental management — are indispensable to political ministers who need to take command of an administrative machine that was in operation long before they rose to power and will function quite well after they have left.

The job of Master is consuming, and includes managing the personnel in the department and, when necessary, advising the executive government departments, the PMO, the PCO, and the Treasury Board about departmental needs and problems. The Master meets often with the deputy ministers of other departments, sometimes over breakfast, to advise and collaborate when necessary with other government departments.

One of the most important skills of a deputy minister is that of human resources manager. "Good government management requires communicating with people, meeting them and consulting with them on a frequent basis," Ms. Hubbard says. Especially at the Mint, people need to feel engaged in the decisions that affect them.

---

absence. This is not the case at all. The deputy minister does not have a partisan position in government; rather, the position is uniquely administrative. In all instances, deputy ministers are career civil servants who have worked their way through the ranks of the public service to become the senior departmental policy adviser, and, in effect, the principal administrator in the department.

Unlike other public servants in the hierarchy of Canada's federal government whose positions fall under the job-protection and collective-bargaining provisions of the Public Service Employment Act, the deputy minister holds his or her position "at the pleasure" of the political executive. Deputy ministers are appointed by the Cabinet upon the recommendation of the prime minister. Because of this executive prerogative, deputy ministers can be shuffled, demoted, or fired by the prime minister (Osbaldeston 1989).

The deputy minister has the dual responsibility of managing administrative affairs in the department and advising the minister on matters of policy development. This is a powerful position to occupy, in terms of our governability. In all of Canada's governing institutions, the expert — the person who knows the history of the organization's problems and possesses the technical and administrative skills to bring solutions to the problems of government — has enormous advantages over the public and the people they elect to represent them in the legislative bodies of the country. In Canada, the more complex and difficult the problems the greater the power of administrative experts, in particular, deputy ministers.

## THE PUBLIC SERVICE AND GOVERNABILITY

Canada's public service does a great deal. If we could compile a list of all of its functions, it would include activities that directly and indirectly touch every conceivable aspect of Canadian life, the production and distribution of wealth, the regulation of business, sport, and the economy, as well as general services to the family, our education system, and the world of artistic endeavours. Yet even these do not provide a vivid sense of the enormous scale and seemingly endless variety of things that the Canadian government does.

Even if we understand the formal organization of Canada's federal government, we do not know how much power and influence a department or agency has, or what effect it

has on the establishment of government priorities. The public service is thrust into the mainstream of Canada's governing activity and has emerged as a major source of power in its own right. To some, the public service is very powerful because it is not elected yet implements policy with discretion.

Canadians expect their appointed public servants to perform their functions under the direct control of elected officials (see Figure 5.3). Under Canada's democracy, once an election takes place, politicians on the government side of the legislature are supposed to be the rulers, and the bureaucracy is supposed to follow their directives.

But is this what really happens? Who really governs in Canada? Do we have an **administocracy** (see Figure 5.4) whereby those whom we expect to carry out the decisions of government also have input into the substance and content of those decisions? The role of the bureaucracy in Canada's governing system — who they are, how they are recruited, what power and resources they command, and how they control outcomes — is at the heart of our governability.

**Figure 5.3 Public Expectations: Flow of Governability**

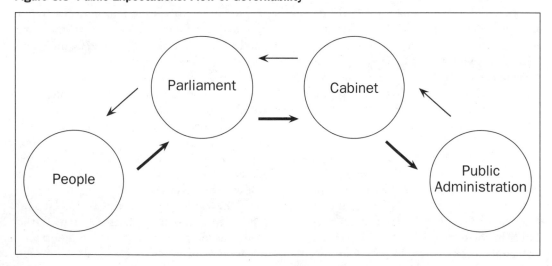

**Figure 5.4  Administocracy**

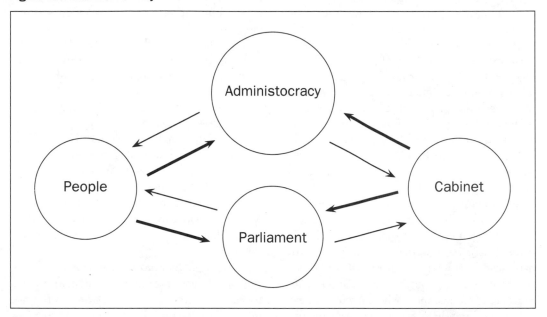

Canadians want their governments to be efficient and to accept the need for a professionalized public service recruited and appointed according to standards of competence. They have no wish to return to the bad old days of rampant patronage. Yet most Canadians also want democracy, with a commitment to the ideal of public control of government and a dedication to the idea that governability needs public consent.

## Policy Implementation

One of the expected roles of Canada's bureaucracy is to convert policies legislated on paper by elected officials into policies in action administered by bureaucrats. This process is **policy implementation**, which means putting specific policies into operation so that the people will respect and benefit from them.

Public policies are rarely self-executing. The Cabinet announces the goals of a policy or a law in broad terms and leaves to the public servants the task of implementing it. A policy or law has no impact until public administrators decide how to implement it. Accordingly, after the rules are made, implementation involves carrying them out in an efficient and responsive way so that the administration of the law becomes routine. For example, officials responsible for old age pensions have elaborate routines for processing claims, hearing appeals, and paying benefits.

But the existence of routine administration does not mean that bureaucrats cannot continue to exercise power, and they do so through administrative "discretion." One of the reasons why implementation is complicated is that the laws and policies to be carried out are not always clearly stated. No set of laws can anticipate every case or exception. Therein lies the considerable discretionary power that bureaucrats often have over their clients. Usually, the details of federal government programs are left to administrators out of political necessity. In this regard, they can play a major role in the governability of the country.

The Law Reform Commission of Canada (1977) catalogued thousands of discretionary powers exercised in Canada's public service. Government employees who have direct and frequent contact with citizens apply their skills at the grass-roots level. They are the Canada Customs official who searches through your luggage, the Revenue Canada agent who conducts an audit on an individual or company, the judge who passes sentence, and the consumer and corporate affairs inspector who examines the accuracy of food and drug labels.

Encounters with public servants are often shaped by books of rules, manuals of procedure, and forms in triplicate — in short, red tape. In many cases, the public becomes frustrated waiting for things to "go through channels." A small business's application for a loan through a government financial agency, the paperwork involved in remitting the GST, and the receiving of goods through Canada Customs are some instances where frustration can occur. And nearly everyone who pays income tax is burdened by the necessity of keeping personal financial records for the potential scrutiny of Revenue Canada. Undoubtedly, at times there can be too much red tape. And an insistence by governments on forms and records often stifles initiative, wastes productive time, and inhibits useful change, although, generally speaking, most programs administered by the public service can, and do, work.

## Regulation

When we think about what our governments do, most of us think of regulations, rules, orders, by-laws, warrants, directives, and the like. Everyday life itself seems to be the target of government control (Strick 1990). All sorts of human activities are subject to government regulations, even something apparently as simple as filling out a census form. Every year, the Department of Justice sends a warning by registered mail to the more than 1000 people who, according to Statistics Canada, do not complete the census form delivered to more than 10 million households. Under the Statistics Act of Canada,

the penalty for failing to return the completed form can be as much as $500, or three months in jail, or both.

Regulations like this one pervade our daily lives in business and finance, universities, hospitals, at airports, and where we fish, camp, and drive our cars. Government regulation of our economy and of our private lives has, of course, grown in recent decades.

Not surprisingly, this situation has led to charges that the federal government is too invasive. Regulations are rarely popular with those who are regulated. They seem to be the most controversial aspects of governing. But, in Canada, by almost everyone's standards, regulations are seen to be in the public interest.

The regulatory process in Canada involves the development of regulatory instruments to carry out the intent of Parliament. One important regulatory instrument used increasingly by governments is licensing. In Canada, a private person, a group, or a corporation can legally conduct certain kinds of activities only after obtaining a licence from the federal government. All public and private broadcasting in Canada is regulated in part through the licensing of stations, which, as licensees, must meet standards set out in legislation as well as by the Canadian Radio-television and Telecommunications Commission (CRTC).

As an administrative device, licensing permits the government to control an activity while gaining revenue from those who engage in it. Licensing enables the government to establish standards of performance for activities having public consequence and certain qualifications of those engaging in them.

Canadians demand certain regulations. They want to drive on highways that are regulated for speed and other violations; they expect that the food products they buy will be properly and honestly labelled as to ingredients and weight; they assume that scales will be honest when they buy products in bulk.

But critics of regulation are fond of pointing out that legislators rarely evaluate the costs of regulation in relation to benefits. They argue that, in an economy that demands increasing competitiveness, regulations raise prices because producers must pass the costs on to consumers. The critics hold that regulations hurt Canada's competitiveness abroad, especially where other economies have fewer regulations on pollution, worker safety, and other business practices. They charge that regulations disrupt the natural reconciliation of market forces and sometimes just do not achieve the results that Parliament intends.

Thus, "deregulation" is a fashionable term in many sectors of the Canadian economy that supply goods and services. These days, many more people believe that governmental regulations have simply gone too far. They insist that it is time to deregulate the economy and other areas of government control to permit the market and human ingenuity to work in their own way.

## Services

Canadians expect their public service to respond to their needs by providing government services. A *government service* is an activity or benefit directly produced by the government and usually made available to people free of charge, or below or at cost. *Bureaucratic responsiveness*, which we also expect, is the trait of a government that does what we want it to.

In a general sense, many of our needs, such as to live in a safe, orderly, and progressive society, have to do with the primary functions of government. From this perspective, the RCMP provides an important public service, and safety at work is served by the Canadian Centre for Occupational Health and Safety. Similarly, Revenue Canada collects taxes that are redistributed in the forms of transfer payments to the provinces and direct payments to qualified individuals. So, in the course of administering the laws of the land,

the federal bureaucracy renders important services to the public.

But some government bodies mainly provide services that are not necessarily primary functions of government, or regulative for all those who wish to use them (see Table 5.4). For example, the National Film Board, established in 1939, serves the public by producing and distributing films and videos that are distinctively Canadian.

Another service is provided by the National Library of Canada which ensures that the published heritage of Canadians is preserved and made accessible to everyone through Canada's libraries. The National Library collects the literary heritage of Canada, its rare books, its music, aboriginal and other cultural documents, theses, dissertations, and general statistics. Canada's national museums are crown corporations that collect and exhibit important information about Canadians and the world for presentation to the public. Museums, as crown corporations are relatively newcomers in the total scheme of government services provided to the general public.

Many Canadians see government as the best available vehicle for providing many of the services that once were regarded as solely the preserve of the private sector in the Canadian economy, and so over the years government has expanded.

## Collecting Information

Statistics Canada provides an important service as a national information-gathering agency. By means of the skills and methodologies of this body, the government collects massive quantities of data, such as the census, and makes this information available for Canadians to use in business, at universities, and in planning communities.

Much of what we know about ourselves comes from the government's collection of data on births, deaths, occupation and income, housing and health, crime, and many other

**Table 5.4 Select Government Bodies Supplying Services to the Public**

| Organization | Year Established | Service |
|---|---|---|
| Canada Council | 1957 | Fosters and promotes the arts |
| Canadian Advisory Council on the Status of Women | 1973 | Undertakes research and public education on women's issues |
| Canadian Centre for Occupational Health and Safety | 1978 | Promotes health and safety |
| Canadian Human Rights Commission | 1977 | Conducts research and public education on human rights |
| Canadian Museum of Civilization | 1990 | Conducts public education |
| Canadian Museum of Nature | 1990 | Conducts public education |
| National Archives of Canada | 1987 | Collects and preserves public historic records |
| National Film Board of Canada | 1939 | Produces and distributes Canadian films and videos |
| National Gallery of Canada | 1990 | Conducts public education |
| National Library of Canada | 1953 | Provides national library services |
| National Museum of Science and Technology | 1990 | Conducts public education |
| Science Council of Canada | 1966 | Conducts research and public education |
| Social Sciences and Humanities Research Council of Canada | 1976 | Funds and promotes social and humanities research |
| Statistics Canada | 1962 | Collects, analyzes, and provides national statistics |

*Source:* Treasury Board Secretariat, Ottawa, 1992. Reprinted with permission of the Minister of Supply and Services Canada, 1994.

things. The information-gathering function of Revenue Canada operates on a massive scale. Revenue Canada receives about 20 million tax returns each year, subjecting everyone to scrutiny by tax accountants or computers. It audits in greater detail thousands of tax returns and investigates thousands of suspected criminal violations of the tax laws. Not only are personal and corporate tax files maintained, but information about the financial transactions of individuals, banking information, legal information, treaty information, and general auditing data are stored for potential use.

The bureaucracy does research too. A prime example is Agriculture Canada, which does research on how to grow bigger and better crops, raise healthier animals, and transport and market products more effectively. The National Research Council of Canada performs scientific and engineering research in the marine sciences, biotechnology, chemistry, physics, and space. Natural Resources Canada conducts geological, geographical, and environmental research, especially in areas related to energy and resources. And Environment Canada does extensive research on all matters related to land, air, water, and wildlife, including maintaining a public database on the management of national parks. Most departments of government, agencies, and crown corporations conduct at least general research in a particular policy area in which they are involved. Federal departments in particular are concerned about the effectiveness of the programs they are providing (Treasury Board 1990).

The Canadian federal government stands at the centre of a complex sociological and technological society. Such a society cannot function well — some might say, cannot even survive — without a continuous flow of accurate data and information on very many aspects of human endeavour, including a great deal of information on what the government does in society. For example, Canadian businesses with international customers need detailed information about markets abroad, tariff regulations, the shipping industry, the official policies of the government toward other countries, and so on. These and many other examples suggest the importance of information to the making of policy in the public and private sectors.

Many government records are the product of self-reporting. Internal evaluations of government departments and the annual reports of departments are usually drafted by the departments themselves. This kind of self-reporting is often biased: Facts that work to the credit of the reporting department or agency are exaggerated, and those that might discredit it are downplayed. This institutional bias by government is understandable: To maintain credibility, government bureaucracies must demonstrate that they are doing what they are expected to do, and that they could do even better if only budgets were increased. But, however understandable from a bureaucratic and political point of view, the institutional bias creates a problem for those who rely on public documents' accurately reflecting the information gathered by the government.

Another factor that relates to information-gathering by the federal government is secrecy. In a democracy such as Canada, the information that government bureaucracies collect is presumably public. In comparison with other governing systems in the world, the Canadian government makes public a considerable amount of information.

Yet a lot of information the government gathers is held in secrecy or in semi-secrecy. This is obviously true, and for understandable reasons, of information gathered by the Armed Forces and by the Canadian Security Intelligence Service (CSIS) because it is a matter of national security. However, nearly all information that goes into the Cabinet is made public only at the discretion of the Cabinet.

Although the debates of the House of Commons are public, many committees meet in private for the critical sessions during which the final drafting of legislation takes place. Supreme Court decisions are announced publicly, but the deliberations of the justices take place in private. Thus, the study of what information the government gathers is always, to some extent, the study of what the government chooses to disclose to an outsider.

## Making Policy

The one bureaucratic function that worries the informed public in a democracy like Canada's is the actual making of policy. Since Confederation, the administrative functions of Canada's civil service have grown to include the formulation of public policy (Kernaghan and Siegal 1991, 113–41). Rapid industrialization, population growth, urbanization, and profound changes in science and technology, transportation, and communications have put problems of a more complex nature on government's agenda. The Cabinet often responds to the complexity of modern policy making by identifying general goals and actions that the government wants to pursue. Then the government engages the department or agency with the relevant expertise to draft, as well as to execute and administer, specific policies.

"Coloured papers" are one of the ways that bureaucrats have a major input into the policy-making process (Doer 1982). They can alert the bureaucracy, members of Parliament, other members of the Cabinet, the media, and the public that a change in public policy is forthcoming. Coloured papers are persuasive and, as prepared by administrators who are knowledgeable and supportive of "departmental" standards, develop policy on behalf of elected politicians. Their role is educative, not only of the general public, but of the politicians as well. They function to stimulate national debate, to act as trial balloons that measure public tolerance of or opposition to a new national course of action, and to encourage interprovincial consultation.

Such is the purpose of a **green paper**, which encourages public and parliamentary reaction about the possibility of changing or modifying a government policy. "Green" papers are sometimes blue, beige, and even orange: "Green paper" is a generic, or sweeping, term that generally covers this kind of administrative correspondence. A **white paper**, which is an announcement of a government policy, is always white. It explains and defends the way the government intends to act or not to act.

Policy that is inspired by the same bureaucrats who implement it is often seen by political scientists as symptomatic of administocracy, and potentially problematic within the framework of a democratic system of government like Canada's. Administration-made policy is as binding as legislated policy, yet it, unlike the latter, is not influenced by the electorate. Legislators are not as permanent a constituency of power in Ottawa as administrators tend to be. Members of Parliament come and go, but administrators do not need regular public consent to do their jobs.

For a variety of reasons, a bureaucrat has a much better chance than has a member of

Parliament of becoming a persuasive expert on government matters. On the one hand, public servants tend to specialize in their knowledge, whether it be the environment, issuing passports, transportation policy, or whatever. On the other hand, the legislator is expected to deal with all matters. Such specialization gives the public servant an enormous advantage over the politician, who at best really has only a general, partial, and probably shaky knowledge of matters for which he or she is responsible. Accordingly, the transient, non-permanent, and most often unspecialized elected representatives are in the position of asking the advice of the permanent, full-time, and specialized administrative experts about the relative merits of policies. More often than not, they take the advice.

The policy preferences of public servants almost inevitably enter into and affect their advice. When administrators are asked their advice, they can hardly avoid making their views known, and when, as often happens, the political representatives and their constituents hold no intense views of their own, the preferences of the public service are likely to become public policy.

Because Canadian statutes and policies are general expressions of the law, no government department, control agency, or crown corporation can avoid developing its own body of rules for determining which specific instances do and do not fall within the terms of the law that it administers. The power of this administrative rule-making has the character of legislation and is sometimes referred to as "administrative legislation."

Many students of public administration are convinced that this involves administrators in the making of public policy. In Canada, a growing body of decision-making research confirms that the vast house of bureaucracy engages in the important tasks of initiating public policy and, in fact, it is often the only place where public policy is made (Adie and Thomas 1987, 142–89).

## CONTROLLING THE PUBLIC SERVICE

Bureaucratic power is sometimes negatively expressed. Just on the basis of their great numbers and legislated mandates, career public servants are elevated to positions of enormous influence and power in the Canadian governing system. It is in the power of these men and women to do Canadians great injury, just as it is in their power to advance the well-being of Canadians. That career public servants are prominent forces in the making of government policy in Canada does not mean that their activities have dominion over the whole parliamentary process and go unchecked.

Within Canada's political system, various governmental, legislative, judicial, administrative, and sociopolitical controls fix very definite limits upon what public servants can and cannot do (see Table 5.5).

### Government Controls

Political control of the public service in Canada is directly exercised by Parliament and the government, both jointly and separately. Jointly, they approve of legislation that creates administrative bodies, defining their objectives and powers and establishing standards of performance. They provide the

bureaucracies with their budgets, audit them, and monitor their actions. They review, criticize, and sometimes intervene in the conduct of administrators. Separately, the government, through its ministers, controls most public servants. Deputy ministers and their assistants are appointed by the Cabinet and are directly responsible to the ministers as well as to Parliament.

### What the Political Executive Can Do

In the executive realm of Cabinet government, the prime minister and other ministers can potentially exercise tight control over administrative action taken by public servants because they are responsible for all of it and for the operations of their departments. In Canada, public servants are considered to be part of the executive branch of government. Ministers can send orders through the administrative hierarchy, expect their executive directives to be complied with, and require reports from government employees to keep them informed on internal matters.

Perhaps the most visible and dramatic form of executive supervision and control of bureaucracy is an investigation. Certain governing instruments are available to the political executive to control the bureaucrats in this regard. If need be, the political executive can

**Table 5.5 Regulating the Regulators**

| Government Controls | Administrative Controls | Sociopolitical Controls |
|---|---|---|
| PM/Cabinet | Professional standards | Public opinion |
| Parliament | Testing | Public access |
| Courts | Ombudsperson | to information |
| Public hearings | Merit principle | Pressure groups |
| Inquiries | Upgrading | Political parties |
| Royal commissions | Performance evaluation | University training |
| Decentralization | | Media |
| Deconcentration | | |
| Deregulation | | |

initiate inquiries under the Federal Inquiries Act for the purpose of departmental investigation into administrative conduct. **Commissions of inquiry** are headed by a commissioner who is appointed by the deputy minister and who instructs the commission to conduct an internal investigation of some administrative problem (Ledoux 1980).

Another governing instrument in the hands of the Cabinet is the **royal commission**, for example, the Dubin Inquiry, which investigated the use of drugs in sports. Royal commissions are mandated by order-in-council and usually comprise people outside the public service who formally and publicly investigate specific administrative problems or look at general policy concerns with the purpose of reporting them to government, to Parliament, and ultimately to the general public.

A **task force** is less formal than a royal commission because it is usually mandated by the prime minister or a minister rather than by order-in-council. Task forces tend to be less visible to the public, and report to the Cabinet. For example, the Task Force on Program Review — Regulatory Agencies, 1985, studied the conduct and procedures of regulatory agencies and recommended that Cabinet should exercise more controls on bodies that regulate and, when necessary, should override their decisions.

## What Parliament Can Do

The powers to create departments and pass legislation give Parliament the opportunity to control the federal bureaucracy. New departments can be formed only by an act of Parliament (Doern and Phidd 1983). In addition, Parliament may exercise controls on the bureaucracy by means of its legislation affecting departments, for example, acts establishing new programs to be administered, and through broad legislation that affects all departments, such as the Public Service Employment Act.

Another important parliamentary control is the annual budget. The Estimates, which list the budget requirements of each department, must be approved by Parliament and defended by ministers and their senior administrators. When the Estimates are passed through the appropriate committees of the House of Commons, members of Parliament can learn what the anticipated activities of the government departments will be, and what they will cost. This is where the "confidence" of the legislators regarding the administrative appropriations of funds is nurtured. Parliament's power to pass the federal budget means that the legislative branch of government can substantially shape both the amount of money bureaucrats can spend and the things they can spend it on.

But parliamentary scrutiny of bureaucratic conduct is most evident when ministers are asked questions about their departments. Ministers must take responsibility for any administrative errors public servants may commit in the government department they formally control. Ministers can take a great deal of heat when their officials engage in the mismanagement of their departments, usually having to withstand opposition calls for their resignation. Parliamentary conventions have dictated that ministers are not answerable to the point of being forced to resign for all administrative errors. But such pressure places the minister in a defensive administrative posture that inevitably has the effect of increasing his or her desire to oversee departmental organization and procedures, and thus to control the actions of government employees.

The role of the opposition to criticize, debate, question, and constantly scrutinize the actions of administrators is an important parliamentary control of the bureaucracy. Inevitably, opposition members build an expertise that can check the whims of administrative activity, not only in the legislature, but in its committee system, where powerful alternatives to government strategies are introduced by members who have acquired specialized knowledge. Committees such as the Public Accounts Committee, and the Standing Joint Committee on Regulatory Scrutiny, exercise greater independence than other parliamentary committees because they are chaired by a member of the opposition. This committee process compels the government to defend its behaviour toward and policies concerning the general public.

Members of Parliament themselves will often play an important part in bringing controls to bear on bureaucratic behaviour and in maintaining the responsiveness of the public service. The role of the member of Parliament as representing his or her constituents provides this kind of service to voters entangled with the police, the courts, the tax collector, or Customs officials. Even today, bureaucratic red tape can be cut with the help of an energetic and competent MP. The representation casework of parliamentarians has greatly increased, because many constituents now realize that their representatives can help straighten out bureaucratic entanglements. MPs who intercede for a constituent are also, in a sense, campaigning for the next election, because constituents who owe their representative a debt of gratitude almost always express it with a vote at election time.

Other parliamentary controls on the federal public service system include decentralization, deconcentration, and deregulation. *Decentralization*, in theory, creates the potential for greater control over the public service by dispersing administrative power throughout the country. *Deconcentration* disperses government workers across the country; by the 1990s, most of Canada's federal government employees lived and worked outside Ottawa. *Deregulation* has been a parliamentary watchword since the early 1980s; for some parliamentarians, especially those in the Cabinet, deregulation has provided the opportunity to downsize the public sector and thus reduce the burden of government on the national budget.

The clamour to cut back on the growth of government has encouraged many politicians to look for ways to show voters that they are responsive. The control of the federal bureaucracy can also be achieved in part by privatization. *Privatization* involves replacing government services with services from the private sector. A body of opinion among parliamentarians argues that some government services could be provided more efficiently in the marketplace.

### What the Courts Can Do

For many people, suing the bureaucracy in the courts is not attractive or even a feasible method of controlling government conduct: It is time-consuming, unpleasant, and costly — and there is no guarantee that the governing system will respond to the case as a model for administrative reform. Judicial control, which leaves the initiative to the aggrieved, is thus more often a last resort than a common device for keeping administrators in line.

If a private citizen feels that the bureaucracy has used its powers maliciously, causing personal harm; has stepped outside its legal jurisdiction; has exceeded its regulatory powers; or has unfairly denied a right under the law, he or she can go to court to seek redress. The remedy may take the form of damages, a writ of *mandamus* (that is, a court order to a public official directing that a particular duty be carried out according to the law), a writ of *injunction* (that is, a court order prohibiting an administrator from performing a specific action), a writ of *certiorari* (that is, a decision quashing one made by a lower court), and so on.

Because courts are important makers and interpreters of public policy, it follows that they are enmeshed in the administrative process of the country. In many ways, all law is public policy, and the various interpretations of the law by the courts can restrict, and thereby control, the conduct of public servants. In the early 1990s, the Supreme Court of

Canada held that police cannot recruit informers to try to obtain a confession from someone accused of a crime. The Court determined that a person's constitutional rights are violated by the police under certain circumstances, such as when the police recruit cellmates or friends of an accused to get a confession or other information that can be used as evidence at a trial.

Canadian courts can review matters flowing from the discretionary powers of public servants, for example, if the provisions of the Clean Air Act were perceived to be administered unfairly by individuals, groups, or companies. Courts may also rule on administrative questions involving breaches of the principle of "natural justice," which includes such rights as the right to hear the other side in a case, the right to cross-examine witnesses, and a guarantee that no one should be a judge in his or her own case.

Accordingly, when administrative abuse is felt to occur because an individual cannot present his or her side of the story, or when the impartiality of the administration to render a fair decision on a matter is seen to be compromised, then the courts can be approached for a ruling. Sometimes public servants will act outside of the scope of authority granted to them under the provisions of a governing statute. Courts will rule on whether the powers of public servants have been exceeded and may determine whether administrative conduct is appropriate.

Finally, the courts can control the conduct of public servants by their interpretations of the Charter of Rights and Freedoms. The charter has had a momentous effect on administrative law in Canada, not only because it constitutionally protects individual rights, but because it builds widespread normative expectations about what the conduct of government employees should be in a democracy.

Judicial decisions shape the actions of the government bureaucracy by directing it to follow legally correct procedures. The courts can

do this by defining the intentions of Parliament when legislation is vague or ambiguous. When Parliament is not precise about what bureaucrats should or can do in a specific instance, the courts ultimately decide the fairness or legitimacy of bureaucratic action.

## Administrative Controls

A number of important administrative controls that perform as effective "watchdogs" of the federal bureaucracy in Canada can be viewed as independent bureaucracies created by Parliament to watch the conduct of other bureaucracies. The openness of government bureaucracies to scrutiny by other bureaucracies is important in making public agencies both responsive and accountable in a society as complex as Canada's.

The Public Service Commission (PSC) is itself one such independent body that was created by Parliament to expunge the exercise of patronage and to control the influence of politics in Canada's government service. As the custodian of the merit principle, the PSC is a special neutralizing instrument that controls political influence and partisan conduct in the federal bureaucracy. That bureaucracy does not operate in a vacuum, but within a constellation of political forces that can influence organizational behaviour in ways that may not always serve the public well. By applying neutral principles to recruitment, hiring, promotion, and firing, a great number of natural political forces can be monitored and controlled.

Another special administrative agency committed to watching the behaviour of administrators is the Office of Auditor General (OAG). The OAG closely examines the efficiency, effectiveness, and financial integrity of government programs and reports its findings to Parliament. The public annual reports of the auditor general focus on the operation and management of randomly selected departments in the federal bureaucracy, often criticizing the lack of controls on spending.

The enormous obstacles that people as private individuals must confront when challenging injustices committed by a government bureaucracy were recognized as long ago as 1809, when the government of Sweden established the special office of ombudsman (parliamentary commissioner) to act as an observer of bureaucratic conduct and to intervene on behalf of individuals or groups, whose rights are violated in an administrative context.

The office of ombudsperson exists in all Canadian provinces except Prince Edward Island, but not at the federal level of government. Instead of a general-purpose ombudsperson, successive Canadian governments have opted to establish several specialized "ombudspersons," usually called "commissioners," who have responsibility for scrutinizing particular areas of administrative powers and jurisdictions (see Table 5.6). These commissioners report to Parliament after investigating each complaint and, on the basis of their independent findings, publicize any instance of administrative abuse or omission. In most cases, public criticism by the commissioner's office is enough to make an erring bureaucracy mend its ways. Through these special administrative offices, most of the initiative for and cost of obtaining a remedy from administrative abuses are born by the governing system rather than by the private citizen.

The federal public service is also subject to a number of internal controls, such as professional standards and upgrading. The Public Service Commission establishes professional selection and conduct standards for government employees. Its Training Programs Branch provides professional upgrading for people in administrative technologies, language, and the protocols of bureaucratic conduct. These are

## Table 5.6 Canada's Mini-Ombuds

| Federal Commissioners | Year Established | Parliamentary Mandate |
|---|---|---|
| Office of the Official Language Commissioner | 1970 | To administer the Official Languages Act and protect language rights |
| Office of Correctional Investigator | 1973 | To investigate complaints made by inmates against prison authorities |
| Canadian Human Rights Commissioner | 1976 | To administer the Canadian Human Rights Act and investigate complaints of human-rights abuse |
| Office of the Information Commissioner | 1983 | To administer the Access to Information Act and investigate complaints of denial of access |
| Office of the Privacy Commissioner | 1983 | To administer the Privacy Act and investigate abuses of privacy rights |

*Source:* Adapted from Public Service Commission of Canada, *Annual Report Statistics, 1992.* Reproduced by authority of the Minister of Industry, 1994.

some of the important ways that the administrative branch of government keeps itself accountable. As long as the federal bureaucracy exists, there will continue to be attempts to make it more open, efficient, and responsive to the needs of Canadians.

## Sociopolitical Controls

Generally speaking, Canadians do not want bureaucrats to treat them as if they are part of a mythical lump called "clients," "society," or "the people," or to treat them like statistics that measure but do not voice responses to their conduct. Ideally, the public wants the bureaucracy to be concerned primarily with the needs of each individual it serves, and to be judged by how well it carries out this service (Bryden 1982).

Realistically, the public wants the bureaucracy to implement rules and to adopt regulation and enforcement practices they favour without the actual experience or appearance of any abuse of administrative authority. Owing to the fact that Canadians have so many interactions with bureaucrats, a number of sociopolitical instruments have evolved to cope with the growing phenomenon of bureaucracy.

Because most federal departments and agencies were created explicitly to serve or regulate some sector of Canadian society — agriculture, business, labour, environment, sports — it is not surprising that the organizations representing those sectors should take a keen interest in, and have a substantial influence over, the government body created to administer to them. Thus, bureaucratic self-preservation is a fundamental characteristic of governability in Canada.

Parliament and the Cabinet are joined by interest groups in wanting to limit and direct the power of bureaucrats. In many cases, interest groups try to influence the bureaucracy and use all means at their disposal to limit its actions. The more successful pressure groups in Canada have never regarded their

work as finished when the legislature or Parliament passes a bill they fought for or when Cabinet issues orders-in-council that they have sought. Many interest groups then shift their attentions to the appropriate government department to ensure that they can control the implementation of the spirit as well as the letter of the laws they pressured for.

Interest groups exercise controls over bureaucracy by rallying public opinion to their side and by pressuring Parliament and the government to do something about perceived or potential abuses of administrative power. In recent times, Canadian interest groups, using their own investigative staffs, have challenged the efficacy of many types of social programs and brought pressure to bear on government officials to change their conduct. Groups can use press conferences or advertising campaigns to control and influence bureaucratic decisions.

Sometimes interest groups will try to control the bureaucracy directly. For example, the Canadian broadcasting industry frequently challenges the decisions and conduct of the Canadian Radio-television and Telecommunications Commission to enable the industry to compete more effectively.

Pressure groups can stimulate reforms in the bureaucracy by bringing administrative abuses to the attention of managing administrators. Pressure groups can make direct appeals to the bureaucrats themselves. But the most likely routes of claims made by pressure group on the bureaucracy are through other institutions, such as the media, the courts, and Parliament.

Many federal departments and agencies, in order to carry out their mandates, gather information on the private lives of individual citizens. The Department of Justice and the Solicitor General are charged with responsibilities to fight crime. The files created on people hold information on even the most intimate aspects of the lives of millions of Canadians. This kind of information can have devastating consequences if it is irresponsibly handled or wrongfully gathered.

Most of the information amassed by a bureaucracy is not so controversial. The census is normally taken every five years to gather information about the general population in order to help government officials make policy choices that fit the needs of individuals and communities.

But, in terms of the individual's rights to privacy when governments, gather and hold information, there is always the potential of abuse. The government comes to know about our family histories, where we reside, our identifying physical marks and fingerprints, our financial affairs, our bank account balances, our reputations for honesty, and our politics. If we apply for a job with the Canadian government, or require security clearance for one of its special agencies, the files in the bureaucracy may detail whatever stories a neighbour, or even a stranger, has told about us.

It is difficult for citizens acting as individuals to deal with government bodies under these circumstances. But individuals do have certain instruments at their disposal that enable them to gain a measure of control over the attitudes, conduct, and internal procedures within the bureaucracy. They can gain access to and change information that the bureaucracy holds on them.

Not surprisingly, a relatively small number of individuals take advantage of the rights to information from a bureaucracy. The Access to Information Act gives people who live in Canada the right to have access to federal government records that are not of a personal nature. The act enhances the ordinary ways that the public can normally gain access to government information. Individuals can ask to see information, no matter what form it is in, including letters, memos, reports, photographs, films, microfilms, and computerized data.

Certain categories of information are more difficult to penetrate and gain access to.

For example, information involving matters of national security, law enforcement, official secrets, and classified information are exempted; however, the withholding of such information can be challenged, and it may, under specific circumstances, be provided to satisfy an individual's legal rights to access.

Another legal instrument, The Privacy Act, gives Canadian citizens and people living in Canada the right to have access to information that is held about them by the federal government. This act also protects unauthorized disclosure of personal information, and strictly controls how the government will collect, use, store, disclose, and dispose of any personal information. The federal government is required to keep personal information collected about you confidential.

At all levels of government in Canada, the bureaucracies of government must work against a public-image problem. The media pay scant attention to public servants, except to publicize their mistakes and slip-ups. Effective and courteous public administration is unfortunately not newsworthy. Nevertheless, the harsh glare of the media can have the effect of checking controversial policy implementation, especially when injustice is reported. Unlike pressure groups and executive, legislative, and judicial bodies, the media confer with a broad and diffuse audience. In the realm of public administration, as in politics in general, the media can be the major source of "heat," shaping and reshaping government processes, policies, and institutions.

Plenty of evidence points to the power of the media in Canadian politics to control the conduct of governing institutions. The media are ubiquitous. Evidence abounds that the news and its presentation are an important influence on the accountability of bureaucrats. The media can shape not only the policy agenda but also policy implementation. By constantly watching the policy-making process in Canada, the media may compress the time available to the public service for achieving results. Media coverage may actually reduce the options open to public administrators by spotlighting expected solutions prematurely, inviting criticism, and eliminating alternatives from consideration.

## CONCLUSION

The way the public service performs has many implications for how we govern ourselves. Bureaucracies are territorial and competitive: They desire to maintain or expand their own turf and, by so doing, sometimes distort the governing potential of the other institutions of government. The bureaucrats themselves compete sharply with each other and contend for administrative influence, seeking to gain the best reputations, the biggest budgets, the largest staffs, and ultimately the favour of the prime minister and Cabinet. For example, the Department of Finance is often quite critical of the ways Revenue Canada enforces the tax laws that Finance designs, and many departments have tussles with Statistics Canada over the gathering, analysis, and interpretation of data that statisticians generate.

But all departments strive to have an immense impact on Canada's public policy. In this regard, we must ask whether the mandates of the bureaucracy are being fulfilled in their own interests or in the national interest. Are the broader needs of Canadians caught up in a maze of bureaucratic infighting and competitions within and among the federal branches of government? Is Canadian democracy threatened by the emergence of an administrative state?

In general, performance in the federal public service has to do with numerous administrative qualities. A government department that is working well can function orderly and predictably, impartially and fairly, responsibly and economically. It keeps a staff of qualified people who advance on merit and maintain a professional standard of conduct. Honesty is another concrete aspect of performance. Corruption — bribes, theft, and using official positions for personal gain — can and does occur in government, ultimately affecting governability.

Perhaps the most important questions about administrative performance relate to values and goals. In a government bureaucracy, whose and what values are pursued? Does the government bureaucracy share the goals of the society to which it is responsible? Is it responsive to those people and groups? Is the government bureaucracy effective in reaching its goals? What procedures does the government use in seeking to achieve its goals? Do those procedures respect individual and group rights?

Assessing Canada's federal bureaucracy is difficult because of its conflicting roles of rewarding and punishing, of regulating and servicing, and of implementing and formulating policies. At times it is perceived as unresponsive, pursuing its own values and self-interests rather than responding to Parliament and the public.

In Canadian society, we know that government bureaucracy is essential but poses serious political problems. Even if our public servants are doing a good job, the enormous size, complexity, and fragmentation of the bureaucracy create obstacles to how well we govern ourselves. As a result, the ability of the governing system to work is related to how well the Cabinet, Parliament, the courts, and the public can monitor the bureaucracy and ensure the effective administration of public policy.

## GLOSSARY

**administocracy**  A term coined by American Guy S. Claire to denote a government effectively run by career public servants.

**administrative law**  The branch of law that governs the relations between the government and individuals and groups, by determining the limitations of government action and by establishing remedies when violations of human and legal rights occur.

**civil service**  Collectively, all non-military employees of the federal, provincial, and municipal governments in Canada.

**commission of inquiry**  Sometimes designated "royal," this investigative body is appointed by government to engage in a formal determination of facts involved in a particular area of concern, usually followed by a report to Parliament or to a government department.

**crown corporation**  A government-owned enterprise with a mandate to engage in commercial, industrial, or financial activities.

**functionaries**  Subordinate officials who follow the orders of their administrative-class superiors and who are usually expected to pay strict attention to the procedures of doing their jobs.

**green paper**  A policy proposal prepared by government to generate reaction that could affect the range of options being considered by decision-makers.

**hierarchy**  A group of individuals or positions of administrative jurisdiction arranged in some rank order, based on specific classifications of personnel to perform special tasks.

**line organizations**  Government units that provide direct services to the public.

**policy implementation**  Translating the goals and objectives of the government into operating, ongoing, and routine procedures.

**political neutrality**  A constitutional convention prescribing that public servants should not obstruct or appear to obstruct the activities and policies of the political executive.

**Public Service Commission**  An independent agency that serves Parliament by providing human resource management in the public service.

**royal commission**  A formal inquiry commissioned by the Cabinet by means of an order-in-council to look into a matter deemed to be of high priority regarding public policy, such as the use of drugs in sports (Dubin Inquiry) or to determine the circumstances surrounding a wrongful conviction (Hughes Commission).

**task force**  A body convened temporarily to investigate a specific problem or general policy concern and to report to a government department.

**white paper**  A declaration of government policy prepared in a statement that explains and defends the course of action taken.

## RECOMMENDED READING

Abele, Frances. 1991. *How Ottawa Spends, 1991–92: The Politics of Fragmentation.* Ottawa: Carleton University Press. This study examines the public administration of Canada from the perspective of the constitution, free trade, interest groups, abortion, and multiculturalism and race.

Albo, Gregary, David Langille, and Leo Panitch, eds. 1993. *A Different Kind of State? Popular Power and Democratic Administra-*

*tion.* Don Mills, Ont.: Oxford University Press. This book addresses the idea of democratic public administration, and reforming the Canadian system of government so as to involve more public participation, improve the design of government programs, deliver the services efficiently and adequately, and provide a better working environment for public employees.

Atkinson, Michael. 1993. *Governing Canada.* Toronto: Harcourt Brace, Canada. This textbook brings together excellent contributions by political science experts in the fields of public administration, public policy, and federalism.

Canada. 1990. *Beneath the Veneer: Report of the Task Force on Barriers to Women in the Public Service,* Vol. 1. Ottawa: Supply and Services Canada. This excellent report discusses the professional obstacles women face in a public service that many take to be free of workplace discrimination against women.

Canada. 1990. *Public Service 2000. The Renewal of the Public Service of Canada.* Ottawa: Supply and Services Canada. This document focusses on what changes are necessary to bring Canada's public service into the next century.

Coleman, William, and Grace Skogstad. 1990. *Policy Communities and Public Policy in Canada.* Mississauga, Ont.: Copp Clark Pitman. This book examines the interaction between organized interests and the state in a range of policy issues in Canada. Using the concepts of policy networks, the book provides readers with a better understanding of group–state relations in Canada.

Davidson, Roger, and Phil White. 1990. *Information and Government: Studies in the Dynamics of Policy Making.* Edinburgh: University of Edinburgh Press. This an interdisciplinary and cross-national study examines aspects of government policies in relation to the gathering of information.

Huddleston, Mark. 1992. *The Public Administration Workbook.* New York: Longman Publishing Group. This book provides students with actual problems of public administration and requires them to think in terms of bureaucratic skills to solve them.

Peters, Guy. 1990. *The Politics of Bureaucracy.* New York: Longman Publishing Group. This book takes a cross-national survey of the role of government bureaucracy in implementing policy, and examines the problem of administrative accountability and control.

Pross, A. Paul. 1992. *Group Politics and Public Policy.* Don Mills, Ont.: Oxford University Press. This book — the most comprehensive analysis of pressure-group activity in Canada — looks at the role of pressure groups in shaping Canadian public policies from the perspective of women's issues, the environment, language, free trade, and other issues.

# LAW AND THE CANADIAN JUDICIARY

Sometimes we ask judges to make life-and-death decisions — for example, on abortion and on the right to die. Like the question of abortion, the issue of assisted suicide invokes strong public reactions concerning the sanctity of life, religious convictions, and especially the role of physicians in the treatment of patients. Do people have the "right to die"? Must every effort be made to prolong life, no matter what the circumstances? The ethical dilemmas of physicians, politicians, and judges are fundamental. When our legislators fail to provide the answers to these questions, people must turn to the courts for decisive action.

Shortly after Sue Rodriguez learned that she had amyotrophic lateral sclerosis (ALS), an incurable muscular disorder also known as Lou Gehrig's disease, she knew she would gradually lose the use of her arms and legs, and develop difficulties swallowing and breathing. She knew that eventually the disease would kill her, but that she would probably retain all her mental faculties throughout the ordeal.

She decided not to die that way but to control the time and the place of her dying by having a physician assist her. While her reasoning seemed proper and dignified, in her case there was the spectre of Section 241 (b) of the Criminal Code that prohibits physician-assisted suicide. In Canada, it is not an offence to commit suicide yourself, but it is an offence to "assist" someone else to.

Sue Rodriguez was asking judges to do what many of them have done in the course of their careers — make new law. But it was not going to be as easy as that. In 1992, Ms. Rodriquez had asked the government of British Columbia to grant immunity from prosecution to any physician who helped her commit suicide. The government of Premier Harcourt denied her that special request. Following this attempt, both the Supreme Court of British Columbia and the B.C. Court of Appeal rejected her contention that the ban on doctor-assisted suicide violated her right to life, liberty, and security of the person guaranteed by the Charter of Rights and Freedoms.

Finally, by a narrow 5-to-4 majority, the Supreme Court of Canada upheld that the prohibition on assisted suicide is based on the interest of the Crown to protect life. The law, they said, was upheld to protect those who, in moments of weakness and depression, might want to take their own lives.

It was the kind of case that most judges dread — whatever was decided would cause a person to suffer who did not deserve to. The judges had to struggle with the legal and human implications of their decision.

The ethical dilemma was at the centre of their deliberations. On the one hand, judges know the law is almost always dedicated to preserving life, and, on the other hand, it is sometimes asked to alleviate suffering. They had to ask themselves, what is the point of maintaining, on a life-support system, the life of a person who may have irrevocable brain damage? Should quality of life not be taken into consideration?

Many people object to recognizing the right to die because a cure may be just around the corner in many cases, the process may be subject to abuse, or it is reminiscent of what happened in Nazi Germany. These are all issues judges must consider when deciding a case like this.

Making judicial decisions on problems of rights in Canada is agonizing for the courts as well as for the people involved. Every day, courts are asked to dismantle de facto barriers and add new dimensions to our rights.

Deep and fundamental differences have polarized many groups, but judicial and governmental institutions try to maintain balances between them. This kind of balancing can be done so long as we recognize that policy choices about rights cannot be absolute and final. Every judicial decision we make contributes to the Canadian conscience. Whatever compromises have to be made in order to govern ourselves without violence, Canadians cannot afford to be satisfied. That is why courts are so important in the real world, and not just in theory. They contribute to our context of rights, defined in the constitution as limits on the powers of government and as the rightful claims of individuals and groups.

# INTRODUCTION

It is impossible to think of Canada as a governable country in the absence of law — that is, without a judicial system, a legal system, or the lawmaking system that prescribes and proscribes the conduct of Canadians. *Law* is the set of rules of conduct established by custom or laid down and enforced by a governing authority. No rational person believes that the intricate problems arising in a complex urban–technological society like ours can be dealt with in the absence of statutes, courts, legislatures, public administration, the police, lawyers, and judges.

Government does not rely solely upon the law to achieve its objectives, but government without the **administration of justice** in Canada would not perform. To govern means to control, and control in a governmental sense requires the regulation of conduct embedded in legal principles, standards, and rules — all enforced by sanctions, whether civil or criminal. High among the ideals of Canadians is that the goal of their democratic governing system will attain law, order, and justice: Laws exist to help reach these goals, although in practice the judicial system often fails to satisfy everybody concerned.

Law also comprises the dos and don'ts of human routines. Parking one's car on the wrong side of the street, disposing of garbage in forbidden places, unlawfully invading the files of computers, insulting or punching a neighbour in a fit of temper, failing to file an income tax return, theft of private or public property — all of these actions lead to legal sanctions.

The law has three main tasks: to make the operations of government predictable, precise, and consistent as a social command and passed by a legitimate authority. The need for predictability of human behaviour is the basic reason for law. People demand from others certain regularities of behaviour, and they must provide to others the expectation that they themselves will behave peacefully and predictably.

Law can be classified in two principal ways: first, according to whom it involves and protects, as in civil law and criminal law; and, second, by source — from the constitution, as in constitutional law; in legislation, as in statutory law; from the public administration of law; from judge-made law; and from international law. Effective laws limit the actions of government itself, so that people can know what the government will and will not do.

Most Canadians tend to see justice as a higher ideal than law, but they also tend to see law as the surest and safest way to achieve justice. Even where they disagree with particular laws, Canadians remain deeply committed to the "rule of law," which goes some way toward explaining why theories of civil disobedience, violence, resistance, and rebellion have not played a significant role in Canadian political ideologies. Unlike people in other political systems, Canadians traditionally direct their efforts toward changing unjust laws instead of resisting or rebelling against them.

Governments must not only make law, but administer it as well. For the political scientist, law means the processes, principles, standards, and rules that are administered, govern the relationships, and help resolve conflicts among human beings through the legal and judicial institutions of society. In Canada, we speak of constitutional, federal, provincial, municipal, and international law. Decisions of the Supreme Court of Canada and of the superior courts of the provinces and territories interpret and proclaim the meaning of the provisions of our constitution and Charter of Rights and Freedoms: Parliament governs the areas of human affairs that the constitution has entrusted to the federal government; laws passed by the provinces blanket the remainder of such relationships, except where they have conferred lawmaking authority over certain matters on counties, cities, towns, and other municipalities; and treaties between Canada and other nation-states constitute a formal source of domestic Canadian law.

In the latter part of the twentieth century, Canadians are increasingly law-conscious. They are prone to engage in litigation and to use the **courts** to resolve disputes at all levels of society, and for all matters involving human interaction. Despite signs to the contrary, especially in times of uncertainty and economic hardship, we hold the rule of law in the highest esteem, as evidenced by the traditional respect Canadians have demonstrated for reasoned conduct and for duly constituted authority. Above all, Canadians view their constitution as a higher law, the ark of the political and social covenant that unites Canada.

## THE FOUNDATIONS OF CANADIAN LAW

Because of its English and French colonial heritage, a great portion of Canadian law is based on the English common-law system, and, in the province of Quebec, on French-Canadian civil law. Quebec's civil law is a **code**, while the common law generally is not **codified law**. Although Canadian society in the 1990s is undoubtedly multicultural, its judicial system is richly bicultural and has a dual character.

National uniformity of law cannot be realized because Quebec will not give up its civil-law system and the other provinces will not relinquish their common-law systems (Brierly 1968). Indeed, the Civil Code of Quebec is, like its language and culture, viewed as a clear illustration of the distinctiveness of Quebec society.

### Common Law

One of the institutions the Normans created to unite the England they conquered in 1066 was the King's Court, or *Curia Regis*. Before the conquest, disputes were settled according to local custom. The King's Court endeavoured to establish a "common," or unified, set of rules for the whole country. Case law was built up through the work of travelling justices of the monarch's superior courts, who were sent from London to apply common or general customs to litigation in various parts of the realm.

Judges deciding in disputes similar to ones that had been dealt with previously used as a basis yearbooks in which were recorded earlier judicial decisions. If a case was unique, judges had to create new law, but they based their decisions on the general principles established by earlier cases. The body of judge-made law that developed under this system is still used today in Canada and is known as the "common law." The practice of deciding new cases with reference to former decisions, that is, according to **precedent**, became a cornerstone of the British and Commonwealth judicial systems, and is embodied in the doctrine of *stare decisis et non quieta movere* (let the decision stand and do not move what has been settled).

In the Canadian legal system, the rule of *stare decisis* performs many useful governmental functions. First, it makes Canadian courts more efficient. It would be time-consuming if every judge had to establish reasons for deciding what the law should be for each case brought before the court. If other courts have confronted the same issue and reasoned through the case carefully, their opinions can serve as guides and build predictability into our judicial system. Second, the rule of *stare decisis* makes for a uniform judicial system of government by building continuity into the administration of the law from province to province. Judges consult precedents not only within Canada, but from other Commonwealth states (such as Australia and New Zealand), the United States, and Europe (McCormick and Greene 1990, 217). In Canada, some variations will occur because different provinces may be adhering to different precedents. But the rule of precedent tends to neutralize the personal prejudices of individual judges to the degree that they feel obliged to use precedent as the basis of their decisions. Finally, the rule makes the law more predictable than it otherwise would be.

Sometimes a Canadian court may depart from the rule of precedent because it has decided the precedent is no longer valid — for example, when it is affected by changes in technology, business practices, or general social attitudes favouring a change in the law. Usually, however, judges are reluctant to overrule precedent, and whether they do so will depend on each case, the number and prestige of previous decisions, the degree of social change that has occurred before the trial, and the identity of the deciding on court. The Supreme Court of Canada, when deciding on a constitutional question, a charter question, or a general principle of Canadian law is the highest authority in the land and is therefore freer to reverse the direction of the law than is a lower court.

Sometimes there is no acceptable precedent on which to base a decision, or precedents conflict. In these situations, a court will: (1) refer to decisions in earlier cases that may be similar to the current case and formulate a decision by reasoning through analogy; (2) look at social factors — changes in the status of women or children, for example — that might influence the issues involved; and (3) apply the principles of **equity** to determine what the fairest result might be. Cases that overturn precedent often receive a lot of publicity, and it might seem that they are quite common; in reality, the great majority of cases are decided according to the rule of *stare decisis*.

Related to this common-law principle is *res judicata* (the matter has been adjudicated) — the idea that, under normal conditions, a judicial determination is final. This judicial axiom holds to the merits of a court's decision that settles the matter before it in a conclusive way. The principle *res judicata* constitutes a fundamental aspect of governability because, if court decisions were not final, the judicial system would fail in its governing role as settler of disputes.

Another fundamental element in the judicial and legal practice of common law is adversarial debate before judges and juries. In the centuries before common law was consolidated in England, trials by combat, **ordeal**, and the swearing of oaths were used to determine the guilt or innocence of the parties before the courts. Modern common law holds that the litigants (those involved in a lawsuit) have the job of persuading the court that their actions are legal, or at least defensible under the law. The facts are heard and weighed, and a decision is rendered that may or may not achieve the justice, fairness, or equity expected by the parties involved, or the community for that matter. The use of reasoned debate in the controlled and peaceful setting of a courtroom permits legal adversaries to present their cases. Judges are not responsible for the quality of these presentations and can make their decisions only from the evidence before them.

Involving, as it does, the central role of the judge, the system is really no better than its judges. The common law assumes that the judge will adhere to reasonable precedents with reasonable frequency and will exercise fairness and avoid arbitrariness. When courts make mistakes, the common-law system permits that dissatisfied litigants may "appeal" to a higher court for a remedy.

Flexibility, which is the best quality of the common-law system, permits a gradual, steady accommodation of change in the legal system. The broad legal and judicial principles, combined with the interpretative role of judges, have enabled the law to change with the times in Canada. Having been established in Canada at an early date, the common law has adapted to conditions different from those existing in England and other common-law states.

While the common-law system has been a unifying force in the economic and political life of Canada, its mere existence has not resulted in the acceptance of common-law principles throughout the country.

## Civil-Law Codes of Quebec

Canada's legal and judicial system comprises the practice and traditions of both the common law and the civil law, although the common law dwarfs the civil law. The civil law of France, based on the **Code Napoléon**, is the historic model of Quebec jurisprudence. Thus, the **private law** of Quebec is French-Canadian civil law, in contrast to the Anglo-Canadian common law. But, in public-law matters, the common law is practised in Quebec, as it is in the other provinces and by the federal government.

Until 1759, Quebec was part of the French Empire. In 1763, the Treaty of Paris, which ended the Seven Years War, brought Quebec under British control. The British guaranteed Quebeckers that the private law of French Canada would be protected under French-Canadian civil law (Cheffins and Johnson 1986). It was a matter of British public policy to accept and preserve French-Canadian language and culture, instead of forcing an assimilation within the culture of Great Britain. The French civil law remained uncodified until 1866, when it was enacted as the Civil Code of Lower Canada (Quebec), with a revision proclaimed in 1981 as the Civil Code of Quebec (Crepeau and Brierly 1981).

In other parts of Canada, and certainly at the federal level, legislators use the word *code* as just another name for an ordinary legislative act, such as the Highway Code or the Criminal Code. But, in Quebec private law, the term "code" is used to mean a unified area of law — a great diversity of legislation that has been compiled and gathered in one place in order to facilitate consultation, as in family law. The code provides clear and precise solutions to practical legal problems in understand-able language. But, unlike the more malleable character of common law, the codified written law brings the risk of rigidity. Codes face the possibility of not always responding to new social problems, and periodically undergo extensive legislative overhauls to bring them up-to-date.

The civil-law tradition in Quebec follows general abstract legal principles that have been substantially codified. The facts of each case are analyzed in relation to these principles and not from prior judicial decisions that comprise common-law tradition in the techniques of binding case-law precedent. The civil-law tradition is essentially "deductive" because it applies general rules to a particular case, whereas the common-law tradition is essentially "inductive" because it builds its rules from particular cases and general principles.

Unlike the common-law system, where judges exercise latitude and flexibility, the civil-law system accords primary responsibility for the interpretation of the law to experts. In fact, their role in giving final meaning to the codes tends to supersede that of judges. In the application of the civil law, judicial decisions are regarded as persuasive rather than as precedents that should be adhered to in future cases. For this reason, the writings of scholars and professors are given pre-eminent attention in the interpretation of civil-law doctrine.

Official bilingualism exists in various degrees throughout Canada and has had particular impact on judicial practices in the country. The federal statute enacted in 1969 as the Official Languages Act requires official bilingualism within all federal government institutions. Included within the act are the federal Parliament, the Supreme Court of Canada, and the federal court system, the departments of the executive branch of government, and federal publications and communications. In matters before the courts, most provinces have voluntarily accepted some measure of official bilingualism.

Quebec's uniqueness as a legal culture was conserved, not only by its governing provincial status, but also in terms of federal public policy. The Supreme Court of Canada is required by law to provide three judges from Quebec because it functions as a civil-law court for private-law appeals from Quebec and as a common-law court for public matters across the country.

Some qualification is required when we explain the actual practice of law in Quebec today. The influx of common-law approaches through the federal and public law of Canada, and the incidence of appeals to the Supreme Court of Canada, have diluted the purity of civil law in Quebec. Currently, the Quebec system of law might best be described as a "hybrid" or "mixed" system (Fitsgerald and McShane 1982). But the differences between common law and civil law are still more than merely a matter of degree and are widely recognized by those who want to preserve the bicultural legal heritage of Canada. It is very unlikely that uniformity of law across all provinces will ever be achieved.

## CANADIAN PUBLIC LAW

Four bodies of law comprise the public-law system: constitutional, criminal, administrative, and international (Waddams 1982). Public law is often concerned with the great issues of public policy, such as wrongful conviction, abortion, the rights of inmates, and so on, although even a minor issue affecting the power of the state qualifies as a matter of public law. Constitutional law, for example, falls within the area of public law, and when the Supreme Court of Canada is confronted with a case in which it must determine the effect of a federal or provincial power on individual rights, it is then concerned with both public law and broad issues of public policy. Similarly, it is a principal function of the courts to protect individuals against

abuses emanating from the actions and conduct of public officials through the application of administrative law.

### Constitutional Law

In Canada, constitutional law is a branch of public law that treats the organization and framework of the various governments in the country; the division of sovereign powers among provinces, the federal government, and aboriginal peoples; the Charter of Rights and Freedoms; and all judicial decisions that interpret the constitution and/or set precedents on how the constitution should be viewed in law (Hogg 1985). All judicial decisions actually confirm constitutional law, but when judges and courts rule directly on the contents of our constitution, they are themselves a major source of constitutional law.

The Constitution Act, 1867, was passed by Great Britain as the British North America Act, 1867, and was renamed in 1982. The primary sources of Canadian constitutional law include all constitution acts after 1867 and other documents, such as federal and provincial statutes, that relate to constitutional matters. Certain conventions and traditions of governments in Canada (such as ministerial solidarity and confidentiality) are elevated to the level of constitutional law by the Supreme Court of Canada (Morton 1984). In addition, the various amendments to the written constitutional documents themselves are a source of Canadian constitutional law. Any formal changes to the constitution create an addition to or deletion from constitutional law. Certain British documents are incorporated into the formal constitutional framework of Canada, such as the Magna Carta; the British Bill of Rights, 1689; and various other statutes and charters, such as the Statute of Westminster, 1931. Included as well are constitutional British orders-in-council, pertaining to Canada's territoriality (such as those admitting Rupert's Land and the North-Western Territory in 1870), and Letters

Patent, which were issued periodically since 1867 as part of the royal prerogative to create the office of governor general and to delegate the powers of the monarch to Canada's governor general.

Certain statutes also form an important part of Canadian constitutional law. Statutes that create the provinces, create courts, change provincial boundaries, and affect the voting franchise are constitutional in form and substance. As well, the Canadian Bill of Rights, 1960, is constitutional in nature, and therefore must be seen as a source of Canadian constitutional law. Certain provincial statutes possess enacted constitutional status as well. For example, Saskatchewan, Alberta, and Quebec have bills of rights.

Another component of Canadian constitutional law is the rules of order by which Parliament and provincial legislatures function. These rules are constitutional in nature because they govern the operation of the legislative branch of government and are used to make laws.

Perhaps more than any other constitutional instrument, the charter has become the most active source of constitutional law in Canada. Especially since the addition of the charter, and at no other time in Canadian history, constitutional law has been focussed to a great extent on the relationship of the state to the individual, minorities, and certain collectivities. The courts define charter rights and freedoms as cases arise. In addition, in interpreting the charter, the judiciary is granted broad discretionary powers under Section 1 to decide what limits to rights and freedoms are "reasonable" in a free and democratic society.

Sometimes the interpretation of these rights will collide, as in the high-profile case of Ernst Zundel, in which free speech and minority rights clashed, and free speech won. In that case, the Supreme Court of Canada decided to throw out a conviction against Holocaust-denial publisher Ernst Zundel for "publishing false news." The result was a decision that left the parties in the dispute about where they began in 1983, when the veracity of the Holocaust was debated. This decision, as well as many others, shows that the charter places in the hands of the courts the potential to play a much greater lawmaking role than they have exercised in the past.

### Criminal law

Because crime is a violation of public order, it constitutes a fundamental component of public law. The Criminal Code is a federal statute enacted by Parliament, as empowered in the Constitution Act, 1867, that provides the federal government exclusive jurisdiction to legislate against criminal offences in Canada. A *crime* is any act that contravenes the Criminal Code and any other offence prohibited and indictable under parliamentary law. The Criminal Code defines the exact nature of an offence; indicates who is prohibited from performing it; and specifies the formal, negative sanctions that may be applied to the offender.

Criminal law enhances governability because it is a powerful instrument for enforcing order and stability in our society. It directly affects the operation of penal institutions, judicial procedures and evidence, as well as the success of police investigative work. The application of the criminal law by police, prosecutors, judges, and juries depends very much on the adaptive capacity of the Criminal Code in response to technological advances in weapons, telecommunications, and surveillance.

Criminal law and its procedures must conform with the Charter of Rights and Freedoms (Monahan 1987). Because criminal law must meet constitutional standards, all courts in Canada apply the criminal law under the provisions laid down in the constitution. Under the charter, courts can never escape the task of reconciling the application of criminal laws to constitutional standards.

## Administrative Law

One aspect of public law that directly affects governability is administrative law (Jones and de Villars 1985). This branch of law is concerned with limiting the actions of governments and their officials. Administrative law involves matters of lawful authority and jurisdiction, what government actions are rightful and wrongful when directed, in particular, at individuals.

Canadian citizens are concerned about effective government but also about the adequate control of bureaucratic power. In Canada, administrative law takes its model from the British parliamentary system, where legislative powers are delegated to administrators who exercise discretion in the implementation of public policy.

Much administrative law is drawn from the regulatory function of Canada's bureaucracy and applies when individuals feel that the discretionary powers of public administrators have been exercised unfairly. Administrative discretion can often deviate from both the spirit and the letter of the law and grate against the rights of citizens. Because of the critical impact of these discretionary freedoms on citizens when government officials implement the substance of legislative, executive, and judicial functions, there is a body of public law, administrative law, to regulate the regulators.

Several factors account for the growth of administrative law. During the last hundred years, all levels of government have been providing scores of new regulations and services to the public. As governments in Canada embarked upon these tasks, it became necessary to develop a genre of law to protect people against government excesses. These standards and rules, which became known as administrative law, have secured recognition and now serve to make administrative procedures more uniform throughout Canada. Most public administrators are, indeed, acutely aware of their legal obligations, and hence mindful of the legal rights of those coming under the jurisdiction of some government body.

Just as criminal law must coexist with the charter provisions, so too must administrative law. The legality of bureaucratic conduct is measured by its accordance not only with statutes but also with the prescriptions of the charter. Just the presence of the charter has already had notable bearing on the professional conduct of public servants at all levels of governments. A great many pieces of legislation have been amended since 1982 to harmonize statutes and regulations with the charter.

The charter has even been used to expand the rights of public servants themselves. For example, in 1988, the Federal Court of Appeal struck down a law that restricted the political rights of some 250 000 federal public servants who were prohibited under the law to work for or against candidates for federal, provincial, or territorial political office.

## International Law

International law is the body of generally accepted principles, standards, and rules that regulate or control the conduct between and among nation-states, individuals, international organizations, and transnational organizations. Since Canada became a recognized independent member of the international community in the early part of the twentieth century, international law has been legally and judicially regarded as a significant area of public law throughout the country. Canada's federal government is empowered to bind Canadians to international legal obligations. As such, international law permeates and shapes the rules of Canadian law. For example, the bilateral treaty signed by Canada and the United States in 1930 was binding on both states to manage the salmon fishery of the west coast by bringing those nationals who fish on both sides of the border under the same law.

Customary law and treaty law are implemented in whole or in part in the Canadian legal and judicial system. Canada's public law incorporates international law when its federal government signs treaties or consents to binding world norms in the councils of international organizations. The doctrine of *incorporation* means that international laws are automatically considered to be part of Canadian public law unless they are in conflict with an act of Parliament. Canadian courts may also give **judicial notice** of international-law decisions made in the courts of other states.

But, like all law, international law must justify its existence by demonstrating its utility. Canadian authorities will give force to international law when they perceive that the rule of law is to be preferred over international chaos. The practical and dynamic qualities of international law assist Canadians in their attempts to govern problems in the environment, human rights, including the rights of those engaged in peacekeeping; space exploration; multinational business; the oceans; the fisheries; and terrorism. As an adopted component of Canadian public law, international law also advances the welfare of Canadians in the international community.

## CANADA'S JUDICIARY

Canadian federalism nurtures two constitutionally distinctive levels of government: federal and provincial (with municipal governments as political subdivisions of the provinces). This federal structure affects Canada's judiciary. A *judiciary* is an institution of government made up of courts that are empowered to determine and regulate the application, implementation, and enforcement of the law in all of its forms, both public and private. It is a body of judges collectively known as the "bench." Separate sets of courts operate in Canada; federal courts exist side by side with courts established by the provinces. The Supreme Court of Canada sits alone at the top of this extensive judiciary. While some provincial courts may fre-

quently exercise the same powers as the Supreme Court, their actions are subject to review by the higher court.

The Constitution Act, 1867, called for a system of separate federal and provincial courts, and permits cases to be appealed from provincial to federal courts: The present Supreme Court is the final court of **appeal**, standing at the summit of the Canadian judiciary (see Figure 6.1). Section 92 (14) gives the provinces exclusive jurisdiction to administer justice within their territorial boundaries. But Section 91 (27) gives the federal Parliament exclusive jurisdiction over criminal procedure, and sections 96, 99, and 100 grant the federal government the powers to appoint, pay salaries to, and remove all superior, county, and district judges in the provinces. However, the federal and provincial governments must co-operate in the administration of justice.

The judiciary is independent of and impartial toward the other branches of government. It is established as a very separate and special type of governmental institution. The procedures followed by the courts and the professional standards that govern them are vastly different from those of the other branches. As such, the courts are bound by a set of norms that is distinctive in the realm of politics.

Because Canada's judiciary is less susceptible to political influence than are the other branches of government, courts can act on behalf of relatively powerless individuals and groups, those who may lack political clout with the executive and legislative branches of government. Courts have extended important legal and **human rights** to these individuals and groups.

In the 1990s, Canadians expect a broader range of governmental services and protections than they did in the past. Like other government institutions, the judiciary has responded — some would say, wisely; others, foolishly — to these increased expectations and demands. As the courts have become involved in a wider range of policy questions, they have attracted the critical eye of the media and the general public. The development of a more active judicial branch is monitored carefully because courts are not responsible, as legislators are, for the costs and effects of their actions.

## Courts in the Provinces

Historically, three levels of courts were created in each province, although actual structures and the names of the courts vary among the provinces (see Figure 6.1). The lower level consists of local courts that range from "inferior" to "county" or "district" courts, although, since 1975, most provinces have merged their county or district courts with their superior courts. The "pure provincial" courts exercise jurisdiction over criminal acts, breaches of regulatory statutes, quasi-criminal behaviour such as traffic offences, young offenders, family-law cases, and small claims (Russell 1987). The small-claims courts are instituted to settle minor civil disputes with minimal formality.

Provincial courts were created to be easily accessible to every citizen. They have become collection agencies for disputes that involve small debts. In Quebec's small-claims courts, corporations cannot initiate proceedings, lawyers are not present, and there is no right of appeal. Provincial criminal courts (staffed by magistrates or provincial judges) hear less-serious criminal crimes. In Quebec, municipal courts hear cases arising under municipal by-laws, and minor traffic offences.

It is also true that the procedures for appeal from lower courts to higher courts vary from province to province (McCormick 1994). Judges of these pure provincial courts are appointed by the provincial lieutenant-governor and paid by the province. Legislation in all provinces except Alberta and Newfoundland requires that provincial court judges are selected from the bar.

The intermediate level of courts is gradually being merged provincially across Canada,

and their jurisdictions are being absorbed by provincial supreme courts, which have taken on the general jurisdiction of superior trial courts. The county or district courts were instituted to hear intermediate civil cases and most of the "serious" criminal cases. Only the most important criminal cases are reserved for the superior courts. Some provinces retain surrogate courts, which are responsible for matters related to probate in the settlement of estates.

At the top is a supreme (superior) **appellate court** that sits with general jurisdiction to determine appeals from the lower courts in the province. This court is the direct successor of the eighteenth-century courts of common law and equity. The name of this court may vary from province to province. In Ontario, it is the High Court of Justice; in Manitoba, Alberta, Saskatchewan, and New Brunswick, it is the Court of Queen's Bench; in Quebec, it is the Cour supérieure; and, in the other provinces, it is the Supreme Court, Trial Division (the other division is the appellate division).

Today, throughout Canada, the most common structure is one superior court divided into trial and appellate divisions. Over the supreme court of original jurisdiction is the appellate court, usually called the Court of Appeal. In all provinces, this court carries unlimited jurisdiction to adjudicate and administer the law, except where a statute gives exclusive jurisdiction to another court.

Apart from the federal processes of appointment and removal of superior and other provincial court judges, and of establishing the rules of procedure, the provinces are granted jurisdiction to administer justice in the province, including determining the structure, organization, and administration of the courts. Hence, the number of judges is determined by the province. In practice, there is consultation before appointments are made between the federal and provincial attorneys general and other interested parties, such as

**Figure 6.1  The Hierarchy of Canadian Courts**

1. Federal Courts —established by federal statutes, with judges appointed by the federal government.

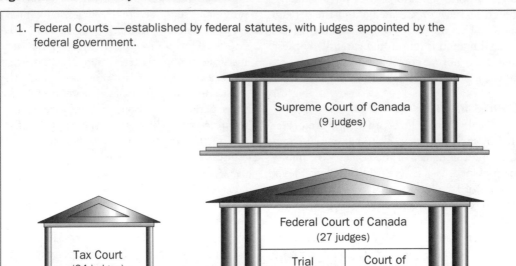

2. Provincial Courts—established by provincial statutes, with judges appointed by the federal government.

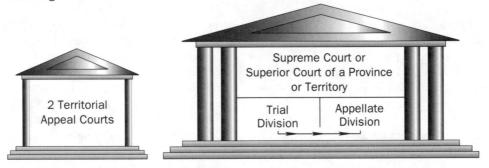

3. Provincial Courts—established by provincial statutes, with judges appointed by the provincial government.

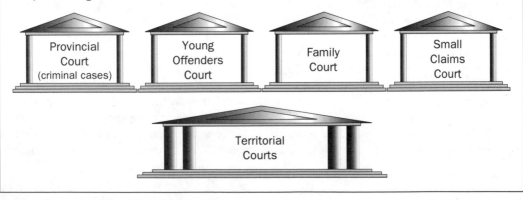

the Canadian Bar Association and, in some provinces, even laypeople.

Under the law, federally appointed judges are chosen from among lawyers who have been qualified to practise law by a provincial or territorial law society for at least ten years. The present arrangement, borrowing from the Meech Lake Accord, has produced agreement that Ottawa should choose Supreme Court nominees from lists supplied by the provinces and the territories.

## The Federal Court of Canada

The Federal Court of Canada is successor to the Exchequer Court of Canada, which was established in 1875, at the same time as the Supreme Court of Canada, by the Supreme Court and Exchequer Court Act, 1875.

In 1971, the Court was constituted by the Federal Court Act, passed by the Parliament of Canada under the authority of Section 101 of the Constitution Act, 1867, which, after authorizing the creation of the Supreme Court of Canada, confers on the Parliament of Canada authority to constitute additional courts for the better administration of the laws of Canada. The Federal Court of Canada is one such additional court. The Tax Court of Canada, a separate court, is another.

The Federal Court of Canada is a court of law, equity, and **admiralty law**, and it is a superior court of record, having civil and criminal jurisdiction. It has two divisions: the Federal Court — Appeal Division, and the Federal Court — Trial Division.

At the present time, the Appeal Division, also called the "Court of Appeal," consists of the Chief Justice and thirteen other judges, of whom three are **supernumerary judges**, that is, those who have attained the age of 65 years and have served more than 15 years as federally appointed judges. The Trial Division consists of the Associate Chief Justice and two other judges, of whom one is supernumerary. Supernumerary judges work at least 50 percent of sitting time.

By law, one-third of the judges of the Court must come from the province of Quebec, and litigants may choose to conduct their cases in either or both of the two official languages.

In addition to providing for full-time and supernumerary judges, all of whom are required to live in or near the National Capital region, Parliament has given to the Chief Justice authority to invite retired federally appointed judges to act as Deputy Judges of the Court in order to assist with the work of the Court on a limited basis, where warranted.

The headquarters of the Court is in Ottawa, and the judges of both divisions sit there from time to time. However, most of the work of the Court is done outside of Ottawa because the Court is required by legislation (the Federal Court Act) to arrange sittings of each division of the Court at places and times that suit the convenience of litigants. As a result of this statutory requirement, the Court has established registry offices in each province, which are linked to the principal Registry in Ottawa through a computer network, and the judges of each division travel to each of the provinces, as required, to sit and preside over trials or appeals, as the case may be.

The Court of Appeal sits in each province in the cities where the Court of Appeal for that province normally sits. For example, in the province of New Brunswick, the Court of Appeal sits only in Fredericton. The Trial Division, on the other hand, sits in Fredericton and in other places in that province that are convenient to the parties in particular cases.

The Court is both itinerant and bilingual, and has jurisdiction from coast to coast. It is sometimes said that the Court has a specialized jurisdiction. This means that the Court has authority to hear cases in a limited number of areas of law. Generally speaking, these include cases involving claims against the Crown; claims by the Crown; claims involving the Crown; claims against or concerning officers or servants of the Crown; injunctions, judicial review (writs of *certiorari*, prohibition, *mandamus*, and *quo warranto*), and declaratory relief against federal boards, commissions, and other tribunals; interprovincial and federal–provincial disputes; industrial property matters (patent, trademarks, copyright, and industrial design); admiralty and maritime matters; income tax; citizenship appeals; aeronautics; and, in limited circumstances, divorce. At the present time, the largest volume of the work of the Trial Division consists of judicial reviews of decisions of the Refugee Determination Division of the Immigration and Refugee Board.

As it has on the Supreme Court of Canada, the Charter of Rights and Freedoms, with its comprehensive constitutional package of rights, has had an impact on the Federal Court of Canada. People are able to raise constitutional challenges against the government and its administrative boards and tribunals. Federal Court judges may now be asked to determine if the actions and conduct of the government or of one of its statutory bodies has violated the charter.

Even though the Court does not receive much publicity, it is busier every year and handles cases that attract wider public interest. In 1993, the number of cases disposed of by the Trial Division was 2347. In addition, another 6018 cases involved questions of immigration. In view of its active docket, the Federal Court now deals with a wide range of charter issues that flow from questions of equality, life, liberty, and security of the person, as well as freedom of association, expression, conscience, and religion. These kinds of legal questions can at any time involve the Court in matters involving immigration, penitentiaries, the public service, and taxation.

## The Supreme Court of Canada

Established in 1875, the Supreme Court of Canada is the creature of ordinary federal legislation. Notwithstanding its enormous power

and prestige in the 1990s, the only reference in the Constitution Act, 1867, to a court of the stature of the Supreme Court is the authority for the federal government to establish a "general court of appeal for Canada" (Section 101). For a considerable time, from 1867 to 1949, the Supreme Court was not the final appellate court for Canada: The Judicial Committee of the Privy Council in the United Kingdom served Canadians in that capacity. Rights of appeal from Canada to the Judicial Committee were abolished in 1949, and the Supreme Court of Canada no longer considers itself bound by earlier Canadian decisions of the Judicial Committee (Snell and Vaughan 1985, 180–190).

From its tenuous and uncertain beginnings, the Supreme Court of Canada gradually assumed a prominent role in the governing of Canada. At most periods in Canadian history, the Supreme Court attracted very little interest, but, since the 1980s, it has become one of Canada's most visible arms of government, making significant decisions affecting the most intimate and private aspects of Canadian lives, on matters such as retirement age, abortion, pornography, and whether Canadians can shop on Sundays.

Comprising a Chief Justice and eight puisne (pronounced "pyoo-ney") justices, the Court now appears to be similar to the U.S. Supreme Court. But, in fact, its jurisdiction is surprisingly greater than that of its U.S. counterpart, which tends to adjudicate primarily in matters arising from federal law. The Supreme Court of Canada has the general powers and responsibilities of the House of Lords in the English system as well as the constitutional power and authority to review, which is analogous to the federal jurisdiction of the U.S. Supreme Court. The Supreme Court of Canada is a court of "general" jurisdiction.

Every category of law — constitutional, statutory, common, civil, criminal, federal, and provincial — can fall within the decisional jurisdiction of the Supreme Court. There are

Inside the Supreme Court of Canada. *Source:* Peter Christopher/Masterfile.

rules of access that must be followed before a case gets on the Supreme Court docket. The idea that anyone can take a case all the way to the Supreme Court is true hypothetically, but not always in fact. For example, in one of many cases, the Supreme Court refused to hear an appeal by a New Brunswick man who wanted a traffic ticket quashed because he was not given a choice of being served with it in English or French.

The Supreme Court follows a number of procedures for deciding what cases it will hear. There is automatic right to appeal for those whose acquittal was reversed by a provincial appellate court on an appeal by the Crown. For example, in the case of Dr. Henry Morgentaler, who was given an acquittal by a Toronto jury on a charge of conspiracy to procure a miscarriage, the Ontario Court of Appeal ordered a new trial. Morgentaler opted instead to exercise his automatic appeal to the Supreme Court of Canada.

A rightful appeal also goes to those whose conviction was upheld by an appellate court but with one of the judges dissenting on a question of law. For example, an automatic right to appeal to the Supreme Court was granted in the case of convicted murderer Colin Thatcher because a member of the Saskatchewan Court of Appeal disagreed with the lower court's ruling, even though a majority of the justices upheld the conviction.

Lawyers prepare legal arguments for an appeal in written documents called **factums** that contain the facts and reasoning of the case. Supreme Court justices review these documents in panels of three, two of whom must concur to grant leave to appeal. Annually, about 500 applications for leave to appeal are reviewed, and only 15 to 20 percent of them are granted.

Once an appeal is granted, the Supreme Court conducts a hearing on a case, sitting in panels of five, seven, or the full court of nine to hear lawyers' arguments. After hearing these arguments, the justices meet in conference to consider the matters in the case and to exchange opinions. Justices rarely discuss cases with each other before going to conference. The opinions of each justice are heard to determine the consensus and differences of opinion among them. After a tentative vote has been taken, the drafting of opinions is assigned to the individual justices. When justices are satisfied with their drafts, they circulate them to each other, exchange memoranda, and confer with others to discuss differences.

When more than one judge must decide a case, internal politicking will inevitably occur. Nowhere is this truer than in the Supreme Court of Canada. The nine justices are keenly aware of one another's views. The highest court in the land operates not only by principled persuasion but also by negotiation, even by bargaining. The justices must agree, although not unanimously, first, which cases to hear; second, the direction of the case (who wins and who loses); and, third, what legal reasoning should be applied to a decision. Negotiation plays a significant role in arriving at decisions as to who wins and who loses.

Because Supreme Court justices reach their decisions in private, it is difficult to pinpoint who persuaded whom to vote in a particular way, but persuasive activity of some intensity undoubtedly takes place. The Chief Justice can be influential in shaping court decisions. On highly controversial issues, the Chief Justice may try to achieve a unanimous decision to enhance the finality of a single judicial opinion, realizing the potentially divisive results that certain decisions can have in society. This may be done by stalling or manoeuvring until everyone agrees, even if it means delaying a decision for a some time.

Negotiation over the nature of the Court's opinions, which formally lay out the reasoning behind a decision, is particularly important. The Chief Justice may exert influence to shape these opinions to suit a personal policy preference. In that regard, the Chief Justice can exert influence to shape opinions by assigning the writing of the opinion to particular justices who are aligned with his (as yet, no woman has been appointed Chief Justice) opinions. Those justices who disagree with their colleagues write dissenting opinions. Justices who agree with the outcome but base their agreement on different reasoning write concurring opinions. But only majority opinions have the force of law.

It is fortunate that the Canadian judicial system invites and respects the function of dissenting opinions. The very process of dissent ensures a rigorous testing of the majority view within the Court itself, and reduces the chances of arbitrary decision making. Those who analyze matters on the highest bench know that the forceful dissent of today may attract a majority vote in some future year.

The Supreme Court is a place where justices and their staffs work extremely long hours, often 80-hour weeks; where the nature of what they do is always tedious, though intellectually challenging; where their responsibilities are handled with utter seriousness; and where there is little or no time for socializing.

Lawyers have some impact on what questions the Supreme Court will consider. They may decide not to appeal certain cases if they think they will get a negative result. In effect, lawyers may choose to keep certain issues from the Court, and instead seek to keep cases at the provincial supreme court level or simply accept a loss rather than risk an unfavourable, precedent-setting decision by the Supreme Court. Those who do not win court suits — even if they lose in the Supreme Court — have other avenues of appeal, mainly Parliament and the provincial legislatures, which can pass new laws favourable to their positions.

Who gets on the Supreme Court plays an important role in what the Court decides. Not surprisingly, the political arguments surrounding the selection of Supreme Court justices are gaining intensity. Supreme Court appointments increasingly attract public attention

because the federal government, as well as informed observers, know that these appointments help shape the general philosophy of the Court, which in turn influences each decision and reflects on the government. Some Supreme Court appointments attract special attention because they are breaking new social ground, as when the first woman justice (Bertha Wilson) was appointed. But as the visibility of the Court grows in Canadian society, the first aboriginal appointment, or other minority appointment, would draw attention as well.

The ideological complexion of the Supreme Court is also gaining more significance in Canada, particularly as the impact of the charter impinges on the role of government and the conduct of government officials. Increasingly, prime ministers seek people for the Supreme Court who are close to them ideologically, and often who have had some connection with the same political party. But prime ministers and their cabinets cannot always predict ideological agreement because of the professional nature of judicial thinking and because of the force of legal precedent in shaping the decision-making ideology of judges. Still, the balance of "liberal" and "conservative" justices is at present an important factor when appointments are being considered. A "liberal" judge would be open to forces of social change, tend to apply principles of affirmative action and equality, take progressive approaches to questions on government programs, and defend individual rights against the traditional powers of the state. In comparison, "conservative" justices would find a logic in preserving and conserving social traditions that have demonstrated their viability, uphold the role and conduct of government, and tend to side with the Crown in criminal matters.

Because it can take many years and a great deal of effort and expense for a case to reach the Supreme Court, the cases that get there tend to represent persistent legal problems in

Canadian society or powerful social concerns, or both. When this happens, the Supreme Court confronts complicated questions of law, usually involving serious ethical and moral questions. No other court in Canada remains so prominently in the public eye, enjoying the greatest indulgence of public trust by Canadians of all the federal institutions of government. For most Canadians, the Supreme Court of Canada symbolizes the principle that no one, including government officials, is above the law.

### The Supreme Court and the Charter

The enacting of the Charter of Rights and Freedoms on April 17, 1982, has resulted in nothing less than a revolution, affecting Canada's judicial system as well as everyone in the country. During the remaining years of the 1980s, the Supreme Court became dramatically visible to the Canadian people because so many of its decisions focussed on their rights. The Supreme Court became "supreme" in its close linkage to the charter and its emergent decision-making authority on the constitutionality of Canadian government. The power to interpret the constitution is a judicial *decision* that carries its weight long into the future and influences the law profoundly (Dickson 1984).

The scope of the Court's political influence has dramatically broadened because the rights and freedoms outlined in the charter touch the most private aspects of our lives as individuals of all ages, parents, employers, employees, and members of many different groups. These rights place limits on what governments can do with their constitutional powers in dealing with individuals and certain groups.

Because of the spirit and letter of the charter, the Supreme Court now can, in many ways, supervise the work of the lawmakers, to make sure acts of Parliament, regulations, provincial statutes, and the rules of administrative and quasi-judicial tribunals do not infringe

on the basic rights of Canadians. For example, in 1992, the Supreme Court held that judges can order government to pay social benefits to individuals in some circumstances when there is clear violation of constitutional rights.

In addition, the Court can decide to strike down laws that violate individual rights, or give its stamp of approval to those laws that may limit the actions of individuals but can be justified as reasonable limits in a democratic society. In 1988, when the Supreme Court struck down the 1969 abortion law as unconstitutional, this charter interpretation triggered a flurry of political reactions across the country. The issues surrounding this decision — the equality of women, the rights of women to control their bodies, the rights of the unborn, and the right to choose whether to carry a life to birth — propelled the role of the Supreme Court as an instrument of government into the mainstream of democratic politics in Canada. The decision forced Parliament to create legislation that amended the Criminal Code to allow a woman to have an abortion at any stage of pregnancy if one doctor agrees that the woman's physical, mental, or psychological health is threatened.

The success or failure of the charter rests with the judiciary, in particular with the justices of the Supreme Court of Canada. The constitutional status of the charter has enabled the courts to apply broadly principled interpretations that, so far, retain the integrity of other branches of government. Much general power comes to the Supreme Court because of its great popular prestige, flowing in particular from charter interpretations. People — including government officials — respect the pronouncements of the Court, in great measure because of its new and dramatic powers of judicial review.

The powers of judicial review have been especially enhanced under the charter: first, that decisions of the federal Cabinet as well as provincial cabinets are subject to review by the courts under the charter; second, that the scope of judicial review is not limited to matters that arise directly from statutes, but also includes matters exercised by the executive branch, even under the royal prerogative powers; and, third, that disputes related to political or foreign policy may be reviewed by the courts.

Does the Supreme Court lead or follow Parliament and public opinion in the kinds of policies that are made by government institutions in Canada? Some might perceive the role of the Supreme Court as just part of a ruling national policy alliance — never far adrift from or far ahead of the general thrust of the expected behaviour of government. Others want the Supreme Court to have a more independent and innovative input into public policy now that the charter has become so prominent an instrument in the lives of Canadians.

## THE COURTS AND GOVERNABILITY

Judicial decisions inevitably intertwine themselves with political and governmental decisions. In the process of deciding cases, Canadian courts perform several functions, including interpreting the meaning of terms in the constitution, clarifying the essence of the Charter of Rights and Freedoms, adjudicating disputes between contesting parties, determining the facts in criminal and civil matters, ascertaining the boundaries of political authority in the conduct of governmental affairs, and applying the fundamental values of Canadian society.

Laws at all levels of government, including constitutional law, are often not self-explanatory in every detail. Judges in different courts must interpret constitutional and statutory provisions constantly when they apply them to specific cases. These interpretations not only decide individual cases, but, when aggregated into lines of legal precedent, also help to decide broader questions of pub-

lic policy, and may even realign the spirit of the constitution. Thus, Canadian courts can be both judicial and political.

The Canadian constitution does not specifically grant courts the powers of judicial review. The Constitution Act, 1867, says nothing at all about the exercise of judicial review by Canadian courts. Nonetheless, through continuing use, judicial review developed into an unwritten rule, a binding convention within the constitutional framework of Canada.

The roots of judicial review in Canada can be traced to practical considerations flowing implicitly from the principle of federalism. The writing of a Charter of Rights and Freedoms gave Canadian courts an instrument on which to build a comprehensive body of precedent for the implementation of judicial review. The increasing use of judicial review by Canadian courts reveals the extent to which government now influences the lives of ordinary people and the increasing abuses of public power and authority by those who have them. When exercising judicial review, Canadian courts place the issue before them on the public agenda, forcing a response from government. Thus, the ever-present possibility that courts may invalidate laws has undoubtedly persuaded legislatures against enacting laws that could be struck down.

The federal judiciary is 100 percent appointed in Canada, giving it the appearance of a government institution that is above politics. But that does not mean that the judicial branch of government is **apolitical**. Indeed, Canadian courts play a major role in making public policy. Scarcely any political question, from abortion to Zionism, arises in Canada that is not resolved sooner or later by a judicial interpretation of the constitution or a decision on a particular case in law.

Some political forces can limit the extent to which courts exercise judicial freedom. When the money is not to be found to carry out court rulings, the court is, to some extent, controlled by the governing system. A court may decide, for example, that prison condi-tions are deplorable and must be improved. But a legislature has to provide the funds to carry out such a ruling. Legislatures can pass new laws to overturn, frustrate, or subvert court decisions.

Courts represent and enforce value choices that define the kind of country Canadians expect to live in. By virtue of that fact alone, courts are an important part of the governance of the country. Canadian courts perform this task in ways that set them apart from other governing institutions. For example, courts deal only with cases in which two or more parties have a specific disagreement that requires **adjudication**.

Courts handle legal questions involving an injury that a party is alleged to have com-mitted against another or others. The parties in a lawsuit may be individuals, classes of people, groups, corporations, or governments. The alleged injury may involve criminal behaviour or result from a civil matter involv-ing property, contracts, or domestic relations. Any party may bring a suit against another in accordance with established procedures, laws, and court jurisdiction. The court focusses on the specific disagreement that is at issue in a specific case.

The courts are that branch of government that is primarily designed to service the needs of individuals in specific cases. It is in this capacity that we say every person has the right to his or her "day in court" — the day when the governing system pays attention to an individual's problems. This function of the courts has often been obscured in practice by the enormous costs and delays of judicial pro-cedures. How the courts act continues to make a difference to the governmental system. The judiciary helps to decide where Canadians and their government will go next.

### Access to the Courts
In Canada's increasingly litigation-prone soci-ety, many individuals want courts to resolve

their disputes. But getting our day in court depends on the type of case it is, how much money we have, and the level of court involved. Criminal cases do not afford indi-viduals or groups much choice. People in-volved in these kinds of matters *must* appear, under penalty of law. Potential civil litigants often cannot get to court, even after they sue others for denying their rights and causing them to incur damages.

Although the courts are supposed to be open to all people, many individuals do not have enough money to hire a lawyer and pay the related costs necessary to pursue a case. Only corporations, people with enough money, or seriously injured victims who sue can gain access to the courts. Sometimes poor victims with a strong case can agree to pay a lawyer a portion of what they win from their suit to take their cases all the way to court. In addi-tion, some individuals qualify for support from legal-aid programs and can pursue a case.

A large part of the expense in gaining access to court is paying a lawyer to defend or research the case. Other expenses include vari-ous kinds of fees for filing the case, summon-ing jurors, paying certain types of witnesses, and general court costs. Even if individuals have enough money to initiate a suit, a dis-parity can reveal itself as the case is presented in court: Those with more money can develop a full case, whereas others must proceed with a skeletal case that may not persuade judges or jurors. This holds true not only for civil litigants but for criminal defendants.

Legal aid — where full-time lawyers defend qualifying clients — is provided by gov-ernments, and in fact is regarded as a public-defender system to enable people with little money to get to court or to defend themselves against charges by the state. While most are inclined to see advantages in this kind of gov-ernment service, there are disadvantages that clients might experience as consumers. One is that, when a lawyer is provided by the state, individuals lose their independence because the judge, the prosecutor, the police, court officials, and the legal-aid lawyer are all "government" employees. The danger of this degree of government influence over the conduct of a case in a public-defender system is higher than when the services of lawyers are paid for privately by the client. The built-in danger comes from the fact that taxpayers are reluctant to approve of spending large sums of public money to pursue technical defences whereby people who are clearly guilty win by means of lengthy and tedious legal strategies in court.

Because of the spiralling expenses of going to court, interest groups will sometimes sponsor and finance certain cases that relate to their goals. Some groups, especially those concerned with civil liberties, such as the Civil Liberties Association; civil- and human-rights organizations, such as the National Action Committee on the Status of Women (NAC); environmental groups, such as Greenpeace; and consumer and safety groups use litigation as a tactic to advance their goals.

Many of the most important cases that get to court are sometimes organized by an interest group, which will find the plaintiffs, develop a legal strategy, and mobilize allies and public support in the community. But, despite their activity and successes, interest groups can and are willing to help only a small number of individuals who may not have the resources to finance their own suits.

Restrictions of access are often imposed by the courts themselves. Not every dispute can gain standing in a court of law. Laws that are on the books may not be enforceable, or damages claimed by litigants may not be demonstrable under the law. Provincial courts of appeal, especially, exercise selective control in hearing cases and in accepting cases for review. Of all the courts in Canada, the Supreme Court has tremendous power to control its docket, and therefore to determine access to the highest court of appeal in the country.

The situation of crowded courts also deters access in the public mind. Responsible for one-third of the country's population, Ontario's courts have become strained under the weight of rapid development and government underfunding, particularly in cities such as Newmarket, Oshawa, Scarborough, Barrie, and Ottawa, where trial delays can be a year or more. In Winnipeg, it takes at least twelve months to get a provincial court trial. In Montreal, where provincial courts handle more than 30 000 cases a year, delays also are quite common. These backlogs in the courts, which allow accused individuals to buy time by demanding a trial and then pleading guilty at the last minute, can have the effect of eroding public confidence in the justice system.

Since the release of the Supreme Court of Canada's landmark **Askov decision** in 1990, more than 50 000 criminal cases in Canada have been stayed, or withdrawn, because accused persons were waiting unreasonable lengths of time before their cases were heard, all resulting from a backlogged court system. The right to a trial within a reasonable length of time became a guaranteed constitutional right in Canada when the Charter of Rights and Freedoms was passed in 1982. The *Askov* decision created a public outcry because cases that involved sexual assault, extreme assault causing bodily harm, theft, and other serious crimes went untried, leaving victims and witnesses frustrated with the judicial system and the accused free from the responsibilities of their defences. In response, the federal and provincial governments were forced to add judges to their existing benches, build new courthouses, appoint more prosecutors, and increase the efficiency of judicial administration everywhere. Using the *Askov* decision as their guide, most judges regard any delay over eight months, if it can be directly blamed on institutional hurdles and not the accused, as unreasonable. Equality of access has become a measure of how people see governability as a judicial function.

## Juries

Access to courts and the judiciary is available to the public by means of juries. The jury system allows for ordinary citizens to take part in the judicial process without being litigants or legal professionals. Most Canadians never serve on juries, and those who do are not representative of the total population. However, although most lawsuits and criminal prosecutions are settled without going to trial, those that do go to trial, particularly civil cases, are often tried solely by a judge, without a jury.

Still, juries are an important symbol of democratic participation in our governing system. Their existence encourages Canadians to accept the way our judicial system works and to believe in its fairness. Those who are called to serve on juries have an opportunity to learn more about how the Canadian justice system actually works. Such service also generates a greater respect for the law.

A trial jury in a criminal case is usually composed of twelve jurors, but juries of six people are used, for example, in the Yukon and Northwest Territories. Juries can function with fewer than twelve members if someone who has qualified gets sick or if a conflict is discovered during the trial. Jurors are responsible for determining what the facts are in the case and how the law should be applied. In both federal and provincial courts, the parties may waive their right to a jury and may have a case tried by a judge alone.

Juries must be randomly selected. Lists of potential jurors are prepared from voters' lists, which tends to ensure that the sample from which jurors are drawn is representative. People from a number of professions and occupations — for example, judges, lawyers, doctors, and police officers — are quite often excused from serving on juries. People on fixed incomes sometimes ask to be excused because the jury fee is seldom equal to their regular pay.

At the beginning of a civil or criminal trial, prospective trial jurors are assembled in a courtroom. The court clerk calls out several names, and those who are called rise and take their places in the jury box. During jury selection (a process sometimes called "voir dire"), the lawyers for both sides take turns questioning the prospective jurors to determine whether they have any biases that would prevent them from serving in an impartial manner. The lawyers may seek to find out whether a prospective juror is biased against certain types of cases. Each side in the case has a small number of "pre-emptory challenges," which permit them to have a few prospective jurors excused from a jury without stating any reason whatsoever. In addition, each side has an opportunity to challenge for "cause" for example, if a prospective juror is an alien, or does not speak the official language of the accused, or has been convicted of an offence for which sentencing to a term of imprisonment exceeding twelve months applies. On the basis of these and "causes," a prospective juror can be excused from serving in the case.

Upon application of one of the parties, a judge can grant a "change of venue" — that is, move the case to some other town or country. This is done when it is shown that it will be impossible to find a sufficient number of impartial jurors in the original jurisdiction, usually because the case has received widespread publicity. During the trial, jurors serve in a passive role: They simply sit and listen. After they have heard closing addresses, they can ask the trial judge to clarify points.

At the conclusion of a trial, and before both sides make their final arguments, the judge "instructs" the jury about the law that governs the case. Federal criminal cases always require unanimous verdicts. When a jury is "hung" — unable to reach a verdict by the required unanimous vote — the judge may first send the jury back to try again. But, if they are deadlocked, the judge must eventually declare a mistrial. The case can be retried, but a new jury must be selected.

Critics of the trial-by-jury system have focussed on the problem of using ordinary citizens to decide technical cases. Juries may be more likely to use their own "common-sense" notions of fairness in deciding a case, but judges often do the same. In any event, most Canadians do not want to eliminate the possibility of having a jury decide their case.

## The Judges

So far we have dealt with courts as if they were things. It is now time to recall that courts are composed of human beings. Detailed analysis of the personal characteristics of judges reveals little that is surprising. As one might expect, some substantial differences can be seen between the backgrounds of judges and those of other political actors, particularly bureaucrats. The Canadian constitution sets no special requirements for judges, but most observers would conclude that the judiciary is composed of a distinguished group of men and women.

Judges tend to come from a wealthier, better-educated, more socially prominent stratum of society than most other government officials. Given the tendency of our economic system to reward professional services, the most distinguished lawyers, even those who have served the underdog, are likely to have achieved financial success before reaching the bench.

Increasingly, in Canada, there is a public perception that who gets appointed to the bench plays an important part in what the courts decide and that, therefore, public concern is warranted. Throughout Canadian history, most judges have come from a narrow social elite. Most have come out of families of Western European stock (especially English, Welsh, Scots, and Irish), are white, and are members of the upper-middle or upper class.

The Canadian judicial establishment includes the courts, court reporters, court administrators, clerks of the court, contending lawyers, and the public. But the most crucial participants are the judges, the men and women, usually dressed in black robes, who preside over the courtrooms and make the decisions that have so much impact on the lives of people.

Today, gender, race, and ethnicity are more salient criteria for Cabinet to consider when selecting judges. The judiciary can no longer be described as a male preserve because the barriers of gender, and those of race and ethnic identity, are being challenged in Canadian courts as well as in other government institutions. More women and people of different ethnic and racial composition are serving on both provincial and federal courts, both because of increased opportunities for legal education and decreased public and official prejudice against their engaging in judicial activity, and because of the growing political empowerment of these groups.

In some ways, the courts in Canada are not very democratic. Judges are not elected, and it is difficult to remove them. Their social and educational backgrounds make the courts an elite-dominated policy-making institution in Canada. They are not "representative" as a government profession, and they especially do not regard themselves as representing the interests of any Canadian constituency. Judges are therefore not subject to the whims of popular majorities or to the electoral processes of democratic politics. In a country that insists so strongly on democratic accountability, the courts are a unique government institution.

In Canada, the recruitment of judges is a somewhat complex process that increasingly involves greater scrutiny of their competence, ethical behaviour, and social and political attitudes. At the federal level, the prime minister consults with provincial attorneys general and the Canadian Bar Association to determine candidates. Usually, the RCMP performs a top-level security check on the candidates, and sometimes the names are floated to the media to ensure that there are no surprises out there.

Likewise, the provincial government, after consulting privately with bar associations, sometimes other provinces, and whomever else it sees fit, considers its choices of who would make a good judicial appointment. Various members of the legal community are contacted for their views on the character and skills of potential candidates. Governments will try to determine the reputation of the judicial candidate for fairness, capacity for hard work, clarity of written judgements, and concern for the underdog. Although the criteria of competence and character screen out some possible candidates, other characteristics play prominent roles as well.

Judges are all lawyers, drawn primarily from other federal and provincial courts, the federal and provincial governments, or law firms. Federal judges are typically selected from among provincial judges, prosecutors, and sometimes prominent lawyers. Skilled and honourable judges reflect well on the governments that appoint them.

Although premiers, the prime minister, and members of their Cabinets would ideally prefer judges with merit, they are sometimes selected on the basis of other factors, such as personal friendship, political loyalty, favouritism, political experience, and philosophical views. Political executives will sometimes select judges so as to balance representation on their courts. They may choose judges from groups who do not have a member on the court. The prime minister and the minister of justice might be urged to give greater representation to certain provinces or regions. Since 1949, Supreme Court appointments have followed a pattern: three justices from Ontario, three from Quebec, two from the Western provinces, and one from the Atlantic region. Canada's enormous size and regional geography will always be persistent criteria for selection of judges for Canada's federal courts, especially the Supreme Court and the Federal Court. In that regard, prime ministers do like to generate a truly national dispersion on the Court.

Once the selection of a candidate is made, there is no lengthy scrutinizing process of confirmation, by either the public or the legislatures, as there is in the United States. The Canadian process spares a nominee from national public humiliation but also cuts short the exposure of flawed or incompetent aspirants. In Canada, there is really no public scrutiny of a candidate's background, character, and qualifications, and no comprehensive sense of where these individuals stand on legal, political, constitutional, or moral questions, or how these characteristics may or may not affect judgements in particular cases. Judicial appointments are not subject to legislative ratification, confirmation, or even recommendation of any kind.

Many judges will deny that they *make* law. They say that it is already there, that they merely find it or interpret it with the help of their education and experience. But when judges exercise discretion, they do make law — when they interpret statutes, the constitution, and the charter, and when they determine which precedents to follow or disregard. In doing so, they reflect their own political and social preferences. In other words, judges are human beings, and, as such, have perceptions and attitudes, even prejudices.

But to say that judges make law is not to say that they make law as legislators do. Judges make law less directly, in the process of resolving disputes that come before them. They usually make it by telling governments what they cannot do and how they must do things. More significantly, judges make law less freely: They do not start with clean slates but with established principles embodied in statutes, the constitution, and precedents.

In the present judicial context, the judge must be an observer of emerging social values and a translator of such observations into law. In most cases, the judge, as a public government official with the force of the state behind his or her proper actions, will ultimately systematize and organize the law.

# Profile: Chief Justice of the Federal Court of Canada

**C**hief Justice Julius Isaac was born in Grenada, in the West Indies, and came to Canada in 1950. He studied law at the University of Toronto and was admitted to the bar of Ontario, and subsequently to the bars of Saskatchewan, Grenada, and Alberta. In addition to practising law in the private sector, Chief Justice Isaac was a legal adviser to the government of Saskatchewan, the Ontario Securities Commission, and the federal Department of Justice. He was Assistant Deputy Attorney General of Canada and, as such, served as principal legal adviser to the attorney general on federal prosecutions across Canada, on the extradition of fugitive criminals to and from Canada, and on other criminal matters. He also represented the Government of Canada in appeals before the Supreme Court of Canada and in all levels of courts in Ontario and Alberta. In 1989, Julius Isaac was appointed Justice of the Supreme Court of Ontario and, in 1991, Chief Justice of the Federal Court of Canada.

The Chief Justice of the Federal Court usually puts in twelve-hour days, administering the affairs of this little-known Canadian court. His extensive experience in Canada's legal and judicial system has earned him the highest regard as someone sincerely dedicated to public service and to the love of law and jurisprudence. He is frequently asked to speak at law schools in Canada, often addresses provincial bar associations, the Canadian Bar Association, and community associations across the country, educating his legal colleagues and the public about the newest developments in the Federal Court, and the latest rules of practice and procedure.

Unlike the job of government officials, which is concerned with the business of the government, the work of a Chief Justice and his colleagues is concerned with pondering legal briefs and Memoranda of Fact and Law, and researching past decisions. A substantial amount of the Chief Justice's time is taken up with reading and writing decisions. He likes to arrive at his office early in the morning, when no one else is around. During this quiet time, he works on matters requiring concentration. He reads cases and replies to letters from the public or memoranda from other members of the Court on current problems. He may also prepare answers to letters inviting him to speak at various functions.

The Chief Justice spends a great deal of time reading and interpreting legislation in order to make decisions that are fair and just. In deciding cases, the Chief Justice and his colleagues must try to ascertain the legislators' intent in passing laws. The production of a judgement of the Court requires co-operation from both judges and staff of the Court, since the judgement must be written, edited, translated, and printed before it is issued. The Chief Justice must manage the process with effectiveness and efficiency.

As the Chief Justice of the Federal Court, Julius Isaac usually meets with other judges and with his executive assistant and the judicial administrator of the Court, who helps to schedule cases, organize the sittings of the Court for the up-coming terms, assign judges, and keep track of their availability. The judicial administrator also keeps track of the cases and the issues involved. On matters of special importance to the Court, such as when additional judges are required to handle the caseload, the Chief Justice will meet with the Deputy Minister of Justice or even the Minister of Justice.

The Chief Justice also confers with the Commissioner for Federal Affairs, and with his or her deputy, the Administrator of the Federal Court, who has responsibility for the Registry of the Court, where documents are filed. The administrator also has responsibility for preparing the annual budget of the Court and for the security of judges both out of town and in Ottawa.

In the afternoons, the Chief Justice may meet with his law clerk to assign research questions or receive reports from him or her. Law clerks of the Federal Court, recent law school graduates who ranked high in their classes, are chosen by the justices each year to help prepare cases before the Court, research statutes and precedents, and edit opinions.

The Chief Justice is also a member of the Canadian Judicial Council, which consists of all federally appointed Chief Justices and Chief Judges in Canada, and has responsibility to ensure uniformity and efficiency in all superior courts in Canada.

For Chief Justice Isaac, the challenges of his job have never been greater, nor the work of the Court over which he presides and which he administers so demanding. At an age when most people want to retire, Chief Justice Isaac puts enormous energy into his work as both administrator of the Federal Court and judicial colleague of the other members on the bench. In the final analysis, Chief Justice Isaac, and his colleagues on the Federal Court bench, are charged with an important task of government — namely, to settle disputes peacefully and justly. Because of the importance of the decisions this Court is asked to make, his professional life is necessarily solitary, but rewarding.

## The Lawyers

To better understand the role of judges and the powers they wield, we need to understand lawyers and the nature of their craft. Lawyers effect our ability to govern the country. They are officers of the courts in Canada, and they state the claims of their clients in such a way that a legal or judicial issue can be resolved within the terms of the law: what constitutional or legal interests are at stake, what legal remedies are sought, and what facts and principles are to guide the resolution of the dispute.

Practising lawyers in Canada are called "the bar" because they are admitted past the low rail, or "bar," in the courtroom, while the general public normally must remain outside it. Lawyers are bound by professional codes that bar associations have developed, and those who violate those codes are subject to disciplinary action by their bar association and can be "disbarred," which means that they can no longer practise law. Bar associations not only police their membership but may also intervene as interest groups in governmental decision making. They are influential in the making of laws that are favourable to their profession as well as those that improve the judicial system.

As members of the legal profession, and often as advocates in the judicial system, lawyers perform a number of functions that relate to governability in matters of the law and justice. At every level of government in Canada, lawyers are employed to advise on a wide range of legal problems. As well, they are employed by the provincial and federal levels as counsel to prosecute criminal cases on behalf of the Crown.

Their contributions to the legal and judicial system are fundamental to the operation and performance of governments. First, they counsel people about the law that is made by legislators and adjudicated and interpreted by judges. This means that lawyers give advice by interpreting the law and the actions of the judicial system to the general public. They are an important educative link among the legislative and judicial branches of government and the citizen. Lawyers play an active role in negotiation within the legal and judicial system to resolve civil and criminal disputes. They assist in the peaceful settlement of social disputes, usually outside the judicial system because most civil cases are settled out of court.

Second, lawyers are mediators between competing interests of their clients. They spend a great deal of their time as conciliators in legal disputes. Successful mediation and arbitration involve reducing the tension between disputants and reconciling their opposing claims.

Third, lawyers draft legal documents and, when they work for governments, write the language of legislation. The contractual character of modern Canadian society requires that agreements be made in light of the law and adhered to according to the rules of law so that individuals and corporations will conduct their affairs legally. Lawyers often have a great deal of knowledge and expertise that is useful in drafting legislation or constitutional provisions. Many conduct research on such matters and present their findings to legislative officials, who convert these legal endeavours into laws.

Fourth, lawyers litigate — the skill most people associate with them. But only a small fraction of all lawyers devote much time to courtroom activities. In fact, the majority of lawyers never venture into a courthouse, except perhaps to file legal papers with a clerk.

Fifth, lawyers perform as assistants to judges. Assisting judges in the courts are law clerks, young men and women often hand-picked by the judges from among the highest-ranking recent law school graduates, who do research, summarize petitions, and write and critique drafts of opinions. Often law clerks will screen petitions and prepare summaries for judges to use in writing their decisions.

In the endless debate over the role of lawyers in society, there is a strong argument to be made that lawyers are the architects of our judicial system, building and repairing it to fit their vision of a better judiciary.

## CONCLUSION

The web of relationships between the judiciary and the rest of Canadian government and politics is extremely complex. The central fact, however, is that Canadians accept the roles of their courts and judges as a central and integral part of the governing process in Canada. The "peace, order, and good government of Canada" requires that, when people quarrel, they are provided with a third-party method of resolving their dispute. The universal appeal of third-party intervention explains the social magic of the judiciary, the special something that earns it popular favour and support. We use voluntary mediation to settle disputes in some areas, such as in labour–management relations and marital problems, but, for many kinds of quarrels, we have developed a governmental system based on law and judicial office.

The judiciary can exercise considerable governing powers; but, it is reactive, or passive. In civil cases, it must wait until one party sues another; in criminal cases, it cannot act until the Crown files a complaint against someone, or the police make an arrest. In contrast, Parliament and the Cabinet may initiate government action without waiting to be asked.

Courts and judges are also the guardians of our judicial system and of our governing culture and structure. They administer the law. As noted earlier, the basis of our legal system is the need for predictability or regularity of behaviour. A large proportion of these accepted standards of conduct have been codified in our constitution, and in acts of Parliament, treaties, and judicial decisions. As guardian of our legal system, the Canadian judiciary is expected to administer these norms. As a branch of government, courts and judges mete out punishments, award damages, issue judicial orders, and oversee the judicial administrative machinery to do so.

The judiciary acts as a guarantor of the government structure. It can direct parliamentarians, bureaucrats, and the members of the Cabinet to comply with Canadian and international law. In this regard, it is expected to be above the politics that drives the other branches of government, and to act independently of political and public pressure in reaching its decisions. As a special branch of government, the judiciary is expected to function as the neutral referee, deciding each case upon its facts and according to the law that applies to those facts. Administration of law, then, is an important function of the judiciary, and thus, of government.

But courts and judges sometimes make law too. They must often make discretionary choices in determining how a particular case should be decided. Although courts and judges only decide actual cases, the decisions and opinions they render can greatly alter the policy landscape of the country.

Canadians believe in the rule of law. They think the law should be impartially administered. Canadians want a neutral judiciary that is independent and representative, and allows citizens to participate. The Canadian judicial system has been criticized because it is not accessible to all — rich and poor, minority and majority — equally. Some point out that there are discrepancies in the way people are treated in regard to arrests, bail, conviction, and sentencing. The overcrowded dockets of some Canadian courts can create too much delay in securing justice.

The courts in Canada provide relief to thousands of people seeking redress for grievances that they could not obtain elsewhere in the governing system. While far from perfect, courts are capable of applying more equal treatment to Canadian citizens than do other social and governmental institutions. The quest for a greater justice will continue to be a principal goal of governability in Canada.

## GLOSSARY

**adjudication**  The settling of a dispute judicially by means of a formal hearing using court procedures and legal rules in the presence of a judge.

**administration of justice**  The provision, maintenance, and operation of the justice system, which includes courts, judicial records, and trained officials who deliver the services of justice to their communities.

**admiralty law**  The law as it relates to ships, harbours, and mariners; in Canada, referred to as "maritime law."

**apolitical**  An orientation to society and social issues that does not have as its main purpose intentions regarding the political or governing order.

**appeal**  In law, the procedure in which a higher court is asked to review a decision of a lower court.

**appellate court**  A court of law that hears appeals from the losing parties in trial-court decisions.

**Askov decision**  The case of Eli Askov, one of four Brampton men who waited more than two years for their trial on extortion charges. The Supreme Court of Canada stayed charges against Askov and his co-accused, declaring that six to eight months would have been a reasonable delay for their trial.

**code**  A legislative enactment or group of statutes and regulations brought together in a single body to provide a more or less complete set of rules on a field or fields of law.

**Code Napoléon**  The systematic collection and compilation of the laws of France as ordered by Napoleon and promulgated in 1804.

**codified law**   A body of law that has been systematically arranged, indexed, and promulgated as such to cover an entire field of jurisprudence.

**courts**   Organs of government, organized under various classes and levels, that belong to the judicial branch of government and adjudicate and administer laws.

**equity**   A branch of English common law developed to cover the limitations of civil law by applying principles of justice and fairness to remedy a judicial dispute.

**factum**   A statement of the facts and law that a party files in an application, appeal, or motion.

**human rights**   Rights that are the entitlement of a person by virtue of his or her status as a human being and not necessarily those rights protected by law or a constitution.

**judicial notice**   The acceptance by a judicial body of the credibility of a state of affairs without requiring evidence to prove its truth. In international law, domestic justices may recognize the decisions that were made by courts in other states to solve matters of international significance.

**ordeal**   The most ancient kind of trial in Saxon and old English law that called upon the "judgement of God" to intervene in human justice to rescue an innocent person from physical harm (fire or water) to which he or she was exposed in the conduct of the trial.

**precedent**   A prior court decision that is cited as an authority by other courts.

**private law**   All law relating to persons, as distinct from public law.

**supernumerary judges**   Semi-retired judges who wish to continue judging on a part-time basis, and who serve at various levels of the judiciary.

## RECOMMENDED READING

Bogart, W.A. 1994. *Courts and Country: The Limits of Litigation and the Social and Political Life of Canada.* Don Mills, Ont.: Oxford University Press. This book looks at the role of courts in the context of the entire Canadian legal system as a product of our political culture. The author examines the impact of the Charter of Rights and Freedoms on our judiciary.

Carrigan, D. Owen. 1991. *Crime and Punishment in Canada.* Markham, Ont.: McClelland & Stewart. This book takes a comprehensive historical view of crime and criminal justice in Canada.

Heard, Andrew. 1991. *Canadian Constitutional Conventions: The Marriage of Law and Politics.* Toronto: Oxford University Press. This book is a valuable contribution to the scanty literature on Canadian conventions and constitutional law.

Kaplan, William, and Donald McRae, eds. 1993. *Law, Policy, and International Justice: Essays in Honour of Maxwell Cohen.* Montreal and Kingston: McGill-Queen's University Press. This collection of essays in honour of Judge Maxwell Cohen addresses international law, public law, legal history, and legal education.

Loo, Tina, and Lorna McLean, eds. 1994. *Historical Perspectives on Law and Society in Canada.* Mississauga, Ont.: Copp Clark Longman. This collection contains interesting articles on law and society, written by historians, lawyers, and anthropologists. The topics range from informal law to the role of the police in enforcing the law.

McCormick, Peter, and Ian Greene. 1991. *Judges and Judging: Inside the Canadian Judicial System.* Toronto: James Lorimer. This penetrating study examines who our judges are and how they make their decisions. The authors discuss judicial appointment, the background of judges, and the role of the Supreme Court.

Manfredi, Christopher P. 1993. *Judicial Power and the Charter*. Toronto: McClelland & Stewart. This book looks at the use of judicial power to review, and sometimes to nullify or modify, policies enacted by Parliament. The author examines the impact of the Supreme Court of Canada on the Charter of Rights and Freedoms.

Morton, F.L., ed. 1993. *Law, Politics and the Judicial Process in Canada*. Calgary: University of Calgary Press. In this book, the author exposes the political dimensions of the judicial process in Canada.

Reesor, Bayard. 1992. *The Canadian Constitution in Historical Perspective*. Scarborough, Ont.: Prentice-Hall Canada. This book is a guide to the constitutional documentation of Canada and the history of the events leading up to their adoption as parts of Canada's constitutional law.

Saywell, John, and George Vegh. 1991. *Making the Law: The Courts and the Constitution*. Mississauga, Ont.: Copp Clark Pitman. This book provides an introduction to the role of the courts within the Canadian federal system and how courts *make* law, rather than discover it or merely interpret it.

# PART

# 3

# POLITICAL PROCESS AND BEHAVIOUR

CHAPTER

# ELECTIONS, CAMPAIGNS, AND VOTER BEHAVIOUR

**W**hat's in a Canadian election campaign? Something borrowed, something blue, a lot of irony and hypocrisy too. When Canadians think back to the federal election campaign of 1993, the memories they call up could be ambivalent, verging on both the hilarious and the tragic. Some of us will remember the lighter moments — Jean Chrétien lugging beer cartons to demonstrate his manliness, Audrey McLaughlin arm-wrestling with Paul (the butcher) Vachon, Kim Campbell revving up a tractor, the Natural Law Party espousing the benefits of yogic flying as a strategy to lower the deficit.

A touch of irony accompanied what was supposed to be nothing more than a "photo op" for former prime minister Kim Campbell. She was trying out a computer-simulated air traffic control tower at a high-tech firm in St. Bruno, Quebec. "I haven't crashed yet, but I have no idea where I'm going" was a remark that proved somewhat prophetic for her entire election campaign. Later that day, in a scrum with reporters, Campbell delivered her now-infamous political contradiction, saying that election campaigns were "the worst possible time to get involved in a debate on very, very serious issues."

The unassuming Chrétien campaign also had its ironic moments. On October 5, 1993, in Montreal, Jean Chrétien's aides told reporters who were following the Liberal leader that he had no

An election campaign is an organized event to persuade voters to choose a particular candidate or political party over others competing in the same riding. There are, however, no guaranteed recipes for political success, and most politicians are willing to try anything. *Source:* Andy Donato, *The Toronto Sun*, September 19, 1993. Reproduced with permission of Andy Donato.

activities that evening. They lied! Instead of getting the good night's sleep they said he needed, Chrétien was really going to attend a $1000-a-head cocktail party in affluent Westmount, Quebec. The invitations that were sent to Montreal's corporate elite offered them privileged access to "the future prime minister." Chrétien applied his own damage control by explaining that the cocktail party was really a fundraiser for the Laurier Club, the Liberals' corporate support group, and that $1000 couldn't buy his attention. Somewhat later, his retort was "I am a member of the Laurier Club. My wife is a member. She is the only one who has privileged access to me. But you know," Chrétien added, "millionaires vote."

With that level of dialogue, Preston Manning could not lose in the debates. All he had to do was show up, ask a few rhetorical questions, and look like a reasonable human being, and his right-of-centre Reform agenda would benefit. All he had to do was not be extreme. But it wasn't all easy going for Reform. John Beck, a Reform candidate in the Toronto-area riding of York Centre, told a college paper that immigrants bring "death and destruction" to Canada. Beck later disclosed that he couldn't get a licence to drive a taxi, owed huge sums of money to creditors, and seemed to have a fixation on Satanism. He also showed his anti-Semitism when he said, "I feel we have lost control of our country here. It seems to be predominantly Jewish people who are running this country."

Blunders, bad ads, voter scepticism, and confusion hampered campaign image-makers in their efforts to influence public opinion. More than in previous federal election campaigns, the strategies of candidates were overshadowed by the influence of public opinion polls. This may have prompted people to vote strategically. With numerous political parties and no appealing choice, voters were faced with many political permutations. New Democratic supporters could vote for the Liberals because they would be a lesser evil than the Reform Party. Quebec federalists could jump to the Liberals to stave off the Bloc Québécois. With the Liberals heading for a majority, the Prairies turned to Reform to counter the rise of the Bloc. It was an election campaign where people wished they could vote "none of the above."

There is an old rule in the campaign business: A bad product with good publicity will only die faster because it will attract more attention and disillusion voters faster. Even before their controversial commercial mocking Chrétien's face, the Conservative party's ad campaign ran into trouble. The first ad — a close-up of Prime Minister Campbell explaining her vision of Canada — was unappealing. Losing steam in the polls, the Conservative party campaign changed themes and slogans and switched to negative ads, which only made things worse for all of the candidates. Even New Democratic Party campaign strategists admitted that their ads, which showed angered responses to government policies, backfired because many of their supporters switched allegiance to Reform. The best ad of the campaign came from the Natural Law Party. What other party could claim to be able to wipe out the deficit and the national debt the way Doug Henning made an elephant disappear on the TV screen?

## INTRODUCTION

The peaceful participation of ordinary people in selecting who governs us is one of the greatest achievements of Canada's electoral system. Its importance cannot be overstated, although it can be misunderstood. Most Canadians, including those who seldom vote, are drawn to elections for two basic reasons. First, we believe elections promote accountability,

that is, that they force those in power to conduct themselves in a responsible manner and to take us into account when they make decisions. Second, Canadians believe elections give them some influence over their governance, that is, that the chance to vote for public officials is also an opportunity to make choices about the policies, programs, and future directions of government action.

Accordingly, elections are powerful events that affect how we are governed in Canada. They command more attention and participation from more people than any other single political event in the country. Thousands of candidates take part in the numerous elections and by-elections that characterize Canada's parliamentary system of government. From these are unleashed the grass-roots forces of election campaigns, the psychology of candidate and voter behaviour, and the application of election rules and regulations.

Elections are misleadingly brief, occurring on one day, and lasting eleven hours. The interval between the opening and closing of the polling booths does not span the entire election process: It starts much earlier, as candidates explore their strategies, and lasts much later, as winners and losers assess election results and begin to position themselves for the next election. But much of what we think is happening during elections is determined by the electoral system we have adopted, the rules that flow from it, and the outcomes it produces.

## WHAT IS AN ELECTORAL SYSTEM?

By definition, an electoral system embodies all of the customs, laws, procedures, methods, and institutions used to conduct campaigns and elections, and to count the votes of a qualified **electorate,** so as to elect the representatives in a political system. The Canadian electoral system includes those specific traditions and practices that regulate the conduct of voters, campaigners, the role of political parties and pressure groups, and institutions that supervise elections, such as the Chief Electoral Office in Canada, also known as "Elections Canada."

The Canada Elections Act and its amendments are the parliamentary instrument that regulates elections, candidates, campaigns, voters, and the operation of the electoral system that is presently in place in Canada. It regulates a great deal of what is involved in the process of voting and campaigning in Canada. For example, Canadian candidates are not permitted to use the services of U.S. radio and television border stations to broadcast their political messages back into Canada. Another act, the Broadcast Act, forbids the broadcast of any advertisement of a party or candidate on the day of an election.

Because the electoral system is employed to choose our political leaders, it is fundamental to the security of the democratic rights of Canadian voters, their access to elected office, and the confidence the public displays in the legitimacy of the political system and how we govern the country (Clarke et al. 1991).

Two important aspects of the electoral system that can affect the fairness and effectiveness of elections involve how the boundaries of ridings are drawn and whether the distribution of seats by province to the House of Commons reflects a proportionate representation of the population.

If the electoral system is to be seen as legitimate, every person's vote should have about equal weight anywhere in the country. But when, for example, a member of Parliament from British Columbia represents about 25 000 more constituents than a member of Parliament from Saskatchewan, the electoral system has generated and sustains inequalities.

Canada's electoral system has built-in biases. When a voter stands alone in a poll booth, apparently exercising the untrammelled right of free choice, many other factors are at work, influencing the effect of that vote, for example, the constitution, federal laws, political traditions of redistribution and redrawing boundaries, and the formula used by the election to declare a winner.

Despite the fact that we pride ourselves on being a parliamentary democracy, most Canadians know very little about their electoral system and the consequences of the **electoral (decision) rules** that govern their elections. For many Canadians, the only interesting outcome of an election is who won. Voters seem content to participate in and enjoy the competitive exhilaration during election campaigns, much as they do watching an exciting hockey game. We do not always recognize or understand that a wide variety of electoral rules govern the outcome of the process of voting and that these rules can greatly affect the choices we make.

Many Canadians may not be aware that the simple fact of holding elections is less important than the specific rules and circumstances that govern the acts of voting and campaigning. We have become so accustomed to our electoral apparatus that few of us think about the consequences of continually using the same system to select our leaders and representatives.

Electoral rules specify *what* a candidate should or should not do, *who* is allowed to vote, *how much* each qualified person's vote counts, and *how many* votes are needed to get elected. The arrangements under which the votes of Canadians are cast and counted exert considerable influence on the outcomes of our elections. The electoral system adopted by Canada is important because no set of electoral mechanics is politically neutral (Blais and Carty 1987).

What if the electoral rules that are in place for choosing our parliamentary representatives make it difficult to represent a majority of Canadian voters, thereby ensuring that the wishes of that majority will become public policy? In Canada, for example, most federal elections do not produce governments with the support of 50 percent of voters. In this regard, our electoral system may distort the results of elections by not giving all of the votes in a riding equal weight. Thus, if someone can get elected with only 30 percent of the popular votes in a riding, that means 70 percent of the voters in that riding do

not support their MP, nor are their interests really represented. When this MP goes to Ottawa, who represents all those who opposed his or her candidacy?

## CANADA'S ELECTORAL SYSTEM

Canada's elections are modelled on the British system of **plurality voting**, in which the member of Parliament for each constituency is elected on the basis of a simple plurality of votes, what is sometimes called the "first past the post" model. Under this principle, the candidate who gets at least one more vote than the second-place candidate in the constituency is awarded the seat on the basis of a single casting of ballots.

In Canadian elections, there is no absolute majority requirement whereby MPs, MLAs, or MNAs must get at least 50 percent of all ballots cast. Elections for seats in the House of Commons and provincial legislative assemblies, and other offices are filled by those winning by simple pluralities (Boyer 1987). Canada, and each of its provinces and territories, are divided into **single-member constituencies**, usually called "ridings," from which a single legislator is chosen by plurality vote to represent everybody in the riding.

Most other democratic governing systems have adopted electoral systems based on some form of **proportional representation**. The effect of proportional representation is to reduce the distortion of election results to a minimum, give competing political parties a national caucus, and distribute the representation of political parties in Parliament according to their proportional success at the polls.

The electoral system in operation in Canada today is essentially the same as it was at Confederation (Irvine 1980). Reforms have been proposed from time to time but were not taken seriously at the federal level until the 1990s, when the report of the Royal Commission on Electoral Reform and Party Financing was tabled in the House of Commons. That report, entitled *Reforming Electoral Democracy*, was the result of extensive nation-wide public hearings and consultations based on a comprehensive research program.

The idea of installing proportional representation (PR) had been seriously studied by the province of Quebec in the 1970s and the early 1980s, with the result that an unsuccessful recommendation for PR was made in 1984. Canada's only experience with PR has been with the **single transferable vote**, used in Winnipeg for the Manitoba elections between 1920 and 1953 and in Edmonton and Calgary up to 1955.

In recent years, there have been signs that Canadians are becoming more interested in the workings of proportional representation (PR) than before (Dobell 1986; Courtney 1980). The Spicer Commission examined PR as a possible alternative to Canada's existing electoral system. And, in Nova Scotia, a government Working Committee on the Constitution reported in 1991 that Nova Scotians support election to the House of Commons by PR. In 1991, the federal government's proposals for constitutional reforms called for the use of PR in an elected Senate.

No electoral system can provide a perfect correspondence between the proportion of votes cast for a party or candidate and the absolute representation it earns in the legislature. However, there are three criteria by which Canada's electoral system can be evaluated for determining its ability to enhance the governability of our political system: efficacy of the vote, effective representation, and effective government.

## Efficacy of the Vote

Efficacy of the vote is evaluated as the capacity of the electoral system to transfer popular votes proportionately into seats in the legislature. In other words, do all the votes *count* in electing parliamentary representatives? If a political party attracts 20 percent of the popular vote, does it occupy approximately 20 percent of the seats in the legislature? Is every elector's vote of equal value, such that a party's strength in Parliament reflects the strength of its actual vote in the electorate?

The principle of "one person, one vote" is reflected in Section 15 of Canada's Charter of Rights and Freedoms, which declares that "every individual is equal before and under the law." However, the adherence to plurality as the central principle in Canadian elections seriously challenges the ability of Canada's electoral system to uphold the ideal of "one person, one vote," even though the constitution embraces it.

Efficacy of the vote is determined by the size of federal constituencies in a vast country such as Canada with its own unique clusters of population. At the time of Confederation, the principle of "representation by population" was thought to promote the equality of each elector's vote, and it was believed that this should be the rule of thumb that guides electoral boundary commissions across Canada. Representation by population was never achieved because ridings evolved differently in different parts of the country, and large disparities in the population size of ridings exist within and among provinces.

The boundaries of federal constituencies are drawn by a boundaries commission appointed for each province. The job of these commissions is to design constituencies with approximately equal numbers of voters (Courtney, MacKinnon, and Smith 1992). The Chief Electoral Officer of Canada provides each commission with population data for its respective province, as well as the "electoral quotient," which is obtained by dividing the population of the province by the number of seats allocated to the province, as stated in the Constitution Act, 1867. For example, Nova Scotia's, population of 899 942 is divided by 11 (seats), which gives it an electoral quotient of 81 813. The commission is then charged with the task of drawing the electoral boundaries so that the population in each district corresponds as closely as possible to the quotient. The commission may deviate from the quotient to take account of historical patterns, community interests, or geographic features.

The efficacy of one's vote is determined by how fairly these boundaries are drawn, by the size and population of each boundary area, and by the character of the riding, be it rural, urban, or suburban. Voter efficacy requires the electoral system to be fair at all strategic points in an election, where the vote is exercised and how the votes are counted.

The fairness of the electoral system also requires equal access to the House of Commons for minor parties and independents, who may not enjoy the popularity or financial resources of the major parties, yet aspire to represent the special interests of their supporters. In this regard, we must ask whether our electoral system creates obstacles to the election of minority candidates, aboriginals, women, and disadvantaged groups, such as the poor and the unemployed.

## Effective Representation

The second criterion for determining the effect of our electoral system on governance is that of effective representation. Does the electoral system enable voters in all provinces to feel represented once the election results have been tabulated? *Proportionate representation* — not to be confused with proportional representation — is the principle, enshrined in the constitution, that a province's number of seats in the House of Commons should reflect the size of its population relative to that of other provinces. *Redistribution* is the process used for allocating House of Commons seats among the provinces. Redistribution occurs every ten years, after the census takes the population of each province.

The current formula is drawn from the Representation Act, 1985, which divides the total population of the ten provinces by 279 to secure an electoral quotient. The quota 279 is derived by subtracting 3 seats, representing the Northwest Territories and the Yukon, from a base number of 282 seats established for the 33rd Parliament in 1976 (see Figure 7.1). The electoral quota, 279, is divided into the popu-

**Figure 7.1 Calculating Representation in the House of Commons**

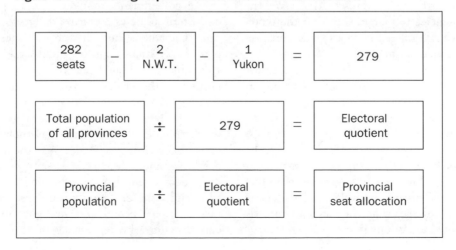

lation of each province, thus giving Ontario 99 seats and Alberta 26 seats. No province may have fewer seats than it has senators, as stipulated in the "senatorial clause," and no province may have fewer seats than it had before the Representation Act, as set out in the "grandfather clause." Accordingly, when the electoral quota is applied to Quebec, the number of seats obtained is 74. But, because of the grandfather clause, one seat is added to this result since, in 1976, Quebec had 75 seats.

Evaluating the criterion of effective representation involves analyzing the relationship voters have with their member of Parliament. Representation is a difficult concept to pin down because it means different things to different people. It can mean anything from who the MP is to how well a representative communicates with constituents or can articulate their needs to other party members or to Parliament in general.

Do the rules of our electoral system permit the average Canadian to have a say over how the government is run and what it does? Do grass-roots party members play a significant role in choosing and campaigning for their representatives? Does the member of Parliament mirror a majority of his or her constituents in qualities of gender, ethnicity, socio-economic status, and so on? Can voters identify with their representative? Are the constituencies too large, such that the representative is hindered from access to constituents and vice versa?

In Parliament, MPs rarely vote contrary to their party caucus, particularly on important issues such as free trade or the Goods and Services Tax (GST), as doing so contravenes the rules of party discipline. Yet, most Canadians want their MP to reflect the majority perspectives of their constituents (see Table 7.1). This can sometimes mean that electors who disagree with the local MP's party position will feel that they are not directly represented in Parliament.

**Table 7.1 How Should Your MP Vote?**

| | Percentage Who Agree |
| --- | --- |
| According to the majority view of constituents | 71 |
| According to the MP's own conscience | 21 |
| According to the MP's party policies | 7 |

*Source: Maclean's/CTV Poll, Decima Research, 1993. Reprinted with permission of Maclean's.*

## Effective Government

The third criterion used to evaluate our electoral system is effective government. In the past, informed Canadians have supported the plurality system because it tends to produce party majorities in Parliament and therefore has a greater potential to provide strong and stable governments. This view was reflected in the Macdonald Commission, which hesitated to recommend changing Canada's electoral system because proportional representation (PR) might lead to more frequent formation of minority governments and weaken the effectiveness of strong federal governments. Effective government refers to the ability of the electoral system to yield strong governments that are able to pursue consistent policies for extended periods of time. Canadians have, in the past, placed a particularly high value on stable and sound government without much reflection on the fairness of the electoral system that delivers their representatives to Parliament.

In analyzing how well we govern ourselves, we should ask whether voters feel their votes draw them closer to or distance them from the governmental process. Does the system make people feel that government is inaccessible and remote? The general sense of distance between people and their governments can threaten the legitimacy of the entire political system, especially if governments do not have to respond to those who voted against them.

All of these hypothetical criteria are potentially in conflict. A parliament that fairly represents the proportion of popular votes cast for different political parties in a general election may be too divided to provide effective government. Minority parliaments may result more frequently if elections were held using the rules of proportional representation. Canada's experience with the minority governments that have been formed from time to time under our plurality electoral system has been that they are productive but short-lived, better liked by voters than by the political parties involved, and prone to come to tenuous, fragile agreements between and among parties.

Much more political competition would result between and among political parties vying to acquire Cabinet positions or to sustain the governing coalition. The back-room deals made by party leaders could affect the expectations of the constituents of MPs caught up in the spiral of compromise and political *quid pro quo*. This can — although it does not necessarily — produce a fragmentation of political parties, unstable coalitions and alliances in Parliament, and governments too weak to make tough decisions.

## The Effects of Plurality Voting

Political scientists have observed that Canada's "first past the post," simple plurality electoral system regularly distorts the results of Canadian elections and ultimately creates a number of problems that affect the governability of the country (Cairns 1968). The disparities (disproportionalities) generated by the electoral system may be a factor behind the general distrust of government that is often expressed by many Canadians.

The plurality principle fosters a mismatch between how Canadians vote and how they are represented in Parliament and their pro-

vincial legislative assemblies. This disparity, which is the inevitable result of the plurality rule, affects the legitimacy of the political system, and ultimately the willingness of some Canadians to accept the decisions it produces.

Examples of disproportionality in Canadian federal and provincial elections are quite common. Very few elections (1940, 1958, and 1984) produce a government that has earned more than 50 percent of the electoral vote. In the 1988 federal election, for example, the Progressive Conservatives were returned to government with 43 percent of the popular vote, but won 58 percent of the seats in the House of Commons. When the Liberals under Jean Chrétien won the federal election in 1993, they polled 41.23 percent of the popular vote, but won 60.0 percent of the seats in the House of Commons. In that election, the Progressive Conservatives, under Kim Campbell, polled 16.04 percent of the popular vote, but won less than 1 percent of the places in the Commons. The Bloc Québécois won 13.52 percent of the popular vote, and sits in about 18 percent of the seats in the House. The New Democratic Party, under Audrey McLaughlin, polled 6.87 percent of the popular vote, and won only 3 percent of the seats in the House. But the Reform Party won 18.69 percent of the popular vote and took about the same percentage of the Commons seats.

These kinds of disproportionalities also occur in provincial elections (see Table 7.2). The most notable example was the 1987 New Brunswick election in which the Liberals won every seat in the provincial legislature with just 60 percent of the popular vote, while the two opposition parties, with 40 percent of the vote, elected no one. In the 1990 Ontario election, the New Democrats took 57 percent of the seats, with only 37 percent of the popular vote, while the Liberals won just 27 percent of the seats, with 32 percent of the popular vote.

**Table 7.2 Disproportionality in Select Provincial Elections**

| Province | Year | Party | Percentage of Vote | Percentage of Seats |
|----------|------|-------|--------------------|--------------------|
| Quebec | 1973 | Liberal | 54.7 | 92.7 |
| | | PQ | 30.2 | 5.5 |
| Alberta | 1982 | PC | 62.3 | 94.9 |
| | | NDP | 18.7 | 2.5 |
| New Brunswick | 1987 | Liberal | 60.4 | 100.0 |
| | | PC & NDP | 39.1 | 0 |
| Ontario | 1990 | NDP | 37.6 | 56.9 |
| | | Liberal | 32.4 | 27.7 |

*Source*: Compiled from reports of provincial Chief Electoral Officers.

Disproportionality can be indexed to monitor the discrepancy between seats won and votes cast for all parties in an election. An index of disproportionality can also be used to compare how differently electoral systems perform to determine whether they meet or fall short of the ideals of democratic representation.

What we call the *index of electoral disparity* is the sum of the difference between the percentage of votes and the percentage of seats for all parties in an election, divided by 2. The direction of the difference (+ or −) is ignored: The index measures the total variance between votes and seats, both positive and negative, but divides by 2 in order to put the index on a base of 100. Because the "disparity" generally favours the elected government and the most successful political parties in the political system, the equality and efficacy of voters is adversely affected when the disparity is pronounced, as it tends to be in Canadian election.

An example of how the index of electoral disparity works can be found in the results of most federal elections, but especially in that of 1984, which gave the Progressive Conservatives a major electoral victory. In that election, the Progressive Conservative party won slightly more than 50 percent of the popular vote, but won 75 percent of the seats in the House of Commons. The Liberals got 28 percent of the vote, but only 14 percent of the seats. The NDP got 19 percent of the votes, and only 11 percent of the seats. Others got 2 percent of the popular vote and no seats.

In this case, the winning party's share of the seats was 25 percentage points more than its share of the vote and the opposition's, that is, the Liberal party's, share was 14 percentage points less, while the NDP's share was 8 percentage points less. The index of electoral bias therefore would be 25 + 14 + 8 + 2 = 49/2, or 24.5.

Table 7.3 shows the difference between the share of the popular vote and the number of seats earned by each of the parties during the past five federal elections, along with the overall index of electoral bias for each election. Over the period from 1979 to 1993, the index of electoral bias between seats and votes in federal elections averaged 16.7, with the bias always favouring the government.

The 1980, 1988, and 1993 election results show the bias of the electoral system in favour of the most successful party is often enough to lift a party to a clear majority of seats in the House of Commons once it exceeds 40 percent of the vote in a multiparty election race.

As a general rule, in our electoral system, any party that wins the popular vote at

**Table 7.3  Disproportionality in Federal Elections, 1979–1993**

| Year | PC | LIB | NDP (percent) | Other | | Index of Electoral Disparity |
|------|-----|-----|------|------|------|------|
| **1979** | | | | | | |
| Votes | 36 | 40 | 18 | 5 | | 12 |
| Seats | 48 | 40 | 9 | 2 | | |
| **1980** | | | | | | |
| Votes | 33 | 44 | 20 | 3 | | 12 |
| Seats | 37 | 52 | 11 | 0 | | |
| **1984** | | | | | | |
| Votes | 50 | 28 | 19 | 2 | | 24.5 |
| Seats | 75 | 14 | 11 | 0 | | |
| **1988** | | | | | | |
| Votes | 43 | 32 | 20 | 4 | | 13.5 |
| Seats | 57 | 28 | 15 | 0 | | |
| **1993** | | | | Bloc | Reform | |
| Votes | 16 | 41 | 7.0 | 13.6 | 18.5 | 21.5 |
| Seats | 01 | 60 | 4.0 | 18.6 | 18.5 | |
| **Average Bias 1979–93** | 14.00 | -9.0 | -6.8 | -3 | | 16.7 |

*Source:* Compiled from Elections Canada data.

40 percent-plus has a good chance of gaining a large majority, and thus unqualified control of the House of Commons for up to five years.

In the past, the Liberals and Progressive Conservatives, being the only parties to ever form governments at the federal level in Canada, have benefited most from this electoral bias in our system. However, this situation is changing because of the political instability created by the establishment of strong new regional parties in Quebec and in Western Canada, and the relative weakening of the two major parties. In effect, the traditional dominance by the two major brokerage parties may gradually be eroding.

These disparities are not just characteristic of Canada's federal elections. The same electoral system governs provincial elections.

Table 7.4 shows the index of electoral bias in provincial elections over the past 27 years. The bias has been greater in provincial elections than in those at the national level because the provincial legislatures have fewer seats, and voting patterns in provincial elections tend to be less affected by regional forces than those for the federal Parliament.

The relationship between popular votes and seats won in the provinces tends to discourage the strategies of minor political parties. Currently, some parties are relatively inactive in areas where their support is weak and their chances of winning elections are small. Examples are the NDP in Quebec and the provincial Liberal parties in most of Western Canada. Minor provincial parties tend to lose the incentive to remain active and

**Table 7.4 Electoral Disparities in Provincial Elections, 1965–1992**

| Provinces | Number of Elections | Index of Electoral Disparities (Average) |
|---|---|---|
| Ontario | 8 | 14.3 |
| Quebec | 7 | 22.7 |
| Nova Scotia | 7 | 19.7 |
| New Brunswick | 7 | 17.4 |
| Manitoba | 8 | 12.9 |
| British Columbia | 8 | 18.1 |
| Prince Edward Island | 8 | 16.5 |
| Saskatchewan | 7 | 22.9 |
| Alberta | 6 | 29.9 |
| Newfoundland | 8 | 17.8 |
| Average for all provinces | 7.5 | 19.2 |

*Source:* Compiled from reports of provincial Chief Electoral Officers.

competitive between elections and thus preserve the effect of the plurality system to overrepresent large parties.

As it does in most other states, the adoption of proportional representation in Canadian elections would significantly reduce the distortions of election results, provide all competing political parties with more national representation, and increase party representation in Parliament (Rose 1991). Governability is enhanced because proportional representation provides the government with a broad political — if not an ideological — mandate. A more representative electoral system would allow a government to claim more legitimately public support for its policies and would foster more public confidence in the governing system.

## The Canadian Electorate

Since the enactment of the Charter of Rights and Freedoms, voting is a right, no longer just a privilege. This right to vote has been sus-

tained by the courts, and by certain provincial codes and charters, such as the Quebec Charter of Rights and Freedoms and the Saskatchewan Human Rights Code (Boyer 1981).

Prior to the charter each legislative body in Canada could enact its own voting requirements and deny certain people the right to vote. Chinese and Japanese people were not permitted to vote in British Columbia, women were excluded from federal elections until 1918, and aboriginal Canadians were denied the right to vote until 1960.

Even today, electoral laws, as outlined in the Canada Elections Act, qualify that right with some limitations, which thus far have not been found to be contrary to the charter. Disqualification of non-citizens to vote conforms with the charter, but Parliament and other legislative bodies no longer have the authority to set arbitrary limits. Any restrictions on the right to vote must meet the tests of charter rights.

The extension of **suffrage**, combined with changes in the process of enumeration, has increased substantially the proportion of Canadians aged eighteen or older qualified to vote in federal elections. Section 3 of the Charter reads as follows:

> Every citizen of Canada has the right to vote in an election of members of the House of Commons or of a legislative assembly and to be qualified for membership therein.

Today the chief and assistant chief electoral officers, returning officers (except in the case of a tie), non-citizens, and minors are the only people **disenfranchised** in federal elections.

For years, the right to vote was denied to many, such as women, persons with mental disabilities, judges, and prison inmates. In fact, most categories of groups in Canada have been involved at one time or another in attempting to gain the right to vote. Like most other governments, the government of

Canada regulated voting so as to influence its effects. The most important forms of regulation still include determining the electorate's composition, and regulating how voters' choices are represented in Parliament.

Since 1867, important developments have altered the right to vote: The electorate has been widened by charter guarantees, acts of Parliament, and Supreme Court decisions. By the 1990s, over 90 percent of adults in Canada (approximately 18 million people) comprised our electorate, and thus were eligible voters (electors).

At Confederation, voting was regarded as a entitlement too important to entrust to the masses. Accordingly, legal restrictions on who can vote have existed since that time. In fact, fewer than 40 percent of adult Canadians were eligible to vote in Canada's first election. The first extensions of suffrage came with the elimination of property requirements for voting (see Table 7.5). The single largest increase in the number of voters in Canada occurred in the early part of the twentieth century, when women got the vote. After nearly 50 years of pressure from the woman's suffrage movement, women received the right to vote. Although opponents feared a massive change in electoral politics if women got the vote, there was no immediate electoral change after 1918.

Canada does not maintain a permanent voters' list. Instead, election officials undertake to compile a list of eligible voters between the 38th and 32nd day prior to election day. Consequently, voting requires registration by enumeration and, in order to be enumerated, a voter must satisfy certain qualifications, such as citizenship, age, residence, and electoral status under Canada's election laws. This statutory requirement serves two electoral purposes: First, it ensures that only qualified voters vote and that they do so only once in an election; second, it promotes the integrity of the vote by projecting its public significance and its importance to the democratic process of government.

## Table 7.5 Chronology of Canadian Voting Rights

| | |
|---|---|
| 1867 | The first federal election was held: Only men who owned a certain amount of property were allowed to vote. |
| 1885 | The Electoral Franchise Act defined a "person" as a male, including Native peoples but excluding a person of Mongolian or Chinese race. |
| 1917 | The Wartime Elections Act disenfranchised Canadian citizens who were born in an enemy state and were naturalized after March 31, 1902, as well as those whose "mother tongue" was the language of the enemy country, regardless of country of birth. |
| 1917 | Wives, widows, sisters, daughters, and mothers of any person, male or female, living or dead, who was serving or had served got the right to vote. |
| 1918 | All adult women won the right to vote. |
| 1948 | The franchise was extended to Canadians of Japanese ancestry. |
| 1950 | The Inuit, explicitly excluded in the Dominion Franchise Act, 1934, became eligible to vote. |
| 1960 | The Indian Act was amended to extend the franchise to Native Canadians living on reserves. |
| 1982 | Charter guarantees. |
| 1987 | Judges became eligible to vote. |
| 1988 | People with mental disabilities were granted the franchise. |
| 1992 | Voting rights were extended to prison inmates, and the Canada Elections Act was formally amended to reflect reversal of disqualifications of mentally challenged people, judges, and prison inmates. |

## A Canadian General Election

The term of a Canadian Parliament is limited by the constitution to a maximum of five years. There must also be a sitting of Parliament and each legislature at least once every twelve months. The House of Commons can prolong the term of Parliament when extraordinary circumstances warrant (such as war, invasion, and insurrection) and not more than one-third of the MPs oppose an extension. This has happened only once in Canadian history, when, as a result of the break-out of the First World War — six years transpired between the federal elections of 1911 and 1917.

Under normal circumstances, the prime minister requests the governor general to dissolve Parliament. Such a request initiates the process and machinery for conducting a federal election in Canada. The Cabinet (governor-in-council) then directs the chief electoral officer to issue **writs of election** for each constituency.

The election procedures in each riding are administered and supervised by a returning officer, who is responsible for preparing the voters' list, appointing deputy returning officers to supervise the procedures in the subdivisions of each riding, receiving the **nomination papers** of candidates, and authorizing the printing of ballots and fixing the location of polling stations in each riding, which can range from just a few to more than 500. At each polling station, a deputy returning officer and a poll clerk supervise the voting process under the scrutiny of two agents representing each candidate.

By election day, the voters' list has been prepared by means of an enumeration process conducted door to door after the election writs have been issued. In urban areas, two enumerators are appointed — one from each of the two parties that obtained the highest pluralities (came first and second) in the riding in the last election — go from door to door to register voters. Only one enumerator is appointed to compile lists in each rural riding.

All provinces but British Columbia now conduct an enumeration to produce a voters' list for provincial elections. British Columbia maintains a register of voters. Generally, in the Canadian electoral system, separate enumerations are conducted for federal, provincial, and municipal elections.

At the polling station, each voter is given a ballot on which are listed the names of the candidates running for seats, two detachable serial numbers on the back, and the initials of the deputy returning officer. To verify the ballot, the deputy returning officer tears off the first serial number. After the voter has marked the ballot in the voting booth with an "X" beside the name of the preferred candidate, he or she folds the ballot paper so that the initials of the deputy returning officer and the remaining serial number on the back of the ballot can be read without unfolding it. The voter gives the ballot back to the deputy returning officer, who verifies the initials and the remaining serial number as those that appear on the original ballot. On confirming that it is the same ballot, the deputy returning officer detaches the other serial number and deposits the ballot in the box.

To be a candidate for election to the House of Commons a person must be a Canadian citizen who is eighteen years of age or older. Section 3 of the Charter of Rights and Freedoms accords every Canadian the right to be "qualified for membership" in the federal House of Commons or in a provincial legislature. To file nomination papers, a candidate needs the endorsement of 100 other electors and must provide a $1000 deposit to the returning office of the riding. Up to half of the deposit is refunded if the candidate submits an election's expenses return within the prescribed time limit, and the remaining half is refunded if the candidate obtains 15 percent of the ballots cast in the electoral district. All unrefunded deposits are forfeited to the Crown.

Approximately one-third of these expenses pay for the preparation, enumeration, revision, and the printing of lists and notices. About 20 percent of the cost of the election is spent on the operation of polling stations and the printing of ballots. Another 20 percent covers the fees and allowances of returning officers, election clerks, and the expenses associated with operating headquarters. About 15 percent pays for postage and wages of assisting staff, and the costs of providing special voting for the armed forces and public-sector electors, such as diplomats and their staffs. Finally, about 12 percent is set aside to reimburse qualifying candidates, and for certain political party expenses.

### Elections and Governability

Elections preserve the stability of parliamentary government by containing and channelling potentially more disruptive or dangerous forms of mass political activity. By establishing formal avenues for mass participation and getting people to rely on them, government reduces the threat that volatile, unorganized, and spontaneous involvement can pose to the established order.

In addition, elections bolster the power and authority of parliamentary government and its traditions in Canada. After all, elections are the means we use to fill Parliament and staff the government. The candidates whom voters choose at the riding level help to organize government as well. Because candidates advocate party policies, elections involve a choice of party platforms and point Canadian society in certain directions on a wide range of fronts, from abortion to the economy, to national defence, to the environment. The winning party will claim a **mandate** (literally, a command) from the people to carry out its platform.

Two other types of elections used in Canada are **plebiscites** and **referendums**. Occasionally, the electorate discloses its opinions on certain public issues specifically placed before it. Plebiscites are direct popular votes on a given subject on which governments want a public response; they are consultative only, and governments are not bound by their results. Referendums can be binding or non-binding.

Three single-issue referendums have been held at the federal level in Canadian history, although the referendum as an electoral device has also been used at the provincial level. In 1898, the government of Sir Wilfrid Laurier held a referendum on alcohol prohibition. In 1942, the government of Mackenzie King held a referendum on conscription. In 1992, the government of Brian Mulroney held a non-binding referendum on the Charlottetown Accord.

Elections, plebiscites, and referendums help to increase popular support not only for political leaders but also for the legitimacy of the governing system itself. Popular elections confer on a government a legitimacy that it can achieve in no other way. Thus, the symbolism of elections as mechanisms to legitimize governmental change is important. The formal opportunity to participate in election serves to persuade voters that the government is responsive to their needs and wishes. Elections facilitate the compliance of people to the laws that the governing system produces. Electoral participation increases popular acceptance of taxes and regulations upon which government depends. Elections substitute consent for coercion as the foundation of governmental power.

## CAMPAIGNS

An election campaign is an organized effort to persuade voters to choose a particular candidate or political party, usually over others competing to represent them in the same riding. In Canada, election campaigns are influenced by the following characteristics. First, candidate selection is controlled by constituency party organizations. Second, the national political parties' organizations control many of the key facets of the campaign, insofar as they provide some of the financing, which is regulated by federal statute, and they execute the campaign strategy. As a result, national party platforms — as well as candidate personalities — play a dominant role in the campaign. These party organizations provide invaluable campaign services — research, media advice, technical support, legal council, and even training for some candidates and their staffs. Finally, the power of the prime minister to call elections as a prerogative produces relatively spontaneous campaigns of short duration.

Throughout Canadian history, political parties have played a central role in developing the traditions of campaigning across the country. Since the nineteenth century, political parties have taken the pulse of the rank-and-file members to learn what was important to voters. They chose the candidates, and then lined up the people to support them and build a campaign strategy. They prepared buttons, banners, and newspaper advertisements, touting their candidates, proudly named under the prominent label of the party. Political parties attracted loyal constituency party organizations to canvass voters before the election, mention the names of their candidates, extol their virtues, and make sure the people get out to vote.

Today, in an election campaign, all actors in the political process come into vigorous interplay: Political parties begin selecting and promoting their candidates; interest groups mobilize their forces to ensure that their interests will be remembered by successful candidates; and the mass media project electoral politics more clearly and consistently onto centre stage. As a result, the public, whose interest in political affairs is normally limited to the headlines, now turns its attention to specifics about the candidates vying for public office.

Because so many people are involved, an election campaign is a complex event. Two principal types of players are involved in the electoral drama: voters and candidates. For voters, the basic questions are whether or not to vote, and for whom. Candidates confront a more complicated set of choices. Their basic decisions are whether to run, and how to attract votes to win. To do this they must make scores of strategic decisions. Candidates must meet the expectations of a more informed electorate, position themselves as serious contenders against other party candidates, and pull together financial resources in their ridings. Canadians have high expectations about their parliamentary leaders and representatives. Candidates should be intelligent but not ivory tower, decisive but reflective, honest but shrewd, articulate but sincere; they should possess a good sense of humour without being frivolous and be politically experienced while appearing fresh and new.

There are no guaranteed recipes for electoral success. However, in all good campaigns, certain ingredients facilitate success at the polls. They are the choice of experienced candidates, timing, money, canvassing, advertising, and the expedient use of the media.

## Experienced Candidates

An important strategy for parties is to attract experienced candidates, preferably those who have been previously successful at winning their seats. Members of the House of Commons seeking re-election have a better-than-average chance of winning in their riding. The nature of parliamentary incumbency has profound implications for constituents, the legislative process, and governability (Krashinsky and Milne 1985).

*Incumbents* are successful at getting re-elected for a variety of reasons, not the least of which are a vast array of political resources they have at their disposal in their ridings. They can tap into a successful pool of organizers who have proved effective in getting votes for their MP. Incumbents have the advantage of pre-election communication with their constituents through subsidized mailings and other contact through their constituency offices.

They are also in an advantageous position to attract campaign contributions to cover the costs of running. They can usually draw upon a network of loyal supporters who fan out by campaigning for their MP in the community.

Despite their better-than-average electoral security, most members of Parliament act as if they were in great danger of losing their jobs. Some even run for re-election between elections by canvassing their constituents regularly (Black 1984). Even though many parliamentary seats are "safe," the ultimate electoral sanction — defeat at the polls — is poised like Damocles' sword, ready to put a quiet end to a parliamentary career.

While parliamentary incumbency is a formidable challenge for opposing contenders, sometimes it can be a handicap, especially when opposition candidates try to lay the blame for national calamities at the incumbent's door. Public antipathy toward government has increased in recent years, nurtured by those who challenge the incumbent in the quest to become a part of it.

In some regions of the country, parliamentary incumbency has become rather like nitroglycerin: a potential liability that needs careful handling. Even the most experienced parliamentarians need well-planned strategies, great timing, money, advertising, the ability to cultivate their images, rhetorical appeal, and sensitivity toward issues that attract the voters.

### Strategies

All would-be candidates and political parties have strategies — plans that they hope will enable them to capture the hearts and minds of the electorate. The goal of every election campaign is the same — to win. In Canada, unlike most other states, there are no rewards for the party candidate who comes in second; the winner takes all. Virtually every major party candidate, and even those who may choose to run as an **independent candidate** or as a representative of a minor party, must plan a strategy to maximize their chances of winning or to reduce the probability that a certain other candidate might win.

Some campaign strategies are highly routine, especially those at the constituency level. Candidates follow traditional patterns, which include unleashing a strong campaign and organizing the poll. Candidates have to put together a reliable team that can provide ideas on strategy, deal with the media, plan personal appearances, and handle advance work. They rent headquarters or turn their constituency offices into headquarters. They buy billboard space, buy buttons and signage, print literature, and appear at numerous public meetings to ensure exposure.

Campaign strategists hope and expect that the usual party vote will remain loyal and that they will be able to convince undecided voters to support them. The unaffiliated must be won over. This set of uncertain Canadian voters is now significant in all constituencies in any election campaign: They constitute the critical margin and can sway an election.

Establishing an organization to handle what are the routine technical requirements of a campaign is a prerequisite to election success at the grass-roots level. Experienced MPs spend a lot of time with their organizers, studying the returns from previous elections in order to be able to use this information for electoral gain. As election day draws near in each constituency, candidates try to appeal to as many voters as possible. The details of organizing the constituency campaigns are usually handled by provincial party organizations. The closing days of the campaign are carefully orchestrated to project the attractive personal qualities of the candidate and to address those issues that build voter consensus.

Another essential aspect of any campaign is for candidates of each party to have a strong poll organization, usually consisting of a poll chairperson, scrutineers, and a poll captain for each polling subdivision in the riding. The poll chairperson is someone who manages the schedules of the candidate and workers at the polling stations. He or she tries to develop a good relationship with the returning officer in the area. The returning officer is important to know because he or she will keep the campaign organization aware of any changes that have been made in the boundaries of the polling subdivisions.

The poll captains get out the known-supportive voters in their subdivision and get to know personally as many of the voters in the subdivision as possible. The ideal poll captain has been working between elections, tracking the stability of party support in the riding at all times. On election day, most of the campaign "machine" becomes the Election Day Organization, which is charged with getting out the voters. They are the drivers, baby sitters, and escorters of voters to the polls.

Not very much can be assumed during a national campaign. At the national level, in Canada, campaigns are the most elaborate, hectic, and expensive. Careful and deliberate choices about party tactics and strategies are necessary for the positive effects of the national campaign to spill over into each constituency to return a majority of members of Parliament.

What is striking about today's campaigns is that many tasks are now put into the hands of paid professionals rather than volunteers or amateur politicians. Most parties hire political consultants, who devise the party's campaign strategy, create a campaign theme, and manage the public relations of the campaign. The training materials and briefing materials for local candidates are usually produced centrally so as to provide consistency in the national campaign strategy. They comprise the brochures, campaign stationery, signage, billboards, bumper stickers, and campaign posters.

A centralized computer communications network is provided by all major parties to local candidates so that they are informed as to policy updates and are consistent with party policy in their campaigns. In a game in which hand-shaking and the personal touch are con-

sidered to be the most important ways of gaining votes, computers have come into their own as important adjuncts for parties and candidates at the national and local levels.

Campaign strategists are aware of the many important tasks that computers can do for them. At election time, many computer sales companies tailor their computer services and provide software packages designed especially to accommodate election campaigns. Computers have taken on an amazing variety of jobs. They can dial voters and give them a tape-recorded message. They can be used to establish a network among constituency offices, with electronic mailboxes for the candidates and their workers. They can organize and analyze voters by category — male, female, residence, income, occupation, ethnicity, and so on. Computers create specialized mailing lists for fundraising, questionnaires, and political advertising.

A key feature of national campaigning in Canada involves party leaders' touring the country to get as much positive media exposure as possible. Each major party leader makes speeches in locations across the country and they are usually supplemented by news releases from national party headquarters. The impact of a visit by the leader of a party can mean the difference between success or failure of the local party candidate at the polls. So-called B-teams of notable party leaders or Cabinet ministers criss-cross the country, helping to elect local party candidates. Their objective is to bring repeatedly the national campaign to local ridings, which is in keeping with the overall strategy and objectives of the leaders' tour. It is almost impossible for a party leader to visit all of the ridings in the country, so efforts are made to disperse B-teams to campaign in ridings where the party leader is not likely to appear.

The goal of all this frantic activity is the same for all campaigns — to convince voters to choose a party candidate or a slate of party candidates to sit in the House of Commons.

Among the three major political parties, the national strategy is to maintain central control of campaigns at all levels, by means of French and English advertising. Canada permits paid political advertising as well as access to regulated free-time broadcasts.

## Timing

The timing of an election is out of the control of most members of Parliament, except the prime minister and the Cabinet. The decision to call an election is usually made on the basis of how the government is performing in political opinion polls or simply because a parliamentary term is ending. Most general elections in Canada are called within four years of the previous election. Taking full advantage of the constitutional five-year limit is perilous for a government because it is often perceived by the media and the public to be a delaying of accountability.

Nevertheless, once the election is called, timing considerations dominate all phases of local campaigns, and most candidates work hard at it. The minimum campaign period is set by the Canada Elections Act at 50 days. The law sets no maximum limit for election campaigns. But, during the last three federal elections, the average length of campaign has been 58 days. The duration of each campaign is determined by how long it takes to compile voters' lists, process candidates' nomination papers, and complete the other administrative tasks of conducting an election.

The Royal Commission on Electoral Reform and Party Financing recommended that federal campaigns be shortened to 40 days, with a maximum of 47 days, in order to maintain public interest, reduce administrative and campaign costs, and ensure the efficient governability of the country.

Election campaigns are full of often very unpleasant surprises, which, once they occur, can be quite difficult to handle. At best candidates can only prepare for the worst ahead of time. The timing behind fundraising in each

riding is crucial, especially in advance of an election. Planning a campaign to raise money early and steadily between elections is a good strategy to discourage potentially strong contenders who are considering running as candidates for other parties. The best time to beat someone is before he or she decides to run.

Once the campaign begins, tactics have to be devised, revised, and sometimes abandoned quickly, in reaction to opponents. At the constituency level in Canada, campaigning is not like playing chess with someone who cannot make a move, or moves slowly and predictably; opponents react and launch their own initiatives. Increasingly, candidates need to be highly reactive; rarely in today's campaigns can candidates just lay out a campaign schedule and follow it.

Every campaign organization designs a "campaign calendar." This strategic timing device shows a countdown of days, ranging from 58-minus-1 to Election Day, permitting organizers to write in the important events to occur on each day. These calendars are pinned to the wall in the committee room, where they can be seen by all workers and used to keep the campaign on target.

## Campaigns and Money

Any election campaign in Canada has four components: the candidates, the issues, the party organizations, and money. The reactiveness of campaigning is demonstrated in the ways parties and candidates raise and spend money. Money is an essential ingredient in successful election campaigns, especially for challenging candidates who need to offset the advantages of parliamentary incumbency. It is sometimes said that money is the mother's milk of politics (Wearing and Wearing 1990). There is still a lot of truth in the saying, but, in Canada, money seems to be the surrogate mother of the electoral process.

At the time of Confederation, Canada's election laws focussed on corrupt practices, such as bribery. Concern about the impact of money on Canadian elections was probably at its peak in the late nineteenth century, when the Pacific scandal of 1872 made the headlines. The scandal, which contributed to the government's defeat, involved a large sum of money donated to John A. Macdonald's campaign by business interests in order to influence their contract bids to build the CPR. A much larger sum of money was involved in the Beauharnois scandal of 1930, in Quebec, when business money was given to the Liberal party to get the contract to build the Beauharnois Dam on the St. Lawrence River.

The legislation to regulate campaign funding — The Dominion Elections Act, 1874, and its subsequent amendments in 1891, 1906, 1908, and 1920 — failed to address the continuing corruption arising out of businesses making large contributions to political parties to procure government contracts. But not until the Elections Expenses Act, 1974, did Parliament respond to the questionable fundraising practices of parties and candidates in Canada (MacDonald 1991).

Over the decades, Canadians have developed a more explicit understanding of the appropriate role of money in electoral politics, but many issues and ambiguities still remain. Canadians know that money can be a corrupting influence on electoral politics. At the least, it can buy access to the electoral system, and ultimately to the institutions of parliamentary decision making. At worst, it can buy the decisions once parliamentary access is achieved.

Today, it is generally true that, because no one is certain what really works in a campaign, money is sometimes spent beyond the point of diminishing returns (Axworthy 1991). Money has become a central problem in contemporary campaigning. Without substantial funding, parties and their candidates know that they will not make effective appeals to the electorate. As the cost of getting elected increases in Canada, public suspicions are raised over the importance attached to money

and the undue influence exerted by corporate interests and advocacy groups that supply it to party campaigns.

Prompted by the continuing possibility of electoral corruption with money, amendments to the Canada Elections Act were introduced in 1983 to make the campaign finance system more open, to limit spending, and to encourage the parties and their candidates to seek contributions from individuals rather than just a few big corporate donors. The law does not set limits on the size of contributions, but places a ceiling on the amounts parties and their candidates can spend.

Money tends to pour into political party coffers around election time. The public is drawn into the excitement of the campaign, and there is much more fundraising activity by political parties as well as by the campaigns of independent candidates.

The law does not put to rest all of the financial contention that lingers in Canada's electoral system. The cost and financing of leadership contests have been sources of controversy. Neither of the two largest parties requires its leadership contenders to provide full public disclosure of who contributed to their campaign and how much. Nor does the Canada Elections Act require disclosure or accountability. Yet, in every election, public funds are involved in party leadership contests because parties have been channelling contributions to leadership campaigns through the parties, thereby making contributors eligible for political tax credits.

At the constituency level, most candidates have a finance or fundraising chairperson in their election campaign committee. This person is usually a resident in the constituency, or someone who conducts business there, and is resourceful in bringing money into the local campaign. Most of the money required to get a candidate elected must be raised at the constituency level. Funds are needed to bridge the gap between the candidate's campaign resources and the amount of support provided by the national party headquarters and Elections Canada on the basis of the number of votes cast. A fundraising chairperson will usually supervise five or six collectors who approach the constituency membership, larger businesses, professionals, and retail establishments in the area.

Most incumbent politicians jealously guard their mailing lists, which contain the names of people who have given money to their campaigns in the past, have written a letter of complaint or praise, are known to be supportive, or have delivered a favour.

The finance chairperson works with the campaign manager and the candidate to determine what the budget should be for the campaign and tries to commit everyone to a budget that should not be changed. In this way, the planning of income is clarified. If the budget is increased halfway through the campaign, it is very difficult for the collectors and other finance people to go back to major contributors a second time. Any indication of poor planning will erode faith in the candidate and nullify the efforts of volunteers.

## Canvassing

A thorough poll-by-poll, door-to-door canvassing plan is essential for election success. The process of canvassing helps campaign organizers to determine which voters support the political party and the candidate, and which might be undecided. When an election is called, about 40 percent of voters belong to the latter group. From the perspective of party campaign strategy good canvassers can swing a significant number of these voters to their candidate.

Canvassing is conducted in waves in most constituencies. The first wave is usually planned for the first week of the election campaign, followed by successive waves approaching the two last weeks of the campaign. Canvassers are aware that, as the campaigns develop, voter opinion, especially among the undecided group, will change.

Canvassers are expected to assess voter opinion accurately. Some voters may already support the party's candidate, for whom the canvassing is being done, or may be leaning toward the candidate. Follow-up canvasses are sometimes made to further persuade those who are leaning toward the party and the candidate, and those who are undecided.

The candidates and their campaign managers brief their canvassers as a group on procedures for using voters' lists; the regulations governing advance polls, including the dates; the methods of ensuring that prospective voters are properly listed; and the securing of aides such as drivers, child-sitters, and so on, for election day.

Canvassers are carefully instructed about what to say or do as they go about their work. They know they can alienate voters by walking across grass and gardens. They never ask the voters directly how they intend to vote but mention their candidate's name often. They are advised not to discuss policy, and usually refer policy questions to the candidate, who will answer them in person or send a representative to talk with the prospective voter.

In Canada, most party canvassing is done in the evening, between 6:45 and 9:15 P.M., which is deemed to be the best time to catch people at home — earlier visits can interrupt a meal and later ones can disturb those who are resting or have retired for the night. Daytime hours are used to reach single parents and married spouses. Saturdays are used to reach all members of the family, except in Jewish communities where Saturday canvassing is avoided. Very few candidates risk canvassing on Sundays.

Each canvasser brings lots of advertising on the campaign trail. Bumper stickers, badges, lapel buttons, and pins are given to potential voters. The idea is to keep the impression and memory of the candidate fresh in the mind of the voter. A handshake and a souvenir can quite often get a vote in return. Canvassers campaign on their feet, knocking on doors; if there is no one home, they leave a brochure or door hanger carrying a positive message about the candidate and a promise to return on another day.

## National and Local Advertising

In addition to producing signs, brochures and billboards, every candidate invests in a steady flow of media advertising. Extensive use of the electronic media, especially television and radio, has become the hallmark of national and constituency advertising strategies of most political parties in Canada. By far the most commonly used broadcast technique is the 30- or 60-second spot advertisement, which permits the candidate's message to be delivered to a target audience before uninterested or hostile viewers can tune it out.

Consistent exposure is essential to a successful campaign. These spot ads and other media techniques are designed by party campaign strategists to establish the name of the candidate for voters, to create a favourable image of the candidate and a negative image of opponents, to link the party's candidate with desirable groups in the local community, and to communicate the party's stands on issues.

Local newspaper insertions in dailies and weeklies, and in publications of farm and ethnic presses, carry the candidate's picture and stress the views of the party on local issues. Most candidates conduct an analysis of the options available in their area and try to select the best media at the lowest possible cost to the campaign. Careful attention is paid to the purchase of local radio and television time, and to the writing of scripts for political commercials that are short enough for broadcast purposes yet comprehensive enough to be effective.

The national advertising campaign of the major political parties tries to cover every riding across Canada, delivering similar messages to millions of voters. This advertising deals with national issues, highlighting poli-cies and supporting the party and its leader. Generally, the national media advertising campaign attempts to follow the party's performance in the polls. Advertisements seek to strike a responsive chord with voters and to reinforce existing loyalties. The broadcast media are now so central to the national campaign that most party activities are tied to their media strategies.

## The Media and Campaigning

From the perspective of the media, election campaigns have all the elements of a good story: conflict and competition, drama, and well-known personalities. Consequently, the media now cover election campaigns from their conception to the end — from the selection of candidates at the local level and the choice of party leaders at conventions to the final tally of votes.

For the majority of Canadian voters, election campaigns have little reality apart from their media versions. The standing of political parties and their candidates today is determined not so much by party identification or voter commitment to a particular leader but, increasingly, by a handful of reporters and commentators who follow the campaign trail (Crouse 1974). The judgement of the media can make or break a political party, its leader, and its candidates across the country. These political commentators, correspondents, and journalists are recognized as experts in their field, work for the largest and most prestigious publishers and networks, and have developed the trust of the Canadian public through stories they have covered in the past.

During Canadian elections, the relationship between party leaders, their slate of candidates, and the media is both symbiotic and adversarial. It is symbiotic because the candidates and the media need each other. Those running for Parliament need the media to get their messages across to Canadian voters, and journalists need the information that the candidates and their campaign strategists have at their disposal. The relationship becomes adversarial during elections because journalists see their role as not just conduits for party platforms and personality projection, but political critics, analysts, and fortune tellers on behalf of the Canadian public.

The major Canadian political parties direct their national campaigns to winning over the press and to getting as much widespread and favourable attention in the public media as possible. More than ever in Canada, a candidate's chances for election success depend on his or her ability to use the media effectively during campaigns, especially radio and television. Somewhat like actors, candidates must be able to project an image that their audience — the voters — will respond to favourably. The media's powerful influence in Canadian elections has changed the kinds of candidates who enter the political and governing arena. Increasingly, unknown candidates can get elected across the country if the media shine their powerful spotlight on them soon enough.

What voters actually see and hear of a candidate is mainly determined by what is called the "free" media (newspaper and television coverage) and the "paid" media (such as television advertising) accompanying an election campaign. The paid media are completely under the control of the campaign, whereas the free media are totally independent.

## WHO VOTES AND WHY

### Voter Turnout

Canadians believe in the ideal of political participation, especially voting (Mishler and Clarke 1990). Among all the ways of participating — voting, campaigning, and giving money — voting is the easiest and the most

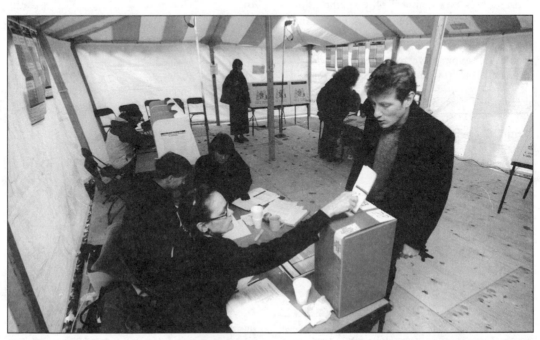

Canadians believe in the ideal of political participation, especially voting. This photograph shows voters in Toronto's Ward Number 13, November 1991. *Source:* Canada Wide.

popular way Canadians choose to connect with their governing system. Canadians believe that their record on voter turnout is quite good, especially compared with the usually low voter turnout among the U.S. electorate. In fact, in terms of voter turnout, Canada ranks low among the world's major democracies (Rose 1991, 244).

Turnout at federal elections has averaged about 75 percent since the Second World War. Average voter turnout in provincial and territorial elections is about the same, or higher, than voter turnout in federal elections (see Table 7.6).

These are not disappointing percentages for a political system that does not have **compulsory voting**. However, research conducted by the Royal Commission on Electoral Reform and Party Financing shows that Canada ranks 28th in a list of 32 democracies in terms of rates of voter turnout.

Even though Canadian voters tend to turn out in greater numbers than the voters of some other states (see Table 7.7), Canadian voters still encounter electoral barriers. For example,

election day in Canada is not a national holiday, as it is in many European states. People are expected to make time in their busy per-

**Table 7.7 Turnout Rates, Canada and 32 Other Democracies, 1980s**

| Rank | Country | Percent |
| --- | --- | --- |
| 1 | Australia | 94.3* |
| 2 | Belgium | 93.8* |
| 3 | Austria | 91.5 |
| 4 | New Zealand | 90.5 |
| 5 | Bahamas | 90.5 |
| 6 | Italy | 89.8* |
| 7 | Iceland | 89.2 |
| 8 | Sweden | 89.1 |
| 9 | Luxembourg | 88.1* |
| 10 | Germany | 87.3 |
| 11 | France | 86.2 |
| 12 | Denmark | 86.1 |
| 13 | Venezuela | 84.3 |
| 14 | Netherlands | 83.4 |
| 15 | Norway | 83.1 |
| 16 | Greece | 82.0* |
| 17 | Mauritius | 80.1 |
| 18 | Israel | 79.0 |
| 19 | Costa Rica | 78.9* |
| 20 | Finland | 78.2 |
| 21 | Barbados | 77.3 |
| 22 | Jamaica | 77.1 |
| 23 | Portugal | 76.8 |
| 24 | Botswana | 76.0 |
| 25 | Ireland | 74.2 |
| 26 | United Kingdom | 74.0 |
| 27 | Spain | 73.4 |
| **28** | **Canada** | **73.0** |
| 29 | Japan | 71.4 |
| 30 | India | 62.0 |
| 31 | Trinidad and Tobago | 58.8 |
| 32 | United States | 54.3 |
| 33 | Switzerland | 47.5 |

* Compulsory voting

*Source:* Thomas Mackie and Richard Rose, *The International Almanac of Electoral History*, 2d ed. (New York: Facts On File, 1982). Reprinted with permission of Facts On File, Inc., New York.

**Table 7.6 Average Voter Turnout in Federal Elections by Province and Territory**

| Province | Percent |
| --- | --- |
| British Columbia | 77 |
| Alberta | 56 |
| Saskatchewan | 83 |
| Manitoba | 71 |
| Ontario | 61 |
| Quebec | 76 |
| New Brunswick | 82 |
| Nova Scotia | 76 |
| Prince Edward Island | 82 |
| Newfoundland | 79 |
| Northwest Territories | 71 |
| Yukon Territories | 78 |

*Source:* Elections Canada, *Report of the Chief Electoral Officer*, selective years: 1975, 1980, 1981, 1985, 1989, 1994.

sonal and profession schedules to get out and vote, although the law requires that workers be given time off from their jobs in order to vote.

Voter turnout in Canadian federal elections might be higher if the election machinery were made more convenient, but Canadians have many reasons for not voting (see Table 7.8).

Those concerned with the electoral system are interested in the reasons why about 25 percent of the electorate do not vote in federal elections. About 5 percent of the electorate are perennial non-voters, that is, people who are too busy or just not interested in casting a ballot. Far more significant are the occasional non-voters — the 20 percent of eligible Canadians who fail to go to the polls for any election.

**Table 7.8 Some Stated Reasons Why Canadians Don't Vote**

Too busy
Couldn't remember
Couldn't decide
Didn't want to
Forgot
I was sick in the hospital
My party would win without my vote
My vote wouldn't make a difference
I never vote
I'm not eligible
I wasn't enumerated
I was on vacation
I was out of town
I'm protesting
I have religious reasons
No particular reason

*Source*: Adapted from Jon Pammett, "Voting Turnout in Canada" in Herman Bakvis, ed., *Voter Turnout in Canada*, Research Studies, Royal Commission on Electoral Reform and Party Financing, Volume 15 (Toronto: Dundurn Press, 1991), 37. Reproduced with permission of the Minister of Supply and Services.

The most striking characteristics of non-voters in Canada are that they are most likely young, between 18 and 24 years of age, and/or of lower socio-economic status than the rest of the electorate. Most of these people are disenfranchised by administrative barriers present in the electoral system. They may fail to get on the voters' list; they may be away from home on election day; they may find the location of the polling station inconvenient.

## Factors Affecting Why People Vote

Explaining why people vote the way they do is quite difficult. In the past, political scientists have relied on surveys that asked people why they voted they way they did, but critics point out that the answers provided to these kinds of survey questions do not always reflect actual voter behaviour. So what are the factors that really motivate us to choose the Parliament we have?

Many of the same factors at work in our learning about the formation of political opinions and ideologies are also at work in making electoral decisions. Generally, the stable factors that influence voting decisions can be divided into three categories: socio-economic, demographic, and psychological.

### Socio-Economic and Demographic Factors

Some influences have to do with the family into which a person is born. The family links us with our racial and ethnic identity, our views on social class, and our basic social and political beliefs. We know that the family is the most pervasive agent of political socialization, and it shapes our political orientations in fundamental ways.

Other influences on voter behaviour may be the result of choices made throughout an individual's life: place and region of residence, occupation or profession, and level of education. Understanding the social milieu of voters is thus helpful in understanding how and why they vote the way they do.

The opinions of a closely knit group to which a voter belongs, such as a peer group, can influence the effect of a campaign message, as can the two-step flow of such a message through an opinion leader with whom we identify. We have long known that the groups with which we identify influence our thinking about politics and can determine our voting choices. Peer groups seem to reinforce already formulated political attitudes. Identifying with groups of people with similar educational attainments, income, region, and race will affect the way we vote.

Age is also a factor in voting behaviour. In Canada, the older a person is, the more likely he or she is to vote. Even though the majority of young Canadians vote, those between the ages of 18 and 21 are three times less likely to vote than those over age 50. Older people tend to be more settled in their occupations and places of residence: They have more time and inclination to participate in politics and, consequently, to build the habit of voting and engaging in other forms of political participation. Younger people know less about the procedures of voting and are more likely to be absent from home when an election is held. It is not unfair to say that young people have not had the time, or have not seen the need to take the time, to develop a strong interest in electoral politics.

As the proportion of older adults has increased in Canada, this segment of the population has become more organized, more active electorally, and more politically conscious. This growing political movement has been called "grey power." In the past, older voters have not tended to vote as a block. However, with the emergence of politically active organizations (for example, the United Senior Citizens of Ontario, One Voice, the National Advisory Council on Aging, Fédération de l'âge d'or du Québec), Canada's older voters are making their concerns

known to politicians and to a younger generation of voters.

Voter turnout is lowest at the beginning of adult life. When they do vote, younger voters are more likely to support equality in matters affecting employment, opportunity, and minorities, as well as wanting a clean environment. They are less likely to identify with a political party. Young voters develop stronger and more fixed political orientations and outlooks around age 30, as they assume the role of taxpayers, parents, and community members.

In recent times, gender has become a factor in how and why people vote. What some call a "gender gap" among Canadian voters involves how differently men and women perceive the same issue. The "feminization" of families living in poverty, an increasing number of women in the work force, and more social awareness of the distinctive character of women's issues (such as abortion, day care, violence against women, and equal pay for equal work) in the Canadian political system have contributed to making gender an emerging and significant factor for analyzing and understanding voter behaviour.

Traditionally, in Canada, there have been no significant differences in the voting patterns of men and women. Gender differences in voting patterns are quite recent in the history Canadian electoral politics. During the 1950s and 1960s, some differences began to emerge as the women's movement became politically organized. Since the mid-1970s, Canadian women have supported the Liberal party more enthusiastically than have men. In the same period, the support of women for the NDP has increased as well. When education is factored into voting behaviour along gender lines, university-educated women are much more inclined to vote Liberal and NDP than are their male counterparts.

A gender gap has also been identified on some important issues, such as the censorship of pornographic materials and movies, legal and judicial remedies for violence against women, and certain employment discrepancies (Wearing and Wearing 1991).

Contemporary knowledge about gender differences and similarities in Canadian politics has been advanced by Kathryn Kopinak's studies (1985; 1987). Generally, she found that women tend to be more liberal than men in the world of politics and government. Canadian women are more likely than men to favour social welfare policies and expect more participatory democracy in the workplace. Women's liberal leanings tend to increase with income, whereas men's support for liberal causes tends to decline with higher incomes.

Region of residence can also make a difference in the way people vote, although this can also be related to other variables, such as immigration patterns, education, and income. Regional differences have been important to the development and maintenance of political opinion and voting behaviour. As Canada grew and developed into an industrial economy, waves of immigrants with new political traditions and customs entered Canada and settled in areas they viewed as hospitable to their way of life. Thousands of Ukrainians in the Prairie provinces; the Irish and the Scots in Newfoundland and Cape Breton; the Poles, Italians, and Jews in Ontario and Quebec — all of them brought unique political attitudes and values that continue to affect voting behaviour regionally.

Generally, voter support for the Liberal party west of Lake Superior is weak. Traditionally, Quebeckers have tended to vote for the Liberal party, even though voter support from Quebec shifted to the Progressive Conservatives in the 1984 and 1988 elections, and to the Bloc in 1993. The NDP has traditionally enjoyed strength in Manitoba, Saskatchewan, British Columbia, and parts of Ontario, but has been a minor political force east of the Ottawa valley. Although a particular region of Canada can be identified with voter support for particular political parties,

one must use caution in assuming region "causes" voters to cast their ballots in a specific direction (Matthews 1983, 17–18). It is not the region as such, but those unique socioeconomic dimensions of life's experiences that happen to vary geographically, that are likely to have a causal impact on voting behaviour.

One potential influence on voter behaviour that relates to place of residence or region is the effect of early returns from eastern Canada on voters in the West. This can create a "bandwagon effect," or what the Royal Commission on Electoral Reform and Party Financing called a "time-zone effect," whereby election results from the East Coast can influence voters in the West to support the local candidate of the party reported to be winning in the East. Canadian voters are dispersed over five-and-a-half time zones and, because polls close during federal elections at 8:00 P.M. local time, poll results in Newfoundland are known shortly after 3:30 P.M. British Columbia and Yukon time.

The current voting day is eleven hours long (9:00 A.M. to 8:00 P.M.) in all parts of Canada. Because of sophisticated computer forecasting, relatively reliable patterns of voter preference can become known in other parts of the country after the easternmost polls close. Cable-satellite feeds can relay such information to the West, and influence voter behaviour there. Under the present system, results from as many as 262 ridings are available before the polls close in British Columbia. The Royal Commission recommended that voting hours across Canada be staggered so that election trends and outcomes are not broadcast in Western Canada before voters in Eastern and Central Canada have finished casting their ballots.

Canadians speak of "social class" with some understandable embarrassment. Our views about equality urge us to regard people as individuals, and not usually as parts of a social group. Social scientists are confused about what class is, and constantly disagree about how to define it: by income? occupation? wealth? prestige?

However class is defined, voting has been less determined by it in Canada than in Europe. Political sociologists have been interested in finding out if Canadians are influenced in how they vote to the extent that they are aware of their membership in a class category, such as one based on occupation or profession (Hunter 1982). R. Lambert and colleagues (1987) found that class orientation accounted for only a small deviation in voting behaviour at the national level, but class was a more significant variable in Western Canada. This study found that class voting tends to be more common in provincial than in federal elections.

But there is no consistent evidence that upper-class Canadians vote for the Progressive Conservative party, middle-class Canadians vote for the Liberal party, or working-class Canadians vote for the NDP. Very few Canadian political parties articulate their positions in class terms, most probably because class consciousness is present only at low levels in Canada. Most Canadians identify themselves with a huge amorphous middle class than with the working classes (Pammett 1987). This identification makes the voting patterns of different social classes somewhat similar, although voters of lower socio-economic status are more likely than voters of higher economic status to hold liberal views on economic and social issues.

Some other socio-economic variables related to class, such as education, can translate into certain manifestations of voter behaviour. Voters with university educations are more likely to vote. Education plays such a big role because it stimulates political interest and provides information that people need to be effective participants in the political process. Education exposes people to more information about politics from all sources. Compared with high school graduates, college and university graduates read more newspapers and magazines, join more organizations and social groups, and participate in more election campaigns.

Attending a college or university has an impact on voting behaviour because our political attitudes are transformed during our experiences of higher education. People develop a more liberal orientation toward politics and are more likely to participate in the political system because of it.

In the final approach to the ballot box, most Canadian voters are simply pragmatic, voting in response to immediate election issues or on the image and winability of some party leader. Voting behaviour is retrospective, measuring how good or bad voters feel at the time the election is called relative to the way they felt after the previous election. Voters also make a rational calculation of the personal rewards of voting for one particular candidate and not voting for others. In this regard, voting is reactive and interpretative, a current response to changing political circumstances and realities of government and politics in Canada. People usually do not vote in conscious reflection of some particular social characteristic, such as ethnicity, or education level they may possess. Rarely can such descriptions adequately explain the complexities of a single voting decision. As the product of a vast middle-class electorate, voting does not pretend to determine Crown policy; it merely provides authorization for those who do control it.

### Psychological Factors

In addition to socio-economic and geographic/locational explanations for the way Canadians vote, some psychological factors, rooted in the attitudes and beliefs held by voters, have an effect. The approach of political sociology to voter analysis looks at group voting patterns without seeking explanations for why people vote the way they do as individuals (Gidengil 1992). Social psychologists study those psychological factors that influence individuals' political behaviour: These are usually expressed as "political efficacy," "party identification," "perception of the candidates," and "issue preferences."

**Political Efficacy** A person's sense of capability in matters of politics and government influences his or her perception, motivation, and participation in many ways. People will tend not attempt to participate in complex political processes when they expect to be ineffectual.

Not surprisingly, the greater a person's sense of efficacy in politics, the more likely he or she is to campaign and vote. Canadians are free to assert whatever demands, views, and grievances they might have through a variety of different legal means of political participation. All it takes is personal motivation. People can, if they wish, demonstrate, lobby, or file a suit in court. Despite the availability of an array of alternatives, in practice, most people feel efficacious when they vote and engage in a small number of other electoral activities, such as campaigning.

The more a person thinks he or she can accomplish in the political system (i.e., the more politically efficacious a person feels), the greater the likelihood that person will vote. Feelings of low political efficacy are often demonstrated by decisions not to vote in any given election (Pammett 1991, 44). Canadians who feel that politics is too complicated to understand, or that governments ignore them, or that their vote is inconsequential, are most likely not to vote.

Those who see little or no gain do not vote. Because one's vote is not likely to determine the election's outcome, a voter must see other personal and group benefits. People who feel efficacious make positive judgements about their competence in the political arena after the votes have been counted and about the responsiveness of the political system beyond the vote.

**Party Identification** Party identification is another observable influence on voter beha-

viour. It is the psychological attachment that many Canadians feel toward a particular political party which provides a strong impetus to voter action. We can assume that election outcomes are influenced by short-term and long-term forces. The short-term forces include candidate appeal and issue preferences. The long-term forces are those voting habits that recur and endure.

Party loyalty is still the most significant of these. It is like a cord that ties certain voters to one party — a cord that is fairly inelastic for strong partisans and more elastic for weak partisans. For the less strongly attached, the cord stretches more easily; short-term influences can cause defections to another political party.

The highest rates of political participation are most frequently observed among people with a strong commitment to a particular political party. To some degree, party identification overlaps with other variables such as religion, socio-economic status, region, and education.

In the past, in Canada, party affiliation tended to be a fairly stable factor in a person's life. Once a person opted for a particular political party, he or she would tend to stick with that party for the rest of his or her life. Party identification has always been a filter through which people receive information, acquire an ideological perspective, and form political opinions. It colours the ways in which voters look at the pivotal elements in an election.

Through a process psychologists call "selective perception," people who identify strongly with a political party look at their party's candidates and see the personification of virtue and look at the opposition's candidates and see the personification of vice. Thus, voters tend to see and hear what they want to see or hear. Related to selective perception in matters of party identification is what psychologists call "reinforcement," which describes a phenomenon whereby voters are receptive only to political messages that reinforce the beliefs and attitudes they already hold.

For some analysts, it is important to ask who "belongs" to a particular party in order to determine genuine party identification (Blake 1982). For them, the political party has weakened as a reference point for many Canadians in recent years (Leduc 1989). As parties become less important to voters, it follows that they will become less important as determinants of voter decisions. Independent voting seems to be most concentrated among new young voters and is growing as a characteristic of general voter behaviour.

**Perception of the Candidates** Another psychological factor that influences voters' choices is their perception of the candidates. If political parties were all that mattered in Canadian elections, candidates would only have to identify themselves as party loyalists. Yet this clearly is not what happens. Increasingly, the personalities and leadership styles of candidates have had more impact as a party influence, especially as television has become the major source of voter information about elections. The perceived competence and integrity of a candidate, and his or her personality, are important facets of voter evaluation. Today, voters are less likely to support local candidates who do not seem capable of handling the job, regardless of their party positions.

In reality, most candidates do not offer voters clear-cut choices on important national controversies. So voters seem to place greater weight on factors such as experience, leadership, and personal qualities. At both the federal and the provincial level, the Canadian public shows a marked preference for the candidate with substantial political experience, someone who has been in politics for some time and who knows the ways things are done in the party and in the legislature.

The voting public also inclines toward candidates who show they are able to take command of a situation, who do not wallow in pessimism or indecision but act when the time is right. At the same time that voters want someone who will be a strong leader, they are also inclined to want honesty, dedication, and perseverance in the person they choose.

The personality and image factors may be very persuasive but, in the final stages of an election, voters size up the performance of the candidates, assess whether they are economically better or worse off since the last election, and take stock of the policy performance of government in the areas that concern them the most.

**Issue Preferences** Still another important psychological influence is the issue preferences of the voter. Since the 1950s, Canadians have become more aware of national issues and problems, in part because education levels have climbed and in part because the media have become much more analytical. As well, Canadians are just more sophisticated politically, better educated, and cognitively more competent on matters of government, as is confirmed by the unmistakable growth in the measurable consistency of our political attitudes on key issues.

The phenomenon of **issue voting** is increasingly evident among the Canadian electorate. Issue voting involves how voters feel about issues and whether they vote for candidates whose positions on issues are the same as theirs. Today, more than ever, issues drive the voting public toward a particular electoral choice. Even observers who have previously minimized the importance of issues now concede that they can make a difference when the public knows and cares about them and when the candidates declare a position on them.

Economic issues usually have the strongest influence on voters' behaviour. The mainspring issue driving most electoral decisions seems to be the economy. The so-called bread-and-butter economic issues of unemployment, inflation, interest rates, and taxes make the most difference. When the economy is doing well, it is very difficult for an opposition party to defeat the government. In contrast, high rates of unemployment, inflation, or high interest rates can work to the disadvantage of governments. Canadians vote on the basis of their personal economic well-being as well as on the economy's overall health. Clearly, the better off people think they are during an election year, the more likely they will be to vote for the party that made them feel that way.

This is not to say that economics spawns the only issues that sway voters. Increasingly, some of the most heated debates in Canadian election campaigns take place over the social issues of abortion, the role of women, the rights of homosexuals, and the treatment of people with AIDS. Most party candidates try to avoid such issues because voters who care about these questions are likely to be offended if the party's candidate does not share their view.

Because of the highly partisan character of Canada's political party system, all parties try to set themselves apart as alternatives to their opposition on important issues in order to attract voters. What is difficult to ascertain is the extent to which issue voting overshadows party identification or personality factors in the voters' minds.

## CONCLUSION

It is easy to see that elections matter in Canada. Elections give Canadians a measure of control over their parliamentarians by enabling them to send one person, or set of persons, to their legislatures instead of another person, or set of persons. They can defeat a government or throw a local constituency representative out of office. Although, on average, Canadians tend to return their local candidates to the legislature rather than throw them out, electoral defeat is always possible, and challengers frequently win seats. Most Canadian politicians regard themselves as unsafe at any margin and are aware that they can be ousted, even after a string of electoral victories in their ridings. They run fearing electoral defeat and attune their strategies to line up with voter preferences.

A more difficult assessment for observers to make is what impact elections have on public policies. Most scholarly research in Canada has been concerned with why people vote in the ways they do. Voters are retrospective: They assess whether they are economically better or worse off than they were before their representatives took their seats, or they

take stock of the policy performance of the government in those realms of life that concern them most. Then they make choices in the election in accord with their dissatisfactions and their feelings of wellbeing.

Elections seem to be the centrepiece of our parliamentary system of government. Although Canadian voters make individual choices among local candidates, elections are also collective decisions. Even though our elections by no means determine everything that Canadian governments do, they have an impact on the direction of public policy, and on the quality of political leadership in our society.

The electoral process is thus central to the operation of our political system. Understanding it is important because the results it produces has a great effect on the governability of the country. The political campaign, with its hoopla, vigorous electioneering, and media blitzes, mobilizes most Canadian voters to participate in elections.

But Canadian elections do not occur under ideal conditions. The country is huge, and population is scattered. A significant number of Canadians do not take part; many who vote are not well informed about the choices or their consequences; most do not know anything about the electoral rules of the election game; and too often candidates and parties cloud the policy issues.

Furthermore, the electoral system is far from perfect. The present system helps maintain unfair political party representation that the public knows very little about and sees as desirable. Election procedures, which are supposed to administer elections impartially, can have partisan effects, favouring the larger traditional parties and their candidates. By discouraging the success of minor parties, the rules of Canada's electoral system have nurtured a dominant two-party system with direct impact on how we govern ourselves.

On the positive side, electoral politics in Canada is quite competitive. Voters are offered many choices by competitive political parties that seek to attract their support. Notwithstanding the powerful influences of the media focus on personalities and on the rivalry among candidates, Canadians have increasingly shown an ability to make their choices on the basis of issues.

The political campaign is a vital part of the competitive process of elections in Canada. Through the campaign, voters are aroused, mobilized, amazed, amused, and educated about the issues — if the campaigners are doing their jobs. But the way in which the electoral system works even shapes the focus, targeting, planning, and conduct of campaigns.

Effective campaigns must be well organized to cope with the complexity of competition at the federal and local levels. More and more, in Canada, money has become essential for the success of campaigns. The increasing importance of money in electoral politics has raised two questions: How should spending be controlled and regulated? and Does money buy electoral success?

Socio-economic status and age can have powerful effects on voting. Voters tend to be older, better educated, and holders of higher-status jobs than non-voters. Social class is a weaker feature of voting behaviour in Canada than in many other countries. In the heat of competition, the candidates and issues variously influence elections. Political issues have become more important in affecting voters' choices among candidates.

At the base of our political system, elections are collective decisions that affect the whole country. These decisions may give analysts a basis for finding patterns in electoral behaviour. But elections are the real stuff of governability because they provide the personnel to run the government.

## GLOSSARY

**compulsory voting**  A legal electoral provision stipulating that citizens must vote in elections or pay a penalty.

**disenfranchised**  Deprived of the right to vote.

**electoral (decision) rules**  The specific methods by which electoral decisions are determined, such as simple majority, absolute majority, plurality, and proportional representation.

**electorate**  All of the eligible voters in a parliamentary election.

**incumbent**  A person who has previously won an election and is offering again, as opposed to a challenger.

**independent candidate**  One who seeks a legislative seat without affiliation with a registered political party.

**issue voting**  Voting for a candidate based on how he or she stands on a particular issue.

**mandate**  A publicly endorsed and permissible course of political or government action, supported by an electorate's votes, for elected officials to carry out their platforms.

**nomination papers**  A form provided by Elections Canada to be filed by the candidate, showing his or her name, a pledge to account for expenses, and the signatures of 25 qualified electors, along with a deposit of $200, all to be sent to the chief returning officer.

**plebiscites**  Direct popular vote of the people on any given subject placed before them by the appropriate authorities.

**plurality voting**  An electoral rule that permits a candidate to win a legislative seat in an election simply by getting more votes than any other candidate, even if that number is less than a majority of the votes.

**proportional representation**  An electoral system that awards legislative seats to a party in proportion to the popular vote which that party wins in an election.

**referendums**  Electoral process in which legislative or constitutional questions are referred to the total electorate for its acceptance or rejection. A referendum may have the force of law or it may be used in an advisory capacity to inform government officials of public feelings on particular subjects.

**single-member constituencies**  An electoral riding in which only one representative is elected.

**single transferable vote**  A system of balloting that combines the principle that voters should have maximum choice of the candidates with a formula that guarantees all votes will be used to select representatives.

**suffrage**  The right to vote; the franchise.

**writs of election**  Formal documents addressed by the chief electoral officer to returning officers requiring that an election be held.

## RECOMMENDED READING

Archer, Keith. 1990. *Political Choices and Electoral Consequences*. Montreal and Kingston: McGill-Queen's University Press. This book presents a lucid analysis of Canada's electoral system, along with discussions of consequences and reforms.

Bakvis, Herman, ed. 1991. *Voter Turnout in Canada*. Toronto: Dundurn Press. This book examines the variables associated with the acts of voting and non-voting in Canada, focussing on the functions and dysfunctions inherent in Canada's electoral system.

Brook, Tom. 1991. *Getting Elected in Canada*. Stratford, Ont.: Mercury Press. This book introduces the reader to the nuance of electioneering in Canada, and presents a masterful analysis of elections that underscores the strategies used by candidates and parties to seek nomination and election.

Ewing, K.D. 1992. *Money, Politics and Law: A Study of Electoral Campaign Finance Reform in Canada*. Don Mills, Ont.: Oxford University Press. This study of electoral expenditure controls in Canada uses frequent comparisons with Great Britain.

Fletcher, Frederick, ed. 1991. *Media, Elections and Democracy*. Toronto: Dundurn Press. This book gives the reader electoral comparisons involving broadcasting, campaigning, and the details of elections in Canada, France, Australia, Germany, and Scandinavia.

Johnson, R., et al. 1992. *Letting the People Decide: The Dynamics of a Canadian Election*. Stanford, Calif.: Stanford University Press. This book examines the linkages among voting, the role of political parties, and elections. It offers a general discussion of the role of elections in society and provides important comparisons for Canada.

Johnston, Paul, and Harvey Pasis. 1990. *Representation and Electoral Systems*. Scarborough, Ont.: Prentice-Hall Canada. This study is an insightful analysis of the effects of sociodemographic variables and electoral laws on voter behaviour.

Renstrom, Peter, and Chester Rogers. 1990. *The Electoral Politics Dictionary*. Santa Barbara, Calif.: ABC-CLIO. This dictionary of electoral language defines more than 400 terms in a concise manner.

Taras, David. 1990. *The Newsmakers*. Scarborough, Ont.: Nelson Canada. This book looks at the events and players in the election game, disclosing the strategies of the campaign and the press room with vivid and insightful analysis.

Wearing, Joseph, ed. 1991. *The Ballot and Its Message*. Toronto: Copp Clark Pitman. This comprehensive anthology collects highly focussed articles on Canadian voting behaviour from the perspective of party identification, ideology, class, the economy, and gender.

CHAPTER

# PARTIES, INTEREST GROUPS, AND GOVERNABILITY

ISSUE EDUCATION
BUILDING THE PUBLIC AGENDA
PUBLIC-POLICY WATCHDOGS

## TYPES OF INTEREST GROUPS

AGRICULTURAL GROUPS
BUSINESS GROUPS
ENVIRONMENTAL GROUPS
LABOUR GROUPS
WOMEN'S GROUPS

## TACTICS OF INTEREST GROUPS

LOBBYING IN CANADA
LEGISLATIVE LOBBIES
ADMINISTRATIVE LOBBYING
CAMPAIGN LOBBYING
LOBBYING THE COURTS
REGULATING THE LOBBYISTS

## CONCLUSION

## GLOSSARY

## RECOMMENDED READING

**A** lone voice is often not likely to be heard. Two voices can at least talk to each other. But a well-organized pressure group can captivate the attentions of an entire public in the world of politics and government. Grass-roots politics takes many forms in Canada because there are so many groups using different tactics to get our attention and influence government policy. And going public is a strategy interest groups use to mobilize the widest and most favourable climate of opinion.

An organized groundswell of opposition to proposed changes in the unemployment insurance (UI) system hit the streets with a bang in cities across Canada soon after the Liberals came to power in Ottawa in 1993. Noisy demonstrations organized by the Canadian Labour Congress (CLC) were held in many provinces. Their purpose was to bring public attention to the plight of union members who would be adversely affected by a government proposal to change the number of qualifying weeks for UI from 10 to 12 and to reduce the benefit period for a claimant with 12 weeks' work from 41 weeks to 32. Many people were threatened by these changes and wanted the government to know how they felt.

In March 1994, Prime Minister Jean Chrétien received an angry reception in his home town of Shawinigan, Quebec. Five hundred unemployed construction workers protested government cuts to unemployment insurance. In Bathurst, New Brunswick, 1200 demonstrators, also outraged by the government cuts, burned Chrétien in effigy.

In Sydney, Nova Scotia, a crowd estimated by police to be about 1500 strong marched through the streets behind a horn-blasting boom truck to the Steelworkers Hall, where a clamorous indoor rally was held. The demonstrators then moved downtown for yet another effigy-burning demonstration outside the constituency office of Liberal MP Russell MacLellan, who was in Ottawa at the time. A number of demonstrators briefly occupied the MP's office while a three-headed effigy representing Prime Minister Chrétien, Finance minister Paul Martin, and Human Resources minister Lloyd Axworthy was burned on the street outside the MP's office.

The demonstrators doused a pile of tires with gasoline and lit a pungent fire that billowed black smoke throughout the centre of the city, leaving a smouldering mess for the civic workers and fire department to clean up. Evidently, the flames were intended to signify a spontaneous outburst of emotion among people driven to desperation by a callous government action. This was the same sort of angered response that overtook demonstrators in other Canadian cities, and the same spasm of outrage that drove unemployed construction workers to smash a glass door and jostle the prime minister in Shawinigan.

Hundreds of marchers then walked another block to the city's Canada Employment Centre (CEC) office, where they were met by locked doors, guarded by three of the extra police officers called out for crowd control.

Such acts of civil disruption, organized in this case by the CLC in response to government cuts or policy changes, reflect the dynamics of protest used increasingly by pressure groups when they go public with their concerns. Pressure groups often fill voids left by the traditional political parties and give Canadians another opportunity to take their claims directly to the government. Groups such as the CLC give those who may be un- or underrepresented an opportunity to have their voices heard, thereby making the government and its policy-making process more representative of their needs. Whether good or bad, the tactics of pressure groups educate Canadians that the policies and actions of government, made ostensibly for the benefit of everyone, can sometimes cause pain and uncertainty among certain segments of the population.

## INTRODUCTION

In the early 1800s, when groups resembling political parties began to take shape and to struggle for control of government in pre-Confederation legislative assemblies, their architects had no blueprints to follow. At the local level, political patronage encouraged like-minded people to form groups and **coalitions** of groups so as to generate majorities in the colonial legislatures. The first organized parties in Canada evolved from these legislative factions and consisted of groups who wanted to work together on a systematic basis (Winn and McMenemy 1976, 1–30).

In the case of the Progressive Conservative party (the Conservative party until 1942), four groups, consisting of Tories, Moderates, business interests, and French Conservatives, mingled and formed a loose coalition to support John A. Macdonald in the 1850s. Two other groups, the French radicals and Clear Grits, joined in a coalition that later would organize the Liberal party under Alexander Mackenzie after the defeat of the Conservatives in the 1870s.

Permanently organized political parties were evident only after Confederation. They operated between elections, maintained a consistent membership, and advocated common viewpoints and policies. National political parties did not exist in Canada until the end of the nineteenth century. They were not mentioned in the Constitution Act, 1867, because Canadians were uncertain as to the purposes of political parties. Nonetheless, Canadians went ahead rapidly building them.

Accordingly, political parties began as "extraconstitutional" institutions in the Canadian political and governing system. Even though political parties did not gain explicit constitutional recognition in Canada, they do have explicit legal status and are very important political institutions that contribute to how we are governed (Courtney 1978, 33–60).

The spread of universal suffrage dramatically altered the nature of political parties, from exclusive institutions representing a few men of property to **mass parties**. Along with this change came the recognition that democratic government depends more and more on groups that seek to include everyone in the political and governing process.

Gradually, people began to think of parties as institutions, as permanent political organizations that link them to their government. Parties became the hallmarks of public representation, where information about government and strategies to reach government would be planned and launched.

## WHAT IS A POLITICAL PARTY?

Although political scientists often disagree on definitions, most will agree that a political party is a voluntary organization that seeks to influence public policy by putting its own members into positions of government authority or positions opposing government authority.

Parties want to win elections and control the offices of government. In pursuing this goal, parties perform many tasks: They nominate candidates, campaign, influence voters' attitudes, bring many interests together under one umbrella organization, and form the government. In order to win, they cannot be choosy about who comes with them, and thus such parties often contain very unlike elements. They rely upon traditional voting support, charismatic candidates, material benefits, and changing positions on issues.

Political parties articulate the interests of their members. They put into words and action the vaguely felt needs, fears, and expectations of their constituents and translate these feelings into specific demands for legislation of government action.

Political parties also transform a social demand into practical political and government action. They do so by aggregating many different interests and groups representing certain interests into a stable coalition that is stronger and more powerful than any single interest group could ever be.

Other definitions of political parties stress the organizational side of parties, their ideologies, or their stands on issues. Still others begin with the various ways in which political parties reveal themselves every day, for example, representing themselves by a label or a coloured emblem that can create a psychological attachment in our mind, as when we say "I am a Progressive Conservative/Liberal/Reform Party member."

The party label is important. It is likely to tell us something about the background, outlook, and views of the person who identifies with the party. The party label is especially important to inexperienced voters, who may be less actively involved in politics and who may find voting choices more confusing than the more experienced and active voters are likely to.

## Party Identification

We gauge the strength of a political party in Canada, its status in government or opposition, on the basis of how large a portion of the electorate identifies with it. Every election is a momentary measure of **party identification**, but elections do not always tell the whole story about how and why Canadians identify with political parties over the long term.

Today, more and more voters in Canada no longer identify with a particular party for a very long time. Such identification is not necessarily reflected by the popular vote, and so disgruntled Conservatives may vote for the Liberal, NDP, or some other party in a particular election. Increasingly, party-identification trends seem to be related to the relative popularity or unpopularity of a party leader or party policies, as well as to events and issues.

Most Canadians do not belong to a political party in the sense of holding formal membership and paying dues. Rather, we become New Democrats or Liberals by thinking of ourselves as adherents of one party or another. A majority of us could almost be said to acquire our party loyalty through inheritance — from our parents, especially if our parents were in agreement on party identification.

Those who retain their original party identification do so partly because, as they grow older, it is reinforced by other agents of identification, such as peers. That is why to say "I am a New Democrat" is to express a commitment deeper and more lasting than what is conveyed by saying "I am going to vote for a New Democratic candidate in the next election."

Over the last two decades, party identification has been more fluid because voter loyalties are weaker than they once were (Blake 1982). Voters are much more uncertain about who they will support, creating a pool of undecided voters before elections. An increasing number of voters — better educated and bombarded by media and interest-group appeals — wear their party mantles lightly. But party loyalty seems to be less shakeable with age, so it is not surprising to find that, when party ties loosen, they loosen mostly among young people, for whom those ties have not yet become as binding as for others.

## WHAT PARTIES DO

Parties do many things, some of them well, some not so well. They pick policy-makers, run campaigns, attract voters, advocate policies, and sometimes govern. They have developed complex structures for recruiting, promoting, and unifying officeholders. For over a century, in Canada, they have virtually monopolized the voting process.

The nominating process for successful candidates to sit in the House of Commons is controlled by Canadian political party organizations. They are pledged to support their party's policies. But in order to win elective office, one must get votes. In the Canadian system of plurality voting, that means simply getting more votes than anybody else. To secure enough votes, a party needs to appeal to a variety of voters. Given the wide range of voters' interests, a single issue will probably not appeal to a plurality of voters.

## Recruiting and Training Leaders and Policy-Makers

Political parties are the primary instruments we use to recruit and train the leaders and policy-makers in our governing system. They persuade people to seek the party's nomination; support their candidate with money, workers, and organizers; and provide publicity and traditional voter loyalty. Canadian politicians who desire to run in elections as independents have a tough time winning parliamentary seats. Above the local level, and often not even there, no one gets elected without a party's support.

In fact, the Canadian party system provides almost the only source of recruitment to political office. In the absence of parties, voters would be confronted with a bewildering array of self-nominated electoral candidates, each seeking a narrow victory over others on the basis of personal friendships, celebrity status, or family name.

To a certain extent, political parties provide a kind of quality control for their candidates through the process of political peer review. Party insiders, the candidates' peers, usually know potential candidates much better than the average voter does, and candidates are often judged by their peers for acceptability as the party's representatives. After all, the only path for political parties to form the government is by putting up an attractive slate of candidates.

The candidates can be the best or worst advertising for parties in an election, and their leaders are the main standards by which voters judge the credentials of competing parties

(Erickson and Carty 1991). Accordingly, in seeking a slate of candidates, political parties do more than just pass judgement on potential office seekers; in effect, they recruit what in their view are the most talented individuals for political and governmental leadership.

Only a small fraction of Canadians are recruited by political parties to become our governing leaders and representatives. Sometimes remarkable leaders are produced, sometimes not. Such a loose and diverse political party recruitment system offers few guarantees that anyone of competence will emerge.

Canada's governing system depends to an extraordinary extent on the individual choices, ambitions, and motivations of millions of people across the country. In our political system, we assume, or hope, that somehow enough good and qualified people will get involved, take responsibility, and run for office to enable us to govern ourselves effectively (see Figure 8.1). It is a huge assumption — by no means always valid, but absolutely central to the quality of our governing system.

## Educating the Voter's Choice

It is trendy to discount the explanations political parties give us of their views of the political world. Many believe that parties cannot be believed and that, like "Tweedledee, Tweedledum, and Tweedledummer," each is no different from the other. But, if one listens to politicians presenting their party platforms, one gains insights into current issues, even though the presentations are biased. Voters are apt to learn at least as much about the issues from the campaign advertising of political parties as they are from media coverage and analysis.

Political parties compete to educate the public about politics and government. Their views are partisan, and thus biased, but nevertheless their ideas structure the choices voters have during elections. Political parties represent alternatives in terms not only of candidates but also of public policy. Parties simplify

**Figure 8.1  Political Party Recruitment: "Many Are Called; Few Are Chosen."**

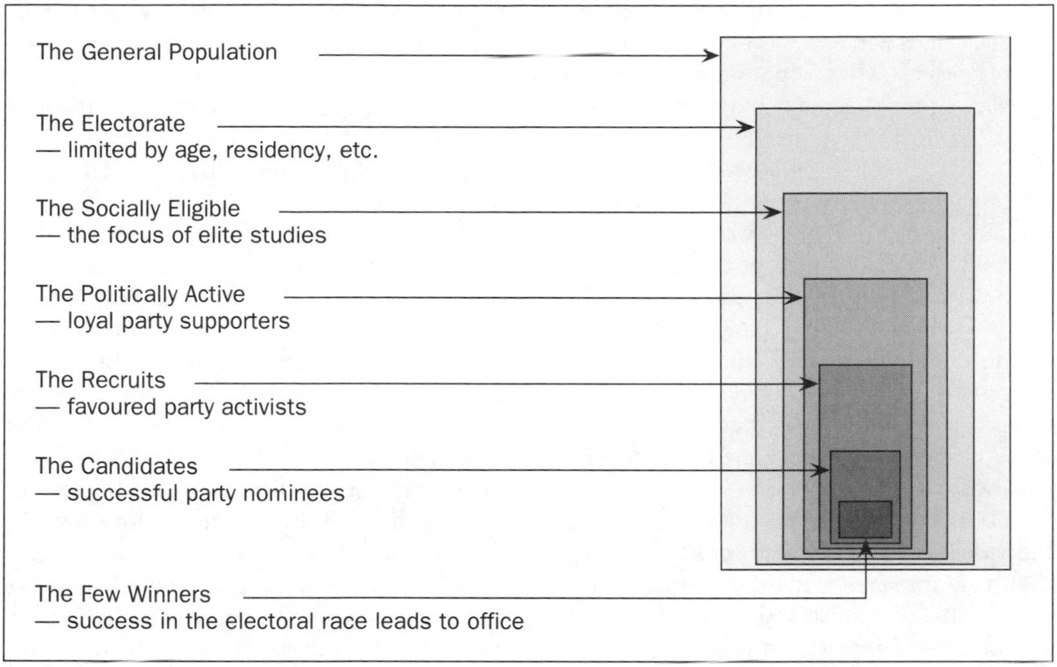

The General Population

The Electorate
— limited by age, residency, etc.

The Socially Eligible
— the focus of elite studies

The Politically Active
— loyal party supporters

The Recruits
— favoured party activists

The Candidates
— successful party nominees

The Few Winners
— success in the electoral race leads to office

the issues for the average voter. In Canada's competing political system, political parties formulate alternative positions and offer criticism of each other's programs. At election time, the voter has a choice and a basis on which to evaluate the performance of government and other political parties.

Political parties provide a way to link events, issues, and candidates so that the voters can fix responsibility (Nevitte, Bakvis, and Gibbins 1989). They make it possible for voters to blame one party for failure or to reward another for success. Although political parties are rarely able to deliver everything they promise, they can be held responsible by the public for what they appear to have or have not done.

## Political Parties as Opposition

The role of opposition parties is to provide informed criticism of the government and pro-pose ways to improve its policies and legislation. Canadians want a political party system that produces criticism, watchfulness, and an effective set of alternatives to the governing party. The political party system is expected to reflect the waves of both supportive and opposing opinion that rise and wash in the world of Canadian politics.

Under the rules of Parliament, the opposition is made up of the political parties not included in the formation of the government. The party that wins the second-largest number of seats in a general election becomes the "official opposition."

In Canada's governing system, the opposition is provided with resources and support facilities paid for by the public. The responsibility of the opposition, official and otherwise, is to discredit the conduct and policies of the government as well as of other opposition parties.

Opposition parties are expected to prepare for governing. Each opposition party appoints members of its party caucus as "critics" of Cabinet ministers. These opposition appointees, known as the "shadow cabinet," specialize in the affairs of the Cabinet ministries, become the watchdogs of the ministers' conduct and performance, and are preparing to assume the Cabinet positions they are watching.

Political parties present options in terms of their candidates, public policies, and tactics in Parliament. They represent the causes of the underrepresented; they articulate the interests of groups that cannot get the attention of government; and they bring together those elements that feel they hold no political anchorage in our society.

Individual politicians come and go, and individual issues burst into prominence and then fade into obscurity. But political parties are among the most stable and long-lived instruments of representation and opposition on the Canadian political scene. Because of the presence of political parties, the public is in a position to supervise every detail of government action.

### Parties as Government

The ultimate test of the party system is its relationship to and influence on the institutions of government. In Canada, we have what is essentially party government. The recruitment, training, and selection of candidates in political parties has but one objective: to control the governing machinery that creates public policy.

The most powerful MP, the prime minister, is the leader of the governing party; he or she exercises extensive prerogatives to appoint party colleagues to the Cabinet and other legislative offices and to call the next election. Only by forming and managing the government can political parties have the opportunity to bring about real political change, or to slow it down, by implementing their programs.

Parliament in particular depends more on the party system than is generally recognized. The committee system of the House of Commons is a product of the party system. Although the rules governing the organization of committees and the rules defining the jurisdiction of each committee are adopted by the whole membership, all other features of the committees are shaped by political parties. For example, committee assignments are party based and reflect the percentage of seats a party has won in the House of Commons.

The party that wins a majority of seats in the House of Commons or in a provincial legislature does not take over the entire government and throw its opponents out on the street, but party control does matter to the various administrative arms of government. Such control matters because each political party and the elected parliamentarians who represent it generally try to turn campaign promises into policies once they get into government. They can also appoint or shuffle key senior administrators in Canada's powerful bureaucracy, where the implementation of, and often the inspiration behind, government policies takes place.

One of the most important functions of the governing party is that of uniting, simplifying, and stabilizing the governing process. This function can be seen in the role of the Cabinet in keeping its members in the House of Commons united in their votes and committed to the policies that flow from Cabinet decisions. Organizing the affairs of government while representing the public interest often places a heavy burden on the party that governs.

## HOW CANADIAN POLITICAL PARTIES ARE ORGANIZED

All Canadian political parties have organizations, even if the organization is limited to a few legislators consulting one another under a shared party label or a primary organization of dedicated workers who build a network of support for party goals across the country before anyone has been elected.

Party organization can be decentralized, with open entry arrangements that permit anyone to join and be nominated as a candidate, as is the case with the Liberal, Progressive Conservative, and New Democratic parties. Then there are the hierarchical and centralized organizations which are more common to doctrinal and **ideological parties**, such as the Communist Party and the Marxist–Leninists, which are very careful who they recruit and allow into the party.

A well-organized national political party requires a tightly controlled party machine staffed by professional party workers (Pelletier, Bundock, and Sarra-Bournet 1991). This machine endorses candidates for election to Parliament and ensures that they will respond to the dictates of the party leadership. The prime minister and the Cabinet exercise tremendous power over their MPs because of the ability promote and demote members in Cabinet positions, expel them from the party, and to call elections. Leaders of the other parties in Parliament have similar controls over their MPs, with the exception of calling elections.

Typically, Canadian political parties comprise a small inner circle of parliamentarians and those seeking to be, along with a professional staff and a few loyal party supporters. This parliamentary wing consists of the party leader and the party **caucus** who are the most visible party representatives in the House of Commons, the Senate and the media (see Figure 8.2).

The staff and loyal supporters come and go, depending on the political fortunes of the party leaders or local candidates. The extra-parliamentary wing consists of the loyal and active supporters who work at the party headquarters, serve on party committees, co-ordinate regional and provincial strategies, and comprise the party bureaucracy throughout the country.

Then there are those who regularly identify with the political party at the constituency level and who cast their ballots for the candidates chosen by the party professionals and party activists. At the grass-roots level, federal candidates are nominated, delegates to national conventions are selected, volunteers and party members are recruited, and money to finance party activities is raised.

The organization and co-ordination of the federal and provincial wings of the same party vary from province to province. Parties of the same name tend to operate independently federally and provincially as well as interprovincially. Among the parliamentary parties, only the NDP and Reform keep a tight linkage among provincial party organizations and the national body.

Party elites and activists in all three major parties come from more privileged social backgrounds. The typical party delegate to a convention is a businessman or a male lawyer of above-average income and education. The same can be said for the candidates the parties send to the House of Commons (Guppy, Freeman, and Buchan 1987, 427). The NDP nominates and elects more people from lower-middle-class groups than does the Liberal or Progressive Conservative party, but middle-class people still predominate. The traditional connection of the NDP with Canadian labour ensures some representation of organized labour in the inner circles of the party, while big business is barely visible (Archer 1991).

We should distinguish between the broad mass of members whose affiliation may only be nominal and whose loyalties may be tentative and the professional workers who hold party positions and the elite of the party who wield the primary power of decision making within the party organization.

## Party Organization and New Technologies

Throughout most of the twentieth century, Canadian party organizations employed rick-

**Figure 8.2 Typical Political Party Organization in Canada**

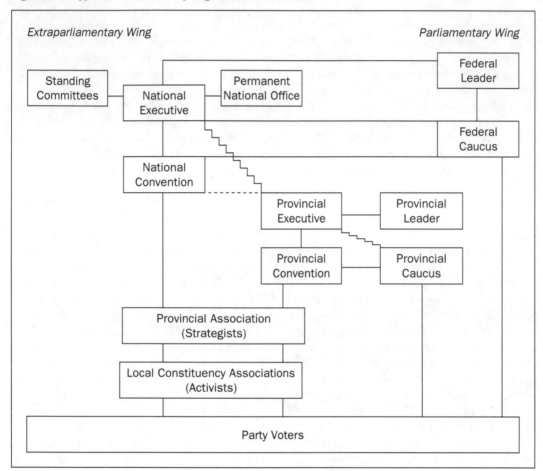

ety methods of communication. By the 1990s, most of the major political parties began to use intricate electronic communications techniques to facilitate intraparty organization and to attract electoral support.

The new political techniques include five basic elements.

1. *Polling*. Surveys of voter opinions provide information that political parties use to craft their campaign strategies. Parties randomly select ridings across the country and conduct polls on the popularity of their candidate or MP. They employ polls to

select issues, to assess their own strengths and weaknesses as well as those of their opposition, to check voter responses to campaigns, and to determine the degree to which certain groups are susceptible to campaign appeals. In recent years, pollsters have become central figures in political party campaigns.

2. *The broadcast media*. Television in particular has become the hallmark of the political party campaign. By far the most commonly used technique is the 30- to 60-second spot, which permits the

party or a candidate to target a certain audience.

3. *Phone campaigns.* Phone campaigns allow party workers to make personal contact with thousands of voters at the constituency level. Personal contacts of this sort are thought to be extremely effective. Especially at election time, staffs of callers, often using computer-assisted dialling systems and prepared scripts, place calls to deliver the candidate's message. The targeted groups are generally those identified by the polls as either undecided or strong supporters who are contacted simply to encourage them to vote.

4. *Direct mail campaigns.* Direct mail serves both as a vehicle for the party to communicate with voters and as a mechanism for raising money. Computerized mailing lists of voters with some particular perspective or social characteristic are prepared by party candidates. Usually the national party organization prepares pamphlets and brochures on behalf of their MPs and returns them to the constituency for distribution, using these lists.

5. *Public relations.* All major political parties in Canada use public relations techniques and professional consultants to promote their party images and to get their candidates elected. Increasingly, political party organizations at the local level have come to rely upon professional campaign management. Consultants offer parties the expertise necessary to conduct accurate public opinion polls, produce television commercials, organize mail campaigns, and interpret complex computer data. Political parties organize their public relations around media advertisements, the preparation and distribution of press releases, public meetings, detailed travel arrangements for candidates, speech writing, and fundraising.

New technologies adopted by political parties not only change the ways parties communicate with the public but also the ways they organize themselves. Technology brings a greater number of experts into the party structure who may not necessarily be loyal party members.

The routine operation of political parties and the conduct of campaigns, once performed by masses of party workers, is changing. These tasks now require fewer personnel but a great deal more money. The new political style depends on polls, computers, and other sophisticated techniques.

The acquisition of new political technologies has far-reaching implications for the balance of power among political parties. Labour-intensive party organizations whose chief support comes from groups near the bottom of the social and economic scale lose the numerical superiority of their forces to other party organizations that can afford the latest technologies. The capital-intensive technological format, by contrast, is given a major boost in parties whose sympathizers are better able to furnish larger sums of financial support to the party organization. Today, the likelihood that political parties without substantial economic or organizational resources can acquire some measure of power is severely diminished.

## Party Organization and the Need for Money

Political parties provide their candidates with expertise and resources to raise money. Levels of contributions are limited by law, but political parties and party campaign organizations can be very helpful by, for example, steering potential donors toward particular candidates. Political parties provide candidates with a base of popular support and party identifiers that, it is hoped, can be converted into votes and donations.

Money is a central problem for all political party organizations. It is needed to pay rent for offices, mortgages on land and buildings, staff salaries, office supplies, copying costs, postage, telephone bills, computers, polls, and advertising. Without money, political parties and their candidates cannot reasonably make their appeals to the electorate. Money can also become too important and used in ways that abuse and bias popular support.

In an increasingly competitive political party system, money has become a very important resource for the major political parties. Some are better at amassing it than are others. Depending on who the leader is and whether the party is the government, the Progressive Conservative and Liberal parties tend to do well at gaining revenues through fundraising dinners.

Direct-mail campaigns are a good method for securing party financing. In such campaigns, people are approached by mail and asked for money in support of a political party. Party organizations know that the best prospects for direct-mail fundraising are those who have given to the group before. So, once a name goes on the party list, that person is solicited repeatedly by the party organization. The first goal of a direct-mail package is to get people to open it rather than just toss it unopened in the wastepaper basket as "junk mail."

Political clubs are organized by political parties in order to solicit the business and professional communities, and young voters. They give people the opportunity to network with elected leaders and other party members who meet from time to time with club members.

Political parties also engage in the direct solicitation of companies and make annual requests for contributions as well as campaign requests during election periods. The Liberal and Progressive Conservative parties still use business circles as a financial resource, whereas the NDP approaches trade unions and small commercial enterprises for funding. Union contributions are significant for the NDP because they flow monthly from union members and members of affiliated organizations.

Another instrument of party funding is the sale of membership cards. Party "membership" is not aggressively pursued by the traditional parties because they represent so many divergent interests. However, the NDP attaches more importance to the sale of party memberships than do the other major parties because it is organized to make rank-and-file decisions.

The Elections Expenses Act provides a legal framework for political parties to raise money through individual and corporate contributions. But it also provides public reimbursements of half the permissible spending for party candidates who win 15 percent of the total votes cast in their ridings.

## THE BASIC FEATURES OF THE CANADIAN PARTY SYSTEM

It is difficult to imagine that a country as large and as socially complex as Canada developed a modified two-party governing system. And considering the range of political ideologies among voters and the variety among provincial political systems, the fact that only two political parties have ever governed Canada is somewhat unusual (Carty 1988).

A powerful tradition of support exists for the two parties that have formed governments at the federal level. However, the federal election of 1993, with the powerful showing of the Bloc Québécois and the Reform Party, suggested a significant realignment of the Canadian party system.

Party leaders in Canada have traditionally organized political conflict around dualistic party positions, such as government economic intervention versus government cut-backs. Beyond these rather basic issue cleavages, the two prominent federal political parties have assembled a broad base of support and have not been that concerned about the internal consistency of their supporters on most issues.

The two traditional governing parties do not simply seesaw after each election, one winning now, the other winning when the next election is called (see Figure 8.3). Throughout our party history, as a general rule each

**Figure 8.3 Two-Party Dominance in Canadian Government, 1867–1993**

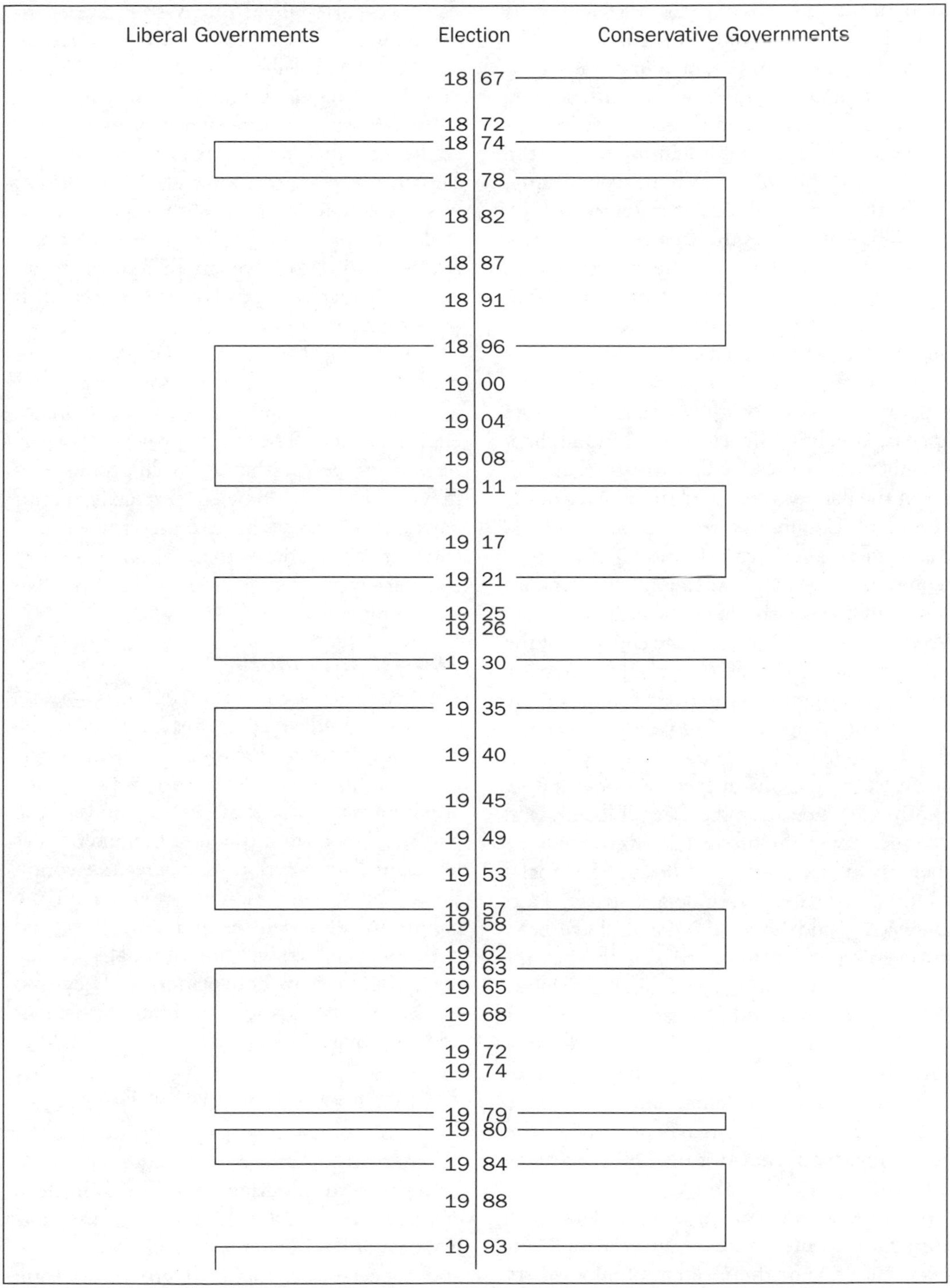

| Liberal Governments | Election | Conservative Governments |
|---|---|---|
| | 18 \| 67 | |
| | 18 \| 72 | |
| | 18 \| 74 | |
| | 18 \| 78 | |
| | 18 \| 82 | |
| | 18 \| 87 | |
| | 18 \| 91 | |
| | 18 \| 96 | |
| | 19 \| 00 | |
| | 19 \| 04 | |
| | 19 \| 08 | |
| | 19 \| 11 | |
| | 19 \| 17 | |
| | 19 \| 21 | |
| | 19 \| 25 | |
| | 19 \| 26 | |
| | 19 \| 30 | |
| | 19 \| 35 | |
| | 19 \| 40 | |
| | 19 \| 45 | |
| | 19 \| 49 | |
| | 19 \| 53 | |
| | 19 \| 57 | |
| | 19 \| 58 | |
| | 19 \| 62 | |
| | 19 \| 63 | |
| | 19 \| 65 | |
| | 19 \| 68 | |
| | 19 \| 72 | |
| | 19 \| 74 | |
| | 19 \| 79 | |
| | 19 \| 80 | |
| | 19 \| 84 | |
| | 19 \| 88 | |
| | 19 \| 93 | |

party has been the dominant governing party for significant periods of time. We might think of each of these periods as a **party era**. The dominant party does not, of course, win everything in sight: Sometimes it suffers from intraparty squabbles, and loses; sometimes its leader is unable to win or maintain support in Quebec or the West. When such failings occur, the opposition cashes in on them.

What punctuates these party eras is a **critical election**, after which the parties realign their support and the governing party is displaced. A critical-election is an electoral earthquake: The ground shakes beneath the governing party; fissures appear in the party's support; it begins to unravel; and new issues appear, dividing the electorate. What happened to the Progressive Conservatives in 1993 when the party was reduced to two MPs in the House of Commons serves as an example. Sometimes a critical-election period may require more than one election before change is apparent (as with Diefenbaker in 1957 and his sweep in 1958), but, in the end, one of the major parties has come to dominate the party system for a significant period of time.

Strong competition between political parties at the federal level has generally filtered down to the provincial level. At one time or another, competition between Liberals and Conservatives has produced governments by them in all provinces, although the Social Credit Party, New Democratic Party, Parti Québécois, and Union Nationale have been intervening governing parties at the provincial level in Ontario, the Prairie provinces, British Columbia, and Quebec.

What is sometimes labelled **one-party dominance** is the rule in many regions of Canada. And, at the federal level, one party — the Liberal party — has dominated the governing institutions for over 80 years since Confederation.

Our electoral system and the laws governing it institutionalize certain structural barriers that prevent the election of minor-party candidates to the House of Commons. Canada's two-party governing system seems to endure mainly because it has always existed.

However, the federal election of 1993 propelled two previous minor parties to formidable opposition status and appears to have challenged the traditional two-party system. But, in the past, this kind of election result was unlikely to happen. Without much hope of developing a base of their own, minor parties tend to die off, resign themselves to an extraparliamentary existence, or merge with one of the major parties.

By the 1990s, Canada had more minor political parties than any other democracy that uses the single-member district and plurality electoral system. The two major governing parties try to be all things to all people, and inevitably fail at doing so. Typically, minor parties in Canada have represented social and economic protests that, for one reason or another, were not given voice by the two governing parties.

## The Traditional Parties

Although they are in a state of flux, Canada's two major traditional parties continue to be important for several reasons. Of all other parties operating in Canada's party system, they are the most institutional in the minds of the public. They furnish the most prominent cues for Canadian voters to compare at election time. The two traditional parties are on the ballots in all provinces and territories, and their national conventions formally decide upon nominations and platforms. They also furnish the organizational focus for Parliament and all provincial legislatures.

### The Progressive Conservative Party

Canada's first political party organized as the "Conservatives" in the early 1860s. A decade before, John A. Macdonald had built a coalition of wealthy conservative interests made up of French Canadians, Ontario Tories, and successful commercial groups to form a short-lived coalition called the "Liberal-Conservatives."

Eventually forming the Conservative party, these interests wanted to build a Canadian Confederation that would produce national unity from sea to sea, and do it by means of a National Policy which encompassed building a national railway and fostering national industry and commerce. To protect themselves against an expansionist U.S. republic, the Conservatives kept their British and French connections and erected high tariffs as protections for the fledgling Canadian economy.

After the death of Macdonald, a rapid succession of new party leaders between 1891 and 1896 (John Abbott, John Thompson, Mackenzie Bowell, and Charles Tupper) destabilized the party. Finally, in 1911, Conservative leader Sir Robert Borden defeated the Liberal government of Wilfrid Laurier. But the party's platform was divisive in the West and in Quebec.

Western farmers did not trust the influence of big business in the party, and the French Canadians resisted the party's obsession with Great Britain. French Canadians were also offended by the murder of Louis Riel and by the **Conscription crisis** of 1917. The Conservatives lost their support in Quebec, only to retain backing in Ontario. Out West, a minor party, the Progressive Party, formed a coalition with the Liberals and eroded the farmers' support of the Conservatives.

The Depression sealed the fate of the party in 1921 and, except for the one-year period between 1925 and 1926, the Conservatives would stay out of power until 1930. The party's new leader and prime minister, R.B. Bennett, was not able to endear his party to Quebec's voters and generated internal divisions among his Cabinet and loyal party supporters. Bennett was defeated in 1935, triggering another succession of unsuccessful party leaders (R.J. Manion, Arthur Meighen, John Bracken, and George Drew). The party would remain in the political wilderness, even though it

merged with the Progressives to become the Progressive Conservative party in 1942.

Not until the late 1950s, under the leadership of John Diefenbaker, Drew's successor, would the Progressive Conservatives regain their credibility as a national political party (Perlin 1980). Forming a minority government in 1957, Diefenbaker was able to appeal to much wider constituency of power than any other previous leader since John A. Macdonald. In 1958, Diefenbaker led the Progressive Conservatives to an unprecedented electoral victory. The party glided on Diefenbaker's charismatic style for six years, but his government was not returned in the election of 1963. Internal divisions within the party forced Diefenbaker to resign his leadership in 1967.

Diefenbaker's successor, Robert Stanfield, failed to rebuild the party's national constituency and was unable to defeat the Liberals in three federal elections — 1968, 1972, and 1974. In 1976, Stanfield was succeeded by Joe Clark, who won the party's leadership in a narrow victory against Claude Wagner. Within three years, Clark would form his minority government, only to suffer defeat eight months later on a budget vote. Clark failed to win the election in 1980 and would not retain the leadership of his party.

Brian Mulroney, the first Progressive Conservative party leadership candidate from Quebec since John Abbott, took the reins of a deeply divided party in 1983 and led it to its largest victory in Canadian history. Mulroney successfully penetrated Liberal party strongholds in Quebec, winning two successive elections, in 1984 and 1988.

His successor, Kim Campbell, became Canada's first female prime minister in 1993, but would serve in that role for only 123 days. Ms. Campbell promised to practise government differently and spent most of the gruelling election campaign distancing herself from the record of successive Mulroney governments. The continuous stumbling of the campaign organization, her inability to distinguish candour from rebuke, and her failure to define her policies in terms of job creation led to the most devastating major-party defeat in Canada's electoral history. Left with only two seats in the House of Commons, the party began to rebuild itself from the ground up, with Jean Charest as leader. Notwithstanding the unprecedented defeat of the party at the polls in 1993, since Confederation, Conservatives have formed more governments in Canada than the Liberals but have governed for less than 50 years (see Figure 8.3, page 281).

### The Liberal Party of Canada

The Liberal party developed slowly out of a coalition of reformers opposing John A. Macdonald's first government. The coalition consisted of Clear Grits from Ontario, Le Parti Rouge from Quebec, and anti-Confederation MPs from Nova Scotia under the leadership of Alexander Mackenzie. These Grits won the election of 1874 with the support of moderate reform groups in Ontario, anti-business and anti-clerical reformers in Quebec, and voters in the small towns and rural areas.

The Liberals would not hold power for very long, suffering defeat in 1878, and subsequently losing two successive elections, in 1891 and 1894. Wilfrid Laurier had become leader of the party in 1887 and, within two years, had unified the diverse supporting groups into a national political party. Laurier won the realigning election of 1896 and thus transformed Canada's political party system from a one-party-dominant (Conservative) system to a **two-party competitive system**. Laurier served the longest continuous term as prime minister until 1911, when he lost the election to the Conservatives, who remained in power until 1920. Laurier retired in 1919, passing party leadership on to William Lyon Mackenzie King.

Mackenzie King won the 1921 election and would serve as prime minister, presiding over majority governments three times, intermittently for more than 21 years, and occupying the position of party leader for 29 years.

Louis St. Laurent succeeded King and sustained the electoral success of the Liberal party by strengthening the support for the party in Quebec. He served as prime minister for nine years, winning two elections, in 1949 and 1953, but was defeated by John Diefenbaker in 1957.

His successor, Lester B. Pearson, was party leader from 1958 to 1968 and prime minister from 1963 to 1968. Pierre Trudeau assumed the party leadership from 1968 to 1984, winning four general elections throughout that period. His successor, John Turner, served as prime minister for 80 days, but failed to win an election, and resigned the leadership of the Liberal party in 1989.

Jean Chrétien was chosen the new party leader in June 1990. Chrétien had to overcome his public image as a relic of past Liberal governments and their former policies. After running a strong campaign, he won the 1993 federal election by promising a government that would be kinder, more prosperous, more sensitive to the needs of unemployed Canadians, and less obsessive about the market-driven economics than Progressive Conservative governments had been in the past. He talked about restoring integrity in government and injecting hope back into the economy.

To achieve his campaign promises, Chrétien advocated a two-year multibillion-dollar program to be cost-shared with provinces and municipalities to rebuild roads, bridges, and transit systems and to build and rebuild other Canadian infrastructures. He promised to make financing available to stimulate small business and increase apprenticeship programs. During the election campaign, Liberals pledged to support universal health care and to oppose user fees. The party sought to amend the North American Free Trade Agreement (NAFTA), to increase trade with the Pacific Rim economies, and to support the thrust of the General Agreement on Tariffs and Trade (GATT) as the cornerstone of its overall trade policy.

## The New Democratic Party

The third-largest national political party with elected representatives to the Canadian House of Commons is the New Democratic Party. Originally formed as a democratic socialist movement in 1932, the Co-operative Commonwealth Federation (CCF) initially attracted the support of farmers and workers in the 1930s and 1940s.

The first electoral successes of the CCF occurred in 1935, when it won 7 federal seats, and in 1940, when it won 8 seats. In 1944, the CCF formed a government in Saskatchewan. On the heels of this provincial victory, the party won 28 seats in the federal election of 1945, making it a credible third-party challenger to the two traditional governing parties.

The economic prosperity that followed the Second World War and the entrenched East–West tensions of the Cold War hurt the CCF as it was a party dedicated to establishing socialist governments in Canada. In the 1950s, the party discarded its doctrinaire socialist positions and adopted a milder political philosophy, embracing a mixed economy in Canada made up of the interplay of private and corporate enterprises. The softer ideological profile of the party encouraged its members to seek a new name. In 1961, the CCF united with major unions in the Canadian Labour Congress and founded the New Democratic Party (NDP).

But its moderate, left-of-centre platforms have not succeeded in winning enough seats for the party to form a government and break the entrenched historical pattern of just two governing parties. On average, the NDP had won 26 seats per federal election from 1962 to 1988. Up to that time, its party caucus constituted about 8 percent of the membership of the House of Commons, and the party rarely gains 20 percent of the popular vote. None of the seven party leaders since 1935 has been able to build a national constituency in the Canadian House of Commons. The party is quite regionalized in comparison with the other parliamentary parties, with concentrated representation in British Columbia, Saskatchewan, and Ontario (Morton 1986).

Under Audrey McLaughlin's leadership, the party's traditional union and intellectual support eroded substantially. The 1993 federal election battered and bruised the NDP across the political landscape, reducing its electoral support from 43 seats to 9, its lowest performance since 1961, and causing it to lose its status as an opposition party in the House of Commons. The long journey back from the political wilderness began with calls for a new leader, a more modernized platform, and a revamped and more accountable organization.

## The Minor Parties

The apparent two-party character of Canada's electoral system has never remained pure for long (Conway 1978). Numerous minor parties, sometimes called "small" or "fringe" parties, have risen to challenge one or all of the traditional dominant political parties. And though often these minor parties disappear with time, their presence is seldom without influence.

Some of Canada's earliest minor parties, which have since disappeared, were the Progressives, the Reconstruction Party, and the Bloc Populaire. But many new minor parties have formed, especially since the early 1980s, and registered with Elections Canada to compete in federal elections (see Table 8.1).

The historical dominance of two parties in government, and the presence of more than twenty other political parties, give Canada the character of a two-party-dominant **multiparty system**. Minor parties must compete within a political party system that has been dominated — at least until 1993 — by three traditional political parties.

None of the minor parties has run a full slate of candidates nationally for seats in the House of Commons. Even the Bloc Québécois, which became Canada's official opposition, ran

**Table 8.1 Registered Minor Parties: 1984, 1988, 1993 Federal Elections**

| Party | Number of Candidates | | |
|---|---|---|---|
| | 1984 | 1988 | 1993 |
| Abolitionist Party of Canada | 0 | 0 | 80 |
| Bloc Québécois | 0 | 0 | 75 |
| Canada Party | 0 | 0 | 56 |
| Christian Heritage Party of Canada (first election 1988) | 0 | 63 | 59 |
| The Green Party of Canada | 60 | 68 | 79 |
| Libertarian Party of Canada | 72 | 88 | 52 |
| Marxist-Leninist Party of Canada | 0 | 0 | 51 |
| National Party of Canada (first election 1993) | 0 | 0 | 171 |
| Natural Law Party of Canada | 0 | 0 | 231 |
| Party for the Commonwealth of Canada | 65 | 59 | 59 |
| Reform Party of Canada | 0 | 72 | 207 |

*Source:* Data from Elections Canada, 1984:69, 1989:59, and 1994:160. Reprinted with permission of the Chief Electoral Officer of Canada.

none of its candidates outside of Quebec. Nonetheless, minor parties have increased their importance as well as their numbers in Canada's political and governing system, as was dramatically witnessed in the federal election of 1993.

Frequently, dissatisfied groups have split within the major political parties to form new political parties, which have acted as barometers of changes in the political mood of the country. The formation of the Bloc Québécois from the rebellious factions of both the Progressive Conservative and the Liberal party in Quebec is a striking case in point. Such barometric indicators have forced the major parties to recognize new issues or trends in the thinking of Canadians.

Minor parties also differ sharply in their aims and their likelihood of success. Some of these parties are narrow and "doctrinal parties," as are the Communist parties, which profess a particular ideology or political doctrine,

or are formed around a single issue or leader. They enter elections mainly to publicize their goals. Others are "transient parties," so named because they tend to last for only a brief period of time and usually emerge out of economic and regional protest movements. Still others are, from a national perspective, able to become powerful contenders in Parliament, as was demonstrated in 1993 by the Reform Party and the Bloc Québécois.

Some persistent minor parties, such as the Marxist–Leninist Party, have a strong ideological foundation that may be at odds with the general ideological mindset present in the traditional parties. In this regard, members of minor parties regard themselves as rebellious outsiders who look to one another for support. Furthermore, these types of minor parties do not necessarily think in terms of winning an election or having even one of their candidates elected. So, a poor showing at the polls does not dissuade either the leadership or the grass-roots members from continuing their quest to change Canadian society. This is particularly true of such parties as the Libertarian Party, which supports a *laissez-faire* capitalist economic program combined with a hands-off policy on regulating matters of morals.

The minor parties that endure have been largely unsuccessful in influencing election results, partly because the Canadian electoral system denies small parties the representation they rightfully earn in the popular vote and because Canadians tend to vote for national parties that are capable of forming strong governments. But minor parties are not to be judged only by their lack of electoral success. The smaller political parties seeking economic and environmental reforms call attention to the new issues, sometimes advocate unpopular policies, and force the major parties to adopt the substance of their platforms.

Accordingly, minor parties must be judged by their impact on the major parties. They have been formed primarily to express discontent with the choices offered by the major parties, working for their own objectives within the electoral system. In advancing their proposals, minor parties convey a warning to the major parties that, if they ignore emerging concerns, they risk losing popular support.

Minor parties are constant reminders of the multidimensional character of Canadian society. They generate new ideas about government and politics, often advocating important reforms to how we conduct our political system. As vote-getters, most minor parties have not performed very well, with some exceptions. In the 1920s, the Progressives, which represented Western farming interests, sent farmers to the House of Common as MPs. In the 1960s the Social Credit and the Créditistes represented their regional interests in Ottawa. In the 1980s, the Reform Party broke into the parliamentary arena, calling for a very different kind of politics. And, in the 1990s the Bloc Québécois gave Quebec's

sovereignist sentiments a formal voice in Parliament, and the Reform Party provided a Western populist reform focus in Parliament.

## Rivals of Political Parties

People who support Canada's traditional party system worry about its future. They fear that we are in an era of significant party transformation, when people gradually disengage from the traditional parties and support new parties, based on a regional, economic, or leadership focus. Yet the electoral system does not guarantee that the votes cast in support of new parties will be fairly represented. People are simply disengaging from the parties between elections, poised as undecided voters until they approach the polling booth. Among the major parties, the national party organizations are stronger and richer than ever before, but the elite segment of each party is stronger and the mass segment more anemic than ever.

In an era of high-tech political information, political parties have been slow to enter the technological revolution affecting the conduct government and politics in Canada. By canvassing door-to-door, the political party is the only political institution that still makes house calls. Yet, increasingly, political communication is not face-to-face; it is conducted through the media. In fact, political parties are no longer the main sources of our political information, attention, and affection.

Among the biggest rivals of political parties are the media. Voters can learn about candidates directly from television, radio, and the print media, and no longer have to listen to the representatives of political parties.

In addition to the media, pressure groups and organizations such as labour unions, associations of manufacturers, boards of trade, chambers of commerce, and farm groups rival political parties. Other racial, ethnic, or religious groups have their own associations: Assembly of First Nations, Jewish, Italian, Polish, and Irish groups are active in Canadian politics. Women press their demands through hundreds of organizations (Galipeau 1989). Still other groups are designed to promote particular policies, such as the Federation of Canadian Municipalities or the National Council of Welfare.

## WHAT IS AN INTEREST GROUP?

Most people who visit Ottawa want to see the monuments of government in Canada, for example, the Parliament Buildings, the Supreme Court building, and the various departments of government that are located close to Parliament Hill. But very few people will walk into the downtown core of the city, where much of the political life of the country also occurs. The capital's sidewalks are lined with rows of office buildings, no different from the ones we find in downtown Toronto or Vancouver.

What is there to see? In some of these buildings, and in similar ones lining nearby streets, are the offices of hundreds of organizations that are represented in Ottawa. These groups are there to participate in the political life of the country. They are the interest groups who pressure the formal institutions of government for the demands they make and for the people they represent.

An interest group is any organization that tries to achieve at least some of its goals by influencing public policy. In Canada, an interest group is often referred to as a pressure group when its activities are concentrated on the change, development, and implementation of public policy (Pross 1975, 10–18). Because it is difficult to determine that a group is always political or always non-political, we can call a group "political" when it uses political tactics to get what it wants. A group becomes a political interest group when it seeks to press its claims on other parts of society by means of political action and influence.

The efforts of interest groups to influence government and parliamentarians are called "lobbying." Lobbying may involve direct contact between a lobbyist, or some group's representative, with a government official or parliamentarian, or it may involve indirect action, such as attempts to sway public opinion that can influence the content and direction of public policy. Listed in the yellow pages under "Government Relations Consultants," lobbyists offering their services to individuals and groups wear attractive names, such as "Alphalink," "Capitol Hill Group," and "Parliamentary Agent."

## CHARACTERISTICS OF INTEREST GROUPS

When an interest group attempts to pursue its goals through involvement in the political process, it becomes a political actor. In this regard, a group's influence must be measured relative to the characteristics of other groups with which it must compete for government attention. Effectiveness depends on how big the group is, how strong its identification is, how closely tied to politics it is, how well organized it is, and how its goals are articulated and received by the general public.

### Size

Interest groups vary dramatically in size. A small group of people petitioning the city council to improve garbage collection services on their block represents one extreme, while all the women in Canada might represent the other.

It would seem that the bigger the group, the more effective it is likely to be. Large groups can mobilize more people, raise more money to support their causes, and swing more votes in an election. Large groups can, of course, be more cumbersome because the diversity of views among their members makes them more difficult to co-ordinate. Being big is not always the most important advantage, but given our reliance on plurality and majority decision making, it is usually better than being small.

## Membership

Interest groups vary as well in membership procedures. Some groups, like the Canadian Jewish Congress, enrol individual members, while others, such as the Canadian Manufacturers' Association, enrol companies as members. Some groups enrol members formally, as when labour unions ask workers to join and pay dues. Other groups rest on a more informal notion of membership in which people just think of themselves as belonging. A person who never goes to church may nonetheless think of herself as a Catholic. Even this informal sense of membership can vary; some groups evoke in their membership a very strong sense of identification with the group, while others do so only weakly.

For still other groups, membership is not even a choice of the individual involved; rather, people belong by the fact of having particular characteristics. Aboriginals and women are often identified as important interest groups. Even though they may not think of themselves as belonging to some large group, they are considered members simply because they possess a particular characteristic — for example, race or gender.

Political scientists refer to such a group as a **latent interest group** — one that is not necessarily organized, but has a commonality of interest that may at some point lead to organization and action within the political system.

Generally speaking, the stronger the bonds of the individual members to the group, the more effective the interest group will be. Group members are more likely to co-operate with one another and respond to their group leaders if they feel a strong sense of identification with the group's goals.

Formal groups can come into existence to represent the interests of an entire category of people, but not all the people in the category may get involved. In fact, this is more often the rule than the exception. For example, the National Action Committee on the Status of Women (NAC) speaks for women, but most women are not members, and some disagree with what the organization advocates.

Such disparities raise some interesting problems. Groups may try to portray themselves as "the voice" of business or women or working people in order to increase the credence given to their efforts, but they may actually represent a minority of the broader group involved. In some cases, members and non-members may even be in dispute with each other, as the organized group seeks to advance its members at the expense of the "members" who do not belong. Unions have attempted to impose unionization on workers who do not want it on the grounds that non-union members should not be "free riders" who reap the benefits gained by the unions, and that all workers will benefit if unionization of workers is universal.

## Organization

Some interest groups are formally organized — with elected leaders, regular meetings, and dues-paying members. Some are large corporations whose leaders are corporate officers hired by boards of directors. Others have just a basic organizational structure, with few, or sometimes no, leaders, and a bare minimum of prescribed rules.

Whatever the outward appearance of pressure groups, internal organization is always a significant variable in preserving and articulating their interests. The success of an interest group in advancing its interests depends on how well it is organized. A strong network of communication and control can amplify the power of the group, while poor internal organization and an inability to co-ordinate common efforts can dissipate the influence the group intends to have.

Leaders and followers emerge in most groups. The noted German sociologist Robert

Michels (1959) termed this the "iron law of oligarchy." In all organizations, power tends to gravitate to a few strong members. Not all groups operate in the same manner. Some are free and lively, with many members taking part, others are dictatorships of the few. Oligarchy, or rule by the select few, is most common in larger groups that have geographically diffuse memberships.

There has been increasing attention in recent years to the importance of formal organization as an interest-group resource — such as using computers in extensive direct-mail campaigns, and building coalitions of groups to better integrate lobbying efforts. Interest groups are better organized today than ever before, and thus the disadvantages of ineffectively organized groups are greater than ever before.

Organization is an even more critical resource because Canadian governments are so decentralized and awash with contending claims and interests. Getting one's case across in this cluttered, diverse, and pluralistic governing system requires planning and systematic effort. The older stereotype of the effective lobbyist as someone who knows the right people and meets them periodically to cut deals is increasingly out of touch with the governing environment that puts a premium on careful organization in group dealings with a big and complex federal government, or even a small provincial one.

## Money

Money is a critical political resource for determining a group's influence on government. Some groups have a lot of it; others, very little. Pressure groups spend huge amounts of money because all organizational efforts require money to attract new members, renew old memberships, educate members about upcoming threats to their interests, mobilize members in attempts to exert pressure on parliamentarians, maintain a professional staff, retain outside expert advice, and conduct pub-

lic relations campaigns. Most interest groups rely heavily on membership contributions, dues, and other fundraising activities. And a growing number of groups rely on direct-mail appeals to raise money for their causes.

Groups use money in a variety of ways to advance their interests, most of which are straightforward and legal. Well-financed associations of business or professional people, like the Canadian Federation of Independent Business and the Canadian Medical Association, employ large and politically astute staffs. They mount effective public relations campaigns, utilizing the mass media to present their positions. In general, they use their financial resources to get their messages before bureaucrats, legislators, and the general public — political resources quite beyond the reach of groups that lack such substantial funding.

Interest groups that draw on large financial resources can also increase their access to officials, often more effectively than political parties, a fact that is troubling to some, even though it is completely legal. One common method of increasing or protecting access is by making campaign contributions to political parties and local candidates. Electioneering can be very expensive for local candidates, and it is becoming steadily more so, especially as the use of television expands. Groups that contribute to campaigns do not think they are buying votes, but they do think their contributions entitle them to get in the door and make their case the next time an issue of importance to them comes along.

## Political Linkage

Interest groups are discernible by the degree to which they have connections to politics and the governing system in Canada. Some interest groups have little, if any, connection to the political system. They are generally not concerned with political issues or involved in political activities. For example, the United Way campaign rarely has anything to do with politics. In fact, it would probably suffer as an organization if it became embroiled in partisan political struggles.

The political significance of this kind of organization lies in its potential to become politically active should its interests somehow be threatened in the political arena. Removing the tax deductions on charitable donations would undoubtedly motivate an organization such as United Way to take up the cudgel of politics. However, under ordinary circumstances, these kinds of interest groups position themselves entirely outside the political system.

Other interest groups operate solely for political purposes. They engage in public displays, inside lobbying at the political and administrative levels, and sometimes disruptive tactics — such as protest marches, picketing, and violence. Some Canadian businesses have used strong-arm tactics against workers to enforce their interests. Likewise, some Canadian unions have used violence against their employers. And an endless array of "anti" groups have all placed their specific political agendas before the public.

Both ends of the political spectrum have demonstrated a capacity for political disruption, even violence. On the Left, feminists, coal miners, autoworkers, welfare mothers, Afro-Canadians, anti-nuclear groups, public-housing groups, the Canadian aboriginal peoples movement, and students are some of the politically charged groups in Canada.

On the extreme Right, the Ku Klux Klan and other racist groups have used terror, intimidation, and political agitation (Robin 1991). Klan agitation has been very effective and contributed to winning amendments to Canada's immigration laws in 1929, which established quotas for targeted less-preferred immigrants and was a force behind the toppling of the Liberal government in Saskatchewan in the same year.

Many other groups comprise the racist Right in Canada — groups such as Aryan Nations, the Aryan Resistance Movement, the Church of the Creator, the Heritage Front, and Final Solution. Most of these groups attempt to recruit young people into their movements by penetrating schools, dispersing hate literature, and engaging in violence against homosexuals, Jews, Afro-Canadians, and aboriginals.

Between these two extremes are many organizations that are involved in politics to a greater or lesser degree. They range from groups that are primarily non-political but engage in political activity to a limited degree to groups that are heavily involved in politics but carry on some non-political activities as well.

An example of the first type is the Roman Catholic Church, which carries on a broad range of non-political activities but does occasionally get embroiled in political issues, such as abortion and the practising rights of women in the church. An example of the second type is the National Firearms Association, which engages in a variety of educational and promotional activities regarding the use of firearms in Canada but concentrates heavily on opposing governmental restrictions on the ownership and use of guns. Some groups focus on just one political issue, while others have long lists of issues they wish to see the political system address in terms favourable to them.

## WHY SO MANY INTEREST GROUPS?

In Canada, groups can organize because of our freedoms to speak, assemble, associate, and petition government, as guaranteed in the Charter of Rights and Freedoms, and in the Canadian Bill of Rights, 1960. Without such freedoms, only groups favoured by the government — or groups whose members are willing to be punished for their actions — could and would exist.

Accordingly, in Canada, every conceivable social interest is organized — even crime. Criminals, however, unlike other groups, cannot claim a constitutional right to engage in their pursuits. In all cases, people organize primarily because organization is one way for them to enhance their influence in our political system. The cliché "in numbers there is strength" applies especially in the political world of interest groups. Whenever people combine their resources, they usually enhance the possibility that they will achieve their goals.

Organizations touch every aspect of our lives; members of the Canadian Medical Association bring us into the world and members of the National Funeral Directors Association of Canada usher us out. The doctors have an interest in managing government policies affecting the delivery of medicare, and the funeral directors want to be free of government controls for the services they provide.

There are three important reasons why interest groups are so commonplace in Canadian society. First, the more diversity there is in society, the greater the variety of interests that will emerge. Canada is culturally, socially, and economically diverse. These characteristics provide an especially fertile soil for the growth of groups. Millions of Canadians live scattered over a vast land made up of many regions with distinctive traditions and cultures. There are at least 85 religions, each claiming thousands of followers. The diversity of races, religions, and ethnic origins makes us more heterogeneous than many other societies. This diversity prompts people to organize to protect their interests.

Canada's parliamentary system of government encourages the growth of group organization by multiplying the points at which such groups can gain access to the government (Pross 1985). Political authority is spread over many individuals and government agencies, the Cabinet, the bureaucracy, the courts, and Parliament. And the more chances there are to influence public policy, the more organizations there will be that seek to exercise that influence.

Recent trends that have fostered such openness and accessibility include a proliferation of minor political parties, electoral financial and broadcasting laws, access-to-information laws, and more accountable decision making that encourages and even sponsors inputs by interest groups at the Cabinet and parliamentary levels.

Our highly decentralized federal system of government reflects and fosters the diversity of the country. Governing authority is spread among ten provinces and two territories, and thousands of municipal structures. This decentralization causes people to organize on a great many levels, and to wage battles over public policy on a variety of fronts. Because provinces and municipal governments exercise significant power so directly over our lives, groups also must organize at those levels to protect their interests.

The inability of our political parties to represent all interests intensely and effectively may help explain the number and strength of interest groups. The media have challenged the role of parties as the primary means of communication between the people and their government and as an institution capable of reaching many people quickly.

Interest groups are an integral part of the political milieu, and their behaviour is conditioned by the nature of political parties and the parliamentary system. The effectiveness of interest groups in influencing the direction of public policy on behalf of a cohesive body of people has challenged the viability of political parties by luring precious political dollars from the public.

Other important differences should be noted. Political parties select, nominate, and elect candidates for public office: If elected, a political party assumes the responsibility of governing the country, and creates and enforces public policy. When out of power, a political party presumably behaves as an alternative government, offering competitive courses of action and criticizing the incumbent opposition. The main arena of political parties is the electoral system.

The interest group pursues much more limited objectives with considerable purpose and intensity of effort. Interest groups are not motivated by the desire to get elected: They focus their energies directly on the people they represent. They can raise and spend money and otherwise initiate political action in ways outside the legal scope of party functions. Interest groups may work through political parties, but when party representation becomes massive and unwieldy, interests operate directly on the structures of government. Interest groups are often experts and specialists in some aspect of public policy. In that regard, an interest group has only a handful of key policies to push, whereas political parties represent and advocate the widest possible range of issues.

Since the 1960s, in Canada, many new groups have organized. No one really knows how many groups there really are. But an ever-increasing number of people are becoming active in protest groups, local organizations, and special interest groups. Along with the perennial issues of unemployment and other economic realities, we are now animated by a variety of social and human-rights issues. Some of these have given rise to powerful broad-based movements that represent the elderly, gays and lesbians, women, consumers, environmentalists, and moralists. Few of these issues sharply divide our political parties. Thus, activists have had to move outside the parties to push their causes most effectively. And therein lies the power of the interest group.

## THE ROLE OF INTEREST GROUPS

Only recently have Canadians debated the nature of interest groups and their role in our democratic society. Do interest groups corrupt the representative process in a parliamentary

system of government, or do they contribute to effective government? Should they be controlled by government, and, if so, to what extent?

Those who strongly defend interest groups see politics as an open democratic process where groups organize and compete for political power. Supporters stress the competitive struggle among groups and find it beneficial in limiting the control of any one group. Opposed to this point of view are those who view the political process as controlled by a more cohesive set of decision-makers. They see the governing structures as adequate to make representative decisions, without so many interests intervening in the system. Those who are opposed to them consider special interests to be already represented by political parties and the roles they play within the parliamentary system of government.

Defenders of interest groups say that they fill voids left by the political parties and give Canadians another opportunity to take their claims to government. Interest groups give underrepresented segments of the population an opportunity to have their voices heard, thereby making government and the policy-making process more representative of the diverse perspectives that exist across the country.

The growing presence of interest groups in the Canadian political system affects the economy of governing. Because so many groups make claims on society, they can increase the cost of public policy. Most interest groups seek to further their own causes with little regard for the demands of other groups, or people who may not be represented by any organized groups. Hemophiliacs who received HIV-tainted blood want government compensation, businesses seek deregulation and tax loopholes, consumers want protections on what they consume, and students want better-subsidized education programs.

Besides enhancing the parliamentary system of government by providing increased representation and participation, interest groups increase public awareness about important issues, help draft the public's political agenda, and act as watchdogs to guarantee the effective implementation of government policy.

## Representation of Interests

Interest groups "represent" people before their government. All sorts of people — physical therapists, professors, campers, gays and lesbians — have found that banding together and hiring a person or group of persons to advocate their interests in Ottawa or in the provincial capitals increases the likelihood that issues of concern to them will be addressed by government and, they hope, favourably acted upon.

Members of Parliament represent a multitude of interests — some of them conflicting — from their own ridings and provinces. Government administrators are also pulled in different directions when they exercise discretion on policy implementation. Interest groups supplement official representation and are directly involved in the legislative process. Interest groups articulate their members' concerns, presenting them directly and forcefully to members of the different branches of government.

Canadians are not equally represented by interest groups. Generally, the rich and educated are better represented than the poor and uneducated. And many segments of the Canadian population are still not organized, or are underorganized, and thus underrepresented by interest groups.

## Political Action and Protest

Interest groups are also vehicles for political action. They provide a means by which likeminded people can pool their resources and channel their energies into collective political action. People organize their interests because they know that it is much easier to get government to listen to a group than to an individual. One farmer asking for govern-

ment supports will not probably get very far, no matter how persuasively the case is made. But thousands of farmers united in an organization stand a much better chance of getting policy-makers to consider their needs.

Political action can take the form of protest — sometimes legal and sometimes illegal. Peaceful but illegal protest activity, where those involved allow themselves to be arrested and punished, can target policy-makers directly or indirectly through public opinion.

Greenpeace (an interest group that links the concept of peace with the environment) attempts to influence public opinion by means of dramatic political participation. They are an environmental and peace interest group that practises protest and civil disobedience. Throughout the 1970s and 1980s, Greenpeace has staged many political protests. The *Rainbow Warrior*, flagship of the Greenpeace organization, represents this action-oriented role. To protest the dumping of toxic wastes and sewage in the ocean, they have rammed sewage vessels, trying to prevent them from reaching the high seas. To protect endangered whales, members of Greenpeace have placed themselves in the path of harpoons, narrowly missing being struck. Others have clung to nuclear-powered ships on the high seas to protest nuclear weapons, or parachuted over coal-powered plants to protest acid rain–causing emissions. Their goal is always to generate publicity and get their activists into dramatic photographs that will rouse the general population into taking action.

## Issue Education

As part of their mandate to represent certain interests, interest groups help educate their members, the public at large, and government officials. With money, an interest group can mount public relations and advertising campaigns that affect public opinion, which, in turn, will affect public officials.

In some instances, interest groups try to produce a groundswell of public pressure to

Greenpeace, an interest group that links the concept of peace with the environment, attempts to influence public opinion by means of dramatic political participation. The photograph shows a Greenpeace Foundation sailing vessel. *Source:* W. Griebeling/Comstock.

influence the government. Computers and satellite links make national communication efforts even more effective. Interests groups may commission polls to find out what the public sentiments are, and then publicize the results. The intent of this activity is to convince policy-makers that public opinion overwhelmingly supports the groups' positions.

Some interest groups, such as Greenpeace, are prepared to propagandize the public on issues that affect the environment. Interest groups usually present only their side of the facts, but this does bring more information out into the open, where it is evaluated and absorbed by the public. The content of their messages can range from very detailed and technical kinds of information to strong rhetorical demands for policy changes.

Groups use public relations techniques to shape public opinion through the media. When a group's political interests are threatened, representatives of the group use the media to make the group's views known. Group leaders will make a special effort to cultivate contacts in the media for such purposes.

In some instances, groups buy time or space in the media to present their points of view to the public. Ads in newspapers and magazines, and on television, educate the public, foster a positive image for the group, and promote a public-policy position. Groups also may stage events, such as rallies or pickets, to attract media coverage to their cause.

Some interest groups, and corporations that act as their own interest groups, engage in strategies to create a favourable public image of what they do. This calls for public relations efforts, often not directly related to a specific political issue, legislation, or bureaucratic regulation. Instead, the efforts are aimed at improving the public image of the industry or group.

Advertising by corporations and groups on radio and television programs, the sponsoring of events such as the participation in the Olympics by Canadian teams, the Canada Games, or commercials extolling the virtues of corporate research in matters of social concern are approaches used more and more by interest groups. By building a reservoir of favourable public opinion, groups believe it is less likely that their legislative goals will be met with opposition by the government.

### Building the Public Agenda

An interest group's role in educating the public on certain issues is related to its role in building the government's policy agenda. As groups mobilize to push their policy goals, they often bring into the public forum issues that might not otherwise have been placed on the agenda of government. Interest groups bring new issues into the public limelight.

The Humane Society, for example, has been around since the turn of the century but has tended to remain low key on issues involving the abuse of animals. But more aggressive groups, such as Ark 11 and the Animal Alliance of Canada, have placed animal rights on the public agenda, pressuring universities and companies to change the ways they treat animals in matters of research or when animal products are commercialized.

Putting issues on the public agenda does not necessarily mean that an interest group pressures a governmental body to act: It can also mean that the public is made sufficiently aware of a certain practice or policy to call for changes to be made. Interest groups make the government aware of problems through their advocacy and try to see to it that something is done to solve them, either directly, involving the government, or indirectly, by getting the public involved.

### Public-Policy Watchdogs

In addition to trying to bring about political action in the form of laws or regulations, interest groups keep a close watch on the administration of laws once they have been passed. In this regard, they analyze in detail legislative and administrative activity. Interest group representatives keep close watch on the rules and regulations administered by Canadian bureaucrats. They follow government programs relevant to their members, keeping abreast of developments where policies are being implemented.

When problems emerge, interest groups push public administrators to resolve them in ways that promote the group's goals. Interest groups are in regular contact with government officials to discuss enforcement and to lobby against regulations that would hinder their interests. When group interests appear to be threatened, representatives swing into action: They publicize the potential threat, mobilize group and public opinion, meet the administrators, and ask members of Parliament sympathetic to the "true intent" of the original legislation to intercede with the erring bureaucrats.

## TYPES OF INTEREST GROUPS

Interest groups come in many shapes and sizes in Canada. Some have large memberships, such as the Canadian Labour Congress with

2 million members. Others have small memberships of fewer than 20. When most people think about interest groups, they immediately think of those groups that have a direct economic interest in governmental actions.

In the most general sense, everyone has an economic interest. But some economic interests are much better organized than other types of groups. In the past, business, labour, and agriculture have been well organized for economic purposes, although recently consumers, environmental groups, and women's groups have organized well for their interests.

All economic interests are ultimately concerned with wages, prices, and profits. Social and political interests are concerned with equality issues, human rights, and quality of life. Public policy in Canada affects all interests through regulations, taxation, subsidies, and grants.

Professional groups such as the Canadian Bar Association and the Canadian Medical Association have been particularly successful in furthering their own interests in federal and provincial legislatures. Financial institutions, such as the Canadian Bankers' Association, often are less visible than other interest groups, but play a key role in shaping fiscal and monetary policy in Canada.

## Agricultural Groups

At the time of Confederation, farming was the predominant industry in Canada. Immigrants were lured to Canada to farm its vast lands and to find prosperity in agriculture. The ideal of the small family farm attracted thousands of European settlers to Quebec, Ontario, and Canada's West.

But the number of farms has dramatically declined, from about 750 000 in the late 1930s to about 250 000 in the early 1990s. Yet, in spite of a reduction in farms and farm workers, agricultural productivity has steadily increased.

Agricultural interests are represented by a variety of general and specialized groups. Farmers and their organizations are a clientele group long recognized as vital to the heritage and economy of the country. The federal Department of Agriculture (Agriculture Canada) was established in 1867 to support and work with farm and agribusiness interests. Its responsibilities cover so many aspects of the agricultural industry that farmers have had to organize into many different groups just to represent their concerns before government. Yet farmers remain independent in many of their demands and have never united or spoken with one voice.

During the 1970s and 1980s, many farmers piled up increasingly heavy debts. By the 1990s, there had been an unprecedented number of farm bankruptcies, notably in Ontario and on the prairies. Large numbers of farmers were forced to leave farming; some went on welfare. The crisis in farming generated a number of new support groups and organizations dedicated to lobbying on behalf of the farmer.

In the 1990s, traditional, old-line farm organizations are being eclipsed by the rising political power of a new constellation of agricultural interests. International trade, agricultural chemicals, and commodity groups have moved to the forefront as farm-based interest groups, while family farms are still disappearing. Farms no longer make up a significant bloc of interests, but these newer agricultural interests are exercising increasing clout.

## Business Groups

In Canada, business groups form the oldest and most heterogeneous kinds of interests, originally representing trades and crafts, banks, insurance companies, and manufacturers. For example, the Canadian Manufacturers Association — which today recognizes the globalization of business and supports free trade — was established in 1871, at first as a group formed to protect Canadian manufacturers by calling on government to erect trade barriers.

The commercial community in Canada has many umbrella groups that speak for the overall interests of business. Today, one of the most prominent of such groups is the Canadian Chamber of Commerce, established in 1925. It is a federation of more than 500 community chambers and boards of trade located throughout Canada. It is the only interest group in Canada with active partner organizations in every federal riding. The National Chamber is also Canada's largest and most representative business association. It already has an extensive organization, expertise, a large membership, and a long-standing relationship with key actors in government.

The Canadian Chamber of Commerce encourages its members across the country to contact their elected officials about issues of concern at the national, provincial, and municipal level. As Canada's premier advocate for business, the Chamber of Commerce provides leadership in anticipating major issues that affect the competitiveness of Canadian businesses both domestically and internationally. It monitors federal, provincial, and international issues, and communicates these views to policy-makers in Ottawa and to the Canadian public (see Table 8.2).

Trade associations are made up of business firms in the same or related activities. They are among the most visible business lobby groups in all parts of the country. Thousands of business groups dispense information and other services to their members. The Canadian Sugar Institute, the Canadian Textiles Institute, and the Air Transport Association of Canada are examples of thousands of such organizations that embrace every type of business or industry and deal with legislators and bureaucrats on a regular basis in Canada. They wage public relations campaigns to win public praise and support for their industry, and they lobby for legislation or for the implementation of regulations to protect and enhance their industry.

Most businesses (97 percent of them) in Canada are small. These business enterprises, the most common business organizations in

**Table 8.2 The Chamber of Commerce as a Pressure Group**

| Expressed Goals |
| --- |

- Maintaining pressure to reduce government deficits
- Promoting the interests of the business sector on economic, social, and constitutional issues
- Lobbying the government to ease the tax burden as a means to improve competitiveness
- Ensuring that reform of legislation affecting employment (such as UI) reflects the best interests of employers as well as employees
- Monitoring the free-trade agreements, the FTA and NAFTA
- Lobbying to dismantle interprovincial trade barriers
- Promoting the adoption by all businesses of environmentally responsible policies and practices

Canada, have never been shy in dealing with government. Their interest is "profit," and their members are managers, workers, and stockholders. In many of Canada's firms, a busy public relations department encourages employees to speak out on issues affecting the company's well-being.

All businesses inevitably affect the politics of the communities in which they are situated. At the federal level, some national companies have offices in Ottawa to maintain contact with officials. Smaller companies call on lobbying consultants and trade associations to speak for them. In Canada, many large businesses are **multinational corporations**, whose business affairs cross national boundaries and whose public relations agents deal with officials in many different countries. The various business interest groups do not always agree on what government policy as it affects them should be. For some, such as those that make computers, favour free trade because foreign sales are very important to them. But others, such as car manufacturers and textile manufacturers, favour restrictions on foreign imports because their market is primarily in Canada and they want to protect it.

In Canada, business groups are quite united on issues such as lower business taxes, fewer government regulations, the restriction of labour unions, and reduced federal and provincial spending on social programs (Coleman and Jacek 1983). Business enterprises want maximum freedom of competition and freedom to determine investments, prices, and output policies, including the freedom to close down and lay off workers when business is unprofitable.

### Environmental Groups

Since the 1960s, rising concerns for the environment have produced a proliferation of environmental interest groups in Canada. The Sierra Club of Canada, incorporated in 1993 (having first established chapters in 1970), has a membership of 5000, and lobbies for clean air and clean water and opposes construction activity that spoils scenic areas. The number of environmental groups grew following the OPEC embargo in 1973 as Canadians considered alternative energy sources, each with its own environmental effects.

Hundreds of groups organized, focussing on the wilderness, forestry, wildlife, and fisheries. The discovery of significant levels of acid rain, the pollution of thousands of Canadian lakes and rivers, ozone depletion, hazardous waste, the greenhouse effect, and oil spills off Canada's coasts generated even more groups across the country. Consumer advocacy groups have expanded at the provincial level, especially in areas where environmental questions affect health and consumer affairs.

But the recession of the 1990s took its toll on the environmental movement. Groups such as the Friends of the Earth, Pollution Probe, the Canadian Wildlife Federation, and the Sierra Club had to lay off some of their

staff in the recessionary economy. The environment fell slowly down the list of priorities Canadians wanted to address, and jobs and the economy quickly rose to the top of the public agenda. Green products, which had flooded the consumer markets in the 1980s, met with much less success than expected in the 1990s.

Despite the apparent lessening of the general public's attention to environmental issues, environmental interest groups continue to grow at the grass-roots level. These are the groups that are instrumental in lobbying the federal, provincial, and municipal governments to establish environmental-protection programs and regulations to preserve clean air and water and other threatened environmental resources.

### Labour Groups

When people think of labour as an interest group in Canada, they usually think first of its more visible side — labour organized into unions. Local trade unions date from before Confederation. The first unions were formed by workers in small crafts and skills guilds in the nineteenth century. Less-skilled workers began to organize in the 1870s as the Canadian affiliate of the Knights of Labor, an American union.

The first widely successful confederation of labour in Canada was the Trades and Labor Council of Canada (TLC), established in 1883 and eventually to become an affiliate of the American Federation of Labor (AFL). The TLC organized skilled workers, representing their interests in issues of pay, the length of the work week, occupational safety, and other labour needs.

There were turbulent times in the Canadian labour movement in the early decades of the twentieth century (Panitch and Swartz 1988). More than a decade of labour unrest, punctuated by increasingly violent strikes, preceded the Winnipeg General Strike of 1919. During that strike, the RCMP were used to

disperse strikers, resulting in dozens of casual-
ties and one death. Coercion against workers
was the norm in Canada prior to the 1940s.
The right of workers to free collective bargaining was not recognized by the federal government until 1945.

During this time, the Canadian Congress
of Labour (CCL) was organized to represent
all workers by plant and industry, rather than
by crafts, and became the affiliate of the U.S.
Congress of Industrial Organizations (CIO).
These two main wings of the Canadian labour
movement merged in 1956, forming the
Canadian Labour Congress (CLC).

Today, in Canada, industrial unions them-
selves function as independent interest groups.
For example, the Canadian Union of Public
Employees (CUPE), the largest union in
Canada, educates Canadians about the public-
interest side of their organization as it would
affect such programs as medicare and the
North American Free Trade Agreement
(NAFTA). And the American Train Dis-
patchers Association, the smallest union in
Canada, with nine members, also engages in
public education.

Unions in the 1990s are more concerned
about the global economy than ever before.
Low wages in other economies have diminished the Canadian job market. Steel once
made by Canadian workers is now made more
cheaply by lower-paid workers in Korea and
Venezuela. The global connection has increased labour's interest in international economic policy. Bargaining over wages and work
conditions is left largely to individual unions.

The voice of unions is firmest on economic
issues that directly touch their members. These
include labour–management relations, occupational health and safety, minimum wage, plant
closings, and unemployment insurance.

Labour has another side, less visible but
numerically much larger than unionized workers in Canada. The majority of Canada's working people (about 62 percent) do not belong
to unions. For example, workers in the new

high-technology industries are much less likely
to be unionized than are workers in the old
smokestack industries they are supplanting.
Because non-union workers are not organized,
they lack political and economic influence.
Although some of their interests are protected
by government labour legislation and by the
examples set by their more organized counterparts, their opportunities for political representation are usually limited to the actions of
individual workers and negotiators.

The problems faced by organized labour
in Canada reflect decades of economic slide.
Labour's share of Canada's work force has been
dwindling, with only about one-third of
all workers counted as union members. The
major membership growth since 1960 has
been in the public sector. This growth has
barely compensated for declining membership
in other areas. Union strength is still highest
in older industries that are declining in numbers, such as the steel and automotive industries. As an interest group, labour's future rests
in part on organizing new industries and workers in the services and public sector.

## Women's Groups

The women's movement is older than the
country if we consider the pre-Confederation
activities of feminists in Canada. But the modern movement began to flourish during the
women's suffrage movement in the early 1900s.
In 1900, women made up only 13 percent of
the labour force, but, by 1990, women comprised the majority of the labour force. Members of the women's movement became active
in social and political reform groups, trade
unions, and human-rights groups.

Groups advocating women's equality have
mushroomed in the past two decades and range
from large, mass-based organizations with a broad
agenda, such as the National Action Committee (NAC), to much smaller groups with very
specific interests, such as groups protesting violence against women, pro-life and pro-choice
groups, and political and economic action groups.

The activities of women's interest groups have shifted from Ottawa to provincial and municipal governments, where issues can gain effective public visibility at the local and regional level. Family and child care have joined more confrontational issues such as abortion and pornography as major concerns. Along with other interest-group organizations, many women's groups take part in protest actions and public demonstrations.

By the 1990s, the goals of the Canadian women's movement had spread to a wide variety of public interests. Women have played pivotal roles in campaigns for their own interests; nuclear disarmament; children's rights; and the legal treatment of drunk drivers, abusers, and those who neglect their family-maintenance and child-support responsibilities.

## TACTICS OF INTEREST GROUPS

Interest groups use a number of tactics to achieve their goals. Some try to influence parliamentarians directly, by means of demonstrations, boycotts, and sit-ins, whereas others seek to mould public opinion and influence them indirectly, by means of campaign activity, grass-roots pressure, and public relations. Sometimes interest groups will form broad coalitions that create a more powerful consensus of interest on an issue.

In Canada, no group has enough staff, money, or time to get everything it wants from the governing system. To assume that interest groups are well-oiled political machines that effectively and regularly move Parliament and its bureaucracies may be to overstate the reality of pressure-group politics. Members of Parliament themselves often have to pressure groups to get them behind their legislation.

The Coalition for Gun Control is an example of a successful Canadian interest group. The group pressured the Ministry of Justice on gun control, which led to a new law requiring tougher standards for storage,

handling, and transportation of firearms. The law places controls on who can buy firearms and imposes stiffer penalties on those who violate the law. Since January 1995, by order-in-council, the AK-47 semi-automatic rifle (the "Rambo rifle"), and the less powerful versions of the paramilitary rifle (the Ruger Mini 14) used by Marc Lepine to kill fourteen women in Montreal in 1989, have been prohibited under federal law in Canada.

Nailing down the specific effects interest groups have is difficult, in part because the influence they have is linked with other policy influences such as party leadership and Cabinet politics. Because the tactics of lobbyists work best with those already on their side of an issue, getting the right people in government to agree is a key strategy of interest groups.

### Lobbying in Canada

Some of the money raised by interest groups is used to pay for the services of lobbyists, who represent the organizations before government. In Canada, some of the large lobby houses have Washington affiliates, and a number of Ottawa firms even have a Washington observer.

Lobbyists make sure that people in government know what their clients want and that the organizations they represent know what government is doing. When the government issues new regulations, lobbyists are ready to interpret their content and implications for the rank-and-file members. In Canada, interest groups tend to lobby bureaucrats about twice as much as they do MPs (Kernaghan 1991, 444). MPs are lobbied less often because elected officials play only a minor role in governing. Ottawa lobbyists focus on the Prime Minister's Office (PMO), key Cabinet ministers, and senior bureaucrats as the key targets of their trade.

Some lobbyists are full-time employees of an organization; others are employees of public relations or government consulting firms who are hired as lobbyists on retainer. Lobbyists are valued for their experience and knowledge of how government operates. Often they are people who have served in Cabinet or in Parliament, where they gained first-hand experience with government.

The primary job of the lobbyist is to inform policy-makers. Lobbyists provide government officials and their staffs with a constant flow of data that support their organizations' policy goals. What lobbyists really try to do is to convince policy-makers that their information deserves more attention and is more accurate than that presented by other lobbyists (see Table 8.3).

The classic interpretation of lobbying involves contacting public officials directly. Making personal contacts in an office or in a more informal setting is probably the most effective lobbying technique. Compared with other lobbying tactics, direct personal contact is relatively inexpensive, and it minimizes problems of misinterpretation by allowing questions to be asked and influence to take place on the spot.

In Ottawa and in the provincial capitals, lobbyists are judged on the basis of their skill in giving information and persuading others. This means speaking with senior bureaucrats, ministers, and their staffs; supplying them with information; and making informal social contacts. Such contacts are usually routine. The job of the lobbyist is to give information to those who make or implement decisions. Lobbyists gain their reputations for the quality of the information they are able to provide and for the issues or groups they represent.

Making contacts with decision-makers is not as simple as it once was. Power is increasingly dispersed on Parliament Hill, and in provincial capitals throughout the executive branch of government and its administration. To some extent, governments have learned to immunize themselves against the interventions of lobbyists. They know that not every citizen belongs to an interest group that lobbies, and that some groups are big and powerful and can dominate the government agenda.

## Table 8.3 What Many Lobbyists Do

- Contact senior bureaucrats, Cabinet ministers, and executive bodies
- Contact informally party leaders, party organizers, and legislators
- Use influential constituents to contact government officials
- Gather information and do technical and scientific research
- Launch letter and telegram campaigns
- Communicate with the press and the media
- Run advertisements in the media
- Publicly endorse certain candidates
- Consult with government
- Public relations
- Shape the public agenda
- Do favours for politicians and administrators
- Take legal action on behalf of clients
- Present public testimony before royal commissions, task forces, and inquiries

## Legislative Lobbies

The exact origin of the practice of lobbying is uncertain. In the mid-seventeenth century, British members of Parliament were frequently approached by constituents and others who wanted government favours. These advocates came to be referred to as "lobbyists" because they waited in lobbies to meet with legislators.

In Canada, lobbying emerged as a natural product of twentieth-century politics, the growth of government and the proliferation of interest groups coinciding in the complex human interactions of a technological society.

At first, lobbying involved just hobnobbing with legislators, providing them with published materials and advisory letters, and testifying before inquiries. Some lobbyists have been indirectly involved in the actual process of drafting legislation by collaborating with Cabinet ministers and their staffs on matters affecting the technical precision of a Canadian law.

### Administrative Lobbying

The idea of lobbying extends far beyond the corridors and offices of Parliament. For many lobbyists, the battle is not won when a bill is proclaimed as law. Lobbyists also try to influence the senior bureaucrats who wield so much power and discretion once a law has been passed. These can be the deputy ministers and those who work closely with them in the federal and provincial bureaucracies.

The effect of a law depends not just on how the legislation is drafted but also on how it is translated into action. Lobbyists keep close watch on how the written rules and regulations are administered by the agencies and departments of government.

For example, regulations outlawing discrimination on the basis of gender and sexual harassment were drafted with very broad guidelines by Parliament and in provincial legislatures. Both women's rights groups and interests opposing them lobbied for years to influence the regulations.

In influencing bureaucrats, interest groups use most of the tactics already described. Some groups will try to influence who gets appointed or shuffled within the bureaucracy to certain senior administrative positions. The influence of lobbyists in the appointment process is especially crucial in the case of regulatory agencies, such as the National Energy Board, the Atomic Energy Board, the Canadian Radio-television and Telecommunications Commission, the Immigration Appeal Board, and the Pension Appeal Board. By influencing appointments to these types of agencies, the regulated industry or group can improve its prospects of favourable treatment when important government actions are conducted that affect them.

### Campaign Lobbying

Most interest groups try to influence government policy, no matter which party forms a government. But some interest groups get involved in elections on a partisan basis. The Canadian Labour Congress has traditionally, for many years, identified with the New Democratic Party, and the Canadian Chamber of Commerce is often identified with the Progressive Conservative party in philosophy and outlook.

The extent of electoral activity depends on the group's resources — that is, its money and votes. Since most political parties and candidates need both, interest groups are a major electoral resource. Within the structure of a political party, interest groups can make demands that the party and its candidates move to the group's position. Parties are useful in organizing the collective energies of many interest groups and aggregate their concerns in the governing system.

Very few groups become involved in campaign politics by embracing only one of the major political parties and giving up access to the others. Many groups use a non-partisan strategy, such as appearing before policy committees of many political parties or providing campaign support to at least the three major parliamentary parties.

### Lobbying the Courts

Most members of the public see the Canadian court system as standing apart from the rest of government in its objectivity, impartiality, and immunity from external pressures. According to this view, interest groups would have little hope for influence in this area.

However, a more realistic appraisal is that the courts, like other branches of government, are susceptible to the influence of interest groups. And, just as MPs and bureaucrats do, judges also make policy. Knowing this, some interest-groups try to achieve their goals by getting involved in cases and persuading the courts to rule in their favour.

Taking legal action may be a more effective interest-group strategy than lobbying senior bureaucrats and legislators. Taking policy goals to court offers a way of neutralizing battles that may have been lost on Parliament Hill. Consumer groups and environmentalists have used suits against government business and polluters to change the direction of public policy or to get certain matters on the public agenda.

Interest groups can file civil suits, represent defendants in criminal cases, or file legal briefs known as *amicus curiae* (friend of the court) briefs. Although the tactic is infrequently used in Canada, interest groups can formally make their interests known to the courts in cases in which they are not themselves parties. Such briefs present argument and evidence in favour of a judgement that will be advantageous to the members of the interest group.

Some groups use the courts to make opposing groups negotiate with them. Environmental groups frequently challenge developers who threaten the environment in order to force them to bear the heavy costs of defending themselves and to delay their projects.

Courts are a special part of the political process, and the etiquette for interest groups to attempt persuasion is different for them than for other governmental institutions. Judges are not supposed to be "lobbied" in traditional ways, and usually are not. Judicial propriety prohibits justices from meeting face to face with interest-group representatives. However, judges do receive mail, watch TV, read the newspapers, and see protests outside their court buildings. Of course, tradition dictates that jurists be oblivious to all this, but they are only human, and it is difficult to imagine that they are totally immune to such influences.

## Regulating the Lobbyists

Lobbying is linked to the cherished democratic rights of assembly and free speech. However, concern that some groups have too much influence or that interest-group representation is biased in favour of certain segments of society has prompted calls for reform (Stark 1992). One effort to apply reforms to a galaxy of interests, all potentially trying to get the attention of governments, is to know who the lobbyists are.

Canada requires lobbyists to register with the government under the Lobbyists Registration Act, 1989. The act is administered by Consumer and Corporate Affairs Canada, which categorizes lobbyists in two tiers: Tier 1 lobbyists are professionals who lobby on behalf of others; Tier 2 lobbyists are employees of companies and associations that lobby the government. In Ottawa, there are about 3000 registered lobbyists (Tier 1, approximately 1000; and Tier 2, approximately 2000) who put pressure on the government on behalf of their clients or interest groups.

The act was implemented in response to allegations that friends of successive prime ministers and Cabinet ministers were gaining access to them on behalf of powerful corporate clients. The registration requirements were supposed to reassure the public that undue influence was not being exerted by the rich or well connected.

Lobbyists are allowed to give only vague descriptions of the government policy or program they seek to influence and do not have to say whom they lobby, either in the bureaucracy or in the Cabinet. Accordingly, the federal registry of lobbyists does not reveal what its registrants are trying to achieve when they huddle in private with ministers and mandarins, nor does it show whom was lobbied.

Another problem is that some lobbyists do not register, and yet these non-registered lobbyists compete with registered lobbyists for the attentions of government. Fines for not registering under the act can be issued. Lack of legal enforcement can adversely affect the credibility of the government to regulate lobbyists in Canada. But, at the same time strict enforcement may call into question the wisdom of trying to regulate contacts between people and their government.

# CONCLUSION

A political party is a broadly based coalition of interests that attempts to form a government by winning elections. All political parties perform vital functions in Canada's political system. The transfer of governing party takes place through political parties. They offer the electorate a choice of rival candidates and platforms, and serve as a link between government and the people by helping to hold parliamentarians and bureaucrats accountable to the voters. They also reconcile conflicting interests in society, staff the government and the opposition, and link the political executive with the legislative branch of government. Relationships among the federal, provincial, and territorial governments depend, to a considerable degree, on ties among party officials and political leaders.

The organizational elements that make up a political party include the voters; the party activists; people who serve as delegates to leadership conventions; those who perform the day-to-day, grass-roots work of party politics; and the party leaders outside the government, who frequently control the party machinery and party leaders.

Throughout most of Canada's history, two major political parties have been arrayed against each other at the federal level. Yet minor parties have been active throughout the twentieth century. Some, such as the Bloc Québécois and the Reform Party, demonstrated after the 1993 federal election that they can be propelled to positions of power and influence in the House of Commons.

Even though they lack explicit constitutional standing, political parties are vital to the functioning of Canada's parliamentary system of government. In the traditions of responsible government, political parties are responsible and accountable to voters and must comply with the rules of Parliament when their members are elected.

Over a period of time, all political parties must respond to the pressures for, or against,

political and social change, or pay the price of extinction. Generally, there are noteworthy differences among parties that are evident from campaign platforms, leadership style, and party organizations. Furthermore, platform promises are often carried out.

The "brokerage" role of Canada's major parties in mediating interest groups (whether such groups are organized or not), and in resolving social conflict, is of tremendous importance in a parliamentary system under pressure. All major political parties try to form a broad national base by appealing to diverse groups in society. The parties that fail to form a government play a valuable role in Parliament as opposition, and in the electorate, by offering alternative policies and serving as rallying institutions for the public.

Interest groups are private groups that attempt to influence the government to respond to the shared attitudes of their members. When people organize to express attitudes held in common, and to influence the government to respond to those attitudes, they become involved in the political system as interest groups. Lobbying, public relations, media relations, and grass-roots pressure are among the techniques employed by interest groups to achieve their objectives. One of the most powerful techniques is lobbying, communicating with the Cabinet, senior administrators, and legislators to try to influence their decisions.

Interest groups perform certain functions in Canada's political system that cannot be performed as well through the conventional structures of government. They provide representation that supplements Parliament and political parties. They facilitate the resolution of group conflict and perform the functions of government watchdogs. They provide an alternative access to government and ultimately affect the quality of how we govern ourselves.

## GLOSSARY

**caucus** A private meeting of members of a political party. The members of a party in Parliament are also referred to as a "party caucus" and meet regularly to discuss legislative strategies.

**coalition** A collection or cluster of distinct groups that join together; agree, at least temporarily, on a desirable outcome; and work together to achieve their goals.

**Conscription crisis** In the 1917 federal election, compulsory military service divided the country along linguistic lines such that every riding in which French was the majority language voted against the government and conscription.

**critical election** An election that heralds a new political alignment, produces a new government, and reveals significant shifts in voter identification with particular political parties.

**ideological parties** Political parties that are organized around some coherent view of the proper relationship of government and society, such as the Marxist–Leninist view of political economy.

**latent interest group** A group of people with a common characteristic who have not yet banded together but who may be led to organization and action when their common interests are threatened.

**mass parties** Political parties that seek to attract the support of anyone in the electorate.

**multinational corporations** Large companies that carry on business in two or more national economies simultaneously.

**multiparty system** A competitive electoral relationship among three or more political parties that contest elections and may win seats, and/or form coalitions with the governing political party of parties.

**one-party dominance** A political party system in which one political party predictably wins successive elections over a significant period of time.

**party era** Periods in which voters sustain a political party in government that tends to win successive elections.

**party identification** The loyalty felt by individuals toward a particular political party.

**two-party competitive system** A competitive political party system that tends to enable two political parties to win seats in Parliament, to form governments from time to time, and to prevent minor parties from gaining legislative representation.

## RECOMMENDED READING

*Associations Canada 1991: An Encyclopedic Directory.* Mississauga, Ont.: Canadian Almanac & Directory Publishing Co. This handy composite contains a comprehensive list of organized groups and associations in Canada.

Bakvis, Herman. 1991. *Canadian Political Parties: Leaders, Candidates and Organization.* Toronto: Dundurn Press. Part of the series of works commissioned by the Royal Commission on Electoral Reform and Party Financing, this thirteenth volume provides articles with a comparative focus on parties and their leaders in Canada, Germany, Great Britain, the United States.

Boardman, Robert, ed. 1992. *Canadian Environmental Policy: Ecosystems, Politics and Process.* Toronto: Oxford University Press. This book attempts the important task of explaining the complex and significant web of political relationships and processes that underlies environmental policy and advocacy in Canada.

Brooks, Stephen, and Andrew Stritch. 1991. *Business and Government in Canada*. Scarborough, Ont.: Prentice-Hall Canada. This book examines the powerful role of business in Canadian politics and government, with a look at the pressure tactics and business–government relations.

Christian, William, and Colin Campbell. 1990. *Political Parties and Ideologies in Canada*, 3rd ed. Toronto: McGraw-Hill Ryerson. This comprehensive study presents and analyzes of traditional Canadian ideologies as they manifest themselves within the confines of Canada's political parties.

Clarkson, Stephen, and Christina McCall. 1990. *Trudeau and Our Times*. Toronto: McClelland & Stewart. Besides being an interesting biography, this book offers an insightful analysis of Liberal party politics as it affected repatriation, the Charter of Rights and Freedoms, and relations with the Parti Québécois during Trudeau's era of political leadership.

Coleman, William, and Grace Skogstad. 1990. *Policy Communities and Public Policy in Canada*. Mississauga, Ont.: Copp Clark Pitman. This book provides a comprehensive collection of articles first presented at a conference at the University of Toronto in 1989, with contributions made by many distinguished Canadian scholars who focus on the public-policy advocacy of agricultural, fishery, forestry, labour, language, and women's groups.

Dobbin, Murray. 1993. *Preston Manning and the Reform Party*. Toronto: James Lorimer. This book traces the development of the Reform Party, examines its policies, and evaluates the leadership qualities of Preston Manning.

Thorburn, H.G., ed. 1991. *Party Politics in Canada*, 6th ed. Scarborough, Ont.: Prentice-Hall Canada. This book compiles excellent essays on topics ranging from the historical background of political parties to the role of interest groups.

Whitehorn, Alan. 1992. *Canadian Socialism: Essays on the CCF and the NDP*. Toronto: Oxford University Press. This book gives an account of the development of social democracy in Canada.

CHAPTER

# THE MEDIA AND PUBLIC POLITICAL OPINION

**A**mong the most important personalities shaping our political opinions are national news reporters. The content and character of national news and public affairs programming — what reporters and producers choose to present and how they present it — can have the most far-reaching effects on how we learn about politics and government. The disclosures of reporters can greatly enhance — or fatally damage — the careers of our political leaders and the institutions they represent. Often, their comments can rally support for — or intensify opposition to — national and provincial policies. Their regular appearance in the media can shape and modify, if not completely form, public perceptions of events, issues, and institutions. They bring a world of political information to us every day.

A common element of most television and radio newscasts is the anchor: the reporter or announcer in charge who leads viewers on the tour of the day's events and who symbolizes trust and stability in a sea of unsettling news. Successful anchors become household names and trademarks of the station or network we watch regularly.

Although anchors, like actors, must put on makeup, read scripts, and be schooled in the arts of professional conduct and show business, these people have special qualifications to do what they do. As executive reporters in their fields, each has had a large say in what stories go on the air, and each writes some of the script. Hovering over their professionalism, however, is the pervasive network, concerned with its ratings, mandate, and profits. Like other journalists, these professional broadcasters must worry about the quality of coverage they provide. After all, they are held responsible by the public and the network.

Lloyd Robertson, of CTV Television Network, is one of Canada's most recognized and respected news anchors. *Source:* David Street/CTV Television Network Ltd.

Because literally thousands of events occur in the world every day, space and time constraints mean that most of them go unreported. Selecting what becomes news is especially critical in television. Some events seem destined to become the news: national disasters and political turning points such as elections, revolutions, and military invasions. Still others, qualify as news because they are "scoops" — attention-getting stories that are likely to become majors news events. There seems to be a substantial agreement among anchors on what, besides a scoop, constitutes the most newsworthy stories.

During the 1990s, two outstanding Canadian journalists have anchored the evening news and parliamentary reports on the major national networks: Don Newman, *Capital Report* for the CBC; and Lloyd Robertson, *CTV News* for CTV.

Don Newman, the senior parliamentary editor of CBC Television news who anchors *Capital Report*, is one of Canada's most experienced and best-known journalists and broadcasters. His program has, as its mainstay, national political news, usually originating on Parliament Hill and often off the floor of the House of Commons. But Ottawa is not the only focus. On his program, he regularly interviews provincial premiers, ambassadors, foreign politicians, and a variety of experts in many fields such as political science, economics, and public administration.

The editorial direction of the program is set by the host, Don Newman who brings more than 30 years' experience to *Capital Report*. During his career, he has covered many federal elections, the Meech Lake and Charlottetown accords, numerous leadership conventions, American presidential elections, the Watergate scandal, and the Camp David peace talks.

Lloyd Robertson is one of Canada's most recognized and respected news anchors, and brings four decades of broadcasting experience to the CTV television network. He is the chief anchor and senior news editor of *CTV News* and *CTV Radio News*. He has excelled at the anchor desk for numerous *CTV News* specials, including CTV's coverage of the Gulf War, budgets, Canadian elections and leadership conventions, political and economic summits, the openings of Parliament, and U.S. presidential elections.

Robertson has been a Gemini Award winner for "Best Anchor/Interviewer" (1992 and 1994) and has been chosen many times by Canadians as the "most trusted TV journalist." Robertson plays an important role in how the news is reported. He knows that television news reporting calls for interpretation of events, rather than just a bare statement of what happened. Every news story has a particular structure that must be portrayed — a beginning, a middle, and an end. These are not only the essentials of narrative, but reflect the character of the reporter — in this case that of the TV anchor.

---

## INTRODUCTION

Most of what Canadians know about politics and government comes to them directly or indirectly, through the mass media (Siegel 1983). Newspapers and television are the primary sources of information, and radio and magazines are secondary mass-media sources. Whatever medium we consume, there is no question that it will probably provide some political information, either directly in a news story, or indirectly in a documentary or a program that addresses a public concern such as unemployment, crime, or government mismanagement. In so many ways, the media reflect and shape our political reality.

Canadians spend nearly half of their leisure time exposed to the media in one form or another. Most of us read newspapers and magazines every day. Just these two media alone consume nearly four hours of our time every week. Even though, in Canada, magazine circulation is tiny compared with exposure to the other three major media, magazine readership is heavily concentrated among educated and informed people. As a result, magazines

may in fact have an impact out of proportion to their numerical readership.

One can also identify "minor" media in Canada, which can expose Canadians to political information of one kind or another. The minor media are everywhere, consumed by us on our way to work, in public places such as malls and airports, and on highways and thoroughfares. Books, many of which focus on political issues, are regularly read by Canadians. Similarly, most people habitually read pamphlets, billboards, and posters on buses and streetcars. The influence of the minor media in presenting political information may also be greater than the size of their audience suggests. For example, opinion leaders, who are often able to influence others, are heavy consumers of books.

Over 80 percent of Canadians have radios, about three for each family, and about 97 percent of us have a television (Statistics Canada 1991a). The average Canadian adult watches television for about three hours each day, and the average child watches for four hours. Children are introduced to the world of politics by TV because, in Canada, the average child spends 15 000 hours (625 full days, or 21 complete months) between birth and age seventeen in front of a TV screen.

Consequently, by the age of ten, Canadian children obtain most of their information about the outside world from TV and school rather than from their parents (Lambert, Yackley, and Hein 1971). By the time a child graduates from high school, he or she has spent more time watching television than in a classroom. By the time Canadians die, they will have spent nearly two years of their lives just watching TV commercials, and about six years watching all kinds of programs.

The mass media are the various forms of communication that reach a large audience without any personal contact between the senders and the receivers of messages: newspapers, magazines, books, television, radio, movies, videos, tapes, and records. These media developed primarily as information technologies within the context of a democratic ideology, especially one that espouses freedom of speech and expression.

But these are only some of what constitute mass communications in Canadian society. Because of the revolutionary changes in communication technologies, the power of the media and their political impact now must also be thought to include communication networks, telephones, satellites, fibre-optic equipment, and home computers.

These technologies are potentially all carriers of news, comparative government data, political debate, and analysis of world affairs. Today, the mass media introduce us to an extraordinarily diverse array of political information, which we now regularly "internalize" as general knowledge on a daily basis.

Although the media do not comprise a branch of government, or even a cluster of organizations established especially to influence government, they are widely credited as having an enormous impact on the performance of governments, and thus on how we are governed. In fact, few analysts will deny that the mass media are as much a part of the governing process as are the formal institutions of government themselves (Black 1982).

For our political and governing systems to work effectively, they must communicate with the very people they claim to represent. Governments must inform their citizens, political groups must persuade their members, and voters must send messages to their policymakers in order for Canada's democratic and parliamentary system to function.

The news promises to reflect the world's reality, and yet the process of mass communication can often distort that reality, by twisting facts or events, or by ignoring or minimizing certain facts or events that could be equally important. Rather than think of the media as a mirror that reflects things as they *are*, it might be more useful to think of them as searchlights that seek out or illuminate some things specifically. From all of the events that occur in Canada, and in the international community, the media can report only a handful as the news of the day. After the media select events to report, they decide where to report them — on the front page, or at the top of the newscast, or somewhere else.

The relationship between the various governments in Canada and the media is shaped by laws and traditions that accord the media a degree of freedom greater than that found in most other political systems. While many politicians and government leaders might secretly want to control the media, they also depend on the media for the advancement of their careers and public policies. At the same time, the media themselves have evolved during this century, attracting a class of experts with unique professional standards and values to the top positions of Canadian journalism.

## THE MEDIA IN CANADA

### Early Canadian Journalism

In the 1990s, Canadians accept instantaneous communications as a fact of life. In the 1860s, it took days, and sometimes weeks, for news to travel just from Ottawa to Halifax and vice versa. In addition to the slowness of communication, the early forms of mass communication were rudimentary and limited (Rutherford 1978, 1).

In the early days of journalism, political opinions were still being expressed in the form of political pamphlets. Writing styles were characteristically pompous and literary, with much emphasis on trivial facts and biased political commentary. Imaginative publishers lured readers with photographs, cartoons, comic strips, and scandalous stories of sex, crime, and political intrigue.

The early Canadian newspapers, some established long before Confederation, were not independent observers of politics. For example, the Halifax *Gazette*, the Quebec *Gazette*, and the Montreal *Gazette du Commerce et Littéraire* depended heavily on government support and were blatantly sympathetic to the governments that backed them.

By the time of Confederation, nearly 300 papers were publishing weekly or biweekly in Canada, most of them allied with some political cause and expecting the patronage of governments. These first creations of a media appealing to the masses were much influenced by political factions and the fledgling political parties that expressed their views to an elite and limited audience (Kesterton 1967).

Although, by the 1860s, most Canadians (80 percent) were literate and liked to read numerous print media, as is still the case today a great deal of political information was carried by rumour. At the time of Confederation, the popular press was in its infancy, but technological changes that allowed faster and cheaper printing were bringing newspapers to larger numbers of people.

The telegraph had just been invented, which led to the establishment of the first news wire service (the Associated Press). The Associated Press provided political information from outside of Canadian localities and gave readers an international perspective. Telegraph wires were used by Canadians to import news from the United States. The installation of an undersea cable across the North Atlantic in 1866 gave Canadians access to the political and commercial world of Europe. The increasing volume of information available to print encouraged many newspapers eventually to publish daily, and thus to find a wider readership.

## Newspapers and Magazines

It was no accident that Canada became one of the world's first media states. Canadians had embraced democracy, creating the climate for a free press and a ready audience for magazines and newspapers. The drive to build a nation from sea to sea promised publishers a growing market with a mass audience. By the turn of the century, newspapers were germinating all over Canada. Most were profitable and popular with the public, many increasing their appeal with sensational stories.

Publishers were beginning to play an important role in Canadian politics, regularly presenting political stories from other papers in other Canadian cities. Although they were independent in the sense that they were privately owned and not affiliated with a political party, newspapers were quite biased and opinionated. These independent papers took sides in political debates. Publishers', editors', and reporters' attitudes seeped — sometimes flooded — into their prose.

Gradually newspapers abandoned their ardour for editorializing and adopted the practice of objectivity so as to reach as many readers as possible. The popular press began to shrink the political world of Canadians, building a common thread of experience and fostering an emergent national political culture. In Quebec, the French-language media were in their infant stages, but they were sensitive to the cultural distinctiveness of the province and wanted to protect French-speaking people from the tidal waves of English and American cultural product flooding Canada.

By the first decade of the twentieth century, magazines such as *Saturday Night, Canadian Home Journal, Messenger canadien,* and *Queen's Quarterly* became important vehicles of opinion on contemporary questions of public policy. Magazines differed — and still do — from newspapers primarily in what they covered, their frequency of publication, and the quality of their production. The first Canadian magazines focussed on narrow topics, such as a political personality or an event. The more permanent character of magazines allowed them to be important as forums for opinion than as news reports. The power of the press had been established, was felt, and increasingly pushed parliamentarians and provincial legislators in one direction or another.

### Radio

Radio broadcast journalism generated another communications revolution in Canada. At first, the news was available only on radio receivers which were owned and operated by small numbers of technical experts. One of the world's great radio pioneers in radio technologies had a unique connection to Canada: Guglielmo Marconi sent the first wireless message across to Europe from Glace Bay, Nova Scotia. Less than twenty years later, the Marconi Company was established in Montreal and began the operation of what is today CFCF.

Radio did not just provide entertainment and military and navigational information: It affected the social fabric of Canada, its culture, its politics, and its economy. It had the power to colonize its listeners across national borders, and to cause them to identify with other national interests and pop cultures, in particular those thriving in the United States. After the formation of two U.S. networks, NBC and CBS, Canada's largest urban stations began to join with them, creating a new and loyal market for American culture.

The development of radio during the 1920s also brought many listeners into direct personal contact with some Canadian politicians, allowing people to hear the words of politicians expressed in their own voices over great distances (Vipond 1992). Radio quickly became an attractive entertainment medium, but it also became a powerful political instrument. In the 1930 federal election campaign, the leaders of the Liberals and the Conservatives appealed to national voters on the radio.

Radio enabled politicians to reach people who could not or did not read, and it allowed them to reach people more directly. No longer did they have to go through political parties or editors. Politicians took radio seriously and delivered their speeches in prepared text written especially for broadcast. By the 1930s, more than 30 percent of Canadians had radios and listened to them faithfully. Radio had gone from novelty to necessity in just ten years.

In 1928, the King government launched the Aird Commission, which reported in 1929, recommending the creation of a Canadian Radio Broadcasting Commission on the model of the British Broadcasting Corporation (BBC). The Radio Broadcasting Act was passed by the Bennett government in 1932, and the Canadian Radio Broadcasting Commission (CRBC) was established in 1936, which then was reorganized as the Canadian Broadcasting Corporation (CBC).

The CBC networks and their private station affiliates quickly made radio the top-ranking source of news in Canada. The Radio-Canada French network was established by the CBC in 1938, becoming an instant success in the province of Quebec. By linking together hundreds of radio stations, the CBC was instrumental in transforming radio into a national medium. Radio reporting, especially during the Second World War, brought home the drama of world events.

The advent of television dramatically affected radio's position as the dominant "mass" medium in Canada. For many, there was scarcely anything radio could do that TV could not do better. By the 1960s, radio had been reduced primarily to a local service medium and, with the exception of CBC, catered only to local audiences. Radio programming tended to specialize more, targeting particular audiences in terms of news and entertainment. AM stations significantly lost listening share, and FM stations filled the void. Unlike the early days of radio, when Canadians listened mostly to American programs, today Canadian-content rules regulated by the Canadian Radio-television and Telecommunications Commission (CRTC), have reduced radio programs produced in the United States and airing in Canada to a very low number. And, by the 1990s, fewer than 5 percent of Canadians were listening to U.S. stations.

Notwithstanding the national power of television to reach millions of Canadians very quickly, politicians still find radio a useful and flexible means for reaching their constituents. Many Canadian stations are beginning to use satellite connections to provide syndicated programming, giving radio a renewed national relevance for political broadcasts. And, during the 1992 referendum campaign, radio was a very successful medium for advocates to deliver their arguments on both the "Yes" and the "No" side and to reach Canadians in their local communities on an important national issue.

Radio and the press are now seen as "the media," to be treated with as much respect as television by politicians and governments across the country. Political parties and government leaders prepare their positions deliberately and formally for either airing or printing. They recognize the political importance of the media and use the media for their own purposes.

## Television

Television was the next stage of technical advance, one that has had profound effects on the conduct of Canadian politics and on the governability of the country. To voices were added pictures, actions, and gestures that were observable simultaneously by millions of people. Such visual dynamics had enormous political advantages.

The onset of the Second World War temporarily froze the development of television technology, but, following the war, growth in the medium exploded (Rutherford 1990). The first party leadership conventions were televised in the 1950s, and the federal campaigns of 1957 and 1958 received extensive TV coverage. By that time, politicians were quick to exploit the dramatic possibilities of television.

Today, television claims by far the largest mass audiences in Canada, with much persuasive evidence that it is the most influential of the media. The Carleton School of Journalism (1979) found that a majority of Canadians (52 percent) reported receiving most of their campaign information from television, followed by newspapers (30 percent) and radio (11 percent).

Television's influence on Canada's political process is thus recognized by all who engage in or study it. Some studies point out that those messages presented live or via TV are more effective than audio-only radio messages, which in turn, are more effective than written messages (Williams 1975). There is also evidence that an individual's understanding of political issues can be significantly influenced by the manner in which television news presentations "frame" them (Iyengar 1987, 815).

In Canada, the influence of American-produced programming affects the type of information Canadians consume (Williams 1986). Over 70 percent of the viewing time of English Canadians, and 65 percent of that of French Canadians, is spent watching American programs.

Cable networks exist that devote more time to news-type programs, and some offer programming in which viewers can "talk back" to participants. Satellites, home computers, home video, and computer phone system technologies all continue the process of rapid change in political communication. For example, in 1992, a "dial-a-leader" system — whereby computer software programs permitted thousands of Nova Scotia Liberal party delegates to communicate their vote for a particular leadership candidate by telephone — was used for the first time in Canada.

The Canadian political system has moved rapidly into the age of high-tech politics, a politics in which the behaviour of citizens and policy-makers, as well as the government agenda, are shaped by the technology of mass communications. Inevitably, this has revolutionized how we do politics and government.

## Ownership of the Media

In Canada, private ownership of most media is an accepted fact. Most Canadians would regard government ownership of the media as unacceptable for the obvious consequences it might have on our political freedoms in a democratic system of government. Private ownership of the media is seen to offer a more stable and continuing forum for government criticism. The print media are privately owned, but, among the broadcast media, the CBC is publicly owned.

The question of media ownership has been the focus of some major studies, including those by J. Porter (1965), W. Clement (1975), and D. Taras (1990). In addition, two federal commissions have documented an increase in concentration of media ownership in Canada. The Davey Commission's report drew attention to the extent of corporate concentration in the Canadian media, and the Kent Commission concluded that the ownership by fewer and fewer large corporations is "entirely unacceptable for a democratic society."

Three of the wealthiest men in the world control vast corporate empires that include the mass media in Canada. K.C. Irving, worth nearly $7 billion (U.S.), owns most media outlets in New Brunswick (Canada 1986).

Another individual, Kenneth Thomson, worth an estimated $6 billion (U.S.), is referred to as a "newspaper magnate." He owns nearly 60 percent of Canada's English-language newspapers. Another billionaire, Conrad Black, controls a chain of daily and weekly newspapers as part of his vast corporate empire. Among his companies, Hollinger Inc. acquired a 23 percent stake in Southam Inc., one of Canada's largest media corporations. In 1994, cable TV magnate Ted Rogers came to control a multibillion-dollar cable and publishing empire of Maclean Hunter Publishing, which holds investments in cable television in Canada and the United States and more than 200 periodicals published in 10 countries. Rogers Communications has extensive investments in cable television, broadcasting, cellular telephones, and long distance telephone service.

Indeed, "concentration" is the word that best applies to the mass media in Canada today. Four large publishing companies control nearly 70 percent of newspaper circulation; two large chains win 80 percent of all movie attendance in Canada; six companies control about 60 percent of cable-TV subscriptions; and four major publishers gain 90 percent of the total revenues in the market for Canadian consumer magazines (Vipond 1992, 79).

This economic reality raises questions about the role of the media in Canada's system of government. Among newspapers, competition for reporting the news has all but disappeared in many Canadian towns and cities. Chain ownership is fast dominating the newspaper and television business. Locally owned newspapers and television stations may soon be a thing of the past.

Aside from the laws of competition that apply to all businesses, the only significant limitations on the broadcast media comes in the form of regulations issued by the Canadian Radio-television and Telecommunications Commission. Does the concentration of ownership increase the political power of these corporations and ultimately affect the governability of the country?

## Government Regulation of the Media

In Canada, governments have regarded the media as — among other things — instruments to foster and protect culture (Meisel 1986). In this regard, the media have been seen by Canadians not only as guarantors of democracy, but also as agents that play an essential public-sector role in the cultural life of the country.

Since 1867, a special role for government was perceived to exist — namely, to promote, monitor, and regulate the cultural industries in Canada (Collins 1990). The one area where the Canadian government has been significantly involved in regulating the mass communications media is radio and television. Outside of radio and television broadcasting, the print media in Canada have not felt the heavy regulatory hand of government to the same extent. Once something is published, a newspaper or magazine may be sued or prosecuted under the laws of libel and obscenity, and those that relate to the truth of what is written. There are also laws to protect the privacy of individuals when they are published.

The federal Department of Communications (Communications Canada) was created in 1969 to encourage the growth of telecommunications and to manage and regulate the airwaves, and was assigned special responsibilities in 1980 for the arts and culture.

In the 1990s, this federal department regulates broadcasting in a way that contributes to Canadian cultural, economic, and social objectives. The national communications system is regarded as a nation-building infrastructure that has crucial bearing on the achievement of Canada's social and economic goals. The minister of communications is responsible to Parliament for formulating and implement-ing legislation governing certain crown corporations, such as the CBC, the National Film Board, the National Archives, the National Library, and museums.

Regulation of the broadcast media arose out of necessity. Today, the Canadian Radio-television and Telecommunications Commission, one of eleven regulatory agencies organized under Communications Canada, licenses radio and television stations. A corporation wanting to establish a television station in Canada cannot simply purchase the necessary equipment, hire staff, and begin broadcasting. It must secure a licence to operate on a particular frequency from the CRTC.

When the first radio stations began to broadcast at any frequencies, the Canadian government learned very quickly that the airwaves are a vital public resource. The now rather detailed provisions of CRTC licensing developed from the premise that some basic regulation of who could broadcast at what frequency was needed to prevent a hopeless scrambling of signals. In contrast, there are no technical limits on the number of newspapers and newsmagazines that can be disseminated in a particular market, other than the limits imposed by the market forces themselves. But the airwaves are a finite common property, defined by the laws of physics, rather than simply by the laws of supply and demand.

Another important area of government regulation affects political advertising. Canada has created rules for the allocation of free-time political broadcasts and paid political advertising. As far back as the 1930s, the Broadcasting Act prescribed equitable time slots for political parties and candidates, paid for by them or their identified sponsors.

By the 1990s, Canada was still one of only four democratic political systems to permit paid political advertising. Free-time advertising on both the public and the private networks is regulated by the Canada Elections Act. A "broadcast arbitrator" negotiates with registered political parties or with referendum committees to determine actual free-time allocations. The position of broadcast arbitrator as authorized by the chief electoral officer was created in 1983 to mediate between broadcasters and political parties and groups to determine a fair allocation of time for political messages.

The development of cable television in Canada has also affected the debate over broadcast regulation because cable companies are bringing many more U.S.–produced programs into Canada. Most Canadian households subscribe to cable television, linking them directly to U.S. networks. Cable offers the possibility of much greater choice and competition in parts of Canada previously served by only a few stations. Cable also boosts the chances for success of news, political analysis, and educational stations in the private sector.

## MASS COMMUNICATIONS AND THE POLITICAL SYSTEM

Two Canadian scholars stand out as having been particularly influential in forming the understanding of mass communications in Canada — Harold Innis and Marshall McLuhan. Innis (1951) focussed on the ways changes in communications technology affect the political and social structures of society. He noted that the media can stimulate institutional and political change and alter the belief systems throughout society.

Innis's work had significant influence on Marshall McLuhan, who noted the physical characteristics of the media (the layout of print, seeing the flow of pictures, hearing the sound of voices and events) as major influences on how we think and what we think about. For McLuhan (1964), the ways we mass-communicate affect the forces of individualism, collectivism, nationalism, and regionalism, and ultimately our ability to govern ourselves.

Most students of mass communications systems have concluded that the relationship between the governing system and the media is best viewed as a two-way street. Political communication in Canada's parliamentary democracy tends to move in two directions: from government and opposition to citizens, and from citizens to government. But, in Canada, mass political communication seldom goes directly from the government or the political system to citizens without first passing through the media.

The media also transmit information from the citizens to the government by reporting the positive and negative reactions of people to political events and government policy.

### The Sources of Political Communication

Political communication usually includes sources, a message, a medium (or channel), an audience, and an effect. At the grass-roots level of "source," politicians, government leaders, and pressure groups communicate with the masses. All these groups consciously try to influence or defend government policy and are political communicators at the source. Cabinet ministers, party leaders, and spokespersons for interest groups spend much time spreading ideas among the masses. Conversely, the people send messages to their representatives in many ways — letters and phone calls, meetings, votes, and so on.

### The Medium and the Message

Politicians and bureaucrats regularly speak to the public by means of speeches, press releases, departmental publications, Statistics Canada reports, party platforms, and so on. The most common form of this kind of mass communication is the *news release* — a prepared text given to reporters, producers, or editors that seeks verbatim presentation in the media. *News briefings* are formal presentations used

News conferences appear to be freewheeling, but they enable politicians to control the presentation of information and to exercise damage control. *Source:* Andy Donato, *The Toronto Sun*, October 19, 1993. Reproduced with permission of Andy Donato.

often by politicians, government leaders, or members of their staffs to enable reporters to ask questions, in controlled surroundings, about news releases. A *news conference* usually involves questioning high-level officials such as members of Cabinet, especially the prime min-

ister or a premier. News conferences appear to be freewheeling, but they enable politicians to control the presentation of information as well as the time allotted to each reply.

Just as important are informal messages, such as off-the-record remarks, information leaks, or political interviews. Leaks are rarely accidental; they are a deliberate release of information by an official to a reporter for a specific purpose. Besides doing the journalist a favour, the official may be trying to embarrass a supervisor, expose bureaucratic waste and bad management in the public service, provide damaging detail to discredit a policy, or test the political waters for a new idea. Leaks may spring from the pettiest personal motives or the loftiest patriotic sentiments, but they are nevertheless an important source of political information. They give reporters an "inside" source and enable the mass media to analyze the events and behaviours of the political world and to transmit the content of political information to the public.

Each of the categories of the media, that is, the print media (newspapers, magazines, and journals) and the electronic media (radio and TV), has certain advantages and disadvantages in putting out a story. Intricate detail and complex political arguments are best stated in print, through newspaper stories, books, and magazine articles.

Television is constrained by its peculiar technical and physical limits, the most important being time; stories must be reported in only a few minutes. But, in Canada, television news enters many more homes than does news from the other media. Emotional and personal aspects of an event are most powerfully conveyed by the medium of television. With TV, the news audience actually sees the broadcasters as well as hears them, giving the presentation of the news a "personalized" character.

Just as the appearance of the newscaster becomes important for television viewers, so does the appearance of the news itself — both phenomena contribute to the special impact of television news coverage and, to a great extent, determine the news that television chooses to cover. Organized protests and spontaneous political clashes perform well on television, so television producers tend to show them. Violent conflict of any kind, especially unfolding dramas that involve weapons, such as the OKA stand-off in 1990, rate especially high for visual impact.

## The Effects of Media on the Political Agenda

The media can intervene in every phase of public life, especially those areas related to government and politics. They are the eyes, ears, and voices of how we govern ourselves. The powers of disclosure and confrontation can have enormous impact on success or failure in the world of politics. The media regularly expose us to the performance of our politicians and to the institutions where they work.

The mass media have historically played an important role in defining the political agenda. The media control "agenda setting," that is, prioritizing issues by emphasizing some and downplaying others with the intention of making the public aware of them and opening them up for discussion (Winter, Eyal, and Rogers 1982). Those who "set" the political agenda are those who define the issues for discussion and debate among government decision-makers. Since this process is selective, the public may not learn all of the facts about a particular political issue, but they can gain general impressions from the media, such as feelings of apathy, cynicism, fear, trust, powerlessness, or support.

Of course, media influence seems most obvious during political campaigns. Candidates for Parliament and provincial legislative assemblies aim their messages at the media, which hold the key to the larger audiences and the attentive publics. Campaign staff and constituency workers must become familiar with the technical aspects of media coverage — camera angles, necessary equipment, timing, and deadlines — to plan their political events to accommodate the media. They must be aware what events are photogenic or telegenic and interesting enough to qualify as newsworthy.

By the 1990s, the art of putting the appropriate **spin** on a story or event had become highly developed in Canada, especially at party leadership conventions and during election campaigns. Spins were especially evident during the constitutional referendum debate of 1992 when the "Yes" side and the "No" side each tried to convince the media, and ultimately the public, that their position was gaining acceptance across the country. Journalists report on the different spins and how politicians try to manipulate news coverage.

## THE FUNCTIONS OF THE MEDIA

Understanding why the media matters with respect to how we are governed requires an examination of the various roles the media play in the Canadian political system. All of them can have political implications and are essential to the democratic and parliamentary processes.

### Entertainment

There may not be a direct and obvious linkage between entertainment and politics, but some programs introduce material that is politically controversial and that may stimulate public discussion. Segments of some programs focus on the right to die, unemployment, and other controversial topics, such as AIDS, incest, child abuse, and wife-battering.

Nearly everyone knows that some programs designed generally to entertain can also affect our political attitudes and beliefs, but not enough is known about how this effect comes about and what its result is. However, it is clear that this role of the media is part of the process of political socialization and is involved in the development of our general political attitudes and beliefs — as well as part of the development of opinion on particular political issues.

### Teaching Us about Politics

The media are now considered to be primary agents of political socialization in Canada, as elsewhere (Fletcher and Taras 1990). They influence the political ideas and beliefs of all adults, but especially young people and recent immigrants. The extensive presentation and coverage of the news from a Canadian perspective is a socializing process for these groups, as it can also be for everyone.

With exposure to the various media, people acquire historical knowledge (sometimes fictionalized); a familiarity with the peculiarities of Canada's political cultures; and an awareness of all the diverse regions, groups, and peoples in Canada, as well as what it means to be a Canadian. The extensive coverage of elections and referenda in Canada are an especially important feature of the socializing process for these groups.

Sometimes the media can dispel myths about the character of Canadian society. The widely publicized case of James Keegstra, the high school teacher from Eckville, Alberta, and those who supported his positions, revealed much about the extent and nature of prejudice and bigotry in Canada. The media, especially the CBC and the *Edmonton Journal*, focussed public attention on this complex case and disclosed the issues involved. Keegstra, who taught his views to his classes, blamed the Jews for almost everything — the cause of the French Revolution, the U.S. Civil War, the Bolshevik Revolution in Russia, and the First World War. He and other Canadians, like New Brunswick teacher Malcolm Ross and Toronto publisher Ernst Zundel, taught that the Holocaust was a hoax designed to gain support for Israel while the Jews clandestinely collaborated with Hitler. The extensive coverage the media gave to this story roused Canadians from the belief that Canada is always and universally a "tolerant society."

Subtle values — transmitted through the movies, popular music, comics, and TV and radio programs — affect our perceptions of ourselves, our governments, and the political process. While not labelled "political," they can transmit certain kinds of information.

Usually the media play a contradictory role in the process of political socialization. In some reports, they can generate public support for government by joining in the celebration of national holidays, the birthdays and accomplishments of prominent historic figures, political anniversaries, and citizens' accomplishments. In other reports, however, the media can erode public confidence in government by reporting problems in the economy, airing investigative reports on political and administrative conduct, and giving front-page and prime-time coverage to political critics and protestors.

### Identifying Political Issues

Producers, news editors, and reporters are said to function as **gatekeepers** because they decide which events to report and how to present those elements of a story they choose to report. They identify the political issues for public consumption, and they are usually selective about what goes through the "gate." Child abuse, violence against women, and water pollution were not major political issues before the media began giving substantial attention to these matters and helped place them on the political agenda.

In this regard, the power of information is important not only in that it reveals what the government is doing or not doing, or doing wrong, but also in that it determines what the government ought to be doing. The media will identify political problems and issues that need government intervention. Canadian journalists work in a long tradition of uncovering public wrongdoing, political corruption, and bribery, and bringing such abuses of the system to the public's attention. Closely related to this kind of **investigative journalism** is the media exposure of policy alternatives.

The media's powers of independent investigation and identification of political issues

have important implications. They not only can force governments at all levels to consider matters they may not have chosen to consider but also play a key role in the public's image of the performance of a government. They can increase or decrease a government's ability to govern by choosing to cover or not cover a particular policy or set of government actions. Little or no coverage can be worse than unfavourable coverage.

### Providing a Political Forum

Another function of the news media is to provide a political forum for political leaders and the public. Because politics is theatre, politicians usually want the events they influence to be "media events." Elaborate party leadership conventions at the national and provincial levels of political debates are events staged purposely for media coverage (Fletcher 1987).

Journalists try to be everywhere, covering everything from the trivial to the momentous. Major addresses, such as a political nomination or acceptance speech, are planned for peak TV viewing hours. Televised debates are the most conspicuous use of the media as political forum (LeDuc and Price 1985). The first televised debate in Canada took place during the Quebec provincial election of 1962, and at the federal level in 1968. Debates have become a key part of the electoral and referendum process in Canada, as witnessed during the 1984, 1988, and 1993 federal election campaigns, as well as the 1992 referendum campaign. The Charlottetown constitutional agreement (1992) touched off publicly staged debates all over Canada, especially one between Premier Robert Bourassa and Parti Québécois leader Jacques Parizeau.

Reporters may see these debates as personal contests. The media will be eager to declare who won or lost the debate, watching who stumbles, who appears uncertain in a response to challenges, or who makes false and inaccurate assertions about political realities. Some Canadian debates tend to be confrontational and emotional. There is often a real clash of personalities or views, heated dialogue between the candidates, sometimes with follow-up from questioners and moderators. The two televised debates of the 1993 election campaign were short on discussion of issues but long on finger-pointing and strident accusations.

Most debates are good media forums because they air challenging views and expose the issues on an equal footing before an election or referendum. Because debates are seen to be educative, attracting an intensive and attentive public, they are elevated to an institutionalized event during contemporary election campaigns. The public expects to see them, and candidates expect to participate in them as part of the ritual of getting elected.

As a political forum, the televised debate has the unique ability to heighten the impact of issues and to give credence to the idea that an issue can be "won" or "lost," all in how it is delivered to the viewer. The crucial fact about the practice of televising debates is that, although debates are now publicly justified as opportunities for voters to learn how candidates differ and perform, what candidates want is to capitalize on the power of television to project an image. They view the debate as a strategic opportunity to improve their images or to weaken the images of their opponents in the public eye.

After some controversy and considerable anxiety, the Canadian House of Commons became the first legislative body in the world to routinely televise its proceedings, beginning 1977. No regular TV coverage of the Senate is conducted. In 1988, the Canadian Radio-television and Telecommunications Commission licensed a Canadian Parliamentary Channel/La Chaîne (CPaC), which, by 1992, had 25 of Canada's largest and smallest cable companies as shareholders, becoming the Cable Parliamentary Channel (CPAC).

As a forum for televised debate, the House of Commons has become much affected by the presentation of its proceedings by the media. The attendance of MPs and their appearance in the House of Commons have improved since the cameras focussed on them.

Normally, the cameras show only the MP who is speaking, so that no empty seats will appear. Often, other MPs of the same party will temporarily sit in the empty seats of absent colleagues around whoever is speaking to give the public the impression that their party's attendance is high. MPs tend to enlarge the number of speeches they make, often gesturing with their hands to their "audience."

CBC and CTV network news programs usually include short segments from Question Period in their national news coverage. However, in the main, the public does not watch the televised House of Commons sessions. Perhaps for this reason, there is not much evidence that a televised forum for some of Parliament's proceedings dramatically increases or decreases the likelihood of the re-election of members. And because a great deal of what happens in the House of Commons at a given time happens in committees, this kind of media forum does not provide Canadians with a full view of legislative politics and decision making in action.

## Reporting the News

Early in Canadian history, much of the work of government and the actions of politicians occurred locally, in small towns and rural areas. Politics and government were "up close and personal": People could see them first-hand and could speak to their representatives in person, and ask them to explain or defend their actions.

Today, the work of government is far more complex and remote. Most Canadians never see in person the federal and provincial government officials whose decisions and actions affect their lives. The information we get about government policies, politicians, and events is reported to us through the media, whose personnel are usually not known personally by us either.

Full-time reporters usually cover local news stories — for example, city hall, the courts, police, business, society, sports, and local political news. The average newspaper rarely assigns its reporters to cover national politics. Many local stories come off the "provincial wires," which are provincial government news services, such as the Nova Scotia Information Services. But a great amount of print information is written out of the country. The newspaper masthead may say "Vancouver," "Regina," "Moncton," or "Quebec City," but when it comes to news of national and international politics, only a few reportorial organizations, with great resources, dominate the scene.

Most newspapers in Canada cover national and world news from syndicated articles or with wire service copy from Canadian Press (CP), founded in 1917. CP is the primary Canadian source of non-local news for most Canadian dailies. This major Canadian wire service connects Canadian newspapers with Associated Press (AP) and United Press International (UPI); with stories written by other reporters who work for other papers in the chain; or, occasionally, with material provided by "stringers" — people who contract to write for a "string" of newspapers. Fewer journalists work in radio and TV than in the print media. CBC and CTV have correspondents who specialize in international reporting, but, beyond that, there is little specialized reporting.

The idea of journalism as an autonomous profession in Canada dramatically altered the ways by which the mass media report the news. All major news media, such as CBC and CTV (Global is an Ontario-based network), seek to cover political events through firsthand reports from professional journalists on the scene. Reporters also rely heavily on sources for their stories — people who have special information about a particular event. Reporters and sources have a mutually dependent relationship. Each has what the other wants: Sources have information; reporters have the power to give it public visibility.

Often journalists will get information they report from other journalists because they work and travel together. This practice of reporting is called **pack journalism**, because of the group character of gathering and sharing stories, and reporting them as news. But sometimes a story hounded by the pack will not provide enough substance to sustain pursuit, and the chase is abandoned as quickly as it began.

## Interpreting Political News

Professional journalism invites many "shoulds." The media should be independent of politicians, reporting on them as fully and fairly as possible. Journalists should be independent of publishers who run the business side of the profession. The media should operate according to the canons of good journalism, seeking accurate and fair reporting. News people should write without fear or favour in the interpretation of facts, subject only to their standards of ethics and professional competency.

But, invariably, the media's interpretation and coverage of government policy and political events will affect the content and delivery of the news. Because the media are more or less free to decide what they cover and how they cover it, they will interpret the political world according to their own value system. And while the media may value their independence from government, many believe that a systemic bias exists wherever there is an interpretation of facts.

## Bias

The media are said to be "biased" whenever they add their own interpretation to their coverage or take sides in reporting the news. Bias may surface because of the political and ideological preferences of the people who work in the medium or because of public or commercial pressures to package the news in certain ways.

In some instances, glaring cases of bias appear in certain media. In most cases, however, bias in the news can even out over a period of time. Reporters may have more liberal or more conservative leanings than the general population, and even personally dislike certain political leaders. But bias counts only when it appears in a newspaper column or comes through a radio or television news program, and when it is just in the minds of those who report, edit, or produce the news.

Bias can also exist in those who read, listen, and watch the media. No one would deny the enormous impact of the media on opinion formation, or how extensively Canadians are tied to their sources of information in a vast continental mass communications system. But most Canadians do not watch TV, read the newspapers, and listen to the radio with minds empty of opinions and prejudices.

Canadians receive information in the context of existing predispositions that lead them, most of the time, to sort out and interpret messages so as to reinforce their opinions rather than to change them. Moreover, people watch, listen, and read in the midst of family and peer group influences that give them interpretations of the political reality. The interpretative frameworks are already there, and, for most of us, the message is quickly absorbed into our existing views of the world.

This is not to say that the media cannot alter our understanding of political events. Often bias may be unavoidable because of limitations on time or space in reporting the news, because of competition in the profession of journalism, and because of the specific training levels and personal biases of reporters.

Bias can result in situations of conflict and chaos, as in times of war and when stories are subject to censor approval. In regard to limitations, the quantity of news is finite: There are limits to what can fit in a newspaper or on an hour-long news program on the radio or television. Limitations on space and time constrain what can be reported and force someone to decide what is newsworthy. In the end, it is the editors, reporters, and publishers who decide what we read, hear, and watch on the basis of their standards of what is news, and on the basis of their preferences about how it should be reported.

The news media's competitive and organizational incentives force a concern with market share and, especially for the private media, with profits. The news, therefore, must be marketable and competitive. Reliance on market share and audience appeal has induced the news industry in Canada to monitor its audience very carefully. The ratings reports have resulted in a "ratings game" in which the media try to increase their ratings by adjusting the delivery, and even the content, of their news.

Gradually, in Canada, a powerful ethos has worked its way into the media, with emphasis on professional standards. University programs are now widely developed to teach journalists the technical tools of their profession and to instill in them professional standards. Today most reporters will acknowledge that their field has become a profession with its own norms and ethical standards, like diplomacy and law.

Other factors may have strong influences on the content of bias in reporting stories. What about media reporting during war? Is it still true that the first casualty of war is the truth? William Christian (1991), asked in a *Globe and Mail* editorial: "in domestic reporting, balanced coverage is fair, reasonable, and just. But is it appropriate in wartime?"

During the Gulf crisis, one CBC reporter made the comment that "our ships are arriving in the Persian Gulf." The report quickly portrayed a we/they dichotomy in the Persian Gulf story, describing Canadian vessels arriving, however late, in a favourable light against the threat of Saddam Hussein's "aggression." This kind of comment raises the question of whether the customary principles of neutral journalism apply in times of war, when Canada is involved and when Canadian reporters are sending the news home.

During the Gulf War, television reporters revealed that their stories were constantly vulnerable to censor approval. CBC and CTV journalists noted that certain governments placed restrictions on some classes of information that could be reported about the war.

The CBC's *The Journal* (February 6, 1992) reported on the role of **propaganda** in the Gulf War. The story, called "Creating Consensus," disclosed that all sides in a war manipulate the media so as to achieve a "fighting justification." During the airing of that night's program the argument was made that the media should not be blamed for inaccuracies in war coverage. CBC reporter Paul McGrath noted that the press was forced to report a standard line from the Pentagon. In that program he stated: "all information therefore is potentially tainted. All of it must be taken with at least a shaker full of salt."

It is interesting to note that, with the exception of CTV, both Canadian and American television focussed a significant amount of

**Figure 9.1 Evaluations of Saddam Hussein**

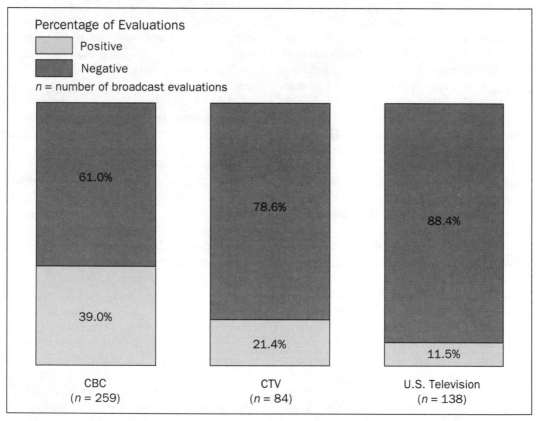

*Source:* National Media Archive, *On Balance*, Volume 4, Issue 6, Vancouver, B.C., 1991. Reproduced with permission of the Fraser Institute.

attention on Saddam Hussein (see Figure 9.1). On U.S. television, reporting of the Iraqi leader was quite usually negative (88 percent). But, on the CBC, although the balance of reporting was more critical than complimentary toward Saddam Hussein, 39 percent of the appraisals were positive. By contrast, only 21 percent of the attention given Saddam Hussein on CTV was approving.

On the CBC network, U.S. president George Bush received less than one-fifth of the amount of attention given Saddam Hussein. CTV, like the U.S. networks, provided less coverage of the U.S. president than of the Iraqi leader. CTV and the U.S. networks also gave less coverage to Bush than Hussein (see Figure 9.2). It is interesting to note that most of the coverage President Bush received on Canadian television networks was negative. The CBC evaluated President Bush adversely about 84 percent of the time, while CTV was somewhat less critical of him, giving 67 percent negative coverage. Only in the United States did the media's positive evaluations of Bush (about 56 percent) exceed negative assessments.

**Figure 9.2  Evaluations of George Bush**

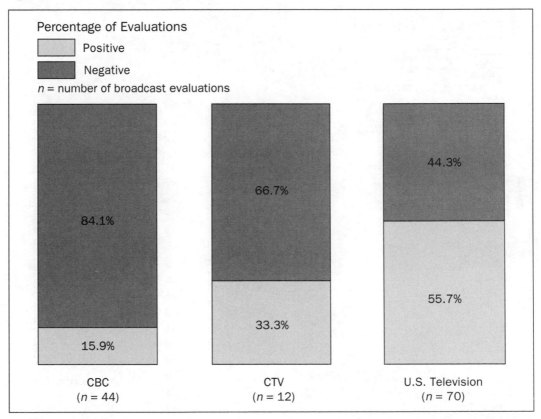

*Source:* National Media Archive, *On Balance,* Volume 4, Issue 6, Vancouver, B.C., 1991. Reproduced with permission of the Fraser Institute.

The one biased mechanism that was used by all North American networks to create a favourable domestic consensus focussed on the military strength of the Allied forces against Iraqi forces (see Figure 9.3).

All networks in both Canada and the United States invariably accorded superiority to the Coalition Forces in their reports throughout the war. North American reporters openly praised the capabilities of the Allied Coalition Forces and diminished the performance of Iraqi military forces. Nearly

three out of four CBC, two out of four CTV, and nine out of ten U.S. network statements about U.S. military capabilities were positive.

In the United States, 95 percent of domestic television reporting on its military was favourable. But it is noteworthy that, while the U.S. networks showed the greatest bias of support toward U.S. military efforts, they also tended to provide more favourable commentary about the performance of the Iraqi military than did Canadian television. In the United States, 46 percent of media evalua-

**Figure 9.3  Evaluating Allied Military Strength**

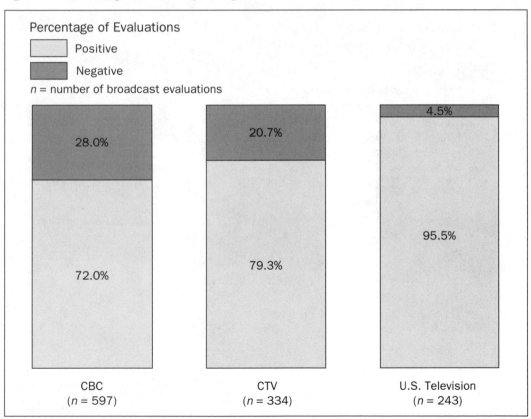

*Source:* National Media Archive, *On Balance,* Volume 4, Issue 6, Vancouver, B.C., 1991. Reproduced with permission of the Fraser Institute

tions were positive, while in Canada only 30 percent of CBC's and 26 percent of CTV's assessments of Iraq's military performance were favourable (see Figure 9.4).

## THE MEDIA AND OPINION FORMATION

Canada's many "publics" hold opinions about many things, and much public opinion comes from our exposure to the media. Our views on premarital sex, the existence of flying saucers, the virtues of jogging, and who manufactures the best car on the road in Canada are usually acquired with the help of the media. "Public opinion" refers to the content and distribution of a population's beliefs about anything. It is a measurable dispersion of individual opinions about issues or objects of general interest, usually those that concern a significant number of people.

In a country as vast as Canada, one cannot usually think of the "public" as a single

**Figure 9.4 Evaluating Iraqi Military Strength**

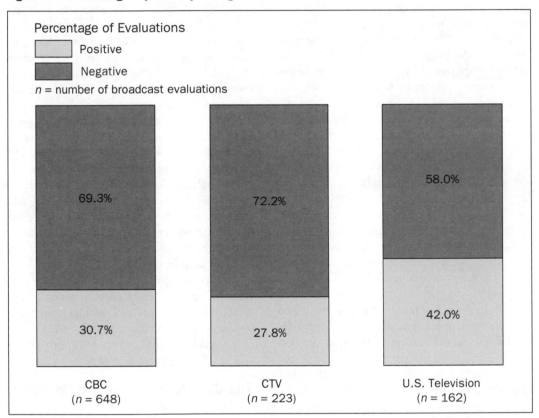

*Source:* National Media Archive, *On Balance*, Volume 4, Issue 6, Vancouver, B.C., 1991. Reproduced with permission of the Fraser Institute.

entity. Canadians tend not to think as a block. Unified public opinion is rare because the Canadian population is so diverse, as are its interests. Some Canadians are inactive in politics; some are active. Some are uninterested in political matters, and some comprise "attentive" publics. Above all, there are fundamental differences in what Canadians think.

Rather than asking about the impact of public opinion as a whole, political scientists ask about the impact of the opinions of special publics. Thus, we can say that public opinion represents the thinking of groups of people concerned about anything that affects them.

Public opinion is usually observed in terms of "direction," "intensity," and "stability." The *direction* of our opinions is demonstrated when we simply like or dislike something or someone. Public opinion is often mixed: Some individuals hold positive opinions; others, negative. *Intensity* is the degree to which we like or dislike something or someone. Intense opinions are most likely to spur action. *Stability* is also an important factor with respect to the impact of public opinions. An individual's opinion is most likely to change when it lacks intensity or information about an issue or object.

We know that the media influence our opinions indirectly, by providing the news and by transmitting the views of various opinion leaders in our society, as well as directly through advertising, editorials, documentaries, and commentaries intended to sway our opinions. We know that different media provide different coverage and reach different audiences.

Because other factors besides the media influence people's knowledge and attitudes about the world around them, it is exceedingly difficult to isolate the impact of a particular medium on a particular group of people. But there is considerable agreement that the media have an enormous impact on the public agenda, and that involves politics and government and the influence on political opinion.

## What Is Political Opinion?

Political scientists are especially interested in those opinions that affect the political and governing systems. The respected American political scientist V.O. Key, Jr., (1961, 14) perhaps said it best when he noted that **political opinion** consists of "those opinions held by private persons which government finds it prudent to heed."

Canadian governments may be more inclined to act in one direction or another when the public expresses strong preferences and perspectives on political issues. Political opinions are expressions of political values in day-to-day terms that political leaders want to know about. They indicate what the people holding them believe to be true or false, right or wrong, desirable or undesirable.

Political opinions have specific content; that is, they refer to identifiable objects or events in the real world of politics and government. They tell us how people feel about their parliamentary and municipal representatives, their decision-making institutions, and their national and provincial goals.

Political opinions reflect our ideologies, our political cultures, our conduct and expectations about how we are governed. Political opinions are significant because they shape and lead to public policy. People act in accordance with their political values and beliefs, and therefore political opinions make a difference. To be sure, many public opinions may lead to no action, but most political opinions direct political behaviour.

Political opinions affect the ability of government and political leaders to govern. They establish the parameters within which our structures of government and the political system operate. Political opinions are both a cause and an effect in the world of politics.

## The Qualities of Political Opinions

As is true of all the opinions Canadians express, political opinions have certain qualities. Each quality can have a consequence for government and the political decision-making process in the country. The qualities political opinions possess are content and relevance, direction and intensity, fluidity and stability, latency, and consensus and divisiveness.

### Content and Relevance

The levels of political knowledge that people carry with them affects the content of their opinions at every turn. People are more likely to express their opinions according to the *content* or knowledge they have on an issue (Pammett and Whittington 1976, Introduction).

When individuals are interested in a particular political question, they will probably take time to read about it and learn details about it. Government leaders know that the more knowledgeable Canadians are about politics, the more active they are likely to be and the more weight they will have to assign to their opinions.

But, for most Canadians, politics and government rank low in *relevance* in terms of position on the daily list of things to think about, well below family matters, jobs, health, personal relationships, sports, and entertainment. As a result, in the general Canadian population, the level of political information tends to be low. Many Canadians are not likely to remember who the members of their provincial and federal cabinets are. Some may not even be able to tell a questioner who their MP is, or their senator, let alone their aldermanic representative. Canadians do not spend much time remembering political facts that may not be relevant in their daily routines. And Canadians are also likely to forget political information quite quickly. Facts that are of vital interest to Canadians at one time tend to lose their importance as time passes.

But Canadians will express their opinions on most political issues, ranging from the competence of politicians to the complexities of the Canadian economy or constitution, even if their level of political knowledge and awareness is low. If opinions flow from little

information, they will change easily when new information is introduced. The result can be a high degree of instability in public opinion poll returns, or a high level of indecision on some political questions.

### Direction and Intensity

Political scientists as well as governments are especially interested in two other general dimensions of opinions: direction and intensity. *Direction* is a measure of whether an opinion is "for" or "against" a policy, candidate, or political event. Political opinion is usually mixed: Some people have positive opinions, others negative.

How strongly Canadians express their preferences comprises the *intensity* of their political opinions. Governments and political leaders in Canada need to know not only what people prefer but how strongly they prefer it.

Opinion analysts try to measure these preferences by tracking them on scales that describe them as "pro" and "con." Often opinions drawn from moral issues such as abortion and capital punishment tend to evoke strong pro and con opinions. Many political issues can likewise rouse strong opinions, such as Quebec's independence, constitutional questions, taxes, and unemployment. Many political issues are not of interest to people. When people are not interested in a particular issue, they may respond to pollsters' questions about an issue by answering "don't know" or "don't care."

### Fluidity and Stability

One of the more interesting characteristics of political opinion is that on some questions it can zig and zag almost overnight, whereas on others, it changes at a glacial pace, if at all. Political opinions are likely to change when people do not feel particularly intense about an issue or when they do not have much information on which to form convictions.

When political opinion changes dramatically in a short period of time, we say it is "fluid." The *fluidity* in political opinions is usually a response to the rapidly changing conditions in the world of politics and government, and in society as a whole. A changing society is one in which attitudes about fundamental political and social beliefs, such as the role of the family, women's rights, minority rights, gay and lesbian rights, the environment, and the distributions of political and governing powers in the constitution, fluctuate.

Many political opinions become constant over time, some even over a lifetime. Taken together, individual opinions about politics and government may gain *stability*, persisting for many years. Arguing that Quebec is potentially an independent nation-state, sovereign and separate from Canada, has become the opinion of a growing number of Québécois in recent years. The "Quiet Revolution" in the early 1960s had a profound effect on the spread of supportive nationalistic political opinions in Quebec. The idea that only Québécois political leaders could be entrusted with looking after the interests of their people and with safeguarding their distinct culture has remained constant since that time.

### Latency

Not all political opinions are outwardly expressed by those who hold them. Some are dormant, and governments and political leaders can only anticipate, and sometimes activate, them. Political analysts call these sleeping opinions "latent," or "quiescent."

*Latency* of political opinions can affect the best-laid plans of governors and politicians because, when they surface, they can reveal widespread public dissatisfaction with the performance of government or political institutions. Latent political opinions are predispositions to react in a particular way. They are unexpressed judgements about what actions are appropriate in relation to issues, institutions, and leaders.

Estimating the possible consequences of latent opinions is a challenging and often momentous task for leaders, and one of the important reasons why governments use polls to take the pulse of opinion across the country, or in a province, on a wide range of issues. How many people now silent and apparently uncommitted will become aroused if action is taken? Will they be supportive or non-supportive of public policy? Will latent opinions flare up and then die away in a short period of time, permitting the government to move unhindered in one direction or another?

While political analysts attempt to understand how latent political opinions are triggered and channelled, hosts of would-be persuaders are interested in directing these opinions as they surface. They want people to think, feel, and be inclined to act in certain directions rather than others.

### Consensus and Divisiveness

To the casual observer, it appears that Canadians do not agree on many political issues. Normally, political opinions are distributed over several different positions. Observing a hypothetical distribution of political opinions can help us understand how divided the public is on a particular issue and to indicate whether compromise is possible. The way a political opinion is distributed can show us what percentage of the population do not even have an opinion.

When a large proportion of the Canadian public appears to agree on an issue, the distribution of their political opinion will show that a *consensus* — at least at the moment an opinion poll was taken — has formed. Figure 9.5 shows hypothetical patterns of opinion that are consensual and conflictive. When most people are in agreement on an issue, governments and politicians have limited options. They can run counter to the will of the majority at high political cost, or they can take no action and hope that the consensus becomes dormant.

Because of the complex nature of Canada's political and governing system, consensus on broad principles is usually difficult to achieve; in practice, consensus often melts into con-

**Figure 9.5 Patterns of Canadian Political Opinions**

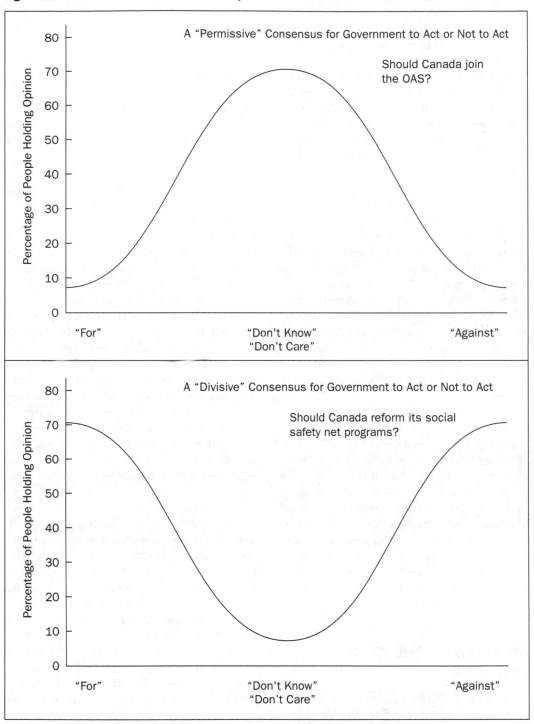

flict and *divisiveness* on specific issues, such as abortion; reconstructing federalism; and constitutional questions involving aboriginal rights, provincial powers, and gender.

When issues divide the public the pattern of political opinion is said to be "divisive," or "conflictive." A divisive distribution reflects political conflict that can have serious consequences for the governability and stability of the country. On the issue of abortion, divisive patterns emerge in many Canadian communities. Politicians, governments, and political parties are forced to take sides on such issues at the risk of distancing themselves from their constituents.

When both the supporters and the opponents of an issue are approximately equally and intensely divided "for" or "against," but most other people either have no knowledge about the issue or simply don't care, the political distribution will reflect a high percentage of latent opinions. Some analysts call this type of distribution "permissive" because governments are able to move in any direction they want without fear of offending a majority of voters.

Such was the opinion distribution that formed in 1989, when Canada joined the Organization of American States (OAS) in Washington. There were small clusters of informed Canadians who felt that joining as a full member was not necessary for Canada at that time, and equally small numbers of Canadians who intensely wanted Canada to become a member. But most Canadians could not tell an interviewer what the OAS is, what it does, and why Canada should or should not belong. So the government was really free to do what it wanted to.

## MEASURING POLITICAL OPINIONS

An **opinion poll**, often just called a "survey," provides governments and the general public with a wealth of information about what Canadians think and do. Pioneered in the early decades of the twentieth century by Americans George Gallup and Elmo Roper, systematic polling has become the dominant tool for opinion measurement. The political opinions of nearly 30 million Canadians can be measured accurately by such polls. The trend in media coverage of political events over the past decade has been to rely on the outcome of polls.

A statistician once remarked: "Must I drink the whole bottle in order to judge the quality of the wine?" What he meant was that a small sample maybe sufficient to judge, providing it has all the important characteristics of the larger unit. Today, this principle of sampling is employed by researchers in the business of measuring political opinions.

Those who conduct scientific polls use what is called **probability sampling**, that is, a national or provincial sample of 1200 to 2000 people is drawn in such a way that everyone has an equal chance of being or not being chosen as part of the sample. This "random" sampling usually involves interviewing a randomly selected number of people within a desired geographical area so as to ensure **representative sampling** of the total population. What is important about an opinion poll is less the size of the sample than how it is chosen.

Sometimes pollsters want to give their sample a particular representative character by using the **quota sampling method**. This involves making sure that the sample reflects the proportional character of the population being measured. For example, a poll wanting to consider Quebec's opinions would set a quota for the sample of 25 percent Québécois to make sure that the proportion of people from that province interviewed is comparable to that of the national population. This approach is often used to build age, ethnicity, gender, and religious compositions into samples so that they are more proportionately representative.

Polls are actually estimates, not precise figures. The results of a sample contain a **sampling error**, that is, the extent to which the answers given in a sample are likely to differ from the responses that would come from the entire population. The sampling error in most scientific polls is about + or – 3 percent. Thus, if a poll indicates that 70 percent of Canadians favour the use of capital punishment for certain crimes, actual support lies somewhere between 67 and 73 percent.

The nature of statistical probability theory is such that increasing the size of a sample may not markedly reduce the sampling error, unless the sample were expanded enormously (see Figure 9.6). If every Canadian could be polled, the sampling error should be *zero*. In fact, the general rule in probability theory is that, if random sampling is conducted, the bigger the sample, the smaller the sampling error, that is, the more closely the estimates obtained from the sample reflect the values in the population as a whole.

**Figure 9.6  With Random Sampling: The Bigger the Sample Size, the Smaller the Sampling Error**

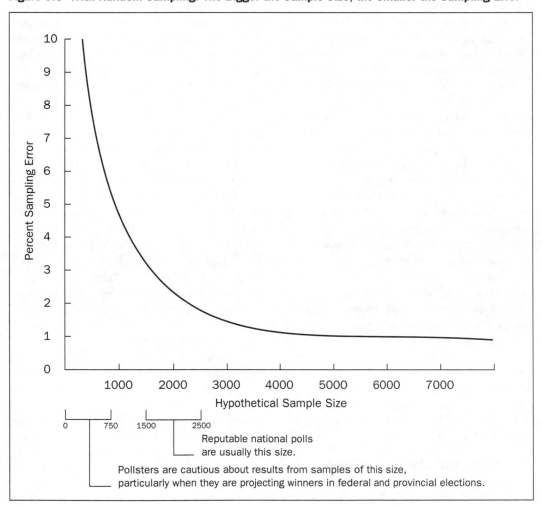

Reputable national polls are usually this size.

Pollsters are cautious about results from samples of this size, particularly when they are projecting winners in federal and provincial elections.

The methods that pollsters use to conduct their polls can affect the accuracy of the responses they receive. The most reliable method is the "face-to-face interview." An interviewer using this method can observe the person being interviewed and ask follow-up questions if the truthfulness or intensity of the opinion is in doubt.

A "telephone interview" is usually less reliable than one conducted face-to-face, but often more reliable than a poll conducted by mail. "Mail polls" are unreliable for most research because the pollster is not certain that the response received is actually from the person selected to respond. As well, they have a low response rate of somewhere between 20 and 40 percent. Most polling is done by telephone because that approach is more cost-effective for the polling company or organization. Today, nearly every Canadian has a telephone, so polling can be done from any place in the country. Pollsters enter people's answers to a questionnaire directly into a computer, allowing analysis to be done instantaneously.

In scientific polling, the way questions are asked is very important. In fact, the results of a survey can be no better than the quality of the questions asked. Pollsters attempt to word questions in a way that will not indicate a bias or desired answer. Value-laden words such as "prohibiting," "protecting," "good," and "bad," should be left out, or used very carefully, so as to achieve neutrality in the interview. A question that leads people to express an opinion that is really not their own tends to incite rather than measure opinion. The type of answers sought in a poll can help gauge the intensity of the feelings of the person being interviewed; response choices, such as "strongly agree" and "strongly disagree," measure intensity of opinion. However, questions that ask only for a "yes" or a "no" answer, do not.

## The Polls and the Politicians

Finding out what Canadians think about politics has become a regular pursuit of governments and politicians. Today, in Canada, there are dozens of commercial research firms, most of which concentrate in the areas of advertising and marketing research. A wide assortment of groups and institutions — including political scientists, the press, business, and other groups — finds polling valuable in their work. Interest groups sponsor surveys on subjects of political importance to them and then introduce these results into their political strategies.

But, increasingly, politicians have been using polls for their own purposes (Gallup 1965, 549). In order to stay in touch with the electorate, governments finance tracking polls on particular issues or events. Politicians have also learned that the polls themselves are persuasive tools. To this end, poll findings are employed, and publicized often quite selectively, on behalf of political and governmental interests.

But polls serve their most important political function during election campaigns (National Election Study 1989). The predictive quality of polls is important at the level of campaign workers. Today, candidates and public officials rely heavily on political opinion polls for deciding their election campaign strategies, and even for making policy decisions once in office. Politicians are interested in polling to find out not only whether they are winning or losing but also what groups support them or not. Learning that he or she is unpopular among particular economic or ethnic groups will enable a politician to make special appeals in that direction.

Despite their limitations, polls are regarded by politicians as the best way to find out about political opinion. The difficulty is determining how the opinions of the public can be translated into public policy, and the degree to which they should be. In a democracy such as Canada's, government policy and the decisions of public officials must in some way reflect public opinion. The Canadian people have an enormous diversity of opinions about political issues. And, as a result, polls are not necessarily valid in predicting what people will think in the future. They frequently show that political opinion fluctuates dramatically in response to events, many of which are created by the politicians themselves.

## CONCLUSION

Almost all of the chapters in this book focus on Canada's political and governmental institutions and the things they do. This chapter has focussed on part of Canada's corporate life called the "mass media." Of special interest to us have been those people who gather, write, edit, report, and produce the news that people read in the newspaper, hear on the radio, and watch on television. Nobody votes for these people. They are not public officials. They do not make our laws. So why do the mass media and those who measure opinions gain special attention in a book on Canadian government?

The mass media and pollsters have a chapter to themselves because newspapers, radio, television, and polls matter politically. They also have an enormous effect on how we are governed. In carving out a specific guarantee for the freedom of the press, Canada's constitution tells us that the media are supposed to matter. They are the means by which political information and political ideas reach and are disseminated among Canadians. They are the forums for clashes between and among competing ideologies in Canada. In short, they help define political realities in the country. Thus, understanding the business of print and electronic journalism is now a necessary part of understanding how Canadian governments perform.

Understanding why the media matters requires a look at the several roles the media play in Canadian politics and government. The media serve as vehicles of direct communication, as gatekeepers of political knowledge and attitudes, as spotlights on issues, and as talent scouts during election campaigns.

The mass media — newspapers, magazines, radio, and television — are vital links between citizens and their government. The relationship between the media and politics and government institutions in Canada is fundamental to the governability of the country. While politicians need the media, those who work in the media depend on candidates, bureaucrats, and political leaders for access to news sources and newsmakers.

In the 1990s, no one denies that polls play a significant role in the operations of Canadian governments, or in the political system in general. Polls recognize that the public is a major source of political power and should not be ignored. Polls have become a staple of political assessment and commentary at every level of government and politics in Canada. Even in the minds of the public, polling is seen to offer a more objective way of gauging political opinion. As a result, polling has become not only the dominant tool for opinion measurement but the most legitimate one as well.

The proliferation of media-initiated polls has altered voter expectations during campaigns, and public perceptions of leaders and policies between elections. Media polls can inject a subtle element of persuasion, creating mindsets, suggesting opinion shifts, and altering the competitive perceptions among leaders and voters. A politics of expectation has been linked to the presence and frequency of polls in Canada. All of this requires us to ask: Can the public be manipulated? Are people who read polls informed about the distortions that can arise from polling? Who is conducting the polls? Are they scientifically designed? How neutral and unbiased are the questions people are asked by pollsters? Are people's political opinions really their own, reflective of their true inner values and interests, or are they manufactured for them by powerful interests?

Before we conclude that the public is incompetent, however, we need to consider the standard by which the public should be judged. Some political scientists argue that people know in general what they like and dislike and can make sound political judgements on that basis. The general public may be more competent than any other group — elitist, expert, or otherwise — to determine what public policies and political leaders they want. It might be more correct to say that the general public lacks competence to determine the best ways of achieving certain governmental goals; to answer technical legal and legislative ques-

tions; or even to prescribe remedies for complex economic, social, and political problems. Elmo Roper, one of the founders of modern public opinion research, noted that we overestimate the amount of information the public has, but we underestimate its intelligence.

Democracy, Canadian style, accords the measurement of political opinion a moral and ethical status. If some form of representative democracy is to exist alongside a technology that promises to report the opinions and will of the people, then a non-distorted reflection of that will is imperative. In the final analysis, the major effects of polls have much less to do with how people vote in an election and much more to do with how we see ourselves and how politics and government are conducted.

## GLOSSARY

**gatekeepers** The media executives, news editors, and prominent reporters who direct the flow of the news.

**investigative journalism** The in-depth research by journalists into a particular social or political problem in order to discover information that may not be immediately evident, and the disclosure of such findings.

**opinion poll** A survey of public thinking conducted by pollsters to measure the opinions of people with speed and precision.

**pack journalism** The tendency of reporters to read one another's work and shape their stories by following the lead of other journalists.

**political opinion** The array of beliefs and attitudes that people hold about politics and government.

**probability sampling** A method by which the characteristics of a general population are estimated by choosing, at random, individuals from that population, such that the responses of those chosen will probably be the same as those of the general population.

**propaganda** A basic device of political persuasion employed in all political systems by which the mass media are used systematically to elicit support for or objections to specific ideas, persons, programs, or national interests.

**quota sampling method** A method of selecting a sample that involves including a certain number of people with specific ethnic, religious, age, gender, and other special population characteristics.

**representative sampling** Choosing a relatively small group of subjects taken to reflect the characteristics of a larger, defined population of interest.

**sampling error** In survey research, the amount by which the results obtained from a sample may, with a specified degree of likelihood, depart from the actual value in the population.

**spin** An interpretation of an event or election result that is most favourable to a particular political strategy.

## RECOMMENDED READING

Desbarats, Peter. 1990. *Guide to Canadian News Media*. Toronto: HBJ-Holt Canada. This concise guide to the Canadian news media provides an in-depth perspective on the structure of the Canadian media and a focus on journalism and politics in Canada.

Lachapelle, Guy. 1992. *Polls and the Media in Canadian Elections: Taking the Pulse*. Toronto: Dundurn Press. This book is one of a series of research studies that emerged from the Royal Commission on Electoral Reform and Party Financing in 1989. The book provides a valuable collection of articles that focus on the role of the media and polls in Canadian election campaigns.

Lorimer, Rowland, and Jean McNulty. 1991. *Mass Communication in Canada*. Toronto: McClelland & Stewart. This is one of the first texts that provides readers with detailed insights on the mass-communications effect on all realms of modern Canadian society — the cultural, economic, educational, political, social, and technological.

Merrill, John C. 1991. *Global Journalism*. New York: Longman Publishing Group. This book provides a substantive picture of the physical aspects of global mass communication, comparing media theories, press freedom, and ethical concepts globally.

Oppenheim, A.N. 1993. *Questionnaire Design, Interviewing and Attitude Measurement*. London: Pinter Publishers. This nuts-and-bolts text informs students about sampling, polling, and gathering information for analysis.

Raboy, Marc. 1992. *Missed Opportunities: The Story of Canada's Broadcasting Policy*. Montreal and Kingston: McGill-Queen's University Press. The author shows how Canadian broadcasting policy has served as an instrument for reinforcing a certain image of Canada as a political entity distinct from the United States.

Shoemaker, Pamela, and Stephen Reese. 1991. *Mediating the Message: Theories of Influences on Mass Media Content*. New York: Longman Publishing Group. The book examines the influences on media content, such as media professionals and ideological perspectives. The authors highlight the similarities among theoretical approaches.

Singer, Benjamin. 1991. *Communications in Canadian Society*. Scarborough, Ont.: Nelson Canada. The author provides a collection of 23 original essays written by authorities in the field of communications in Canada. The book examines the role of the new media in an age of information and develops the evolution of Canadian media in response to technological change.

Taras, David. 1990. *The Newsmakers: The Media's Influence on Canadian Politics*. Scarborough, Ont.: Nelson Canada. This book addresses the controversial topic of media influence on politicians in Canada and examines how the development of journalism has affected the political system.

Vipond, Mary. 1990. *The Mass Media in Canada*. Toronto: James Lorimer. This readable history of the Canadian mass media considers the economic, cultural, and technological forces that have affected government policy-making. Vipond concentrates on the five major media: newspapers, magazines, movies, radio, and television.

# 4

# BRANCHES OF CANADIAN POLITICS

CHAPTER

# PROVINCIAL AND TERRITORIAL INSTITUTIONS

**P**remier Bob Rae said, "This is not the way we run Canada." Dr. Ron Stewart, Nova Scotia's Minister of Health, said that "the federal government was running roughshod over the provinces by letting criminals and the tobacco industry dictate provincial health policy." Manitoba's premier, Gary Filmon, threatened "to counter whatever the feds do with a special provincial tax by the amount of the federal cut, thus wiping out the price advantage." Other premiers asked why they had to toe the line on nation-wide measures imposed on them by the federal government for an issue that was primarily a Quebec problem. What was all of this harsh rhetoric about? It was all about cigarettes and the widespread controversy associated with them.

All of these remarks came as a result of Jean Chrétien's decision to lower federal taxes on a carton of smokes, to take the incentive out of smuggling contraband into Canada, and to reclaim some of the government revenues lost from the booming illegal trade in cigarettes. It seemed like such a simple thing to do. Just lower the federal tax by $5 a carton and offer to match further cuts by the provinces to a maximum of $10 a carton. The smugglers would go away, and Canada's federal system could return to normalcy. But, instead, government actions generated a major political crisis in Canada's federal system and challenged the credibility of the fledgling Liberal government of Prime Minister Jean Chrétien.

How could cigarettes have so much of an effect on how we are governed? How could a change in cigarette tax policy produce so much uncertainty and confusion within Canada's federal structure? How could this kind of change in policy generate tensions among aboriginal communities, the provinces, and the federal government, and between and among the provinces themselves? How could changing a policy on cigarettes damage federal–provincial relations, infuriate the tobacco industry, outrage pressure groups, split political parties, and spark a contentious national debate on how we are governed? After all, this was just about cigarettes. Or was it?

Before the change in federal policy, governments were badly split on how to end cigarette smuggling, which had grown to a multibillion-dollar illegal business, was threatening to spread everywhere in the country, and was significantly eroding government tax revenues. Police forces in all provinces were unable to handle the growing problems, and the illegal cigarette trade was promising to spread to liquor, and perhaps lead to a wider tax revolt.

The ongoing debate about smoking makes Canadians consider so many issues that are central values in their political culture — freedom of choice, jobs, the economy, the social safety net, personal responsibility, the role of government, life, death, and taxes. Governments are constantly facing a moral and political dilemma on the issue of smoking.

Every year, billions of dollars are transferred from the federal government to the provinces to help pay for health-care costs. Provinces try to collect taxes to pay for hospitals, doctors' fees, medical technologies, and research. Yet, all governments are under a major fiscal squeeze to maintain the integrity of the health programs they deliver in the face of serious tax-revenue shortfalls.

Lowering the tax on cigarettes meant less revenues and larger shortfalls. Yet, all governments know that reducing the price of cigarettes will introduce more people to smoking at a younger age and prolong their smoking habit. They also know that eventually many of those who smoke will develop diseases that drive up the costs and effectiveness of their health-care systems.

So the issue will not go away. More people are now smoking and will begin to smoke. Many of them will eventually develop the symptoms of illnesses associated with smoking. The provinces will have to pay for the health care of these smokers. Health advocates will demand that the federal and provincial governments increase taxes on cigarettes to deter smokers. The federal government will be asked to respond, and their actions will no doubt touch off another crisis in our federal system. Perhaps the warning label on cigarettes should also read that "Smoking is dangerous to the heath of federal politics."

## INTRODUCTION

Canada is a nation-state of provinces and territorial governments. In 1867, the British North America (BNA) Act created the provinces of Ontario and Quebec by dividing the **United Province of Canada**, and brought these new provinces into a union with Nova Scotia and New Brunswick. In this way, the BNA Act, formed a confederation of colonies.

The political and governing institutions of the British and French colonies thus foreshadowed the shape of Canada's federal system under the Constitution Act, 1867 (Levy and White 1989). In fact, the shape and form of provincial governments were already here long before the construction of a set of federal governing institutions under the BNA Act. They grew in number as the Canadian frontier was pushed westward to the Pacific, and also eastward to eventually include the great island of Newfoundland.

The Fathers of Confederation had made it clear in the 1867 act that other British North American colonies were welcome to join Canada. And, in 1870, Canada bought **Rupert's Land** from the Hudson's Bay Company and took over the rest of the North-Western Territory from Britain. A small part of this vast territory became the province of Manitoba, which included the rich agricultural colony along the Red River. British Columbia joined Canada in 1871, enticed by the promise of a railway to connect the west coast with eastern Canada. Prince Edward Island followed in 1873. The provinces of Alberta and Saskatchewan were created in 1905, as wheat farmers flooded onto the prairies.

The goal of creating a country from "sea to sea" had been achieved. Newfoundland, which includes Labrador on the mainland, became Canada's tenth province in 1949. Over the years, the Yukon and Northwest Territories have operated with a limited amount of self-government. But they are controlled mainly by the federal government. The division of the Northwest Territories to create new provinces in the North remains a possibility for the future.

Canadian federalism divides powers and **jurisdictions** between the federal government and the provinces. Provinces were never mere administrative or geographic units established for the convenience of the federal government. Rather, the provinces began as key governing institutions rooted in Canada's economic and political development, sharing some important powers under the federal system with the national government in Ottawa.

## A MUCH-GOVERNED FEDERAL SYSTEM

Today, the federal government in Ottawa is, of course, the biggest and the most powerful, but it is just one in a vast array of governments. There are also provincial; territorial; and a bewildering complexity, variety, and multitude of municipal governments, which together total 6009.

While the federal government is the most prominent, the provinces have continued to be central to the Canadian system of government. Provinces are the original building blocks of our federal system of government, and there is a rich diversity of governments among them.

Throughout Canadian history, the provinces have sought, through federalism, to constrain the federal government from direct interference in their administration (Milne 1986). And all have sought financial interaction with the federal government to help pay for the government programs they offer their residents.

In the contemporary federal system, the provinces are constitutionally overshadowed by the federal government. Still, Canada's provinces and their legal subdivisions — cities, counties, towns, and other municipal and

**regional governments** — are very important in the lives of all Canadians. Whether the Fathers of Confederation intended it, the constitution demonstrates without any question that the most fundamental governing in Canada would be done provincially.

The federal government cannot abolish the provinces, and the provinces cannot abolish the federal government. Each level of government can raise and spend money; each has power over certain aspects of our lives. Neither level of government is completely subordinate to the other, and each is, in some real way, independent of the other.

## Separate Spheres of Government

Two separate sets of governments rule over the same territory and over the same citizens. Can such an arrangement be possible without constant clashes over which has jurisdiction over what or which is responsible for developing or reducing the areas of government involvement in our lives? The designers of this system of government at the time of Confederation thought that it was possible as long as the spheres in which governments would be active were differentiated: Some powers were allocated to the provincial governments, some to the federal government, and a number of areas were to be concurrent.

Indeed, it has been possible: The provinces and the federal government have operated side by side with one another since Confederation. But the pattern of their relationship has never involved a simple division of labour, with the provinces dealing with some problems, the federal government with others. Rather, the history of the relationship is one of constant change, of complex interaction and shifting responsibilities; the relationship has involved shared and overlapping powers more often than purely separate and distinct ones.

Provincial capitals are active centres of government business. Government has become a powerful and pervasive force in all provincial capitals. Today, provincial governments run programs and make policies reaching into every corner of our lives. They oversee the provinces' economies; they are usually the provinces' largest employers; they provide residents with a host of essential social services; and they regulate a wide range of business and commercial activities.

Each of the ten provinces permits a wide diversity of political participation and action. There are, of course, the legislators and public administrators who perform their roles and functions in our governments, but there are also countless boards, commissions, and agencies that engage in provincial governmental activity.

In many regards, most Canadians are likely to feel a closer affinity with provincial officials and bureaucrats than with the federal government. Most of the contacts that ordinary Canadians have with government are at the provincial and municipal levels: They regularly interact with and use the services of public schools, colleges, and universities; welfare programs; roads; provincial and local parks; municipal services, such as garbage collection and sewage disposal; water supplies; police and fire protection; and traffic control. Most of the law courts that Canadians encounter, from municipal traffic courts to others that deal with divorces, civil suits for damages, and most criminal matters, are part of provincial judicial systems. All of these are primarily the responsibility of provincial governments.

Beyond providing services in these areas, the provinces regulate marriage, divorce, and child custody; drivers' licences; auto inspection; transfer of property; wills and estates; and many other matters. All of this means that Canada's highly decentralized federal system permits diversity in governmental organization, political structures, and public policies.

In recent decades, provinces have become more important in the federal system. But their capacity to remain viable governing entities is threatened by the enormous costs of the very federal system in which they must compete. The underlying expectation has been that, with time, the federal government could redistribute wealth so that "have-not" provinces could eventually become "have" provinces. But this wealth redistribution has not been forthcoming for most provinces (Stevenson 1989).

One reason for inequity in wealth is that provincial and municipal governments rely heavily on property and consumer taxes, which do not necessarily reflect the general growth in the economy as rapidly as federal income and other taxes do. Provinces are careful not to raise their taxes, in part because they must compete with one another for new industries, services, and technological enterprises, and because Canadians are already highly taxed. Accordingly, they must be wary of increasing taxes in such a way that consumers stop spending or join the underground economy, or businesses resist investing in the provincial economy.

During the 1980s and early 1990s, the provinces felt the effects of economic recession and revenue limitations, which in some cases were harsher than federal government transfer-payment cuts. This combination of factors was to increase fiscal strain in the federal system. To provide their services, the provinces and municipal governments together employ more people than does the federal government — with all of the accompanying challenges associated with organized labour, management–labour disputes, strikes, and the control of bureaucracy. But the shift of the financial burden of government to the provinces, and their growing deficits and debts, made it extremely difficult for them to keep delivering their services with the same level of personnel.

## Political Geography of the Provinces

Geography is one of the most important factors to influence the character and quality of Canada's federal system. Each province has a distinctive geographical position in North America, affecting its governability, its economic growth, and its power within the federal structure of government.

One salient feature of provincial geography conditions their economic and political vitality within Canada as well as internationally (Krueger and Corder 1982): namely, that most provinces share their geographical environment with other provinces and also with one or more American states. Accordingly, in order to understand the politics and economics of each province, one must take into consideration the significance of its geographical location.

It is a fact in Canada that where provinces are located will affect their capacity to do business; to produce and deliver goods and services efficiently; and to trade with one another, the United States, and the world.

Another geopolitical characteristic of most provinces, is the urban primacy of the capital city. In many provinces, the capital city is the largest and most economically developed. Provincial capitals concentrate political and economic decision making, usually to the disadvantage of other urban communities. Within the provincial economy, they draw a disproportionately larger number of jobs, more business and government investment, a more generous tax base, and a higher level of economic efficiency than do other towns and cities within the province. Concentration of economic and political power in one **core area**, such as the capital city, generates problems for regional economic development from the provincial perspective.

All provinces put a premium on transportation. In a country where many of the provinces are larger than most other countries in the international system, roads, railways, air transportation, and waterways are important. Some provinces are coastal, with access to ocean trade routes, or are located on the Great Lakes, while others, such as Alberta and Saskatchewan, are landlocked and confined geographically, in large measure, to trading and interacting with other provinces and the United States or transporting the commodities they produce to other provinces that are able to ship abroad. For example, much of the grain grown in these two landlocked provinces is exported to other countries, but must be brought by train to Thunder Bay, one of the largest grain-handling ports in the world. Some of the grain is stored in elevators and is then loaded onto lake freighters for transport to ports on the lower Great Lakes and the St. Lawrence River, where it is then shipped to Europe. Quebec's transportation system includes ports on the St. Lawrence River and its Seaway, serving Quebec City, Montreal, Trois-Riviérès, Sept-Iles, and Port Cartier.

Natural resources are also important to every province. Primary industries, such as agriculture, fishing, forestry, mining, and petroleum, are significant examples of provincial resource inventories. All are export industries that can enrich provinces when times are good but also can leave provinces vulnerable to international market forces when volatile demands and fluctuating exchange rates are unfavourable. The collapse of Newfoundland's fishery in the early 1990s leaves that province in near destitution as it has few other resources to fall back on.

## Provincial Political Cultures

A drive along the Trans-Canada Highway reveals licence plates of many hues and slogans. But the differences among provinces go beyond mottoes, trees, birds, and flags. Provinces vary in political traditions and governing personality — what political scientists call "political culture" (Elkins and Simeon 1980). In terms of provincial politics, political culture can be simply defined as the way people within the boundaries of a province orient themselves to politics and government.

Population migrations in the eighteenth and nineteenth centuries brought peoples with various cultural heritages to different parts of Canada: the Irish and English to Newfoundland, the Scots and French to Nova Scotia and New Brunswick, the French to Quebec, and the Germans and Ukrainians to the Western provinces.

These many cultural heritages have made for abundant diversity in the political cultures and political traditions among, and within, Canadian provinces. Nova Scotia, Quebec, and British Columbia, for example, exhibit distinct political cultures in their interiors. While people in all provinces share similar political ideals, procedures of government, and patterns of political behaviour that are passed on from one generation to the next, every provincial political system has developed its own particular pattern of political action.

The most obvious example is Quebec, where francophone nationalism has produced distinctive features in the province's governing institutions. For example, Quebec's lieutenant-governor (a symbol of British colonialism) is all but ignored by the political and government system. The Throne Speech has been replaced by the prime minister's (premier's) Inaugural Address. The Speaker is called "le Président" and wears no formal British-style government robes. Bills introduced by the government are often sent directly to committee after the first reading, rather than after approval-in-principle at the second stage of parliamentary procedure.

Each province in Canada is therefore unique. Despite our national media networks, which report stories from the Canadian perspective; franchises and chains that bring the same stores and their products to all parts of the country; and transportation systems that carry us across the country in only a few hours, there are still significant differences among us.

In different provinces, we have developed somewhat different political styles and attitudes. In effect, politics in each province, like those at the national level, have been profoundly shaped by local attitudes and beliefs as to the nature and scope of government.

These divergent beliefs help explain the differences among provincial governments and between the provincial and the federal governments.

Ways of looking at politics and government, political party platforms, appropriate ways of organizing political action, and other exhibitions of political behaviour thus vary across this country. Even next-door neighbours like Alberta and Saskatchewan have different political cultures (Gibbins 1989). Alberta has a history of social conservatism, low taxation, and low-spending fiscal conservatism, while, right next door, Saskatchewan has tended to be more of a welfare-state province, with much higher taxes providing more generous social programs, and an electorate more inclined to support left-of-centre governments.

In Quebec, unlike in other provinces, many politicians see its institutions as national ones that make laws and administer justice for a sovereigntist and distinct society. They are part of a political culture of independence that focusses on the boundaries of the province as those of an independent nation-state. These political-cultural differences among Canadian provinces affect how provincial governments perform, how they relate to one another, and what diplomatic skills they use in relating with the federal government.

Thus, all provinces have preserved distinctive political cultures, traditions, and institutions. Most have produced unique levels of public trust. People also tend to feel more or less efficacious in our various provincial political systems. For example, residents of Ontario tend to show higher levels of political trust and political efficacy than do residents of P.E.I. who display significant levels of cynicism and pessimism about their governing institutions and the people who occupy them (Smitherman, Milne, and Dasgupta 1982; Elkins and Simeon 1980).

Political scientists know that many of the sharpest political differences between provinces are related to their level of economic development. To put it simply, there are rich provinces and poor provinces. The rich ones tend to have more tax and other revenue money to spend, and they spend it on somewhat different things. The precise nature of the economy also makes a difference. The agricultural provinces, such as Manitoba and Saskatchewan, tend to have public policies that differ significantly from those of the most industrialized one, that is, Ontario, and the newly industrialized ones, such as Alberta and British Columbia.

## THE PROVINCES AND FEDERALISM

The Fathers of Confederation did not foresee a federal system like the one we have now. The federal government has maintained the enormous range of governing powers they wanted it to have. But, over the years, the politics of Canadian federalism has produced one of the most decentralized federal systems in the international community.

One of the paradoxes of our political system is that the great expansion of government powers has conferred important jurisdictions on the provincial governments. In fact, all levels of government have expanded the services they administer to an extent never imagined by the original nineteenth-century architects of federalism.

The federal and provincial governments have grown hand and hand. Canadians have come to believe strongly that their provincial government is the cradle of local control and grass-roots governing. In many ways, Canada's federal system is a logical outcome of the contradictory impulses of Canadians who want to find national solutions for building a large nation-state yet who fiercely want to retain local and regional control over their lives.

The role of the provinces in how we govern ourselves is fundamentally that they can meet regional and local demands. Federalism also assumes that, when provinces get rich, they contribute to national wealth. At the same time, provincial governments provide opportunities for experimentation on a small scale as a counterweight to extensive national standards that can be imposed on the provinces by the federal government. In 1994, the federal government began to dismantle the Department of Indian Affairs and Northern Development, beginning with the province of Manitoba so as to monitor the effects that change might have on aboriginals living in the other provinces.

Provincial governments can usually act more swiftly than the federal government in response to local problems. Provinces and their municipal government structures keep government closer to the people and provide more opportunities for residents to participate in how they are governed. Canada's federal system creates multiple points of public access to federal and provincial government bodies to satisfy the political demands of the people.

But, while federalism as it has evolved here created many opportunities to expand the role of our governments, it has also created many road blocks to achieving national unity. The relations between the provinces and the federal government have been a source of continuing conflict and controversy in the Canadian political system and raise a number of questions of fundamental importance.

Who benefits from and who loses in our federal system is an important question to ask if we want to know how effective our governments are. Do the advantages of federalism outweigh the price of fragmented government and a sovereigntist and independent Quebec? Because of the enormous debts our governments have racked up serving our needs, must Canada reconstruct its federal system? Are there better ways of governing ourselves, using different rules and structures? Should we consider these or proceed to reform the existing parliamentary system?

Canadian-style federalism has placed its stamp on a broad range of informal activities in Canadian society. The nature of representation in the Canadian House of Commons reflects the consequences of federalism from the provincial perspective. Each province, no matter how small, has a certain number of MPs and senators who represent ridings within the province (see Table 10.1).

MPs also constitute an informal political delegation to the federal government from their province. Similarly, senators are appointed, but they make up a provincial constituency in Parliament and can influence the dynamics of government in Ottawa as well as their provinces.

Our court system reflects our federal system. Provincial and municipal courts exist side by side with federal courts. However, because provincial courts handle the vast majority of cases, the provincial court system is much larger and busier than the federal system. The federal courts appear distant, and beyond the range of most Canadians. Contact with a fed-

**Table 10.1 Legislative Representation in Parliament**

| Province/ Territory | House of Commons Seats | Senate Seats |
|---|---|---|
| Newfoundland | 7 | 6 |
| Nova Scotia | 11 | 10 |
| P.E.I. | 4 | 4 |
| New Brunswick | 10 | 10 |
| Quebec | 75 | 24 |
| Ontario | 99 | 24 |
| Manitoba | 14 | 6 |
| Saskatchewan | 14 | 6 |
| Alberta | 26 | 6 |
| British Columbia | 32 | 6 |
| Yukon | 1 | 1 |
| Northwest Territories | 2 | 1 |
| Total | 295 | 104 |

eral court in Canada is thus a much rarer occurrence than contact with a provincial court.

Interest groups respond to Canada's federal system as well. Many of them are federations of provincial associations and groups. It is at the provincial level that interest groups build their membership, raise their money to organize and advertise, and create strategies for lobbying the federal government. This is true of the Canadian Medical Association and the Canadian Bar Association, which take their membership from the provincial and territorial organizations.

The contours of Canadian party politics are also driven by **intergovernmental relations**. Political parties reflect federal politics because political parties are organized along federal lines. To a party out of power nationally, the existence of provincial party organizations takes on special importance. By building the strength of a political party from the provincial level and demonstrating its governing ability there, a political party can consolidate its position and prepare for the next federal election. Sometimes a strong premier or former premier will emerge as a contender for national party leadership.

Since the adoption of the Constitution Act, 1867, the single most persistent source of political and governing conflict in Canada has been relations between the federal and the provincial governments. The basic political fact about Canada's federal system is that it has created separate, self-sustaining centres of governing power across the country.

The Constitution Act, 1867, gave the federal government enormous governing powers and control over all areas that are both national and provincial in interest and scope. These areas include navigation, fisheries, the fiscal and monetary system, public debt, aboriginal territories, and defence (see Table 10.2). The provincial governments were given important powers as well — over resources, education, health services, busi-

### Table 10.2  What the Federal Government Can Do

- Amend the Canadian constitution
- Control public debt and property
- Regulate trade and commerce
- Administer unemployment insurance
- Raise monies by any means of taxation
- Borrow money on public credit
- Operate the postal service
- Take the census and gather statistics
- Raise an Army, Navy, Air Force, and Militia
- Fix salaries for all public officials
- Establish and maintain all beacons, buoys, lighthouses, and Sable Island
- Control navigation and shipping
- Declare quarantines and maintain marine hospitals
- Manage seacoastal and inland fisheries
- Operate ferries
- Coin money, incorporate banks, and set national fiscal and monetary policy
- Set national weights and measures
- Set interest rates
- Establish policy on bankruptcy and insolvency
- Register patents and discoveries
- Register copyrights
- Administer for aboriginal peoples and lands reserved for them
- Grant citizenship
- Legalize marriage and divorce
- Establish and codify criminal law
- Establish, maintain, and manage penitentiaries
- Administer agriculture and immigration
- Administer old-age pensions

ness, industry, transportation, and municipal governing institutions (see Table 10.3).

Over the years, Canada's federal system has greatly decentralized our politics and government. The federal system decentralizes not only our politics but also our policies. The history of the federal system is one of tension between the provinces and the federal government about jurisdictions of public policy — who controls it and what it should be. Most of our public-policy issues in Canada are based on federalism.

**Table 10.3 What Provincial Governments Can Do**

- Propose amendments to the constitution except as regards the lieutenant-governor
- Determine direct taxation within the province
- Borrow money on the credit of the province
- Establish the payment and appointment tenure of public servants and public officials
- Management and sale of public lands and forests
- Establish, maintain, and manage hospitals, asylums, charities, and eleemosynary institutions in and for the province, other than marine hospitals
- Municipal institutions within the province
- Grant shop, saloon, tavern, auctioneer, and other licences issued for the raising of provincial and municipal revenues
- Fund and administer local public works
- The incorporation of companies with provincial business interests
- The solemnization of marriage in the province
- Property and civil rights in the province
- The administration of justice in the province, including the maintenance, and organization of provincial courts, both of civil and of criminal jurisdiction, including procedure in civil matters in these courts
- The imposition of punishment by fine, penalty, or imprisonment in enforcing any law of the province relating to any of the aforesaid subjects
- Generally all matters of a merely local or private nature in the province
- Administer education
- Administer agriculture and immigration

## An Evolving Federalism

Since 1867, the Canadian federal system has changed significantly. But, from the start, a sizable part of the transactions among Canadian governments involved money (Cody 1977). The federal government began extending grants to the provinces early in the country's political history. This involved using the enormous economic resources, derived from the extensive taxing powers of the federal government, to transfer money to the provinces or to absorb their debts. For example, in 1867, the federal government absorbed pre-Confederation provincial debts and agreed to pay the provinces certain subsidies and annual grants to fund provincial programs and services.

Early in this century, the federal government gave conditional grants to the provinces, the "condition" being that the money was to be spent on federally approved projects and to meet national standards. However, it soon became evident that these grants would not eliminate the fundamental weakness of Canada's federal system — namely, that the provinces' capacity to produce wealth is not uniform. Moreover, the provinces were quick to resent the paternalistic manner in which these grants were provided.

Conditional grants were supposed to give the provinces some freedom in deciding how to spend the money while helping many provinces to relieve their tax burdens and raise the living standards of their residents. But the amount of money available for conditional grants did not grow as fast as the provinces had hoped. Furthermore, the federal government attached numerous strings to these grants in terms of how the money could be spent (Moore, Perry, and Beach 1966).

The Fathers of Confederation initiated a quasi-federal system because, in 1867, Ottawa assumed major administrative responsibilities for the bulk of public services. The constitution had deliberately centralized how we govern Canada, such that the federal government dominated, exercising national governing authority. At that time, federalism seemed to be all about the division of powers. It was the belief of many of the Fathers of Confederation that the provinces might even wither away.

Less than 30 years after Confederation, Canadian federalism had already evolved beyond its quasi-federal origins. In the period between 1896 and 1914, the provinces demanded more power and consultation from the federal government. Emergency federalism characterized the war period, when Parliament delegated sweeping authority to Ottawa to levy personal and corporate income taxes, to apply wage and price controls, and to prohibit strikes in wartime. The federal government was now expected to play a central role in the economic and social life of the country. This quality of federalism would return just prior to the Depression and last until the end of the Second World War.

In Canada, federal powers have always grown in wartime. During both world wars, Ottawa made heavy use of the federal powers granted by the constitution. In fact, federal powers actually expanded under the state of emergency.

But, during the 1920s, provincial autonomy grew as a result of revenues drawn from licensing automobiles, and taxing gasoline and liquor. During the Great Depression, many of the provinces were not able to deal with the trauma of economic and social decline. By the 1930s, it was necessary to restructure the fiscal relations between the provinces and the federal government because tensions were mounting over how to undertake economic recovery and how to deal with the high levels of unemployment.

In 1937, the Royal Commission on Dominion–Provincial Relations (the Rowell–Sirois Commission) was established. For the next three years, this commission studied the problems of Canadian federalism. Its recommendations included, among others, that the federal government should collect personal and corporate income tax, assume the accumulated debt of the provinces, and support the unemployed through a social security program. The commission also recommended that certain grants provided by the federal government be used to assist the poorer provinces and standardize government services across the country.

The advent of the Second World War enabled the federal government, under certain emergency powers, to assume some of the responsibilities recommended in the Rowell–Sirois Commission's report. The war solidified the central role of the federal government in fiscal and monetary matters. Wartime prosperity produced strong economic growth almost everywhere in the country and eased the financial squeeze on the provinces. The federal government consolidated its powerful centralist position, steering the national economy and taking responsibility for our economic well-being.

What has been called "Father knows best" federalism resulted from the enormous postwar taxing powers of the federal government and its ability to penetrate the jurisdictions of the provinces by funding certain shared-cost programs. The federal government entered into a series of taxation agreements with the provinces, preparing the way for fiscal co-operation in the federal system.

Co-operative federalism began in the 1960s as provincial governments experienced unprecedented demands for expanded services in health, education, welfare, and resource development. Today, all provinces spend more than half their budgets on these areas. Since the 1960s, personal income taxes have been collected by Ottawa, and the provincial portion is transferred back to the province, except in Quebec, where the government collects its own personal income tax. For this reason, Quebeckers must complete two income tax forms. As well, the rise of nationalism in Quebec spawned the concurrent spread of provincial autonomy in the other provinces.

Since the 1940s, shared-cost programs in the form of conditional grants and block grants have continued to be a source of provincial revenues. Examples are the block grants to provinces for post-secondary education (established in 1952), the conditional grant for hospital insurance (1957), the conditional grant for the Canada Assistance Plan (1966), and the conditional grant for medical insurance (1968).

Provinces also gain substantial revenues through equalization payments. Equalization is an instrument used to reduce disparities between the rich and poor partners in the Canadian federal family. The idea of equalization payments came out of the Rowell–Sirois Commission, but it was not implemented in Canada's federal system until 1957.

Equalization payments are unconditional grants to the so-called have-not provinces — there are seven — in order to bring them up to the national average in terms of tax yield per capita. The equalization formula tries to ensure that the seven have-not provinces enjoy roughly the same services as Ontario, British Columbia, and Alberta.

The formula used to determine whether a province qualifies takes the base average of per-capita revenues of the provinces of Quebec, Ontario, Manitoba, Saskatchewan, and British Columbia. If any province has a total per-capita revenue below this base average, the federal government prepares a payment based on the per-capita shortfall multiplied by the province's population. So payments vary from province to province. At the high end of the scale, in 1994 Newfoundland received $1655 per capita, and Saskatchewan, at the low end, received $521 per capita.

During the late 1960s and early 1970s, another federal style emerged in Canada, usually referred to as "executive federalism." Executive federalism changed the conduct of federal–provincial relations, transforming them from negotiations among provincial and federal bureaucrats who met behind closed doors to formal meetings among premiers and the prime minister at **First Ministers' Conferences** to resolve problems of federalism in front of television cameras. This convention format, in which eleven political executives work out "deals" on intergovernmental affairs, was largely the framework used in the Constitutional Conferences that produced what came to be known as the Meech Lake and the Charlottetown accords.

First Ministers' Conferences have addressed many of the issues at the root of federal–provincial differences over the years. One persistent issue has been regionalism. Because Canadians are so regional in outlook, it is difficult for the federal and provincial governments to find coast-to-coast agreement on every issue. Because the regions are host to such different economic and political cultures, it has been natural for disagreements to occur. Other contentious issues have involved transfer payments, cable and pay TV, energy prices, offshore resources, and the state of the economy.

Executive federalism has been criticized for creating public political forums that give First Ministers the opportunity to appeal to their voters rather than to negotiate in the national interest. Premiers have also used the conference format to oppose the federal government as a group, often appearing to be an extraparliamentary opposition.

But, by the early 1980s, the public began to view the federal system as bloated and out of control. Successive governments promised to reduce the deficit and debt, and the size and cost of the federal government. They began to criticize the contemporary version of federalism, charging that it concentrated too much authority at the federal level of government. The federal government was indeed the senior partner in intergovernmental relations, but it was being asked to pay for too many services provided under provincial jurisdiction. The share of provincial costs footed by the federal government began to fall, and Ottawa became very reluctant to take on any new funding programs.

Eventually the provinces were expected to pick up the costs themselves for the new programs they wanted to offer and to cut funding to existing programs to pay for them. Federal attempts at downsizing government aroused intense opposition at the provincial level. If the Progressive Conservative governments of the 1980s did not achieve a wholesale reorganization of the federal system, they did prompt a re-evaluation of the role of the federal government in that system.

By the time Prime Minister Mulroney left office in 1993, the federal government was no longer a benefactor, bestowing generosity on worthy provinces. The debt and deficit pressures on the provinces had mounted enormously, such that many provinces began to speak of their treasuries as being in crisis. The sober reality of federal budget deficits erased the hopes among provincial governments that the rest of the country could come to their assistance. For the first time in decades, provinces had to consider raising taxes as well as initiating major cuts in health, education, and welfare services.

## Quebec and Federalism

The reality of Quebec's distinctiveness has deep historical roots, as does the legal recognition of its cultural identity within the federal system (Young 1991). Long before Confederation, in 1838, Lord Durham described "Lower Canada" (Quebec) as "two nations warring in the bosom of a single state." Concern with Quebec as a distinct society has been a powerful force throughout Canada's federal history.

When Confederation was being debated, the pattern for key protections of the French language and aspects of Quebec's distinctiveness had already been set. Almost immediately, the unique political culture of Quebec began to alter the federal landscape of Canada. The British North America Act recognized the status of French as an official language in the Parliament of Canada and the Assembly of Quebec. Latent within the legalistic language of the constitution was the basis for Canadian bilingualism, and for the status of French as an official language equal to English in federal, Quebec, and New Brunswick law.

From the beginning, Quebec challenged one of the main underpinnings of the Canadian federation — the equality of the provinces. As the argument has been made through the years, treating any province differently

under the constitution leads to "special status." However, Confederation did confer special status on a number of provinces, including Quebec.

In 1871, under its terms of union, British Columbia agreed to join Canada if a transcontinental railway was built to link it to the East within ten years. And Newfoundland, under its terms of union in 1949, protected denominational schools and colleges. The equality of the provinces may have been a wish of the Fathers of Confederation, but the terms of the union laid the foundations for something quite different.

But what was to have a significant affect on the dynamics of Canadian federalism was the emergence and strengthening of Quebec nationalism. Although Confederation tied French-speaking Quebeckers to the rest of British North America, it also provided them with a separate province in which they were the majority and could eventually use provincial governing institutions to protect their distinctive culture. For many Quebeckers, Confederation did not mean assimilation into the larger English community of provinces and federal institutions; rather, it meant the opportunity to remain distinctive and free to develop a political culture that might one day launch itself on a separate course.

In the era of Premier Jean Lesage, the so-called Quiet Revolution of the 1960s, this sentiment was expressed in the idea that Quebec was not "une province comme les autres" (a province like the others). Lesage altered the spirit of Canadian federalism with the phrase "maîtres chez nous" (masters in our own house), a doctrine that would eventually challenge the federal assumption that all provinces are equal entities within Canada.

In the 1970s, the victory of the Parti Québécois showed the strength of Quebec nationalism in the province and reflected the challenges that Canada's federal system would come to face (Posgate and McRoberts 1976). Quebec's claim to be a distinct society within

Canada led the Quebec government to propose "sovereignty association." Under this policy, the province would be a separate state but remain associated with Canada with respect to currency and defence.

A referendum on the issue was held in 1979 to see if the Quebec voters wanted their government to negotiate sovereignty association. The "Non" vote won, and by 1985 a federalist government, headed by Liberal leader Robert Bourassa, was returned to power.

In 1987, the question of Quebec as a distinct society in the Canadian federation came to a head. Quebec had not signed the Canada Act, 1982, the act patriating and amending the constitution, because the constitution did not recognize Quebec as a "distinct society within Canada."

But, in 1987, the federal government and the provinces agreed upon amendments to the constitution, recognizing Quebec's distinctiveness. The Meech Lake Accord would have made it more difficult for the federal government to encroach on areas of exclusive jurisdiction. The accord's recognition of Quebec's distinctiveness would have increased the decentralization of Canadian federalism as it involves all provinces.

In the failed Charlottetown Accord, the recognition of Quebec's distinctiveness was included as one of only eight "fundamental characteristics" in the Canada Clause. But in a subsection that followed the list of fundamental characteristics, the accord confirmed Quebec's distinctiveness: "The role of the legislature and Government of Quebec to preserve and promote the distinct society of Quebec is affirmed."

Within Canada's federal structure, the distinctiveness of Quebec extends beyond its major language and cultural uniqueness. Its distinctiveness is a considerably broader canvas. This was recognized even in the 1960s, when the Royal Commission on Bilingualism and Biculturalism referred in its preliminary report to Quebec's political and economic institutions and its "autonomous network of social institutions."

The flexibility of Canada's federal system has permitted Quebec to do a number of important things its way. Quebec has, in the past, chosen to take a different route from the rest of Canada in several areas of public policy and public administration. Quebec is the only province that has its own public pension plan, which came into effect in 1965, a few months before the Canada Pension Plan. Both plans emerged from a period of lively public debate and intergovernmental negotiations. A number of elements in the original Canada Pension Plan were strengthened in response to the Quebec's government's proposal for its own plan.

The Quebec government has also developed what most agree is a unique approach to encouraging economic development, particularly to strengthen the province's economic infrastructure. At the forefront has been the *Caisse de dépôt et placement*, created in 1965 to manage the funds of various Quebec insurance plans. The *Caisse* also invests in government bonds — both inside and outside Quebec — and in Quebec businesses. It provides assistance to Quebeckers seeking to acquire control over Quebec corporations. The *Caisse* is the largest of any Canadian corporation to invest on the stock exchange.

Quebec's special character in Canada's federal system is also exemplified by its participation in international affairs (Munton and Kirton 1992, 156–74). As the homeland and mainstay of the majority of French-speaking people in North America, Quebec has assumed responsibilities peculiar to it alone by its active participation in the international community. Bolstered by the 1867 constitution, which gave the provinces formidable powers in economic and cultural areas, Quebec has taken initiatives in external affairs with many of the francophone nation-states in Europe, Africa, and the Caribbean. The efforts by Quebec to conduct its own external relations as a province of Canada by participating in international conferences, and by developing independent agreements in the educational and cultural fields with France and La Francophonie, are examples of Quebec's ability to act as a special entity in Canada's federal system.

## PROVINCIAL GOVERNING SYSTEMS

There is more to provincial government than federalism. Constitutionally, the provinces have developed as separate governing entities, acquiring their own institutional and political legitimacy, what some people call a "provincial state" (Brownsey and Howlett 1992). Provinces all make and implement laws for the people and organizations located within their territorial jurisdictions.

In the context of their constitutional powers, provinces are truly Canada's welfare states. They deliver most of the government's programs that directly affect the welfare of our citizens. But, by the 1990s, because of their burgeoning debts and deficits, all provinces had abandoned direct state intervention in favour of loan guarantees, privatization, and cutbacks in social programs.

### Provincial Executives

All provinces have the formal institutions of executive government that operate in a parliamentary system. They have the office of lieutenant-governor which represents the monarchy, as does the governor general at the federal level (Saywell 1957). Originally, the lieutenant-governor was the head of the local government, Queen Victoria's representative in the colony. Before Confederation, this person was appointed by the British government. The job of the office was to carry out administrative work, such as corresponding with officials in London from the residence usually called Government House.

The Fathers of Confederation were quite emphatic about the need to retain the principle of constitutional monarchy in the provinces and to separate the provincial executive into a ceremonial representative and a head of government. John A. Macdonald envisioned lieutenant-governors as federal officers, keeping a close eye on the provinces; they were to be the intermediaries between the federal government in Ottawa and the local administrations in the provincial capitals.

That Macdonald saw the lieutenant-governors simply as agents of the federal government becomes clear when we examine the pertinent sections of the Constitution Act, 1867. In that document, the lieutenant-governor is appointed, not by the monarch, but by the governor general–in–council, paid by the federal treasury, and removable from office by the governor general–in–council.

In the early years of Confederation, this threat of removal was not an idle one. Two lieutenant-governors were removed from office by the governor general–in–council. In 1879, Luc Letellier de St-Just was removed as lieutenant-governor of Quebec for dismissing his Cabinet ministers arbitrarily, just prior to a provincial election, and replacing them with members of the Liberal opposition. And Thomas McInnes, in British Columbia, was himself dismissed in 1900 for removing two premiers, one after the other.

The courts clarified the status of lieutenant-governors in two cases, *Hodge V. the Queen* (1883) and *Maritime Bank V. the Receiver-General of New Brunswick* (1892). These two judgements ensured that, from then on, lieutenant-governors, like the governor general, were to be looked upon as the Crown's personal representatives, and not as mere agents of the federal government.

Today, all formal acts of provincial governments are carried out in the name of the Crown, and therefore of the lieutenant-governor of the province in the exercise of his or her constitutional jurisdiction. Lieutenant-governors are appointed by the federal government on the advice of the prime minister for a five-year term. As the agents of the Crown, they have the executive power to reserve provincial legislation for the federal Cabinet to consider, which could decide to approve or reject it. They can veto legislation, dismiss provincial governments, and refuse to dissolve the legislature when requested by a premier who wishes to call an election. They summon, prorogue (temporarily discontinue), and dissolve provincial legislatures, and assent to provincial legislation in the name of the Crown. They also deliver the **Speech from the Throne**.

Like the governor general, lieutenant-governors ensure that there is always a government in office. The power of reservation has been used once since the 1930s, provincial legislation has been vetoed fewer than 30 times, only 3 lieutenant-governors refused to dissolve their provincial legislatures, and 5 have dismissed their provincial governments. Almost always, lieutenant-governors perform ceremonial and social functions, such as dedicating a public building or receiving a royal visitor.

## Premiers

The head of a provincial political party which succeeds in electing the greatest number of members is invited by the lieutenant-governor to become premier. When no party has a majority, the premier is the person most likely to hold the confidence of the members. The premier is the head of government and chooses a Cabinet, traditionally from members of the Assembly, usually the premier's party.

Premiers are analogous to prime ministers in many respects. They all operate under parliamentary systems of government. Their power comes from their personal and political skills, the strength of their political parties, and their ability to use the media and win elections. Most premiers have considerable influence over policy but also must co-ordinate policy matters with the cabinets they appoint.

In each province, the premier, who heads the provincial government, leads an essentially unified party and can usually count on the loyal support of its parliamentary members. But party loyalties alone are rarely enough to guarantee success for a premier in a provincial legislature.

To a premier, it may be just as important to have strong public support. With it, the premier can win elections. And he or she must be able to convey to executive subordinates, administrators, and party colleagues alike the fact (or convincing illusion) of continuing popular support. Beyond the strength a government derives from the public is the existence of a widespread popular mood of confidence in the premier that he or she is knowledgeable, politically skilful, and, to use a colloquialism, "in charge."

The public prestige of a premier depends, not only on the actual accomplishments of his or her government, but on the skill of the premier in public relations. While it is true that the former depends on the latter, premiers must handle press conferences well, give countless addresses competently, make innumerable personal appearances, and project positive images of themselves and their policies.

All premiers have prime minister-like powers to appoint top executive officials, such as deputy ministers; propose legislation; and sign bills to be passed by the legislative assembly. They possess discretion in deciding which laws to use, when, as often is the case, alternative laws can be invoked. They have options in deciding how vigorously to enforce existing legislation. Moreover, they derive strength from a popular expectation that they will use all powers available to them when there is an emergency, such as a flood or drought, a crippling strike in the public sector, or a pattern of violence that they regard as threatening the well-being of the province.

Ultimately, the greatest potential source of power for a premier is the political skill he or she uses in maximizing and using official power and in activating public support for the

**BEST ACTOR**
*for a Socialist in a Conservative Role*
and **BEST SUPPORTING ACTOR**
*for a Conservative in a Socialist Role*

This cartoon of Ontario premier Bob Rae demonstrates that a premier must be able to convey the idea (or a convincing illusion) of continued popular support. *Source:* Andy Donato, *The Toronto Sun,* March 30, 1993. Reproduced with permission of Andy Donato.

government. A premier is not a mere clerk, administering a provincial bureaucracy, but a leader. He or she will have an agenda for the fulfilment of certain policy goals. To be effective, the premier no less than the prime minister must be a successful persuader, and to be a successful persuader he or she must be a good politician.

## *Cabinets*

It is Cabinet that formulates government policy (Kornberg, Mishler and Clarke 1982, 171–75). Cabinet members are known as "ministers," and the premier is, in fact, the "First Minister." Each minister is responsible for one or more government departments or other

provincial agencies. In the provincial Assembly, it is the custom for ministers to occupy the two front rows of seats to the right of the Speaker. The premier's place is normally in the centre of the first row.

Typically, provincial cabinets are small, decisive governing bodies that range in size from 11 to 30 ministers (see Table 10.4). Traditionally, provincial cabinets have been called the "Executive Council." They do what the federal Cabinet does; they plan legislation, co-ordinate provincial government policies, draft provincial laws, supervise government departments, and issue orders-in-council under provincial statute.

Provincial Cabinets reflect their constitutional jurisdictions, usually with ministers holding portfolios in health, education, labour, human resources, social services, energy, environment, natural resources, economic development, agriculture, highways, tourism, municipal affairs, consumer protection, housing, finance, and justice. Most coastal provinces also have departments of fisheries. Others have a minister for the status of women, and some, such as Alberta and Quebec, have ministers for international trade. More recently, cabinets have been given special ministerial assignments for intergovernmental relations. In choosing their cabinets, premiers are concerned about appointing people who repre-

**Table 10.4 Size of Provincial Cabinets, 1993**

|  | Cabinet Size |
| --- | --- |
| Quebec | 30 |
| Ontario | 27 |
| Alberta | 27 |
| New Brunswick | 24 |
| British Columbia | 23 |
| Nova Scotia | 16 |
| Saskatchewan | 20 |
| Manitoba | 18 |
| Newfoundland | 15 |
| P.E.I. | 11 |

sent gender, language, certain regions or municipalities, racial and ethnic groups, and religions, and have working-class backgrounds.

Since the 1960s, the growth of provincial governments has spawned the use of committees to help plan and co-ordinate the legislative process. No less so than their federal colleagues, members of provincial cabinets must often deal with complex issues that require much consideration. Cabinet committees are modelled after their federal counterparts, usually with a Treasury Board (for finance and personnel), a planning and priorities committee, and committees on social policy and resource development.

## Provincial Legislatures

The passage of laws is the function most commonly attributed to provincial legislative assemblies (Atkinson and White 1980). As in the federal House of Commons and the Senate, each piece of legislation is introduced in the Assembly, and given effective consideration. Once introduced, a bill goes through the same stages as a federal bill. After a bill is passed, it becomes an act or statute.

Each year, a budget is proposed to the legislative assembly by the provincial minister of finance. Expenditure estimates are tabled so that members may review the budget in detail. This process usually takes place in a Committee of Finance (comprising all members of the Assembly except the Speaker), where the minister must answer questions and hear the opinions of members before the money is approved.

Once the Assembly has concluded its consideration of the estimates, an appropriation bill is introduced to grant the amount of money the provincial Committee of Finance has agreed to supply. Provincial governments have no authority to spend public money until this process is completed, unless, in the meantime, the Assembly allows temporary financing by passing an interim supply bill.

An audit process begins upon the passage of such bills, and at the conclusion of the fis-

cal year the government must table the Public Accounts. Usually a provincial auditor, an officer of the Assembly, makes a final report. All of these matters are referred to the Standing Committee on Public Accounts, which determines whether all expenditures were done with proper legislative authority and with value for money spent.

All provinces have unicameral provincial legislatures that vary significantly in size, usually called the Legislative Assembly or House of Assembly (the Assemblée nationale in Quebec) (see Table 10.5). Provincial laws are made as in the federal Parliament, usually introduced as government bills that proceed through three readings, deliberation by an appropriate committee, and royal assent represented by the lieutenant-governor.

Members of the provincial legislatures are usually elected from single-member districts for five-year parliamentary terms. However, the premiers can call elections at any time before the five-year term expires. A majority of provincial legislators come from the legal profession and some from farming or teaching, or from businesses — such as insurance or real estate — that allow them to take leave for parliamentary duties. Most provincial legislatures meet for only a fraction of the year, but

**Table 10.5 Size of Provincial Legislative Assemblies, 1993**

|  | Assembly Size |
| --- | --- |
| Ontario | 130 |
| Quebec | 125 |
| Alberta | 83 |
| British Columbia | 69 |
| Saskatchewan | 64 |
| New Brunswick | 58 |
| Manitoba | 57 |
| Newfoundland | 52 |
| Nova Scotia | 52 |
| P.E.I. | 16 |

members are expected to consult with their constituents and act upon their problems and requests year-round.

Unlike in the federal House of Commons, provincial cabinets take up a much larger proportion of the members. In fact, most of Canada's provincial cabinets are larger than that of Great Britain, a country with a population of more than 60 million. And even after former prime minister Kim Campbell reduced the size of the federal Cabinet to 24, and her successor, Jean Chrétien, to 23, the cabinets of four provinces were larger or equal to that of the federal government — Quebec 30, Ontario 27, Alberta 27, and New Brunswick 24. Because provincial cabinets are large in comparison with the number of legislative members, they tend to be much more decisive. Many use orders-in-council much more frequently than does the federal government.

Provincial legislative assemblies are parliaments that play a vital role in the life of every resident in the province. In essence, government power must be exercised through the legislative assembly. Therefore, members of the provincial Assembly have a vital role to play in the development of the province.

## The Opposition

The head of the political party that forms the official opposition is given the parliamentary rank at the provincial level of "Leader of the Opposition." The leader of the opposition has the same parliamentary status as a Cabinet minister. In the Assembly, the leader of the opposition sits directly opposite the premier.

The role of the opposition has traditionally been much weaker in provincial legislatures than in Parliament, where procedures of debate give the opposition more power against the government. Legislative procedures have evolved in all provinces where legislatures have adopted question period as a tool for the opposition. About one half-hour of each day of sitting, members have the opportunity to direct oral questions to a provincial

Cabinet minister on any topic within the minister's responsibility. Members can also direct written questions to a minister, who has the option to answer directly, usually within 48 hours, or to convert the question into a "return." A return is necessary when a response would be too detailed to prepare within the normal time limit.

Some provinces use standing committees to scrutinize government bills and to offer amendments. Opposition members can affect the spirit and content of legislation in these committees. Standing committees are appointed to undertake specialized tasks, such as the examination of the Public Accounts or the activities of provincial crown corporations. These committees meet on a regular basis to hear witnesses and gather evidence. Given the evolving role of the opposition in provincial legislatures, the entire lawmaking process has become much more complex and variable. Despite the apparent dominance of provincial cabinets over the lawmaking process, more recently legislative procedures have become an obstacle course to any minister introducing a piece of contentious legislation.

## The Speaker

Central to the political rivalry in provincial assemblies is the Speaker, who exercises a significant role in all provincial legislatures. The Speaker is a member of the Legislative Assembly (MLA or MNA), usually elected by secret ballot by all other members to maintain order in the Assembly in an impartial manner. The selection of a Speaker takes place after each general provincial election, or when a Speaker dies or retires. The Speaker must be prepared to treat all members of the Assembly equally. As the person of highest authority in the Assembly, the Speaker usually sits on a raised chair at the end of the provincial Chamber, with the government members on his or her right and opposition members to the left.

The provincial Speaker is responsible for controlling the flow of House business and acts as referee during debates. The importance of this role in ensuring the proper working of the Assembly is emphasized at the beginning of each sitting of the Assembly in the Speaker's parade.

The Speaker, accompanied by the **Clerk** and the **pages**, is escorted into the legislative chamber by the Sergeant-at-Arms, carrying the mace. The Speaker's traditional robes help to emphasize his or her neutrality, while the mace is the symbol of the Speaker's authority in the provincial Assembly. It is the Speaker's duty to ensure that the rules of the Assembly for conducting its business are followed and that all members have the opportunity to take parts in debates.

Balancing the right of the majority to conduct business with the right of the minority to be heard is one of the Speaker's most difficult tasks. Because it is essential that the Speaker be seen to be above party politics, he or she does not take part in the debates or votes, unless there is a tie. All remarks made in the provincial legislature must be made to the Speaker, and normally, no members may stand when the Speaker is standing.

The Speaker has an additional, very important role in overseeing a range of services — financial, administrative, legal, and informational — in the provincial legislative assembly. The Speaker is responsible for the costs involved in operating the legislature, and usually chairs a board that directs the internal economy of legislative work. Such a board establishes policies and spending levels for all services and funds provided to MLAs and MNAs.

The Speaker is also required to represent the provincial legislature on all ceremonial and formal occasions, including dealings with the Crown, and other parliaments and legislatures. This may involve playing the role of host to visiting foreign dignitaries, or premiers and MLAs from other provinces at parliamentary gatherings in Canada.

Finally, like the Speaker of the federal House of Commons, the Speaker of the Assembly does not cease to be an MLA or MNA. The Speaker must continue to listen to concerns of constituents and effectively represent them. Acting as Speaker requires a broad range of personal and professional skills. A Speaker needs to be sympathetic and firm, fair and honest at all times, and must have the ability to remain aloof from the fray of the legislature, and to be a convivial host when the need arises.

## The Roles of Provincial Members

At sittings of provincial legislative assemblies, Members oversee government activities and they represent the interests of their constituents. The average session for provincial legislatures is about 90 days annually.

Most members take their role very seriously because the laws they pass affect the lives of every citizen in the province. In provincial assemblies, members debate, analyze, and amend bills on a wide variety of issues in provincial politics.

Often members draw on their own life experiences when they consider legislation. It is not uncommon, however, for certain members to have expertise in some field, such as health or education, which they will apply in debate. More often, preparation for a debate involves research, consultation with experts, and listening to constituents; invariably, it involves writing a speech.

Consideration of legislation is only part of the Assembly's role in maintaining constant scrutiny of a provincial government. Whether members are reviewing the clauses of a bill or making a line-by-line examination of the provincial budget, the publicity they bring to issues helps to form public opinion and bring pressure to bear on government. Therefore, the effectiveness of members in their support of, or opposition to, government has a critical effect.

Debate is as rigorous at the provincial level as it is in Ottawa. There is a formidable amount of work involved in debate, including long hours spent listening to what other members have to say and preparing for a chance to speak in the Assembly.

Each member is entitled to speak in each debate, but members also have the opportunity to initiate debate. Normally, one day is set aside on a province's legislative calendar for members to raise issues of their own choosing. Members are usually assigned to one or more of the legislative committees in the provincial legislature.

Debates are opportunities that members use to express concern or agreement with government policy. As in the federal House of Commons, the Throne Speech debate is often used by members to relate policy issues to the well-being of their constituencies.

In their constituencies, members must be able to explain the legislation they have discussed in the provincial legislature, and therefore must understand it.

When constituents bring problems, members' knowledge of government ministers and officials, and contacts with other levels of government and community groups, enable them to choose the best route to a resolution. When constituents feel they have been treated unfairly or improperly represented in some manner, they look to their member to understand and defend their interests. Members often require mediation skills to resolve a clash of interests within their constituencies, or between constituents and other groups. Sometimes constituents will bring personal problems to members, requiring them to have the skills of a social worker to be effective in their role. And within their constituencies, members must display leadership qualities when local issues are addressed.

## The Cost of Government

The **decentralization** of governing responsibilities in Canada has made provincial governments busier places. Legislatures sit for longer sessions, and individual members are swamped with constituency work. The job of a provincial legislator is undoubtedly a full-time one, with all of the complexities of that of a member of Parliament in Ottawa. Over the years since Confederation, the expansion of provincial governments has increased the need for legislators to seek the support of administrative and clerical staff to get the job done. Salaries, pensions, and services have increased the cost of governing at the provincial level (see Table 10.6).

The bureaucracy of governing and representation has become significant in recent years. Legislatures in most provinces spend more money now on their offices, secretaries, research staffs, travel, computer services, telephones, committee work, and the process of making laws than ever before. These services have driven up substantially the cost of governing in all provinces.

## The Courts

Each of the provinces has a court system that only occasionally comes into contact with federal courts. Most Canadians never see the inside of the Supreme Court of Canada and are never parties to a case resolved by the Federal Court. But many have been to provincial and municipal courts, for example, paying a fine in traffic court, or serving as a juror in a case before the supreme court of a province. Provincial courts handle many more cases than the federal courts do. The quality of justice in Canada therefore depends to a great extent on the quality of justice administered in the provinces and local communities. These courts, rather than the federal courts, are the most visible to the average citizen.

The federal government retains important controls on provincial courts: Decisions made by provincial courts can be reviewed and appealed to the Supreme Court of Canada. It is the federal government, not the provinces, that generates the Criminal Code. And provincial supreme court or superior court judges are federal government appointments.

**Table 10.6 The High Cost of Governing Canada's Provinces and Territories, 1992**

|  | Legislative Budget | Population | Total Cost Per Capita |
|---|---|---|---|
| Newfoundland | $6 752 700 | 571 700 | $21.91 |
| P.E.I. | $2 542 100 | 129 900 | $29.67 |
| Nova Scotia | $7 648 600 | 897 500 | $18.62 |
| New Brunswick | $6 602 000 | 725 600 | $19.20 |
| Quebec | $76 000 000 | 6 811 800 | $21.26 |
| Ontario | $129 131 700 | 9 840 300 | $23.22 |
| Manitoba | $9 749 800 | 1 092 600 | $19.02 |
| Saskatchewan | $14 435 700 | 995 300 | $24.60 |
| Alberta | $23 346 717 | 2 501 400 | $19.43 |
| B.C. | $24 711 000 | 3 185 900 | $17.86 |
| N.W.T. | $9 209 000 | 54 000 | $180.64 |
| Yukon | $2 196 000 | 26 500 | $91.43 |

*Source:* Robert Flemming, *Canadian Legislatures, 1992* (Agincourt, Ont.: Global Press, 1992), 70. Reproduced with permission of Robert Flemming.

Each of the provinces has its own judicial hierarchy and rules. Each has a complex system of courts that usually includes a supreme court, **small claims courts**, family courts, and courts that can handle minor criminal charges. Judges who serve in these courts are appointed by the provincial government. Like federal judges, provincial judges are involved in conflict resolution, administration of provincial and federal laws, and the interpretation of laws passed by both the provincial and the federal governments. Provincial court rulings must conform to the Canadian constitution as interpreted by the Supreme Court of Canada.

## PROVINCIAL POLITICAL SYSTEMS

The opportunities for effective political participation by Canadians would be greatly reduced if we had only a centralized national government (Bellamy, Pammett, and Rowat 1976, Chap. 1). Each province has developed its own political system wherein non-govern-

mental forces, such as pressure groups and political parties, place demands on or give support to the governing system. These are the groups that can affect how provincial governments perform because they show what people want from their government, covering most matters of concern to people, whether it be more provincial autonomy, outright sovereign independence, a more efficient health care system, or the control of provincial deficits and debts.

## The Provinces and Pressure Groups

Aside from differences of size and scale, there is little that sharply differentiates interest-group tactics at the provincial level from those used with the federal government. All provincial governments must deal with these so-called interest groups, pressure groups, or lobbyists. There may be some disagreement over which label best describes their purpose, but it is always much the same — to influence provincial government policies and actions.

Although interest groups vary tremendously from province to province in terms of size, goals, budget, and scope of interest, they employ the same techniques to accomplish their objectives with provincial governments as they do with the federal government.

Despite a remarkable similarity to the Ottawa scene, lobbying provincial governments is somewhat different from lobbying at the federal level. One reason is that leadership in the provincial legislatures tends to be more concentrated — in the hands of the premier, the Cabinet, party leaders, and provincial bureaucrats — than in the federal House.

Because provincial governments deliver some of the most basic services to Canadians — for example, health, education, and welfare — pressure groups that represent these interests can have a profound effect on the direction of public policy. **Institutional pressure groups**, such as those representing provincial public servants, schools, universities, and doctors and hospitals, continually make a stream of specific demands on provincial governments. The British Columbia Government Employees Union, the Nova Scotia Teachers Union, the Manitoba Medical Association, and the Ontario Hospital Association are examples of some pressure groups that reflect the diversity of provincial politics.

The first job of groups like these is to identify which of the several government departments needs to be persuaded. The second is to discover whether the provincial government can do what is wanted at all, without having to lobby in Ottawa as well. Contacts at social functions are always of considerable importance and rank as significant elements in the total patterns of interest group–provincial government interaction. Other indirect modes of influence include attempts to manipulate the selection of provincial government appointees with an eye to securing a "friend in the Cabinet" or the provincial public service.

Some provinces have long been regarded as having strong pressure-group systems. In Ontario and Quebec, public policy appears to be largely the end-product of the pulling and hauling of organized groups in the province. In many provinces, dozens of groups, such as farmers, real estate interests, labour unions, teachers, and public servants, seek to put pressure on the provincial government. In some provinces, such as Quebec (sovereigntists, paper, textiles, hydro-electric power) and Alberta (oil and gas), a few powerful interests may play a pervasive and dominant role in shaping basic provincial policies. In other provinces, interest groups tend to represent a wider variety of interests.

### Provincial Political Parties

The provinces are important elements in Canada's evolving political party system. They are often the barometers of national politics and are the proving grounds for ambitious politicians (Thorburn 1991, 363–506).

Each province has developed its own party system, somewhat distinctive from all the others. There are ten provincial party systems and two territorial systems, no two exactly alike. In all provinces, most political parties are well organized and have permanent staffs who control budgets. Almost all provincial parties maintain a permanent headquarters office, typically in the capital city.

Most provinces have produced two party competitive systems, wherein, over significant periods of time, two political parties tend to form governments intermittently. The provinces of Atlantic Canada have provided the best and most stable examples of party systems in which political power and governmental office tend to fluctuate between two major political parties — namely, the Liberals and the Conservatives. This structure has not precluded the presence of minor parties in electoral competition within each province. In most of the other provinces, **third parties** have formed and competed to challenge one or both of the dominant provincial governing parties.

Once we leave the Atlantic region, provincial political party systems become more kaleidoscopic. On examination, Quebec deviates from a pure two-party model not only because third parties have formed governments but because one party — the Liberal party — has dominated the office of government since the turn of the century. The Union Nationale governed for about 25 years, and the Parti Québécois governed for more than 10 and was reelected in 1994. Ontario shows the dominance of the Conservative party, peppered with governments formed by the United Farmers Party, the Liberals, and the NDP.

The typical dichotomy of strong Liberal- or Conservative-dominated provincial party systems changes considerably once we reach the political landscape of Manitoba. A greater transformation of this province's party system is evident than in all provinces east of Ontario. Manitoba's party system has generated Liberal governments; United Farmers; coalitions with United Farmers and Progressives; and Liberal-Progressive, Conservative, and NDP.

Saskatchewan has exhibited long intervals of one-party dominance, as when the Liberal party formed a succession of governments from 1905 to 1944, and the CCF/NDP from 1944 to 1964. But, since the mid-1960s, Saskatchewan has produced a more competitive two-party system, changing between the Liberals and the Conservatives, the Liberals and the NDP, and the Conservatives and the NDP. Other parties, such as the Progressives in the 1920s and Social Credit from the late 1930s to the mid-1950s, have competed credibly in Saskatchewan's party system.

In Alberta, the Liberal, United Farmers, Social Credit, and Conservative parties have formed governments at various times throughout this century. Each of these parties has produced governments at different times, reflecting a trend toward one-party dominance.

British Columbia nurtured a two-party competitive system early in its provincial history, beginning in 1903, with the Liberal and Conservative parties alternating in power until the 1940s. In 1941, these two parties formed a unique coalition government that lasted until 1952. Social Credit emerged as the party of protest and succeeded in unravelling the electoral support for the coalition, eventually leading to the decline of the Liberals and the Conservatives. The Social Credit Party was instrumental in building a one-party dominant trend in British Columbia, which, except for the NDP government of Dave Barrett from 1972 to 1975, remained predominant until the early 1990s, when the NDP again formed the government.

Most provinces have retained a biparty character of some kind, despite the intermittent presence of third parties — although there are always exceptions, such as in some of the Prairie provinces and British Columbia. The case of Quebec served to illustrate how a provincial minor party — the Parti Québécois — could stun itself, as well as the rest of the country, by springing to power, weathering political storms, recovering from defeat, and going on to form another government in 1994.

## The Provinces and the Electoral System

The constitution of Canada requires that a provincial general election be held five years from the date of the previous election. Within that period, the premier names a specific day as election day, sometimes called "dropping the Writ." This formally starts the election period, which lasts on average for 30 days. The Writ has the effect of immediately dissolving the Assembly, that is, there are no members of the Assembly during this period. However, the political executive — the premier, Cabinet ministers, and the prerogatives of the lieutenant-governor — remain in place throughout the election period. Thus, while there is no elected Assembly during this period, there is still continuous provincial government.

According to the Elections Act, any person eighteen years of age or older who has been living in a province for at least six months, who is a Canadian citizen, and who is not disqualified from voting (a convicted criminal serving time in a penitentiary, for example) is eligible to become a candidate for election to a provincial legislative assembly.

The chief electoral officer is the person responsible for co-ordinating an election on a province-wide basis, but it is the returning officer for each constituency who makes the detailed arrangements for holding the election in that particular provincial riding. Persons called "enumerators" call door-to-door to make lists of eligible voters, voting places are established, ballots and ballot boxes are pro-

vided, and notices are issued regarding the location of polling stations.

The fundamental rules of Canada's electoral system apply in all provinces. The act of choice performed by provincial voters on election day takes place within the legal and structural framework that strongly influences the result. Provincial electoral systems are not neutral; they affect the dynamics of voting all along the way. All provinces except P.E.I. (which still has dual-member ridings) elect one candidate in each riding, determined by his or her having won a plurality of votes. The candidate who wins one or more votes than anyone else in the riding represents the whole constituency. This first-past-the-post and winner-take-all electoral formula has tended to produce strong provincial governments, often with fewer than 50 percent of voters supporting them.

## CONCLUSION

Since 1867, Canada's provinces have become very significant players in how we govern this country. The Fathers of Confederation designed a federal system that favoured the central government in Ottawa so that the provinces would follow the lead of the federal government and the country could be built decisively from the national perspective. And even though two world wars and the Depression further empowered the federal government, the provinces gradually claimed an equal partnership with Ottawa. Meanwhile, social and structural changes in Quebec produced all of the necessary political ingredients in that province for the creation of a new independent nation-state in North America.

As with so many issues in Canadian political life, the constitution did not settle the issue of federalism. Rather, it provided a framework within which future changes would be worked out. No one reading the Constitution Act, 1867, which outlined the jurisdictions giving the federal government and the prov-

inces certain powers, would be able on that basis alone to predict the state of Canadian federalism in the 1990s. The basic framework was a strong and unified federal government in Ottawa and a group of partially independent provinces. Its peculiar evolution depended on historical forces.

The balance of power between the federal government and the provinces has changed significantly over time. But the constitutional framework which created a strong central government and an independent group of provinces has survived. As federalism has evolved, government responsibilities have been sorted out through a political and legal, but not a procedural, process.

Strong and demanding premiers have pulled and tugged powers to their provinces. The enduring nationalism of Quebec and its unique political culture have kept the federal government sensitive to provincial autonomy and made it reluctant to use its constitutional powers to keep the provinces subordinate.

Canadian courts have also contributed to the transfer of authority between the federal and provincial governments, tending to empower the provinces as the level of government most capable of serving the local and regional needs of Canadians.

Federal–provincial relations have thus undergone marked changes through the twentieth century. Today, there are relatively few governmental functions that are carried out in Canada exclusively by one level of government. Health, education, the environment, public works, and even law enforcement are examples of government services provided through federal, provincial, and even municipal co-operation.

Each province has developed distinctive patterns of economic growth and social development. Distinguishing political cultures also flourish among the provinces and territories. But provincial government institutions are quite similar in every respect, having been modelled after the parliamentary traditions of Great Britain, which include the Crown, Cabinet government, and legislative and judicial accountability.

The federal and provincial governments share common problems of too much government deficit and debt, too much foreign-owned debt financing, and high borrowing requirements to meet public demands. All levels of government place the burden of these debt problems on the same taxpayer who is subject to taxes on income, capital, and consumption, and who faces charges for licences, permits, user fees, and additional payroll deductions. Current provincial and provincial deficits are already at the point where they are not sustainable for very much longer.

There are competing theories about the best ways for Canadian governments to deal with these monumental economic challenges. And there are disagreements among politicians and political economists about what the solutions might be and on the consequences of acting in accord with any of them.

Canada's federal system has evolved to become one of the most striking examples of the fragmentation of government power and jurisdiction. Many believe that a natural consequence of the obstacles to governing in Canada under the current federal system has been inconsistency in policy and enormous public debt. Some might say that Canada's institutions of government are too fragmented to manage a modern political economy. Key economic choices are linked to co-operation or conflict between the federal and provincial governments.

The prominence of economic concerns, and the relationship between governability and policy effectiveness, recur as themes in Canadian federalism. How these and countless other problems are addressed in the coming decades depends on how well Canadian federalism works and how effectively the country's leaders are able to govern.

## GLOSSARY

**Clerk**   The Clerk of the Legislative Assembly is responsible for co-ordinating the procedural, administrative, financial, and support services required by the MLAs, the Assembly, and the committees. The Clerk reports to the Speaker.

**core area**   A small portion of a province in which the political and economic power is concentrated, usually the capital city.

**decentralization**   The tendency to devolve government responsibilities to subgovernments, such as those of provinces and municipalities.

**First Ministers' Conferences**   A feature of Canadian federalism, which can be traced, first, to 1887, that brings together premiers or Cabinet ministers of provincial governments, the prime minister, and members of the federal Cabinet at a meeting of summitry among Canadian governments to discuss and negotiate problems and issues facing the country.

**institutional pressure groups**   Pressure groups that represent well-established social structures in society, such as businesses, bureaucracies, churches, and universities.

**intergovernmental relations**   The workings of the federal system of government, by which is meant the entire set of interactions among the federal, provincial, and municipal levels of government.

**jurisdictions**   The constitutional right of a level of government to make public policy in a certain domain of societal need.

**pages**   The men and women who work while the legislative assembly is in session to carry messages between members, run errands, and perform other tasks related to legislative responsibilities. Before each day's session, they place the day's agenda and other necessary papers on members' desks.

**regional governments**   Governing structures created by provinces under which municipalities are regrouped with a regional administration.

**Rupert's Land**   Vast territory controlled by the Hudson's Bay Company until 1870 when Canada bought it and took over the rest of the Northwest Territory from Great Britain.

**small claims courts**   Courts that are established by provinces to hear civil cases that involved small amounts of money, up to $10 000 in Quebec and $1000, $2000, and $3000 in other provinces.

**Speech from the Throne**   As it occurs in a province, it is a statement of government policy for the legislative session, read by the lieutenant-governor at the start of each session of the legislative assembly.

**third parties**   At the provincial level, a term used somewhat inaccurately to refer to political parties that have formed (i.e., Social Credit in Alberta and British Columbia) to challenge the dominance of the traditional parties (the Liberals and the Conservatives).

**United Province of Canada**   The union of the former provinces of Upper Canada and Lower Canada on the recommendation of the Durham Report of 1839.

## RECOMMENDED READING

Bickerton, James. 1990. *Nova Scotia, Ottawa, and the Politics of Regional Development.* Toronto: University of Toronto Press. This book traces the history of Ottawa's regional development policies as they have affected Nova Scotia and the other Atlantic provinces.

Brownsey, Keith, and Michael Howlett, eds. 1992. *The Provincial State.* Toronto: Copp Clark Pitman. This excellent collection gathers interpretations by well-known Canadian political scientists who analyze the politics and government of Canada's provinces and territories.

Coates, Ken, and William Morrison. 1992. *The Forgotten North: A History of Canada's Provincial Norths.* Toronto: James Lorimer. This book analyzes the history and politics of northern development in six provinces, from British Columbia through the Canadian Shield and Labrador.

Drache, Daniel, and Roberto Perin, eds. 1992. *Negotiating with a Sovereign Quebec.* Toronto: James Lorimer. This collection gathers essays that focus on the ramifications of Quebec sovereignty. The collection is divided into six sections that address the cultural, economic, political, and social dimensions of this question.

Dyck, Rand. 1991. *Provincial Politics in Canada*. Scarborough, Ont.: Prentice-Hall Canada. One of the most authoritative texts on provincial politics in Canada, this book contains an in-depth portrayal of each province's political culture, institutions, political leadership, electoral system, and relationship with the federal government and other provinces.

Forbes, E.R., and D.A. Muise. 1993. *The Atlantic Provinces in Confederation*. Toronto: University of Toronto Press. This book tells the story of the diverse character of Canada's four easternmost provinces and the development of their economies and provincial governing systems.

Gagnon, Alain. 1992. *Quebec: State and Society*. Scarborough, Ont.: Nelson Canada. This collection of original interdisciplinary articles serves as an introduction to Quebec history, politics, and economics.

Gagnon, Alain, and M.B. Montcalm. 1990. *Quebec: Beyond the Quiet Revolution*. Scarborough, Ont.: Nelson Canada. This book provides the uninitiated reader with a comprehensive analysis of the political transformations that have occurred in Quebec society since 1960, with a focus on the constitutional agenda of Quebec's leaders from Lesage to Bourassa.

White, Graham, ed. 1990. *The Government and Politics of Ontario*. Scarborough, Ont.: Nelson Canada. This book provides an integrated analysis of Ontario politics and government, the political culture, and legislative and bureaucratic institutions.

Young, Robert. 1991. *Confederation in Crisis*. Toronto: James Lorimer. This book analyzes the state of the Canadian federation from the perspective of constitutional politics.

# CANADA'S MUNICIPAL GOVERNMENTS

Ron Martelle had no idea that being mayor of Cornwall could be a life-threatening experience. He decided to run for that office in the fall of 1991 and, never thought at the time that, within a year of taking on the job, he and members of his family would go into hiding under 24-hour police protection. In his words, "having my personal safety and that of my family's threatened was not in the mayor's job description." While campaigning for mayor, he focussed on curb and gutter issues: street maintenance, traffic lights, beautification, parks, recreation, and garbage collection. He never thought his job would make him a target of violence.

How could the mayor of a small law-abiding Canadian city get entangled in a scenario reminiscent of a *Miami Vice* rerun? It had something to do with death, taxes, and smuggling. But it also had something to do with the responsibilities of governments. When problems become more than one level of government can handle, how do the other levels respond? What does it take to make them co-operate? And, do they respond fast enough?

Geography placed Cornwall in a strategic position for criminals who wanted to smuggle contraband into Canada. Cornwall is just across the St. Lawrence River from the Akwesasne Reserve, which straddles the Canada–U.S. border. Nearly all of the $8 billion worth of cigarettes exported to the United States each year (before the Canadian government lowered taxes) crossed the border tax-free at Buffalo, New York, where they were sold to distributors. From Buffalo, large shipments were transported up the U.S. side of Lake Ontario, to Akwesasne.

At the reserve, the cigarettes were loaded onto boats and smuggled back into Canada from the many secluded bays around the City of Cornwall. About 50 000 cartons of cigarettes were being smuggled through Cornwall every day, where millions of dollars were changing hands on the St. Lawrence shoreline. From Cornwall, the cheaper cigarettes were shipped to other provinces, finding their way as far west as British Columbia and as far east as Newfoundland. It was not surprising that anyone who wanted to put a stop to this lucrative trade would incur the wrath of the profit-seeking smugglers and those who made the initial large outlay of cash to pay for the cigarettes.

Mayor Ron Martelle crawled out on a limb in an attempt to prod the federal government into doing something about the smuggling in the Cornwall region. The mayor issued the federal government an ultimatum, threatening to cause a "spectacle on Parliament Hill" if they didn't act quickly to stop the smugglers and bring an end to the violence in his city. Martelle demanded a much greater federal and provincial police presence in the Cornwall region and called on all governments concerned to implement anti-smuggling policies that would reduce the price of domestic cigarettes by cutting federal and provincial taxes, and at the same time increasing the domestic export tax by $10 a carton.

Almost without warning, in 1992, Cornwall erupted in the kind of violence that Chicago saw during prohibition days of the 1920s and 1930s, and was seen more recently in the towns and cities controlled by the drug lords of Colombia. Suddenly, in this sleepy Ontario mill town, homes, businesses, and civic property were sprayed with automatic weapons' fire by vengeful cigarette smugglers who didn't like one another's competition, and especially didn't like Mayor Martelle's insistence that the federal government do something about the illegal cartels using Cornwall as their major redistribution depot for other cities in Canada.

Drive-by shootings, sniper fire, car-jackings, car-shootings, theft, extortion, and acts of random violence were occurring every day in Cornwall. The threat level to citizens became intolerable when gunmen on a boat travelling past the city fired shots into the Civic Complex. The incident sent shivers up the spines of many Cornwall citizens who could see the problem escalating into routine shoot-outs.

The mayor of this small Canadian city and members of his family were drawn into the centre of Canadian politics and government. They were to learn the hard way how interconnected the challenge of governing Canada is. For Mayor Martelle, the division of powers and responsibilities between the federal and provincial governments carries momentous significance for ordinary Canadians who just want to do their jobs and live their lives peacefully. He learned that municipal problems are often national problems and that, in the words of Sir Ernest Simon, how we run our cities can "mean the difference between savagery and civilization."

## INTRODUCTION

The Canada that most Canadians see when they start their day is not always the romantic one of pristine forests, mountains, lakes, rivers, ocean shores, and broad expanses of land. The landscape most of us see is one of highrise buildings, busy paved streets and boulevards, complex signage, parking lots, factories, service industries, and urban and suburban sprawl. Most Canadians have no other life than that of the city. In fact, more than three-quarters of Canada's population is concentrated in **urban centres** that take up only about 1 percent of its land area. Although the population of Canada is relatively small, especially in relation to its geographical size, Canadian people are concentrated in localities that are predominantly urban in character.

Municipal governments were the first that settlers established in Canada; some, such as Montreal, Quebec City, and Trois-Riviérès date back to the seventeenth century (Kennedy 1983). Local systems of government emerged gradually and unevenly across the country, primarily because of the early patterns of settlement. British immigrants had little experience in the practice of local government. The French tended toward authoritarian local administrative bodies strongly influenced by the Catholic Church. New France, which was a commercial centre based on the fur trade, was — by the standards of the day — highly urbanized, with about 25 percent of its population clustered in large settlements; by contrast, in the thirteen American colonies, fewer than 10 percent of the population lived in "urban" areas.

The American Loyalists, skilled in the democratic practices of local self-government,

influenced Canada's municipal systems, especially in Ontario but also in many other provinces. By 1825, Fort York (Toronto) had about 2000 residents. By the mid-1800s, Montreal was a **city** of more than 50 000, and Quebec City and Toronto had grown to over 30 000. Most municipal systems were already formed or well underway when Canada's provinces were established under the terms of the British North America Act.

Since Confederation, the degree of **urbanization** has increased in each decade. In 1871, less than one Canadian in five lived in a **town** or a city. By the turn of the century, advances in agricultural technology led to dramatic changes in the community life of Canadians (see Table 11.1). By 1901, one in three Canadians lived in an urban setting.

**Table 11.1 Canadians as Urban Dwellers**

| Year | Percentage of Population |
|------|--------------------------|
| 1871 | 18.3 |
| 1881 | 23.3 |
| 1891 | 29.8 |
| 1901 | 34.9 |
| 1911 | 41.8 |
| 1921 | 47.4 |
| 1931 | 52.5 |
| 1941 | 55.7 |
| 1951 | 62.4 |
| 1961 | 69.7 |
| 1971 | 76.1 |
| 1981 | 75.8 |
| 1986 | 76.5 |
| 1991 | 76.6 |

Source: Adapted from F.H. Leacy, ed., *Historical Statistics of Canada* (Toronto: Macmillan Company of Canada, 1983).

Nineteenth-century industrialization brought the application of non-animal sources of power to labour tasks, causing a wide range of effects on people's lifestyles as well as on the political institutions and government structures in their local **communities**. Canada's emerging urban settlements became centres not only of industry but also of artistic endeavour, banking, education, finance, government, labour, management, and professional expertise. Towns and cities are where political parties and interest groups emerged to place demands on the formal institutions of government.

The great waves of immigrants coming to North America (many of whom sought to live in urban places despite the avowed government policy of favouring farmers, miners, and railway workers) drove the proportion of Canadian citizens living in cities to over 50 percent by 1931. By 1971, 76.1 percent of the population were urbanized; in 1991, 76.6 percent were city dwellers.

Some analysts forecast that as much as 90 percent of Canada's population could be urban by the early decades of the next century (Gertler and Crowley 1977). Already nearly half of Canada's current population live in three major cities — Montreal, Toronto, and Vancouver. This has implications for the future of how we govern ourselves in Canada because, with high levels of urbanization, national problems are directly related to municipal problems. Some might say that city problems *are*, in fact, national problems.

It makes sense to think of Canada as an urban society rather than as a **rural** one in the 1990s, even though, in some provinces, more people live in the country than in urban centres (see Table 11.2). Generally, however, across Canada, most people live in large cities, and even those who live in rural settings have adopted many of the elements of an urban lifestyle. As a result, many of the traditional differences between city folks and country folks have disappeared.

**Table 11.2 Percentage of Urban Dwellers in the Provinces and the Territories, 1991**

| Province | Percentage of Population |
| --- | --- |
| Newfoundland | 53.6 |
| Prince Edward Island | 39.9 |
| Nova Scotia | 53.5 |
| New Brunswick | 47.7 |
| Quebec | 77.6 |
| Ontario | 81.8 |
| Manitoba | 72.1 |
| Saskatchewan | 63.0 |
| Alberta | 79.8 |
| British Columbia | 80.4 |
| Yukon | 58.8 |
| Northwest Territories | 36.7 |

*Source:* Adapted from *Profiles of Rural and Urban Areas*, Part A, Statistics Canada, Cat. No. 93-339, 1991. Reproduced by authority of the Minister of Industry, 1994.

This generalized character of Canadian society affects how we relate to each other in every way, including economically, politically, and socially. In urban centres, relations among people are often transitory, impersonal, superficial, and anonymous, and fundamentally more competitive in matters of politics and economics. We expect our municipal governments to be "efficient" and "business-like," free of favouritism and corruption. Further, it is perceived that municipal governments should be bureaucratic and practical in the delivery of their services and the administration of their regulations, and urban planning is highly desirable and is viewed as a job of municipal governments, not of private citizens.

## PATTERNS OF URBAN GROWTH

Historically, the largest cities in Canada were eastern ports for ocean-going ships, settled because of a good harbour and navigable waterways. Examples are Halifax, Thunder Bay, Toronto, and Vancouver. The St. Lawrence River allowed ocean-going vessels to go much farther inland than they could in the United States. This access encouraged the westward movement of settlers and their location on waterways along the U.S. border. Some Canadian cities began as collection points for the shipping of local produce, especially the small grain cities such as Winnipeg and Regina. These cities still function as commercial and government service centres for the same **hinterland** where they govern, manage resources, and do business.

**Industrialization** was also a factor in the location of Canada's first industrial cities, such as Toronto and Edmonton. In turn such factors as specialized resources such as labour pools, the availability of raw materials, the proximity to profitable markets, minimal costs associated with shipping and taxes, and access to government services became important as well. Some Canadian cities originally had strategic importance; Calgary, Winnipeg, and Sydney had police and military significance.

Cities were also formed for political reasons, as is evident from the selection of Ottawa as the national capital, and that of the capitals of the provincial and territorial governments. Most of Canada's provincial capitals have great advantages over other cities because the presence of government provides stability to the local economy.

As well, government attracts well-educated people with special skills and professional expertise who are usually highly paid and whose disposable income facilitates strong urban economic growth. A capital city is an urban centre of public-administrative activity, attracting the most advanced information and communications technologies into a concentrated area and helping to diversify the economy.

## MODELS OF URBAN GROWTH

### Concentric Zone Theory

Most of the classical models of urban growth were expounded by theorists in the twentieth century (see Figure 11.1). The "concentric zone theory" was first proposed by Ernest Burgess (1925). He pictured the growth of North American cities as represented by a concentric series of increasingly larger rings, each of which is the centre of different social, economic, or political functions.

Natural barriers, such as hills, rivers, and lakes, would distort this ideal pattern, but some urban communities approximate the concentric zone pattern to a significant degree. The zones, one by one, spread out from the central city area. The central business district, with stores and offices, is the first zone. The second zone is one of transition, where businesses and industry encroach on residential neighbourhoods, often causing housing standards to degenerate. The third zone is for working people. The fourth zone is a residential area for middle-income people. The city limits encompass the commuters' zone, where small towns and suburbs provide the political organization for people. Some older and larger Canadian cities seem to reflect this model of urban development (Guest 1969).

### Sector Theory

Another theorist, Homer Hoyt (1939), found weaknesses in the Burgess model and offered his own hypothesis — the "sector theory," based on sectors rather than concentric zones. Hoyt found sectors in many North American cities that formed along principal transportation routes (rail, water, highways). You may have noticed that, in many Canadian cities, the earliest housing and commercial buildings are found along major railway lines or facing a harbour.

Each sector provides a particular function for land use, for example, commercial, indus-

**Figure 11.1 Theories of Urban Growth**

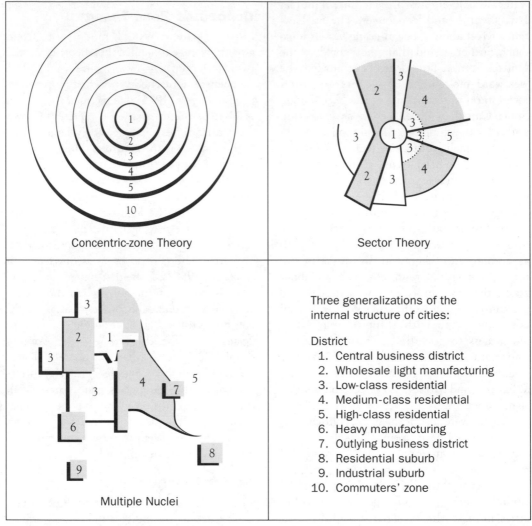

Concentric-zone Theory

Sector Theory

Multiple Nuclei

Three generalizations of the internal structure of cities:

District
1. Central business district
2. Wholesale light manufacturing
3. Low-class residential
4. Medium-class residential
5. High-class residential
6. Heavy manufacturing
7. Outlying business district
8. Residential suburb
9. Industrial suburb
10. Commuters' zone

*Source:* Chauncy D. Harris and Edward L. Ullman, "The Nature of Cities," *Annals of the American Academy of Political and Social Science* 242 (November 1945): 7–17. Reproduced with permission of the American Academy of Political and Social Science and Chauncy D. Harris.

trial, residential, even recreational. High-income residential neighbourhoods develop initially near the central business district in a kind of wedge-shaped sector. Factories and other businesses also settle into various wedge-shaped sectors. Calgary is often cited as an example of a city that grew within the logic of the sector theory.

## Multiple Nuclei Theory

By the middle of the twentieth century, in Canada, urban populations had spilled beyond the traditional city limits. Significant numbers of people were abandoning the old city centres to live in suburban areas. By 1970, many more people in **metropolitan** Toronto, Montreal, and Winnipeg were migrating to live outside the city limits. In many cities, this trend has gradually increased over the past two decades.

In response to the emergence of more than one focal point in some metropolitan areas, C.D. Harris and Edward Ullman (1945) presented their "multiple nuclei theory." In their view, urban growth in North America does not necessarily radiate outward from a central business district. Instead, a metropolitan area can have many centres of development, each of which reflects a particular urban need or activity.

Accordingly, a city may have a financial district, a manufacturing area, a waterfront zone, and a recreational and entertainment centre. Business and commerce will naturally cluster around each distinctive nucleus. The rise of **suburban** shopping malls is a vivid example of the phenomenon of multiple nuclei within Canada's growing metropolitan areas (see Table 11.3).

Historically, most major retail activity in Canadian cities was located in the central business district. Each residential neighbourhood had its own grocers, bakers, and butchers, but people travelled to the centre of the city to make major purchases at "department stores." However, as metropolitan areas expanded, the suburbs became more populous and an increasing number of Canadians began to shop closer to their homes. Today, the suburban mall is a significant retailing and social centre for communities all over Canada. Increasingly, politicians at all levels see malls as good places to campaign, and some even have their offices in them.

### Regional Government

Suburbanization, or "metropolitanization," as the process is also called, affects the political

**Table 11.3 Growth Rate of Selected Canadian Metropolitan Areas, 1986–1991**

| City | Growth Rate Percentage |
| --- | --- |
| Oshawa | 18 |
| Vancouver | 16 |
| Kitchener | 14 |
| Toronto | 13 |
| Victoria | 12.5 |
| Ottawa–Hull | 12 |
| Calgary | 12 |
| Edmonton | 9 |
| Halifax | 9 |
| Quebec | 7 |
| Montreal | 7 |
| St. John's | 6 |
| Saskatoon | 4.25 |
| Winnipeg | 4 |
| Windsor | 3 |
| Saint John | 3 |
| Regina | 2.75 |
| Thunder Bay | 2 |

*Source:* Adapted from Statistics Canada, *Canadian Social Trends,* Cat. No. 11-008E, Summer 1992. Reproduced by authority of the Minister of Industry, 1994.

sociology of all major urban areas in Canada. As a result, the concept of metropolitan government or regional government has become more popular in Canada. Under this approach, overlapping levels of government are reduced, and a central authority is established with wide responsibilities for policymaking and administration. In effect, the regional government approach attempts to overcome the fragmentation and decentralization of **municipal** centres that are unable to deal independently with area-wide social and economic problems, such as pollution, transportation, crime, recreation, and taxation.

From the perspective of efficiency, regional governing control lends itself most easily to the management of municipal services common to a large urban area. Thus, across Canada, metropolitan-wide services have occurred in such areas as waste disposal; museums; public transportation; and the co-ordination of health, police, and fire protection.

In political terms, metropolitanization increases the representation and power of the suburbs. Political power radiates outward from the heart of the urban community to the peripheral communities. Until recent times, most suburbs were tiny communities almost totally dependent on these urban centres for jobs, shopping, recreation, and even services such as water, garbage collection, and police protection.

Today, Canadian suburbs defy any easy definition. But the term generally refers to any community near a large city — or any municipality within a metropolitan area that is not included in the city centre. Whatever the precise definition of the term, it is clear that suburbs have changed the political landscape of local government and have altered the demography of provincial politics. Shifts in the economic base of cities have exacerbated the problems of their governments.

Many of Canada's older cities are ringed by communities that owe them no allegiance. The growing power of the suburbs also produces an environment of tension between urban and suburban legislators in all political parties on matters related to the revitalization of cities and questions of who should pay for crime prevention, pollution control, deteriorating housing, and municipal services.

The proliferation of municipal governments throughout Canada has led to many proposals for provincial reforms in order to rationalize the costs and operations of services and regulation. The more drastic the changes required, the more likely they are to affect the established interests of elected, appointed, and administrative municipal leaders. The tendency is for local politicians and public servants to resist the restructuring and realignments of municipalities as rationalized by provincial Cabinets.

# WHAT MUNICIPAL GOVERNMENTS DO

## Providing Services

In Canada's federal system, the primary unit of government is the **municipality**. Municipalities govern a specific geographical region, choose most of their representatives in regular elections, and exercise certain powers of local government. Most of the governments in Canada are municipal governments, which are either urban or rural. The vast majority of Canadians live within the jurisdiction of a municipal government, which is usually contained within another municipal boundary, be it a county or region.

Rural municipalities are called "counties," "communities," "hamlets," "parishes," "townships," and "districts." Urban municipalities are called "cities," "towns," and "villages." All are creatures of the provincial governments with whom they are engaged in a constant and unevenly matched power struggle.

Every day, municipal governments carry out an extraordinarily wide array of services that have vital impacts on the lives of Canadians. They are the governments that deliver the basic housekeeping services necessary to ensure the survival of Canadians in organized communities of densely concentrated populations, sometimes rivalling in size the entire populations of foreign nation-states. These services include police and fire protection; water supply; collection and disposal of garbage and sewerage; maintenance of streets and sidewalks, including streetlights; and the maintenance of other public places, such as boardwalks and sports arenas. They operate buses, subways, and streetcars; run airports; manage food and farmers' markets; and participate in the administration of port facilities. They also operate schools and libraries.

In matters of public health, municipal governments are understandably concerned with the detection, control, and prevention of communicable diseases; the safety and availability of water; emergency measures; and the maintenance of public health standards. The planning and development of adequate public health services and facilities are usually beyond the fiscal competence of many Canadian municipalities, and thus require a regional or provincial policy rationale.

But, in addition, municipal governments have gradually come to provide various services and facilities that go far beyond merely guaranteeing survival. Over the years, municipal governments have gradually and selectively taken on the operation of recreational and cultural facilities such as museums, art galleries, concert halls, municipal parks and playgrounds, swimming pools, skating rinks, and even ski slopes, in an attempt to provide enjoyment, and thus enhance the quality of urban life.

At the same time that municipal governments are expected to deliver housekeeping services and certain amenities, they are also expected to take on a variety of intensifying social problems that have become disproportionately concentrated within the spreading boundaries of Canadian cities. They provide public housing; shelters for women, children, and animals; day-care centres, homes for the aged and the homeless; and general counselling services.

Some of the most serious of these problems associated with concentrated urban living include the interrelated ones of poverty, unemployment, blighted and dilapidated housing, racial and ethnic discrimination, drug abuse, and young offender and adult crime.

Municipalities also provide services that are less tangible, particularly in the forms of honours, awards, prizes, the celebration of commemorative holidays, and special recognition to special citizens and groups, honouring their achievements. They also entertain their citizens in all seasons.

## Acting as Regulator

In the course of providing necessities and amenities as well as coping with social prob-

lems, most municipal governments make and enforce a wide variety of regulations prohibiting or requiring certain kinds of behaviour. The most elemental form of municipal regulation is the enforcement of federal and provincial criminal laws, local ordinances, and by-laws that declare illegal certain kinds of conduct — such as homicide, assault, theft, and break and enter — that are usually injurious to life, person, and property. But there are many other regulations that affect our everyday lives that are enforced with municipal by-laws. Regulations tell us about littering, parking, smoking, walking, running, sitting, eating, waiting, and so on.

This regulatory role of municipal governments is necessary to protect citizens from danger, violence, and general chaos, whether it be standard crime in the streets or, more sporadically, social disruptions, such as riots, and threats from disgruntled groups, even terrorists. Protection of life and property is, of course, a basic function of all governments at all levels. But municipal governments are usually directly involved and are most affected by such crimes.

City and town governments also regulate and license certain kinds of businesses, such as restaurants, coffee houses, dance halls, taxi cabs, private garbage collection companies, and parking lots. Many businesses must meet municipal standards of hours of operation, Sunday closing, **zoning** codes, beautification codes, signage, master plans, and other land-use restrictions. For example, in Victoria, British Columbia, unsightly gardens are rearranged by city gardeners, whose services are then billed to the property owner.

Increasingly, municipal governments have had to cope with threats to the environmental quality of their towns and cities. Indeed, many Canadian cities are environmental disaster areas. Sydney, Nova Scotia, has an area known as the Tar Ponds that, for years, absorbed the toxic emissions and discharges of the Sydney Steel Corporation,

Municipalities provide services that are related to public spirit; they recognize the contributions of special citizens by establishing parks and monuments. The Terry Fox Monument in Thunder Bay, Ontario, is an example. *Source:* W. Griebeling/Comstock.

becoming one of the most concentrated polluted areas in North America.

In general, the affects of unbridled metropolitan growth have been damaging to the delicate ecology within and around high concentrations of people. The conversion of agricultural land to urban use has altered the quality of the land itself, the underground water table, and the exposure of air to automotive and industrial pollutants. All of these environmental issues are now on the agenda of municipal councils, which, in addition to attending to traditional governmental concerns, need to devise administrative, fiscal, and legal ways of protecting the air, land, and water within city limits.

## Collecting Taxes

In an era of federal and provincial government cutbacks and public-sector austerity, municipal governments must extract the increasing costs of providing their services, attending to their civic responsibilities, and regulating the behaviour of their corporate and private citizenry. Furthermore, the amount of money that must be raised grows larger every year as the costs of delivering even a constant level of services spiral. Municipal governments cost more every year not only because of salary increases and the costs of supplies, and maintaining and rebuilding physical plants, but also because all municipalities are taking on an ever-expanding range of functions.

The single largest chunk of revenues raised by municipal government administrations comes from taxes on property. Some municipalities tax business inventories, utilities, theatre tickets, hotel room occupancies, and the rental of commercial property. Another method used by municipal governments to raise revenues is by imposing user charges for the provision of certain services and the use of their facilities.

Examples of these types of charges are admission prices for zoos, recreational facilities, amusement parks, and museums; bridge and tunnel tolls; and bus and subway fares. Fees for certain franchises, licences, and permits would fall into such a category as well. For example, a special permit to demolish a building would bring revenues to the municipal government that issued it. Still another source of revenue for municipal governments is the fines and penalties they collect for violations of their regulations, ordinances, by-laws, and statutes.

Canadian municipalities still rely heavily on property taxes, which are not very growth-responsive, meaning that they do not have the capacity to generate additional revenues faster than the growth of the economy, or to match increases in the costs of living. In times of recession, municipalities suffer erosions of property values, loss of retail sales, and the emigration of their citizens to other municipalities. New and steadily increasing taxes, excises, fees, and user charges have had to be regularly imposed to raise revenues.

But these increases and additions are too small and incremental to give municipalities the fiscal elbow room they need to function efficiently. For the larger cities, the cycle is vicious. The inability to raise sufficient tax revenues has caused cities to become steadily less attractive to those with middle and higher incomes, who see themselves constantly paying higher taxes for what they perceive to be a deteriorating physical, social, and economic environment.

# PROBLEMS OF GOVERNABILITY

## Creatures of Dependence

A 1976 study by the Canadian Federation of Mayors and Municipalities (CFMM; now called the Federation of Canadian Municipalities) referred to municipal governments as "puppets on a shoestring," disclosing that they were creatures of dependence on other levels of government in Canada.

Neither cities nor any other kinds of local governments enjoy the constitutional right to self-government. Local governments are mentioned in Canada's constitution only as an appendage of provincial jurisdictions. According to Canada's constitutional scheme, all governmental authority is divided between the federal government and the provinces. Legally, cities, towns, and other local government creations are *de jure* municipal corporations, supervised by their provinces and assigned the rights to perform certain governmental functions within specified, relatively densely populated, geographic areas (Tindal and Tindal 1984, 157–81). As creatures of their provinces, municipalities can exercise only those governmental powers expressly granted to them, and such powers can be contracted or taken away by the provincial government, even without the consent of the municipality. In effect, cities, towns, and other municipal inventions are political subdivisions of the province, created as convenient administrative agencies for the exercise of certain governmental powers the province has entrusted to them (Higgins 1986, 70–74).

The federal government has constitutional superiority over many matters that have a major impact on how we govern our municipalities. For example, the federal government controls aviation, navigation, and shipping, which prevents local authorities from making decisions in these areas as they might affect their municipalities. Even federal crown property is exempt from local taxation. And because provinces are always on guard regarding the intrusions of the federal government in their areas of jurisdiction, the municipalities are shielded from the possible benefits of a federal–municipal relationship.

For example, from 1971 to 1979, the federal government operated the Ministry of State for Urban Affairs (MSUA) in an attempt to address urban problems from a national perspective, with the enormous financial resources of the federal government. The attempt failed to launch a coherent federal urban policy largely because of the constant bickering between the provinces and the federal government.

There are also important federal constitutional constraints on municipal governments found in the various guarantees flowing from the Charter of Rights and Freedoms, such as procedural due process and equality protections. These constraints require municipalities to provide their citizens the rights that are, in fact, prescribed by other levels of government. Restrictions on municipal governments are also derived from judicial interpretation, especially in relation to the charter and the Bill of Rights. Admittedly, the federal court system, capped by the Supreme Court, is part of the federal government, and court decisions affect the governability of municipal governments.

For example, in a unanimous decision, the Supreme Court ruled that Ottawa has the authority to reduce its share of welfare transfer payments, thus potentially affecting every municipality in Canada. Another example is that the Supreme Court upheld the requirement that the public must obtain a city permit in order to conduct planned demonstrations on city property.

Most of the federal government's actions have, however, been either not constraining or positively helpful to municipalities. The federal government itself imposes less statutory regulation on municipal governments than do provincial governments. And, in the past, the federal level of government has provided a growing variety of grants, loans, and funding, in increasing amounts, as direct and indirect subsidies for municipal government operations. These kinds of federal subsidies result in higher levels of municipal government performance than would otherwise be possible with their own locally raised and provincial revenues.

But the fate of municipalities is directly tied to the wealth of their provincial treasuries and the competence of provincial governments in providing solutions for urban problems. A province may modify or even withdraw municipal governing powers, expand or contract the territorial area of a municipality, unite the whole or parts of it as amalgamations with other municipalities, and repeal the charter of a town or city and dissolve its corporation.

All of this may be done conditionally or unconditionally, with or without the consent of the citizens. In all these respects, the provinces are supreme, and their legislative bodies may do as they will. As a matter of course, municipal governments are constitutionally, and thus legally, inferior to the provincial and federal governments.

Because cities, towns, and other municipal organizations can perform only those functions for which they have clear mandates expressed in their charters or in provincial statutes, provincial governments can influence municipal council decisions by placing restrictions on or setting requirements for the exercise of whatever authority is granted.

Clearly, the most onerous restrictions on the decision-making ability, and ultimately on how well we govern our municipalities, are those related to financial matters. All provinces can exercise control over various municipal tax rates, particularly with respect to the property tax rates that municipal councils set.

With the costs of operating municipal governments on the rise, the ability of provincial treasuries to assist their municipalities is quite crucial. Provincial financial assistance has great impact on the level of services and the quality of performance local governments can provide their citizens. But, in the final analysis, the capacity of provincial governments to channel enough money to municipalities is always largely dependent on the federal government's ability to provide increased transfer payments to the provinces.

In the 1990s, the federal government has turned over more and more responsibility for funding to the provinces since money — or, more accurately, the lack of it — is seen to be at the centre of Canada's urban problems. Although the provinces exercise their powers using some federal money, most municipal leaders question the depth of Ottawa's commitment to continue current levels of funding and the willingness of the provinces to honour their new obligations.

Provincial governments can also influence municipal decision-making institutions by determining suffrage requirements in municipal elections, election procedures, voter registration methods, the operation of polls, and the timing of elections. Provinces generate the training and standards for police services, firefighting services, and emergency health services. In addition to these, and a host of other procedural and housekeeping details for municipalities, the provinces control the substance of many programs offered within municipal jurisdictions, through provincial welfare laws, provincial education programs, and provincial health laws and standards.

It should be emphasized that the exercise of provincial influence on municipal governments is not always denying, limiting, or otherwise unhelpful. Provincial governments have, over the years, permitted their municipalities to undertake an increasingly broader range of service and regulatory functions. They have also authorized the tapping of new sources of revenue and, from time to time, raised the limits on traditional ones, such as the property tax.

The most challenging obstacles confronting municipal governments have to do with the simple fact that cities are where most people live and where most human problems occur. In Canada's urban environments, social problems are closely intertwined with the physical aspects of city living and the ability of governments to address them under constrained fiscal and jurisdictional circumstances (Frisken 1986).

Those who raise questions about the governability of Canada's urban communities point to the sociological dynamics of crime, the constant surfacing of racism, concentrated poverty, neighbourhood decay, unemployment, environmental hazards, the decline in the ability of urban governments to deliver basic housekeeping services, and the erosion of their tax bases.

## Service Delivery

In the 1990s, few people who live, work, or even visit Canada's large urban centres can deny that there has been a general decline in the quality of service delivery. This decline is the result of chronic underfinancing and understaffing and, increasingly in recent years, interruptions by municipal labour–management problems.

Canadians lament that traffic congestion seems to get worse; streets appear dirtier, neglected, and more cluttered; and mass-transit facilities such as subways, buses, and commuter trains are less reliable and increasingly present dangers to passengers. A growing number of municipal properties are left to deteriorate, and city equipment is often inadequate or in disrepair.

There is room for argument whether this decline in municipal services is really occurring or whether it is simply perceived to be by a public with higher expectations of services. But whether it is absolute or only apparent, it is how people feel about their municipalities that will determine whether they will want to live, work, or play there, and whether they will make demands for new government structures and policies.

The fiscal restraints of the 1990s have created problems for local governments with respect to the quality and upkeep of parks, zoos, museums, libraries, and municipal gardens. Because such services are commonly regarded as less essential or of lesser priority than the more standard municipal government services, such as poverty-related problems or law enforcement needs, these kinds of services are the most vulnerable targets for cutbacks during budgetary crunches.

## Urban Poverty

Another indication of the difficulties municipal governments have in governing their jurisdictions is the failure of governments to eliminate, improve, or even reverse the deterioration of neighbourhoods across Canada in which people with low incomes are concentrated. Poverty leads to deteriorating neighbourhoods in urban communities, where high unemployment negatively affects the ability of people to maintain property or to afford property that has been maintained.

In such circumstances, many of the buildings people live in are overcrowded, dilapidated, and often unsafe for residents (Priest 1983). Buildings may even lack heat or functional plumbing. Many single-parent families dependent on welfare are forced to live in these kinds of properties.

In recent years, an additional problem faced by city governments has been created by numbers of buildings being "abandoned" by their owners. Some of these buildings have homeless families living in them because there is no other place for them to go. These gutted buildings become loci for criminal activity and are often vulnerable to arson. Abandonment contributes to further deterioration because often people who live near neglected buildings will flee to safer neighbourhoods.

Urban poverty breeds its own culture. Not surprisingly, most unemployment in Canada occurs in cities; most poverty occurs in cities; and most crime occurs in cities. People in difficult circumstances may develop attitudes of helplessness, hopelessness, despair, and criminal aggression, and are compelled to adopt the same practices that led to their parents' generation becoming trapped in poverty.

## Crime

Opinion surveys suggest that what Canadians consider to be the most critical evidence of

Homelessness is a serious problem in Canadian cities. Here, a homeless man sleeps inside an urban bus shelter. *Source:* O'Neill/Canada Wide.

municipalities becoming ungovernable is the increasing incidence of crime in their communities (Krahn and Kennedy 1985). During the 1990s, the kinds of crime that have been of major public concern include acts committed by individuals, such as the various forms of robbery and assault, and, increasingly, forms of mass riots in response to conflictive issues that may generate rioting, looting, and large forcible demonstrations.

The public's satisfaction with the competence of municipal governments to control crime is affected by the most recent crime statistics. Crime is considered by many to be evidence of ungovernability in Canada's larger cities because statistics on crime show that these cities have a disproportionately larger share than their population warrants, making the risk of victimization there higher than the national average.

Theft, robbery, and assault are consistently associated in Canada with urbanization and are found to increase as city size increases (Gabor and Gottheil 1984). Moreover, levels of violence in large cities no doubt appear unacceptably high because of the awareness that rates of such conduct in the surrounding suburbs, or in small urban areas, are significantly lower.

Higher crime rates in Canada's larger urban centres affects the governability of these cities and drains the budgets of the province. City governments are under public pressure to expand police forces and increase expenditures for policing in an effort to contain, if not reduce, the crime rate. And because police forces are labour intensive, the costs of trying to strengthen law enforcement efforts consume funds that would otherwise go to housekeeping or welfare services.

The most serious consequences of escalating crime rates is the pressure on governments to react bureaucratically, which increases costs to the ratepayer. Once these costs are incurred, it is difficult to reduce them, even when statistics reflect some success in handling the threat.

Fear of becoming a victim of crime changes the behaviour of citizens living close to each other. Because people are afraid, they avoid public places, and thus avoid doing business, enjoying cultural events, and participating in community life, such as attending a PTA meeting or assisting with local political campaigning. In short, more and more people sit behind locked doors and feel besieged rather than enjoying the amenities of urban life as citizens of well-governed municipalities.

## Raising Revenues

Another problem for many city governments in Canada is their eroding tax bases. In their heyday, Canada's larger cities had strong and vigorously expanding tax bases. This advantageous position derived from the fact that valued manufacturing, commercial, and residential properties; high-volume retail sales; new construction; and an increasing pool of citizens with well-paying jobs were concentrating in urban centres. As these sources of municipal funding were growing, large additional amounts of revenue became available automatically as a spin-off each year, without tax rates having to be raised beyond the rate of annual inflation.

In recent years, the tax bases of many large cities have either been growing very slowly relative to expenditures or have declined in absolute terms. In Canada, suburbanization generated a decline in the populations of many city centres, and thus shifted revenues to the outskirts of urban areas. Job opportunities, new construction, and middle- and upper-income families have all been moving to the suburbs. This **decentralization** has had an effect on retailing, manufacturing, warehousing, wholesaling, and service occupations.

Toronto's city centre decreased in population significantly (16 percent) between 1971 and 1981, and grew back only marginally (2 percent) between 1981 and 1991. Between 1971 and 1991, Montreal's inner-city population dropped by more than 20 percent and shows no signs of growth in the immediate future (Statistics Canada 1991b).

Modern communications and transportation systems have obviated past needs for a central city location near seaports, freight terminals, rail lines, and mass-transit facilities. All of this has weakened or eroded the tax base of cities, forcing their governments to constantly raise tax rates, increase their borrowing, and persistently seek additional provincial funding in order to meet the steadily increasing costs of providing services.

### Recommendations for Improving Municipal Government

The fact that Canadian municipalities are not constitutionally empowered to make self-governing decisions adversely affects their abilities to function proactively in the presently configured federal system. Over the years, all provincial governments have studied the problems of their municipalities, as did the federal government's Macdonald Commission in 1985.

The Macdonald Commission made a number of proposals that, if implemented, would change local governments across Canada. One important recommendation was to untie the conditions upon which current provincial grants are made to municipalities. Making provincial money conditional on its targeted uses restricts the ability of local governments to plan their expenditures and to manage the resources they have. The commission found that local governments are better able to judge for themselves the best applications for provincial funding.

The commission also recommended that other levels of government with more advantageous taxing powers designate a special portion of their tax revenues for local government financing. To enhance the co-ordination of a federal strategy on the governability of municipalities, the Macdonald Commission recommended more tri-level conferencing

among public officials in order to gain greater national visibility for the problems of municipalities.

### THE DYNAMICS OF LOCAL DECISION MAKING

The major job of governing a Canadian city or town is the making and implementing of decisions about what services, regulations, and taxes will be administered. The making of these decisions is fundamentally a political process: It takes place in a context of disagreement, competition, and conflict, where numerous individuals and groups support different, and often contradictory, positions about what municipal government should do to address a particular issue. Part of this political process involves the city officials and their employees themselves, who must deal with the constant lobbying of private and corporate interests in the community.

Much of the activity of any municipal government is routine administration of previously established policies and civil programs. The process of local decision making begins with a "demand," "claim," or "proposal" that is asserted from within the community, affecting the ability of the municipal government to deliver. Such demands normally arise when some individual or group perceives that a solution is possible through local government action.

Often problems consist of people feeling neglected because a service does not meet their expectations: Parents want their children to play in better-maintained park grounds with better equipment; people want to walk the streets safely at night; individuals want better-quality water in their homes and apartments. Sometimes problems arise because of a threatened interruption of a satisfactory state of affairs, as in a fall-off in the frequency of garbage collection or a city decision to relocate stop signs and street lights, slowing or changing the direction of traffic in a neighbourhood.

Local decision-making problems are experienced not only when conditions change, but also when public expectations change. In recent decades, Canadians have adopted different lifestyles, reflecting a more athletic and active population at every age level. To accommodate some of these new lifestyle expectations, many cities have instituted bike lanes on their streets for the safety of cyclists. Some communities have similar arrangements for walkers and joggers. In more and more Canadian neighbourhoods, people expect their local governments to provide life trails, or aerobic and gymnastic exercise spaces, in municipal parks.

Most demands for local government action grow out the public's desire to solve social problems or respond to social needs. Demands may be implicit in general complaints that municipal officials receive about urban blight or traffic congestion. Occasionally, however, municipal government actions are generated by the perception of opportunities to achieve new or additional goals or satisfactions. For example, a neighbourhood pond or lake may already give aesthetic satisfaction every day, but at some point it may be seen as an opportunity to provide a recreational service, such as ice-skating or canoeing; if so, a new policy demand is made. The individuals involved in recognizing a problem, developing a local remedy, or pressing for a solution will usually approach municipal officials and employees.

Money is ultimately what people fight about in municipal politics. Almost every local government decision either directly or indirectly takes money out of one person's personal or official pocketbook and puts it into someone else's. In the ultimate sense, conflict over spending involves decisions about how the municipal government will distribute its benefits to various individuals and groups. Examples include the eligibility criteria for, and size of, welfare payments, salaries, and other monetary ben-

efits for municipal employees; the companies and contractors patronized by the local government for goods and services; and the buying and leasing of space to provide government services.

Political decisions about what business activities to regulate, what standards to require, and what levels of enforcement are needed affect the monetary well-being of many corporate and private citizens. Such regulations as minimum standards governing the cleanliness of restaurants or public food markets, and for the construction of buildings, almost always raise the costs of operation and reduce the profits of those engaged in these businesses. They also raise the costs of government itself because regulations need people to enforce them. Municipal government decisions to change traffic patterns by establishing one-way streets or no-parking areas may alter the business patterns in the community positively or negatively.

Another political decision-making obstacle encountered by municipal government is that the activities of adjacent local governments, in the form of villages, cities, towns, townships, districts, and so on, spill over and have a *de facto* effect on the governing of cities. Often, city governments must absorb the costs of those municipal services being used by residents of other municipalities. However, the constellation of town, county, and regional governments that operate collaterally to city governments can have both positive and negative effects.

On the positive side, when people from other municipalities pay bridge tolls and parking fees, use subways, pay entrance fees to zoos and museums, and shop in another municipality, the benefits to that municipality are obvious. But, on the negative side, when citizens from neighbouring municipalities use the services and facilities provided by another government, the host government will absorb the spill-over problems of traffic congestion; air pollution; crime; and wear and tear on roads, streets, transportation systems, and other physical components of the city's **infrastructure**. Much of the contact between a large city and its immediate adjoining municipal neighbours requires co-operative agreement that concerns routine administrative matters, for example, construction and maintenance of facilities such as roads, bridges, mass-transit lines, traffic-control signals, and parks that straddle or connect the boundaries between or among governments.

Other relations between or among neighbouring governments involve the joint construction and operation of expensive public works, such as water-supply and -distribution systems, or sewage treatment facilities and airports, that are more economic to build on a scale that will meet the combined needs of two or more municipal jurisdictions.

Still other relations can consist of the large city providing standard services — such as supplying water — to some or all of its neighbours from its own facilities for a fee, established on a contractual basis, and sometimes within limits specified by provincial law. Special agreements also frequently involve police and firefighting services to help cope with emergency situations with other jurisdictions.

## Instruments of Governability

### Charters

One of the traditional sources of municipal governmental authority is a charter. Prior to Confederation, cities were incorporated, and their charters granted by colonial authorities, acting in the name of the monarch. The charter was regarded as a contract between the Crown and the municipality, and was not subject to amendment without the consent of both parties.

After Confederation, charters were granted by provincial legislatures and came to be regarded as ordinary legislative acts, subject to amendment and appeal by the legislature alone. Today, two types of provincial

statutes are used as instruments for incorporating municipalities: special charters and general municipal acts. Because of the unique historical circumstances of Canada's urbanization prior to 1867, most Canadian cities have retained special charters, which are amended by special acts of the provincial legislature. In the latter part of the twentieth century, the traditional practice of incorporating new urban communities has given way to the uniform provisions contained in general municipal acts.

The charter serves as organic law, somewhat like a constitution does for a country, specifying in varying degrees of detail, depending on the municipality, the form, the composition, the specific powers, and duties of the governing unit. Charters also outline procedures to be followed by the various decision-making officials and governing bodies. Normally, a charter will summarize the methods of selecting different government decision-makers, the kinds of matters to which a city's authority extends and various limits on that authority, the boundaries of the city, and methods for amending the charter itself.

In defining the powers of a particular city government, the charter usually does not stand by itself: The authority granted and the limits imposed by the charter are supplemented by relevant provincial legislation — in particular, provincial statutes applicable to municipalities. Thus, legislation controlling police enforcement, health and welfare services, urban and municipal planning, social services, and electoral rules and regulations affect the governability of cities.

Many analysts view the dependence of municipalities on a provincial governing executive, and on a province's legislative power, as indicative of inferior status in the realm of governability in Canada. Under the law, as perceived by one analyst, municipalities are not very different from liquor licence boards (Makuch 1983, 107).

# MUNICIPAL GOVERNMENT LEADERSHIP

Municipal officials such as mayors, city managers, and councillors are unique among governing actors. These officials possess the authority to make legally binding decisions about the content of municipal policies and programs, and also have the right to direct and supervise the performance of municipal employees who implement the decisions that become policy outputs, the taxes, the regulations, and the services.

In making and supervising the implementation of municipal government policies, these officials function in a twofold capacity: first, as independent decision-makers, bringing their personal preferences, goals, needs, and interests to government; and second, as targets for and reflectors of the interests of other actors in the system. Collectively, they comprise the top decision-making element of local governments.

## The City Manager

City managers, sometimes called "chief administrative officers" (CAOs), are officials who are usually appointed by a city council to supervise and direct the operation of city government. Not being an elected official, managers are administrative heads of the municipal governments that employ them. They supervise the administration of the affairs of the city and enforce its resolutions and by-laws.

City managers usually have the power to recommend to council such measures as administrative experience deems desirable, to report on the financial condition of the city, to submit a proposed budget, and to prepare any other reports the council may request (Plunkett 1968, 38).

In many cities, the manager is permitted to attend council meetings, and even to take part in discussions, although without voting privileges. In effect, the city manager acts as a source of information and recommendations for the council's deliberations. The manager's recommendations are an important part of the council's agenda and generally are approved. But there has always been some uneasiness about the extent to which managers who are appointed public officials actually participate in making city policies. Normally, the manager plays a leading role in the process by which municipal policies are eventually made.

Given the manager's near monopoly of information about problems and alternatives, relative to the often part-time and sometimes less experienced councillors, who are motivated by political pressures, the manager is in a strong position on most issues to be very influential on the range of possible policies the council considers.

## Municipal Councillors

It is in the city and municipal councils that city charters and provincial statutes vest the legislative powers of municipal governments. City councillors are primarily involved in enacting laws and resolutions and establishing new or changed regulative policies or services. They vote on ways to increase municipal revenues, to authorize the borrowing of money, and other matters, such as condemning certain buildings and taking private property for public use.

They are also involved in fixing the administrative details of municipal government, such as the salaries of officials and employees, and appropriating money for capital expenditures and current operations. Councillors have the power to conduct investigations of any aspect of municipal government. They can compel witnesses and request to see various papers, records, and other evidence relevant to an inquiry.

Members of municipal councils most often routinely adopt policies proposed by mayors, managers, and other CAOs; occasionally, they delay, amend, or reject such proposals; and rarely do they adopt policies originating from their own membership.

But they frequently influence the policy process by intervening on behalf of their constituents to bring about some specific administrative decision. These interventions may be for such things as improving certain services and facilities in their neighbourhoods, getting exemptions for constituents in the application of certain municipal regulations, or providing some disputed benefit to a private or corporate citizen. In some municipalities, councillors have the power to withhold approval on administrative decisions, share in the preparation or changing of the budget, and serve on committees responsible for supervising the operations of particular departments.

Every municipal council is attached to standing, *ad hoc*, or special committees that are struck to debate the issues of the day; to make recommendations to council, the mayor, and other administrative officers; and to keep a close watch on the operations of the departments that serve the public.

Committees are where the accountability of municipal government is seen to take place. Unlike councils, which are bodies of people with general knowledge and interests in municipal affairs, committees allow a municipal government to specialize in certain pressing matters and to build a pool of expertise that can be called upon to advise the government. They are the pulse of the government, the eyes and the ears of municipal planners, and the vehicles through which the public can formally make a plea to the council on matters of urgency. Committees conduct research on every kind of municipal problem, like homelessness, prostitution, housing, the populations of certain domestic animals, and the planning of special events such as the Canada Games and the Olympics.

Councillors are, of course, primarily interested in the problems of their wards. They must deal with complaints from their constituents about anything having to do with the responsibilities of the municipal government. They must contend with such mundane things as flooded basements, backed-up sewers, street lighting, storm drains, snow removal, and stray animals. They must be able to represent the needs of their constituents with the appropriate civic department.

## The Role of Mayors

The mayor of any Canadian city or town is likely to be its single most influential political actor. The mayor is like the head of state of a city or town, and symbolizes the unity of the municipality as an organized community. Public expectations have resulted in the mayor being viewed as the chief problem-solver, a crisis manager, and the person in charge of the overall operation of the municipal government.

Although the exact legal specifications of the mayor's total powers vary from city to city in Canada, he or she may be seen to play four major roles — ceremonial head of civic government, community ambassador, chief executive, and legislative leader. In the performance of each of these roles, the mayor usually has opportunities to make an impact on the content of the local government's policies and programs.

### Ceremonial Head of Municipal Government

As the ceremonial head of municipal government, the mayor acts as the community's pre-eminent formal representative on a variety of ceremonial occasions: The mayor greets and receives distinguished guests and visitors at city hall, and will often give them a "key" to the city. Mayors also lay cornerstones and place time capsules in major public and private buildings, and cut ribbons when important projects are complete and ready to be opened for use. The mayor attends numerous luncheons, dinners, meetings, celebrations, and testimonials in honour of prominent citizens.

Mayors issue proclamations, celebrate anniversaries, launch charity drives, and open sports events.

Although the mayor's time-consuming ceremonial activities may not immediately appear to offer opportunities for influencing policy output, they do so in a number of ways. The mayor can use ceremonial activities to build up generalized goodwill, from which political rewards may result, and he or she very often has a chance to make remarks in support of government policies, reaching the media, a target audience, or the wider public, even the international community.

### Community Ambassador

By custom, because the mayor is regarded as the official most capable of speaking for the community as a whole, the mayor serves as ambassador to outside entities. He or she is its paramount negotiator with neighbouring municipalities, and especially with the officials of provincial and federal governments. Given the dependent constitutional and legal status of local governments, many of the initiatives a mayor might want to take need authorization by provincial politicians and administrators. In addition, mayors must make regular pilgrimages to the provincial capital, usually "hat in hand," to plead for increased funding for municipal programs.

The potentialities for provincial governments to help or hinder the mayor are great. And other than as a result of having a persuasive and affable personality, the influence a mayor working as an individual can have on the actions of the provincial government is close to non-existent.

Even for a mayor with enormous skills in municipal negotiation, normally the only success he or she can have is in helping to keep the government from losing ground on most problems, while managing, with some good fortune, to inch ahead in persuading provincial authorities that certain issues need to be addressed immediately. Yet to accomplish even this, a mayor needs to possess the talents of a diplomat.

### Chief Municipal Executive

The mayor of every large Canadian city is designated by charter or provincial statute to see that laws, by-laws, ordinances, and resolutions are implemented. These bits of formal governing authority give the mayor some power to direct and supervise, within the limits of local, provincial, and federal legislation, the municipal officials and employees in the operating departments that carry out the government's existing policies and programs.

In most urban municipalities, the mayor will have appointed the heads of departments and other key executive officials with or without the necessity of seeking approval of the council. As a result, these officials will most often share the mayor's general policy outlook and governing style, and perhaps even feel some further obligation to comply with the mayor's wishes out of a sense of political loyalty. Because the mayor's formal powers might include responsibility for the preparation of the budget, he or she has a powerful sanction for keeping executive officials in line.

The array of formal powers a mayor has to perform his or her job as chief executive is subject to community restraints. Even the strongest mayors have various independent community agencies, boards, and commissions that are not under formal municipal executive control and perform important functions within the urban municipality (e.g., school boards, housing authorities, crown corporations, development agencies, unions, and community corporations).

The mayor's influence on the activities of the operating departments is usually marginal. Most departmental activities simply go on unchanged, or changes are introduced without any reference to the mayor. Occasionally, the mayor does intervene in the operations of a department on his or her own initiative. The mayor may direct that some specific item that has come to the attention of the mayor's office must be handled in a certain way.

The public has come to expect their mayor to deal personally with threatening or damaging situations. Municipal emergencies, such as riots, crime waves, natural or human-made disasters, breakdowns in city services, or scandals in civic government are situations in which the public expects the mayor to take charge.

Some mayors see their role as that of caretaker and administrative mediator and will make no strong attempt to impose their personal policy preferences on the operations of civic government. Their overriding concern is to preside over the continuation of programs the municipal government has traditionally carried out and to ward off interruptions to ongoing routines. Such a mayor avoids demands for change unless changes are legislated by the provincial government.

Other mayors are oriented to respond assertively to problems with policies, incorporating solutions based on personal preferences. This kind of mayor not only exercises the legal responsibilities of the office, but also provides political, and sometimes moral, leadership to mobilize the conscience of the community. Somewhere midway between the passive and active mayors are those who see themselves as brokers. Their main objectives are to win the approval of those who can help and avoid displeasing those who can damage their personal power position, especially their chances for re-election.

### Legislative Leader

In Canada, the legislative and policy-making function of municipal governments is centred in the council, where mayors usually take a legislative leadership role. No city charter actually terms the mayor a "legislative leader," but the mayor's usual charter-based duties give her or him a formal share of the city's legislative authority. Mayors sometimes

hold the power of veto over council motions and amendments to by-laws, and they usually cast the deciding vote when a tie occurs.

In many cities the mayor reports to the council in an annual "blue book," which contains a message from the mayor on the state of the city or municipality and contains information and recommendations that the mayor considers necessary or expedient in the operations of government. It is also the mayor's right in a majority of large Canadian cities to submit an executive budget, once financial statements are audited, deliberated, and debated.

Because of the inability of contemporary councils in complex, rapidly changing municipalities to generate their own agendas, mayors are the chief continuing sources of major proposals that councils must consider. It is the mayor who speaks for the operating departments, which are front-line receptors of information about the nature of current civic problems. These departments have the staff for developing, reviewing, and integrating ideas for legislative proposals, which must proceed through three readings before they become law.

Mayors are often elected on platforms that reflect their personal political agendas, which might focus on beautification, commercial expansion, crime control, fiscal responsibility, tax reduction, or some combination of these. Mayors must formulate and submit a constant stream of legislative proposals to council in order for their agendas to materialize.

However, the council does not always approve. It is true that in many communities most of the mayor's legislative proposals are of such a routine nature that they are quickly adopted. But if the mayor does have real interest in a proposal and that proposal is controversial, he or she might have to exercise considerable influence on the passage of certain resolutions into by-laws. And, in any municipality, if the mayor is highly popular and does not mind running the risk of turning occasional opponents into permanent enemies, the mayor's access to the mass media can turn the tide positively for his or her agenda on council. In the final analysis, the only tool available for converting the council to legislate the mayor's agenda is, simply, persuasion.

## TYPES OF MUNICIPAL GOVERNMENTS

Municipal decisions are made and carried out by various parts of a formal governmental structure. Because the governmental structure of any particular municipality is determined by the instruments of provincial law, they vary across Canada. Municipalities differ in name, legal powers, and the responsibilities of their civic officers, decision-making bodies, and other components of their governmental structures. Municipalities also differ from province to province in the procedures they use to engage in governing.

All municipalities are alike in that their building blocks consist of an array of "line," sometimes called "operating," and "administrative," or "staff," departments. These departments carry out particular specialized governmental functions — for example, Recreation, Social Services, Public Works, Roads, and Property Standards are "line" departments, and City Manager, City Solicitor, City Treasurer, City Clerk, and City Engineer are "staff departments."

Local governmental decisions are made and carried out by various formal structures. Municipal governments are differentiated and categorized as "council–committee," "council–chief administrative officer," "council–commission," "council–board of control," and "council–executive committee" models.

### Council–Committee

This model is most easily adapted for use in smaller municipalities across Canada. It has its roots in the British traditions of local government and is the oldest model of a municipal government structure (Plunkett and Betts 1978). The council–committee model comprises an elected mayor and council who also serve on the standing committees that supervise and monitor key administrative and policy areas of municipal government. Sometimes special *ad hoc* committees are struck on a short-term basis to address exceptional problems, such as prostitution or environmental hazards. The various municipal departments, such as Recreation or Public Works, report to the appropriate standing committee, and through it to the council as a whole (see Figure 11.2).

Committees play a central role in this model of municipal government because they are the means by which connections are made between the government and the public. Sometimes committees hear public briefs, thus providing access to the decision-making process to groups and individuals who want their concerns reported to council. Committees are usually specialized in what they consider, drawing their expertise from interested and experienced councillors and using it to focus on administrative or policy problems. The power and legitimacy of these committees flow from their ability to influence all of the members of council. Once their recommendations are tabled, council usually accept them.

One reason why this model has been abandoned by larger municipalities is that it lacks a mechanism for co-ordinating the work of the committees with the council as a whole, and with the departments affected by their recommendations. So the potential effect of a particular committee's recommendations on the whole of the municipal government is often not immediately perceivable. It is up to the mayor, who usually sits *ex officio* on all committees, to catch any problems that might result from contradictory or conflicting committee work. In a large community, it would be quite burdensome for one person to assume that responsibility.

**Figure 11.2 Council–Committee Model of Municipal Government**

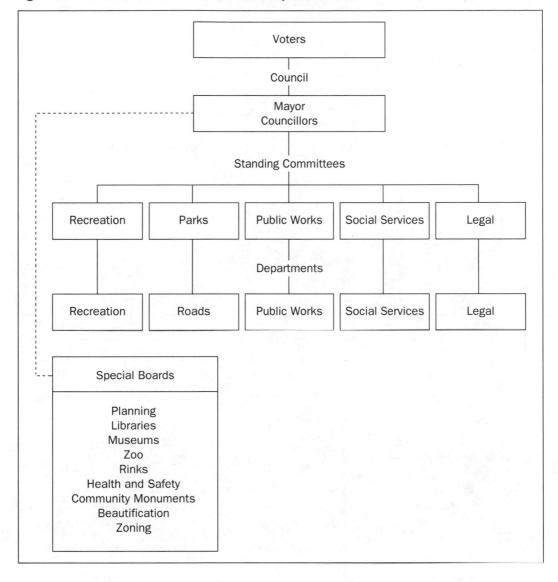

## Council–Chief Administrative Officer

A growing number of Canadian municipalities have found the council–chief administrative officer (CAO), or council–city manager, model of government attractive and have adopted it, particularly in Quebec (see Figure 11.3), although it is also found in such cities as Vancouver, Regina, Windsor, Mississauga, St. Catharines, Thunder Bay, Halifax, and Sydney. Originating in the United States around the turn of the century, this model was first successfully implemented in Canada in Westmount, Quebec, in 1913.

**Figure 11.3  Council–Chief Administrative Officer Model of Government**

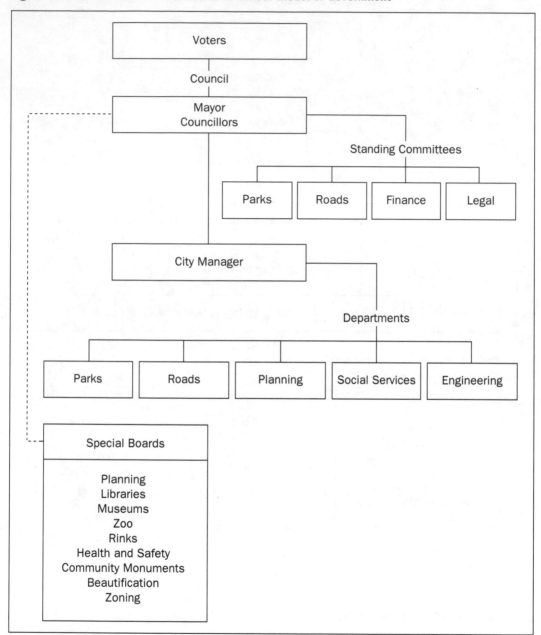

The widespread adoption of the council–city manager municipal structure grew out its efficient business approach to municipal management, which in practice diminished the occurrences of political corruption, nepotism, and other kinds of favouritism witnessed at local levels of government.

The council–manager system was seen as an alternative to the dominant-mayor form, which tends to emerge in the council–committee model, because it overcomes the fragmentation of authority in the various committees and provides an approach for introducing a business-like economy into the operation of local government. The idea was that the council would function in the manner of a business corporation, setting general policies. The manager would perform the role of an administrator responsible for seeing that those policies were implemented in a technically neutral and efficient manner. "Politics" would thus be separated or distanced from the everyday administration of municipal government.

Under this model, a noticeable separation of function is made between the legislative and policy-making branch of municipal government and its executive-administrative branch. The centralization of administrative responsibility is achieved by the council hiring a professionally trained manager to supervise the daily operations of the departments. The city manager acts as the liaison, the link between the council and the departments and between the council and the committees. The flow of information affecting decisions concentrates in the manager or CAO, who is in the position to co-ordinate and influence all levels of government.

In effect, a great amount of trust and expectation is placed in one individual, who is not elected yet is at the forefront of local decision making. Because the manager is usually the only full-time governmental official who oversees all departmental activities (the councillors serve on a part-time basis), the manager's advice to the council is crucial in the formulation of policy.

## Council–Commission

A modified version of the council–chief administrative officer model is the council–commission form of government, which is concentrated in the Prairie provinces, particularly in the cities of Edmonton, Calgary, Saskatoon, and Winnipeg, but is also found in other communities such as Fort McMurray and Medicine Hat (see Figure 11.4). The major difference between them is the substitution of a multimember board of commissioners, usually chaired by the mayor, but sometimes by a chief commissioner. Normally, there are as many commissioners as there are standing committees, and each commissioner meets with his or her standing committee on a regular basis. The board of commissioners links the council with the departments and acts as a co-ordinating mechanism between the council and the committees. The departments are responsible to council through the appropriate commissioner, and sometimes through the entire board when that body functions as a unified body.

The council hires and fires commissioners, who, like the city manager or CAO, are interposed between the legislative (council) and administrative (departments) branches of government. The use of a board of commissioners makes this mode more effective at coordinating because it does not rely on the abilities of just one person, as does the council–CAO model. Because commissioners function as equals, they tend not to criticize or review each other's activities for fear that their own budgetary allotments or departmental responsibilities would then be open to scrutiny.

## Council–Board of Control

The council–board of control model appears to be concentrated in Ontario, but it has been adopted elsewhere, as in Montreal between 1909 and 1921. Statutory law in Ontario prescribes that municipalities with a population of more than 100 000 should adopt this form of government. However, some cities and boroughs, such as Toronto and Ottawa, have abandoned this model and opted instead for council–commission and other structures.

**Figure 11.4 Council–Commission Model of Municipal Government**

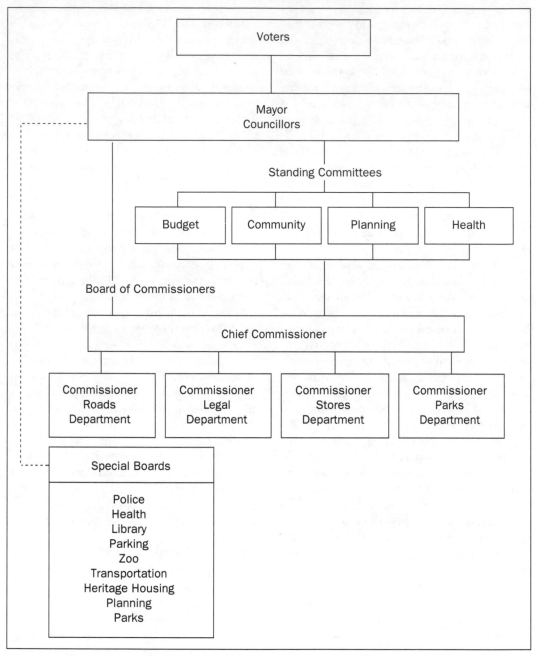

Both the council–commission model and the council–board of control model offer the municipality a collective co-ordinating mechanism; in other words, a board is in control of the lines of communication between the council and the departments (see

**Figure 11.5  Council–Board of Control Model of Municipal Government**

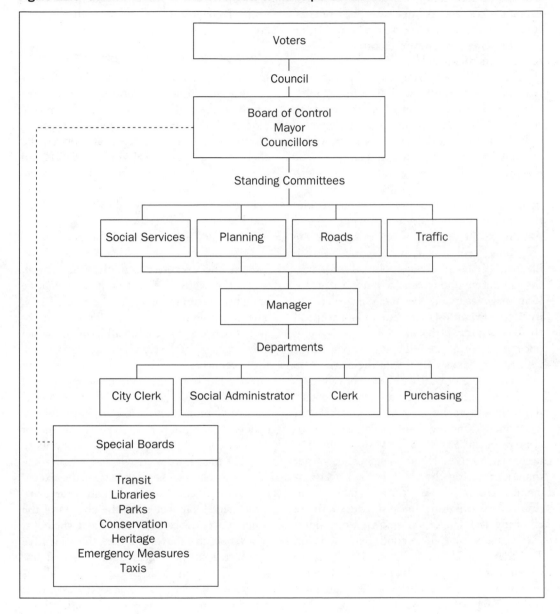

Figure 11.5). The council–board of control model elects rather than appoints controllers on a city-wide platform, while other members of council are elected in wards.

Controllers perform the same representative and policy-making functions that other members of council do, but they also carry out executive tasks that are not performed by aldermanic representatives (councillors). For example, controllers supervise departments, nominate individuals to key administrative positions, negotiate union contracts, prepare tenders, and draft budgets.

The task of preparing budgets places controllers at the centre of the policy-making process. Recommendations from the board to the council on these matters can be rejected only by a two-thirds majority of the whole council. Because the council comprises the mayor, controllers, and aldermanic representatives, a two-thirds-majority dissension is difficult to achieve, and most decisions require the support of the board in any event.

As in all models of government, there are some weaknesses in this one as well. Electing the board creates political tension in the legislative and executive branches of this form of government. Because controllers run in city-wide contests, they are in fact political rivals, not just during the campaign, but also once they are elected. They are competitive with each other as well as with the mayor, who also runs as a city-wide candidate for office.

Mayors know that controllers are potential competitors for that office in the next election. Ultimately, this can affect governability, because political rivals usually distance themselves from one another rather than joining together as a unified decision-making group. Those who are ambitious in their jobs are sometimes suspected to be climbing the ladder of success, from aldermanic representative to controller, to mayor. The mayor is always watching closely those who might be grooming themselves to become successors. In effect, this wariness can limit the ability of governing personnel to co-operate and co-ordinate for the public good. Controllers wield more power than do aldermanic representatives because they perform advisory and supervisory roles in relation to the departments and can claim superior electoral status because they are elected city-wide. Thus, the structures of this form of government can be conflictive and are often highly charged politically.

## Council–Executive Committee

In recent years, a growing number of communities in Ontario and other provinces have adopted the council–executive committee model of municipal government. In Quebec, Montreal has used it since it abandoned the council–board of control model in 1921, and more recently Quebec City and Laval have adopted it. Toronto took it on in 1969, and Winnipeg in 1971, followed by Ottawa in 1980 and Hamilton in 1981.

The model has some of the characteristics of Cabinet in the parliamentary system, because the executive committee is central, fusing the legislative and political-executive branches within the council (see Figure 11.6). The executive committee comprises the mayor and usually up to five councillors, all of whom are elected officials. However, the members of the executive committee are not elected directly but are chosen from among elected councillors. Individual members of the executive committee hold responsibility for the operations of one or more departments, or exercise control over a specific area of policy.

The mayor is directly elected, and in some cities can choose the members of the executive committee; elsewhere the mayor can make recommendations but takes the choices of the committee of the council, voting as a whole.

When the mayor chooses the executive committee, its members tend to see themselves as a team loyal to the mayor, who is the leader. Under this scenario, the executive can function better as a co-ordinating body in dealing with the council and the administration. More competitive politics results when the mayor does not directly choose the executive committee because the members are more independent and representative of interests other than the mayor.

**Figure 11.6 Council–Executive Committee Model of Municipal Government**

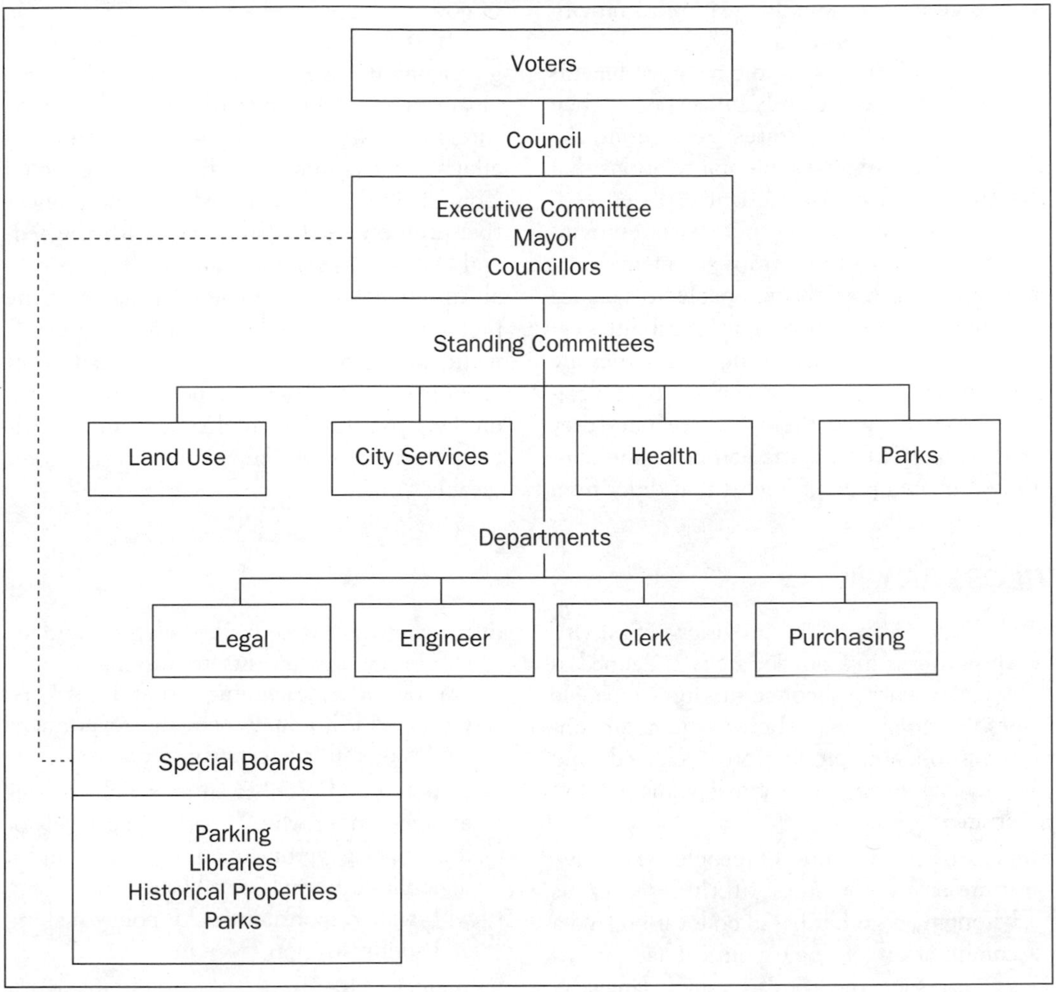

## CONCLUSION

While the formal structures of Canadian municipalities influence the process of decision making, they are not sovereign governing units in the ways that the federal and provincial governments are. Indeed, most political decision making in Canadian municipalities consists of the attempt on the part of citizens to influence the relevant decision-makers to exercise some discretion in their authority in some way.

The various structures of local government set the general framework within which the community may exert political influence on municipal authorities. And the only way ordinary citizens, who themselves may lack legal decision-making power, can influence the decision-making process is by influencing those who have legal powers in relation to provincial and federal politicians.

The evolution of municipal governments in Canada has been greatly influenced by their lack of constitutional status. As a result, the character of intergovernmental relations that this third level of government experiences is that of superior to subordinate within provincial and federal jurisdictions. In many ways, municipalities have been unable to balance revenues with their growing responsibilities because, as legitimate governing bodies, they are not empowered to make the kinds of decisions that can give them the revenues they need. In particular, Canadian cities are confronted by complex problems that differ from those that must be addressed by other levels of government.

If the present structures of municipal governments are strengthened, and municipalities take the initiative in adopting an integrated approach to intergovernmental affairs, as recommended by the Macdonald Commission, they could secure a more effective position in their relations with the federal and provincial governments. The proposals for change may help alleviate some of the problems experienced by municipal government, but, given the present combination of provincial domination and public apathy, it is unlikely that fundamental change in municipal government will be achieved in the foreseeable future.

## GLOSSARY

**city** Depending on the provisions of provincial statutes in Canada, a city is defined as a place where a concentration of people reside and interact, where a market for consumption and production is created, and where an organized system of municipal government exists.

**communities** Groups of people who have some consciousness of themselves as belonging together based on location, and a combination of socio-political factors involving such qualities as values, language, and ideology.

**decentralization** The tendency to move away from the central focus of a city, with the result that the activities and buildings are spread throughout the urban area.

**hinterland** Land and territory within the jurisdiction of a nation-state that is interior to coastal areas, often far from big cities and towns, and considered to be the core land mass that makes up a country.

**industrialization** The economic process in a society that relies chiefly on mechanization for the production of goods and services.

**infrastructure** A network of physical and institutional instruments to sustain the operation of a community, that is, streets, power grid, hospitals, schools, government facilities, and emergency services.

**metropolitan** Describes an approach to governance under which overlapping levels of municipal governments are reduced and a regional authority is established in an area with wide responsibilities for policy-making and administration.

**municipal** Used to describe any sizable community where people live within certain boundaries of an incorporated area possessing powers granted to it by the province.

**municipality** A body of government formed by the local residents of a particular region and empowered to exercise certain powers of government autonomously.

**rural** Describes areas of low population density, in small settlements located some distance from urban communities.

**suburban** Describes the result of a migration of people and businesses to the fringes of a city.

**town**  A particular category of municipality as defined by provincial statute, distinct from a city, county, borough, district, region.

**urban centres**  Locations in which populations of significant density cluster, attracting factories, stores, banks, modern technologies, and other features of a city.

**urbanization**  The growth of cities by means of rural transformation, natural population increase, or populations' migrating to and settling in a concentrated area.

**zoning**  Legal provisions stipulating land use and architectural design to ensure that certain standards of housing and general building construction are maintained; usually applied to separate industrial, commercial, and residential areas, but also employed to distinguish wealthy property owners from poorer residents in the municipality.

## RECOMMENDED READING

Andrews, Vian, ed. 1991. *The Encyclopedia of Canadian Municipal Governments*. Burnaby, B.C.: Venture Page Design. This work lists all Canadian municipalities and includes basic information on each, such as population, type of municipal government and structures, and other aspects of urban government.

Bourne, Larry, and David Ley, eds. 1993. *The Changing Social Geography of Canadian Cities*. Montreal and Kingston: McGill-Queen's University Press. This book contains nineteen articles that analyze the social and economic transformations that have taken place in Canadian cities from the 1960s to the 1990s.

Bunting, Trudi, and Pierre Filion, eds. 1992. *Canadian Cities in Transition*. Don Mills, Ont.: Oxford University Press. This collection brings together a national, regional, and intra-urban perspective on local government in Canada.

Driedger, Leo. 1991. *The Urban Factor: Sociology of Canadian Cities*. Don Mills, Ont.: Oxford University Press. This book draws on an eclectic contribution of perspectives from geography, anthropology, economics, and political science. The author examines the demography, ecology, organization, and planning of Canada's urban communities.

Fowler, Edmund. 1992. *Building Cities That Work*. Montreal and Kingston: McGill-Queen's University Press. This book examines how Canadians think about their cities, what their expectations are, and what they are prepared to do to change how their cities develop.

Hampton, William. 1991. *Local Government and Urban Politics*. Essex, U.K.: Longman Group. Examines the tensions between local and other governments in Great Britain.

Loreto, Richard, and David Price. 1991. *Urban Policy Issues: Canadian Perspectives*. Toronto: McClelland & Stewart. This collection of original readings examines policy development and service delivery in Canada's major urban areas. The book offers a wide range of exposure to the diversities of urban government, from economics, urban planning, social work, and medicine.

Maclaren, Virginia. 1992. *Sustainable Urban Development in Canada: From Concept to Practice*. Toronto: ICURR Press. This book examines the kinds of urban development that produce the least social and ecological stress.

Roy, Jean-Hugues, and Brendan Weston. 1990. *Montreal: A Citizen's Guide to City Politics*. Montreal: Black Rose Books. This book takes a unique analytical view of Montreal's City Council and provides an interesting analysis of Montreal urban politics since the era of Mayor Jean Drapeau, scrutinizing every aspect of urban Montreal: housing and planning, ecology, public transportation, public health, civic government, and so on.

Tindal, C.R., and S. Nobes Tindal. 1990. *Local Government in Canada*. Toronto: McGraw-Hill Ryerson. This widely used book provides a comprehensive survey of municipal structures and local politics in Canada.

CONCLUSION

# THE POLITICAL ECONOMY OF GOVERNABILITY

### INTRODUCTION

### THE ECONOMIC ROLE OF GOVERNMENT

What Governments Do in the Economy
Business and Government

### CANADA IN THE GLOBAL ECONOMY

The FTA and NAFTA

### MANAGING THE ECONOMY: POLICY OPTIONS

What Is Economic Policy?
The Influence of Economic Theories on Government
How Governments Monitor Economic Health

### INSTRUMENTS OF ECONOMIC POLICY

Economic Tools

### CONCLUSION

### GLOSSARY

### RECOMMENDED READING

406 ■ Conclusion THE POLITICAL ECONOMY OF GOVERNABILITY

**B**rian and Teresa were having fun ... avoiding taxes. In just one year, they had bought a refrigerator, replaced the railing on their old deck, had a new toilet installed, and paid their house cleaner with cash, all "under the table." Now, without even thinking, when they purchase anything of significance, out of habit they simply ask the salesperson, "Will you take cash, or does your price include the tax?" Is the underground economy healthier than the legal one? Does avoiding taxes really mean avoiding government, and does it ultimately affect how we are governed?

Brian and Teresa are just two of millions of Canadians who are deliberately evading taxes and participating willingly in the "underground," or as it is sometimes called, the "invisible" or "unrecorded economy." Especially since the introduction of the Goods and Services Tax (GST) in 1991 and the continuing economic slump from the recession, a much larger number of Canadians are evading taxes. In fact, the whole underground economy is growing at an alarming rate to the displeasure of Revenue Canada and Finance Canada.

Louis XIV of France had one of the most resourceful finance ministers in modern history, J.B. Colbert. He is famous for his remark that "the art of taxation consists of so plucking the goose as to elicit the least amount of hissing." He is also famous for the answer he got from the business people of the day when he asked them: "How can I help you?" Their answer was "Please, *laissez-nous faire*" (leave us alone), and hence the term *laissez faire* to describe those who believe that government should have a limited role in the economy.

The federal government is admitting for the first time that Canadians are hissing against the unwanted effects of the tax system, and that Revenue Canada is coping with shrinking tax revenues. Due to the reluctance of governments to control spending, tax rates of all kinds have been escalating — tax revenues have not. Canadians are bartering, cross-border shopping, "do-it-yourself" cheating, smuggling, working without declaring income, and evading taxes on services at unprecedented levels. In 1992, when cigarettes were still taxed in excess of 60 percent, about three out of ten cigarettes puffed by Canadians were illegal. Over 30 percent of all jewellery bought by Canadians escaped taxation. In that same year, about three-fourths of house cleaners were paid under the table. And nearly 60 percent of all home renovations were paid for in cash that avoided being taxed.

In addition, businesses are fleeing to tax-friendly havens in "other" economies. Those who have not, as yet, have an increasing incentive to do so. Although understandably difficult to measure, recent Canadian estimates based on activities conducted in cash suggest that the unreported economy might be as low as 3 percent and as high as 22 percent of the measured economy. If the unreported economy is greater than 10 percent of the Canadian economy, as many economists now suspect, an amount of money greater than $60 billion is annually creating jobs, purchasing goods and services, and is taking a free ride on Canada's tax system. An underground economy as large as 10 percent of the Canadian economy is as big or bigger than the gross national products (GNPs) of many states, such as Egypt, Israel, the Republic of Ireland, and New Zealand, to name but a few. In fact, most economies in the developing world are smaller than Canada's unrecorded economy.

What happens to a government system when an expanding number of patrons avoid paying their fair share of the deficit and debt burden? Well, government coffers take a double blow when people evade taxes. The income on the tax money is not reported, and the taxes are not paid. Social welfare programs are adversely affected. These programs include unemployment insurance, old age pensions, welfare, and other transfer payments. Their funding shrinks because they take the largest share of total taxes, which are shrinking from the effects of a growing underground economy.

While Canadians have long regarded their governments as kinder and gentler than their American counterparts, they are increasingly confronted with the fact that the best instrument of public charity is being abused by tax evasion. If we add this to the fact that our health system is deteriorating, our schools cannot afford to pay as many teachers or buy new teaching technologies, and, in many areas of the country, roads, bridges, and other infrastructures are rapidly degrading, it is not surprising that the underground economy is booming and the public sector is reeling.

# INTRODUCTION

In the late nineteenth century, the federal government and the provincial governments that comprised Confederation were minuscule actors in the Canadian economy by present-day measures. The economic activities of these governments were quite limited. There were no social programs, no health programs, no unemployment insurance, no welfare programs, no business assistance or regional development programs, and no programs to meet the needs of the elderly or the disabled. The federal and provincial governments taxed very little, spent very little, and did very little.

There were few government programs to cushion the shock of economic hardship. Governments were mere shadows rather than dominant players in the economy. The pervasive presence of governments in the Canadian economy at the end of the twentieth century symbolizes the drastic changes in the relationship between government and the economic well-being of Canadians over the past 130 years.

Today, questions about how we govern ourselves have as much to do with the managing of Canada's economy as they do with the constitution, federalism, or the bureaucracy. And in this era of downsizing and cutbacks, of all the factors we use to judge the performance of our governments, the state of the economy — particularly unemployment — is the most closely watched. We, and foreigners who invest in this country, continue to hold governments responsible for how the economy performs.

Accordingly, economic relationships are a fundamental part of the successful operation of all Canadian governments. Our parliamentary institutions are at the heart of how we manage our economy. The efficiency of these institutions bears directly on the capacity of our economy to perform and grow in a world of powerful competitors. How our governments wrestle with inflation, recession or depression,

and unemployment will make it possible or impossible for Canadians to compete with the Americans, the Mexicans, the Asians, and the Europeans.

The Constitution Act, 1867, created a federal structure in which different levels of government have responsibilities for different matters affecting the Canadian economy. The federal government has legislative jurisdiction over all matters of "national" economic interest. Provincial governments have jurisdiction over all matters of "local" economic import.

The federal–provincial sharing of certain responsibilities has been controversial. The roles of the levels sometimes overlap, as in the cases of agriculture, immigration, and old-age pensions. Social, technological, economic, and political developments have created new problems to be addressed, including aviation, payment for medical services, telecommunications, and energy shortages. Problems have risen over provincial control of natural resources. Disputes have brewed around how mining tax revenues are to be collected and allocated between the federal and provincial governments.

To manage the economy, the federal government has much more extensive taxing powers to raise money than do the provincial governments. Because the costs of some provincial responsibilities, such as education and health care, exceed their revenue-raising capacity, the federal government has instituted revenue sharing; for example, the federal, provincial, and municipal governments share education expenses.

The ways our governments manage and conduct themselves in the economy provide an important foundation for subsequent analysis of Canada's political processes and public policies. The major issues facing Canadians over the budget, tax policy, regulation, and the "social safety net" can be better understood in the context of the kind of relationship that has evolved between the government and the economy.

Parliament itself is obsessed with economic issues. Most of the daily debates reflect economic concerns. The bureaucracy's rule-making, servicing, and regulation affect the economy every day. Even the courts exercise economic influence in refereeing disputes between employers and employees, and government and business. Although many complex factors shape politics in Canada, and many diverse issues compete for the attention of decision-makers, economic concerns are a common thread.

In the exploration of the nature of Canadian politics around the theme of governability, "political economy" — the close relationship between the political and governing system and the economy — provides important examples and insights.

## THE ECONOMIC ROLE OF GOVERNMENT

Throughout the twentieth century, Canadians have increasingly come to believe that the federal and provincial ministers of finance can affect the state of the economy in significant ways. Economic concerns at the personal level are crucial to many voters most of the time.

Such concerns are especially prominent at election time. Canadian politicians are well aware that good economic times usually favour them for re-election and that bad economic times spell trouble for parliamentarians (Carmichael 1990). Politicians are also aware that voters expect their public officials to talk about and offer solutions to perceived problems.

Everyone wants economic prosperity, but the views on how that can be achieved in a country as large and as complex as Canada conflict. Because voters now hold governments responsible for the state of the economy, ministers of finance must be concerned with how their governments raise and spend money, and the kinds of decisions they make to attract investment, create jobs, and manage the public debt.

The federal and provincial governments must also confront both domestic and international market forces that limit the impact of the measures they take. There is never agreement between politicians and professional economists on what the role of governments should be or on what government measures will produce the most favourable economic results.

Questions about the Canadian economy and the government's role in it have been central to political debate in Canada since 1867. What is the most efficient organization for the Canadian economy? What is the fairest way to distribute wealth? How involved should the government be in managing and directing the economy?

Political conservatives, mostly in Canada's business community, say the people should work out their own economic relations and make their own choices with only a minimum of government involvement in the economy. Political liberals say that often the market does not work very well, frequently producing unacceptable inequalities and distortions that must be rectified by government action and policy. Socialists require considerable public ownership and government intervention, but some are willing to leave a significant portion of economic activity in the hands of private decision-makers. Communists have adopted the perspective that all the means of production should be collectively owned, and very little should be permitted to remain in the hands of private entrepreneurs.

Within the confines of these views, debates about economic policies are ongoing. These debates are spirited because the stakes are so high. Decisions about spending, taxing, and government regulation not only affect the material interests of each of us but also involve our deepest beliefs about the kind of government and society that we want to have.

Often, no consensus exists among us about these fundamental questions.

The role of government in the economy defines the kind of economic system we have. The present central economic role of government is a far cry from what it was during the first decades of Confederation. To a lesser or greater extent, Canada's economic system, as it has evolved across the country and in each province, has always been based upon capitalism.

But economic systems are not static; they grow, adapt, and change. The Canadian economy of the 1990s is quite different from the economy of the 1890s and will, by the year 2090, predictably have changed even more. Under *capitalism*, the means of production are privately owned by individuals and corporations, rather than being publicly owned by the government or some governmental unit. When an economy takes on this free-market philosophy, the private sector owns the businesses, the manufacturing enterprises, and the farms.

Canada's original economic system was based on the concept of *free enterprise*, or competitive capitalism — that is, the right of people to start or invest in whatever business or other enterprise they please, and the right of workers to move from job to job as they please, without government interference.

Another kind of economic system is *socialism*. This system has had some applicability in Canada as well. Although, in theory, it refers to collective ownership of the productive units in the economy, in practice, it commonly refers to a system in which government owns the banks, the factories, the businesses, and the farms, and has the power to control the supply and demand of goods and services. Socialists argue that government-owned industries are more efficient and serve the public better.

The Canadian economic system is a *mixed economy* because both the private sector and the government have developed significant

roles to play. The private-sector organizations provide the majority of Canada's employment, wealth, and productivity, while the governments are responsible for maintaining the economic equilibrium to accelerate or slow down economic growth. The government protects workers employed by private companies with social welfare programs, labour standards, health insurance, unemployment and workers' compensation. It also protects consumers of products from the private sector from exploitation and safety problems.

Canada moved toward a more active government economic role because of the perceived inability or unwillingness of the private sector to address nation-building demands and because of the abuses perpetrated by business in the late nineteenth century: child labour was used, workers were paid a pittance, working conditions were unsafe, and markets were overshadowed by producers who controlled prices and wages.

Over the years, all governments in Canada intervened in the economy to redistribute wealth. By taxing and spending, they came to exercise responsibility for the "welfare" of their citizens in such areas as education, health care, and housing, building what came to be called the **welfare state**. The term is often used in the criticism that there is too much government in Canada.

Because of the huge level of government debt across the country, Canadians are now re-examining the role of government in the economy. All government services require spending, and thus the cost and size of government programs are directly related to the level of taxes people must pay, and this affects Canada's competitive position in the world economy.

## What Governments Do in the Economy

Since Confederation, all Canadian governments have developed an array of governing instruments by which the behaviour of individuals and companies are motivated, regulated, or controlled in the interest of the economy (see Figure 12.1).

The first is *persuasion*, whereby governments, by means of ministerial speeches, advertising campaigns, royal commissions, task forces, and departmental reorganization, try to induce businesses and organizations to comply voluntarily with the goals of government. Sometimes such methods work; sometimes they fail. But governments try to steer the **private sector** in the direction of national and provincial economic goals.

Governments in Canada have come to play many specific roles in its complex economic system. These roles, which influence the way people make economic decisions in business, as professionals, and as private individuals, are: competitor, economic administrator, regulator, taxer, investor, customer, and housekeeper.

### Government as Competitor

Governments can be competitors in the economy and participate directly in the business of the country. This occurs when government becomes involved as a crown corporation, either by owning a public company that competes with private companies in the economy or by having the crown corporation regulate private companies in a certain sector of the economy (Pritchard 1983). A crown corporation is one that is accountable, through a minister, to Parliament for the conduct of its affairs (see Table 12.1). Government cor-

**Table 12.1 Canada's Top Ten Crown Corporations**

|  | Revenues (thousands of dollars) |
| --- | ---: |
| 1. Petro-Canada | 5 001 354 |
| 2. Canadian National Railway | 4 876 230 |
| 3. Canada Post | 3 987 075 |
| 4. Canadian Wheat Board | 2 974 907 |
| 5. Bank of Canada | 2 744 889 |
| 6. Canada Mortgage and Housing | 988 443 |
| 7. Royal Canadian Mint | 965 622 |
| 8. Canadian Commercial | 704 265 |
| 9. Export Development | 679 587 |
| 10. Farm Credit | 399 022 |

*Source: Canadian Business*, June 1992.

porations exist at the provincial level as well. Public ownership of the means of production may be undertaken for many reasons. When private investors are unwilling to assume the risk in some kinds of business investment, the government may decide to do it. In other cases, the investment needed may be too great for private investors, or the potential payoff may be too intangible. Sometimes a government operates a crown corporation to provide employment in an impoverished area. The government may also come to believe that certain businesses in the private sector are not providing a product or service adequately, or are charging too high a price for it, so they will become competitors to those firms.

### Figure 12.1 Governing Instruments of the Canadian Economy

| **Least Coercive** | | | | | | **Most Coercive** |
| --- | --- | --- | --- | --- | --- | --- |
| Persuasion | Money | Deregulation | Privatization | Taxation | Regulation | Public Ownership |

### Government as Economic Administrator

Another government economic role is that of economic administrator. Governments wanting to control certain aspects of the economy have alternatives to crown corporations. Governments can set up administrative boards, tribunals, or commissions to screen decisions of private companies before they are implemented. There are many examples of these organizations, including Investment Canada, the Canadian Radio-television and Telecommunications Commission, the Canadian Transport Commission, the National Energy Board, and provincial boards. Some administrative agencies and boards issue and review licences for a particular industry. Others have important roles in establishing prices and or production levels for producers.

### Government as Regulator

There are also many government policies that can affect the anticipated conditions in the economy. One effect of government regulatory policy is to limit the options available to businesses and economic organizations. About one-third of all the federal and provincial statutes in force are regulatory, in other words, statutes that seek to alter the economic behaviour of individuals in the private sector. Three important areas of regulation are competition policy, consumer protection, and environmental policy.

*Competition policy* as outlined in the Combines Investigation Act, seeks to eliminate restrictive trade practices and thereby stimulate maximum production, distribution, and employment through open competition. Competition policy is used to regulate the practices of Canadian businesses. The underlying belief is that, if there is vigorous competition, all Canadians will benefit from permanent jobs, efficient production systems, lower prices, and a healthier economy.

*Consumer protection* covers the gamut of consumer relations in the Canadian economy. A number of important pieces of legislation protect people from an unregulated private sector. The Hazardous Products Act regulates products that have been determined to be dangerous by consumers and government, such as poorly designed toys, inflammable products, paints containing lead and other dangerous chemical compounds, poisons, and explosives. The Food and Drug Act prohibits the sale of a food that contains any poisonous or harmful substances, is unfit for human consumption, consists in whole or in part of any rotten substances, is adulterated, or was manufactured under unsanitary conditions. The Consumer Packaging and Labelling Act provides a comprehensive set of rules for packaging consumer products, and seeks to ensure that full and factual information appears on product labels. Another fundamental regulatory regime is implemented under the Weights and Measures Act, which sets standards of accuracy for weighing and measuring devices.

In *environmental policy*, most of the industrial sources of industrial pollution are regulated by the provinces. But the federal government plays a limited role when environmental problems affect interprovincial and international affairs. An example is the Canada Water Act. Under it, the federal government can control water quality in fresh and marine waters when there is a formal federal–provincial agreement, when federal waters are involved, or when there is sufficient national urgency to warrant federal action. Acid rain is handled by the federal government because international dealings are necessary. Two other important environmental regulations are the Fisheries Act, which controls the discharge of any harmful substance into any water, and the Environmental Contaminants Act, which establishes regulations for airborne substances that are a danger to human health or the environment.

### Government as Taxer

Governments can also tax for economic control and regulation. Taxes are imposed and collected by government at the federal, provincial, and local levels. "Revenue taxes" have as their main purpose the funding of government services and programs. These represent the majority of taxes raised in Canada. But another class of taxes, called "restrictive taxes," are levied to control certain activities that legislative bodies feel should be controlled. The federal government collects most of the important revenue taxes, especially the income tax. Revenues from income taxes directly reflect economic growth, providing the federal government with increased tax receipts in an expanding economy. By contrast, provincial governments depend heavily on sales taxes and other sources of revenue that grow less rapidly than the economy as a whole. Provincial and municipal taxes are not nearly as "progressive" (based on the ability to pay) as federal taxes. Provincial sales taxes are "regressive" because they fall heaviest on the poor.

### Government as Investor

Federal, provincial, and municipal governments invest in the economy by offering "incentive" and "information programs" to businesses, and organizations that play a productive role in the economy. Incentive programs help to stimulate economic development. They are designed to encourage owners and managers to make certain decisions and take certain actions desired by governments. They sometimes try to encourage businesses to locate in underdeveloped regions of the country, to invest new-product development, or to engage in export activities.

The Federal Business Development Bank (FBDB) offers incentive programs for the development of new products and processes, to establish new production facilities, and to market products domestically and internationally. Foreign Affairs and International Trade Canada provides businesses with the Trade Commissioner Service to assist Canadian exporters and foreign importers with marketing and sales problems in more than 70 countries. The Export Development Corporation was designed to improve Canadian export insurance for Canadian exporters against non-payment by foreign buyers; to give long-term loans to foreign purchasers of Canadian products or guarantees of private loans to purchasers; and to offer insurance against loss of, or damage to, a Canadian company's investment abroad arising from expropriation, revolution, or war.

Natural Resources Canada provides geological maps of Canada's potential mineral-producing areas. This service gives companies interested in mineral exploration much better geological information about Canada than is available about most other countries. Provincial governments also provide geological services to the mining industry. Statistics Canada is yet another valuable government service to businesses. Its data and analysis describe almost every aspect of social and economic life in Canada and provide information used in government policy formulation and decision making by the private sector.

### Government as Customer

Governments are also major customers in the Canadian economy. By spending on programs and administration, governments can influence the economy by attracting many businesses to locate near them and to provide products and services that meet the needs of the public sector. Millions of dollars are spent every year on office equipment, pencils, paper, computers, and so on. Many industries are dependent on government purchasing decisions, if not for their survival, at least for their level of prosperity, as are construction and architectural firms, and companies in the aerospace industry.

### Government as Housekeeper

Finally, governments do the housekeeping that keeps the economy functioning from day to day. Cities and towns provide streets, lighting, sewers, and sanitation services. They also provide security for stores, insurance agencies, wholesalers, and factories through police and fire protection. Educational opportunities for people are provided by the school, university, and community college systems. The federal government provides highways and postal services as well as a wealth of statistical data that help business firms. It also attempts to maintain economic stability through fiscal and monetary policy. Federal government involvement in minting coins and money also provides a stable environment in which the economy can operate.

## Business and Government

In Canada, what governments do in the economy will directly influence how businesses perform. The relationship between business and government is crucial because both are involved in providing Canadians with the basic necessities of life, from health care, education, transportation and communications to water, food, entertainment, waste disposal, and jobs (Starke et al. 1990, 613–39). Almost everything produced in Canada is an output of private businesses. About 95 percent of these businesses are classified as "small" in comparison with the intermediate and large national corporations, as well as multinational corporations.

Business is owned and operated by individuals and groups that fall within the private sector. Although they may provide and duplicate similar services, business, unlike government, strives for profit. Non-profit organizations and agencies, such as churches, charities, and government, can be considered to be the **public sector**, which is "public" because it is owned and operated by the people in the interest of Canadians.

The roles of government and business in Canada are different but not necessarily incompatible or antagonistic. The goods and services produced in Canada may not be essentially useful in fulfilling social or human needs, but the federal and provincial governments have entered and intervened in the Canadian

economy so as to meet the needs of Canadians, when in their view, the private sector has not met public needs.

Accordingly, governments have influenced the conduct of business in many ways. As noted, in addition to passing laws, and using the tax system and moral suasion, governments have influenced businesses by establishing their own corporations, sometimes called "public enterprises." Governments can engage in the substantial management of a particular sector of the economy by exercising complete or partial control over the production, distribution, and consumption of goods and services.

Some academics have argued that the term "corporatism" best characterizes the use of these kinds of governing instruments. Corporatism is a conception of society that permits private individuals, organizations, and groups to do what they do but guided by social and economic policy (Panitch 1988). Government has the main responsibility in managing the business–government relationship.

Corporatism views society as an organic whole and not simply comprised of disparate beings, groups or classes in conflict. Under corporatism, business is seen as an essential partner, along with labour, in the management of Canada's economy. Government, business, and labour must co-operate to ensure that policies are arrived at that serve the best interest of Canadians as a society.

## CANADA IN THE GLOBAL ECONOMY

The Canadian economy is increasingly intertwined with the world economy. The ability to manage an economy is no longer exclusively under the control of federal and provincial governments. The economic events that culminated in the North American stock market crash of 1987 showed how susceptible Canada was to economic forces, many of which happen outside of its own economy.

As the first signs of the **globalization** of the economy began to appear in the 1960s, economists began to see Canada's political and economic health as being directly linked to its ability to compete in the global economy. The trend toward globalization has altered the map of the world economy, and Canada's place in it. Evidence of the growing importance of world business is everywhere. Canada is both a seller and purchaser in the world marketplace. Many Canadian companies, like their counterparts elsewhere, depend heavily on their ability to buy inventories and sell their products abroad.

Canada is a major participant in the international marketplace, even though its economy is relatively small by industrialized standards. It is the seventh-largest exporter in the world, the eighth-largest importer, and a major recipient of foreign direct investment. The five major Canadian chartered banks (see Table 12.2) are among the world's top 50 banks. All of these banks derive a large part of their revenues from their foreign operations and operate in a multitude of foreign economies.

Canada's wealth in natural resources is frequently seen as its main international strength. Many Canadian companies have added technological know-how and marketing expertise to the kinds of benefits they can draw on from a resource-rich country. For example, Abitibi-Price, the world's largest producer of newsprint, owes a large part of its success to Canada's abundant timber resources. Generally, Canada's unique characteristics in terms of large land area, cold climate, and resource wealth can provide advantages to companies that export their goods and services abroad.

The globalization of the Canadian economy is affected by international trade. Foreign trade is important to Canada from two viewpoints — exporting, or selling goods and services abroad, and importing, or buying foreign goods, services, and raw materials. The United States has long been Canada's best trading partner, and in 1991 provided 71 percent of Canada's imports. Consumers in the U.S. economy bought 74 percent of Canadian exports.

For Canada, trade has grown dramatically since the Second World War, both in absolute-dollar terms and as a percentage of the **gross domestic product**. Canada has been very successful in exporting its products, as well as being a major importer. Except for the motor vehicles and parts that flow across the border under the Auto Pact, signed with the United States in 1965, machinery has been the leading import, and wheat and paper products have been the leading exports.

Canada's **balance of trade** is determined by the relationship between its exports and its imports (see Figure 12.2). The federal government, in particular, wants to develop economic policies that produce a favourable balance of trade, or export surplus, which occurs when exports exceed imports. When governments are successful at promoting trade, new money flows into the economic system and generates growth. An unfavourable balance of trade, or import surplus, occurs when imports exceed exports, because the net flow of money is outward, which ultimately can cost jobs.

## Table 12.2 The Largest Banks in Canada, 1992

|  | Assets (thousands of dollars) |
| --- | --- |
| 1. Royal Bank of Canada | 132 367 342 |
| 2. Canadian Imperial Bank of Commerce | 121 000 366 |
| 3. Bank of Montreal | 98 745 211 |
| 4. Bank of Nova Scotia | 88 731 178 |
| 5. Toronto Dominion | 68 968 899 |

*Source:* Adapted from *Financial and Taxation Statistics*, Statistics Canada, Cat. No. 61-219, 1993. Reproduced by authority of the Minister of Industry, 1994.

**Figure 12.2  An Ideal Balance of Trade for Canada**

A net trade surplus or a small deficit on the difference in the value of Canada's total annual imports and exports constitutes an ideal balance of trade. Ideally, total trade flows in should be less than trade flows out.

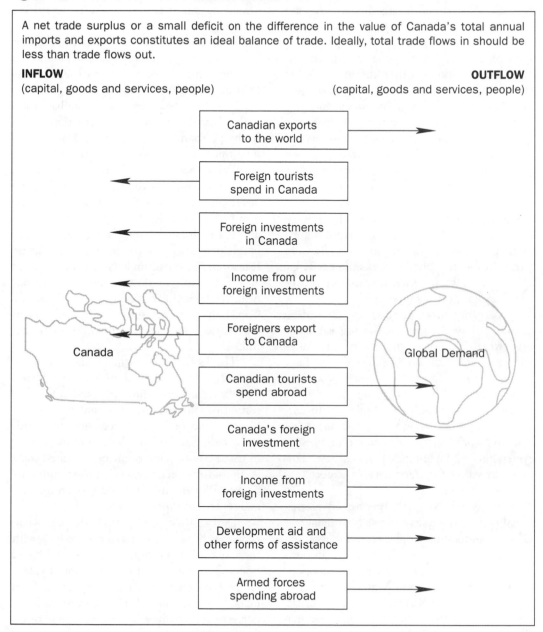

**INFLOW**
(capital, goods and services, people)

**OUTFLOW**
(capital, goods and services, people)

Canadian exports
to the world

Foreign tourists
spend in Canada

Foreign investments
in Canada

Income from our
foreign investments

Foreigners export
to Canada

Canada

Global Demand

Canadian tourists
spend abroad

Canada's foreign
investment

Income from
foreign investments

Development aid and
other forms of assistance

Armed forces
spending abroad

All of this is part of Canada's **balance of payments**, which, depending on how Canada's economy performs, determines the flow of money into or out of the country. A favourable balance of payments leaves money in the economy, which contributes to investment, growth, and debt reduction; an unfavourable balance of payments means money flows out of Canada to the benefit of other economies.

Canada's competitive global economic position is determined by the value of its currency in relation to other currencies. What the Canadian dollar is worth depends on government action in terms of policy and promotion, and market conditions. A deliberate government policy of **devaluation** would reduce the value of Canada's currency in relation to some other currency. Such a policy would have the effect of lowering the cost of Canadian goods and services abroad and making trips to Canada cheaper for foreign tourists. A **revaluation** is the upward adjustment in the value of Canada's currency. In either situation, Canada adjusts the **exchange rate** — the rate at which its currency can be exchanged for other currencies.

Most national economies, including Canada's, have adopted a **floating exchange rate**, which is allowed to vary in accordance with market conditions. Exchange rates have a considerable impact on trade flows and reflect the health of the economy. As the Canadian dollar declines in relation to currencies in other economies, the prices of Canadian products are lower for Europeans, Americans, or Japanese, to name a few. This makes it easier for Canadians to export into other economies.

Closely related to the growth of international trade is the role of the multinational corporation. A multinational corporation is an enterprise that owns, controls, and manages income-generating assets in more than one economy. Since the Second World War, the growth of multinationals in Canada has been dramatic. Some of the better-known Canadian multinationals are Alcan Aluminium, Seagram, MacMillan Bloedel, Moore, National Sea Products, Northern Telecom, and Bombardier.

In terms of investment, multinational corporations demonstrate the globalization of the Canadian economy. The power of the Canadian parent company is used to market Canadian products on a world-wide basis. The company must think in global rather than domestic terms as it develops its production strategy and manages its business affairs (Mittelstaedt 1988).

Another component of the globalization of the Canadian economy is international debt. In the 1970s, many Canadian banks and many investment companies were making loans to developing economies. The financial health of these lending institutions is affected by the developing economies' ability to pay, which points to how the Canadian economy is affected by financial shocks abroad. The global debt contributes to the world economic recession, which ultimately affects Canada's ability to find markets overseas. Without healthy, financially prosperous markets, the Canadian economy suffers. Thus, Canadian and world economic growth are inextricably linked.

The 1990s signalled major shifts in world trade and monetary relations. As a result, Canada led moves to lift **tariffs** and other trade restrictions in the international system. For Canada, the General Agreement on Tariffs and Trade (GATT) has been a primary focus of that activity. One result of increased trade is increasing economic interdependence: Today, all economies rely on foreign markets and sources of supply.

During this same period, the Canadian economy became more interdependent with those of other countries, especially the United States. This meant not only that many Canadian export industries relied increasingly on markets abroad, but also that, even more so, domestic companies faced stiff competition from foreign producers, in particular, Japanese and European competitors, which were especially effective in penetrating Canadian markets for textiles, steel, autos, machine tools, and electronic goods.

## The FTA and NAFTA

In 1992, the government leaders of Canada, Mexico, and the United States signed a trilateral agreement establishing the North American Free Trade Association (NAFTA). The original agreement leading to NAFTA was the Canada–U.S. Free Trade Agreement (FTA) signed in Ottawa in 1988, which committed Canada and the United States to eliminating economic barriers to their economies by 1999 (Woodside 1989). At that time, the two economies will have eliminated most of the barriers to the exchange of almost all goods and many financial services between them.

In Canada, there was particularly vigorous debate, culminating in heated rhetoric during the elections called in 1988 and 1993. The Liberal and NDP parties strongly opposed the deals, while the Conservatives supported them. The FTA has prompted many Canadian companies to think in continental terms rather than solely on the basis of the Canadian economy. Although much less integrative than the European Communities (EC), the FTA and NAFTA have made North America a free-trade area that will rival the EC into the twenty-first century. The free-trade area encompassed by NAFTA includes 380 million people and a $6-billion international economy. NAFTA accounts for nearly 30 percent of the global economy.

Free trade between Canada and the United States began the process of gradually removing market barriers, eventually enabling duty-free access to a market of more than 280 million people. The economic philosophy behind the FTA supports the belief that the dynamic spin-off from a North American marketplace will produce greater efficiency of production and distribution, lower prices, and more employ-

# The Great Debate on Free Trade

## ARGUMENTS FAVOURING FREE TRADE

The far-reaching hemispheric free-trade agreements signed by Canada in 1988 and 1992 capped a long series of trade agreements that have been made with the United States over the past 100 years. The first free-trade agreement Canada signed was with the United States in 1854, but it was terminated by the United States in 1866. In the latter half of the nineteenth century, several other attempts at free-trade agreements were made, but none was successful. In 1935, a modest **most-favoured-nation** agreement was ratified with the United States. This agreement marked the start of serious trade liberalization between the United States and Canada. In 1948, Canada became part of the General Agreement on Tariffs and Trade (GATT), which laid the foundation for the dramatic expansion of world trade. GATT agreements helped reduce trade barriers between Canada and the Unites States. In 1965, Canada and the United States concluded the Auto Pact agreement, which provided for duty-free trade in cars, trucks, buses, and parts. With the success of this "sectoral" free-trade agreement, the Canadian government developed an interest in gaining more secure access to the large U.S. market, and ultimately to the Mexican market. Those who favour free trade say that it would have a positive impact on Canada's economy in the following ways:

1. **Employment.** Canada's economy is built on trade, especially with the United States. No longer can economic nationalism create and protect Canadian jobs. Free-trade agreements give Canada access to other economies and expand jobs opportunities for Canadians. The North American economy provides many more job opportunities for Canadian workers than does a Canadian economy surrounded by high tariff barriers, quotas, and customs restrictions on the exit and entry of goods and services. Such protections erode Canadian jobs because the United States will apply its own protectionism on goods and services produced in Canada that enter into the American market. Canadian companies will learn to compete successfully with foreign firms.

2. **Canada's Social Safety Net.** During the twentieth century, Canada entered into more than 200 trade agreements with the United States. There is no evidence that any of these agreements threatened social services in Canada, such as unemployment insurance and universal medicare. Without free trade in North America, the Canadian economy will perform so poorly that the Canadian government will not be able to afford the current levels of social programs.

3. **Corporate Takeovers.** The parties to free trade maintain controls on foreign investment. Approximately 75 percent of Canada's corporate assets will remain subject to government approval before a takeover from Mexico or the United States is permitted.

4. **Energy and Resources.** Nothing specific in the free-trade agreements refers to energy or natural resources (e.g., water). There are, however, specific articles giving the Canadian government the right to take action to protect health, safety, essential security, the environment, and consumer interests.

5. **Employment for Women.** Women are heavily employed in the service sector of the Canadian economy. The negotiating parties to free trade argue that many of the new jobs created under the agreements will be in the service sector.

6. **The Environment.** The environment is not covered in the agreement. The federal government retains the right to take whatever actions are necessary to protect against negative environmental consequences to the free-trade agreements.

7. **National Sovereignty and Cultural Identity.** Canada's cultures are not even mentioned in the agreements, and its sovereignty will be strengthened by a growing and competitive economy.

8. **Access to Treaty Markets.** The free-trade agreements formalize and expand Canada's access to the U.S. and Mexican markets.

## ARGUMENTS AGAINST FREE TRADE

1. **Employment.** Canadian workers will be laid off because U.S. companies will cut down their production activities in Canada and ship duty-free goods produced at U.S. plants across the border.

2. **Canada's Social Safety Net.** In order to compete in NAFTA, Canadian companies will lobby Canadian governments to decrease spending on social programs and to redirect tax revenues to lower the deficit and the national debt. This will result in the elimination of universality in the administration of Canada's social programs.

3. **Corporate Takeovers.** U.S. and Mexican corporations will buy many Canadian companies in whole or in part because, under the terms of free trade, the Canadian government will not screen takeovers that are valued at less than $150 million. Foreign ownership in the Canadian economy will thus significantly increase.

4. **Energy and Resources.** As the terms of NAFTA are expanded, Canada will lose control of its valuable natural resources such as oil, coal, gas, and perhaps even water.

5. **Employment for Women.** Many Canadian women who are employed in the service sector will lose their jobs because free trade permits foreign firms to deal in services.

6. **The Environment.** As the standards of corporate conduct are lowered to harmonize corporations within NAFTA, Canada will lose its right and ability to control environmental standards.

7. **National Sovereignty and Cultural Identity.** Because of all of the policy changes that will be required to implement free trade, Canada will surrender much of its economic sovereignty and political independence.

8. **Access to Treaty Markets.** Access to foreign markets does not automatically guarantee that Canadian companies will be able to compete and produce successfully. Jobs will be lost because many small and medium-sized corporations will go out of business or transfer their assets to foreign markets.

---

ment on both sides of the border. The idea of a binding free-trade arrangement between the two most-developed economies in the Western hemisphere is seen to prepare and strengthen Canada and the United States for a more competitive advantage in the global economy (Doern and Tomlin 1991).

Not only do the authors of free-trade agreements perceive that economic benefits will result, but they argue that political gains are inevitable. Strong economies enhance political systems and governments because they can deliver rewards to their constituents. For Canadians, national unity is considered to be a by-product of a vibrant economy. Provinces are less likely to sustain separatist movements when economic growth is taking place and jobs are available.

The trilateral negotiations culminating in the signing of NAFTA in San Antonio resulted in 2000 pages of detailed trade conditions. More than 20 000 products are governed by this international treaty. Under the agreement, most tariff and **non-tariff barriers** would be eliminated over a fifteen-year period. Many rules and regulations require "domestic content" in order for products to be made within NAFTA. Cars and trucks must have 62.5 percent domestic content to meet the requirement of being "made in NAFTA."

The treaty removes many restrictions on cross-border investments and other financial transactions. Advertising, banking, and insurance will flow much more freely. Commercial transportation will be much less impeded at the border points. Any trade disputes among the parties will be settled by an international commission with representation from all three signatories. There are provisions for other states in Central and South America and the Caribbean to eventually join NAFTA, potentially creating a regional economic association stretching from the Arctic to Antarctica.

Canada and the United States already conduct the largest commercial bilateral trade relationship in the world, annually totalling about $200 billion. Canada's trade with Mexico has been much smaller, not exceeding 1 percent of Canadian imports and 2 percent of Canadian exports. By comparison, only 3 percent of Mexico's exports go to Canada, and 1 percent of Canada's imports come from there. Whether the overall economies of each state will be strengthened or weakened is very controversial and will not be evident for decades.

## MANAGING THE ECONOMY: POLICY OPTIONS

### What Is Economic Policy?

Public policies aimed at improving the economy as a whole are examples of economic policy. Economic policies are redistributive tools governments use that have a common purpose — namely, to control people by manipulating the entire economy rather than regulating people directly and individually. Economic policies are redistributive when they seek to control conduct more indirectly by altering the conditions of conduct and manipulating the environment of conduct.

The Canadian economy is an extraordinarily complex and poorly understood set of human interrelationships. It rests its beliefs on the competitive marketplace, where the exchange of goods and services between and among private individuals generates income and wealth.

The Canadian marketplace is widely known for its efficiency, but it also generates an unequal distribution of income and wealth. Thousands of Canadians do not have jobs, and millions fall below the poverty line in the economy. Because our governing process has decreed that too much inequality is undesirable, the government uses its policy-making power to redistribute income in order to provide a measure of equality.

In fact, all Canadian governments — collectively, the public sector — play a major role in our economy. Government taxing and spending in Canada account for over 40 percent of the economy's total yearly value, the **gross national product**. Government legislation and administrative regulation help define what businesses, private individuals, and groups may or may not do in the economy.

Most of us think of economics and politics as separate spheres. On the one hand, economic decisions are primarily made through markets, that is, by private, self-interested consumers, firms, and workers. Political decisions, on the other hand, are primarily made through elections, legislatures, and public bureaucracies. While politics includes self-interested behaviour, it also involves generating agreement on the broader "public interest,"

which expects governments to provide jobs and positive economic conditions.

But it is by no means clear that, despite campaign promises, the federal and provincial governments can or will do whatever is necessary to reduce unemployment, cut inflation, lower interest rates, and increase incomes. For one thing, governments do not know how to produce all these desirable outcomes. Moreover, doing one of these things may be possible only at the cost of not doing another.

For example, reducing unemployment can, in many cases, require governments to act so as to increase public spending, which increases inflation, debt, and taxes. This, in turn, can slow down the economy by making it harder sell automobiles, houses, and other commodities that are purchased with borrowed money. All this means that politicians must make choices about economic policy, choices that are affected by uncertainty and ignorance, and by conflicting public demands. Those choices are shaped by the pressures of interest groups and the ideological platforms of the political parties in and out of Parliament.

## The Influence of Economic Theories on Government

Over the years, governments of all political persuasions have been guided by the great economic ideas of our time. In recent Canadian history, several philosophies of economic policy have vied for acceptance as official government doctrine.

At least four major schools of economic thought about how best to manage the economy have influenced government decision-makers in Canada. Each school of thought, supported by the logic of economic theory, has found considerable political appeal within the confines of our competitive political party system. Each economic theory has clear political consequences, and so it is no accident that people embrace a theory, in part, because of their political beliefs. Should the government promote business and economic growth by its taxing, spending, and regulatory policies, or should it be neutral? Should it focus its efforts on helping individuals or helping businesses? Not surprisingly, monetarists, Keynesians, planners, and supply-siders prescribe different solutions.

### The Monetarist School

Pure "monetarism" is most often associated with the American economist Milton Friedman, whose conservative economic theories won him the Nobel Prize in Economics in 1976. In Friedman's view, because governments do not understand that economic problems result from their own start-and-stop habit of printing money, they will try to solve some of these problems with policies that make matters worse — such as having an unbalanced budget or creating new welfare programs. He believes that the free workings of the market and the equality of opportunity will produce the best economy, and ultimately the best society (Friedman and Friedman 1980).

Monetarism puts singular emphasis on controlling the **money supply** and the price of money (the interest rate) to secure a growing and inflation-free economy. While every economist recognizes that the supply of money in the economy is important, only monetarists give it supreme importance.

The Bank of Canada, established in 1935, is the primary monetarist instrument. The job of the Bank of Canada is to set and enforce long-range targets for growth in the money supply that matches the rate of growth in productivity. If the government allows the amount of money to grow too large and the cost of money falls too low, consumers of money will borrow and spend so much that demand will exceed supply, and **inflation** will result. If money is in short supply and interest rates are high, consumer, business, and government spending and borrowing will decline, supply will exceed demand, and unemployment will result.

Because the federal government has the power to create money, inflation occurs when it prints too much of it. One important monetarist prescription is that the growth in money supply should be steady and gradual, roughly in pace with the growth in the amount of goods and services the economy produces. Anything more will heat up the economy; anything less will cool it down, and perhaps dip it into recession.

Thus, the Bank of Canada keeps watch regularly on the supply of money and takes steps to alter that supply. This central bank is the lender of last resort to chartered banks. The rate at which chartered banks can borrow from the Bank of Canada is called the **bank rate** and is the base used for establishing the prime interest rates. When inflation becomes rampant and the government tries to do something about it, it usually cuts back sharply on the amount of money in circulation. When this happens, a **recession** can occur, with slowed economic growth and an increase in unemployment.

Those who adhere to the monetarist school of thought believe that the proper thing for government to do is to permit a steady, predictable increase in the supply of money at a rate about equal to the growth in the productivity of the economy. Beyond that, government should leave matters alone and let the free market manage its own affairs.

### The Keynesian School

If anyone can be called the "intellectual founder" of modern government intervention in the economy, it is the British economist John Maynard Keynes. Keynes (pronounced "kanes") revolutionized economic thinking by overturning orthodox (i.e., *laissez faire*) economic theories that were dominant before the 1930s.

In his classic work, *The General Theory of Employment, Interest, and Money*, he showed that capitalist economies do not consistently operate at a level that fully employs an economy's workers or keeps its factories operating. What Keynes provided was crucial —

an intellectual justification for government intervention in the economy.

Keynes believed that the health of an economy is dependent on the relationship between overall supply and demand in the economy. *Supply* is the total amount of goods and services produced in the economy; *demand* is the total amount of goods and services consumed. Economic problems arise, according to Keynes, when supply and demand are not in balance.

If supply exceeds demand, businesses build up a backlog of unsold goods, cut back production, and lay off workers. But if demand exceeds supply, buyers bid up the price of goods, and inflation results. Only when supply and demand are in close balance do maximum employment and minimum inflation result.

But Keynes also believed governments must use their policy-making powers to bring supply and demand into balance. When supply exceeds demand and unemployment threatens, the government should spend more than it receives in taxes — that is, engage in *deficit spending* and bring total demand, and hence employment, to the optimal level. If demand exceeds supply and inflation looms, the government should collect more taxes than it spends — that is, run a *surplus* and bring total demand, and hence inflation, down.

Until Keynes, most economists believed that the economy was guided by the "hidden hand" of the price mechanism, which would automatically bring to the economy the full use of its human and capital resources. Unemployment was considered a temporary phenomenon that would disappear when workers realized that their wage demands were too high, and that, in order to be hired by employers, they would have to accept less.

Keynes argued that no automatic mechanism would allow the economy to recover from the Great Depression on its own. What was needed was for the government to create deliberately a large deficit, which would pump

resources back into the economy, and thus spur its recovery. The stimulus would produce income that, in turn, would be spent creating additional jobs and income, and so on. Such a policy would not only stimulate recovery from a depression but could also be used to prevent economic downturns at the first sign of trouble.

Notwithstanding the logic of Keynes's theory, there is still the problem of how to make deficits (budget shortfalls when expenses exceed revenues) which most policy-makers regard as irresponsible, politically appealing. Keynesian economists understand that, for many conservatives and members of the business community, deficits could be made more palatable if they were created by cutting taxes rather than by increasing spending. Moreover, a tax cut gives the advantage of increasing private consumption because, with lower taxes, consumers have more money to spend, creating a higher demand for what the private sector produces.

Keynesians know that both a cause and an effect of economic expansion is greater spending on domestic programs. It became conventional wisdom of governments in Canada during the 1940s, 1950s, and 1960s to believe that the growing prosperity of the times would produce the necessary tax revenue to reduce deficits and debt.

But, by the 1970s, policy-makers faced an unprecedented economic problem — *stagflation*, which is simultaneously high rates of inflation and of unemployment. This was primarily the result of a series of "supply shocks" that buffeted the economies of the industrialized world. The most important was the quadrupling of oil prices and the embargo launched by the international oil cartel OPEC (the Organization of Petroleum Exporting Countries) in 1973. The shock of sudden oil-price rises rippled throughout the entire economy, and the transfer of income from the industrial countries to OPEC reversed economic growth, creating unemployment and inflation.

Stagflation rendered the conduct of macroeconomic management much more difficult. As the "misery index" — the sum of the inflation and unemployment rates — remained in double digits, the tools of modern economic management suddenly appeared obsolete. Policy-makers were on the horns of a dilemma.

## The Planners

Many economists have too little faith in the workings of the free market to be pure Keynesians and pure monetarists. These "planners" say government has a role to play in economic planning, and economic planning has a role to play in successful economies. They believe that, for economies to survive or succeed in a competitive international environment, governments must plan, in varying ways, many of the economic activities in the economy. Planning is not just something for the public sector: It is essential to the smooth functioning of the private sector.

Canadian-born John Kenneth Galbraith is one of the most prominent economists to advocate an important planning component in the governing of the economy. For Galbraith, government must map out the stability of the economy, by managing its expansion and growth. Planning by government has its counterpart in the corporate sector of the economy; economic stability is necessary for long-term planning by large corporations and small and medium-size businesses; planning facilitates corporate profits, trained workers and managers, research and development, and time to build an industrial strategy.

One kind of economic planning governments can do is to control prices and wages. For Galbraith, this is sometimes necessary because big corporations can raise prices when the forces of competition are too weak to restrain them, and labour unions can force up wages when management finds it easier to pass the increases along to consumers. In times of inflation, governments should regulate the maximum prices that can be charged and wages that can be paid.

Another kind of planning involves an industrial strategy whereby the government addresses the declining health of certain basic industries, such as steel and automotive manufacturing. In his aptly titled *The New Industrial State* (1967, 304), Galbraith spells out the chief goals of the state: "The state is strongly concerned with the stability of the economy. And with its expansion or growth. And with education. And with technical and scientific advance." In the emerging technological economies of the 1990s, "smokestack" industries — those that continue to rely on outmoded technologies — can no longer recover through market forces; it is necessary for government to direct or plan investments so that these industries can recover or newer industries can grow and compete.

## Supply-Side Economics

Monetarists are usually catalogued as economic conservatives because they stress the ability of the competitive marketplace to allocate resources efficiently. But not all conservative private-market economists are monetarists. In the 1970s, a new emphasis took shape among conservative economic theorists in North America that was christened "supply-side economics."

By the late 1980s, the perception had become widespread that much of the problem with the Canadian economy was a government that had grown too large and intrusive, especially for business. At best, it appeared that the government was incapable of dealing with stagflation and international competition; at worst, government itself was to blame for the economic problems besetting the Canadian economy. The economic conservatives who rose to power in the Progressive Conservative party in the 1980s were anti-Keynesian because they rejected the notion of governments practising "discretionary" fiscal management and because they sought a reduction in the size of the public sector.

Supply-side economists focus on how much is produced in the economy rather than on how much is demanded, as in the Keynesian and monetarist perspectives. According to supply-side economists, government can affect the balance of supply and demand in the economy better by adjusting supply than by adjusting demand. In fact, supply-siders blame the government for creating the imbalances by setting taxes so high that people have little incentive to work or to invest, and thus to produce. Only if government reduces taxes sufficiently to restore incentives and make money available will people begin to work harder, invest more, and produce more.

According to supply-siders, the stimulus to economic activity created by lower tax rates will be so great that tax revenues will actually increase as a result of higher employment and consumption. Paradoxically, a reduction of the tax rate can actually create an increase in total tax revenues. The role of government in all this is to reduce taxes and domestic spending, and encourage investment to produce balanced budgets.

By the late 1960s, in Canada, an enormous array of government regulations affecting prices and determining which firms could enter certain markets were in place — governing airlines, transport, railways, oil and natural gas, banks, and other financial institutions. Regulations had been imposed early in the development of these industries to promote their orderly growth. By the 1980s, however, economists and other observers felt that much of this regulation was no longer needed, and that its principal and continuing effect was to limit competition. In 1981, the former Economic Council of Canada (ECC) published a study recommending a reduction of government regulation so as to reduce business costs, and therefore reduce prices. In its view, government controls on prices and market entry simply preserved comfortable niches in which businesses could operate free from competitive challenge. The ECC recommended that many regulatory barriers should be removed, and free-market controls substituted.

## How Governments Monitor Economic Health

### The Indicators

Federal and provincial governments in Canada are especially interested in the performance of the economy. Knowing how the economy is performing is crucial to ministers of finance across the country who must decide what actions to take to stabilize economic conditions. Such knowledge is also useful to those who evaluate the effectiveness of the government's economic policies.

Although political scientists use a large number of indicators to examine the economy in detail, a few general economic indicators are visible to the Cabinet, members of Parliament, and the general public. These indicators receive regular coverage in the media, and so are easily accessible to everyone. The most important indicators to both governments and the public are:

1. *Employment and unemployment.* The unemployment rate in the civilian work force is the best-known indicator of all. Statistics Canada releases a new figure monthly, and it receives wide media attention. Canadians are concerned about how much their governments should attempt to reduce unemployment. Governments are concerned about how much joblessness is tolerable. Full employment in Canada is considered to be 5 percent unemployment.

2. *Prices and wages.* The consumer price index (CPI) is widely used as the single best measure of price stability. Rapid price increases lead politicians and consumers to worry about inflation. Wage gains are

compared to price increases to calculate how much "real wages" affect purchasing power.

3. *Economic growth.* The most commonly used indicator of growth in the total economy is the gross national product (GNP) — the value of all goods and services that the economy produces within a year (see Figure 12.3). Economic growth is measured as the percentage change in the GNP. For the economy to grow, the percentage change in the GNP must be higher than the percentage change in prices. When GNP is analyzed for inflation, it measures "real" growth.

4. *Interest rates.* The demand for money in the economy generates a market that sets the cost of borrowing for all those who need it. There are numerous interest rates in the economy that involve many different lenders and many different borrowers.

The prime interest rate is the rate that banks charge their best customers. A variety of other rates charged by banks and other lending institutions determine interest rates on mortgages, treasury bills, and other fiscal instruments.

5. *Investments.* In addition to private individuals, many groups, such as businesses, governments, and foreign buyers, spend money in the Canadian economy. They are the investors whose investments provide for future economic growth by bringing capital to the economy. In addition to investments made by Canadians, governments are particularly interested in foreign direct investment, whereby foreigners control the managerial level of businesses operating in Canada.

6. *Balance of trade.* Canada's net annual trade surplus or deficit is based on the differ-

**Figure 12.3 Economic Growth in Canada**

*Source:* Adapted from *Canadian Economic Observer,* Statistics Canada, Cat. No. 11–210, selected years. Reproduced by authority of the Ministry of Industry, 1994.

ence in the values of its total imports and exports. Generally a surplus of exports over imports is considered "favourable," while a surplus of imports over exports is "unfavourable" in the balance of trade. The balance of trade is to be distinguished from the balance of payments, which includes, in addition to trade, transfers of money between Canada and other economies, such as external assistance, tourist expenditures, and currency transfers.

7. *Budget deficit*. A budget deficit occurs when the spending of the federal or a provincial government exceeds its revenue. A surplus results in the unlikely event that government revenues exceed spending. The national deficit became very visible politically in the 1980s in Canada. In addition to looking at the deficit, political scientists and economists look at the size of the total national debt, that is, all money borrowed by the federal government over the years that it must repay.

Almost invariably, none of the indicators in the above categories has a fixed or unambiguous meaning for either academics or politicians. Economists often disagree on the precise meaning and implications of these indicators; politicians and governments agree even less. In parliamentary debates, politicians with different sets of partisan beliefs will come to very different conclusions about the policy implications of the same set of statistics. There is also no consensus on how best to reverse these kinds of economic difficulties.

How much reliance should be placed on Canada's market system to address economic problems? When is it appropriate for governments to intervene in the economy? How much regulation to protect businesses and consumers in the economy is necessary to generate healthy economic growth?

# INSTRUMENTS OF ECONOMIC POLICY

## Economic Tools

In attempting to achieve and stabilize the economy for high employment, growth, and price stability, governments in Canada have an array of instruments at their disposal. These may be divided into two broad categories — macroeconomic and microeconomic. Macroeconomic instruments affect the overall level of economic activity by regulating aggregate flows of income and expenditure. The two most important of these are fiscal and monetary policies. Fiscal policies are concerned with raising revenues for government purposes, largely through taxation and by controlling or expanding government expenditures. Monetary policies are directed to interest rates and the money supply.

Fiscal policy is conducted through the federal budget, although all provincial budgets address fiscal problems. Governments may decide to raise or cut taxes and increase or decrease spending in the public sector. What is important here is not the composition of the budget (how the government spends the money), but the overall, or "aggregate," levels of spending and revenue and, in turn, the size of the deficit or surplus that is produced.

Fiscal tools are not easy to use, however. Federal spending, for instance, cannot be easily adjusted up or down as economic conditions change. The legislative process is cumbersome and time-consuming, with many interests involved. So, for example, changes in tax policy cannot be done annually. Also, changes in spending and taxing take so long to implement that it is possible they will be inappropriate by the time they filter into the economy. A tax cut to stimulate a sluggish economy, for instance, may kick in just as the economy is entering a period of inflation.

A budget deficit occurs when a government's expenditures exceed its revenues. When total revenues (what the government absorbs from all taxes, customs duties, and user fees) equals total spending, there is a balanced budget. When revenue exceeds spending, the budget is in surplus; and when spending exceeds revenue, a deficit is created. In the case of a deficit, the government must finance the shortfall by borrowing money. The unpaid portion of deficits accumulated over time constitutes Canada's "national debt," sometimes called the "public debt," and it represents the indebtedness of governments at a specific time.

Over the years, the national debt can accumulate because governments spend money, usually without having to balance revenues with a deficit. Some government spending is voluntary, such as deciding to clean up national harbours or build a fixed link to Prince Edward Island. But a large amount of government spending is involuntary, such as operating Parliament and paying pensions to parliamentarians.

### Spending

During the nineteenth and early twentieth centuries, Canada's government expenditures covered little more than the costs of operating the armed forces, police, some public works programs, and the salaries of judges, parliamentarians, and a small number of bureaucrats.

Except for wartime periods, when governments spent money for munitions, weapons, and personnel, public spending was small and under control. With the Depression of the 1930s, there came a major increase in government involvement in the economy. The Depression brought widespread unemployment and suspicion that the private market economy operating on its own steam could improve the lot of Canadians. Public-sector spending increased rapidly as all levels of government tried to alleviate the burden on the unemployed and to create jobs for them in the public sector.

But, until the 1970s much of Canada's national debt stemmed from financing its involvement in the Second World War and from the deep recession of 1958–62. Recessions cause the government to lose tax revenues and to borrow to make up shortfalls. The energy crisis of the 1970s, a succession of severe recessions in the 1980s, and the enormous growth in annual government spending created the largest deficits ever, and sent Canada's national debt skyrocketing. By the 1990s, the combined provincial and federal debts had come to equal the annual gross national product, at about $630 billion dollars.

Hypothetically, if such a debt was generated in one year, all governments in Canada would have had to spend about $20 000 every second (see Figure 12.4). As Canada readies itself to enter the next century, the national debt accounts for almost all of the economy. About 43 cents out of every dollar pays the interest and other carrying charges on the federal and provincial deficits and the national debt.

There have been two major features of government spending patterns in Canada. The first is that the process has historically been incremental; that is, each annual budget is usually slightly larger than the previous year's.

Incrementalism means simply that the best predictor of this year's budget is last year's budget plus a little bit more. Normally, Cabinet does not radically alter the allocation of money from one year to the next; members of Cabinet assume that agencies should get about what they received the previous year. On the surface, this simplifies the work of all concerned. Government departments do not have to defend, or Cabinet members scrutinize, all aspects of the budget. A second feature is that governments tend to spend more in election years. This tendency is more marked in times of unemployment and less so in times of inflation and recession.

**Figure 12.4 The National Debt Clock**

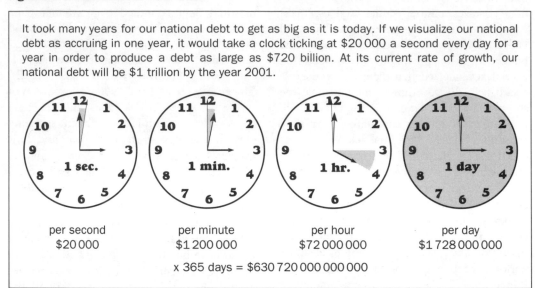

It took many years for our national debt to get as big as it is today. If we visualize our national debt as accruing in one year, it would take a clock ticking at $20 000 a second every day for a year in order to produce a debt as large as $720 billion. At its current rate of growth, our national debt will be $1 trillion by the year 2001.

| per second | per minute | per hour | per day |
|---|---|---|---|
| $20 000 | $1 200 000 | $72 000 000 | $1 728 000 000 |

x 365 days = $630 720 000 000 000

Precisely because so much of government spending appears incremental, there is a never-ending quest for the control of government spending. In Canada, incrementalism has made it very difficult to pare and cut government spending. In 1992, the federal government passed the Spending Control Act in an effort to control its program spending. The act limits the government to spending levels according to its budget projections, and makes the process more visible to the general public, and therefore more accountable.

But there is another reason government spending got out of control in the past few decades: More and more of it has become uncontrollable. Uncontrollable spending results from public policies that make certain groups automatically eligible for some benefit, such as public-sector pension plans. The fact that those who become ill, or unemployed, or qualify for pensions and other federal and provincial government payments are entitled to these benefits is a matter of public policy. As well, government cannot decide this year, for example, that it will not pay the interest on

the federal debt, or that it will chop by half the pensions of MPs.

There is a growing public perception that government spending in Canada is "out of control." But, in 1992, the federal government showed its lowest program spending in more than twenty years.

Spending by the federal and provincial governments generally has a threefold effect on Canadians and their economy. The first is the *fiscal effect*, which can cause employment or unemployment and pressures on prices to rise and decline as a result of what governments demand. Second, spending can also have a *regulatory effect*. If the federal government subsidizes an airline, it may require the airline to service cities or regions that might not otherwise be served. Third, there is the *distributional effect*, whereby spending can redistribute wealth from one group to another.

Most of us tend to think that this distribution is from wealthy to poor people. But redistribution also goes from working-class people in Canada to the more wealthy by means of taxes that generate federal and provincial grants and assistance programs to businesses, many of which are profitable. How the government decides to spend our money may have great impact on the economy, and spending may also produce dramatic results regarding the distribution of wealth and income in Canada.

### Taxation

Nothing can raise the dander of Canadians more than taxes. Bleary-eyed, millions of Canadian taxpayers struggle to the post office before midnight every April 30 to mail their income tax forms. Taxes take a share of money earned in the economy.

Like spending, taxes can also have important effects. First, taxes raise revenues for the government. They are the primary instruments by which governments get money to operate their programs and pay their debts. Second, the fiscal effect of taxes may increase or decrease unemployment or inflation, as money is taken out of the hands of consumers, or left in the hands of consumers to use for product or service consumption or investment. Third, the level of taxation can affect the compliance of people with the tax system. If taxes are too high, people will want to avoid them, and will generate an underground, tax-free economy.

The regulatory effect of taxes may discourage or promote certain kinds of activities, to control smokers and drinkers of alcoholic beverages, or to encourage the installation of high-tech equipment. The distributional effect results from tax decisions about who will pay the taxes, and whether some taxpayers will pay more or less than others.

How high are taxes in Canada? Among comparable states, Canada's burden of taxation as a percentage of 1993 GDP was exceeded by only four other economies — Sweden, Denmark, France, and Italy.

Many Canadians think our present tax system is unfair — benefiting the rich to the detriment of the ordinary working person. Public discontent with taxes has become an important feature of Canadian politics. There are two reasons for this: a rise in the level of taxes other than the federal income tax; and the continuation of tax loopholes that benefit corporate taxpayers and taxpayers in the higher-income brackets.

The total tax bite in Canada involves the installation of the Goods and Services Tax (GST) at the federal level and considerable recent increases in provincial and municipal taxes. On the one hand, these taxes are largely regressive, because they take a larger share from low-income groups than from high-income groups. A progressive tax, on the other hand, does the opposite, and is supposed to be based on the ability to pay. Whether a tax is progressive or regressive, then, depends on what percentage of income the tax takes from various income groups.

When deficits are created by governments, they can stimulate economic growth by expanding incomes and increasing the number of jobs. When this happens, consumers are able to spend more money, which allows business to expand production and hire more workers. Conversely, when taxes are raised and/or spending is cut, the budget moves into balance or surplus. In this case, the rate of economic growth may slow down, and the GDP will decline. If it slows too much, the economy will experience recession, and incomes will stagnate or shrink, and people may be put out of work. If the economy recedes dramatically for a long period of time, whereby the GDP declines for many successive quarters, the economy may be in depression.

Hence, *macroeconomic* tools have powerful impacts on levels of unemployment, prices, and economic growth. When fiscal and monetary policies are too "tight" (i.e., restrictive), they can slow economic growth and increase unemployment; when they are too "loose" (i.e., expansionary), they can "overstimulate" the economy and lead to inflation. In theory, monetary and fiscal policies are supposed to be co-ordinated so that they are moving the economy in the same direction. For any number of reasons, however, such co-ordination is often difficult.

When the government uses *microeconomic* instruments, it seeks to intervene at the level of specific sectors of the economy and particular industries. These tools come in a variety of forms. For instance, government may provide loans to new small businesses that are unable to borrow capital from private banks, subsidies in the form of grants to local governments to help create jobs in areas where unemployment is high, or tax incentives ("tax expenditures") to encourage businesses to invest in new plant and equipment.

### The Budget

Budgeting is at the heart of government in Canada. It sets priorities and limits for government action. It is a tangible expression of what governments want to do. And, politically, it provides a highly visible focus for competition among varying interests, both in and out of government.

Government **budgets** are essential because the wants of Canadians must be tamed by the scarcity of our national and provincial resources. If the wants of Canadians were limited and resources unlimited, budgets would be unnecessary. However, because neither condition exists, all governments in Canada are inevitably forced to wrestle with the necessity of preparing budgets, which can be thought of as planned statements of revenues and expenditures.

Most Canadians are ambivalent toward public money. They know very little about the details of the federal budget or how various government departments work together to arrive at specific taxing and spending policies; however, they are acutely aware of the degree to which their salaries are reduced by withholding taxes, and beneficiaries of public programs notice even small changes in their ben-

efits. They are also aware that where the government gets its money and how the government chooses to spend or not to spend its money impact on their lives every day (see Figure 12.5).

From the individual's perspective, the politics of budget making is about maintaining or increasing the benefits of government spending while shifting the tax costs to someone else. Given the presence of economic inequality, governments are subject to a crossfire of conflicting demands on taxing and spending policies, for no such policy can affect everyone in the same way.

Everyone has some idea about making a budget. Budgets are strategies for handling our needs, for spending and saving, and for coping with debt. But public budgets are only superficially like individual budgets. A budget is a document that contains proposed expenditures for certain objects and purposes. But there is more involved than just bookkeeping: Government budgeting is concerned with translating financial resources for human purposes.

Every politician in Canada has a stake in the federal and provincial budget-making process. Mayors want to keep federal and provincial funding flowing into their towns and cities so they can operate their programs. Provincial politicians are concerned that the downloading of government fiscal responsibilities will affect their ability to govern at the provincial level.

Individual members of Parliament act as a kind of policy entrepreneur for new ideas — which cost money — because they want larger budgets to support benefits to their constituents (Savoie 1990). Cabinets try to use budgets to manage the economy and leave their imprint on the policy agenda. Almost invariably, government departments pad their requests, hoping that the virtually inevitable cuts will be more bearable. Interest groups try to protect and defend their favourite programs in the national interest.

**Figure 12.5  The Federal Government Dollar**

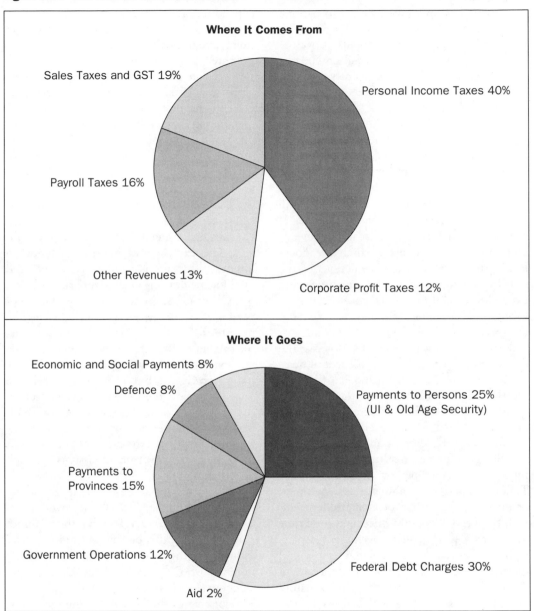

In Canada, the preparation of a national budget is a complex process involving hundreds of bureaucrats, professional economists, and politicians (Doern, Maslove, and Prince 1988). In Parliament, the Standing Committee on Finance serves as the main contact point for business with the House of Commons. The Standing Committee on Banking, Trade and Commerce receives input from the representatives of the business community.

Preparing a budget is one of the most important acts any government can perform (Brown-John, LeBlond, and Marson 1988, especially Chap. 8). Governments, as well as the country itself, can rise or fall on budgets. The economic fate of the country is determined by the ability of ministers of finance to prepare financial plans that are credible to Canadians and international bankers and investors. Yet, for all of the expectations we attach to a government budget, it is always an exercise of some uncertainty.

Determining how much our governments will collect in taxes and how much they will spend in a given year is largely a matter of estimation. In fact, in Canada, the government prepares Estimates, which are documents that contain their predictions of the net inflow and outflow of revenues and expenditures. All provincial governments use Estimates and Public Accounts documents in the preparation of their budgets. Budget-makers cannot always accurately forecast the flow of dollars into and out of the federal treasury in a particular year. Such dollar flows are greatly influenced by the performance of the economy in a world of other economies and unforeseen events — matters over which a Cabinet has little short-term control.

Six government institutions have direct input in the development of the budget: the Treasury Board, the Cabinet, the Department of Finance, the Office of Comptroller General, the Privy Council Office, and the Prime Minister's Office. These government departments and agencies are privy to the most vital information concerning the economic fate of the country. Because of the complex nature of Canadian society, federal budgets address many national objectives at the same time, some of which are not consistent with one another.

The minister of finance devises the federal government's revenue budget, which includes the setting of individual and corporate tax rates, sales taxes, and customs duties,

in order to meet the Canadian government's expenditure requirements.

Part of the process of devising the budget involves extensive consultations with various pressure groups and interested parties. Business pressure groups are well known to be very active in persuading Cabinet at budget time because the profitability of business is often determined by government policies, contracts, and budgets (Young 1983).

During this consultation phase, the minister of finance meets with business leaders and interest groups across the country, while the Department of Finance receives and considers hundreds of briefs on proposed tax changes and other suggested economic policies. The exchange of information between business associations and the government is vital for the drafting of an appropriate budget.

Other ministers can play important supporting roles for the minister of finance. The minister for Industry Canada, and the minister for Human Resources Development Canada are some of those whose advisory roles are most significant. But every minister has a vital interest in the impact of the budget on his or her department. Much of the competition for power and prestige at the ministerial level is determined by the amount of money the government assigns to each department.

The Cabinet represents the economic philosophy and policies of the government. Collectively and individually, the Cabinet contributes to the budget by advising and influencing the minister of finance and the minister who is appointed president of the Treasury Board. The prime minister also plays a major role in the budget-making process. It is the prime minister who can set the tone for the Cabinet and make critical public-policy decisions that bear on the government's relationship to the economy.

The Treasury Board, which is mandated by the Financial Administration Act, is a Cabinet committee that has a major input into the

The minister of finance devises the federal government's revenue budget, which includes the setting of personal and corporate tax rates, sales taxes, and customs duties. *Source:* Andy Donato, *The Toronto Sun*, April 27, 1993. Reproduced with permission of Andy Donato.

budget process because it oversees the expenditures of government, represents the government in its collective agreement with public servants, and generally manages the government with the goal of improving administrative efficiency. The president of the Treasury Board has the task of compiling the expenditure budget for the government of Canada. The expenditure budget considers all the monies spent by government in a fiscal year, including that spent on programs that directly support business.

Another major player is the Office of the Comptroller General (OCG), which is headed by a deputy minister who reports to the president of the Treasury Board. This body contributes to the public budgeting process by recommending how government performance in financial matters can improve. Its role is in the evaluation of how government spends. It has the mandate to advise and impose certain operating rules on departments. The OCG helps departments evaluate themselves and maintains the integrity of the internal audit function within each department. This is important for how the budget is put together, because the actual needs of each department are more easily recognizable when internal evaluations, based on standard procedures are conducted.

Two other executive bodies that serve the Cabinet and are involved in the budgetary process are the Privy Council Office (PCO) and the Prime Minister's Office (PMO). Because they have such an important advisory role in the Cabinet, their input into the budget process is essential. The PMO plans new policies with an eye to their political impact and electoral consequences. Unlike the PMO, the PCO is staffed by career civil servants rather than partisan appointees. The PCO prepares the agenda of Cabinet meetings and co-ordinates the business among government departments. The duties of the PCO earn it the right to become involved in the financial affairs of every government department, and thus to be aware of the budgetary needs and politics of the Cabinet.

The budget addresses macroeconomic policy questions of government, such as what the levels of government revenues will be, how much the government will expend, and whether the government accounts will show a surplus or a deficit. The macroeconomic dimension of a budget can stimulate the economy, slow it down, or keep it on course. The federal budget also influences microeconomic behaviour. Taxes not only raise money for government but can change individual behaviour by encouraging people to do or stop doing certain things. Higher taxes can depress consumer spending, and higher government spending can increase the rate of inflation.

The budget speech of the minister of finance attracts more public and official attention than any other speech made in Parliament. Since the early 1980s, budgets usually stress the theme of expenditure control, cutting the deficit, and reducing government debt. Through the budgetary process the minister of finance decides what to do about the deficit. This is certainly a political issue with economic consequences. Historically, governments in Canada have never believed that fiscal restraint wins votes. It has been a strategy only recently adopted by governments throughout the country, regardless of their political persuasion.

All involved in the preparation of budgets know that government borrowing to cover deficits means that the public sector competes with all other potential borrowers in the economy, such as small businesses and big corporations that want to build new plants, or individuals who want to buy houses or cars. Budgets that encourage investment from abroad to help cover the debt strengthens the dollar, but this can make Canadian goods more expensive to buy in the global economy. When the dollar strengthens, the result is a rise in imports and a drop in exports, which usually hurts domestic industries. This trade imbalance places strain on some sectors of the economy, especially exporters, whose products become less competitive in international markets and who might have to lay off workers because their sales are adversely affected.

Despite political commitments to balance budgets, no government in Canada has been unable to eliminate its deficits or to pay down its debts. How serious a problem are deficits? Some analysts argue that, given a healthy economy, the current large deficits would not be a serious problem, that sooner or later economic growth will allow the budget to be balanced. However, the persistently large deficits of the 1980s and 1990s, during a long, painful recession, clearly demonstrate that large deficits limit the government's ability to offer fiscal stimulation to a downward-trending economy and that, like all debt, large federal deficits represent borrowing against the future for the present. Another problem with large deficits is that they discourage new government investment aimed at making the economy more productive in the long term.

In this last decade of the twentieth century, economic life has become highly politicized. Many of the battles fought in Parliament and in most of our election campaigns revolve around how the economy should be managed and in whose interest it should be run. How far should government go in reshaping the workings of the marketplace? Should we protect the domestic auto industry? Save failing airlines? And how far should government go in altering the composition of the work force? Is it government's responsibility, for example, to make sure that everyone who wants to work is able to find a job? What part should government play in making sure that people who work can earn a decent wage?

## CONCLUSION

Canadian governments play a substantial role in the management of their economies at the provincial and federal levels. However, most of these governments have proved unsuccessful in easing many of the problems generated by market economies and by the federal system itself.

The federal government's macroeconomic responsibilities entail applying policies that affect growth, inflation, and employment across the Canadian economy. The goal of macroeconomic policy is a growing economy, with low unemployment and stable prices for goods and services. Canadian government policy-makers try to meet these goals using fiscal and monetary tools.

There is no consensus among Keynesian, monetarist, supply-side, and planning economists on how to meet the economic responsibilities of government. Each approach embodies a conception of the proper role for government. Keynesian and planning economists favour large and interventionist governments; monetarists and supply-side theorists favour a small and non-interventionist one.

Canada's parliamentary system ensures that political and governmental factors have powerful influences on the development of economic policy. The constitution structures the federal rules of the game in the economic policy-making process. Political parties and interest groups play a particularly central role, many taking different approaches to economic questions.

The growth of deficits and the national debt has been a by-product of the unwillingness of the federal government to take on responsibility for the economy and for developing both the will and the capacity to balance federal budgets.

Early economic wisdom in Canada believed that government spending should be cyclical: that levels of government spending should follow levels of economic activity. If the economy grows, more revenues will flow into the coffers of government, and it would thus have more to spend. Similarly, if the economy was in a slowdown, government revenues would fall, and it would not be able to spend money.

This economic wisdom preached that governments could reverse an economic slowdown by spending money itself and by encouraging consumers to spend their money, thus putting people back to work to produce what was demanded. Thus, when the economy and government revenues fall, the government should increase spending (even though that would create a deficit) or cut taxes so that consumers could increase their spending (even though that, too, would create a deficit). Government spending should counter the economic cycle by increasing when the economy slows down, and decreasing after economic activity picks up, so that the deficit is wiped out.

Federal and provincial debts in Canada have grown in increments — specific additions that result from annual budget deficits (each year's difference between revenues and expenditures). It would be a mistake to think that government deficits each year and the total national debt are natural phenomena, like the beginning of the Ice Age or the end of the dinosaurs. They are not. Rather, deficits and debts are human inventions, the product of incremental budgeting, political pressure, and supply-side economics.

These explanations for the growth of annual deficits and the national debt suggest some basic insights about the behaviour of governments in Canada as they go about trying to make economic policy. The first insight is that government deficits are a product of both economics and politics. There are competing economic ideas about the proper relationship of government to the economy and about which policies will achieve desired goals without compiling huge deficits.

## GLOSSARY

**balance of payments**  The relationship between an economy's inward and outward money flows.

**balance of trade**  The relationship between exports and imports.

**bank rate**  The rate at which chartered banks can borrow from the Bank of Canada.

**budgets**  Policy statements allocating burdens (taxes) and benefits (expenditures).

**devaluation**  The reduction in value of a national currency in relation to gold or some other currency.

**exchange rate**  The rate at which a currency can be exchanged for other currencies or gold.

**floating exchange rate**  A exchange rate that varies according to market conditions.

**globalization**  The process of focussing the resources of a national economy on the global opportunities in marketing and production.

**gross domestic product**  The money value of all goods and services produced in an economy in a particular year.

**gross national product**  The market value of all the country's goods and services produced in a given year.

**inflation**  The state of an economy in which prices are steadily rising, resulting in a steady fall in the value of money and the potential collapse of the monetary system.

**money supply**  The amount of purchasing power available in the economy.

**most-favoured-nation**  A clause in a trade agreement that commits a government to impose no greater barriers on imports from a second economy than it imposes on imports from any other country.

**non-tariff barriers**  Impediments to trade other than tariffs, such as import quotas.

**private sector**  In a mixed economy such as Canada's, it is that part of the economy that is not managed by the government or publicly-financed enterprises; economic decisions are made by enterprises under private ownership, using privately-owned capital, with a view to private gain.

**public sector**  All of the institutions of government and their spending to purchase the goods and services needed to keep government operating.

**recession**  A period during which the total output of the economy declines.

**revaluation**  The upward adjustment in the value of a national currency.

**tariff**  Taxes levied on imported products.

**welfare state**  Government taking an active role in providing for the economic security and social well-being of its citizens.

## RECOMMENDED READING

Chodos, Robert, Rae Murphy, and Eric Hamovitch. 1993. *Canada and the Global Economy*. Toronto: James Lorimer. This book takes a critical look at the FTA and NAFTA and considers the implications of globalization for Canada.

Doern, Bruce, and Brian Tomlin. 1991. *Faith and Fear: The Free Trade Story*. Toronto: Stoddart. This book provides a political and economic analysis of how and why events leading up to the free-trade agreement transpired as they did. It shows that the FTA was more than a bilateral treaty but the basis for the restructuring of Canada's economy and Canada's role in the North American continental economic community.

Gillespie, W. Irwin. 1991. *Tax, Borrow and Spend: Financing Federal Spending in Canada, 1867–1990*. Ottawa: Carleton University Press. This book provides a historical perspective on Canada's tax structure and government approaches to deficit spending, financing, and accountability, from Confederation to the present.

Grinspun, Ricardo, and Maxwell Cameron, eds. 1993. *The Political Economy of North American Free Trade*. Montreal and Kingston: McGill-Queen's University Press. The contributors to this collection examine the economic, social, political, and environmental implications of NAFTA.

Hart, Michael. 1992. *Trade ... Why Bother?* Ottawa, Ont.: Renouf Publishing. This book describes Canadian policy and practice, and Canada's place in the international trading system, with focus on the role of GATT, the FTA, and NAFTA.

Johnson, David. 1993. *Public Choice: An Introduction to the New Political Economy*. Toronto: McClelland & Stewart. This book brings together the subject matter of political science and the methodology of economics and provides a lucid introduction to the complex government decisions that affect the economy.

Quarter, Jack. 1992. *The Social Economy*. Toronto: James Lorimer. This book examines the role played by co-ops, credit unions, non-profit organizations, and alternative businesses as important components of the social economy in Canada.

Rosell, Steven. 1992. *Governing in an Information Society*. Ottawa, Ont.: Renouf Publishing. This thought-provoking short book gives the reader insight into the problems of governing an economy that is undergoing revolutionary transitions in how it communicates and networks.

Starling, Grover. 1993. *Managing the Public Sector*. New York: Nelson. This book offers an excellent theoretical introduction to the problems of public-sector management in the 1990s, from the fundamentals of public administration to the information revolution in contemporary bureaucracies.

Williams, Glen. 1993. *Not for Export: Toward a Political Economy of Canada's Arrested Industrialization*. Toronto: McClelland & Stewart. This book probes the reshaping of Canada's economic priorities and argues in favour of a more nationalistic approach to Canadian manufacturing and a stronger emphasis on exports.

# THE CONSTITUTION ACT, 1867
## 30 & 31 VICTORIA, C.3.
### (Consolidated with amendments)

An Act for the Union of Canada, Nova Scotia, and New Brunswick, and the Government thereof; and for Purposes connected therewith.

*(29th March, 1867.)*

Whereas the Provinces of Canada, Nova Scotia and New Brunswick have expressed their Desire to be federally united into One Dominion under the Crown of the United Kingdom of Great Britain and Ireland, with a Constitution similar in Principle to that of the United Kingdom:

And whereas such a Union would conduce to the Welfare of the Provinces and promote the Interests of the British Empire:

And whereas on the Establishment of the Union by Authority of Parliament it is expedient, not only that the Constitution of the Legislative Authority in the Dominion be provided for, but also that the Nature of the Executive Government therein be declared:

And whereas it is expedient that Provision be made for the eventual Admission into the Union of other Parts of British North America:

## I. PRELIMINARY

1.  This Act may be cited as the *Constitution Act, 1867.*
2.  Repealed.

## II. UNION

3.  It shall be lawful for the Queen, by and with the Advice of Her Majesty's Most Honourable Privy Council, to declare by Proclamation that, on and after a Day therein appointed, not being more than Six Months after the passing of this Act, the Provinces of Canada, Nova Scotia, and New Brunswick shall form and be One Dominion under the Name of Canada; and on and after that Day those Three Provinces shall form and be One Dominion under that Name accordingly.

4.  Unless it is otherwise expressed or implied, the Name Canada shall be taken to mean Canada as constituted under this Act.

5.  Canada shall be divided into Four Provinces, named Ontario, Quebec, Nova Scotia, and New Brunswick.

6.  The Parts of the Province of Canada (as it exists at the passing of this Act) which formerly constituted respectively the Provinces of Upper Canada and Lower Canada shall be

*Source: A Consolidation of the Constitution Acts 1867–1982,* Justice Canada. Reproduced with permission of the Minister of Supply and Services Canada, 1994.

deemed to be severed, and shall form Two separate Provinces. The Part which formerly constituted the Province of Upper Canada shall constitute the Province of Ontario; and the Part which formerly constituted the Province of Lower Canada shall constitute the Province of Quebec.

7. The Provinces of Nova Scotia and New Brunswick shall have the same Limits as at the passing of this Act.

8. In the general Census of the Population of Canada which is hereby required to be taken in the Year One thousand eight hundred and seventy-one, and in every Tenth Year thereafter, the respective Populations of the Four Provinces shall be distinguished.

## III. EXECUTIVE POWER

9. The Executive Government and Authority of and over Canada is hereby declared to continue and be vested in the Queen.

10. The Provisions of this Act referring to the Governor General extend and apply to the Governor General for the Time being of Canada, or other the Chief Executive Officer or Administrator for the Time being carrying on the Government of Canada on behalf and in the Name of the Queen, by whatever Title he is designated.

11. There shall be a Council to aid and advise in the Government of Canada, to be styled the Queen's Privy Council for Canada; and the Persons who are to be Members of that Council shall be from Time to Time chosen and summoned by the Governor General and sworn in as Privy Councillors, and Members thereof may be from Time to Time removed by the Governor General.

12. All Powers, Authorities, and Functions, which under any Act of the Parliament of Great Britain, or of the Parliament of the United Kingdom of Great Britain and Ireland, or of the Legislature of Upper Canada, Lower Canada, Canada, Nova Scotia, or New Brunswick, are at the Union vested in or exerciseable by the respective Governors or Lieutenant Governors of those Provinces, with the Advice, or with the Advice and Consent, of the respective Executive Councils thereof, or in conjunction with those Councils, or with any Number of Members thereof, or by those Governors or Lieutenant Governors individually, shall, as far as the same continue in existence and capable of being exercised after the Union in relation to the Government of Canada, be vested in and exerciseable by the Governor General, with the Advice or with the Advice and Consent of or in conjunction with the Queen's Privy Council for Canada, or any Member thereof, or by the Governor General individually, as the Case requires, subject nevertheless (except with respect to such as exist under Acts of the Parliament of Great Britain or of the Parliament of the United Kingdom of Great Britain and Ireland) to be abolished or altered by the Parliament of Canada.

13. The Provisions of this Act referring to the Governor General in Council shall be construed as referring to the Governor General acting by and with the Advice of the Queen's Privy Council for Canada.

14. It shall be lawful for the Queen, if Her Majesty thinks fit, to authorize the Governor General from Time to Time to appoint any Person or any Persons jointly or severally to be his Deputy or Deputies within any Part or Parts of Canada, and in that Capacity to exercise during the Pleasure of the Governor General such of the Powers, Authorities, and Functions of the Governor General as the Governor General deems it necessary or expedient to assign to him or them, subject to any Limitations or Directions expressed or given by the Queen; but the

Appointment of such a Deputy or Deputies shall not affect the Exercise by the Governor General himself of any Power, Authority or Function.

**15.** The Command-in-Chief of the Land and Naval Militia, and of all Naval and Military Forces, of and in Canada, is hereby declared to continue and be vested in the Queen.

**16.** Until the Queen otherwise directs, the Seat of Government of Canada shall be Ottawa.

## IV. LEGISLATIVE POWER

**17.** There shall be One Parliament for Canada, consisting of the Queen, an Upper House styled the Senate, and the House of Commons.

**18.** The privileges, immunities, and powers to be held, enjoyed, and exercised by the Senate and by the House of Commons, and by the Members thereof respectively, shall be such as are from time to time defined by Act of the Parliament of Canada, but so that any Act of the Parliament of Canada defining such privileges, immunities, and powers shall not confer any privileges, immunities, or powers exceeding those at the passing of such Act held, enjoyed, and exercised by the Commons House of Parliament of the United Kingdom of Great Britain and Ireland, and by the Members thereof.

**19.** The Parliament of Canada shall be called together not later than Six Months after the Union.

**20.** Repealed.

### The Senate

**21.** The Senate shall, subject to the Provisions of this Act, consist of One Hundred and four Members, who shall be styled Senators.

**22.** In relation to the Constitution of the Senate Canada shall be deemed to consist of *Four* Divisions:

1. Ontario;
2. Quebec;
3. The Maritime Provinces, Nova Scotia and New Brunswick, and Prince Edward Island;
4. The Western Provinces of Manitoba, British Columbia, Saskatchewan, and Alberta;

which Four Divisions shall (subject to the Provisions of this Act) be equally represented in the Senate as follows: Ontario by twenty-four senators; Quebec by twenty-four senators; the Maritime Provinces and Prince Edward Island by twenty-four senators, ten thereof representing Nova Scotia, ten thereof representing New Brunswick, and four thereof representing Prince Edward Island; the Western Provinces by twenty-four senators, six thereof representing Manitoba, six thereof representing British Columbia, six thereof representing Saskatchewan, and six thereof representing Alberta; Newfoundland shall be entitled to be represented in the Senate by six members; the Yukon Territory and the Northwest Territories shall be entitled to be represented in the Senate by one member each.

In the Case of Quebec each of the Twenty-four Senators representing that Province shall be appointed for One of the Twenty-four Electoral Divisions of Lower Canada specified in Schedule A, to Chapter One of the Consolidated statutes of Canada.

**23.** The Qualification of a Senator shall be as follows:

(1) He shall be of the full age of Thirty Years:

(2) He shall be either a natural-born Subject of the Queen, or a Subject of the Queen naturalized by an Act of the Parliament of Great Britain, or of the Parliament of the United Kingdom of Great Britain and Ireland, or of the Legislature of One of the Provinces of Upper Canada, Lower Canada, Canada, Nova Scotia, or New Brunswick, before the Union, or of the Parliament of Canada, after the Union:

(3) He shall be legally or equitably seised as of Freehold for his own Use and Benefit of Lands or Tenements held in Free and Common Socage, or seised or possessed for his own Use and Benefit of Lands or Tenements held in Franc-alleu or in Roture, within the Province for which he is appointed, of the Value of Four thousand Dollars, over and above all Rents, Dues, Debts, Charges, Mortgages, and Incumbrances due or payable out of or charged on or affecting the same:

(4) His Real and Personal Property shall be together worth Four thousand Dollars over and above his Debts and Liabilities:

(5) He shall be resident in the Province for which he is appointed:

(6) In the Case of Quebec he shall have his Real Property Qualification in the Electoral Division for which he is appointed, or shall be resident in that Division.

**24.** The Governor General shall from Time to Time, in the Queen's Name, by Instrument under the Great Seal of Canada, summon qualified Persons to the Senate; and, subject to the Provisions of this Act, every Person so summoned shall become and be a Member of the Senate and a Senator.

**25.** Repealed.

**26.** If at any Time on the Recommendation of the Governor General the Queen thinks fit to direct that Four or Eight Members be added to the Senate, the Governor General may by Summons to Four or Eight qualified Persons (as the Case may be), representing equally the Four Divisions of Canada, add to the Senate accordingly.

**27.** In case of such Addition being at any Time made, the Governor General shall not summon any Person to the Senate, except upon a further like Direction by the Queen on the like Recommendation, to represent one of the Four Divisions until such Division is represented by Twenty-four Senators and no more.

**28.** The Number of Senators shall not at any Time exceed One Hundred and twelve.

**29.** (1) Subject to subsection (2), a Senator shall, subject to the provisions of this Act, hold his place in the Senate for life.

(2) A Senator who is summoned to the Senate after the coming into force of this subsection shall, subject to this Act, hold his place in the Senate until he attains the age of seventy-five years.

**30.** A Senator may by Writing under his Hand addressed to the Governor General resign his Place in the Senate, and thereupon the same shall be vacant.

**31.** The Place of a Senator shall become vacant in any of the following Cases:

(1) If for Two consecutive Sessions of the Parliament he fails to give his Attendance in the Senate:

(2) If he takes an Oath or makes a Declaration or Acknowledgement of Allegiance, Obedience, or Adherence to a Foreign Power, or does an Act whereby he becomes a Subject or Citizen, or entitled to the Rights or Privileges of a Subject or Citizen, of a Foreign Power.

(3) If he is adjudged Bankrupt or Insolvent, or applies for the Benefit of any Law relating to Insolvent Debtors, or becomes a public Defaulter:

(4) If he is attainted of Treason or convicted of Felony or of any infamous Crime:

(5) If he ceases to be qualified in respect of Property or of Residence; provided, that a Senator shall not be deemed to have ceased to be qualified in respect of Residence by reason only of his residing at the Seat of the Government of Canada while holding an Office under that Government requiring his Presence there.

**32.** When a Vacancy happens in the Senate by Resignation, Death or otherwise, the Governor General shall by Summons to a fit and qualified Person fill the Vacancy.

**33.** If any Question arises respecting the Qualification of a Senator or a Vacancy in the Senate the same shall be heard and determined by the Senate.

**34.** The Governor General may from Time to Time, by Instrument under the Great Seal of Canada, appoint a Senator to be Speaker of the Senate, and may remove him and appoint another in his Stead.

**35.** Until the Parliament of Canada otherwise provides, the Presence of at least Fifteen Senators, including the Speaker, shall be necessary to constitute a Meeting of the Senate for the Exercise of its Powers.

**36.** Questions arising in the Senate shall be decided by a Majority of Voices, and the Speaker shall in all Cases have a Vote, and when the Voices are equal the Decision shall be deemed to be in the Negative.

## The House of Commons

**37.** The House of Commons shall, subject to the Provisions of this Act, consist of two hundred and eighty-two members of whom ninety-five shall be elected for Ontario, seventy-five for Quebec, eleven for Nova Scotia, ten for New Brunswick, fourteen for Manitoba, twenty-eight for British Columbia, four for Prince Edward Island, twenty-one for Alberta, fourteen for Saskatchewan, seven for Newfoundland, one for the Yukon Territory and two for the Northwest Territories.

**38.** The Governor General shall from Time to Time, in the Queen's Name, by Instrument under the Great Seal of Canada, summon and call together the House of Commons.

**39.** A Senator shall not be capable of being elected or of sitting or voting as a Member of the House of Commons.

**40.** Until the Parliament of Canada otherwise provides, Ontario, Quebec, Nova Scotia and New Brunswick shall, for the Purposes of the Election of Members to serve in the House of Commons, be divided into Electoral districts as follows:

## 1.—Ontario

Ontario shall be divided into the Counties, Ridings of Counties, Cities, Parts of Cities, and Towns enumerated in the First Schedule to this Act, each whereof shall be an Electoral District, each such District as numbered in that Schedule being entitled to return One Member.

## 2.—Quebec

Quebec shall be divided into Sixty-five Electoral Districts, composed of the Sixty-five Electoral Divisions into which Lower Canada is at the passing of this Act divided under Chapter Two of the Consolidated Statutes of Canada, Chapter Seventy-five of the Consolidated Statutes for Lower Canada, and the Act of the Province of Canada of the Twenty-third Year of the

Queen, Chapter One, or any other Act amending the same in force at the Union, so that each such Electoral Division shall be for the Purposes of this Act an Electoral District entitled to return One Member.

## 3.—Nova Scotia

Each of the Eighteen Counties of Nova Scotia shall be an Electoral District. The County of Halifax shall be entitled to return Two Members, and each of the other Counties One Member.

## 4.—New Brunswick

Each of the Fourteen Counties into which New Brunswick is divided, including the City and County of St. John, shall be an Electoral District. The City of St. John shall also be a separate Electoral District. Each of those Fifteen Electoral Districts shall be entitled to return One Member.

**41.** Until the Parliament of Canada otherwise provides, all Laws in force in the several Provinces at the Union relative to the following Matters or any of them, namely,—the Qualifications and Disqualifications of Persons to be elected or to sit or vote as Members of the House of Assembly or Legislative Assembly in the several Provinces, the Voters at Elections of such Members, the Oaths to be taken by Voters, the Returning Officers, their Powers and Duties, the Proceedings at Elections, the Periods during which Elections may be continued, the Trial of controverted Elections, and Proceedings incident thereto, the vacating of Seats of Members, and the Execution of new Writs in case of Seats vacated otherwise than by Dissolution,—shall respectively apply to Elections of Members to serve in the House of Commons for the same several Provinces.

Provided that, until the Parliament of Canada otherwise provides, at any Election for a Member of the House of Commons for the District of Algoma, in addition to Persons qualified by the Law of the Province of Canada to vote, every Male British Subject, aged Twenty-one Years or upwards, being a Householder, shall have a Vote.

**42.** Repealed.

**43.** Repealed.

**44.** The House of Commons on its first assembling after a General Election shall proceed with all practicable Speed to elect One of its Members to be Speaker.

**45.** In case of a Vacancy happening in the Office of Speaker by Death, Resignation, or otherwise, the House of Commons shall with all practicable Speed proceed to elect another of its Members to be Speaker.

**46.** The Speaker shall preside at all Meetings of the House of Commons.

**47.** Until the Parliament of Canada otherwise provides, in case of the Absence for any Reason of the Speaker from the Chair of the House of Commons for a Period of Forty-eight consecutive Hours, the House may elect another of its Members to act as Speaker, and the Member so elected shall during the Continuance of such Absence of the Speaker have and execute all the Powers, Privileges, and Duties of Speaker.

**48.** The Presence of at least Twenty Members of the House of Commons shall be necessary to constitute a Meeting of the House for the Exercise of its Powers, and for that Purpose the Speaker shall be reckoned as a Member.

**49.** Questions arising in the House of Commons shall be decided by a Majority of Voices other than that of the Speaker, and when the Voices are equal, but not otherwise, the Speaker shall have a Vote.

**50.** Every House of Commons shall continue for Five Years from the Day of the Return of the Writs for choosing the House (subject to be sooner dissolved by the Governor General), and no longer.

**51.** (1) The number of members of the House of Commons and the representation of the provinces therein shall on the coming into force of this subsection and thereafter on the completion of each decennial census, be readjusted by such authority, in such manner, and from such time as the Parliament of Canada from time to time provides, subject and according to the following rules:

1.  There shall be assigned to each of the provinces a number of members equal to the number obtained by dividing the total population of the provinces by two hundred and seventy-nine and by dividing the population of each province by the quotient so obtained, counting any remainder in excess of 0.50 as one after the said process of division.

2.  If the total number of members that would be assigned to a province by the application of rule 1 is less than the total number assigned to that province on the date of coming into force of this subsection, there shall be added to the number of members so assigned such number of members as will result in the province having the same number of members as were assigned on that date.

(2)  The Yukon Territory as bounded and described in the schedule to chapter Y-2 of the Revised Statutes of Canada, 1970, shall be entitled to one member, and the Northwest Territories as bounded and described in section 2 of chapter N-22 of the Revised Statutes of Canada, 1970, shall be entitled to two members.

**51A.** Notwithstanding anything in this Act a province shall always be entitled to a number of members in the House of Commons not less than the number of senators representing such province.

**52.** The Number of Members of the House of Commons may be from Time to Time increased by the Parliament of Canada, provided the proportionate Representation of the Provinces prescribed by this Act is not thereby disturbed.

## Money Votes; Royal Assent

**53.** Bills for appropriating any Part of the Public Revenue, or for imposing any Tax or Import, shall originate in the House of Commons.

**54.** It shall not be lawful for the House of Commons to adopt or pass any Vote, Resolution, Address, or Bill for the Appropriation of any Part of the Public Revenue, or of any Tax or Impost, to any Purpose that has not been first recommended to that House by Message of the Governor General in the Session in which such Vote, Resolution, Address, or Bill is proposed.

**55.** Where a Bill passed by the Houses of the Parliament is presented to the Governor General for the Queen's Assent, he shall declare, according to his Discretion, but subject to the Provisions of this Act and to Her Majesty's Instructions, either that he assents thereto in the Queen's Name, or that he withholds the Queen's Assent, or that he reserves the Bill for the Signification of the Queen's Pleasure.

**56.** Where the Governor General assents to a Bill in the Queen's Name, he shall by the first convenient Opportunity send an authentic Copy of the Act to one of Her Majesty's Principal Secretaries of State, and if the Queen in Council within Two Years after Receipt thereof by the Secretary of State thinks fit to disallow the Act, such Disallowance (with a Certificate of the Secretary of State of the Day on which the Act was received by him) being signified by the

Governor General, by Speech or Message to each of the Houses of the Parliament or by Proclamation, shall annul the Act from and after the Day of such Signification.

**57.** A Bill reserved for the Signification of the Queen's Pleasure shall not have any Force unless and until, within Two Years from the Day on which it was presented to the Governor General for the Queen's Assent, the Governor General signifies, by Speech or Message to each of the Houses of the Parliament or by Proclamation, that it has received the Assent of the Queen in Council.

An Entry of every such Speech, Message, or Proclamation shall be made in the Journal of each House, and a Duplicate thereof duly attested shall be delivered to the proper Officer to be kept among the Records of Canada.

## V. PROVINCIAL CONSTITUTIONS

### Executive Power

**58.** For each Province there shall be an Officer, styled the Lieutenant Governor, appointed by the Governor General in Council by Instrument under the Great Seal of Canada.

**59.** A Lieutenant Governor shall hold Office during the Pleasure of the Governor General; but any Lieutenant Governor appointed after the Commencement of the First Session of the Parliament of Canada shall not be removeable within Five Years from his Appointment, except for Cause assigned, which shall be communicated to him in Writing within One Month after the Order for his Removal is made, and shall be communicated by Message to the Senate and to the House of Commons within One Week thereafter if the Parliament is then sitting, and if not then within One Week after the Commencement of the next Session of the Parliament.

**60.** The Salaries of the Lieutenant Governors shall be fixed and provided by the Parliament of Canada.

**61.** Every Lieutenant Governor shall, before assuming the Duties of his Office, make and subscribe before the Governor General or some Person authorized by him Oaths of Allegiance and Office similar to those taken by the Governor General.

**62.** The Provisions of this Act referring to the Lieutenant Governor extend and apply to the Lieutenant Governor for the Time being of each Province, or other the Chief Executive Officer or Administrator for the Time being carrying on the Government of the Province, by whatever Title he is designated.

**63.** The Executive Council of Ontario and of Quebec shall be composed of such Persons as the Lieutenant Governor from Time to Time thinks fit, and in the first instance of the following Officers, namely,—the Attorney General, the Secretary and Registrar of the Province, the Treasurer of the Province, the Commissioner of Crown Lands, and the Commissioner of Agriculture and Public Works, with in Quebec, the Speaker of the Legislative Council and the Solicitor General.

**64.** The Constitution of the Executive Authority in each of the Provinces of Nova Scotia and New Brunswick shall, subject to the Provisions of this Act, continue as it exists at the Union until altered under the Authority of this Act.

**65.** All Powers, Authorities, and Functions which under any Act of the Parliament of Great Britain, or of the Parliament of the United Kingdom of Great Britain and Ireland, or of the Legislature of Upper Canada, Lower Canada, or Canada, were or are before or at the Union vested in or exerciseable by the respective Governors or Lieutenant Governors of those Provinces, with the Advice or with the Advice and Consent of the respective Executive Councils thereof, or in conjunction with those Councils, or with any Number of Members thereof, or by those Governors or Lieutenant Governors individually, shall, as far as the same are capable of being exercised after the Union in relation to the Government of Ontario and Quebec respectively, be vested in and shall or may be exercised by the Lieutenant Governor of Ontario and Quebec respectively, with the Advice or with the Advice and Consent of or in conjunction with the respective Executive Councils, or any Members thereof, or by the Lieutenant Governor individually, as the Case requires, subject nevertheless (except with respect to such as exist under Acts of the Parliament of Great Britain, or of the Parliament of the United Kingdom of Great Britain and Ireland,) to be abolished or altered by the respective Legislatures of Ontario and Quebec.

**66.** The Provisions of this Act referring to the Lieutenant Governor in Council shall be construed as referring to the Lieutenant Governor of the Province acting by and with the Advice of the Executive Council thereof.

**67.** The Governor General in Council may from Time to Time appoint an Administrator to execute the office and Functions of Lieutenant Governor during his Absence, Illness, or other Inability.

**68.** Unless and until the Executive Government of any Province otherwise directs with respect to that Province, the Seats of Government of the Provinces shall be as follows, namely,— of Ontario, the City of Toronto; of Quebec, the City of Quebec; of Nova Scotia, the City of Halifax; and of New Brunswick, the City of Fredericton.

## Legislative Power

### 1.—Ontario

**69.** There shall be a Legislature for Ontario consisting of the Lieutenant Governor and of One House, styled the Legislative Assembly of Ontario.

**70.** The Legislative Assembly of Ontario shall be composed of Eighty-two Members, to be elected to represent the Eighty-two Electoral Districts set forth in the First Schedule to this Act.

### 2.—Quebec

**71.** There shall be a Legislature for Quebec consisting of the Lieutenant Governor and of Two Houses, styled the Legislative Council of Quebec and the Legislative Assembly of Quebec.

**72.** The Legislative Council of Quebec shall be composed of Twenty-four Members, to be appointed by the Lieutenant Governor, in the Queen's Name, by Instrument under the Great Seal of Quebec, One being appointed to represent each of the Twenty-four Electoral Divisions of Lower Canada in this Act referred to, and each holding Office for the Term of his Life, unless the Legislature of Quebec otherwise provides under the Provisions of this Act.

**73.** The Qualifications of the Legislative Councillors of Quebec shall be the same as those of the Senators for Quebec.

**74.** The Place of a Legislative Councillor of Quebec shall become vacant in the Cases, *mutatis mutandis*, in which the Place of Senator becomes vacant.

**75.** When a Vacancy happens in the Legislative Council of Quebec by Resignation, Death, or otherwise, the Lieutenant Governor, in the Queen's Name, by Instrument under the Great Seal of Quebec, shall appoint a fit and qualified Person to fill the Vacancy.

**76.** If any Question arises respecting the Qualification of a Legislative Councillor of Quebec,

448 ■ Appendix A THE CONSTITUTION ACT, 1867

or a Vacancy in the Legislative Council of Quebec, the same shall be heard and determined by the Legislative Council.

**77.** The Lieutenant Governor may from Time to Time, by Instrument under the Great Seal of Quebec, appoint a Member of the Legislative Council of Quebec to be Speaker thereof, and may remove him and appoint another in his Stead.

**78.** Until the Legislature of Quebec otherwise provides, the Presence of at least Ten Members of the Legislative Council, including the Speaker, shall be necessary to constitute a Meeting for the Exercise of its Powers.

**79.** Questions arising in the Legislative Council of Quebec shall be decided by a Majority of Voices, and the Speaker shall in all Cases have a Vote, and when the Voices are equal the Decision shall be deemed to be in the Negative.

**80.** The Legislative Assembly of Quebec shall be composed of Sixty-five Members, to be elected to represent the Sixty-five Electoral Divisions or Districts of Lower Canada in this Act referred to, subject to Alteration thereof by the Legislature of Quebec: Provided that it shall not be lawful to present to the Lieutenant Governor of Quebec for Assent any Bill for altering the Limits of any of the Electoral Divisions or Districts mentioned in the Second Schedule to this Act, unless the Second and Third Readings of such Bill have been passed in the Legislative Assembly with the Concurrence of the Majority of the Members representing all those Electoral Divisions or Districts, and the Assent shall not be given to such Bill unless an Address has been presented by the Legislative Assembly to the Lieutenant Governor stating that it has been so passed.

## 3.—Ontario and Quebec

**81.** Repealed.

**82.** The Lieutenant Governor of Ontario and of Quebec shall from Time to Time, in the Queen's Name, by Instrument under the Great Seal of the Province, summon and call together the Legislative Assembly of the Province.

**83.** Until the Legislature of Ontario or of Quebec otherwise provides, a Person accepting or holding in Ontario or in Quebec any Office, Commission, or Employment, permanent or temporary, at the Nomination of the Lieutenant Governor, to which an annual Salary, or any Fee, Allowance, Emolument, or Profit of any Kind or Amount whatever from the Province is attached, shall not be eligible as a Member of the Legislative Assembly of the respective Province, nor shall he sit or vote as such; but nothing in this Section shall make ineligible any Person being a member of the Executive Council of the respective Province, or holding any of the following Offices, that is to say, the Offices of Attorney General, Secretary and Registrar of the Province, Treasurer of the Province, Commissioner of Crown Lands, and Commissioner of Agriculture and Public Works, and in Quebec Solicitor General, or shall disqualify him to sit or vote in the House for which he is elected, provided he is elected while holding such Office.

**84.** Until the legislatures of Ontario and Quebec respectively otherwise provide, all Laws which at the Union are in force in those Provinces respectively, relative to the following Matters, or any of them, namely,— the Qualifications and Disqualifications of Persons to be elected or to sit or vote as Members of the Assembly of Canada, the Qualifications or Disqualifications of Voters, the Oaths to be taken by Voters, the Returning Officers, their Powers and Duties, the Proceedings at Elections, the Periods during which such Elections may be continued, and the Trial of controverted Elections and the Proceedings incident thereto, the vacating of the Seats of Members and the issuing and execution of new Writs, in case of Seats vacated otherwise than by Dissolution,—shall respectively apply to Elections of Members to serve in the respective Legislative Assemblies of Ontario and Quebec.

Provided that, until the Legislature of Ontario otherwise provides, at any Election for a Member of the Legislative Assembly of Ontario for the District of Algoma, in addition to Persons qualified by the Law of the Province of Canada to vote, every male British Subject, aged Twenty-one Years or upwards, being a Householder, shall have a vote.

**85.** Every Legislative Assembly of Ontario and every Legislative Assembly of Quebec shall continue for Four Years from the Day of the Return of the Writs for choosing the same (subject nevertheless to either the Legislative Assembly of Ontario or the Legislative Assembly of Quebec being sooner dissolved by the Lieutenant Governor of the Province), and no longer.

**86.** There shall be a Session of the Legislature of Ontario and of that of Quebec once at least in every Year, so that Twelve Months shall not intervene between the last Sitting of the Legislature in each Province in one Session and its first Sitting in the next Session.

**87.** The following Provisions of this Act respecting the House of Commons of Canada shall extend and apply to the Legislative Assemblies of Ontario and Quebec, that is to say,—the Provisions relating to the Election of a Speaker originally and on Vacancies, the Duties of the Speaker, the Absence of the Speaker, the Quorum, and the Mode of voting, as if those Provisions were here re-enacted and made applicable in Terms to each such Legislative Assembly.

## 4.—Nova Scotia and New Brunswick

**88.** The Constitution of the Legislature of each of the Provinces of Nova Scotia and New Brunswick shall, subject to the Provisions of this Act, continue as it exists at the Union until altered under the Authority of this Act.

**89.** Repealed.

## 6.—The Four Provinces

**90.** The following Provisions of this Act respecting the Parliament of Canada, namely,—the Provisions relating to Appropriation and Tax Bills, the Recommendation of Money Votes, the Assent to Bills, the Disallowance of Acts, and the Signification of Pleasure on Bills reserved,— shall extend and apply to the Legislatures of the several Provinces as if those Provisions were here re-enacted and made applicable in Terms to the respective Provinces and the Legislatures thereof, with the Substitution of the Lieutenant Governor of the Province for the Governor General, of the Governor General for the Queen and for a Secretary of State, of One Year for Two Years, and of the Province for Canada.

## VI. DISTRIBUTION OF LEGISLATIVE POWERS

### Powers of the Parliament

**91.** It shall be lawful for the Queen, by and with the Advice and Consent of the Senate and House of Commons, to make Laws for the Peace, Order, and good Government of Canada, in relation to all Matters not coming within the Classes of Subjects by this Act assigned exclusively to the Legislatures of the Provinces; and for greater Certainty, but not so as to restrict the Generality of the foregoing Terms of this Section, it is hereby declared that (notwithstanding anything in this Act) the exclusive Legislative Authority of the Parliament of Canada extends to all Matters coming within the Classes of Subjects next hereinafter enumerated; that is to say,—

    1. Repealed.

  1A. The Public Debt and Property.

    2. The Regulation of Trade and Commerce.

  2A. Unemployment insurance.

    3. The raising of Money by any Mode or System of Taxation.

    4. The borrowing of Money on the Public Credit.

    5. Postal Service.

    6. The Census and Statistics.

    7. Militia, Military and Naval Service, and Defence.

    8. The fixing of and providing for the Salaries and Allowances of Civil and other Officers of the Government of Canada.

    9. Beacons, Buoys, Lighthouses, and Sable Island.

  10. Navigation and Shipping.

  11. Quarantine and the Establishment and Maintenance of Marine Hospitals.

  12. Sea Coast and Inland Fisheries.

  13. Ferries between a Province and any British or Foreign Country or between Two Provinces.

  14. Currency and Coinage.

  15. Banking, Incorporation of Banks, and the Issue of Paper Money.

  16. Savings Banks.

  17. Weights and Measures.

  18. Bills of Exchange and Promissory Notes.

  19. Interest.

  20. Legal Tender.

  21. Bankruptcy and Insolvency.

  22. Patents of Invention and Discovery.

  23. Copyrights.

  24. Indians, and Lands reserved for the Indians.

  25. Naturalization and Aliens.

  26. Marriage and Divorce.

  27. The Criminal Law, except the Constitution of Courts of Criminal Jurisdiction, but including the Procedure in Criminal Matters.

  28. The Establishment, Maintenance, and Management of Penitentiaries.

  29. Such Classes of Subjects as are expressly excepted in the Enumeration of the Classes of Subjects by this Act assigned exclusively to the Legislatures of the Provinces.

And any Matter coming within any of the Classes of Subjects enumerated in this Section shall not be deemed to come within the Class of Matters of a local or private Nature comprised in the Enumeration of the Classes of Subjects by this Act assigned exclusively to the Legislatures of the Provinces.

## Exclusive Powers of Provincial Legislatures

**92.** In each Province the Legislature may exclusively make Laws in relation to Matters coming within the Classes of Subject next hereinafter enumerated; that is to say,—

    1. Repealed.

2. Direct Taxation within the Province in order to the raising of a Revenue for Provincial Purposes.
3. The borrowing of Money on the sole Credit of the Province.
4. The Establishment and Tenure of Provincial Offices and the Appointment and Payment of Provincial Officers.
5. The Management and Sale of the Public Lands belonging to the Province and of the Timber and Wood thereon.
6. The Establishment, Maintenance, and Management of Public and Reformatory Prisons in and for the Province.
7. The Establishment, Maintenance, and Management of Hospitals, Asylums, Charities, and Eleemosynary Institutions in and for the Province, other than Marine Hospitals.
8. Municipal Institutions in the Province.
9. Shop, Saloon, Tavern, Auctioneer, and other Licences in order to the raising of a Revenue for Provincial, Local, or Municipal Purposes.
10. Local Works and Undertakings other than such as are of the following Classes:—
    (a) Lines of Steam or other Ships, Railways, Canals, Telegraphs, and other Works and Undertakings connecting the Province with any other or others of the Provinces, or extending beyond the Limits of the Province;
    (b) Lines of Steam Ships between the Province and any British or Foreign Country;
    (c) Such Works as, although wholly situate within the Province, are before or after their Execution declared by the Parliament of Canada to be for the general Advantage of Canada or for the Advantage of Two or more of the Provinces.
11. The Incorporation of Companies with Provincial Objects.
12. The Solemnization of Marriage in the Province.
13. Property and Civil Rights in the Province.
14. The Administration of Justice in the Province, including the Constitution, Maintenance, and Organization of Provincial Courts, both of Civil and of Criminal Jurisdiction, and including Procedure in Civil Matters in those Courts.
15. The Imposition of Punishment by Fine, Penalty, or Imprisonment for enforcing any Law of the Province made in relation to any Matter coming within any of the Classes of Subjects enumerated in this Section.
16. Generally all Matters of a merely local or private Nature in the Province.

## Non-Renewable Natural Resources, Forestry Resources and Electrical Energy

92A. (1) In each province, the legislature may exclusively make laws in relation to
    (a) exploration for non-renewable natural resources in the province;
    (b) development, conservation and management of non-renewable natural resources and forestry resources in the province, including laws in relation to the rate of primary production therefrom; and
    (c) development, conservation and management of sites and facilities in the province for the generation and production of electrical energy.
    (2) In each province, the legislature may make laws in relation to the export from the province to another part of Canada of the primary production from non-renewable natural resources and forestry resources in the province and the production from

facilities in the province for the generation of electrical energy, but such laws may not authorize or provide for discrimination in prices or in supplies exported to another part of Canada.

(3) Nothing in subsection (2) derogates from the authority of Parliament to enact laws in relation to the matters referred to in that subsection and, where such a law of Parliament and a law of a province conflict, the law of Parliament prevails to the extent of the conflict.

(4) In each province, the legislature may make laws in relation to the raising of money by any mode or system of taxation in respect of

(a) non-renewable natural resources and forestry resources in the province and the primary production therefrom, and

(b) sites and facilities in the province for the generation of electrical energy and the production therefrom, whether or not such production is exported in whole or in part from the province, but such laws may not authorize or provide for taxation that differentiates between production exported to another part of Canada and production not exported from the province.

(5) The expression "primary production" has the meaning assigned by the Sixth Schedule.

(6) Nothing in subsections (1) to (5) derogates from any powers or rights that a legislature or government of a province had immediately before the coming into force of this section.

## Education

93. In and for each Province the Legislature may exclusively make Laws in relation to Education, subject and according to the following Provisions:—

(1) Nothing in any such Law shall prejudicially affect any Right or Privilege with respect to Denominational Schools which any Class of Persons have by Law in the Province at the Union:

(2) All the Powers, Privileges, and Duties at the Union by Law conferred and imposed in Upper Canada on the Separate Schools and School Trustees of the Queen's Roman Catholic Subjects shall be and the same are hereby extended to the Dissentient Schools of the Queen's Protestant and Roman Catholic Subjects in Quebec:

(3) Where in any Province a System of Separate or Dissentient Schools exists by Law at the Union or is thereafter established by the Legislature of the Province, an Appeal shall lie to the Governor General in Council from any Act or Decision of any Provincial Authority affecting any Right or Privilege of the Protestant or Roman Catholic Minority of the Queen's Subjects in relation to Education:

(4) In case any such Provincial Law as from Time to Time seems to the Governor General in Council requisite for the due Execution of the Provisions of this Section is not made, or in case any Decision of the Governor General in Council on any Appeal under this Section is not duly executed by the proper Provincial Authority in that Behalf, then and in every such Case, and as far only as the Circumstances of each Case require, the Parliament of Canada may make remedial Laws for the due Execution of the Provisions of this Section and of any Decision of the Governor General in Council under this Section.

## Uniformity of Laws in Ontario, Nova Scotia and New Brunswick

**94.** Notwithstanding anything in this Act, the Parliament of Canada may make Provision for the Uniformity of all or any of the Laws relative to Property and Civil Rights in Ontario, Nova Scotia, and New Brunswick, and of the Procedure of all or any of the Courts in Those Three Provinces, and from and after the passing of any Act in that Behalf the Power of the Parliament of Canada to make Laws in relation to any Matter comprised in any such Act shall, notwithstanding anything in this Act, be unrestricted; but any Act of the Parliament of Canada making Provision for such Uniformity shall not have effect in any Province unless and until it is adopted and enacted as Law by the Legislature thereof.

## Old Age Pensions

**94A.** The Parliament of Canada may make laws in relation to old age pensions and supplementary benefits, including survivors, and disability benefits irrespective of age, but no such law shall affect the operation of any law present or future of a provincial legislature in relation to any such matter.

## Agriculture and Immigration

**95.** In each Province the Legislature may make Laws in relation to Agriculture in the Province, and to Immigration into the Province; and it is hereby declared that the Parliament of Canada may from Time to Time make Laws in relation to Agriculture in all or any of the Provinces, and to Immigration into all or any of the Provinces; and any Law of the Legislature of a Province relative to Agriculture or to Immigration shall have effect in and for the Province as long and as far only as it is not repugnant to any Act of the Parliament of Canada.

# VII. JUDICATURE

**96.** The Governor General shall appoint the Judges of the Superior, District, and County Courts in each Province, except those of the Courts of Probate in Nova Scotia and New Brunswick.

**97.** Until the laws relative to Property and Civil Rights in Ontario, Nova Scotia, and New Brunswick, and the Procedure of the Courts in those Provinces, are made uniform, the Judges of the Courts of those Provinces appointed by the Governor General shall be selected from the respective Bars of those Provinces.

**98.** The Judges of the Courts of Quebec shall be selected from the Bar of that Province.

**99.** (1) Subject to subsection two of this section, the Judges of the Superior Courts shall hold office during good behaviour, but shall be removable by the Governor General on Address of the Senate and House of Commons.

(2) A Judge of a Superior Court, whether appointed before or after the coming into force of this section, shall cease to hold office upon attaining the age of seventy-five years, or upon the coming into force of this section if at that time he has already attained that age.

**100.** The Salaries, Allowances, and Pensions of the Judges of the Superior, District, and County Courts (except the Courts of Probate in Nova Scotia and New Brunswick), and of the

Admiralty Courts in Cases where the Judges thereof are for the Time being paid by Salary, shall be fixed and provided by the Parliament of Canada.

**101.** The Parliament of Canada may, notwithstanding anything in this Act, from Time to Time provide for the Constitution, Maintenance, and Organization of a General Court of Appeal for Canada, and for the Establishment of any additional Courts for the better Administration of the Laws of Canada.

## VIII. REVENUES;
## DEBTS; ASSETS; TAXATION

**102.** All Duties and Revenues over which the respective Legislatures of Canada, Nova Scotia, and New Brunswick before and at the Union had and have Power of Appropriation, except such Portions thereof as are by this Act reserved to the respective Legislatures of the Provinces, or are raised by them in accordance with the special Powers conferred on them by this Act, shall form One Consolidated Revenue Fund, to be appropriated for the Public Service of Canada in the Manner and subject to the Charges of this Act provided.

**103.** The Consolidated Revenue Fund of Canada shall be permanently charged with the Costs, Charges, and Expenses incident to the Collection, Management, and Receipt thereof, and the same shall form the First Charge thereon, subject to be reviewed and audited in such Manner as shall be ordered by the Governor General in Council until the Parliament otherwise provides.

**104.** The annual Interest of the Public Debts of the several Provinces of Canada, Nova Scotia, and New Brunswick at the Union shall form the Second Charge on the Consolidated Revenue Fund of Canada.

**105.** Unless altered by the Parliament of Canada, the Salary of the Governor General shall be Ten thousand Pounds Sterling Money of the United Kingdom of Great Britain and Ireland, payable out of the Consolidated Revenue Fund of Canada, and the same shall form the Third Charge thereon.

**106.** Subject to the several Payments by this Act charged on the Consolidated Revenue Fund of Canada, the same shall be appropriated by the Parliament of Canada for the Public Service.

**107.** All Stocks, Cash, Banker's Balances, and Securities for Money belonging to each Province at the Time of the Union, except as in this Act mentioned, shall be the Property of Canada, and shall be taken in Reduction of the Amount of the respective Debts of the Provinces at the Union.

**108.** The Public Works and Property of each Province, enumerated in the Third Schedule to this Act, shall be the Property of Canada.

**109.** All Lands, Mines, Minerals, and Royalties belonging to the several Provinces of Canada, Nova Scotia, and New Brunswick at the Union, and all Sums then due or payable for such Lands, Mines, Minerals, or Royalties, shall belong to the several Provinces of Ontario, Quebec, Nova Scotia, and New Brunswick in which the same are situate or arise, subject to any Trusts existing in respect thereof, and to any Interest other than that of the Province in the same.

**110.** All Assets connected with such Portions of the Public Debt of each Province as are assumed by that Province shall belong to that Province.

**111.** Canada shall be liable for the Debts and Liabilities of each Province existing at the Union.

**112.** Ontario and Quebec conjointly shall be liable to Canada for the Amount (if any) by which the Debt of the Province of Canada exceeds at the Union Sixty-two million five hundred thousand Dollars, and shall be charged with Interest at the Rate of Five Per Centum per Annum thereon.

**113.** The Assets enumerated in the Fourth Schedule to this Act belonging at the Union to the Province of Canada shall be the Property of Ontario and Quebec conjointly.

**114.** Nova Scotia shall be liable to Canada for the Amount (if any) by which its Public Debt exceeds at the Union Eight million Dollars, and shall be charged with Interest at the Rate of Five per Centum per Annum thereon.

**115.** New Brunswick shall be liable to Canada for the Amount (if any) by which its Public Debt exceeds at the Union Seven million Dollars, and shall be charged with Interest at the Rate of Five Per Centum per Annum thereon.

**116.** In case the Public Debts of Nova Scotia and New Brunswick do not at the Union amount to Eight million and Seven million Dollars respectively, they shall respectively receive by half-yearly Payments in advance from the Government of Canada Interest at Five per Centum per Annum on the Difference between the actual Amounts of their respective Debts and such stipulated Amounts.

**117.** The several Provinces shall retain all their respective Public Property not otherwise disposed of in this Act, subject to the Right of Canada to assume any Lands or Public Property required for Fortifications or for the Defence of the Country.

**118.** Repealed.

**119.** New Brunswick shall receive by half-yearly Payments in advance from Canada for the period of Ten years from the Union an additional Allowance of Sixty-three thousand Dollars per Annum; but as long as the Public Debt of that Province remains under Seven million Dollars, a Deduction equal to the Interest at Five per Centum per Annum on such Deficiency shall be made from that Allowance of Sixty-three thousand Dollars.

**120.** All Payments to be made under this Act, or in discharge of Liabilities created under any Act of the Provinces of Canada, Nova Scotia, and New Brunswick respectively, and assumed by Canada, shall, until the Parliament of Canada otherwise directs, be made in such Form and Manner as may from Time to Time be ordered by the Governor General in Council.

**121.** All Articles of the Growth, Produce, or Manufacture of any one of the Provinces shall, from and after the Union, be admitted free into each of the other Provinces.

**122.** The Customs and Excise Laws of each Province shall, subject to the Provisions of this Act, continue in force until altered by the Parliament of Canada.

**123.** Where Customs Duties are, at the Union, leviable on any Goods, Wares, or Merchandises in any Two Provinces, those Goods, Wares, and Merchandises may, from and after the Union, be imported from one of those Provinces into the other of them on Proof of Payment of the Customs Duty leviable thereon in the Province of Exportation, and on Payment of such further Amount (if any) of Customs Duty as is leviable thereon in the Province of Importation.

**124.** Nothing in this Act shall affect the Right of New Brunswick to levy the Lumber Dues provided in Chapter Fifteen of Title Three of the Revised Statutes of New Brunswick, or in any Act amending that Act before or after the Union, and not increasing the Amount of such Dues; but the Lumber of any of the Provinces other than New Brunswick shall not be subject to such Dues.

**125.** No Lands or Property belonging to Canada or any Province shall be liable to Taxation.

**126.** Such Portions of the Duties and Revenues over which the respective Legislatures of Canada, Nova Scotia, and New Brunswick had before the Union Power of Appropriation as are by this Act reserved to the respective Governments or Legislatures of the Provinces, and all Duties and Revenues raised by them in accordance with the special Powers conferred upon them by this Act, shall in each Province form One Consolidated Revenue Fund to be appropriated for the Public Service of the Province.

## IX. MISCELLANEOUS PROVISIONS

### General

**127.** Repealed.

**128.** Every Member of the Senate or House of Commons of Canada shall before taking his Seat therein take and subscribe before the Governor General or some Person authorized by him, and every Member of a Legislative Council or Legislative Assembly of any Province shall before taking his Seat therein take and subscribe before the Lieutenant Governor of the Province or some Person authorized by him, the Oath of Allegiance contained in the Fifth Schedule to this Act; and every Member of the Senate of Canada and every Member of the Legislative Council of Quebec shall also, before taking his Seat therein, take and subscribe before the Governor General, or some Person authorized by him, the Declaration of Qualification contained in the same Schedule.

**129.** Except as otherwise provided by this Act, all Laws in force in Canada, Nova Scotia, or New Brunswick at the Union, and all Courts of Civil and Criminal Jurisdiction, and all legal Commissions, Powers, and Authorities, and all Officers, Judicial, Administrative, and Ministerial, existing therein at the Union, shall continue in Ontario, Quebec, Nova Scotia, and New Brunswick respectively, as if the Union had not been made; subject nevertheless (except with respect to such as are enacted by or exist under Acts of the Parliament of Great Britain or of the Parliament of the United Kingdom of Great Britain and Ireland), to be repealed, abolished, or altered by the Parliament of Canada, or by the Legislature of the respective Province, according to the Authority of the Parliament or of that Legislature under this Act.

**130.** Until the Parliament of Canada otherwise provides, all Officers of the several Provinces having Duties to discharge in relation to Matters other than those coming within the Classes of Subjects by this Act assigned exclusively to the Legislatures of the Provinces shall be Officers of Canada, and shall continue to discharge the Duties of their respective Offices under the same Liabilities, Responsibilities, and Penalties as if the Union had not been made.

**131.** Until the Parliament of Canada otherwise provides, the Governor General in Council may from Time to Time appoint such Officers as the Governor General in Council deems necessary or proper for the effectual Execution of this Act.

**132.** The Parliament and Government of Canada shall have all Powers necessary or proper for performing the Obligations of Canada or of any Province thereof, as Part of the British Empire, towards Foreign Countries, arising under Treaties between the Empire and such Foreign Countries.

**133.** Either the English or the French Language may be used by any Person in the Debates of the Houses of the Parliament of Canada and of the Houses of the Legislature of Quebec; and both those Languages shall be used in the respective Records and Journals of those Houses; and either of those Languages may be used by any Person or in any Pleading or Process in or issuing from any Court of Canada established under this Act, and in or from all or any of the Courts of Quebec.

The Acts of the Parliament of Canada and of the Legislature of Quebec shall be printed and published in both those Languages.

## Ontario and Quebec

**134.** Until the Legislature of Ontario or of Quebec otherwise provides, the Lieutenant Governors of Ontario and Quebec may each appoint under the Great Seal of the Province the following Officers, to hold Office during Pleasure, that is to say,—the Attorney General, the Secretary and Registrar of the Province, the Treasurer of the Province, the Commissioner of Crown Lands, and the Commissioner of Agriculture and Public Works, and in the Case of Quebec the Solicitor General, and may, by Order of the Lieutenant Governor in Council, from Time to Time prescribe the Duties of those Officers, and of the several Departments over which they shall preside or to which they shall belong, and of the Officers and Clerks thereof, and may also appoint other and additional Officers to hold Office during Pleasure, and may from Time to Time prescribe the Duties of those Officers, and of the several Departments over which they shall preside or to which they shall belong, and of the Officers and Clerks thereof.

**135.** Until the Legislature of Ontario or Quebec otherwise provides, all Rights, Powers, Duties, Functions, Responsibilities, or Authorities at the passing of this Act vested in or imposed on the Attorney General, Solicitor General, Secretary and Registrar of the Province of Canada, Minister of Finance, Commissioner of Crown Lands, Commissioner of Public Works, and Minister of Agriculture and Receiver General, by any Law, Statute, or Ordinance of Upper Canada, Lower Canada, or Canada, and not repugnant to this Act, shall be vested in or imposed on any Officer to be appointed by the Lieutenant Governor for the discharge of the same or any of them; and the Commissioner of Agriculture and Public Works shall perform the Duties and Functions of the Office of Minister of Agriculture at the passing of this Act imposed by the Law of the Province of Canada, as well as those of the Commissioner of Public Works.

**136.** Until altered by the Lieutenant Governor in Council, the Great Seals of Ontario and Quebec respectively shall be the same, or of the same Design, as those used in the Provinces of Upper Canada and Lower Canada respectively before their Union as the Province of Canada.

**137.** The words "and from thence to the End of the then next ensuing Session of the Legislature," or Words to the same Effect, used in any temporary Act of the Province of Canada not expired before the Union, shall be construed to extend and apply to the next Session of the Parliament of Canada if the Subject Matter of the Act is within the Powers of the same as defined by this Act, or to the next Sessions of the Legislatures of Ontario and Quebec respectively if the Subject Matter of the Act is within the Powers of the same as defined by this Act.

**138.** From and after the Union the Use of the Words "Upper Canada," instead of "Ontario," or "Lower Canada" instead of "Quebec," in any Deed, Writ, Process, Pleading, Document, Matter, or Thing shall not invalidate the same.

**139.** Any Proclamation under the Great Seal of the Province of Canada issued before the Union to take effect at a Time which is subsequent to the Union, whether relating to that Province, or to Upper Canada, or to Lower Canada, and the several Matters and Things therein proclaimed, shall be and continue of like Force and Effect as if the Union had not been made.

**140.** Any Proclamation which is authorized by any Act of the Legislature of the Province of Canada to be issued under the Great Seal of the Province of Canada, whether relating to that Province, or to Upper Canada, or to Lower Canada, and which is not issued before the Union, may be issued by the Lieutenant Governor of Ontario or Quebec, as its Subject Matter requires, under the Great Seal thereof; and from and after the Issue of such Proclamation the same and the several Matters and Things therein proclaimed shall be and continue of the like Force and Effect in Ontario or Quebec as if the Union had not been made.

**141.** The Penitentiary of the Province of Canada shall, until the Parliament of Canada otherwise provides, be and continue the Penitentiary of Ontario and of Quebec.

**142.** The Division and Adjustment of the Debts, Credits, Liabilities, Properties, and Assets of Upper Canada and Lower Canada shall be referred to the Arbitrament of Three Arbitrators, One chosen by the Government of Ontario, One by the Government of Quebec, and One by the Government of Canada; and the Selection of the Arbitrators shall not be made until the Parliament of Canada and the Legislatures of Ontario and Quebec have met; and the Arbitrator chosen by the Government of Canada shall not be a Resident either in Ontario or in Quebec.

**143.** The Governor General in Council may from Time to Time order that such and so many of the Records, Books, and Documents of the Province of Canada as he thinks fit shall be appropriated and delivered either to Ontario or to Quebec, and the same shall thenceforth be the Property of that Province; and any Copy thereof or Extract therefrom, duly certified by the Officer having charge of the Original thereof, shall be admitted as Evidence.

**144.** The Lieutenant Governor of Quebec may from Time to Time, by Proclamation under the Great Seal of the Province, to take effect from a Day to be appointed therein, constitute Townships in those Parts of the Province of Quebec in which Townships are not then already constituted, and fix the Metes and Bounds thereof.

## X. INTERCOLONIAL RAILWAY

**145.** Repealed.

## XI. ADMISSION OF OTHER COLONIES

**146.** It shall be lawful for the Queen, by and with the Advice of Her Majesty's Most Honourable Privy Council, on Addresses from the Houses of the Parliament of Canada, and from the Houses of the respective Legislatures of the Colonies or Provinces of Newfoundland, Prince Edward Island, and British Columbia, to admit those Colonies or Provinces, or any of them, into the Union, and on Address from the Houses of the Parliament of Canada to admit Rupert's Land and the North-western Territory, or either of them, into the Union, on such Terms and Conditions in each Case as are in the Addresses expressed and as the Queen thinks fit to approve, subject to the Provisions of this Act; and the Provisions of any Order in Council in that Behalf shall have effect as if they had been enacted by the Parliament of the United Kingdom of Great Britain and Ireland.

**147.** In case of the Admission of Newfoundland and Prince Edward Island, or either of them, each shall be entitled to a Representation in the Senate of Canada of Four Members, and (notwithstanding anything in this Act) in case of the Admission of Newfoundland the normal Number of Senators shall be Seventy-six and their maximum Number shall be Eighty-two; but Prince Edward Island when admitted shall be deemed to be comprised in the Third of Three Divisions into which Canada is, in relation to the Constitution of the Senate, divided by this Act, and accordingly, after the Admission of Prince Edward Island, whether Newfoundland is admitted or not, the Representation of Nova Scotia and New Brunswick in the Senate shall, as Vacancies occur, be reduced from Twelve to Ten Members respectively, and the Representation of each of those Provinces shall not be increased at any Time beyond Ten, except under the Provisions of this Act for the Appointment of Three or Six additional Senators under the Direction of the Queen.

# THE CONSTITUTION ACT, 1982
## SCHEDULE B
## PART 1, CANADIAN CHARTER OF RIGHTS AND FREEDOMS

Whereas Canada is founded upon principles that recognize the supremacy of God and the rule of law:

## Guarantee of Rights and Freedoms

**1.** The *Canadian Charter of Rights and Freedoms* guarantees the rights and freedoms set out in it subject only to such reasonable limits prescribed by law as can be demonstrably justified in a free and democratic society.

## Fundamental Freedoms

**2.** Everyone has the following fundamental freedoms:
(a) freedom of conscience and religion;
(b) freedom of thought, belief, opinion and expression, including freedom of the press and other media of communication;
(c) freedom of peaceful assembly; and
(d) freedom of association.

## Democratic Rights

**3.** Every citizen of Canada has the right to vote in an election of members of the House of Commons or of a legislative assembly and to be qualified for membership therein.
**4.** (1) No House of Commons and no legislative assembly shall continue for longer than five years from the date fixed for the return of the writs at a general election of its members.
(2) In time of real or apprehended war, invasion or insurrection, a House of Commons may be continued by Parliament and a legislative assembly may be continued by the legislature beyond five years if such continuation is not opposed by the votes of more than one-third of the members of the House of Commons or the legislative assembly, as the case may be.
**5.** There shall be a sitting of Parliament and of each legislature at least once every twelve months.

## Mobility Rights

**6.** (1) Every citizen of Canada has the right to enter, remain in and leave Canada.

*Source: A Consolidation of the Constitution Acts, 1867–1982*, Justice Canada. Reproduced with permission of the Minister of Supply and Services Canada, 1994.

(2) Every citizen of Canada and every person who has the status of a permanent resident of Canada has the right

    (a) to move to and take up residence in any province; and

    (b) to pursue the gaining of a livelihood in any province.

(3) The rights specified in subsection (2) are subject to

    (a) any laws or practices of general application in force in a province other than those that discriminate among persons primarily on the basis of province of present or previous residence; and

    (b) any laws providing for reasonable residency requirements as a qualification for the receipt of publicly provided social services.

(4) Subsections (2) and (3) do not preclude any law, program or activity that has as its object the amelioration in a province of conditions of individuals in that province who are socially or economically disadvantaged if the rate of employment in that province is below the rate of employment in Canada.

## Legal Rights

**7.** Everyone has the right to life, liberty and security of the person and the right not to be deprived thereof except in accordance with the principles of fundamental justice.

**8.** Everyone has the right to be secure against unreasonable search or seizure.

**9.** Everyone has the right not to be arbitrarily detained or imprisoned.

**10.** Everyone has the right on arrest or detention

    (a) to be informed promptly of the reasons therefor;

    (b) to retain and instruct counsel without delay and to be inforrned of that right; and

    (c) to have the validity of the detention determined by way of *habeas corpus* and to be released if the detention is not lawful.

**11.** Any person charged with an offence has the right

    (a) to be informed without unreasonable delay of the specific offence;

    (b) to be tried within a reasonable time;

    (c) not to be compelled to be a witness in proceedings against that person in respect of the offence;

    (d) to be presumed innocent until proven guilty according to law in a fair and public hearing by an independent and impartial tribunal;

    (e) not to be denied reasonable bail without just cause;

    (f) except in the case of an offence under military law tried before a military tribunal, to the benefit of trial by jury where the maximum punishment for the offence is imprisonment for five years or a more severe punishment;

    (g) not to be found guilty on account of any act or omission unless, at the time of the act or omission, it constituted an offence under Canadian or international law or was criminal according to the general principles of law recognized by the community of nations;

    (h) if finally acquitted of the offence, not to be tried for it again and, if finally found guilty and punished for the offence, not to be tried or punished for it again; and

    (i) if found guilty of the offence and if the punishment for the offence has been varied between the time of commission and the time of sentencing, to the benefit of the lesser punishment.

**12.** Everyone has the right not to be subjected to any cruel and unusual treatment or punishment.

**13.** A witness who testifies in any proceedings has the right not to have any incriminating evidence so given used to incriminate that witness in any other proceedings, except in a prosecution for perjury or for the giving of contradictory evidence.

**14.** A party or witness in any proceedings who does not understand or speak the language in which the proceedings are conducted or who is deaf has the right to the assistance of an interpreter.

## Equality Rights

**15.** (1) Every individual is equal before and under the law and has the right to the equal protection and equal benefit of the law without discrimination and, in particular, without discrimination based on race, national or ethnic origin, colour, religion, sex, age or mental or physical disability.

(2) Subsection (1) does not preclude any law, program or activity that has as its object the amelioration of conditions of disadvantaged individuals or groups including those that are disadvantaged because of race, national or ethnic origin, colour, religion, sex, age or mental or physical disability.

## Official Languages of Canada

**16.** (1) English and French are the official languages of Canada and have equality of status and equal rights and privileges as to their use in all institutions of the Parliament and government of Canada.

(2) English and French are the official languages of New Brunswick and have equality of status and equal rights and privileges as to their use in all institutions of the legislature and government of New Brunswick.

(3) Nothing in this Charter limits the authority of Parliament or a legislature to advance the equality of status or use of English and French.

**17.** (1) Everyone has the right to use English or French in any debates and other proceedings of Parliament.

(2) Everyone has the right to use English or French in any debates and other proceedings of the legislature of New Brunswick.

**18.** (1) The statutes, records and journals of Parliament shall be printed and published in English and French and both language versions are equally authoritative.

(2) The statutes, records and journals of the legislature of New Brunswick shall be printed and published in English and French and both language versions are equally authoritative.

**19.** (1) Either English or French may be used by any person in, or in any pleading in or process issuing from, any court established by Parliament.

(2) Either English or French may be used by any person in, or in any pleading in or process issuing from, any court of New Brunswick.

**20.** (1) Any member of the public in Canada has the right to communicate with, and to receive available services from, any head or central office of an institution of the Parliament or government of Canada in English or French, and has the same right with respect to any other office of any such institution where

(a) there is a significant demand for communications with and services from that office in such language; or

(b) due to the nature of the office, it is reasonable that communications with and services from that office be available in both English and French.

(2) Any member of the public in New Brunswick has the right to communicate with, and to receive available services from, any office of an institution of the legislature or government of New Brunswick in English or French.

**21.** Nothing in sections 16 to 20 abrogates or derogates from any right, privilege or obligation with respect to the English and French languages, or either of them, that exists or is continued by virtue of any other provision of the Constitution of Canada.

**22.** Nothing in sections 16 to 20 abrogates or derogates from any legal or customary right or privilege acquired or enjoyed either before or after the coming into force of this Charter with respect to any language that is not English or French.

## Minority Language Educational Rights

**23.** (1) Citizens of Canada
(a) whose first language learned and still understood is that of the English or French linguistic minority population of the province in which they reside, or
(b) who have received their primary school instruction in Canada in English or French and reside in a province where the language in which they received that instruction is the language of the English or French linguistic minority population of the province,
have the right to have their children receive primary and secondary school instruction in that language in that province.

(2) Citizens of Canada of whom any child has received or is receiving primary or secondary school instruction in English or French in Canada, have the right to have all their children receive primary and secondary school instruction in the same language.

(3) The right of citizens of Canada under subsections (I) and (2) to have their children receive primary and secondary school instruction in the language of the English or French linguistic minority population of a province
(a) applies wherever in the province the number of children of citizens who have such a right is sufficient to warrant the provision to them out of public funds of minority language instruction; and
(b) includes, where the number of those children so warrants, the right to have them receive that instruction in minority language educational facilities provided out of public funds.

## Enforcement

**24.** (1) Anyone whose rights or freedoms, as guaranteed by this Charter, have been infringed or denied may apply to a court of competent jurisdiction to obtain such remedy as the court considers appropriate and just in the circumstances.

(2) Where, in proceedings under subsection (1), a court concludes that evidence was obtained in a manner that infringed or denied any rights or freedoms guaranteed by this Charter, the evidence shall be excluded if it is established that, having regard to all the circumstances, the admission of it in the proceedings would bring the administration of justice into disrepute.

## General

**25.** The guarantee in this Charter of certain rights and freedoms shall not be construed so as to abrogate or derogate from any aboriginal treaty or other rights or freedoms that pertain to the aboriginal peoples of Canada including

(a) any rights or freedoms that have been recognized by the Royal Proclamation of October 7, 1763; and

(b) any rights or freedoms that may be acquired by the aboriginal peoples of Canada by way of land claims settlement.

**26.** The guarantee in this Charter of certain rights and freedoms shall not be construed as denying the existence of any other rights or freedoms that exist in Canada.

**27.** This Charter shall be interpreted in a manner consistent with the preservation and enhancement of the multicultural heritage of Canadians.

**28.** Notwithstanding anything in this Charter, the rights and freedoms referred to in it are guaranteed equally to male and female persons.

**29.** Nothing in this Charter abrogates or derogates from any rights or privileges guaranteed by or under the Constitution of Canada in respect of denominational, separate or dissentient schools.

**30.** A reference in this Charter to a Province or to the legislative assembly or legislature of a province shall be deemed to include a reference to the Yukon Territory and the Northwest Territories, or to the appropriate legislative authority thereof, as the case may be.

**31.** Nothing in this Charter extends the legislative powers of any body or authority.

## Application of Charter

**32.** (1) This Charter applies

(a) to the Parliament and government of Canada in respect of all matters within the authority of Parliament including all matters relating to the Yukon Territory and Northwest Territories; and

(b) to the legislature and government of each province in respect of all matters within the authority of the legislature of each province.

(2) Notwithstanding subsection (1), section 15 shall not have effect until three years after this section comes into force.

**33.** (1) Parliament or the legislature of a province may expressly declare in an Act of Parliament or of the legislature, as the case may be, that the Act or a provision thereof shall operate notwithstanding a provision included in section 2 or sections 7 to 15 of this Charter.

(2) An Act or a provision of an Act in respect of which a declaration made under this section is in effect shall have such operation as it would have but for the provision of this Charter referred to in the declaration.

(3) A declaration made under subsection (1) shall cease to have effect five years after it comes into force or on such earlier date as may be specified in the declaration.

(4) Parliament or the legislature of a province may re-enact a declaration made under subsection (1).

(5) Subsection (3) applies in respect of a re-enactment made under subsection (4).

## Citation

**34.** This Part may be cited as the *Canadian Charter of Rights and Freedoms*.

# PART II
## RIGHTS OF THE ABORIGINAL PEOPLES OF CANADA

**35.** (1) The existing aboriginal and treaty rights of the aboriginal peoples of Canada are hereby recognized and affirmed.

(2) In this Act, "aboriginal peoples of Canada" includes the Indian, Inuit, and Métis peoples of Canada.

(3) For greater certainty, in subsection (1) "treaty rights" includes rights that now exist by way of land claims agreements or may be so acquired.

(4) Notwithstanding any other provision of this Act, the aboriginal and treaty rights referred to in subsection (1) are guaranteed equally to male and female persons.(94)

**35.1** The government of Canada and the provincial governments are committed to the principle that, before any amendment is made to Class 24 of section 91 of the *"Constitution Act, 1867"*, to section 25 of this Act or to this Part,

> (a) a constitutional conference that includes in its agenda an item relating to the proposed amendment, composed of the Prime Minister of Canada and the first ministers of the provinces, will be convened by the Prime Minister of Canada; and
>
> (b) the Prime Minister of Canada will invite representatives of the aboriginal peoples of Canada to participate in the discussions on that item.

# PART III
## EQUALIZATION AND REGIONAL DISPARITIES

**36.** (1) Without altering the legislative authority of Parliament or of the provincial legislatures, or the rights of any of them with respect to the exercise of their legislative authority, Parliament and the legislatures, together with the government of Canada and the provincial governments, are committed to

> (a) promoting equal opportunities for the well-being of Canadians;
>
> (b) furthering economic development to reduce disparity in opportunities; and
>
> (c) providing essential public services of reasonable quality to all Canadians.

(2) Parliament and the government of Canada are committed to the principle of making equalization payments to ensure that provincial governments have sufficient revenues to provide reasonably comparable levels of public services at reasonably comparable levels of taxation.

# PART IV
## CONSTITUTIONAL CONFERENCES

**37.** (1) A constitutional conference composed of the Prime Minister of Canada and the first ministers of the provinces shall be convened by the Prime Minister of Canada within one year after this Part comes into force.

(2) The conference convened under subsection (1) shall have included in this agenda an item respecting constitutional matters that directly affect the aboriginal peoples of Canada, including the identification and definition of the rights of those peoples to be included in the Constitution of Canada, and the Prime Minister of Canada shall invite representatives of those peoples to participate in the discussions on that item.

(3) The Prime Minister of Canada shall invite elected representatives of the governments of the Yukon Terriotry and the Northwest Territories to participate in that discussion on any item

on the agenda of the conference convened under subsection (1) that, in the opinion of the Prime Minister, directly affects the Yukon Territory and the Northwest Territories.

# PART IV.I
## CONSTITUTIONAL CONFERENCE

**37.1** (1) In addition to the conference convened in March 1983, at least two constitutional conferences composed of the Prime Minister of Canada and the first ministers of the provinces shall be convened by the Prime Minister of Canada, the first within three years after April 17, 1982 and the second within five years after that date.

(2) Each conference convened under subsection (1) shall have included in its agenda constitutional matters that directly affect the aboriginal peoples of Canada, and the Prime Minister of Canada shall invite representatives of those peoples to participate in the discussion on those items.

(3) The Prime Minister of Canada shall invite elected representatives of the governments of the Yukon Territory and the Northwest Territories to participate in the discussions on any item on the agenda convened under subsection (1) that, in the opinion of the Prime Minister, directly affects the Yukon Territory and the Northwest Territories.

(4) Nothing in this section shall be construed so as to derogate from subsection 35(1).

# PART V
## PROCEDURE FOR AMENDING CONSTITUTION
## OF CANADA

**38.** (1) An amendment to the Constitution of Canada may be made by proclamation issued by the Governor General under the Great Seal of Canada where so authorized by

(a) resolutions of the Senate and House of Commons; and

(b) resolutions of the legislative assemblies of at least two-thirds of the provinces that have, in the aggregate, according to the then latest general census, at least fifty per cent of the population of all the provinces.

(2) An amendment made under subsection (1) that derogates from the legislative powers, the proprietary rights or any other rights or privileges of the legislature or government of a province shall require a resolution supported by a majority of the members of each of the Senate, the House of Commons and the legislative assemblies required under subsection (1).

(3) An amendment referred to in subsection (2) shall not have effect in a province the legislative assembly of which has expressed its dissent thereto by resolution supported by a majority of its members prior to the issue of the proclamation to which the amendment relates unless that legislative assembly, subsequently, by resolution supported by a majority of its members, revokes its dissent and authorizes the amendment.

(4) A resolution of dissent made for the purposes of subsection (3) may be revoked at any time before or after the issue of the proclamation to which it relates.

**39.** (1) A proclamation shall not be issued under subsection 38(1) before the expiration of one year from the adoption of the resolution initiating the amendment procedure thereunder, unless the legislative assembly of each province has previously adopted a resolution of assent or dissent.

(2) A proclamation shall not be issued under subsection 38(1) after the expiration of three years from the adoption of the resolution initiating the amendment procedure thereunder.

**40.** Where an amendment is made under subsection 38(1) that transfers provincial legislative powers relating to education or other cultural matters from provincial legislatures to Parliament, Canada shall provide reasonable compensation to any province to which the amendment does not apply.

**41.** An amendment to the Constitution of Canada in relation to the following matters may be made by proclamation issued by the Governor General under the Great Seal of Canada only where authorized by resolutions of the Senate and House of Commons and of the legislative assembly of each province:

> (a) the office of the Queen, the Governor General and the Lieutenant Governor of a province;
>
> (b) the right of a province to a number of members in the House of Commons not less than the number of Senators by which the province is entitled to be represented at the time this Part comes into force;
>
> (c) subject to section 43, the use of the English or the French language;
>
> (d) the composition of the Supreme Court of Canada; and
>
> (e) an amendment to this Part.

**42.** (1) An amendment to the Constitution of Canada in relation to the following matters may be made only in accordance with subsection 38(1):

> (a) the principle of proportionate representation of the provinces in the House of Commons prescribed by the Constitution of Canada;
>
> (b) the powers of the Senate and the method of selecting Senators;
>
> (c) the number of members by which a province is entitled to be represented in the Senate and the residence qualifications of Senators;
>
> (d) subject to paragraph 41(d), the Supreme Court of Canada;
>
> (e) the extension of existing provinces into the territories; and
>
> (f) notwithstanding any other law or practice, the establishment of new provinces.

(2) Subsections 38(2) to (4) do not apply in respect of amendments in relation to matters referred to in subsection (1).

**43.** An amendment to the Constitution of Canada in relation to any provision that applies to one or more, but not all, provinces, including

> (a) any alteration to boundaries between provinces, and
>
> (b) any amendment to any provision that relates to the use of the English or the French language within a province,

may be made by proclamation issued by the Governor General under the Great Seal of Canada only where so authorized by resolutions of the Senate and House of Commons and of the legislative assembly of each province to which the amendment applies.

**44.** Subject to sections 41 and 42, Parliament may exclusively make laws amending the Constitution of Canada in relation to the executive government of Canada or the Senate and House of Commons.

**45.** Subject to section 41, the legislature of each province may exclusively make laws amending the constitution of the province.

**46.** (1) The procedures for amendment under sections 38, 41, 42 and 43 may be initiated either by the Senate or the House of Commons or by the legislative assembly of a province.

(2) A resolution of assent made for the purposes of this Part may be revoked at any time before the issue of a proclamation authorized by it.

**47.** (1) An amendment to the Constitution of Canada made by proclamation under section

38, 41, 42 or 43 may be made without a resolution of the Senate authorizing the issue of the proclamation if, within one hundred and eighty days after the adoption by the House of Commons of a resolution authorizing its issue, the Senate has not adopted such a resolution and if, at any time after the expiration of that period, the House of Commons again adopts the resolution.

(2) Any period when Parliament is prorogued or dissolved shall not be counted in computing the one hundred and eighty day period referred to in subsection (1).

**48.** The Queen's Privy Council for Canada shall advise the Governor General to issue a proclamation under this Part forthwith on the adoption of the resolutions required for an amendment made by proclamation under this Part.

**49.** A constitutional conference composed of the Prime Minister of Canada and the first ministers of the provinces shall be convened by the Prime Minister of Canada within fifteen years after this Part comes into force to review the provisions of this Part.

# PART VI
# AMENDMENT TO THE CONSTITUTION ACT, 1867

**50.** *The Constitution Act, 1867* (formerly named the *British North America Act, 1867*) is amended by adding thereto, immediately after section 92 thereof, the following heading and section:

### *"Non-Renewable Natural Resources,*
### *Forestry Resources and Electrical Energy*

**92A.** (1) In each province, the legislature may exclusively make laws in relation to
(a) exploration for non-renewable natural resources in the province;
(b) development, conservation and management of non-renewable natural resources and forestry resources in the province, including laws in relation to the rate of primary production therefrom; and
(c) development, conservation and management of sites and facilities in the province for the generation and production of electrical energy.
(2) In each province, the legislature may make laws in relation to the export from the province to another part of Canada of the primary production from non-renewable natural resources and forestry resources in the province and the production from facilities in the province for the generation of electrical energy, but such laws may not authorize or provide for discrimination in prices or in supplies exported to another part of Canada.
(3) Nothing in subsection (2) derogates from the authority of Parliament to enact laws in relation to the matters referred to in that subsection and, where such a law of Parliament and a law of a province conflict, the law of Parliament prevails to the extent of the conflict.
(4) In each province, the legislature may make laws in relation to the raising of money by any mode or system of taxation in respect of
(a) non-renewable natural resources and forestry resources in the province and the primary production therefrom, and
(b) sites and facilities in the province for the generation of electrical energy and the production therefrom, whether or not such production is exported in whole or

in part from the province, but such laws may not authorize or provide for taxation that differentiates between production exported to another part of Canada and production not exported from the province.

(5) The expression "primary production" has the meaning assigned by the Sixth Schedule.

(6) Nothing in subsections (1) to (5) derogates from any powers or rights that a legislature or government of a province had immediately before the coming into force of this section."

**51.** The said Act is further amended by adding thereto the following Schedule:

## "THE SIXTH SCHEDULE

### *Primary Production from Non-Renewable Natural Resources and Forestry Resources*

1. For the purposes of section 92A of this Act,

(a) production from a non-renewable natural resource is primary production therefrom if
  (i) it is in the form in which it exists upon its recovery or severance from its natural state, or
  (ii) it is a product resulting from processing or refining the resource, and is not a manufactured product or a product resulting from refining crude oil, refining upgraded heavy crude oil, refining gases or liquids described from coal or refining a synthetic equivalent of crude oil; and

(b) production from a forestry resource is primary production therefrom if it consists of sawlogs, poles, lumber, wood chips, sawdust or any other primary wood product, or wood pulp, and is not a product manufactured from wood."

## PART VII
## GENERAL

**52.** (1) The Constitution of Canada is the supreme law of Canada, and any law that is inconsistent with the provisions of the Constitution is, to the extent of the inconsistency, of no force or effect.

(2) The Constitution of Canada includes

(a) the *Canada Act 1982*, including this Act;

(b) the Acts and orders referred to in the schedule; and

(c) any amendment to any Act or order referred to in paragraph (a) or (b).

(3) Amendments to the Constitution of Canada shall be made only in accordance with the authority contained in the Constitution of Canada.

**53.** (1) The enactments referred to in Column I of the schedule are hereby repealed or amended to the extent indicated in Column II thereof and, unless repealed, shall continue as law in Canada under the names set out in Column III thereof.

(2) Every enactment, except the *Canada Act 1982*, that refers to an enactment referred to in the schedule by the name in Column I thereof is hereby amended by substituting for that name the corresponding name in Column III thereof, and any British North America Act not referred

to in the schedule may be cited as the *Constitution Act* followed by the year and number, if any, of its enactment.

**54.** Part IV is repealed on the day that is one year after this Part comes into force and this section may be repealed and this Act renumbered, consequentially upon the repeal of Part IV and this section, by proclamation issued by the Governor General under the Great Seal of Canada.

**54.1** Part IV.I and this section are repealed on April 18, 1987.

**55.** A French version of the portions of the Constitution of Canada referred to in the schedule shall be prepared by the Minister of Justice of Canada as expeditiously as possible and, when any portion thereof sufficient to warrant action being taken has been so prepared, it shall be put forward for enactment by proclamation issued by the Governor General under the Great Seal of Canada pursuant to the procedure then applicable to an amendment of the same provisions of the Constitution of Canada.

**56.** Where any portion of the Constitution of Canada has been or is enacted in English and French or where a French version of any portion of the Constitution is enacted pursuant to section 55, the English and French versions of that portion of the Constitution are equally authoritative.

**57.** The English and French versions of this Act are equally authoritative.

**58.** Subject to section 59, this Act shall come into force on a day to be fixed by proclamation issued by the Queen or the Governor General under the Great Seal of Canada.

**59.** (1) Paragraph 23(1)(a) shall come into force in respect of Quebec on a day to be fixed by proclamation issued by the Queen or the Governor General under the Great Seal of Canada.

(2) A proclamation under subsection (1) shall be issued only where authorized by the legislative assembly or government of Quebec.

(3) This section may be repealed on the day paragraph 23(1)(a) comes into force in respect of Quebec and this Act amended and renumbered, consequentially upon the repeal of this section, by proclamation issued by the Queen or the Governor General under the Great Seal of Canada.

**60.** This Act may be cited as the *Constitution Act, 1982*, and the Constitution Acts, 1867 to 1975 (No. 2) and this Act may be cited together as the *Constitution Acts, 1867 to 1982*.

**61.** A reference to the "*Constitution Acts, 1867 to 1982*" shall be deemed to include a reference to the "*Constitution Amendment Proclamation, 1983*".

# CANADIAN PRIME MINISTERS
# SINCE 1867

| | Party* | Years in Office |
|---|---|---|
| 1. Rt. Hon. Sir John A. Macdonald | Liberal Conservative | 1867–1873 |
| 2. Hon. Alexander Mackenzie | Liberal | 1873–1878 |
| 3. Rt. Hon. Sir John A. Macdonald | Liberal Conservative | 1878–1891 |
| 4. Hon. Sir John J.C. Abbott | Liberal Conservative | 1891–1892 |
| 5. Rt. Hon. Sir John S.D. Thompson | Liberal Conservative | 1892–1894 |
| 6. Hon. Sir Mackenzie Bowell | Conservative | 1894–1896 |
| 7. Rt. Hon. Sir Charles Tupper (Baronet) | Conservative | 1896–1896 |
| 8. Rt. Hon. Sir Wilfrid Laurier | Liberal | 1896–1911 |
| 9. Rt. Hon. Sir Robert L. Borden | Conservative | 1911–1917 |
| 10. Rt. Hon. Sir Robert L. Borden** | Conservative | 1917–1920 |
| 11. Rt. Hon. Arthur Meighen | Conservative | 1920–1921 |
| 12. Rt. Hon. William Lyon Mackenzie King | Liberal | 1921–1926 |
| 13. Rt. Hon. Arthur Meighen | Conservative | 1926–1926 |
| 14. Rt. Hon. William Lyon Mackenzie King | Liberal | 1926–1930 |
| 15. Rt. Hon. Richard Bedford Bennett (became Viscount Bennett, 1941) | Conservative | 1930–1935 |
| 16. Rt. Hon. William Lyon Mackenzie King | Liberal | 1935–1948 |
| 17. Rt. Hon. Louis Stephen St. Laurent | Liberal | 1948–1957 |
| 18. Rt. Hon. John G. Diefenbaker | Progressive Conservative | 1957–1963 |
| 19. Rt. Hon. Lester B. Pearson | Liberal | 1963–1968 |
| 20. Rt. Hon. Pierre Elliott Trudeau | Liberal | 1968–1979 |
| 21. Rt. Hon. Charles Joseph Clark | Progressive Conservative | 1979–1980 |
| 22. Rt. Hon. Pierre Elliott Trudeau | Liberal | 1980–1984 |
| 23. Rt. Hon. John Napier Turner | Liberal | 1984–1984 |
| 24. Rt. Hon. Martin Brian Mulroney | Progressive Conservative | 1984–1993 |
| 25. Rt. Hon. Kim Campbell | Progressive Conservative | 1993–1993 |
| 26. Rt. Hon. Jean Chrétien | Liberal | 1993– |

\* Individual's party affiliation during tenure as prime minister.
\*\* During his second period in office, Prime Minister Borden headed a coalition government.

# CANADIAN GOVERNORS GENERAL SINCE 1867

| | Assumed Office |
|---|---|
| 1. The Viscount Monck, GCMG | July 1, 1867 |
| 2. The Baron (Lord)* Lisgar of Lisgar and Bailieborough, GCMG | Feb. 2, 1869 |
| 3. The Earl of Dufferin, KP, GCB, GCSI, GCMG, GCIE | June 25, 1872 |
| 4. The Marquess of Lorne, KT, GCMG, GCVO | Nov. 25, 1878 |
| 5. The Marquess of Lansdowne, KG, GCSI, GCMG, GCIE | Oct. 23, 1883 |
| 6. The Baron (Lord)* Stanley of Preston, KG, GCB, GCVO | June 11, 1888 |
| 7. The Earl of Aberdeen, KT, GCMG, GCVO | Sept. 18, 1893 |
| 8. The Earl of Minto, KG, GCSI, GCMG, GCIE | Nov. 12, 1898 |
| 9. The Earl Grey, GCB, GCMG, GCVO | Dec. 10, 1904 |
| 10. Field Marshal H.R.H. The Duke of Connaught and Strathearn, KG, KT, KP, GMB, GCSI, GCMG, GCIE, GCVO, GBE, TD | Oct. 13, 1911 |
| 11. The Duke of Devonshire, KG, GCMG, GCVO, TD | Nov. 11, 1916 |
| 12. Gen. The Baron (Lord)* Byng of Vimy, GCB, GCMG, MVO | Aug. 11, 1921 |
| 13. The Viscount Willingdon of Ratton, GCSI, GCMG, GCIE, GBE | Oct. 2, 1926 |
| 14. The Earl of Bessborough, GCMG | Apr. 4, 1931 |
| 15. The Baron (Lord)* Tweedsmuir of Elsfield, GCMG, GCVO, CH | Nov. 2, 1935 |
| 16. Maj.-Gen. The Earl of Athlone, KG, GCB, GCMG, GCVO, DSO | June 21, 1940 |
| 17. Field Marshal The Viscount Alexander of Tunis, KG, GCB, OM, GCMG, CSI, DSO, MC, ADC | Apr. 12, 1946 |
| 18. The Rt. Hon. Vincent Massey, PC, CC, CH | Feb. 28, 1952 |
| 19. Maj.-Gen. The Rt. Hon. Georges-Philias Vanier, DSO, MC, CD | Sept. 15, 1959 |
| 20. The Rt. Hon. Daniel Roland Michener, PC, CC, CMM, CD, QC | Apr. 17, 1967 |
| 21. The Rt. Hon. Jules Léger, PC, CC, CMM, CD | Jan. 14, 1974 |
| 22. The Rt. Hon. Edward Richard Schreyer, PC, CC, CMM, CD | Jan. 22, 1979 |
| 23. The Rt. Hon. Jeanne Sauvé, PC, CC, CMM, CD | May 14, 1984 |
| 24. The Rt. Hon. Ramon John Hnatyshyn, PC, CC, CMM, CD, QC | Jan. 29, 1990 |
| 25. The Rt. Hon. Romeo LeBlanc, PC, CC, CMM, CD | Feb. 8, 1995 |

\* Common designation during tenure as governor general (e.g., Lord Stanley of Preston).

Note: In certain cases, some of the titles and honours listed above were conferred after the individual's tenure as governor general.

# CANADIAN SPEAKERS OF THE HOUSE OF COMMONS SINCE 1867

|  | | Party* | Years in Office |
|---|---|---|---|
| 1. | Hon. James Cockburn | Conservative | 1867–1874 |
| 2. | Hon. Timothy Warren Anglin | Liberal | 1874–1879 |
| 3. | Hon. Joseph-Godéric Blanchet | Liberal Conservative | 1879–1883 |
| 4. | Hon. George Airey Kirkpatrick | Liberal Conservative | 1883–1887 |
| 5. | Hon. Joseph-Aldéric Ouimet | Liberal Conservative | 1887–1891 |
| 6. | Hon. Peter White | Conservative | 1891–1896 |
| 7. | Hon. Sir James David Edgar | Liberal | 1896–1899 |
| 8. | Hon. Thomas Bain | Liberal | 1899–1901 |
| 9. | Hon. Louis-Philippe Brodeur | Liberal | 1901–1904 |
| 10. | Hon. Napoléon Antoine Belcourt | Liberal | 1904–1905 |
| 11. | Hon. Robert Franklin Sutherland | Liberal | 1905–1909 |
| 12. | Hon. Charles Marcil | Liberal | 1909–1911 |
| 13. | Hon. Thomas Simpson Sproule | Conservative | 1911–1915 |
| 14. | Hon. Albert Sévigny | Conservative | 1916–1917 |
| 15. | Hon. Edgar Nelson Rhodes | Conservative | 1917–1922 |
| 16. | Hon. Rodolphe Lemieux | Liberal | 1922–1930 |
| 17. | Hon. George Black | Conservative | 1930–1935 |
| 18. | Hon. James Langstaff Bowman | Conservative | 1935–1936 |
| 19. | Hon. Pierre François Casgrain | Liberal | 1936–1940 |
| 20. | Hon. James Allison Glen | Liberal Progressive | 1940–1945 |
| 21. | Hon. Gaspard Fauteux | Liberal | 1945–1949 |
| 22. | Hon. William Ross Macdonald | Liberal | 1949–1953 |
| 23. | Hon. Louis René Beaudoin | Liberal | 1953–1957 |
| 24. | Hon. Daniel Roland Michener | Progressive Conservative | 1957–1962 |
| 25. | Hon. Marcel-Joseph-Aimé Lambert | Progressive Conservative | 1962–1963 |
| 26. | Hon. Alan A. Macnaughton | Liberal | 1963–1966 |
| 27. | Hon. Lucien Lamoureux | Liberal | 1966–1974 |
| 28. | Hon. James A. Jerome | Liberal | 1974–1979 |
| 29. | Hon. Jeanne Sauvé | Liberal | 1980–1984 |
| 30. | Hon. Lloyd Francis | Liberal | 1984–1984 |
| 31. | Hon. John W. Bosley | Progressive Conservative | 1984–1986 |
| 32. | Hon. John Allen Fraser | Progressive Conservative | 1986–1994 |
| 33. | Hon. Gilbert Parent | Liberal | 1994– |

\* Individual's party affiliation during tenure as Speaker.

# CANADIAN SUPREME COURT JUSTICES

|  | Date of Appointment |  |
|---|---|---|
| **Chief Justice** | | |
| The Rt. Hon. Antonio Lamer | Mar. 28, 1980 | (to Supreme Court) |
| | July 1, 1990 | (Chief Justice) |
| **Puisne Judges** | | |
| Hon. Gerard V. La Forest | Jan. 16, 1985 | |
| Hon. Claire l'Heureux-Dubé | Apr. 15, 1987 | |
| Hon. John Sopinka | May 24, 1988 | |
| Hon. Charles Doherty Gonthier | Feb. 1, 1989 | |
| Hon. Peter de Carteret Cory | Feb. 1, 1989 | |
| Hon. Beverley McLachlin | Mar. 30, 1989 | |
| Hon. Frank Iacobucci | Jan. 7, 1991 | |
| Hon. John C. Major | Nov. 13, 1992 | |

# *CANADIAN BILL OF RIGHTS*
## *S.C. 1960, c. 44*

The Parliament of Canada, affirming that the Canadian Nation is founded upon principles that acknowledge the supremacy of God, the dignity and worth of the human person and the position of the family in a society of free men and free institutions;

Affirming also that men and institutions remain free only when freedom is founded upon respect for moral and spiritual values and the rule of law;

And being desirous of enshrining these principles and the human rights and fundamental freedoms derived from them, in a Bill of Rights which shall reflect the respect of Parliament for its constitutional authority and which shall ensure the protection of these rights and freedoms in Canada:

THEREFORE Her Majesty, by and with the advice and consent of the Senate and House of Commons of Canada, enacts as follows:

## PART I
## BILL OF RIGHTS

1.   It is hereby recognized and declared that in Canada there have existed and shall continue to exist without discrimination by reason of race, national origin, colour, religion or sex, the following human rights and fundamental freedoms, namely,

(a) the right of the individual to life, liberty, security of the person and enjoyment of property, and the right not to be deprived thereof except by due process of law;

(b) the right of the individual to equality before the law and the protection of the law;

(c) freedom of religion;

(d) freedom of speech;

(e) freedom of assembly and association; and

(f) freedom of the press.

2.   Every law of Canada shall, unless it is expressly declared by an Act of the Parliament of Canada that it shall operate notwithstanding the Canadian Bill of Rights, be so construed and applied as not to abrogate, abridge or infringe or to authorize the abrogation, abridgment or infringement of any of the rights or freedoms herein recognized and declared, and in particular, no law of Canada shall be construed or applied so as to

(a) authorize or effect the arbitrary detention, imprisonment or exile of any person;

(b) impose or authorize the imposition of cruel and unusual treatment or punishment;

(c) deprive a person who has been arrested or detained

(i) of the right to be informed promptly of the reason for his arrest or detention,

(ii) of the right to retain and instruct counsel without delay, or

*Source: Canadian Bill of Rights*, Justice Canada. Reproduced with permission of the Minister of Supply and Services Canada, 1994.

(iii) of the remedy by way of *habeas corpus* for the determination of the validity of his detention and for his release if the detention is not lawful;

(d) authorize a court, tribunal, commission, board or other authority to compel a person to give evidence if he is denied counsel, protection against self crimination or other constitutional safeguards;

(e) deprive a person of the right to a fair hearing in accordance with the principles of fundamental justice for the determination of his rights and obligations;

(f) deprive a person charged with a criminal offence of the right to be presumed innocent until proved guilty according to law in a fair and public hearing by an independent and impartial tribunal, or of the right to reasonable bail without just cause; or

(g) deprive a person of the right to the assistance of an interpreter in any proceedings in which he is involved or in which he is a party or a witness, before a court, commission, board or other tribunal, if he does not understand or speak the language in which such proceedings are conducted.

**3.** (1) Subject to subsection (2), the Minister of Justice shall, in accordance with such regulations as may be prescribed by the Governor in Council, examine every regulation transmitted to the Clerk of the Privy Council for registration pursuant to the *Statutory Instruments Act* and every Bill introduced in or presented to the House of Commons by a Minister of the Crown, in order to ascertain whether any of the provisions thereof are inconsistent with the purposes and provisions of this Part and he shall report any such inconsistency to the House of Commons at the first convenient opportunity.

(2) A regulation need not be examined in accordance with subsection (1) if prior to being made it was examined as a proposed regulation in accordance with section 3 of the *Statutory Instruments Act* to ensure that it was not inconsistent with the purposes and provisions of this Part. (1)

**4.** The provisions of this Part shall be known as the *Canadian Bill of Rights*.

**5.** (1) Nothing in Part I shall be construed to abrogate or abridge any human right or fundamental freedom not enumerated therein that may have existed in Canada at the commencement of this Act.

(2) The expression "law of Canada" in Part I means an Act of the Parliament of Canada enacted before or after the coming into force of this Act, any order, rule or regulation thereunder, and any law in force in Canada or in any part of Canada at the commencement of this Act that is subject to be repealed, abolished or altered by the Parliament of Canada.

(3) The provisions of Part I shall be construed as extending only to matters coming with the legislative authority of the Parliament of Canada.

(1) Section 3 was repealed and replaced by S.C. 1985, c. 26, s. 105.

# REFERENCES

ABERCROMBIE, NICHOLAS, STEPHEN HILL, and BRYAN TURNER. 1980. *The Dominant Ideology Thesis*. London: George Allen and Unwin.

ADIE, R., and P. THOMAS. 1987. *Canadian Public Aministration*. Scarborough, Ont.: Prentice-Hall Canada.

ANDERSON, DORIS. 1991. *The Unfinished Revolution*. Toronto: Doubleday Canada.

ARCHER, K. 1991. "The New Democrats, Organized Labour and the Prospects of Electoral Reform." In Herman Bakvis, ed., *Canadian Political Parties: Leaders, Candidates and Organization* (pp. 313–45). Toronto: Dundurn Press.

ATKINSON, MICHAEL. 1990. "Parliamentary Government in Canada." In Michael Whittington and Glen Williams, eds., *Canadian Politics in the 1990s* (pp. 336–58). Scarborough, Ont.: Nelson Canada.

ATKINSON, MICHAEL, and GRAHAM WHITE. 1980. "The Development of Provincial Legislatures." In Harold Clarke, ed., *Parliament, Policy and Representation* (pp. 255–75). Toronto: Methuen.

AUCOIN, P. 1991. "Cabinet Government in Canada: Corporate Management of a Confederate Executive." In C. Campbell and M.J. Wyszomirski, eds., *Executive Leadership in Anglo-American Systems* (pp. 139–59). Pittsburgh: University of Pittsburgh Press.

AXWORTHY, THOMAS. 1991. "Capital-Intensive Politics: Money, Media and Mores in the United States and Canada." In F.L. Siedle, ed., *Issues in Party and Election Finance in Canada*, Vol. 5 of the research studies of the Royal Commission on Electoral Reform and Party Financing (pp. 172–225). Ottawa and Toronto: Dundurn Press.

BAKVIS, H. 1991. *Regional Ministers: Power and Influence in the Canadian Cabinet*. Toronto: University of Toronto Press.

BANTING, K.G. 1987. "The Welfare State and Inequality in the 1980s." *Canadian Review of Sociology and Anthropology* 24: 309–38.

BECK, P.A. 1977. "The Role of Agents in Political Socialization." In Stanley Allen Renshon, ed., *Handbook of Political Socialization: Theory and Research* (pp. 115–41). New York: Free Press.

BELL, D., and L. TEPPERMAN. 1979. *The Roots of Disunity: A Look at Canadian Political Culture*. Toronto: McClelland & Stewart.

BELLAMY, D., J. PAMMETT, and D. ROWAT, eds. 1976. *The Provincial Political Systems*. Toronto: Methuen.

BIBBY, R.W., and D.C. POSTERSKI. 1985. *The Emerging Generation*. Toronto: Irwin Publishing.

BLACK, E.R. 1982. *Politics and the News*. Toronto: Butterworths.

BLACK, J. H. 1984. "Revisiting the Effects of Canvassing on Voting Behaviour." *Canadian Journal of Political Science* 17: 351–74.

BLAIS, A., and R.K. CARTY. 1987. "The Impact of Electoral Formulae on the Creation of Majority Governments." *Electoral Studies* 6: 209–18.

BLAKE, D. 1982. "The Consistency of Inconsistency: Party Identification in Federal and Provincial Politics." *Canadian Journal of Political Science* 11 (December): 691–710.

BLISS, J. MICHAEL, ed. 1966. *Canadian History in Documents, 1763–1966*. Toronto: Ryerson Press.

BOARDMAN, R. 1992. *Canadian Environmental Policy*. Toronto: Oxford University Press.

BOWDEN, F. 1983. *Canadian Industrialization*. Toronto: McGraw-Hill Ryerson.

BOYER, J.P. 1981. *Political Rights*. Toronto: Butterworths.

———. 1987. *Election Law in Canada: The Law and Procedure of Federal, Provincial, and Territorial Elections*, Vols. 1 and 2. Toronto: Butterworths.

BRADSHAW, L. 1991. "Political Rule, Prudence and the 'Woman Question' in Aristotle." *Canadian Journal of Political Science* 24, no. 3 (September): 557–73.

BRAZIER, RODNEY. 1989. *Constitutional and Administrative Law*, 6th ed. Harmondsworth: Penguin Books.

BRIERLY, J.L. 1968. *The Law of Nations*. New York: Oxford University Press.

BROOKS, STEPHEN, and ANDREW STRITCH. 1991. *Business and Government in Canada*. Scarborough, Ont.: Prentice-Hall Canada.

BROWN-JOHN, C. LLOYD, A. LEBLOND, and B. MARSON. 1988. *Public Financial Management: A Canadian Text*. Scarborough, Ont.: Nelson Canada.

BROWNSEY, KEITH, and MICHAEL HOWLETT. 1992. *The Provincial State Politics in Canada's Provinces and Territories*. Mississauga, Ont.: Copp Clark Pitman.

BRYDEN, KENNETH. 1982. "Public Input into Policy-Making and Administration." *Canadian Public Administration* 25 (Spring): 94–105.

BRYDEN, PHILIP, STEVEN DAVIS, and JOHN RUSSELL. 1993. *The Charter*. Toronto: University of Toronto Press.

BRYM, R., ed. 1986. *Regionalism in Canada*. Toronto: Irwin Publishing.

BURGESS, E.W. 1925. "The Growth of the City." In R.E. Park, E.W. Burgess, and R.D. McKenzie, eds., *The City* (pp. 44–61). Chicago: University of Chicago Press.

BURT, SANDRA. 1990. "Rethinking Canadian Politics: The Impact of Gender." In Michael Whittington and Glen Williams, eds., *Canadian Politics in the 1990s*, 3rd ed. (pp. 208–20). Toronto: Nelson Canada.

CAIRNS, ALAN. 1968. "The Electoral System and the Party System in Canada." *Canadian Journal of Political Science* 1 (March): 55–80.

———. 1970. "The Living Canadian Constitution." *Queen's Quarterly* 77, no. 4 (Winter): 483–98.

CAMPBELL, COLIN, and GEORGE SZABLOWSKI. 1979. *The Superbureaucrats: Structure and Behaviour in Central Agencies*. Toronto: Macmillan.

Canada. 1986. Task Force on Broadcasting Policy. *Report*. Ottawa: Supply and Services Canada.

Canadian Bar Association. 1978. *Towards a New Canada* (pp. 34–35). Ottawa: Canadian Bar Association.

Canadian Federation of Mayors and Municipalities. 1976. *Puppets on a Shoestring*. Ottawa (April 28).

CARDINAL, H. 1969. *The Unjust Society: The Tragedy of Canada's Indians*. Edmonton: Hurtig.

Carleton School of Journalism. 1979. CBC Poll, 30 April to 10 May 1979. Ottawa.

CARMICHAEL, C.M. 1990. "Economic Conditions and the Popularity of the Incumbent Party in Canada." *Canadian Journal of Political Science* 23: 713–26.

CARTY, K. 1988. "Three Canadian Party Systems: An Interpretation of the Development of National Politics." In George Perlin, ed., *Party Democracy in Canada: The Politics of National Party Conventions*, (pp. 15–30). Scarborough, Ont.: Prentice-Hall Canada.

CAYLEY, DAVID. 1991. *The Age of Ecology*. Toronto: James Lorimer.

CHEFFINS, R.I., and P.A. JOHNSON. 1986. *The Revised Canadian Constitution*. Toronto: McGraw-Hill Ryerson.

CHRISTENSON, R.M., et al. 1971. *Ideologies and Modern Politics*. New York: Dodd, Mead.

CHRISTIAN, W. 1991. "Some News Just Isn't Fit to Print." *Globe and Mail* (February 12): A17.

CHRISTIAN, W., and C. CAMPBELL. 1990. *Political Parties and Ideologies in Canada*. Toronto: McGraw-Hill Ryerson.

CLARK, S.D. 1968. *The Developing Canadian Community*. Toronto: University of Toronto Press.

CLARKE, H., et al. 1991. *Absent Mandate: Interpreting Change in Canadian Elections*, 2nd ed. Toronto: Gage.

CLEMENT, W. 1975. *The Canadian Corporate Elite*. Toronto: McClelland & Stewart.

CODY, HOWARD. 1977. "The Evolution of Federal-Provincial Relations in Canada: Some Reflections." *American Review of Canadian Studies* 7, no. 1 (Spring): 55–83.

COLEMAN, W, and H.J. JACEK. 1983. "The Roles and Activities of Business Interest Associations in Canada." *Canadian Journal of Political Science* 16: 257–80.

COLLINS, R. 1990. *Culture, Communication and National Identity*. Toronto: University of Toronto Press.

CONVERSE, P. 1964. "The Nature of Belief Systems in Mass Publics." In David Apter, ed., *Ideology and Discontent* (pp. 206–61). New York: Free Press.

CONWAY, J.F. 1978. "Explaining the Roots of Canada's Third Parties." *Canadian Journal of Political Science* 11, no. 1 (March): 99–124.

COURTNEY, J. 1978. "Recognition of Canadian Political Parties in Parliament and in Law." *Canadian Journal of Political Science* 11: 33–60.

———. 1980. "Reflections on Reforming the Canadian Electoral System." *Canadian Public Administration* 23, no. 3 (Fall): 427–57.

COURTNEY, J.C., P. MACKINNON, and D. SMITH. 1992. *Drawing Boundaries: Legislatures, Courts and Electoral Values*. Saskatoon, Sask.: Fifth House.

CREIGHTON, D. 1966. *John A. Macdonald*. Toronto: Macmillan.

CREPEAU, PAUL A., and JOHN E.C. BRIERLY. 1981. *Code Civil—Civil Code: 1866–1980*. Montreal: Quebec Research Centre of Private and Comparative Law.

CROUSE, TIMOTHY. 1974. *The Boys on the Bus*. New York: Ballantine.

DAHL, R. 1957. "The Concept of Power." *Behavioural Science* 2 (July): 201–15.

D'AQUINO, T. 1984. "The Public Service of Canada: The Case for Political Neutrality." *Canadian Public Administration* 27, no.1 (Spring): 14–23.

DAWSON, R.M. 1933. *Constitutional Issues in Canada, 1900–1933*. London: Oxford University Press.

———. 1947. *The Government of Canada*. Toronto: University of Toronto Press.

Decima Research. 1986. *The Decima Quarterly Report* 12, no. 2 (Summer).

DEUTSCH, K. 1967. "On the Concept of Politics and Power." *Journal of International Affairs* 21, no. 2: 334.

DICKSON, J. 1984. In *Hunter v. Southam Inc.*, 2 S.C.R., 145 at 155.

DOBELL, W.M. 1986. "Updating Duverger's Law." *Canadian Journal of Political Science* 19, no. 3 (September): 585–95.

DOER, A.D. 1982. "The Role of Coloured Papers." *Canadian Public Administration* 25 (Fall): 370–76.

DOERN, G. BRUCE, ALLAN MASLOVE, and MICHAEL PRINCE. 1988. *Public Budetging in Canada*. Ottawa: Carleton University Press.

DOERN, G. BRUCE, and RICHARD W. PHIDD. 1983. *Canadian Public Policy: Ideas, Structures and Process*. Toronto: Methuen.

DOERN, G. BRUCE, and BRIAN W. TOMLIN. 1991. *Faith and Fear: The Free Trade Story*. Toronto: Stoddart.

DWIVEDI, O.P. 1982. *The Administrative State in Canada*. Toronto: University of Toronto Press.

DYE, THOMAS R. 1978. *Understanding Public Policy*. Englewood Cliffs, N.J.: Prentice-Hall.

———. 1984. *Understanding Public Policy*, 5th ed. Englewood Cliffs, N.J.: Prentice-Hall.

EASTON, D. 1965. *A Framework for Political Analysis*. Englewood Cliffs, N.J.: Prentice-Hall.

EASTON, D., and J. DENNIS. 1969. *Children in the Political System*. New York: McGraw-Hill.

Economic Council of Canada. 1981. *Reforming Regulation*. Ottawa.

ELKINS, D., and RICHARD SIMEON, eds. 1980. *Small Worlds: Provinces and Parties in Canadian Political Life.* Toronto: Methuen.

ERIKSON, L., and R.K. CARTY. 1991. "Parties and Candidate Selection in the 1988 Canadian General Election." *Canadian Journal of Political Science* 24: 331–49.

FITSGERALD, P., and K. MCSHANE. 1982. *Looking at Law: Canada's Legal System,* 2nd ed. Ottawa: Bybooks.

FLETCHER, F. 1987. "The Mass Media and the Selection of National Party Leaders: Some Explanations." In George Perlin, ed., *Party Democracy in Canada* (pp. 97–123). Scarborough, Ont.: Prentice-Hall Canada.

FLETCHER, F., and D. TARAS. 1990. "Images and Issues: The Mass Media and Politics in Canada." In Michael Whittington and Glen Williams, eds., *Canadian Politics in the 1990s,* 3rd ed. (pp. 221–46). Scarborough, Ont.: Nelson Canada.

FORSEY, EUGENE. 1985. "The Role and Position of the Monarch in Canada." In Ronald Landes, ed., *Canadian Politics: A Comparative Reader* (pp. 53–62). Scarborough, Ont.: Prentice-Hall Canada.

FOUCAULT, M. 1980. *Power/Knowledge: Selected Interviews and Other Writings 1927–1977.* Colin Gordon, trans. New York: Pantheon.

FRANK, B. 1987. "Hegemonic Heterosexual Masculinity." *Studies in Political Economy* 24 (Autumn): 159–70.

FRANKS, C.E.S. 1987. *The Parliament of Canada.* Toronto: University of Toronto Press.

FRIEDMAN, M., and R. FRIEDMAN. 1980. *Free to Choose.* New York: Harcourt Brace Jovanovich.

FRISKEN, F. 1986. "Canadian Cities and the American Example: A Prologue to Urban Policy Analysis." *Canadian Public Administration* 29: 345–97.

GABOR, T., and E. GOTTHEIL. 1984. "Offender Characteristics and Spatial Mobility: An Empirical Study and Some Policy Implications." *Canadian Journal of Criminology* 26: 267–81.

GALBRAITH, J.K. 1967. *The New Industrial State.* Boston: Houghton Mifflin.

GALIPEAU, C. 1989. "Political Parties, Interest Groups, and New Social Movements." In Alain Gagnon and Brian Tanguay, eds., *Canadian Parties in Transition* (pp. 404–26). Scarborough, Ont.: Nelson Canada.

GALLUP, G. 1965. "Polls and the Political Process—Past, Present, and Future." *Public Opinion Quarterly* (Winter): 544–49.

GÉRIN-LAJOIE, PAUL. 1950. *Constitutional Amendment in Canada.* Toronto: University of Toronto Press.

GERTLER, L., and R. CROWLEY. 1977. *Changing Canadian Cities: The Next 25 Years.* Toronto: McClelland & Stewart.

GIBBINS, ROGER. 1989. "The Prairie Provinces." In Michael Whittington and Glen Williams, eds., *Canadian Politics in the 1990s* (pp. 60–75). Scarborough, Ont.: Nelson Canada.

GIDENGIL, E. 1992. "Canada Votes: A Quarter Century of Canadian National Election Studies." *Canadian Journal of Political Science* 25. no. 2 (June): 219–48.

GRABB, EDWARD. 1988. "Conceptual Issues in the Study of Social Inequality." In J. Curtis, E. Grabb, N. Guppy, and L. Gibbert, eds., *Social Inequality in Canada: Patterns, Problems and Policies* (Chapter I). Scarborough, Ont.: Prentice-Hall Canada.

GRACEY, D.P. 1985. "The Real Issues on the Crown Corporations Debate." In Kenneth Kernaghan, ed., *Public Administration in Canada: Selected Readings,* 5th ed. (pp. 122–40). Toronto: Methuen.

GRANT, G. 1965. *Lament for a Nation.* Toronto: McClelland & Stewart.

GUEST, A. 1969. "The Applicability of Burgess' Zonal Hypothesis to Urban Canada." *Demography* 6: 271–77.

GUIDON, H. 1964. "Social Unrest, Social Class and Quebec's Bureaucratic Revolution." *Queen's Quarterly* 71: 150–62.

GUPPY, N., S. FREEMAN, and S. BUCHAN. "Representing Canadians: Changes in the Economic Backgrounds of Federal Politicians, 1965-1984." *Canadian Review of Sociology and Anthropology* 24: 417–30.

GWYN, RICHARD. 1980. *The Northern Magus*. Toronto: McClelland & Stewart.

HARE, K. 1968. "Canada." In John Wartenkin, ed., *Canada: A Geographical Interpretation* (pp. 3–12). Toronto: Methuen.

HARMON, M., and R. MAYER. 1986. *Organization Theory for Public Administration*. Boston: Little, Brown.

HARRIS, C.D., and E.L. ULLMAN. 1945. "The Nature of Cities." *Annals of the American Academy of Political and Social Science* 242: 7.

HEARD, ANDREW. 1991. *Canadian Constitutional Conventions: The Marriage of Law and Politics*. Toronto: Oxford University Press.

HIGGINS, D.J.H. 1986. *Local and Urban Politics in Canada*. Toronto: Gage Educational Publishing.

HODGETTS, J.E. 1955. *Pioneer Public Service: An Administrative History of the United Canadas, 1841–1867*. Toronto: University of Toronto Press.

HODGINS, B.W. 1955. "Attitudes Toward Democracy During the Pre-Confederation Decade." M.A. thesis, Queen's University.

HOGAN, G. 1963. *The Conservative in Canada*. Toronto: McClelland & Stewart.

HOGG, P.W. 1985. *Responsible Government: Constitutional Law of Canada*, 2nd ed., Toronto: Carswell.

————. 1992. *Constitutional Law of Canada*. Toronto: Carswell.

HOLSTI, K.J. 1988. *International Politics: A Framework for Analysis*. Englewood Cliffs, N.J.: Prentice-Hall.

HOYT, H. 1939. *The Structure and Growth of Urban Areas*. Washington, D.C.: Federal Housing Authority.

HUNTER, A.A. 1982. "On Class, Status, and Voting in Canada." *Canadian Journal of Sociology* 7: 19–39.

INNIS, H. 1951. *The Bias of Communication*. Toronto: University of Toronto Press.

IONESCU, GHITA, and ISABEL DE MADARIAGA. 1972. *Opposition*. Harmondsworth: Penguin.

IRVINE, W.P. 1980. *Does Canada Need a New Electoral System?*, 2nd ed. Kingston: Queen's University Institute of Intergovernmental Relations.

IYENGAR, S. 1987. "Television News and Citizens' Expectations of National Affairs." *American Political Science Review* 81 (September): 815–31.

JACKSON, ROBERT, and MICHAEL ATKINSON. 1980. *The Canadian Legislative System*, 2nd rev. ed. Toronto: Gage.

JACKSON, R., D. JACKSON, and N. BAXTER-MOORE. 1986. *Politics in Canada*. Scarborough, Ont.: Prentice-Hall Canada.

JOHNSON, M., and K. ARCHER. 1988. "Inflation, Unemployment and Canadian Federal Voting Behaviour." *Canadian Journal of Political Science* 19, no. 3 (September): 569–84.

JONES, D.P., and A.S. DE VILLARS. 1985. *Principles of Administrative Law*. Toronto: Carswell.

KENNEDY, L.W. 1983. *The Urban Kaleidoscope: Canadian Perspectives*. Toronto: McGraw-Hill Ryerson.

KERNAGHAN, K., and J. LANGFORD. 1990. *The Responsible Public Servant*. Toronto: Institute of Public Administration of Canada; Halifax: Institute for Research on Public Policy.

KERNAGHAN, K., and DAVID SIEGAL. 1991. *Public Administration in Canada*. Scarborough, Ont.: Nelson Canada.

KESTERTON, W.A. 1967. *A History of Journalism in Canada*. Toronto: McClelland & Stewart.

KEY, V.O., JR. 1961. *Public Opinion and American Democracy*. New York: Knopf.

————. 1966. *The Responsible Electorate*. Cambridge, Mass.: Harvard University Press.

KIRK, R. 1960. *The Conservative Mind*, rev. ed. Chicago: Henry Regnery.

KIRK, R., ed. 1982. *The Portable Conservative Reader*. New York: Penguin.

KOPINAK, KATHRYN. 1985. "Women in Canadian Municipal Politics: Two Steps Forward, One Step Back." *Canadian Review of Sociology and Anthropology* 22: 394–410.

————. 1987. "Gender Differences in Political Ideology in Canada." *Canadian Review of Sociology and Anthropology* 24: 23–38.

KORNBERG, ALLAN, JOEL SMITH, and HAROLD CLARKE. 1979. *Citizen Politicians—Canada: Party Officials in a Democratic Society.* Durham, N.C.: Carolina Academic Press.

KORNBERG, ALLAN, WILLIAM MISHLER, and H.D. CLARKE. 1982. *Representative Democracy in the Canadian Provinces.* Scarborough, Ont: Prentice-Hall Canada.

KRAHN, H., and L.W. KENNEDY. 1985. "Producing Personal Safety: The Effects of Crime Rates, Police Force Size and Fear of Crime." *Criminology* 23: 697–710.

KRASHINSKY, M., and W.J. MILNE. 1985. "Additional Evidence on the Effect of Incumbency in Canadian Elections." *Canadian Journal of Political Science* 18: 155–65.

KRUEGER, R., and R. CORDER. 1982. *Canada: A New Geography.* Toronto: Holt, Rinehart and Winston of Canada.

LAFRAMBOISE, H.L. 1983. "The Uncomfortable Bedfellows of Accountability." *Canadian Public Administration* 26 (Fall): 325–43.

LALONDE, MARK. 1971. "The Changing Role of the Prime Minister's Office." *Canadian Public Administration* 14, no. 4 (Winter): 509–37.

LAMBERT, R., J. CURTIS, S. BROWN, and B. KAY. 1987. "Social Class Left/Right Political Orientations and Subjunctive Class Voting in Provincial and Federal Elections." *Canadian Review of Sociology and Anthropology* 24, no. 4: 526–49.

LAMBERT, W., A. YACKLEY, and R. HEIN. 1971. "Child Training Values of English Canadian and French Canadian Parents." *Canadian Journal of Behavioural Science* 3: 217–36.

LASSWELL, H. 1936. *Politics: Who Gets What, When, and How?* New York: McGraw-Hill.

LAUNDY, P. 1984. *The Office of Speaker in the Parliaments of the Commonwealth.* London: Quiller Press.

LAUX, J., and M. MALOT. 1988. *State Capitalism: Public Enterprise in Canada.* Ithaca, N.Y.: Cornell University Press.

Law Reform Commission of Canada. 1977. *A Catalogue of Discretionary Powers in the Revised Statutes of Canada.* Ottawa: Information Canada.

LEDOUX, D. 1980. *Commissions of Inquiry Under the Inquiries Act, Part 1: 1967 to Date.* Ottawa: Library of Parliament.

LEDUC, L. 1990. "The Changeable Canadian Voter." In Alan Frizzell, Jon Pammett, and Anthony Westall, eds., *The Canadian General Election of 1988* (pp. 103–113). Ottawa: Carleton University.

LEDUC, L., and R. PRICE. 1985. "Great Debates: The Televised Leadership Debates of 1979." *Canadian Journal of Political Science* 18, no. 1 (March): 135–53.

LEVITT, J. 1969. "Henri Bourassa and Modern Industrial Society, 1900–1914." *The Canadian Historical Review* 50: 37–50.

LEVY, G., and G. WHITE, eds. 1989. *Provincial and Territorial Legislatures in Canada.* Toronto: University of Toronto Press.

LIPSET, S.M. 1964. "Canada and the United States: A Comparative View." *Canadian Review of Sociology and Anthropology* 1: 173–85.

————. 1986. "Historical Traditions and National Characteristics: A Comparative Analysis of Canada and the United States." *Canadian Journal of Sociology* 11 no. 2: 133–55.

LOWER, A.R.M. 1977. *Colony to Nation: A History of Canada.* Toronto: Macmillan Canada.

LUCAS, C., ed. 1912. *The Durham Report.* Toronto: Oxford University Press.

McCORMICK, PETER. 1991. "Canada Needs a 'Triple E' Senate." In Paul Fox and Graham White, eds., *Politics: Canada*, 7th ed. (pp. 435–39). Toronto: McGraw-Hill Ryerson.

———. 1994. *Canada's Courts*. Toronto: James Lorimer.

McCORMICK, P., and I. GREENE. 1990. *Inside the Judicial System: Judges and Judging*. Toronto: James Lorimer.

MACDONALD, D.C. 1991. "Election Finances Legislation in Canada." In Hugh Throburn, ed., *Party Politics in Canada*, 6th ed. (pp. 68–79). Scarborough, Ont.: Prentice-Hall.

MACGUIGAN, MARK. 1978. "Parliamentary Reform: Impediments to an Enlarged Role for the Backbencher." *Legislative Studies Quarterly* 3 (November): 671–82.

MACLELLAN, M. 1971. "The History of Women's Rights in Canada." In *Cultural Tradition and Political History of Women in Canada*, Studies of the Royal Commission on the Status of Women in Canada, no. 8 (pp. 1–31). Ottawa: Information Canada.

McLUHAN, M. 1964. *Understanding Media: The Extensions of Man*. New York: Mentor Books.

MACPHERSON, C.B. 1965. *The Real World Of Democracy*. Toronto: Canadian Broadcasting Corporation.

MACRIDIS, R.C. 1983. *Contemporary Political Ideologies*, 2nd ed. Boston: Little, Brown.

———. 1992. *Contempory Political Ideologies*, 5th ed., New York: HarperCollins.

McWHINNEY, EDWARD. 1957. "Prerogative Powers of the Head of State." *Canadian Bar Review* (January): 92–96.

MAINGOT, JOSEPH. 1982. *Parliamentary Privilege in Canada*. Toronto: Carswell.

MAITLAND, F.W. 1908. *The Constitutional History of England*. Cambridge: Cambridge University Press.

MAKUCH, S.M. 1983. *Canadian Municipal and Planning Law*. Toronto: Carswell.

MALLORY, JAMES. 1984. *The Structure of Canadian Government*. Toronto: Gage Educational Publishing.

MANDEL, M. 1989. *The Charter of Rights and Freedoms and the Legalization of Politics in Canada*. Toronto: Wall & Thomson.

MARCHAK, M.P. 1988. *Ideological Perspectives on Canada*, 3rd ed. Toronto: McGraw-Hill Ryerson.

MARCUSE, H. 1964. *One-Dimensional Man*. Boston: Beacon Press.

MATTHEWS, RALPH. 1983. *The Creation of Regional Dependency*. Toronto: University of Toronto Press.

MEISEL, J. 1986. "Escaping Extinction: Cultural Defence of an Undefended Border." *Canadian Journal of Political and Social Theory* 10, no. 1–2: 248–65.

MICHELS, R. 1959. *Political Parties*. New York: Dover Publications; first published in 1915.

MILL, J.S. 1958. *Considerations on Representative Government*. Indianapolis: Bobbs-Merrill.

MILNE, DAVID. 1986. *Tug of War: Ottawa and the Provinces under Trudeau and Mulroney*. Toronto: James Lorimer.

———. 1990. "Canada's Constitutional Odyssey." In Michael Whittington and Glen Williams, eds., *Canadian Politics in the 1990s*, 3rd ed., (pp. 313–35). Toronto: Nelson Canada.

MISHLER, W., and H. CLARKE. 1990. "Political Participation in Canada." In Michael Whittington and Glen Williams, eds., *Canadian Politics in the 1990s*, 3rd ed. (pp. 158–81). Scarborough: Nelson Canada.

MITTELSTAEDT, M. 1988. "World Learns to Love Multinationals." *Globe and Mail*, October 20, B32.

MONAHAN, PATRICK. 1987. *Politics and the Constitution: The Charter, Federalism and the Supreme Court of Canada*. Toronto: Carswell.

MONAHAN, PATRICK, and KEN McROBERTS. 1993. *The Charlottetown Accord*. Toronto: University of Toronto Press.

MOORE, M., J.H. PERRY, and D.I. BEACH. 1966. *The Financing of Canadian Federalism: The First Hundred Years*. Toronto: Canadian Tax Foundation.

MORTON, D. 1983. *A Short History of Canada*. Toronto: McClelland & Stewart.

————. 1986. *The New Democrats, 1961–1986: The Politics of Change*. Toronto: Copp Clark Pitman.

MORTON, F.L., ed. 1984. *Law, Politics and the Judicial Process in Canada*. Calgary: University of Calgary Press.

MORTON, W.L. 1950. *The Progressive Party in Canada*. Toronto: University of Toronto Press.

MUNTON, DON, and JOHN KIRTON. 1992. *Canadian Foreign Policy: Selected Cases*. Scarborough, Ont.: Prentice-Hall Canada.

*National Election Study*. 1989. Toronto: Institute of Social Research, York University.

NEVITTE, N., H. BAKVIS, and R. GIBBINS. 1989. "The Ideological Contours of 'New Politics' in Canada: Policy, Mobilization and Partisan Support." *Canadian Journal of Political Science* 22, no. 3 (September): 475–504.

NEWMAN, P.C. 1963. *Renegade in Power*. Toronto: McClelland & Stewart.

OAKESHOTT, M. 1991 (1962). "On Being Conservative." In Terence Ball and Richard Dagger, eds., *Ideals and Ideologies: A Reader* (pp. 154–62). New York: HarperCollins.

OLSEN, D. 1980. *The State Elite*. Toronto: McClelland & Stewart.

ORNSTEIN, MICHAEL. 1986. "Regionalism and Canadian Political Ideology." In Robert Brym, ed., *Regionalism in Canada*. Toronto: Irwin.

OSBALDESTON, G.F. 1989. *Keeping Deputy Ministers Accountable*. Scarborough, Ont.: McGraw-Hill Ryerson.

PAGE, B.I., R. SHAPIRO, and G.R. DEMPSEY. 1987. "What Moves Public Opinion?" *American Political Science Review* 81 (March): 23–44.

PAL, LESLIE, and DAVID TARAS, eds. 1988. *Prime Ministers and Premiers: Political Leadership and Public Policy in Canada*. Scarborough, Ont.: Prentice-Hall Canada.

PAMMETT, J.H. 1987. "Class Voting and Class Consciousness in Canada." *Canadian Review of Sociology and Anthropology* 24: 269–90.

————. 1991. "Voting Turnout in Canada." In Herman Bakvis, ed., *Voter Turnout in Canada* (pp. 713–20). Toronto: Dundurn Press.

PAMMETT, J.H., and JEAN-LUC PÉPIN, eds. 1988. *Political Education in Canada*. Halifax: The Institute for Research on Public Policy.

PAMMETT, J.H., and M. WHITTINGTON. 1976. *The Foundations of Political Culture: Political Socialization in Canada*. Toronto: Macmillan of Canada.

PANITCH, LEO. 1988. "Corporatism: A Growth Industry Reaches the Monopoly State." *Canadian Journal of Political Science* 21: 813–18.

————. 1990. "Elites, Classes, and Power in Canada." In Michael Whittington and Glen Williams, eds., *Canadian Politics in the 1990s.*, 3rd ed. (pp. 183–207). Toronto: Nelson Canada.

PANITCH, L., and D. SWARTZ. 1988. *The Assault on Trade Union Freedoms*. Toronto: Garamond Press.

PELLETIER, R., F. BUNDOCK, and M. SARRA-BOURNET. 1991. "The Structures of Political Parties." In Herman Bakvis, ed., *Canadian Political Parties, Leaders, Candidates and Organizations* (pp. 265–311). Toronto: Dundurn Press.

PERLIN, G.C. 1980. *The Tory Syndrome: Leadership Politics in the Progressive Conservative Party*. Montreal and Kingston: McGill-Queen's University Press.

PLUNKETT, T.J. 1968. *Urban Canada and its Government*. Toronto: Macmillan of Canada.

PLUNKETT, T.J., and G.M. BETTS. 1978. *The Management of Canadian Urban Government*. Kingston: Institute of Local Government, Queen's University.

POPE, JOSEPH, ed. 1895. *Confederation: Being a Series of Hitherto Unpublished Documents Bearing on the British North America Act*. Toronto.

PORTER, J. 1965. *The Vertical Mosaic: An Analysis of Social Class and Power in Canada.* Toronto: University of Toronto Press.

POSGATE, DALE, and KENNETH MCROBERTS. 1976. *Quebec: Social Change and Political Crisis.* Toronto: McClelland & Stewart.

PREECE, R. 1984. "The Political Wisdom of John A. Macdonald." *Canadian Journal of Political Science* 7 (September): 459–86.

PRIEST, G.E. 1983. "1981 Census Population (Part 4): Housing Highlights." *Canadian Statistical Review* (September): xiii–xxi.

PRITCHARD, R., ed. 1983. *Crown Corporations in Canada.* Toronto: Butterworths.

PROSS, A.P. 1975. *Pressure Group Behaviour in Canadian Politics.* Toronto: McGraw-Hill Ryerson.

———. 1985. "Parliamentary Influence and Diffusion of Power." *Canadian Journal of Political Science* 27, no. 2 (June): 235–66.

REDEKOP, J. H. 1983. *Approaches to Canadian Politics,* 3rd ed. Scarborough, Ont.: Prentice-Hall Canada.

REESOR, BAYNARD. 1992. *The Canadian Constitution in Historical Perspective.* Scarborough, Ont.: Prentice-Hall Canada.

ROBERTSON, R.G. 1971. "The Changing Role of the Privy Council Office." *Canadian Public Administration* 14, no. 4: 487–508.

ROBIN, MARTIN. 1991. *Shades of Right: Nativist and Fascist Politics in Canada, 1920–1940.* Toronto: University of Toronto Press.

ROSE, RICHARD. 1991. *International Almanac of Electoral History,* 3rd ed. Washington, D.C.: Congressional Quarterly.

ROSS, W.D., ed. 1924. *The Works of Aristotle.* Vol. XI, *Rhetorica,* trans. W.R. Roberts. Oxford: Oxford University Press.

RUSSELL, PETER. 1987. *The Judiciary in Canada: The Third Branch of Government.* Toronto: McGraw-Hill Ryerson.

RUTHERFORD, P. 1978. *The Making of the Canadian Media.* Toronto: McGraw-Hill Ryerson.

———. 1990. *When Television Was Young: Primetime Canada 1952–1967.* Toronto: University of Toronto Press.

SAVOIE, D. 1990. *The Politics of Public Spending in Canada.* Toronto: University of Toronto Press.

SAYWELL, J.T. 1957. *The Office of Lieutenant-Governor.* Toronto: University of Toronto Press.

SCOTT, FRANK R. 1977. *Essays on the Constitution: Aspects of Canadian Law and Politics.* Toronto: University of Toronto Press.

SHACKLETON, D. 1977. *Power Town: Democracy Discarded.* Toronto: McClelland & Stewart.

SIEGEL, A. 1983. *Politics and the Media in Canada.* Toronto: McGraw-Hill Ryerson.

SIMEON, R. 1976 "The 'Overload Thesis' and Canadian Government." *Canadian Public Policy* 11, no. 4: 541–52.

SIMEON, R., and D. ELKINS. 1974. "Regional Political Cultures in Canada." *Canadian Journal of Political Science* 7: 397–437.

SMITH, A.D. 1979. *Nationalism in the Twentieth Century.* Oxford: Martin Robertson.

SMITH, D.E. 1975. "An Analysis of Ideological Structures and How Women Are Excluded: Considerations for Academic Women." *Canadian Review of Sociology and Anthropology* 12, no. 4: 353–69.

SMITH, G. 1891. *Canada and the Canadian Question.* London: Macmillan.

SMITH, J. 1983. "The Origins of Judicial Review in Canada." *Canadian Journal of Political Science* 16 (March): 115–34.

SMITHERMAN, V., D. MILNE, and SATADAL DASGUPTA, eds. 1982. *The Garden Transformed, 1945–1980.* Charlottetown, P.E.I.: Ragweed Press.

SNEDDON, B. 1979. "The Westminster Convention and the Speaker." *The Parliamentarian* 60, no. 3: 129–32.

SNELL, J.G., and F. VAUGHAN. 1985. *The Supreme Court of Canada.* Toronto: University of Toronto Press.

STARK, A. 1992. "Political Discourse: Analysis and Debate over Canada's Lobbying Legislation." *Canadian Journal of Political Science* 25: 513–24.

STARKE, F.A., et al. 1990. *Introduction to Canadian Business,* 4th ed. Toronto: Allyn and Bacon.

Statistics Canada. 1991a. *Household Facilities and Equipment,* Catalogue 64-202. Ottawa.

———. 1991b. *National Overview: Population and Dwelling Counts.* Ottawa.

STEINBERG, STEPHEN. 1981. *The Ethnic Myth: Race, Ethnicity, and Class in America.* Boston: Beacon Press.

STEVENSON, GARTH. 1989. *Unfulfilled Union,* 3rd ed. Toronto: Gage.

STRICK, J.C. 1990. *The Economics of Government Regulation: Theory and Canadian Practice.* Toronto: Thompson Education.

TARAS, D. 1990. *The Newsmakers: The Media's Influence on Canadian Politics.* Scarborough, Ont.: Nelson Canada.

TARNOPOLSKY, W.S. 1975. *The Canadian Bill of Rights,* 2nd ed. Toronto: McClelland & Stewart.

TENNANT, P. 1984. "Indian Self-Government: Progress or Stalemate?" *Canadian Public Policy* 10, no. 2: 211–15.

*The Privy Council Office.* 1991. Ottawa.

THORBURN, HUGH. 1991. *Party Politics in Canada.* Scarborough, Ont.: Prentice-Hall Canada.

TINDAL, C.R., and S.N. TINDAL. 1984. *Local Government in Canada.* Toronto: McGraw-Hill Ryerson.

TOFFLER, A. 1990. *Powershift.* New York: Knopf.

Treasury Board. 1990. *Public Service 2000 Task Force Report on Staff Training and Development,* Executive Summary. Ottawa: August 8.

TRUDEAU, P.E. 1968. *Federalism and the French Canadians.* Toronto: Macmillan of Canada.

VIPOND, M. 1992. *Listening In: The First Decade of Canadian Broadcasting, 1922–32.* Montreal and Kingston: McGill-Queen's University Press.

WADDAMS, S.M. 1982. *Introduction to the Study of Law,* 3rd ed. Toronto: Carswell.

WAITE, PETER. 1962. *The Life and Times of Confederation 1864-1867,* 2nd ed. Toronto: University of Toronto Press.

———. 1963. *The Confederation Debates in the Province of Canada/1865.* Toronto: McClelland & Stewart.

WARD, N. 1987. *Davison's The Government of Canada,* 6th ed. Toronto: University of Toronto Press.

WALZ, G., ed. 1986. "Flashback: People and Institutions in Canadian Film History." *Canadian Film Studies* 2. Montreal: Mediatexte Publications.

WATSON, P., and B. BARBER. 1988. *The Struggle for Democracy.* Toronto: Lester and Orpen Dennys.

WEARING, J. 1991. "Does Gender Make a Difference in Voting Behaviour?" In *The Ballot and Its Messsage: Voting in Canada* (pp. 342–49). Toronto: Copp Clark Pitman.

WEARING, J., and P. WEARING. 1990. "Mother's Milk Revisited: The Effect of Foreign Ownership on Political Contributions." *Canadian Journal of Political Science* 23, no. 1 (March): 115–23.

WELLER, P. 1985. *First Among Equals: Prime Ministers in Westminster Systems.* London: Allen & Unwin.

WHITE, RANDALL. 1990. *Voice of Region: The Long Journey to Senate Reform in Canada.* Toronto: Dundurn Press.

WILBUR, J.H.R., ed. 1968. *The Bennett New Deal: Fraud or Portent.* Toronto: Copp Clark.

WILLIAMS, E. 1975. "Medium or Message: Communications Medium as a Determinant of Interpersonal Evaluations." *Sociometry* 38: 119–30.

WILLIAMS, T.M., ed. 1986. *The Impact of Television.* Toronto: Academic Press.

WILSON, J., and D. HOFFMAN. 1974. "The Canadian Political Cultures." *Canadian Journal of Political Science* 7: 581–93.

WINN, C. 1985. "Affirmative Action for Women: More than a Case of Simple Justice." *Canadian Public Admininstration* 28 (Spring): 24–46.

WINN, C., and J. McMENEMY. 1976. *Political Parties in Canada.* Toronto: McGraw-Hill Ryerson.

WINTER, J., C. EYAL, and A. ROGERS. 1982. "Issues-Specific Agenda Steering: The Whole Is Less than the Sum of Its Parts." *Canadian Journal of Communication* 8, no. 2: 1–10.

WOODSIDE, K. 1989. "The Canada-United States Free Trade Agreement." *Canadian Journal of Political Science* 22: 155–70.

YOUNG, ROBERT. 1983. "Business and Budgeting: Recent Proposals for Reforming the Revenue Budgetary Process." *Canadian Public Policy* 9 (September): 347–51.

———. 1991. *Confederation in Crisis.* Toronto: James Lorimer.

# NAME INDEX

# SUBJECT INDEX

## READER REPLY CARD

We are interested in your reaction to *How We Are Governed: The Basics of Canadian Politics and Government*, by James John Guy. You can help us to improve this book in future editions by completing this questionnaire.

1. What was your reason for using this book?
   - ❏ university course
   - ❏ professional development
   - ❏ college course
   - ❏ personal interest
   - ❏ continuing education course
   - ❏ other (please specify) _____
   _____

2. If you are a student, please identify your school and the course in which you used this book.

3. Which chapters or parts of this book did you use? Which did you omit?

4. What did you like best about this book?

5. What did you like least about this book?

6. Please identify any topics you think should be added to future editions.

7. Please add any comments or suggestions.

8. May we contact you for further information?

Name: _____

Address: _____

_____

Phone: _____

(fold here and tape shut)

------------------------------------------------------------------------

MAIL ➤ POSTE

Canada Post Corporation / Société canadienne des postes

**Postage paid**
If mailed in Canada

**Port payé**
si posté au Canada

**Business Reply**

**Réponse d'affaires**

0116870399          01

0116870399-M8Z4X6-BR01

Heather McWhinney
Publisher, College Division
HARCOURT BRACE & COMPANY, CANADA
55 HORNER AVENUE
TORONTO, ONTARIO
M8Z 9Z9